THE SOVIET GULAG

Pitt Series in Russian and East European Studies
Jonathan Harris, Editor

Kritika Historical Studies

THE SOVIET
GULAG

EVIDENCE, INTERPRETATION, and COMPARISON

edited by **MICHAEL DAVID-FOX**

University of Pittsburgh Press

Published by the University of Pittsburgh Press, Pittsburgh, Pa., 15260
Manufactured in the United States of America
Printed on acid-free paper
10 9 8 7 6 5 4 3 2 1

ISBN 13: 978-0-8229-4464-5
ISBN 10: 0-8229-4464-2

Cataloging-in-Publication data is available from the Library of Congress

Cover art: Soviet photoalbum pastiche using interior photographs
Cover design: Joel W. Coggins

CONTENTS

LIST OF ABBREVIATIONS   VII

FOREWORD   IX
DAVID R. SHEARER

CHAPTER 1.   Introduction: From Bounded to Juxtapositional—
New Histories of the Gulag   1
MICHAEL DAVID-FOX

PART I.   Evidence and Interpretation

CHAPTER 2.   The Gulag and the Non-Gulag as One Interrelated
Whole   25
OLEG KHLEVNIUK

CHAPTER 3.   Destructive Labor Camps: Rethinking Solzhenitsyn's Play
on Words   42
GOLFO ALEXOPOULOS

CHAPTER 4.   Lives in the Balance: Weak and Disabled Prisoners and the
Biopolitics of the Gulag   65
DAN HEALEY

CHAPTER 5.   Scientists and Specialists in the Gulag: Life and Death in
Stalin's *Sharashka*   87
ASIF SIDDIQI

CHAPTER 6.   Forced Labor on the Home Front: The Gulag and Total War
in Western Siberia, 1940–1945   114
WILSON T. BELL

CHAPTER 7. (Un)Returned from the Gulag: Life Trajectories and Integration of Postwar Special Settlers 136
EMILIA KOUSTOVA

CHAPTER 8. A Visual History of the Gulag: Nine Theses 162
AGLAYA K. GLEBOVA

PART II. Comparison

CHAPTER 9. Penal Deportation to Siberia and the Limits of State Power, 1801–1881 173
DANIEL BEER

CHAPTER 10. Britain's Archipelago of Camps: Labor and Detention in a Liberal Empire, 1871–1903 199
AIDAN FORTH

CHAPTER 11. Camp Worlds and Forced Labor: A Comparison of the National Socialist and Soviet Camp Systems 224
DIETRICH BEYRAU

CHAPTER 12. "Repaying Blood Debt": The Chinese Labor Camp System during the 1950s 250
KLAUS MÜLHAHN

CHAPTER 13. The Origins and Evolution of the North Korean Prison Camps: A Comparison with the Soviet Gulag 268
SUNGMIN CHO

CHAPTER 14. The Gulag as the Crucible of Russia's Twenty-First-Century System of Punishment 286
JUDITH PALLOT

CHAPTER 15. The Gulag: An Incarnation of the State That Created It 314
BETTINA GREINER

NOTES 321

CONTRIBUTORS 415

INDEX 419

LIST OF ABBREVIATIONS

ASSR—Associated Soviet Socialist Republic

GKO—State Committee on Defense

GPU, OGPU—State Political Administration/Unified State Political Administration

Gulag (GULag)—Main Administration of Corrective Labor Camps and Colonies

MGB—Ministry of State Security

NKVD, MVD—People's Commissariat of Internal Affairs, Ministry of Internal Affairs

NKIu—People's Commissariat of Justice

OITK—Department of Corrective Labor Colonies

RSFSR—Russian Soviet Federated Socialist Republic

spetsposelentsy—special settlers

TsIK SSSR—Central Executive Committee of the USSR

UITLK—Administration for Corrective Labor Camps and Colonies

UMVD—Administration of the MVD

zek—prisoner

FOREWORD

DAVID R. SHEARER

FORTY-THREE YEARS have passed since Alexander Solzhenitsyn authorized publication of his monumental study of the Soviet forced labor camp system, *Arkhipelag Gulag*.[1] That publication not only offered a searing indictment of the Soviet regime but also created the image of the camp system as an archipelago, an image that has dominated scholarly and popular discussion of Soviet penal practice for a number of decades. This image went hand in hand with discussions of secrecy and the separateness of the Gulag system. This was a closed system, not discussed in wider Soviet society—one that, having ensnared a victim, devoured that victim. In Solzhenitsyn's Gulag world there was little or no trafficking between inside and outside. The Gulag was a separate world with its own rules, habits, and culture.

Since then a number of scholars have questioned the metaphor of the Gulag camps as an isolated world within Soviet society. Their work emphasizes a more dynamic and interactive relationship between the Gulag system and the rest of Soviet society. Scholars have coined new metaphors to characterize this relationship—revolving doors, porous boundaries, mirror images, and continuums. The majority of essays in this collection reflect this more dynamic understanding of the Soviet Gulag. At the same time, they also cover the spectrum of discussion that has made the field of Gulag studies so evocative.

There are many studies of the Soviet forced labor camp and colony system, both by individual authors and as collective enterprises, but none with the acumen, breadth, and archival depth of the essays brought together in this collection. The editor is to be congratulated on his judicious selection of essays. None of the selections disappoint, and all work to produce a complex whole. Especially valuable, and almost unprecedented, is the inclusion of comparative essays on British concentration camps, Chinese forced labor systems, the North Korean prison camps, and German prisoner of war camps. As with all things Soviet, the Gulag system reflected many of the contradictions inherent in Soviet history, and the comparative essays in this volume highlight a history that both fits and does not fit general trends of the nineteenth and twentieth centuries.

The collection is not only comparative spatially but also comparative over time. Essays span at least two centuries, situating the Soviet system within a continuum of experience from early nineteenth-century Russian exile practice to the present-day prison system. This kind of coverage provides rich material for reflection, as does the breadth of topics examined. The editor has been diligent to gather work that covers the whole range of Soviet penal and coercive practices, from political "isolators" to well-endowed scientific research institutes to the nearly unguarded penal settlement colonies. The diversity of topics is remarkable. Essays examine the experience of prisoners as well as administrators, micro as well as macro histories of the Gulag system, food rationing as well as brute, deadly exploitation, war mobilization as well as the memories of post-Second World War exiles. Ethnic historians will be interested in the treatment of nationalities within the Gulag world. Historians of warfare will find the essays on mobilization and prisoner of war camps intriguing. The remarkable similarities in practice and ideological justifications will strike readers as they peruse the chapters on British, Soviet, North Korean, and communist Chinese concentration camps. The essays here capture the contradictions and complexity of Soviet coercive practices and, in so doing, they say much about the complexities of Soviet society and the state that created such an elaborate system. This volume is not just a series of essays on Soviet labor camps. It is a social history of the twentieth century. As Bettina Greiner remarks in her conclusion, the Gulag system was an incarnation of the state that created it. It was also an integral part of the society in which it existed.

This collection originated in a conference held at Georgetown University in April 2013. That conference brought together an international group of scholars and resulted in a special issue of *Kritika: Explorations in Russian and Eurasian History* in the summer of 2015.[2] The present volume builds on the *Kritika* issue by expanding the number of authors and topics, and the editor has taken special care to broaden the comparative and international context of Soviet penal practices. As a result, the chapter configuration of the book collection differs from that of the journal issue. The book edition is also welcome, since it will reach a potentially broader audience of interested readers than the journal edition, particularly those who have no or only limited access to the electronic forms of the journal and those who examine the growth of state coercive practices in the modern era but who do not peruse specialized field journals. Solzhenitsyn's famous study focused the world's attention on the Soviet Gulag. These essays situate the Soviet Gulag within that larger world.

THE SOVIET GULAG

INTRODUCTION

From Bounded to Juxtapositional—New Histories of the Gulag

MICHAEL DAVID-FOX

THE GULAG HAS long been approached as a bounded system, a network of camps isolated in the remote corners of the Soviet space. The main metaphor behind Solzhenitsyn's epochal 1973 *Arkhipelag GULAG* (Gulag Archipelago) of a vast chain of islands was, in part, intended to bridge the veil of silence that surrounded the camps much like water surrounds enclaves of land. Solzhenitsyn popularized the previously little-known acronym (Glavnoe up-ravlenie ispravitel´no-trudovykh lagerei i kolonii, or the Main Administration of Corrective Labor Camps and Colonies of the GPU/NKVD and later MVD), turning it into a metonym for not just the NKVD network of labor camps but, by extension, all Soviet camps—and later, in its most expansive usages, Stalinist repression writ large. This symbolic meaning attached to the term no doubt helped reify the Gulag as a discrete entity separated from the Soviet mainland.

Early scholarly contributions to the history of the Gulag were not only heavily influenced by Solzhenitsyn's metaphor but often took a systemic approach by treating the network of camps and colonies as a whole. The most significant examples of this came before the "archival revolution" of the 1990s, which was marked by a statistical war over the total number of victims.[1] In addition, the history of the Gulag was very much bounded chronologically, largely by the years of Stalinism, since the camps as a mass system of forced labor arose under secret police supervision in 1930, shortly after Stalin consolidated sole power, and were radically reduced several years after his death during Khrushchev's Thaw.[2] Finally, there was little if any comparison to the history of camps or forced labor in other times and places.

Solzhenitsyn's archipelago metaphor was inspired by an actual archipelago, the White Sea islands of Solovki that were home to the Solovetskii lager´ osobogo naznacheniia (SLON). This camp complex remained under secret police control during the New Economic Policy (NEP) and became the prototype for the expanding system of camps at the outset of the Stalin period. It assumed this role because it had first developed the mission and methods aimed at economically exploiting prisoner labor and colonizing the Far North, and its staff along with its model were exported to other camps during the rapid expansion of the Gulag network. One of the many famous inmates of Solovki, the future academician Dmitrii Likhachev, was arrested in 1928 and served five years. He recalled a much later time when he shared his notes on the history of the camp in the White Sea archipelago with Solzhenitsyn, who spent eleven years in the camps, as both were preparing their respective publications on the topic. In the course of three days, he told Aleksandr Isaevich about the Latvian camp boss Degtiarev, the self-styled "surgeon-in-chief" and "head of the troops of the Solovetskii archipelago." Solzhenitsyn exclaimed: "That is what I need!" Thus, Likhachev recounted, "in my office the name for his book 'The Gulag Archipelago' was born."[3]

This volume contributes and adds weight to an approach to the Gulag that is in many respects quite different from the one that reigned for a quarter-century after Solzhenitsyn's magnum opus. Scholarship on the Soviet camp system, which began to grow relatively slowly after the opening of the former Soviet archives, has gained a momentum never before achieved. A noteworthy impetus to the field was the publication in 2004–2005 of a landmark, seven-volume, Russian-language documentary history, *The History of the Stalinist Gulag*.[4] Since then, the pace in Gulag studies has accelerated internationally as new scholarship, especially in Russian, English, French, and German, has stimulated new vectors of analysis.

If one were to characterize the most novel element in the new wave of Gulag research, it could be dubbed juxtapositional. Even as much of the new scholarship is built on in-depth case studies rather than systemic coverage, scholars have become, first of all, acutely aware of just how many different types of camps with very different regimes the Soviet Union maintained. In 2007 Lynne Viola drew attention to the "unknown Gulag" of special settlements set up during forced collectivization, a peasant world quite different from the camps but also part of the Gulag.[5] The camps themselves also differed greatly. To cite just one striking example of the range of camp regimes involved, Viazemlag (named after the city Viaz´ma in Smolensk oblast) was tasked in the mid-1930s to build the strategically important Moscow-Minsk highway. It was in many ways on the opposite end of the spectrum from such remote camps as Kolyma, within the Arctic Circle, the horrific and extreme conditions of which were described by Varlam Shalamov. Centrally located, Viazemlag in fact became a moving settlement that traveled as the highway was constructed. There was contact with the local population and minimal security, due to relatively privileged conditions and utilization of prisoners about to be released.[6] Future works will undoubtedly be concerned with further synthesizing the mounting number of case studies and juxtaposing the different types of camps.

Second, Solzhenitsyn's metaphor, so widely adopted and so longlasting, has been productively called into question in this later scholarship. Although by suggesting that Soviet life was made up of bigger and lesser zones, Solzhenitsyn in a way prefigured current approaches, the archipelago metaphor was often taken to presuppose a world that was as closed off as it was physically remote. By contrast, twenty-first-century scholarship emphasizes the "porous" boundaries of many camps and the mixing of free and nonfree populations.[7] It also raises a significant comparative issue, discussed below: the blurred boundaries between free and unfree labor.

The scholarship of juxtaposition thus moves the Gulag, to use Kate Brown's phrase, "out of solitary confinement" and into the mainstream of Soviet history.[8] To do this implies understanding connections, tracing interactions, and making parallels with the broader Soviet civilization beyond the barbed wire. This volume begins with an important effort by the eminent Russian historian of Stalinism, Oleg Khlevniuk, to think through the interconnections between the Gulag and the "non-Gulag." Khlevniuk therefore furthers the juxtapositional approach most explicitly and systematically, but it is also supported by almost all the other chapters in the book. For example, Wilson Bell discusses how the Siberian Gulag was integrated into the total war economy; Asif Siddiqi situates the scientific *sharashki* (teams of engineers and scientists in the Gulag) within the broader history of Soviet "specialists." Siddiqi describes how the illusion of cost-free forced labor even prompted the secret police to target members of the scientific and technical intelligentsia in professions "useful" for Gulag activities, such as geologists "recruited" through arrest to work in mining or industrial operations. Dan Healey, in turn, considers Gulag physicians and camps for invalids in the context of broader Soviet approaches to disability. Insofar as such connections are an intrinsic part of the authors' interpretations, they serve to "bring the Gulag back in" to Soviet history.

Finally, the sharpness of the 1956–1958 divide in historical treatments of Gulag-related topics has also eroded with scholarly treatments of Gulag returnees, the integration of Gulag survivors into Soviet society, and the intertwined history of Gulag camps with their surroundings. All three factors were present, notably, in settlements and even cities that sprang up around the camps and that lived on after the era of Stalinist mass incarceration was over.[9] In this volume, Emilia Koustova's exploration of the reintegration of special settlers from Lithuania and western Ukraine into Soviet society and Judith Pallot's discussion of the afterlife of the Gulag in post-Soviet penal policies both make juxtapositions that transcend long-standing chronological boundaries in Gulag studies.

Perhaps the most novel and far-reaching set of juxtapositions in the current volume, however, derives from its inclusion of a richly suggestive comparative element. Perhaps because of the relative isolation of Soviet studies from other fields, perhaps because of the totalitarian paradigm's stress on exceptionalism (beyond the comparison with National Socialism and Fascism), and certainly because of the long dearth of empirically rich, archival studies, the history of the Gulag has been surprisingly, even startlingly underinformed by comparative history. One of the major purposes of this book is to begin to rectify this situation. Because German scholarship in recent years has become the pacesetter in pursuing the comparative history of concentration camps, a noted participant in this literature, Bettina Greiner, was invited to write the conclusion.[10]

Two chapters, those of Daniel Beer and Judith Pallot, further what might be called temporal comparisons in the Russian context. Their examination of the tsarist exile system and the post-Soviet Russian penal system—that is, the prehistory and posthistory of the Gulag—necessarily affect our understanding of the Soviet era by forcing us to reckon with some of the Gulag's features that predated and outlasted communism. Aidan Forth's work on British camps in Africa and India, exploring a "liberal empire" in the long nineteenth century, well before the era of "high modernism," was quite deliberately selected for inclusion here. Certain uncanny parallels with the Gulag —what Forth memorably calls a "family resemblance"—may well be the most revealing and, perhaps, unexpected part of this book for Soviet historians, who rarely look beyond twentieth-century history and who have grown up for so long on the Nazi-Soviet comparison.

If there is one comparative fact that Soviet historians do know about the Gulag, it is that Soviet camps were not extermination camps, and thus can be distinguished from the industrial killing camps of the Nazis. Dietrich Beyrau, however, returns to the hoary Nazi-Soviet comparison with a consideration of all the camps in the Third Reich, not only what he calls the "pure extermination camps" of Chelmo, Sobibor, Treblinka, Majdanek, and Auschwitz-Birkenau. The creation of these death camps came with the outbreak of the Second World War, roughly coinciding with the Final Solution; all the Nazi camps "before Auschwitz," however horrific, were not extermination camps.[11] Juxtaposing a more comprehensive coverage of the range of

German camps to a Soviet case considered on the basis of the new histo-riography, Beyrau is then able to identify many other similarities and differ-ences. This reconsideration also comes at a time when our understanding of the Holocaust as primarily associated with "industrial" murder in the death camps has been transformed by newer understandings of the "Holocaust by bullets" in the East.[12]

For any updated comparison with the Nazi case, moreover, scholars will wish to take into account Golfo Alexopoulos's powerful new material on how the Gulag camps systematically "managed, utilized, and discarded" people, releasing many on the verge of death in order to reduce mortality rates. Alex-opoulos observes that "there exists a legitimate desire to avoid false equiva-lencies between the Nazi extermination camps and the Soviet labor camps," and she acknowledges the differing severity of camp regimes. At the same time, Alexopoulos concludes that "exhaustive labor and punitive starvation rations" were a form of destruction that was systematic and, to the degree that it was predicated on total exploitation of human bodies, intentional: "The Stalinist leadership may not have planned to exterminate its camp pris-oners, but it intended to extract all available energy, to physically exploit prisoners to the maximum degree possible." Two other comparative cases explored here, those of China and North Korea, both show how camp sys-tems that originally were heavily influenced both by the Soviet example and Soviet advisers diverged from the Gulag in noteworthy respects. The Laogai in China went far down the road of ideological reeducation and frenzied mass mobilization, for example, even as it largely replicated heavily econom-ic functions of the Gulag, while North Korea has emphasized stigma and, evidently, could not replicate the economic role that forced labor played in Soviet forced industrialization.

A key issue that runs through the chapters of this volume, one that cries out for more comparative treatment, has to do with the modernity of the Gulag. Nineteenth-century innovations, both ideological and technological, were preconditions for twentieth-century camps. As Forth argues in his chapter, "British rule helped foster the structural and conceptual preconditions for the development and management of camps." As Beyrau suggests, the First World War was, as in so many other areas, an international watershed in both the scale and duration of the camp experience that, like the Gulag itself, was quite diverse and encompassed many different types of camps. Forth makes a direct connection from the nineteenth to the twentieth century via the con-cept of modernity, arguing: "At a fundamental level, British and Soviet camps materialized within the structural conditions of a shared Western modernity. They developed according to similar frameworks of purity and contagion and emphasized productive labor, fiscal restraint, and fears of social and political danger." The Gulag, like the concentration camp, is quite often seen as a quintessentially twentieth-century, totalitarian, and therefore, by extension, modern phenomenon. Mark Levene's comparative work on genocide in the European "rimlands" from 1939 to 1953 explicitly labels the NKVD, because of its relative efficiency and logistical capabilities in comparison to the Nazi SS, the "cutting edge of Soviet high modernism."[13]

At the same time, when it comes to features of Stalinism that have not infrequently appeared as a prima facie argument about the atavism of the Soviet system, the sheer extent of Soviet political violence and the nature of the Gulag have loomed large. The fact that a significant sector of the Soviet economy and population were tied to what was essentially a form of slave labor, often using nonexistent or primitive tools, led Viktor Berdinskikh, a historian of the Gulag, to begin a paper with an analogy to the Egyptian pyramids. Alexander Etkind, to give a different example, views the Soviet system as "definitively anti-modern." Operating in no small part on the history of the Gulag, Etkind advances the "concept of 'counter-modernities' or perhaps 'anti-modern forces of modernity,' modeled after Isaiah Berlin's concept of Counter-Enlightenment."[14]

Within the chapters of this book alone, there appears to be a spectrum of opinion on the modernity of the Gulag. Wilson Bell, for example, emphasizes the pragmatic adaptation of the Gulag into the wartime economy after 1941, and in his dissertation the large gap between central planning and on-the-ground realities in the Gulag leads him to label it a form of "neo-traditionalism."[15] On the other end of the spectrum, Beyrau, deploying notions of total institutions and absolute power, implicitly emphasizes illiberal modernity, even as for him the concept of camp "underlife" is needed to explain the inevitable gap between intentions and implementation. Alexopoulos's description of a systematized, Gulag-wide regime of extreme physical exploitation necessarily affects our understanding of the Gulag's modernity, because it could only be implemented on such a widespread scale by political authorities, camp administrations, and medical personnel—even while much of the labor was carried out with the most primitive of tools.

I would suggest that attentive readers of these chapters will find it possible to break the vexed issue of modernity into more manageable historical and conceptual problems. One such issue that assumes key importance revolves around state capacity. Beer's chapter on deportation to Siberia and the tsarist exile system is precisely about the "limits of state power" in the prerevolutionary Russian Empire. Even though the nature of both Gulag camps and special settlements was fundamentally about minimizing the number of guards and personnel needed to produce forced labor from a large number of prisoners, the contrast between the tsarist and Soviet states was enormous. The ambitions of the Soviet state were, needless to say, far greater than its own capacity, but without those ambitions the sheer scale of the Gulag is also hard to imagine. A second issue relevant to the question of the modernity of the Gulag has to do with the significant role of science, medicine, and specialists, taken up in the chapters of Alexopoulos, Healey, and Siddiqi. A third issue revolves around the distinctive economic-ideological missions attached to Gulag forced labor from the First Five-Year Plan on. While the British camps, as Forth shows, not only used prisoner labor but reflected an entire ideology of labor, the centrality of the Gulag's forced labor to forced industrialization and internal colonization—what Christian Gerlach and Nicholas Werth have termed "developmental violence"—have to be considered a major facet of Soviet communism.[16] Mühlhahn suggests in his contribution that the Chinese Laogai (the abbreviation for "reform through labor") system shared a "strong, even dominant emphasis on the economic functions of camps" with the Gulag. This is yet another reason to consider Maoism a variation on Stalinism.

Perhaps the greatest issue deriving from the new juxtaposition between the Gulag and the non-Gulag within the Soviet system that cries out for more comparative investigation is the relationship between "free" and Gulag labor. Many of the chapters in this volume contain material that supports Barenberg's recent conclusion: "the straightforward distinction between 'free' workers (*vol´ nonaemnye*) and prisoners (*zakliuchennye*) that one often encounters in archival documents and memoirs, and in much of the historiography of the Gulag, falls short of being able to describe the social intricacy of camp complexes and their surrounding communities."[17] For example, Khlevniuk discusses a "liminal space between the Gulag and non-Gulag" made up of tens of millions of people he describes as "half-free." By "free" in this context one conventionally means, of course, a nonprisoner. However, the notion that it is hard to consider any labor in the Stalin period as truly free, in the sense of not being directly linked to coercion and compulsion, is hardly a novelty in the historiography of the non-Gulag. The entire collective farm system resulting from the collectivization of agriculture, carried out at the very same historical moment the Gulag was created, can be seen as a form of forced labor for the rural population. There is a large comparative dimension to this question, as well. Not just the authors of the new wave of scholarship on the Gulag (including Khlevniuk, Bell, and Siddiqi in this volume) but economic historians investigating other times and contexts are questioning a stark dichotomy between free and forced labor.[18]

Ultimately, the juxtapositional approach furthered here provokes reflection on the myriad ways in which the Gulag was intertwined with Stalinism—the definition and nature of which is in itself an important problem—and why the Gulag became an integral part of the Soviet system in the Stalin period.[19] A good place to begin is the feedback loop between politics and economics, or more specifically the way the persecution of political enemies reinforced the exploitation of forced labor, and vice versa. Soviet authorities became addicted to a constant, seemingly inexhaustible flow of Gulag labor, even though camp administrators often underestimated the number of prisoners the political authorities would produce. To be sure, the Gulag, despite its huge size, was in all-union terms but one rather small part of the emergent command economy. But the importance of Gulag forced labor derived from the Gulag's place as a high-priority sector of that economy run by the powerful secret police: it was used for gold and mineral extraction, the monumental construction sites of the era, and strategically important projects. In the command economy, moreover, prisoner labor contractually supplied by the secret police was regularly directed to fill all sorts of needs outside the Gulag.[20]

The broader point is that in the Stalin period the Soviet system became linked to the Gulag at the hip. This was in no small part because their entire worldview led the Stalinist leadership and Soviet authorities of the period into the illusory trap of assuming that forced labor came at little or no cost—or, perhaps more accurately, for decades operating as if those costs that existed were worth assuming.[21] It is also because the cycles of revolutionary attack or crackdown, alternating with periods of retrenchment as the regime lurched from crisis to crisis starting with the unexpected consequences of collectivization circa 1930, were deeply intertwined with the conditions and population growth of the Gulag.[22] Under Stalinism, there was rarely a shortage in the "supply" of prisoners produced by arrests and the campaigns that generated them. Did Stalinist political violence, which originally created the supply of Gulag slave labor and endowed the NKVD with its own economic empire, ultimately stimulate, in a cruel mimicry of market forces, the "demand" for arrests? Here causal relationships and levels of intentionality remain open to more research and interpretation. But the bigger point is that there existed an interlocking political-economic nexus in which political violence and forced labor were two sides of the Stalinist coin. The result was a camp system that exceeded all antecedents. This must be considered a component feature of the Soviet system as it crystallized under Stalin, and it therefore must be considered no small part of the construction of Soviet socialism as a noncapitalist shortcut to modernity.

It matters greatly, however, whether one investigates the modernity of the Gulag simply in terms of features the Soviet case shared with other modern phenomena or whether one instead conceives a particular, alternative Soviet modernity with its own particular characteristics, at once recognizably modern and part of a distinctively Russian-Soviet historical trajectory.[23] This book can only hope to stimulate thought on such theoretical problems, since the comparative history surrounding the Gulag is at a nascent stage. The comparative agenda, moreover, is complemented by questions raised most explicitly in this volume by Forth about an equally underdeveloped research agenda: to what extent did countries that organized camps and forced labor learn from one another's experiences and practices? Any answer to this question demands a shift from comparative to transnational investigation.

Lev Trotskii, as is well known, was familiar with the British concentration camps in South Africa from his coverage of the Boer War. The first references to "concentration camps" in Russia, as Peter Holquist has shown, derived from the attention paid by both Russian military personnel and the Russian press to the British precedent. By the time the Cheka and military commissariats were tasked with creating concentration camps for defeated White officers and Cossacks in the Don in 1920, for example, Soviet authorities shifted to class analysis of suspect populations and "vastly expanded the use of such camps."[24] These particular linkages, however, represent just tiny pieces of a vast phenomenon. As Mühlhahn has suggested in a discussion of the "dark side of globalization," the "global spread of institutions of mass internment illustrates how, within a relatively short time span, these institutions and their underlying concepts were appropriated across borders, as ruling elites around the globe looked for potent strategies to end opposition and resistance to their projects of expansion and consolidation." He goes on to state, "The simultaneous emergence of modern institutions of mass confinement in Latin America, Africa, Russia, Japan, and China was not a belated replication of a European model so much as the synchronous appropriation of a globally circulating idea."[25] At the same time, the appropriation of practices and models always involves interpretation, domestication, and, almost certainly, adaptation as those practices are implemented in a different context. Any transnational agenda in Gulag studies does not only concern precedents that influenced the Russian and Soviet experience in the era of wars and revolutions. It also concerns the export of the already formed Gulag model to countries, such as China, North Korea, and East Europe, where Soviet advisers, Communists who had spent time in the Soviet Union, and the model of Stalin's USSR were influential.

Both the transnational and comparative history surrounding the Gulag stands at a nascent stage. As we acknowledge how much work remains to be done, let us turn in more detail to the contributions of the individual chapters that compose this book.

Oleg Khlevniuk opens the volume with the biggest juxtaposition of all: a sweeping, big-picture reinterpretation of the relationship between the Gulag and the Soviet system, "The Gulag and the Non-Gulag as One Interrelated Whole." The scale of the question he raises prompts Khlevniuk to divide it into four manageable vectors of analysis: the Gulag's boundaries, its channels of interaction with the outside world, its role as model for the non-Gulag, and its place in a stratified, hierarchical Soviet society. Among Khlevniuk's principal conclusions are that those boundaries contained a large, liminal zone of semifree laborers; the channels of connection were "robust," as tens of millions moved between Gulag and non-Gulag; and the Gulag-as-model inspired a broader strategy of internal colonization in the Soviet periphery as the Gulag's distinctive subculture was spread through concentrations of former prisoners. But it is in terms of the last vector of analysis, the sociopolitical hierarchy of the Gulag, that Khlevniuk advances his most far-reaching conclusions. The way the Gulag produced various strata of victims, beneficiaries, and party-state "prosecutors" inside and outside its borders, he suggests, did not only affect the period from the 1930s to the 1950s but held consequential long-term ramifications. The aftereffects played themselves out in cycles of de-Stalinization and re-Stalinization, in turn creating constituencies of apologists and critics of Stalinism. This legacy, he suggests, has survived and directly influences the conservative revival in Putin's Russia.

Golfo Alexopoulos's important intervention on mortality, rationing, and health policy in the camps raises no fewer far-reaching questions than the work of Khlevniuk. She argues that Solzhenitsyn's grim yet clever *bon mot*, revising the official term *ispravitel'no-trudovye lageria* (corrective labor camps) as *istrebitel'no-trudovye lageria* (destructive labor camps), was in fact an accurate description of a camp regime that was destructive by design. Bringing to bear new material on the Gulag Sanitation Department's "List of Illnesses" over time, Alexopoulos describes a ladder-like and evolving system by which weaker inmates with declining work abilities were allocated fewer calories. The class of inmates at the bottom of the ladder, the so-called "goners," or *dokhodiagi*, were routinely released from the camps before death, leading Alexopoulos into an extended discussion of Gulag mortality rates and the percentage of prisoners released as incurables. Alexopoulos describes a regime of medico-political exploitation (in the sense that Gulag physicians were subordinated to administrative and camp authorities) that escalated in brutality over the course of the Stalin period, peaking in the postwar expansion of the Gulag to its greatest size in the years before Stalin's death. But the framework itself was stable and was put in place at the beginning of the Stalin period with the birth of the Gulag.

Among the many issues for further debate and research that Alexopoulos's chapter should spark, I will mention only two. First, the systematic destruction that Alexopoulos describes as embedded in the system prompts us to reexamine the ideology of *perekovka*, or reforging, which became a kind of official ideology of correctional (as opposed to destructive) labor. Turning this into the official orthodoxy was in no small part the contribution of Maksim Gor'kii, the architect of Stalinism in culture, after his visit to Solovki in 1929.[26] Alexopoulos does not explicitly address how her findings should influence our understanding of the ideology of rehabilitation surrounding the Gulag.[27] In his book Alan Barenberg points to a camp director's cynicism about the uses of this ideology. He quotes a screenwriter who recalled his visit to Vorkutlag in 1946 and was met by the camp director, Mal'tsev: "So, you're going to write—pause—about *perekovka* [reforging]? . . . In response I muttered something incomprehensible. . . . 'That's right,' the general snorted and added measuredly, 'This is a camp. Our task is the slow murder of people.'" Barenberg's conclusion: "If Mal'tsev truly said this, it was a remarkably accurate assessment of the camp, although the destruction of human life was hardly 'slow.'"[28] However, even if Mal'tsev did utter these words, it hardly means that the ideological justification for the Gulag was irrelevant despite the growing, blatant disparity between pervasive ideology and pervasive practices. It means, rather, that we must reinterpret their relationship and the gulf between them.[29]

Second, as Alexopoulos mentions in passing, the politics of food distribution in the non-Gulag became especially acute during the unprecedented crisis of the Second World War on the Eastern Front. In those years in particular, Soviet administrative decisions about food supply held life-and-death ramifications for nonprisoner populations. Yet in a new and illuminating book on the politics of food on the Soviet home front, the Gulag is only rarely mentioned.[30] Clearly, there is room for more juxtapositional research.

Dan Healey also looks at a previously almost unstudied topic, Gulag doctors, but his chapter takes an in-depth look at the camps' significant medical infrastructure, specifically the Gulag's large-scale Sanitation Department, which included significant numbers of imprisoned physicians, nurses, and paramedics. Healey takes great care in explaining and qualifying his adaptation of the Foucauldian notion of biopolitics to the Stalinist case. Despite the obviously illiberal, noncapitalist, and even irrational nature of the Gulag's penal-economic regime, Healey maintains that the concept of biopolitics can encompass the rationale Gulag medicine pursued in allocating resources relating to food, shelter, clothing, sanitation, and medicine in order to optimize camp populations for production. While there certainly is overlap in the chapters of Alexopoulos and Healey—she acknowledges differing camp regimes, while he highlights atrocious mortality rates and brutal exploitation of weak and disabled prisoners—the differences between the two treatments are impossible to ignore. Alexopoulos sees Solzhenitsyn as fundamentally right about the destructive nature of the camps, while Healey takes issue with Solzhenitsyn's contempt for Gulag medicine by describing the extent of weak-prisoner and recovery teams, as well as separate camps for invalids. Perhaps this divergence will stimulate future research that will shed light on the issues raised.

Lurking behind these disagreements is, in fact, one rather fundamental issue: if the Gulag was so geared around the exploitation of prisoner labor, would it not have some interest in at least prolonging *zek* health? Alexopoulos emphasizes how the "meat grinder" of the Gulag treated humans as raw material that could be utterly depleted, in part because there was an inexhaustible supply. By contrast Healey, discussing how weak and disabled prisoners were almost always required to be involved with production, is implicitly emphasizing that Gulag "biopolitics" was still geared around not their destruction per se but their utilization. Thus "refeeding of the exhausted" and medical care for the weak and disabled, however constrained, was sometimes possible; but feeding people back to health was remorselessly reserved for the "recoverable worker body, and if possible, on a prophylactic basis to avoid long-term convalescence." Healey portrays the Gulag's prioritizing of production and harshness toward the disabled as an even crueler, criminal variation of the "bleakness of official policies applied to the disabled in civilian Soviet society." Thus he concludes, "Soviet civilian biopolitics and the Gulag version came to resemble each other in important ways."

Asif Siddiqi's chapter represents the most substantive exploration to date of the *sharashki*, or camps for scientists, the existence of which has been widely noted but that have rarely been examined in depth. Siddiqi attracts our attention to intelligentsia and other relatively privileged inmates and, by examining scientists and applied "specialists" often working on projects with military applications, calls attention to the role of intellectual labor more generally in the Gulag. This role originated in the 1920s at Solovki, which became famous for its imprisoned intellectuals and clergy, and was not only limited to scientists, engineers, and technical specialists. But several developments at the outset of the Stalin period and the birth of the Gulag shaped the mobilization of imprisoned scientists and specialists for high-speed, high-priority, applied projects. Around 1930, the year of the Industrial Party (Prompartiia) show trial, the Soviet engineering corps was decimated. This attack coincided with a broader crackdown on "bourgeois specialists." Indeed, the entire academic and scientific establishment was under siege in the era of forced industrialization, as it was reoriented toward an emphasis on applied, state-driven priorities even as it was wracked by a sociopolitical assault on enemies. The NEP-era specter of an independent-minded, specialist "technocracy," as Loren Graham so memorably described, was crushed and replaced by a breakneck, myopic, Stalinist-style technocracy aimed at the monumental transformation of nature.[31] The sharashki were one reflection and byproduct of this fateful shift.

One of Siddiqi's key findings is that the sharashka phenomenon was a practice that peaked and reoccurred during distinct moments in the Stalin period, which corresponded to intense purging of the intelligentsia: the early 1930s, the Great Terror, and the late 1940s. In the early 1930s, Siddiqi shows, the secret police system of using scientists and specialist prisoners led to conflicts with industrial management, and the period of relative relaxation after 1931 led to the temporary disbandment of the sharashki. A second and a third wave of coercive renewal came in the late 1930s and late 1940s. The fact that imprisoned scientists worked alongside nonprisoner specialists in the prison science system only underscores the relevance of this discussion for the blurred boundaries between carceral and noncompulsory labor. But Siddiqi's most far-reaching conclusions have to do with the way the sharashka phenomenon "cast a long shadow over the Soviet economy" long after it was gone. A generation of elite scientists and engineers during the Cold War were "alumni" of the Gulag and dominated research and development in the Soviet military-industrial complex. This transmitted what Siddiqi calls a distinct organizational mentality: "Their adoption and occasional enthusiasm for certain traits of the organizational culture of the Soviet scientific and engineering system—extreme secrecy, strict hierarchies, coercive practices, rigid reporting protocols—owed much to their shared experiences with similar peculiarities characteristic of the sharashka system."

Wilson Bell's chapter adds to the scholarship on the Gulag at war.[32] Its focus on western Siberia, in particular, gives us a regional perspective on the mass mobilization of forced labor for the most total of total wars. But Bell's chapter also engages most explicitly the scholarly debate about the function of the Gulag—how we should understand the multiple functions and characterize the nature of the network of camps and colonies over time. Indeed, this deceptively simple problem appears to inform many recent scholarly interventions. Bell does not downplay the penal, political, and repressive roles of the camp system, which punished and "isolated," in Soviet parlance, a broad variety of criminal, ethnic, and political categories of people. He notes, for example, that while many prisoners were released to fight on the front, political prisoners received harsher treatment and were barred from release. But on balance Bell emphasizes the economic function as the Siberian Gulag immediately shifted to wartime production after the Nazi invasion. At the same time, he also concludes that Gulag labor, incredibly inefficient first and foremost because of atrocious conditions and high mortality, was still only a relatively marginal part of the region's home front economy.

Bell is well aware that the economic, penal, and ideological functions of the Gulag "are, of course, not mutually exclusive." However, while economic factors are certainly distinguishable for analytical purposes, it is easy to lose sight of how thoroughly economic missions were intertwined with the core ideological agendas of state socialism. One must add that there were multiple economic missions associated with the Gulag, some far more utopian than others. These ranged from dreams of internal colonization of vast swaths of the periphery, which were salient and even decisive when the Gulag crystallized, to the immediate crisis of wartime production that Bell describes. Economic motivations were therefore multiple and are hard to fully disaggregate from the Gulag's other functions. The interconnection of multiple functions, as opposed to their analytical separation, is worth further exploration in the debate about the nature of the Gulag.

Bell's chapter also contains a noteworthy comparative dimension. He maintains that the Gulag "appears to have been *less* important to issues of state power and control than other camp systems in wartime"; he questions whether the Gulag fits into Giorgio Agamben's fashionable description of concentration camps as an extralegal "state of exception" brought into being using the pretext of war or emergency. As Bell notes, much of Agamben's concept derives from the writings of Carl Schmitt, later the crown jurist of the Third Reich, whose theories are frequently and strangely dehistoricized rather than understood as deriving from their political-ideological context. Here it is worth reflecting on the fact that Bolshevism and Stalinism were already engaged in a kind of ersatz, internal class war, or a mobilization against political and social enemies reminiscent of wartime. The scale of the Great Terror in peacetime, albeit in anticipation of war, is also extraordinary in comparative perspective. Considering the relationship more generally between the subperiod of the war and Stalinism writ large is quite revealing.

Stalinism responded to war in at least three distinct ways. First, it made certain ideological and political compromises in the general tradition of long-established cyclical patterns. Second, it matched those concessions with repressions and adaptation to the war of annihilation on the Eastern Front. Finally, it mobilized for the new demands of the most total war to date with a scale and intensity that brought to new levels those features that it had already displayed before. What Stalinism did *not* do during the Second World War was somehow reveal its true nature, find an outlet for long-standing aspirations, or attain a culmination of deep-seated ideological trends that needed the spark of war to be released. Here the contrast with Nazism is at its most stark. If the radical or revolutionary energies in Bolshevism and Stalinism became directed primarily inward, toward a profound, revolutionary reordering of society, the racist and martial revolutionary dreams of National Socialism were from the start thoroughly intertwined with war and became primarily directed outward toward domination, racial colonization, and *Lebensraum*.[33]

Emilia Koustova's exploration of special settlers from Lithuania and western Ukraine turns our attention to the ethnic dimension of Soviet repression. Based on an interview project carried out in Irkutsk, the chapter uses oral history to restore the voices and recover the lived experience of former special settlers. Most of the interviewees were born in the 1930s and were deported to special settlements after the Second World War, when they were children or adolescents. Many of them were talking about their deportations for the first time and lacked big-picture collective narratives to structure their stories. These special settlers, in sum, were not part of the collectivization-era peasant Gulag described by Lynne Viola. They were nationally distinct as well as strangers to the area, but they perceived that the surrounding locals in the non-Gulag "lived only marginally better than the settlers." These deportees had a chance at integration into Soviet society and at overcoming stigma.

How these postwar special settlements could become a vehicle for Sovietization, in fact, represents the little-studied central topic of the chapter. It is concerned, first and foremost, with the "mechanisms and limits of the integration of postwar deportation victims into Soviet society." The chapter's concern with the conditions of the special settlements, labor, the national dimensions of the deportees' outlooks and, not least, their long, arduous attempts to improve their conditions opens up a realm in the history of Soviet everyday life. The reader of Koustova's work will find both a fluid line between the *spetsposelentsy* and Soviet citizens—that is, between the deported and the locals, between Gulag and non-Gulag—and evidence that stigma and the discriminatory logic behind the repressions persisted even in the late 1980s, long after the special settlements were disbanded. One feature of Koustova's contribution, therefore, is that it asks us to look beyond the boundaries of a Gulag strictly conceived.

Aglaya Glebova's "theses" on visual history and the Gulag bring us primarily into the realm of representations, and her contribution thus stands out from the other chapters. But it is a necessary inclusion that originated during a search for images of the Gulag for this volume. As Glebova states in her first sentence: "We have no photographs of the Gulag as atrocity." In this essay, Glebova explains why this is the case. The "archival revolution" after 1991 has made accessible abundant visual records of the Gulag, but the comprehensiveness of the Soviet ideological-cultural regime assured that none of the photographs were about human destruction and all were to some extent staged. Glebova's essay, however, opens up a way to engage and not simply discard the visual record that does exist. First, she uses it as a means to analyze a certain mode of visuality that was not only strongly imprinted by Socialist Realism but extended the late imperial legacy of "curating visuality." She argues, for example, that the Russian models and displays of the Fourth International Penitentiary Congress in 1890 prefigured the kind of crafted images later used by Soviet propaganda. As she describes it, the Stalinist visuality that did emerge was a function of Socialist Realism and of modernism, and therefore was reflected in both the "little zone" and the "big zone" (the Gulag and non-Gulag). Second, Glebova notes that the two types of visual sources most often displayed in post-Soviet publications about the Gulag—mug shots of prisoners and records from the propaganda extravaganza surrounding the Belomor Canal—only scratch the surface of the visual record now available. Even staged, curated, and filtered photographs are "unruly," as she puts it, open to contextualization and signification that is "up to us." The photographs displayed throughout this book were selected by Glebova in conjunction with the texts of the other chapters. They assume meaning in conjunction with the texts and in this way receive the contextualization for which Glebova calls. They become a useful if inherently limited kind of historical source.

The comparative section of the volume begins with Daniel Beer's research on the tsarist exile system, a work that does not make explicit comparisons with the Gulag but allows us to consider significant continuities between tsarist and Soviet penal practices. By focusing on deportation convoys to Siberia, Beer's work provokes consideration of a spatial dimension in the history of penal practices in Russia, and by extension the Soviet Union and the Russian Federation. Historical geography, notably the "Mapping the Gulag" project, has established what Judith Pallot calls a striking "spatial continuity" in the topography of incarceration lasting especially from the 1930s to the present day.[34] Beer takes us back to more long-term continuities. His concentration on deportation convoys within the tsarist exile system vividly evokes how movement across great space—forced mobility or coerced movement—was itself a deeply entrenched component of Russian penal practice. This continuity existed despite the fact that in the tsarist era, as Beer demonstrates, the state did not conceive of the convoy in and of itself as punishment, viewing it merely as a logistical preamble to exile and hard labor (*katorga*).

The harsh and brutal "processions of misfortune" that the convoys represented, so impervious to much improvement through technocratic reform since the days of Mikhail Speranskii, thus highlight the coercion of spatial displacement that continued in the Soviet (and post-Soviet) era. But in the course of his discussion Beer identifies other key continuities between tsarist precedents and the Gulag. For example, he points to the use of incarceration in labor sites beginning with Peter the Great, to the aim of using imprisonment to further colonization in Siberia starting under Catherine the Great, and to rehabilitation as an explicit justification for the penal system beginning with the Great Reforms. Beer also pursues the revealing and, in both the Russian and Soviet contexts, necessary topic of differing and overlapping modes of penality (which he labels, in terms of the tsarist exile system, sovereign, economic, colonial, and disciplinary). In the end, what Beer describes most vividly will be familiar to any Soviet specialist: the yawning gulf between state intentions and unexpected consequences, continually reinforced by inadequate resources and leading directly to disease and overcrowding, corrupt and self-interested local officialdom, and informal practices that grew up alongside official ones. In the end, Beer's chapter inspires reflection on how geography—great distances, the ample availability of remote space for any system of punishment, often extreme environmental conditions, and lack of infrastructure—informed the penal systems that arose under tsarism and in later periods.

In "Britain's Archipelago of Camps," Aidan Forth provides a genealogy of the birth of the concentration camp in the British colonial context. In terms of the British Empire, the storyline moves from workhouses for the poor in the imperial metropole, which became a "template" for future camps, to British India as the "primary arena of encampment" in the nineteenth century. The criminal tribal camps, after the famine and plague emergencies of the 1890s, in turn produced models for the first places to be called concentration camps in the Anglo-Boer War. From this genealogy emerge several important corollaries. First, there was a live interplay between the metropole and the colonial periphery, between workhouses in the center and camps in the periphery, between discourses of class and race. This can provide an analogy, mutatis mutandis, for further investigation of the interplay between Soviet center and periphery, between Gulag and non-Gulag. Second, it was not only Britain but other colonial powers that "assembled many of the cultural, material, and political preconditions of forced encampment" in the long nineteenth century. Notably, army camps in the Napoleonic Wars provided some of the organizational framework for concentration camps for civilians. Third, as in the Soviet case, those cultural preconditions encompassed powerful metaphors of purity and pollution.

The distant yet noticeable "family resemblance" stretching from the nineteenth to the twentieth centuries that Forth lays out, even as he aptly warns against simplistic comparisons, thus includes not only administrative and organizational technologies but cultural and ideological motivations that stretched from centers of power to peripheral sites of the abuse of power. Camps were created by states across the political spectrum, but despite radically different political ideologies the deeper cultural-ideological logic underpinning the camps appears eerily similar. At the same time, to extend Bell's discussion of "states of exception," Forth makes clear that the British camps were "expedient products of emergencies" such as famine, disease, and war, and they were predicated on extrajudicial exemption. They appear, therefore, to uphold the argument about modern camps as "states of exception" in a way the Gulag, arguably and anomalously, does not. Either way, Forth is on target when he calls for comparative agendas that go beyond the "usual suspects" and for comparative agendas that might unsettle "comfortable distinctions" between liberal and illiberal states.

In addition to prompting us to rethink the Nazi-Soviet comparison, as discussed above, Dietrich Beyrau contributes to the tradition of analyzing camps as a "total institution" that became a linchpin and symbol of the two most totalizing dictatorships in the short twentieth-century age of extremes. One feature of his chapter is the attention paid to quantitative estimations of the size of the two camp systems. The overall size of the Gulag grew steadily in the Stalin years, from 1.2 million in camps and colonies in 1936 to 1.7 million in 1940 and 2.3 million in 1953. All in all, in the Soviet case, Beyrau reports that 18–19 million people passed through the Gulag between 1934 and 1953, and in the war years prisoners made up 3–4 percent of the overall Soviet labor force. The well-known exception to linear growth in the size of the Gulag was in fact the period of the war, when invalids were released from camps and penal battalions composed of released prisoners were sent to fight at the front. By contrast, a mere four thousand inmates were held in German concentration camps in 1935 and thirty thousand in 1939. But war and external racial domination directly triggered the murderous right-wing revolutionary and utopian potentialities of National Socialism. According to the figures cited by Beyrau, the total population of the twenty-four concentration camps and one thousand satellite camps in the Reich and occupied Europe is estimated between 2.5 and 3.5 million. While Forth effectively argued that we must move beyond the Nazi-Stalinist comparison alone, the sheer scale of these two systems and their importance to their respective movement-regimes demand continuing comparative attention.

With his concept of "camp worlds," Beyrau attempts an overview and comparison of the Nazi and Soviet camps that, despite the range of camps in each system, synthesizes their main features as institutions. Both were striking in the small numbers of guards and staff used to oversee large numbers of prisoners—effectively subcontracting out power to often criminal gangs. Even in what Beyrau describes as total institutions, then, genuine total control remained elusive and central authorities remained far from fully directing the space inside the barbed wire. However, those in charge certainly were instrumental in establishing the hierarchies in the camps that are the centerpiece of Beyrau's analysis. Those hierarchies in the Nazi case were primarily racial, but those with delegated authority, the "prison functionaries," had greater privileges. In the Soviet case, nationality certainly played an increasing role, and the distinction between politicals and criminals is well known.[35] In the camps of both highly ideological regimes, which became locked in mortal combat in the ideological war on the Eastern Front, Beyrau also concludes, "special conditioning in the form of ideological indoctrination played no major role." Beyrau's evocative analysis of broad similarities between Nazi and Soviet camps includes a number of specific differences: Soviet class and political classification of prisoners was "less rigid" than the Nazis' racial categorization, and in the Soviet case the status of prisoners was more "fluid." The gulf between guards and personnel and the imprisoned, so vast in the German case, was smaller in the Soviet context. Last but not least, camps explicitly dedicated to genocide or outright extermination did not exist under communism.

Mühlhahn's contribution in this volume, together with his other investigations into the Chinese penal system and camps in the twentieth century, allows us to consider Soviet influence along with several key factors shaping the formation and evolution of the Laogai. In his *Criminal Justice in China*, Mühlhahn explained that certain "broad approaches and basic concepts" were "learned from the Soviet example, even if these elements were later partly modified in China." The Soviet model, accepted by Chinese Communists as valid, was never "imitated blindly and uncritically." In Chinese penal policy, such broad approaches deriving from the Soviet model included combining incarceration with economic functions, specifically a major role for penal labor in industrialization, as well as the stress on reeducation and a functionalist approach to law.[36]

Other influences in the shape of the Laogai, however, loomed as large or larger than Soviet influence. The Chinese Communists, for one thing, fought for decades in a revolutionary movement that provided formative experiences long before they came to power. As early as the late 1920s, and then more systematically after the Long March in 1934–1935, they developed their own revolutionary courts and law.[37] Equally important were historical legacies from precommunist China. Nationalist China cooperated closely with Nazi Germany in 1933–1936; Guomindang figures were interested in Nazi camps and attempted to imitate them in China. Leading Shanghai juridical experts and criminologists looked to both Germany and the USSR, praising corrective labor in internment camps as progressive. Camp Xifeng (Alarmfire), created in 1938 and disbanded in 1946, was a major concentration camp that Mühlhahn portrays as a key precedent. It was not just the "totalitarian" powers that influenced it, moreover, since US intelligence agencies visited concentration camps in Republican China and the Guomindang relied on US intelligence cooperation. The techniques and practices of Xifeng resembled those of the later Laogai and lived on after the camp was disbanded.[38]

The results of these various influences, as Mühlhahn concludes in his chapter, were at least three major differences between the Laogai and the Gulag. First, there was no central Chinese administration of the camps equivalent to that of the NKVD. Second, practices of reeducation and ideological remolding became crucial to the way the Chinese camps were run, to a vastly greater extent than in the Soviet case. Third, and related to these other points, "frenzied mass mobilization," while finding "some analogues" in Stalinism and Soviet history, was present to a qualitatively greater extent and constituted a "decentralized method of coercion and pervasive voluntarism among both victims and victimizers." Here, once again, a comparative perspective on the Gulag leads us into thought-provoking reflections on the broader nature of Stalinism. It also raises questions about the formative decades of Chinese communism at a time when Sino-Soviet transnational and comparative history remains, for linguistic and historiographical reasons, far too rare.

Sungmin Cho adds an even rarer, indeed unique treatment of the camps of North Korea in comparative contrast with the Soviet experience. The North Korean prison camp system still exists today and, at the time of this publication, has persisted roughly twice as long as its Soviet antecedent. While some documentation from the early postwar years of North Korea is available to scholars, most of the information about this highly secretive and isolated regime comes from testimonies of those who escaped. Cho sets what is known about the North Korean camps against the history of the Soviet Gulag. While his approach is therefore by necessity synthetic and comparative, he does add some intriguing details on how the Soviet model influenced the North Koreans. When Moscow set up a communist government in Pyongyang in 1945 and dispatched an advisory group there, it included security personnel and a Soviet-born chief of North Korean security, Pang Hak-se, who took a leading role in setting up the North Korean camp system in the years that followed. In the end, Cho concludes that the economic role of the North Korean camps has been far more modest than it was in the context of Stalin-era industrialization. The North Korean camp system also seems to have diverged from the Soviet model as a result of the familial-based tenets of the ruling *juche* ideology.

Judith Pallot's chapter on the legacy of the Gulag for the post-Soviet penal system in the Russian Federation is a fitting conclusion to the volume, for it gives us tools to look at continuities in Russian penal practices stretching back before 1917 and persisting after 1991. Indeed, her long-standing interest in geographical displacement as a form of punishment links directly with Beer's chapter on the Siberian exile system, since the boundary between exile and imprisonment was blurred well before the Bolshevik revolution. Collectivism, encompassing communal housing and administratively overseen prisoner self-organization as the basis of group management of prisoners, can be traced back to the principle of collective responsibility (*krugovaia poruka*) that was a key feature of Russian serfdom. Russian regimes of incarceration were "harsh," a condition Pallot defines in explicit and comparative terms, before 1917 and after 1991. But Pallot makes clear that the specific "geographical division of labor" in the contemporary Russian penal system and the physical organization of carceral space is rooted in the 1930s–1950s.

If the Gulag in its scale, multiple functions, and integration into Stalinism's non-Gulag can be seen in many ways as exceptional or distinctive in both Russian and indeed world history, how can we explain these long-term continuities? Pallot's chapter, notable for its depth in positioning itself theoretically, considers the assumptions of modernization theory, Foucauldian discipline, and the cultural turn in penology. Tilting toward the latter in accounting for harsh punishment and other Russian-Soviet continuities, Pallot suggests that they cannot be easily explained as part of teleologies of either modernizing penal systems or waxing disciplinary power. They become more comprehensible, she suggests, if punishment is seen as rooted in cultural values and penal institutions are understood as sites of ritual performance. However, Pallot avoids making "culture" into the cause of causes, hastening to add that economic and political factors as well as technology clearly shape penal regimes.

Perhaps the most thought-provoking dimension to Pallot's work is the section on how "collectivist" practices present across the boundaries between imperial, Soviet, and post-Soviet history have been "polyvalent," or explained and recoded in very different ways across the different regimes of the nineteenth to the twenty-first centuries. This phenomenon gives insight into how similar penal practices have been justified and presented in different ways and couched in very different ideological formulations. I would add that such recodings can potentially serve to disguise continuities but also, as in the recent conservative turn in Putin's Russia, invoke and thus perpetuate "tradition." Pallot's chapter thus assumes significance for anyone grappling with the complicated conceptual questions surrounding continuity and change across the major turning points of Russian and Soviet history. It is one of the conceptual dividends resulting from this volume's attempt to juxtapose the Gulag—chronologically, geographically, and thematically.

PART 1

EVIDENCE AND INTERPRETATION

2. THE GULAG AND THE NON-GULAG AS ONE INTERRELATED WHOLE

OLEG KHLEVNIUK

TRANSLATED BY SIMON BELOKOWSKY

ONE WOULD BE hard-pressed to identify a question of the Soviet past that has been studied with the same intensity over the past few decades as the history of Stalin's Gulag.[1] Thousands of works have been written on the basis of manifold interviews, published memoirs, and archival documents from both state and private collections. The long list of thoroughly examined topics includes aspects of the Stalinist repressive political apparatus, the structure of the Gulag, the functioning of its administrative bureaucracy from the lowest rungs to the central leadership, and the principles undergirding forced labor and camp life. Many data concerning the magnitude of the camp system, its population, and indicators of production have been published and circulated. Scholars are investigating key moments in the history of the Gulag, such as prisoner uprisings. Increasingly, the object of study has become various aspects of Gulag society itself.[2]

The historiography of the Gulag is, broadly speaking, approaching the point at which we merely begin to reproduce or touch up a well-illustrated picture; one now senses a pressing need to reconsider the literature with the aim of identifying lacunae and new directions for research. Indeed, the advent of new approaches for studying the Gulag is to some extent predicated on the development of new source bases.[3] At the same time, the "archival revolution" has inevitably contributed to ever-growing specialization, and therefore much will still depend on our ability to sharpen our perspective on the most fundamental questions and problems of Gulag scholarship.

The present chapter highlights several complex questions regarding the Gulag's history. In particular, I draw attention to the task of defining the Gulag's boundaries, identifying the channels of its interaction with the broader Soviet society, and specifying the consequences of these interactions in both short- and long-term perspective. Such questions are not entirely novel; one need only recall Alexander Solzhenitsyn's journey through implicitly bounded circles of the Gulag hell or his conception of the Soviet world as bifurcated between greater and lesser zones.[4] At the same time, as they bring to bear previously unknown facts and new methods, historians are in a position to refine and even to challenge established perspectives, or at the very least to articulate new directions for research.

DEFINING BOUNDARIES

Recent archival work has contributed to a vivid and compelling picture of Soviet society under Stalin as composed of several interrelated layers. The first is the Gulag itself—a flourishing system of camps, colonies, prisons, special settlements, and other more fleeting and specialized units of isolation and forced labor. The preponderance of available data indicates that between 1930 and 1952, nearly twenty-five million people passed through the Gulag system, eighteen million to twenty million of whom were sentenced to imprisonment in camps, colonies, and prisons.[5] Meanwhile, no fewer than six million people, mostly kulaks and members of repressed nationalities, were sent into internal exile, living under conditions approaching those of the camps themselves in special settlements.[6] In addition, the Second World War saw several million Soviet citizens interned, quarantined, or subjected to forced labor.

The Gulag "population" was notable for its diversity and for an internal hierarchy that mirrored the hierarchy of Soviet society beyond the Gulag. There were inversions as well: political prisoners, many of whom occupied high positions outside the Gulag, frequently found themselves at a much lower level on the Gulag's social ladder, often yielding to common criminals.[7] The world of special settlements was similarly diverse. The groups most typically liable to deportation included peasants, Baltic and Ukrainian partisans, persecuted peoples of the North Caucusus, and city dwellers expelled during the passportization process.

The delineation of the Gulag's internal boundaries in the Stalin period and the classification of its victims pose problems that have assumed a sharply political tone in Russia over recent years. One widely influential perspective holds that the victims of the Terror include "only" the four million people persecuted for "counterrevolutionary offenses" between 1921 and 1953.[8] Does this mean that the rest—millions of prisoners—were common criminals who deserved their fate?

As a starting point for properly appreciating the true status of nonpolitical prisoners, we can invoke the conclusion of Peter Solomon, a preeminent scholar of the Soviet justice system and the politics of punishment under

Stalin. He finds that exceptionally harsh penalties "made the administration of criminal justice in the USSR less fair" generally.[9] Camps and colonies were mainly populated by those whose punishments were entirely out of proportion with their crimes or transgressions. The majority of prisoners were either common Soviet citizens made examples under demonstrative "law and order" campaigns or those who had run afoul of draconian laws on account of the grim conditions of daily life. It was particularly for these reasons that women accounted for a significant share of victims.[10] The bulk of those imprisoned for nonpolitical (*bytovye*) crimes were thus de facto political prisoners of the regime.

At the other extreme of the Soviet hierarchy were those among the notionally free population. The dearth of actual freedoms and the exceeding harshness of Soviet laws make it difficult to define this social space beyond the borders of Stalin's camps. In Jacques Rossi's lexicon the world outside of camp imprisonment was "freedom" (*volia*); to escape to freedom was to *vyskochit' na voliu*.[11] It is readily apparent that those undergoing horrific suffering in the camps would view liberation as a reprieve, an escape to freedom. Yet Rossi, like Solzhenitsyn and many others, held that the "Soviet Gulag was . . . the epitome of the regime that had wrought it. There is a reason it was said of the freed prisoner that he was being transferred from the 'little' zone to the 'great' one" (*iz "maloi" zony v "bol'shuiu"*).[12] Taking these circumstances into account, it seems more accurate to describe Soviet society outside the camps as the "non-Gulag," consisting of Soviet citizens not subject to the most extreme forms of state terror: summary and extrajudicial executions, confinement in camps, colonies, prisons, and remote exile.

The inadequacy of defining those parts of Soviet society external to the Gulag as "free" is evidenced by the miscellaneous categories of partial freedom. This was a particularly significant layer of the Soviet social hierarchy, and it is entirely appropriate to include these in the non-Gulag sphere. Between 1930 and 1952, judiciary and extrajudiciary organs issued nearly thirty million sentences (including repeat sentences for "recidivists") for punishments that fell short of imprisonment. These were largely sentences of corrective labor without confinement to a camp or colony.[13] In many cases those receiving such sentences faced grim conditions, and the punitive garnishment of wages pushed their families to the brink of starvation—not to mention the ever-present threat of the camps themselves in the case of any further brushes with the law, particularly in the case of those receiving suspended sentences.

To the category of the partially free we can add several other groups. Soviet punitive and defense organs were unusually quick to launch invasive investigations and to obtain arrest warrants even in cases where there were few prospects for a successful prosecution. Data on arrests and convictions maintained by organs of the security apparatus consistently show the former to be noticeably higher—2.3 million arrests to 1.4 million convictions over the six years beginning in 1930.[14] Police files indicate a similar propensity. In 1935 alone criminal proceedings were initiated against 2.4 million, of whom nearly 600,000 were arrested and 800,000 formally declared innocent.[15] This means that, in practice, millions of people unaccounted for by court records were nonetheless subjected to the brutality of Stalinist law enforcement, which could include time spent in custody under horrific conditions.

Several more million faced persistent discrimination based on social, political, or national criteria. Their persecution could take forms including exclusion from their fields of work, exile from major cities, or eviction from their homes. The main context of such discrimination was the practice of collective punishment (based on kinship, nationality, or class), which served as an important element of repression.[16]

Taken together, tens of millions of half-free people (those sentenced to punishments beyond imprisonment and those not sentenced but persecuted) lived in a peculiar liminal space between the Gulag and the non-Gulag. Without becoming prisoners of the Gulag proper, their experiences could approach its terror. Subject to acute material want, political discrimination, and provisional arrest, those in this category often served as the paramount objects of repression and terror and faced a particularly high risk of winding up in the Gulag itself.

The existence of such an enormous zone of half-freedom illustrates the indeterminate character of the boundaries between Gulag and non-Gulag. The haziness and permeability of these boundaries should, of course, not be taken as absolute. It is a given that life outside the camps was, under any circumstance, better than life within them. Likewise, even if purely a formality in many senses, the status of "free" citizen was preferable to prisoner status. Yet closer examination of daily life under Stalin complicates even these a priori truths.

Most important, the Gulag, just like the non-Gulag, was neither socially nor economically homogenous. There were salient differences among the Gulag's various subsystems: camps were not colonies, which in turn were not labor settlements; regimes and conditions differed between the older, established camps and newer ones more commonly susceptible to especially high death tolls. There were wide disparities, moreover, in the rights and freedoms enjoyed by prisoners of a given camp. There were also wide disparities outside the Gulag realm. City dwellers could avail themselves of privileges

TABLE 2.1. Gulag and non-Gulag rations, 1939

Ration	Peasants' consumption (grams per day)	Workers' consumption (grams per day)	Minimal rations for prisoners of labor camps and colonies (grams per day)
Bread, flour, pasta	565	549	610
Groats	36	24	100
Vegetables (including potatoes)	465	393	500
Meat	70	114	30
Fish	4	26	128
Fats (vegetable oil, butter, lard)	18.8	18	Not stipulated
Dairy	176	79	Not stipulated
Sugar & confectionary products	18.6	76	10
Eggs	3.6	3	Not stipulated

unavailable to peasants, and half-free, "socially alien" (*sotsial´no chuzhdye*) contingents of the population faced far greater discrimination than the young *vydvizhentsy* who filled the bureaucratic vacancies created by purge and terror.

It is no exaggeration to say that the more "benign" spheres of the Gulag converged with the crueler spheres of the non-Gulag. Moreover, conditions within the Gulag could, in certain cases, surpass those outside it. A well-known example involves the conditions in the special settlements of internally deported peasants. Here the skill sets and practices of former kulaks afforded them a higher standard of living than local, native peasants could enjoy.[17]

The extreme poverty of the Soviet population, especially among peasants squeezed to pay for the country's recklessly wasteful industrialization, had a decisive effect on the convergence of Gulag and non-Gulag. It was largely on account of the dire conditions faced by the peasantry that several indicators of well-being among the non-Gulag population could approach those of the Gulag. For example, we observe the relationship among Gulag and non-Gulag rations in 1939 (table 2.1).[18]

As the table indicates, daily consumption among the "free" population—in particular, peasants—converged in both volume and makeup with that of prisoners, a tendency that continued in succeeding years.

The blurred boundary between Gulag and non-Gulag further applied to the application of forced labor, not only in camps and special settlements but also in the "free" sector of the economy. From the early 1930s on, peasants became largely bound to their kolkhozes, a process that was repeated from 1940 onward with workers' industrial enterprises. To leave one's position voluntarily was to risk imprisonment as a social parasite, which, in effect, meant the enserfment of formally free workers. Among the more extreme manifestations of this system were the so-called "labor reserves" and schools of working youth, a scheme aimed at mobilizing the young for industrial work. Conditions within these institutions were exceptionally difficult and led to massive desertion despite the very real threat of imprisonment.[19]

CHANNELS OF INTERACTION

In attempting precisely to delineate the boundaries between Gulag and non-Gulag, we are forced instead to recognize their close interconnection. Residential buildings and prisons were located side by side, and the space between them was minimal in both a geographical and a legal sense. An impenetrable wall separated Gulag and non-Gulag, punctuated by legal gates and semilegal breaches. Conceding this much is merely a starting point for the historian. The main challenge is rather to understand the actual practices of interaction between Gulag and non-Gulag, as well as the consequences of these over the long and short term.

Interest in these problems has inevitably grown as basic research defining the Gulag's basic parameters has been completed. Scholars have above all sought to understand the channels through which Gulag and non-Gulag interacted, particularly by examining the release and limited reassimilation of prisoners after Stalin's death.[20] A series of important works has explored the size of prisoner releases, which were in part the product of formal and informal amnesties.[21] Per official data, nearly seven million camp prisoners were freed between 1934 and 1952 (including some who were released more than once).[22] The release figures for colonies or prisons are so far entirely unknown, but they may have been substantial (fig. 2.1). This is especially true for the colonies, which typically held prisoners sentenced to shorter terms. Likewise, many in internal exile, particularly the young, received official permission to leave their place of exile. Hundreds of thousands who did not receive such permission left illicitly.

It is apparent that the massive transfers of population out of the Gulag and

Figure 2.1. Two former Gulag inmates recognize each other based on their identical suitcases. *Source:* Screen capture from *Kholodnoe leto piatdesiat´ tret´ego* (Aleksandr Proshkin, 1987).

into the non-Gulag served as an important channel between these parts of Soviet society. As Golfo Alexopoulos notes, "The traffic through the [Gulag's] revolving door indicates that the gulag and non-gulag worlds regularly came into contact, and that Stalin's penal labor system affected the larger system in many ways."[23] Alan Barenberg came to similar conclusions in his work on the phenomenon of *zazonniki*, prisoners permitted to live outside the camp zone.[24] Sanctioned far more often by local officials than by central authorities, this practice was widespread at several moments in the Gulag's history. On one hand, it was motivated by narrow economic interests. On the other hand, it represented a legal ratification of the tight links between Gulag and non-Gulag.

Zazonniki most fully represented the Gulag's prioritization of economic interests over political and regime interests. Their status resembled that of the so-called "deconvoyed" prisoners (*bezkonvoinye*), who resided within the camp but worked at various production sites beyond its borders.[25] Various studies of the economics of forced labor have focused on the widespread phenomenon of forced laborers who worked alongside freely hired workers, in many enterprises under the direction of the NKVD/MVD and other ministries. In 1950, for example, the MVD assigned a full quarter of camp

Figure 2.2. Inmates and free laborers at the construction site of the Chum-Labitnangy railway, 1954. *Source:* Memorial Society.

and colony prisoners to labor on projects outside its direct purview.[26] The flow of labor in the opposite direction was likewise significant. For the first half of the same year, MVD industrial enterprises and construction projects employed 662,000 free laborers, who comprised nearly 40 percent of their overall labor force, not including camp staff (fig. 2.2).[27]

This last figure serves to remind us that a major channel of interaction between Gulag and non-Gulag was the noteworthy share of the Soviet population serving the penal camp system in a civilian capacity. Facing adverse conditions in distant, barely habitable regions, they occupied one of the lowest layers of Soviet society. It is no accident that, on occasion, disgraced or corrupt Cheka (political police) officials and bureaucrats were appointed as heads of camp subdivisions. Camp guards, too, had to be strategically deployed, and shortages persisted, leading to creative solutions like the *samo-okhrana*, the use of nonpolitical prisoners as guards. Guards were party to a particular sort of professional and life experience that reinforced instincts toward violence and the abuse of authority and furthermore encouraged the acceptance of the criminal world's conception of "maintaining order" (*podderzhanie poriadka*).[28] A simple product of moral hazard amid the absence of incentives for competent execution or professional growth, these phenomena can be interpreted as the social consequences of Gulag/non-Gulag interaction.

Robust channels of connection between Gulag and non-Gulag, allowing tens of millions to move between them and their exploitation for reasons of economic need, suggest that the Gulag had significant influence on Soviet society, as well as its political and economic systems. The main difficulty in applying this principle lies in the need to identify concrete parameters and attributes by which to assess the influence of the Gulag.

THE GULAG AS MODEL

Between the 1930s and the 1950s, the Gulag became a critical component in the development of the Soviet system. This point is best evidenced by the rapid expansion of forced labor throughout the Soviet economy, which suggests that the Gulag economy was thoroughly integrated into the broader Soviet economic mechanism. At Stalin's death, the MVD dominated the construction industry and was responsible for no less than 10 percent of all capital investment in the USSR. The agency consolidated control of the production of all gold, silver, platinum, and cobalt in the postwar period and, by 1952, produced 70 percent of the country's tin as well as a third of its nickel. For 1953, MVD projects were slated to produce 15 percent of the Soviet logging industry's output.[29]

A sizable unfree labor contingent allowed the Soviet economy to maintain its mobilizing character. The state administration and government ministries regularly availed themselves of prisoner labor to address urgent needs in inhospitable environments. This widespread use of coerced labor confounded economic stimuli, encouraged despotic methods of control, and even retarded the growth of infrastructure: camp barracks appeared instead of civilian housing, camp clinics stood in the place of an integrated system of public health, and so on. Furthermore, the labor force itself was degraded by mass arrests and executions. Millions of men and women of working age had their lives artificially shortened or were disabled. This number included a large contingent of skilled workers, few of whom were employed in their professions (as in the so-called *sharashki*, laboratories of prisoner-scientists); the engineer wielding a shovel was a common phenomenon in NKVD/MVD enterprises. Such misapplication of vast labor resources could only slow the pace of industrial expansion. Finally, the use of forced labor was a key factor in grandiose but economically unfeasible projects, which were sometimes abandoned partway during construction. Whether ultimately completed or not, these were the most vivid markers of the degree to which both the Gulag economy and the broader Soviet economy inefficiently exploited labor.[30]

As the existing literature has noted, the Gulag was the principal instrument and in large measure a continuation of the Soviet model of internal

colonization.[31] The Gulag system inspired a particular strategy of colonization in the broader Soviet periphery, as the economic and social infrastructure of distant regions developed in the framework of large camp complexes.
These regions were, relatively speaking, sparsely populated, and camp prisoners quickly became a significant share of the local labor force. At the end
of the 1930s, for example, prisoners and their guards constituted approximately a quarter of the population in the Komi and Karelian republics and
up to 20 percent of the population of the Far East.[32] Freed prisoners likewise
padded the population of these regions, in large measure as a function of
discriminatory policy, which banned former prisoners from living in several
oblasts and persecuted others for leaving the region where they had been
confined. In addition, recent research indicates that areas surrounding camp
complexes represented a more hospitable environment for prisoner reac-
climation, both prior to and after Stalin's death.[33] As a result, "gray zones"
constituting interim spaces between the Gulag and the non-Gulag tended
to develop around major camp clusters in Siberia, the Far East, and the
northeastern part of the Soviet Union (the Komi and Karelian republics and
Arkhangel´sk oblast). Few studies have focused on such zones in the Stalin
period, but demographic data indicate that these were socially underdeveloped regions that experienced high rates of mortality among both infants
and the general population.[34]

Although the concentrations of former prisoners were most dense in far-
flung regions of Russia, harsh laws meant that millions from all parts of the
country became implicated in the subculture of the Gulag. The vast Gulag
contributed significantly to the increase of crime across the Soviet Union: for
example, to "recidivism" among those who had been previously sentenced
to long stretches for petty crimes committed in the context of hardship and
privation. The scale and nature of organized crime in the USSR, as well as
its connections to both Gulag and non-Gulag, require further investigation,
though this is made difficult by the near-total inaccessibility of MVD documents.[35] For now, we can say with certainty that the many who had been
freed or had escaped from the Gulag (chief among them kulaks) greatly
worried the Stalinist leadership. This was a significant motivator of periodic
purges, including the mass operations of 1937–1938.[36]

Cruel and arbitrary repression resulted in a conflicted and even hostile
relationship between the state and a large share of Soviet society. A large segment of the population viewed Soviet punitive politics as unjust. For example,
the Presidium of the Supreme Soviet elicited an irate reaction with its 4 June
1947 decrees on embezzlement of government and private property. Those
decrees prescribed exceedingly harsh punishments for relatively trivial trans-

gressions, many of which were precipitated by material want in the context of postwar destruction. It is precisely the deprivation that is invoked in surviving letters to the Soviet leadership. A. E. Bagno, a pupil at a village school, wrote openly of the difficulties his family experienced in a letter to Stalin:

> You won't steal anything here, but you also can't live without outside means. And now two *kolkhoznitsy* . . . what, did they go stealing to support some kind of plush lifestyle? Maybe their children won't have anything to eat this winter. And the kolkhoz will give you only a tiny bit. Yes, maybe if they held the status of "elevated conditions" [*povyshennyi byt*], then it would be a different matter entirely. Maybe give them ten years. But in this case, where they were basically forced into it, to give them ten years? It's just not right. Create bearable conditions and then go putting people on trial.

The contents of this letter along with similar examples were reported to Stalin without any result.[37]

Other circumstances of mass consciousness helped habituate the public to state violence and legal nihilism, cultivating contempt for law enforcement and judicial systems, as well as passivity within Soviet society. These traits of the average Soviet citizen predetermined the development of the country in the decades that followed, both before and after the fall of socialism. In January 1934 a correspondent for *Krest'ianskaia gazeta* described such a conversation in a note to his editors: "On the road to Leningrad, I came to talking with some kolkhozniks. I was amazed that they do not consider being sentenced *na prinudilovku* [to forced labor] at all shameful. They continuously made statements to the effect of, 'I just returned *s prinudilovki*,' 'I was sent out *na prinudilovku*,' and so on, as if *prinudilovka* is some kind of sanatorium or resort."[38] Furthermore, Elena Zubkova has described the idolization of the recidivist criminal in postwar youth culture.[39] A contemporary scholar, John Round, has encountered the long-term effects of state violence in conversation with former prisoners of the Magadan camps: "Despite almost half a century passing since their release, interviewees still feel that other sectors of society despise them, and they remain extremely fearful of the government. They try to live as anonymous a life as possible, interacting little with government structure."[40]

Mass repressions based on nationality and the tragic experience of internal deportation faced by some Soviet peoples had similarly long-term effects on interethnic relations. It is widely held that "the revenge of the past," including the Stalinist legacy, was a significant factor in the acute interethnic conflicts of the 1980s and ultimately the collapse of the USSR.[41] Interethnic conflict, including armed violence amid the growing discontent of "punished peoples" in exile, was a characteristic feature of the Stalinist system, and a reflection of its crisis nature.[42] The reform of Soviet nationalities policy after Stalin's death managed to alleviate building tension, but it could not remove the underlying contradictions precipitated by the ethnically motivated purges of the 1930s through the early 1950s.

GULAG STRATA

Ultimately, the Stalinist Terror and the development of a vast Gulag gave rise to a new structure of Soviet society. This was a distinctive hierarchy of stratified layers, differentiated in status by the level of government violence to which they were subjected. We can sketch a provisional schematic of this structure:

- those imprisoned and internally exiled;

- those sentenced to punishments other than imprisonment or exile, as well as those under investigation or subject to short-term arrest;

- the "suspect"—relatives of the purged; those subject to discrimination on the basis of class or nationality but able to avoid the Gulag;

- those who had avoided the Gulag in one way or another but who were not party to any obvious social or material privilege;

- the "*vydvizhentsy* of the Terror"—those who had benefited from the purges of the cadres but were not directly party to the planning or execution of the Terror; and

- the prosecutors of the Terror—those staffing the penal system and other rungs of the party-state implicated in the planning and/or execution of the Terror.

Interactions and opposition among these strata are observable over the ensuing decades in the sociopolitical evolution of Soviet and Russian society. Exerting a degrading influence on Soviet politics and morality, the Gulag experience could in certain circumstances become a significant factor in the triumph over Stalinism. The duty of the witness to demand justice and warn of peril became a raison d'être for many of the Gulag's victims.[43] Such testimonies were the strongest, most emotional, and most convincing argument that anti-Stalinists could wield in the fight for the future of their country.

Of course, the possibility of bearing witness depended on the overall political situation. The Stalinist state expended great effort to ensure that knowledge of the Gulag's horrors did not travel beyond its limits. Prisoners' letters were subject to censorship. Visits by relatives were severely limited and tightly controlled. The fear of witnesses' testimony was among the most significant reasons leading the authorities to isolate former prisoners to the maximum practical extent. Having completed their sentence, they were barred from settling in major cities and other special locales, exiled to faraway regions, and/or kept under constant surveillance.

The isolation and punishment of those who had witnessed the Gulag's enormity undoubtedly had its own consequences. For many years, a habit of silence prevailed among former prisoners. In suppressing what they could of their frightful experiences, many attempted above all to protect themselves and their children: "They have lived in hiding and silence for almost seventy years. One of the participants of the interviews emphasised that she had not told anybody, not even her own children, about her experiences," writes Michael Kaznelson of his 2003 interviews with the children of Siberian internal exile.[44]

The possibility of bearing witness greatly expanded after the death of Stalin. Social activism among former political prisoners was a significant element of Khrushchev's thaw. It is true that official criticism of Stalinism in the 1950s and 1960s had its own political motivations, but for former prisoners of the Gulag it nonetheless served as a sort of social recrimination. Such an orientation could count on support from the countless victims of Stalin's despotism and their relatives, irrespective of whether they had personally been arrested or imprisoned. Although the state continued to support the rehabilitation of victims of Stalin's Terror so long as they remained faithful to the Party and the tenets of socialism, it was difficult to contain the flow of testimonials and revelations within a narrow framework of the acceptable.[45] The appearance of Solzhenitsyn's *Gulag Archipelago*, based on a significant number of unorthodox memoirs, demonstrated the long-term futility of Soviet censorship. The testimony of former prisoners shaped several generations' conception of Stalinism and facilitated criticism that gradually became more and more radical; Stalinism increasingly seemed a manifestation of socialism, and Lenin's use of terror was compared with Stalin's.

The swing of the political pendulum back toward re-Stalinization occurred simultaneously with de-Stalinization and was boosted by Khrushchev's removal.[46] To a significant extent, re-Stalinization was rooted in the interests and perspectives of those who had benefited from political terror without perpetrating it directly. It was this group in particular that reached the heights of power between the early 1960s and the early 1980s. Not intending to rehabilitate Stalinism or mass terror fully, they preferred to minimize its excesses and to emphasize the difficulty of building a new society in a hostile geopolitical environment. This formula was entirely satisfactory to those who had actually executed the Terror. There are also few signs that this "quiet re-Stalinization" generated many protests from those who had managed to avoid the brunt of the Stalinist Terror. The predictable authoritarian evolution of the Soviet system, even without bursts of state violence, cultivated indifference toward the crimes of the past. From among these various groups, a community of Gulag apologists developed.

Yet the seeds of misgiving sown by witnesses of the Gulag sprouted in the late 1980s in a way that easily surpassed the experience under Khrushchev.[47] Mass rehabilitations and the increased opportunities for anti-Stalinist forces to organize created a new situation epitomized by the founding of the Memorial Society. The ranks of this movement were filled not only by traditionally active former political prisoners but also by those representing the wider range of victims of Stalinist and post-Stalinist terror. The losers of this turn in the fight for memory were both those who had benefited professionally from the Terror and especially those who were responsible for its prosecution. Several significant scandals during the perestroika period were fed by revelations concerning former Chekists (members of the political police) living out their lives under comfortable conditions and in high esteem.

Gulag apologists were afforded their own opportunity for revanche in the first decades of the present century. The multifarious socioeconomic factors contributing to the return of "soft authoritarianism" are in themselves a topic for close study. As far as the present chapter is concerned, we should emphasize that a contributing factor to this turn is particular broadly held historical conceptions about Stalinism and the Gulag.[48] Despite their diversity and distinct nuances, these viewpoints can be understood with reference to the schematic stratification of Soviet society outlined above.

The mind-set of Gulag survivors and other victims of state terror is evident in an unbroken legacy of condemning Stalinism. At the same time, contemporary Russia also reveals an inert indifference toward the topics of terror and the Gulag. This indifference probably reflects a broader fatigue from political and emotional trials, as well the retreat of Stalinism into the past as the years elapse and thus its growing irrelevance to the practical concerns of a modern Russian citizen. In terms of the stratification noted above, those holding these views may be from families that neither suffered significantly nor benefited substantially from the Terror.

The Terror's *vydvizhentsy*—those who benefited from but did not perpetrate the Terror—can be identified with popular theories of "Stalinist modernization" that recognize the many victims as an unfortunate fact but insist

Figure 2.3. Celebration of seventy-five years of Usol´lag. *Source:* Frame enlargement from televised news report, YouTube.com.

that repression was historically necessary. The perspectives of those directly responsible for the Terror and perhaps a share of the *vydvizhentsy* are represented by countless examples of simple apologia. Calculated Gulag denial in contemporary Russia takes two major forms. The first is the political-propagandistic, declaring Stalin's course to have been entirely correct. The second might be termed the bureaucratic-parochial and argues that Stalin's Gulag was a regular penitentiary system, while emphasizing the heroic feats of the Soviet penal system both in the fight against crime and in the economic sphere.[49]

Adherents to this parochial interpretation of the Gulag in modern Russia include, above all, historians and bureaucrats with ties to the Russian Ministry of Internal Affairs and penitentiary system. Among the most recent examples of this mind-set was the celebration in Perm´ oblast of the seventy-fifth anniversary of the founding of the Usol´skii Camp in 1938, which was designed to facilitate mass punishment (fig. 2.3). The Usol´skii Camp was a symbol of the Terror; prisoners at this hastily organized camp were subject to particularly harsh conditions, and they died and became debilitated at rates far exceeding Gulag averages.[50] Disregarding these well-known historical facts, the current leadership of the Usol´skii Camp and the administration of the Federal Prison Service for Perm´ oblast celebrated the camp's anniversary with a triumphant slogan, "In January 1938 at the Usol´skii ITL NKVD SSSR, traditions were instituted that persist in our times. These are loyalty to the Motherland, mutual aid, and respect for veterans. Usol'lag is thousands of miles of road, hundreds of parcels of forestland, more than sixty thousand staff, workers, and employees laboring over a span of seventy-five years; it is schools, day care centers, clubs."[51]

For many years, the thesis holding that the Gulag was a formative element of the Soviet system was premised on its enormous size, and on the fact that it contained millions or even tens of millions of prisoners. In the last two decades, in connection with growing archival access, it has become possible to reach a relatively high degree of clarity on this matter: at its greatest extent, the Gulag imprisoned about 5.5 million. Does this mean that Gulag terror did not play such a significant role within the Stalinist system after all? In fact, new evidence indicates that Stalin's Terror and Soviet state violence were much more complex in structure than historians previously appreciated. Along with the mass executions and confinement in camps, millions were internally deported, subject to temporary arrests and interrogations without being sentenced, and so forth. Beyond this, tens of millions were sentenced to forced labor outside the context of imprisonment, and various groups were subject to persistent discrimination and lived under the perpetual threat of arrest (e.g., suspect national groups or relatives of "enemies of the people"). Taken together, this means a significant proportion of the Soviet population was affected by repression in some form.

The expansive scope and complex structure of state violence likewise had manifold and complex consequences for the subsequent evolution of the Soviet system; these can be roughly divided into short- and long-term. At its height between the 1930s and the 1950s, Stalin's Gulag exerted significant influence over the development of almost all spheres of Soviet society. The many examples of this influence, only a few of which are discussed in this chapter, afford us an opportunity to study the channels by which the Gulag penetrated the non-Gulag and, in turn, to understand the parameters of their close interconnections. The widespread use of prisoner and deportee labor supported the vigorous top-down involvement of the state and its violence in the Soviet economy. By casting a wide web of camps and colonies across the Soviet landmass, the state could far more easily employ violence with the aim of maintaining social stability (despite the catastrophic collapse in the quality of life). As is often the case, the Terror limited the country's intellectual potential, deforming public morality and encouraging what might be termed adverse social selection—since within systems built around violence, the cruel and indifferent tend to have a higher chance at success and survival.

The gradual dismantling of the Gulag and Stalin's broader apparatus of repression after his death was a necessary but not a sufficient condition for coming to terms with the legacy of Stalinism. Having overcome despotism, the country remained authoritarian, and many of the social effects stemming from terror and the Gulag turned out to be deeply entrenched. The creation of a hefty and intricate penal apparatus, unrestrained by law in its terror, proved to have significant, lasting effects on mass consciousness. The public was desensitized to acts of despotism and state violence and conditioned to accept arbitrary and pernicious limitations on its freedom. Over the long term, the boundaries between Gulag and non-Gulag reveal their conditional character and their permeability.

DESTRUCTIVE LABOR CAMPS
Rethinking Solzhenitsyn's Play on Words

GOLFO ALEXOPOULOS

ALEXANDER SOLZHENITSYN HAS been called "one of the great truth-tellers of the twentieth century," and a breaker of the Soviet regime's "blockade of silence."[1] The writer who first revealed to his countrymen and the world the inhumanity of the Soviet penal labor system was also a master of language. Like Jacques Rossi, whose *Gulag Handbook* exposed the camps' alternative conceptual universe, Solzhenitsyn focused attention on the Gulag lexicon.[2] He rejected the Stalinist term for the slave labor system, corrective labor camps (*ispravitel'no-trudovye lageria*), in favor of his own term: destructive labor camps (*istrebitel'no-trudovye lageria*).[3] This pun or play on Soviet words stressed that Gulag labor was more lethal than corrective. According to Solzhenitsyn, "the camps were designed for destruction" (*izobreteny lageria—na istreblenie*).[4] The writer highlighted the Gulag's destructive elements, like the inhumane transport of prisoners and the draconian rules governing food and work. Solzhenitsyn did not have access to official Soviet sources, yet the archives support his assertions regarding the Gulag's destructive capacity. I argue that Stalin's Gulag constituted an institution of extreme physical exploitation at its core, and that human exploitation in the camps was destructive by design. Moreover, as the present work illustrates, the system of physical exploitation in the camps grew more severe from the 1930s to the 1950s. Under Stalin, the Gulag produced an enormous population of prisoners on the verge of death, the so-called goners (*dokhodiagi*). To unburden the camps, conserve resources, and artificially reduce Gulag mortality rates, the Stalinist leadership routinely released these nearly dead inmates. Not only was Stalin's Gulag destructive, but it deliberately concealed its destructive capacity.

Gulag literature catalogues the causes of human suffering and mortality, but scholars do not generally argue that the Stalinist camps were designed for destruction.[5] We know that the Soviet security police (OGPU/NKVD/MVD), which managed the arrest, deportation, and detention of millions in labor camps and settlements, was distinctly uninterested in preserving human life. Nonetheless, no plan of destruction has emerged from our initial reading of declassified state and party documents. Thus, although historians have emphasized the brutality of the system, few have argued that the Gulag was deliberately destructive.[6] More common is the view that the Gulag represented an institution of mass death but not mass murder. Scholars have demonstrated that people died from the brutal journey in sealed railcars to their remote camps; the hostile Arctic environment; and the neglect, incompetence, and cruelty of camp officials and fellow inmates. Memoirs and the historical literature underscore the nonsystemic causes of Gulag mortality: deaths resulting from underdevelopment (poor sanitation and infrastructure), violent criminal gangs, shortages and theft of food, sadistic guards, or factors external to the system, such as the harsh climate and war. Taken together, these do not produce an image of a labor camp system that was destructive by design. Although Solzhenitsyn remains the towering figure in Gulag studies, his analysis of "destructive labor camps" has not been widely embraced in the historical literature.

There are many reasons why. As noted, no statement from the Stalinist leadership has emerged that expresses a high-level intention or state-sponsored plan to destroy prisoners; quite the contrary, we have found many official complaints concerning elevated rates of illness and mortality and attempts by party leaders to incentivize forced labor and improve productivity through material rewards. Moreover, the Nazi-Soviet comparison looms large. There exists a legitimate desire to avoid false equivalencies between the Nazi extermination camps and the Soviet labor camps.[7] Moreover, a vast memoir literature appears to underscore the survivability of the Soviet camps; some memoirists, like Eugenia Ginzburg, endured nearly two decades in detention.[8] The Gulag maintained hospitals and clinics, and camp doctors were not tasked with experimental and "mercy" killing, as in the Nazi case.[9] Rather, many camp doctors viewed themselves as healers and often struggled to improve prisoners' chances of survival.[10] The NKVD-Gulag leadership regularly criticized camp administrators when illness and mortality rates exceeded mandated norms. In addition, the Stalinist regime invested greatly in the message of rehabilitation through labor or reforging (*perekovka*) in its "corrective labor camps."[11] The serious economic functions of the Stalinist camps seem to belie any notion that these institutions were designed for destruction.[12] Why would an economic system deliberately destroy its own capital? Such objections and contrary evidence have caused many to disregard Solzhenitsyn's analysis, as if the writer exaggerated purposefully, perhaps for dramatic effect, in his "experiment in literary investigation." Yet open archives enable us to turn our attention from nonsystemic to systemic violence and to reconsider the Gulag's destructive design. Forty years after the initial publication of the *Gulag Archipelago*, it is time to revisit Solzhenitsyn.

As I demonstrate at greater length in my forthcoming book (from which this chapter is derived), the above paradoxes of the Gulag regime do not necessarily undermine the validity of Solzhenitsyn's argument. Stalin created a vast hierarchical network of labor camps and colonies that functioned not unlike a developed system of slavery. Individuals were managed as commodities and exploited for their labor. Although camp administrators had some incentive to preserve human capital, this desire largely existed under conditions of labor scarcity. In an environment where camps received a constant influx of more able-bodied prisoners, there was little incentive to preserve the lives of existing inmates. The Gulag Sanitation Department or health service, grossly understaffed and relatively powerless in the camp hierarchy, was constrained by quotas on the number of allowable sick and nonworking prisoners. Moreover, memoirists who survived years in the camps attributed their survival to indoor jobs. They worked as doctors, nurses, artists, or accountants and did not experience heavy physical labor (mining, logging, or construction) for extended periods of time. In its orders and directives the NKVD-Gulag may have urged camps to preserve human capital, but the Stalinist leadership exerted much stronger countervailing pressures. Camps had to minimize costs, maximize economic production, and meet very high quotas for working prisoners.

The Gulag represented a system of human exploitation and institutionalized violence and epitomized what Slavoj Žižek has called objective, systemic, anonymous violence, inherent in the normal state of things.[13] The dehumanization and exploitation of Gulag prisoners constituted the normal state of things. One cannot understand the Gulag fully without appreciating the centrality of its exploitative function. Gulag scholars have examined eruptions of camp violence such as inmate strikes, clashes between ethnic groups, hardened criminals preying on politicals, the willful neglect of children, and the abuse of women.[14] My work sheds light on the Gulag's systemic violence, which was not episodic but relentless and arguably more consequential in its impact on human suffering. Gulag health records expose an elaborate regime of acute physical exploitation, one that ensured prisoners would be exhaustively used up or thoroughly wrung out. This exploitation regime was common to all camps across the vast Gulag system. To be sure, there were differences in implementation. Some camps proved more deadly than others, and some commanders more sadistic than others. Nonetheless, the system of physical exploitation established by the Stalinist leadership applied to all camps. It is this common operating system that is the focus of the present work.

Unlike the camps under Vladimir Lenin or Leonid Brezhnev, Stalin's Gulag was in many ways less a concentration camp than a forced labor camp and less a prison system than a system of slavery. Throughout the Stalin years, counterrevolutionary offenders or political prisoners constituted a minority population. Ordinary Soviet courts, not the notorious secret police, condemned most Gulag prisoners. Peasants and workers who constituted petty criminal offenders (*ukazniki, bytoviki*) represented the majority of prisoners, the backbone of Stalin's prison labor force.[15] If we examine the regime of human exploitation in the Stalinist camps, then the Gulag resembles New World slavery, with its routine dehumanization and institutionalized violence.[16] The total exploitation of prisoners' labor represented one of the Gulag's primary functions in the Stalin years. As Oleg Khlevniuk has explained: "for leaders not concerned with morality the advantages of forced labor were indisputable. Exploitation of prisoners was a natural element of an economic system aimed at extensive growth at any cost . . . the possibility of its unlimited exploitation, including working people to death, was highly valued by the top political leaders and economic managers."[17]

Iosif Stalin used the Gulag to construct new cities and hydroelectric dams and to acquire exportable and profitable resources, such as gold, nickel, timber, coal, aluminum, and copper. The Gulag system generated tons of raw materials and vast construction projects, yet no less systematically the camp regime destroyed prisoners through exhaustive labor and punitive starvation rations. Moreover, the Stalinist regime concealed the Gulag's destructive capacity and conserved resources by systematically releasing emaciated and disabled prisoners. As Alexander Etkind explains, "Solzhenitsyn understood [the camp's] functioning by analogy with the body, which cannot exist without getting rid of its waste products; thus the gulag developed a means by ejecting 'its principal form of waste,' the goners."[18] The unloading (*razgruzka*) and medical discharge (*aktirovanie*) of the camps' *dokhodiagi* served to reduce costs and lower mortality rates. The Gulag physically destroyed prisoners and then discarded them en masse.

THE HUMAN BEING AS RAW MATERIAL

In the Stalinist labor camp system, people were managed, utilized, and discarded as capital inputs in a production process. Gulag administrators needed people who could perform hard manual labor in logging, mining, and construction, so they examined the bodies of prisoners for their fitness. The labor of prisoners proved highly mobile and efficient, for inmates could be directed to inhospitable locations and forced to do work that would not attract civilian laborers. As Paul Gregory explains, prisoners constituted about one in five construction workers in the Soviet Union in 1940 and 1951, and represented roughly 40 percent of laborers in nickel and copper mining, 70 percent in tin mining, and a staggering 85–100 percent of all Soviet labor in gold, diamond, and platinum mining.[19] The Stalinist camps sought the maximum labor utilization of prisoners for industrial development, as the Soviet leader insisted—to overtake and outstrip the advanced capitalist countries.

Gulag laborers represented critical capital inputs in the country's industrialization plan. According to Solzhenitsyn, the Stalinist leadership viewed the prisoner as a commodity (*tovar*) or as human raw material (*chelovecheskoe syr´e*).[20] Gulag prisoners were assessed for their muscle. Gustaw Herling described how "the chief of the Yercevo camp section . . . with a smile of satisfaction felt the biceps, shoulders, and backs of the new arrivals."[21] The Soviet security police registered prisoners as criminals and state enemies but also documented the bodies of inmates to determine who was fit for physical labor (*godnye k fizicheskomu trudu*). As soon as prisoners entered the camps, they were subjected to the medical examination (*meditsinskoe osvidetel´stvovanie*) and assigned to formal categories of physical labor capability (*kategoriia fizicheskoi trudosposobnosti*).[22] With the emergence of the Stalinist camps, the task of determining prisoners' physical labor capability ceased being the sole responsibility of physicians, as was the case in Lenin's concentration camp system.[23] This represents a powerful symbol of Stalin's break with the past.

Under Stalin, the production authorities at the camps had a greater say over health policy than the doctors themselves. Gulag officials in charge of production led the medical-labor commission (*vrachebno-trudovaia komis-siia*), which assigned the categories of physical labor. The head or assistant head of the camp division or camp section served as head of the medical-labor commission. Representatives from the accounting and distribution unit (*uchetno-raspredelitel´naia chast´*), the camp's main industrial section, and the medical staff also had a voice on the commission. However, certification of a prisoner's health (*akt o sostoianii zdorov´ia*) was issued by camp administrators and only confirmed by the head of the sanitation section (*sanchast´*) and the attending physician.[24] The OGPU/NKVD/MVD bosses in charge of production largely controlled the health assessments of prisoners' bodies.

Gulag survivors say relatively little about the general medical examination and the assignment of categories of physical labor capability. Scholars have called attention to such omissions in the testimonies of former prisoners. According to Leona Toker, ex-prisoners maintained certain silences and did not describe the worst of their Gulag experiences: "though Gulag memoirists have witnessed atrocities that they could never have imagined, there usually remains some 'untidy spot' where they fear to tread, some Orwellian room 'one-oh-one.' Each author is reluctant to face some special type of suffering, depravity, or horror. . . . This is one of the reasons Gulag memoirs are never felt to be self-sufficient, finished works."[25] The reluctance of many Gulag survivors to speak of the routine medical examination appears to reflect the exam's deeply degrading and humiliating quality. A former prisoner and camp doctor described how medical examinations and the assignment of categories of physical labor capability were done visually, without medical devices: "among the deciding factors in the examination were skin elasticity and the layer of fat under the skin. Therefore they always pinched our buttocks. The certification process constituted an inhumane and humiliating spectacle. . . . The prisoners stripped naked and lined up in long rows."[26]

In Stalin's Gulag, prisoners were worked to the point of utter depletion. The Stalinist leadership may not have planned to exterminate its camp prisoners, but it intended to extract all available energy, to physically exploit prisoners to the maximum degree possible. As Mark Mazower wrote regarding Nazi prison laborers: "like Hitler himself, German business never saw them as a scarce or valuable resource, still less as human beings to be nurtured and preserved. Rather they were cheap commodities to be worked until they were worn out."[27] Stalin, no less than Hitler, believed in exhaustive labor. In a letter to Lavrentii Beria one observer captured the goal of Gulag bosses: "to wring out [*vyzhat´*] more use for the government from [the camp population]."[28] This implied the maximum exploitation of prisoners at each stage of their declining health. In May 1939 Gulag leaders asserted, "all invalids in the camps or colonies who are able to work in some sort of job must be utilized."[29] A woman who served her sentence at a camp in Kazakhstan in the late 1930s described how severely ill prisoners who were unable to get out of bed were given work that they could do lying down.[30] The Stalinist leadership insisted on the "maximum utilization" of prisoners. A former Gulag boss described the perception of the central administration of his camp, Pechorlag: "the plan for constructing the rail line was a sacred matter. . . . The feeling was: You can do it all. Just work each and every prisoner as hard as you can."[31] As Solzhenitsyn noted, "the supreme law of the Archipelago" was "to squeeze everything out of a prisoner."[32]

PHYSICAL EXPLOITATION AND THE LIST OF ILLNESSES

The Gulag's system of "labor utilization" and "physical labor capability" exposes the severity of human exploitation in the Stalinist camps. On 3 February 1931 the first boss of Stalin's Gulag and soon the director of the White Sea-Baltic Sea Canal project, L. I. Kogan, issued new instructions on the exploitation of prisoners, including redesigned categories of physical labor.[33] Guidelines on how to identify prisoners' physical labor classification were drafted by Isaak Ginzburg, the Gulag's Sanitation Department director.[34] Category 1 referred to labor that was "valuable [polnotsennaia] and fit to perform any kind of productive physical labor." Category 2 applied to the "defective [nepolnotsennaia] workforce with reduced capacity for unskilled physical labor; fit for skilled physical labor according to his profession." Category 3 physical labor was reserved for "invalids who are fit for light forms of physical labor and complete invalids who are not capable of any kind of work."[35] Lynne Viola describes a similar system of labor classification for kulak laborers living in the special settlements in the early 1930s.[36]

The Gulag Sanitation Department's "list of illnesses for early release" (perechen' boleznei po uslovno-dosrochnomu osvobozhdeniiu)—hereafter, the List of Illnesses—provides the clearest evidence of Gulag policy to "wring out" the camp population. The List of Illnesses indicated that the labor of even severely ailing prisoners must be exploited, and that only the most depleted "human raw material" could be released early as "incurables." The List of Illnesses is a creation of the Stalinist camp system.[37] It told camp officials how to assign prisoners to the three categories of physical labor capability. In particular, the document focused on the lowest tier or category 3—"invalid, fit to perform light forms of physical labor or complete invalid, unable to do any kind of work." Prisoners could be classified as invalids only if they suffered from the most severe ailments, such as "clearly pronounced senile infirmity and decrepitude," "organic illnesses of the heart," "extremely large hernias that inhibit walking," and pulmonary tuberculosis involving "impaired functions of the heart and lungs and sharply diminished appetite."[38] The middle category of physical labor capability applied to prisoners with only "reduced capacity for unskilled physical labor," yet these inmates were not healthy. Category 2 included inmates with incurable nutritional disorders or malnutrition, heart disease, pronounced emphysema, anemia, tuberculosis, severe forms of gonorrhea, and progressive muscular atrophy, as well as inmates who experienced "movement impeded by malformations, chronic disease, or a curvature or other changes in the shape of the pelvis." Category 2 also applied to persons with "incurable illnesses, significant damage to and defects of the bones and soft tissue of the face, tongue, palate, nose, larynx, windpipe, throat, or esophagus, accompanied by impaired functions that are important for life." Such were the inmates believed to possess only a reduced capacity for heavy physical labor, according to the Stalinist leadership. Category 1 inmates considered capable of performing all forms of physical labor were not necessarily healthy, either. The Gulag's "valuable" workforce included those with milder forms of bronchial asthma, heart trouble, tuberculosis, benign tumors, and many other ailments.[39]

Classifications did not depend on the presence of illness, for the health of all prisoners was severely compromised. Rather, ascribed physical labor categories in Stalin's Gulag reflected the perceived severity of prisoners' ailments. In general, illnesses described as "treatable" would place a prisoner in category 2, "reduced capacity for unskilled physical labor," while more severe ailments would result in a category 3 or invalid ascription. For example, prisoners with severe malnutrition such as pellagra were category 2 if the illness appeared "significant but curable."[40] Those blind in one eye were considered category 2, while completely blind prisoners were classified as category 3 or invalids. The List of Illnesses reveals that many of the most ailing prisoners were forced to continue working. The Gulag assigned severely disabled prisoners to perform "work for invalids."[41] Prisoners had to continue working even as their health declined. As Steven Barnes writes, "brutality was itself part and parcel of the ideology of labor in the Gulag."[42]

Three simple categories failed to capture the full extent of Stalin's emaciated prison labor force. In the course of the 1930s the Gulag generated more "categories of physical labor capability" for its sick and disabled workforce. Inmates less capable of heavy physical labor were assigned to "medium physical labor." The weakest inmates, who once occupied a single category, were now divided into two categories—those capable of light forms of labor and invalids. Four categories of physical labor capability emerged by the late 1930s—inmates capable of heavy physical labor, medium physical labor, light physical labor, and not work-capable or invalid.[43] At the same time, there appears to have been little uniformity in the categories prior to the end of the Second World War. The number of severely ill and emaciated prisoners increased sharply following the 1939 Soviet invasion of Poland and the 1941 Nazi assault on the Soviet Union. Like the civilian Soviet population, Gulag prisoners increasingly experienced starvation-related diseases.[44] As a result, new physical labor categories were generated to capture the growing population of Stalin's emaciated Gulag workforce. An NKVD order of August 1940 identified six distinct categories of physical labor capability: capable of physical labor; limited labor capability; weakened; sick; invalid; and prisoners requiring constant assistance.[45] During the war, Gulag authorities generated more descriptors for their disabled labor force. One NKVD wartime memo placed invalids and chronically ill camp prisoners into five physical labor classifications: "hospitalized invalids"; "invalids who require constant care"; "invalids who are completely unable to work"; "invalids whose work capability is limited to 25 percent"; and the "mentally ill."[46] As the population of severely ill prisoners grew, the categories of physical labor capability for the Gulag's emaciated workforce proliferated in number and description.

Eventually, the multiple descriptors for prisoners' physical labor capability became simplified and standardized. In a 1944 report to Beria Gulag Director V. G. Nasedkin divided prisoners into four categories: category 1, capable of heavy physical labor; category 2, capable of medium physical labor; category 3, capable of light physical labor; and category 4, invalids and weakened prisoners.[47] Category 3, light physical labor, included a subcategory of "individualized" light labor, thus essentially producing five distinct classifications. The new categories of physical labor capability required new guidelines concerning their application. The lengthy document of 14 June 1944 produced by the director of the Gulag's Sanitation Department, D. M. Loidin, was titled "The List of Main Illnesses, Physical Disabilities, and Defects for Determining Prisoners' Category of Labor Capability or Classifying Them as Invalids."[48] The 1944 iteration of the List of Illnesses paired over a hundred ailments with a corresponding labor category, and it communicated two key elements of Gulag policy. Prisoners would be dispatched to do heavy physical labor even when severely ill, and only persons certified as invalids (the *dokhodiagi* or nearly dead) could be released as "incurables."

The 1944 List of Illnesses illustrates not only the severity of human exploitation that took place in the Gulag but the ways in which sick prisoners were physically exploited at each stage of their debilitating illnesses. The question was not whether someone with heart disease, asthma, or tuberculosis should work in the Gulag, for they must. Rather, medical-labor commissions were supposed to assess the degree to which an illness had progressed and, adhering to the List of Illnesses, place sick prisoners in their appropriate category of physical labor capability. A prisoner with a "general nutritional disorder (pellagra, acute dystrophy, or malnutrition)" that was subject to treatment would be deemed category 3 light labor, while invalids in category 4 had acute malnutrition and starvation-related diseases that were considered incurable or necessitated months of treatment. Prisoners with malignant tumors that had not metastasized were category 3 light labor, while category 4 invalids had advanced or inoperable malignant tumors. In the

1944 iteration, like the 1930s version, categories of physical labor capability depended on the degree of deterioration in a prisoner's health.

Gulag labor classifications reflected stages in the degeneration of an inmate's physical condition, and each category was flagged by particular words and phrases. Medium physical labor applied to illnesses perceived as "lacking changes in pathology" or "lacking marked objective signs and dysfunctions." Light physical labor included notations such as "moderate impairment" and "subject to treatment." The invalid classification referred to prisoners whose prognosis was grim and included the tag lines "incurable," "requiring long-term specialized treatment," "sustained loss of labor capability," "severely limited or complete loss of labor strength," "sustained and profound functional disruption," "complete loss of movement," and "clearly pronounced dysfunction." Moreover, the recurrent phrases that flagged the categories of medium, light, and invalid labor also suggested the physical state of the prisoners assigned to perform heavy physical labor. Evidently a prisoner could have any illness or disease and still be forced to perform arduous work, so long as there was little apparent functional impairment or symptoms were not "clearly pronounced" (*iasno vyrazhennye*). Medical assessments were concerned with prisoners' functionality rather than health, and they constituted matters of perception.

Moreover, the Gulag medical establishment functioned in a highly constrained environment. There were chronic and severe shortages of doctors, medicines, instruments, and rations for sick prisoners. Many health-care workers who treated inmates were prisoners themselves, and all were under intense pressure to keep everyone working. The camps had to comply with impossible quotas for sick and nonworking prisoners. Doctors were required to place their fellow inmates in the most strenuous form of work, to keep everyone maximally "utilized." The NKVD-Gulag leadership expected "labor utilization" rates in the basic work of the camp to be no less than 70 percent of the prisoners. Such quotas, together with high production targets (fig. 3.1), forced doctors to assign weak and emaciated prisoners to perform difficult physical labor that only caused their conditions to worsen. Pressure was built into the system to revise prisoner classifications upward, in favor of more strenuous classifications of physical labor ability. Categories of physical labor capability were not simply assigned once and forgotten but constantly revisited and reassessed.[49] Doctors had to push the limits of prisoners' physical capacities, for they would be held responsible for all classifications.

Doctors and the medical-labor commissions could not apply their independent judgment and reclassify prisoners downward where the medical evi-

Figure 3.1. Overfulfilling the plan on the White Sea-Baltic Sea Canal. *Source:* Aleksandr Rodchenko in *SSSR na stroike* (December 1933).

dence warranted it. As Donald Filtzer explains, in Stalin's civilian health-care system, there existed "a strong punitive dimension" that required doctors to be "extremely stringent when deciding whether or not to grant a sick note" to laborers. Still, many civilian doctors chose to treat workers more mildly than the regime would have preferred.[50] In the Gulag doctors faced much greater pressures to keep people working and much greater risks for perceived leniency. Prisoner doctors avoided any action that might cause them to leave the survivability of a camp clinic and return to heavy physical labor. Indoor jobs were highly coveted in the Gulag. Prisoner doctors would not run the risk of challenging the regime's policy of maximum labor utilization. For this reason, Solzhenitsyn noted that Gulag doctors became complicit in the violence of exploitation: "When quarterly commissioning took place—that comedy known as the general medical examination of the camp population, where prisoners were assigned to categories TFT, SFT, LFT, and IFT (that is, heavy, medium, light, or individualized physical labor)—were there many good doctors who opposed the evil chief of the medical-sanitation department, who was kept in his job only because he supplied columns for heavy labor?"[51]

"THE INVERSE RATIO BETWEEN SOCIAL POSITION AND HUMANENESS"

Comparing the List of Illnesses from 1931 and 1944, it is evident that the severity of Gulag exploitation continued unabated. Very sick and disabled prisoners remained in physically demanding work that further eroded their health. Nonetheless, the Gulag top brass touted the 1944 List of Illnesses for improving the physical condition of prisoners. Sanitation Department Director Loidin insisted that the 1944 List of Illnesses "introduced a degree of clarity in determining the category of prisoners and to a large degree enabled the elimination of vagueness and confusion that existed in this area. This document, which the sanitation organization created in the course of many years, has played an enormous role in improving and preserving the physical condition of the contingents."[52] Similarly, in May 1947 Gulag Director Nasedkin praised NKVD Order no. 00640 for reducing illness and mortality and fundamentally improving the physical profile of prisoners. For Nasedkin this decree introduced a radical change (*korennoi perelom*) in camp conditions.[53]

Not everyone agreed. Camp sanitation department directors, who had to apply the List of Illnesses on the ground, viewed the 1944 document as a harsh revision. In a September 1945 meeting with Loidin the sanitation department director for the Novosibirsk oblast camps and colonies, a certain Prokhorov, criticized the List of Illnesses. He drew attention to the instructions governing the most common illnesses—such as item 38, which referred to "extensive scars that are inclined to be ulcerations or grow into tissue that inhibit movement or putting on clothes and shoes: category 3, individualized labor."[54] According to Prokhorov, most of these prisoners were not work-capable but "practically invalids, practically bedridden," who should be certified as invalids and released as incurables. He also cited item 43, which designated as category 3 light labor those whose ailments included "complete immobility or inactivity of the large joints, significantly limited movement of the limbs that is inherent and the result of traumatic injury or chronic illness of the bones, muscles, tendons, joints."[55] Prokhorov insisted that in most cases these prisoners "aren't capable of anything" and "aren't able to do anything," so they did not belong in category 3 light physical labor. Loidin pushed back at the criticism and suggested that the List of Illnesses was, in fact, *too lenient*. He told Prokhorov: "Take the collective farms. You'll find the elderly there with [acute] hernias, and they're working!"[56] Undaunted, Prokhorov persisted. He cited item 67, which referred to the "absence, complete reduction, or immobility of two fingers or one thumb or the index finger on the right hand. The absence of phalanx bones on two or more fingers on the right hand without eliminating the functions of the extremities—category 2."[57] He argued that such prisoners are severely limited without a thumb and did not always belong in category 2 medium physical labor.[58]

Despite criticism from his subordinates, the Gulag health director refused to accept the argument that the new List of Illness represented a more severe revision of earlier practice. Solzhenitsyn called this "the universal law of the inverse ratio between social position and humaneness."[59] Loidin's defense reveals the mentality of the Stalinist leadership. He argued that it would be very easy to place someone with severe nutritional decline (*pri vyrazhennom upadke pitaniia*) in category 3 light physical labor instead of category 2 medium physical labor, as the List of Illnesses dictates. But he cautioned his "comrades who are panicking" to consider the ramifications of such a change: "We thought about this, Comrades. But think of how many people experience nutritional decline. I'm telling you, this change can be made easily, but if we do it, we'll be making a big mistake. . . . We'll turn our contingent upside down [*perevernem kontingent*]. Our entire useful [*polnotsennyi*] contingent would fall into the not-useful [category]. It was so much work to draw up these instructions. You yourselves know that we lived without instructions. . . . A [change in the List of Illnesses] might have little impact on your own contingent, but for another contingent, like one in a forestry camp, it would be a big deal."[60] Loidin's comment is stunning, for it represents an admission that classifying prisoners according to the true metrics of their ill health, especially in the most brutal sectors like timber, would deny the Gulag its labor force.

Solzhenitsyn called the Gulag "a meat grinder for the worthless millions" (*miasorubka dlia negodnykh millionov*), and this too appears well supported by the evidence.[61] According to the Gulag's own categories and definitions, which probably understate the health crisis, the labor camp experience produced emaciated and disabled prisoners on a truly massive scale. In 1930 only 44 percent of prisoners were deemed fit for all forms of labor, and by 1940 only about a third of inmates were considered capable of heavy physical labor, the principal work of the Gulag.[62] During the war, the physical condition of prisoners declined further. In 1941–1945 roughly half of all Gulag prisoners were classified as either invalids or fit for only light physical labor. Invalid and light labor categories applied to the most emaciated and debilitated inmate population. The physical destruction of prisoners continued well after the war, for evidence suggests that Gulag brutality increased over time. In 1947–1948 a staggering 60 percent of all prisoners in Stalin's labor camps and colonies were designated as either invalid or capable of only light physical labor.[63]

THE MEAT GRINDER GRINDS ON

The Gulag expanded significantly after 1947 and in many ways reached its apogee in the years prior to Stalin's death in 1953. The prisoner population increased sharply, and the MVD took on greater economic tasks. In the late Stalin years the number of Gulag prisoners nearly doubled to about 2.5 million. Sentences grew longer for both political and criminal offenses. The twenty-five-year sentence, rarely meted out in the prewar years, became common for counterrevolutionary offenders after the war.[64] Stalin's decrees of 4 June 1947 concerning the theft of state and personal property condemned ordinary peasants and workers to camp sentences of up to twenty-five years.[65] Largely as a result of these draconian theft decrees, new prisoners flooded into the camps and colonies, resulting in severe overcrowding and deteriorating living conditions, such as food shortages and poor sanitation, which worsened prisoners' health and labor productivity. In the late 1940s, according to Yoram Gorlizki and Oleg Khlevniuk, "the cumulative impact of Stalin's penal policies threatened to push the scale of the Gulag beyond sustainable limits."[66]

At the same time, the Gulag's regime of exploitation did not ease but rather intensified in the late Stalin years. Memoirists describe how the camps in the 1940s "began to take on a mass character . . . things became harsher . . . as the camps grew bigger, the regime grew crueler."[67] In the late 1940s Stalin initiated new campaigns of political repression at home and in Eastern Europe.[68] At the same time, the regime produced another List of Illnesses that intensified Gulag exploitation. On 25 June 1949 the MVD issued Order no. 0418, the latest revision to the categories of physical labor capability and the List of Illnesses. It began with MVD Director S. N. Kruglov praising the earlier iteration and announcing its irrelevance. Kruglov touted NKVD Order no. 00640 of 1944 for having "introduced the practice of placing prisoners into various categories of physical labor consistent with their physical condition" and other "measures to improve the conditions of their detention and their labor utilization."[69] Remarkably, the MVD director characterized the 1944 decree as lenient or indulgent and appropriate only to wartime and immediate postwar conditions. Kruglov continued with the false assertion that "at the present time . . . the condition of prisoner detention has improved overall" and claimed that the supply of food, clothing, and other goods to prisoners takes place "without interruption."[70] So, he argued, the time had come to streamline the categories of physical labor capability.

The new List of Illnesses reveals the escalating brutality of the Gulag regime. MVD Order no. 0418 returned to the older three-tiered system and defined the three categories more severely than the 1931 edition.[71] In 1949 category 1 applied to "all prisoners who are basically fit for physical labor" (*vse zakliuchennye, prakticheski godnye k fizicheskomu trudu*). Prisoners simply had to be functional or usable, meaning that a larger population could be forced to perform heavy physical labor. This new category 1 applied to all prisoners who used to be assigned to heavy and medium labor under the 1944 revision. Thus prisoners who had been previously assigned to medium labor would no longer receive an accommodation but would instead do heavy physical labor. The new category 2 now captured a more disabled population. Category 2 applied to "physically inferior prisoners [*fizicheski nepolnotsennye zakliuchennye*] who could not perform heavy physical labor. They would be placed in light labor with a 15 percent reduction [*skidka*] [in their production targets], or in medium labor with the application of a 30 percent reduction, or in special forms of work without any kind of reduction."[72] It is unclear whether the Gulag issued guidelines concerning the kinds of jobs that should be assigned to the weaker prisoners.[73]

The Gulag regime grew more exploitative in the late 1940s. The 1949 List of Illnesses collapsed the older categories of heavy, medium, and (to a lesser degree) light labor into a single category 1—"basically fit for physical labor." It reserved category 2 for the severely weakened, those who had been classified previously as "category 3 individualized labor," but who were still a notch above the invalid category. To a large degree, category 2 of 1949 corresponded to "category 3 individualized labor" of 1944, a population that was even weaker than those typically assigned to light labor.[74] As in earlier instructions, weaker prisoners would be reevaluated every three months to see whether they could be pushed into a more strenuous physical labor category, while prisoners deemed fit for heavy physical labor remained stuck in their classification for six months.[75] Finally, the invalid category applied to "prisoners suffering from severe chronic illnesses or physical limitations who can neither work nor be utilized in work consistent with their residual labor capability" (*ostatochnaia trudosposobnost´*).[76] Thus the invalid category constituted the final stage in the process of "wringing out" prisoners for their labor. The 1949 List of Illnesses forced all but the most severely weakened prisoners into heavy physical labor.

In the late Stalin years the MVD-Gulag leadership grew especially concerned with maximizing labor utilization rates, and this is reflected in the document. The 1949 List of Illnesses stressed labor exploitation rather explicitly. The full title of the document—"The Listing of Main Illnesses, Physical Deficiencies, and Defects in Development That Prevent the Assignment of Prisoners to Category 1 Labor"—signaled a shift in emphasis. The Stalinist leadership became more focused on ensuring that camps did not easily excuse prisoners from heavy physical labor. Earlier editions of the List of Illnesses had different titles, which drew attention to the invalid classification and early release, for example: "The List of Illnesses for Early Release" (1931) and "The List of the Main Illnesses, Physical Deficiencies, and Defects in Development for Determining the Appropriate Categories of Prisoners' Labor Strength or for Classifying Them as Invalids" (1944). In previous years the center focused on minimizing the number of prisoners classified as invalids and thereby entitled to early release. Now the goal of keeping prisoners in heavy labor appears central. The guidelines sought to instruct camp officials on which prisoners could be excused from heavy physical labor. Heavy physical labor remained the assignment for all but the most emaciated and disabled prisoners. The 1949 List of Illnesses aimed to increase the camps' labor utilization rates by forcing weaker prisoners into harder labor.

The Gulag reserved the invalid designation for its most diseased and debilitated prisoners. To be so classified, a prisoner would have to be completely blind or have third-stage silicosis or no fewer than four asthma attacks per month. The invalid category also included those with "disfiguring inflammation" and chronic illness of the tendons, muscles, and joints that resulted in the "complete loss of movement," as well as inmates who demonstrated the "pronounced effects of senile decrepitude." Category 2 could also be rather graphic in its definition, and for good reason. The MVD used these instructions to send a strong message to camp officials that only the most ailing prisoners could be released from heavy physical labor. The following illnesses would justify a category 2 classification: "benign tumors that make it hard to wear clothing or impair organ functions," "extremely large hernias," "goiter that impairs the functions of nearby organs," and loss of vision in one eye.[77] The evolution of various iterations of the List of Illnesses demonstrates that the 1949 iteration increased considerably the physical exploitation of prisoners. Nearly all prisoners would be forced to do heavy physical labor.

From the 1930s to the 1950s the practice of "utilizing" prisoners in heavy physical labor regardless of their health only intensified. MVD-Gulag leaders grew increasingly unwilling to offer work accommodations for sick and disabled prisoners. In a 4 November 1950 letter to Kruglov Gulag Director G. P. Dobrynin argued that the categories of physical labor capability should be largely discarded and considered only when transferring prisoners to other camps. He believed that it was no longer necessary for the Gulag to continue the practice of matching prisoners with work based on their health. Nor should the camps assign weakened prisoners to less strenuous labor. Dobrynin told his MVD boss:

> At the present time, in connection with the introduction of paid work for prisoners and with the general improvement in the physical condition of prisoners, prisoners' interest in the results of their labor has increased significantly. Thus the need to divide prisoners into categories according to

their physical condition is disappearing. The MVD USSR Gulag, therefore, considers it expedient to eliminate the division of prisoners according to the categories of physical condition that were established in MVD Order no. 00418. [We] no longer need to provide any kind of discount for the less work-capable contingent that is being utilized at work in camps and colonies. Abolishing the categories would allow us to improve the utilization of prisoners in production.[78]

This represented a departure from previous Gulag policy and an escalation in the regime of human exploitation in the camps. There would be no easing of heavy labor requirements for emaciated prisoners.

The system of exploitation in the Gulag intensified in the late Stalin years as the Gulag director rejected any work accommodation for weakened prisoners. Once again, the inverse ratio between social position and humaneness reveals itself. Dobrynin believed that prisoners in declining health should be placed in basic work rather than lighter forms of labor. Camp officials must aim for the maximum utilization of prisoners in basic work. In July 1951 the Sanitation Department was instructed "to review the existing system for the labor utilization of camp prisoners, in light of the change in the categories, the utilization of a large number of contingents in basic work, and the maximum use of their labor."[79] Even severely weakened prisoners would be drawn into the basic work of the camp and assigned to heavy physical labor. In the late Stalin years the MVD-Gulag leadership increased the intensity of physical exploitation in the camps.

Following the 1949 revision to the categories of physical labor capability, a larger population of prisoners was forced into heavy physical labor. As the screws were tightened on prisoners, their health declined further. According to the Gulag's own statistics, only about 60 percent of people detained in Stalin's labor camps and colonies could meet the very low bar of health that would qualify them as "basically fit for physical labor." In 1949–1951 the physical profile of prisoners across the Gulag system appeared as follows: roughly 60 percent in category 1, 30 percent in category 2, and 9 percent invalids.[80] For individual camps the picture was often worse. For example, in March 1950 camps and colonies operated by the Khabarovsk krai MVD detained 24,235 prisoners, and fewer than half were considered "basically fit for physical labor."[81]

Recently declassified Gulag archival documents concerning prisoners' health expose the consequences of severe physical exploitation and the impossibility of achieving utopian production goals with a diseased and emaciated workforce. A great deal of secrecy surrounded Gulag health documents of all kinds. Like the special camps, invalid camps were given cryptic or euphemistic names. In telegram communications any mention of prisoners' illnesses, deaths, or labor capabilities had to be masked using code words.[82] The Gulag maintained a vast regime of secrecy that included data not only on mass starvation and illness but on the very nature and location of the camps. The institution used code words to describe the deadliest camps and prohibited the production of printed maps. As Mark Harrison explains, "printed maps were not wanted because the information they would have carried was among the top state secrets of the Soviet era."[83] Information concerning prisoners' mortality in the camps was similarly concealed and distorted. Stalin systematically masked the destruction of his forced labor camp prisoners by applying article 457-8 of the Criminal Code, which made possible the routine release of the Gulag's "incurables."

"UNLOADING THE BALLAST" TO "ELIMINATE THE DEATH RATE"

In Vladimir Voinovich's dystopian novel *Moscow 2042*, the future Soviet state of Moscowrep has managed to "eliminate the death rate" through "reliable and economic means." One of the so-called Communites explains: "It was simply that critically ill people, as well as pensioners and invalids . . . were resettled to the First Ring and lived out their days there. All that remained here were rare instances of death in accidents and of course heart attacks and strokes. But those were also isolated instances, because people with cardiovascular diseases were also dispatched beyond the limits of the Moscowrep in good time, and if someone should happen to suffer a heart attack or appendicitis, the ambulance would rush him to the First Ring."[84] Perhaps not surprisingly, the Soviet Union's brilliant literary satirist accurately described how the Gulag reduced its mortality rate. As in Moscowrep, the Stalinist forced labor camp system routinely dispatched its weakest and dying population beyond the limits of the zone.

Since the opening of the archives, the official data on Gulag mortality has surprised many historians. Mortality rates, which were generated as monthly and yearly averages, appear largely in the area of 1–6 percent of the total inmate population, with significant fluctuations in certain years. Sometimes, these fluctuations seem logical, as when the Gulag recorded mortality as high as 15 percent during the 1933 famine, and 22–25 percent during the worst years of the war, 1942–1943. At other times, the data are distinctly puzzling. Some of the lowest rates of mortality were recorded in years when camp conditions were known to have plummeted, such as during the 1936–1937 purges (under 3 percent), the 1947 famine (under 4 percent), and the late Stalin years, during the "crisis" of the Gulag.[85] In 1950–1953, when the camps reached their maximum of roughly 2.5 million prisoners, the official death rate remained under 1 percent each year, a truly incomprehensible figure in light of the data on prisoners' physical labor capability.[86]

Gulag scholars have been justifiably cautious when citing NKVD/MVD statistics on camp mortality. The camps were compelled to keep mortality rates within established quotas. Gulag bosses experienced intense pressure of all kinds—to maximally "utilize" their inmate labor, to meet or exceed production targets, to eliminate epidemics and "lost labor days." Directives from Gulag and NKVD/MVD leaders, wholly untethered to the realities of camp life, were not uncommon. In 1945, following a devastating war and a period when the Gulag recorded its highest rates of mortality, Sanitation Department Director Loidin told a meeting of his subordinates that mortality rates had to be kept below 2 percent and rates of illness could not exceed 5 percent.[87] Thus, not surprisingly, the mortality rate for 1946 came in at around 2 percent. Under immense pressure to stay within unworkable quotas, camp officials more often reported figures that were mandated rather than accurate. The Gulag maintained low mortality rates through falsification and deceptive accounting practices but, more important, through mass releases. Routine releases of emaciated and enfeebled prisoners represented the principal method for reducing mortality rates in the Stalinist camps.

The Gulag constantly released inmates. Declassified Gulag archives reveal that 20–40 percent of prisoners were released annually from 1934 to 1953.[88] Prisoners were granted early release consistent with the camps' stated mission of reeducation and as a reward for exceptional labor productivity.[89] The regime freed many prisoners through special amnesties and as caregivers for disabled or underage relatives, especially in the postwar years.[90] At the same time, many prisoner releases resulted from the institution's destructive capacity. The discharged were often inmates who had become thoroughly depleted. As Anne Applebaum writes, "both archives and memoirs indicate that it was common practice in many camps to release prisoners who were on the point of dying, thereby lowering camp death statistics."[91] Historians are now looking more closely at this problem. Recent work by Mikhail Nakonechnyi demonstrates that Gulag mortality figures were highly distorted by the systematic release of *dokhodiagi*. According to Nakonechnyi, "camp statistics only accounted for those prisoners who died within the confines (gates) of the camp or in camp medical institutions. Those who died shortly after their release as 'complete invalids' or 'seriously ill' did not spoil camp statistics, although their deaths resulted from Gulag detention."[92]

The Gulag systematically discarded prisoners it could no longer "utilize" and those considered too costly to support. From its inception Stalin's Gulag routinely released severely ill prisoners, with the exception of most political offenders and recidivist criminals. Invalid certification or medical discharge was largely limited to routine criminal offenders, a population that consistently represented the majority of inmates in Stalin's labor camps and colonies. Those certified as invalids could be freed under article 457-8 of the RSFSR Criminal Procedural Code, which allowed camps to release inmates with "severe, incurable, or psychological illness."[93] The Stalinist leadership used the criminal code to artificially reduce Gulag mortality. Not only did the Gulag release prisoners on the verge of death, but it may have counted some of the dead among those released.[94] Medical discharge (*aktirovanie*) removed terminally ill and disabled prisoners from the Gulag books. People freed as incurables were often terminally ill, and this was widely understood among camp officials. V. A. Isupov notes that prisoners were certified and released as invalids "in order to die."[95] In March 1934 Gulag Director M. D. Berman denounced a medical worker in Belbaltlag who failed to document a sick prisoner's release before that prisoner died at the worksite.[96] On 28 February 1935 the procurator of Dmitlag in the Moscow region asked the USSR Procuracy about prisoners who were being released early for reasons of illness, consistent with the Criminal Code.[97] He complained that sometimes it took months for these prisoners' cases to be processed, by which time the prisoners had often died. He argued that if the local people's court or oblast court could handle these cases for Dmitlag, they could be processed in two to three days, and sharp increases in the camp's mortality rate could be avoided.[98] OGPU/NKVD/MVD officials released inmates deemed no longer useful. As the Gulag survivor Oleg Volkov described:

> So many prisoners without strength and worn out from work accumulated —the elderly with joints that could no longer bend, with crooked fingers and tons of hernias, inmates who developed dementia, deafness, and blindness. They had to be disposed of. The GULAG's creaky laboring body had to be freed of this ballast. . . . So they began to pack them up in bunches and toss them out. Let them find themselves a hole they can crawl into like old dogs sensing imminent death, and where they can await the Great Redeemer. I saw how camps released and sent beyond the zone the veterans of Gulag labor.[99]

Gulag officials knew what they were doing. To quote Michael Ellman, "The policy of releasing 'unfit for work ballast' was a cost-cutting measure which was intended to save on food consumption and on guards and other personnel, and hence reduce the deficit and improve productivity in the Gulag."[100] Camp officials often transferred their sick and disabled prisoners to other camps to improve their data on illness and mortality. In 1945 the Sanitation Department director for the Khabarovsk krai camps and colonies, a certain Khodakov, accused another camp of intentionally dumping its tuberculosis and other ailing prisoners on them. The Primorskii Camp, he complained, "freed itself of its ballast and thereby improved its statistics."[101] The Sanitation Department director for the Molotov oblast UITLK, a certain Toma, explained that her institution's mortality rate would have been lower had she been allowed to release sick prisoners: "Since August 1944 we almost never released people as incurables [po neizlechimosti]. . . . We would have a lower mortality rate, if we had released people a bit earlier than we were able to."[102] Those released were literally dying. A former prisoner and nurse in the Gulag told of how the medical staff was under orders to prepare the dying prisoner for release: "Before their exit [pered exitus], we had to inject camphor under the skin of the dying person."[103]

As the invalid label applied to the nearly dead, many died soon after their release. Ekaterina Gol´ts was released early for reasons of poor health in 1944 and returned from her camp in Komi to the home of her brother in Moscow. Her niece recalled the joy of Katia's release: "Her face was glowing, she was incredibly happy. But she couldn't stay in Moscow. She stayed with us for one night. . . . The next day, Katia went to the home of relatives of a fellow camp prisoner, somewhere about 100 kilometers outside Moscow. After a few days there, she died suddenly. I think it was a stroke." Less than one week following her release, Katia collapsed. Her niece remarked, "Of course, they released her from the camp in order to die at home. Such was the vile custom [podlyi obychai]."[104] Indeed, "unloading the ballast" constituted a Gulag custom. As Solzhenitsyn wrote, "The higher-ups were sly bastards. They released ahead of time on health grounds those who were going to kick the bucket in a month anyway."[105]

A number of Gulag scholars—Khlevniuk, Applebaum, Ellman, Isupov, and Nakonechnyi, among others—have brought to light the fact that the Gulag kept mortality rates low by releasing prisoners on the verge of death. New data reveal that "release-to-die" constituted a Gulag policy of immense proportion. It appears that on a quarterly basis alone, anywhere from 10 to 50 percent of the inmate population in Stalin's labor camps and colonies was released as incurable. In the camps roughly 10 percent of prisoners were released quarterly as invalids from the 1930s to the 1950s, yet the figure appears higher when one takes into account special amnesties and releases from the colonies, where the sickest prisoners were concentrated. For example, in the fourth quarter of 1952 over ninety thousand Gulag prisoners were freed as medically discharged invalids (*aktirovannye invalidy*), representing 10 percent of all inmates released from the camps and as many as 56 percent of all releases from the colonies.[106] At regional camps or colonies, where the Gulag concentrated its weakest inmates, the rate of releases for sick and disabled prisoners appears extraordinarily high. In the third quarter of 1952 approximately 18 percent of the nearly six hundred thousand prisoners detained in the system of regional labor colonies (UITLK/OITK MVD/UMVD) were released as incurables according to article 457 of the Criminal Code. This represented nearly two-thirds of the roughly 169,000 prisoners freed that quarter.[107] The number may be even higher, as many *dokhodiagi* may have been formally released for other reasons, such as completing their sentences. Stalin's Gulag systematically "unloaded" prisoners who could no longer be exploited for their labor due to poor health. Camps certified severely ill prisoners for release as a way of reducing costs and improving their mortality data.

Human exploitation—unrelenting, punitive, and increasingly brutal—constituted the defining feature of Stalin's Gulag. Once we examine the Gulag through the lens of physical exploitation, then its willfully destructive capacity becomes apparent. In Stalin's Gulag prisoners had to be worked to the point of utter depletion. Whereas the Nazi death camps sought total annihilation, the Stalinist labor camps pursued total exploitation. The Gulag's purpose was not the extermination of prisoners but their "maximum utilization," and this system of labor utilization was itself destructive. Gulag exploitation shattered the health of prisoners and produced millions of *dokhodiagi*. Stalinist leaders concealed the Gulag's destructive capacity and kept death rates low by releasing millions of prisoners on the verge of death.

Within the barbed wire, prison laborers were constituted, managed, and discarded as human raw material. To thoroughly wring prisoners of their productive capacity, the Gulag established categories of physical labor capability. With each iteration of the physical labor categories and each revision of the List of Illnesses, the OGPU/NKVD/MVD and Gulag leadership tried to force a larger population of ailing prisoners into heavy physical labor. The exploitation of inmates' labor only intensified over time, while officials concealed the Gulag's brutality through the routine release of invalid and chronically ill prisoners. They freed prisoners to die outside their jurisdiction. Even in the late 1940s, when war no longer provided an excuse, only a minority of prisoners was deemed capable of heavy physical labor. Unmoved by the destructive capacity of the system, the MVD-Gulag leadership altered its bureaucratic classifications so that prisoners only had to be "basically fit" for labor. Then it abandoned even this very low threshold and blamed prisoners for their physical decline. The Gulag system exhaustively depleted and inhumanely discarded its prison laborers or, as Varlam Shalamov wrote, its "human waste, remnants, trash" (*liudskie otkhody, ostatki, otbrosy*).[108] These were destructive labor camps.

LIVES IN THE BALANCE
Weak and Disabled Prisoners and the Biopolitics of the Gulag

DAN HEALEY

DID THE GULAG have a biopolitics? The linked concepts of "biopower" and "biopolitics" were sketched by Michel Foucault and have been taken up by historians of medicine and the body examining diverse historical contexts.[1] It may sound counterintuitive to suggest that the Soviet forced labor camp system operated policies (a "biopolitics") to manage the quality and character of life at the level of the individual and at the collective level of the populations housed in the camp. The scale of mortality in the camps was extraordinary, apparently belying any official concern about prisoner health. Despite a lack of agreement over the precise numbers of prisoners lost to malnutrition, exhaustion through labor, disease, and violence, the death toll in the camps was very high, especially during the Second World War and famine years.[2] Nevertheless, medical facilities existed in the Gulag to monitor and ostensibly to improve the physical condition of prisoners, and the work of these institutions was framed by regulations and norms that merit systematic scrutiny. Declassification and scholarly publication of Gulag administrative archives have given us a previously inaccessible view of what camp administrators said and did, and a majority of scholars now accept these documents as a flawed but credible record of Gulag practices (including those of concealment and dissimulation).[3] Careful reading from a critical perspective can help us assess what these bosses and the doctors who worked for them thought they were doing with prisoner labor. Understanding the history of medicine in the camps begins with a close examination of official rationales and actions.[4]

Simply put, histories of the Gulag have failed to analyze the camps' significant medical infrastructure that from the early 1930s was subordinated to the OGPU/NKVD/MVD. The Gulag's Sanitation Department, or Sanotdel, served both the system's prisoner and free employee populations.[5] Although never as well resourced as civilian medical services, its representatives and facilities were ubiquitous within the camp system. Archival records suggest the scale of activity of this "embedded" medical service—a dedicated (*vedomstvennaia*) service similar to "medico-sanitary" services operating in the People's Commissariats of War, the Navy, and Railroads. The Sanotdel's central Moscow apparatus was run by a physician who directed a cadre of doctors and lay bureaucrats acting as medical inspectors, sanitation specialists, and statisticians; on the eve of the Second World War, they constituted 8.6 percent of central Gulag personnel.[6] By 1939 the Gulag Sanotdel network in the camps counted 1,171 infirmaries, clinics, and hospitals with 39,839 beds. During the Second World War, it expanded to 165,000 beds, and by 1953, on the eve of Stalin's death and the subsequent release of millions of prisoners, the Gulag medical service had 111,612 beds at its disposal.[7] In 1938 it employed 1,830 qualified doctors, of whom perhaps one-third were prisoners; at the same time, 7,556 nurses and paramedics worked in the system, and a large proportion of these were prisoners, too.[8] As the camp system expanded, the system's appetite for medical professionals grew inexorably. Prisoner-physicians were plucked from transports and put to work as medics, thereby avoiding life-exhausting "general labor" in the Gulag's mines and forests; such was the demand that prisoner-medics were (from 1939, at least) allowed to use their professional skills more often than engineers or other skilled technicians.[9] They were supervised locally by "freely hired" doctors and medical bureaucrats who were Sanotdel employees. There were lower-level "free" employees, too. From 1938 on Gulag representatives recruited newly qualified doctors, nurses, paramedics (*fel'dshera*), dentists, and pharmacists directly from the graduate assignment commissions of medical institutes and training colleges.[10] Many prisoners were trained as paramedics and nurses in the Gulag's in-house courses, which varied in quality and geographic distribution.[11] Prisoners taught themselves medical basics and forged careers in the camp infirmaries.[12] The medical service was a variegated and dynamic element of the Gulag system, distinctive from Soviet civilian and other institutionally "dedicated" medical systems because of the prisoner status of most of its patients and many of its operatives.

For survivor-memoirists and historians the existence of a medical service in the Gulag has been a politically and morally ambiguous fact, a puzzle for those who spoke out against Stalinist terror. Alexander Solzhenitsyn regarded Gulag medicine with contempt. In *The Gulag Archipelago*, a work analyzing life in the camps in encyclopedic detail, there is no chapter devoted to medicine. Solzhenitsyn dismissed medical care in passages scattered throughout the work. For him the medical services were cut from the same cloth as the rest of the camp power structure, "born of the devil and filled with the devil's blood."[13] He condemned what he saw as Varlam Shalamov's positive view of the camp sanitation sections (*sanchasti*) as mythologizing legend.[14] Shalamov survived the Kolyma camps thanks to their medical services and to his work from 1946 as a Gulag-trained paramedic. A less jaundiced reading of Shalamov's documentary fiction and autobiographical sketches yields a much more ambivalent view of Gulag medicine, but historians have not systematically analyzed this commentary on labor-camp medical ethics and personalities.[15] Similarly, the perceptive and gifted memoirist Evgeniia Ginzburg, a self-taught Gulag nurse, only episodically reflected on the meaning of penal medical work, apparently bemused by its ambiguous significance.[16]

Despite enjoying access to archival sources, recent authorities on the Gulag continue to skirt this question. Anne Applebaum offers only a cursory sketch of clinics and doctors, avoiding like Solzhenitsyn any sustained analysis of the meaning of medicine behind barbed wire. It was one "of the many absurdities of camp life," a bureaucratic "paradox . . . built right into the system" that she implies was riddled with perversions of medical ethics.[17] Steven Barnes has argued provocatively that Gulag authorities instrumentalized the threat of death as a spur to compel prisoners to greater productivity and the reforging of the self; however, he does not consider what role the camps' medical infrastructure played in the process of sorting prisoners between "death and redemption."[18] The existence of the Sanotdel and its impact on the Gulag prisoner requires closer analysis, preferably from comparative perspectives, but this is beyond the scope of the present chapter.[19]

The concept of biopolitics can help us appreciate the calculus of life and death in the Soviet penal-economic complex. Foucault chiefly defined "biopolitical" concerns as focused on the adjustment of the human body to the needs of modern economies.[20] Capitalism, he wrote, "would not have been possible without the controlled insertion of bodies into the machinery of production and the adjustment of the phenomena of population to economic processes."[21] Drawing on the notions of the surveillance and training of the body that he had described in his history of the modern prison, *Discipline and Punish*, Foucault first argued that "biopower" consisted of two polarities: a focus on the individual body that enabled authorities to optimize its capabilities and integrate it into systems of production and control; and a focus on populations, with expertise that allowed for optimal reproduction, health, and capacity for labor.[22] He later drew a stronger distinction between these polarities, even giving them separate names: "disciplinary power" imposed norms and spatial regimes on individual bodies, while "biopower" used norms to foster the growth and productivity of entire populations.[23] Even in this later refinement, the ultimate aims of biopower remained the same. Through biopower, authorities attempted to exert "a positive influence on life, that endeavors to administer, optimize, and multiply it, subjecting it to precise controls and comprehensive regulations." The rise of medical and scientific expertise gave authorities the power to shape life to the requirements of a particular political economy, relying on norms of administration, public health, hygiene, and planning. Biopower turned less on the force of law and more emphatically toward "regulatory and corrective mechanisms" that "qualify, measure, appraise, and hierarchize" bodies and their disposition. Indeed, so powerful were these new norms in comparison to legal mechanisms in crafting lives that, for modern societies as imagined by Foucault, the norm began to overtake law as a key instrument of power.[24]

The distinctiveness of a socialist penal economy, and critiques of Foucault's writing by historians of Russia, means that notions of biopolitics cannot be applied to the Gulag without significant qualifications.[25] The Soviet state aspired to total control of society; drawing on prerevolutionary radical precedents, it adapted and deployed disciplinary knowledge without the moderating influence of liberal rule-of-law restraints. The productive symbiosis between law and disciplinary norms discerned by Laura Engelstein for liberal democracies (and mistrusted by Foucault and others) did not take hold in Russia.[26] Foucault himself could not decide if the Gulag represented a pre-Enlightenment form of punishment or an example of modern (in his characteristically Eurocentric sense) incarceration. Jan Plamper demonstrates how productively Foucault generated compellingly paradoxical characterizations of Soviet penality without ever deciding where the Gulag fit in his schemes of historical progress. In particular, Foucault was puzzled by the spectacle of a presumptive socialist workers' state that used labor to define citizenship but also as a punishment and pathway to rehabilitation.[27]

Here I consider the Gulag's biopolitics as a dynamic rationale that lay behind sanitary and medical norms and surveillance mechanisms deployed by the Gulag Sanotdel. Fundamental to biopolitics are decisions taken about resources related to sustaining and enhancing life (food, shelter, clothing, sanitation, medicine). I argue that the Sanotdel's activity, rather than representing one "of the many absurdities of camp life," in Applebaum's phrase, was in fact intended, with a shifting degree of conscious deliberation, to achieve "the controlled insertion of bodies into the machinery of production" using Gulag medicine's specific norms and mechanisms. It is self-evident in this historical context that the relationship between norms and the law followed Soviet rather than liberal-democratic patterns. There was less productive symbiosis between law and norms, although it is premature to dismiss the possibility entirely, and there were plenty of cases when "sovereign power" (the right to kill or let live, in Foucault's formulation) bluntly trumped norms of disciplinary power or biopower.[28] The noncapitalist and, for many observers, the nonrational nature of Gulag economic activity must also be confronted. Foucault recognized the symbolic dissonance of a nominal workers' state punishing outcasts with forced labor. Many critics of Stalinism have asserted emphatically, with entirely understandable motives, that the Gulag yielded little of value: shallow canals, useless railways, faked production figures. The imperative of punishment and the desperately high cost paid in human lives overwhelmed any genuine value created. Moreover, careful scholars have also cast doubt on the efficiency of Soviet forced labor.[29] Despite these reservations, and while deploring the criminality of Stalinist forced labor, economic historians drawing on archival sources describe the significant proportion of key commodities that the NKVD's penal empire did contribute to the Soviet economy.[30] Meanwhile the survival of Gulag towns after 1953 illustrates the de-Stalinizers' reluctance to abandon as useless the industrial complexes built by prisoner labor, even if MVD Director Lavrentii Pavlovich Beria declared them bankrupt.[31] We must imagine a penal-economic model that made at least some sense to those NKVD–MVD officials who tried to run it. Their management of resources, including their biopolitical decisions, evidently strove to enhance productivity, even in the face of deprivation, neglect, and misinformation. Moreover, Gulag bosses and the Sanotdel did not devise the biopolitics of the camps in a vacuum. Rather, they adapted to the penal setting many of the political decisions about resources applied to Soviet civilian society. This adaptation of civilian norms to penal contexts and the promiscuous crossing of the "Gulag/non-Gulag" border have been noted by Oleg Khlevniuk for the Gulag economy and by Wilson Bell for labor camp society more broadly.[32]

In this chapter I focus on the Stalin-era Gulag from approximately 1929 to the mid-1950s. The peculiar biopolitics of the Gulag evolved rapidly and mutated radically in the era of the Great Break and the establishment of the major penal-construction projects of the early 1930s. Preexisting medical surveillance and norms inherited from the Solovetskii Islands Camp of Special Purpose (SLON) contributed to the shape of later regulation, but from 1929 on wider Soviet civilian biopolitics and the Gulag version came to resemble each other in important ways. In that year Soviet civilian medicine (under Health Commissariat control) was officially redirected away from the unachieved revolutionary aspiration to provide universal care toward a "mobilized" agenda prioritizing "productive" populations, principally urban workers.[33] Prisoners experienced a particularly harsh form of mobilized medical care, but as will be shown it shared many characteristics with civilian provision. The end of the period studied here marked a shift in civilian and penal biopolitics, with the party leadership making more generous decisions about consumption, for example, and with the embrace of "socialist legality." The Gulag Sanotdel saw corresponding reform after Stalin's death, including a name change to Medical Department (Meditsinskoe otdelenie) that adumbrated an ostensibly more humane view of the prisoner as meriting medical rather than merely sanitary attention.

The discussion that follows concentrates on Gulag treatment of weak and disabled prisoners as a useful window on the biopolitics practiced by camp managers. The treatment of impaired prisoner-workers set baselines that in part defined who was worth saving from the many hazards of Gulag life. The biopolitics of disability in the Gulag was directly related to the camps' economic activity: the burden represented by invalids and nonworking prisoners would become a constant concern for those administrators who managed perceptions of the profitability of Gulag production. Through various forms of regular medical surveillance and norm setting, prisoners were classified in a labor balance or inventory. The labor inventory system identified, sorted, and removed weak and disabled prisoners from camp balances. An examination of this system of surveillance and classification can reveal some of the features of Soviet penal biopolitics. There are major aspects of Gulag experience that a focus on administrative activity and biopolitics cannot address. One is the closed-door decision making in the Sanotdel, which is scantily documented, and therefore intention must often be inferred from the timing, authorship, and language of instructions, directives, and decrees. Another obvious absence is the prisoners' experience of incarceration. The norms and regulations produced by the Sanotdel only hint at weakened and disabled prisoners' victimization and agency. Here I use memoir sources from disabled prisoners that illustrate features of particular regimes and prisoner responses to them. These are primarily the recollections of members of the intelligentsia who were imprisoned unjustly for political crimes, and as such the voices of less privileged inmates, both political and criminal (and the indeterminacy of these boundaries is notorious), are less audible. What follows is not a social history of Gulag invalids, but as an attempt to trace the biopolitical regime that contained them, it will make a "history from below" more feasible.[34]

SOVIET CIVILIANS AND PRISONERS AS INVALIDS

Stalin-era medicine defined the "invalid" as someone who had lost the capacity for labor by virtue of illness or accident; the loss of other life potential was scarcely recognized.[35] The Soviet approach to disability emphasized the individual's functional capabilities and sought to maximize labor capacity in particular.[36] In 1932, as industrialization accelerated, complicated Health Commissariat schemes devised in the 1920s to classify the injured and disabled civilian worker were scrapped in favor of a three-category system that severely limited access to a disability pension; most invalids were to be re-deployed in support roles in the industries they knew. Although the Stalin Constitution of 1936 guaranteed the incapacitated worker the theoretical right to state support, Welfare Commissariat experts promoted the "application of invalid labor" both in rehabilitation and in the general economy. By 1937 welfare officials wrested control from the Health Commissariat of the medical-labor expertise commissions (*vrachebnye-trudovye ekspertnye komissii*, VTEK) which examined invalids and classified them. Financial constraints, generated by five-year plan pressures, overshadowed Hippocratic or humanitarian values on these commissions.[37] VTEK doctors in the Welfare Commissariat devised exercises, treatments, and "labor therapy" (with short work periods and adaptive physical arrangements) to rehabilitate tuberculosis patients and invalids capable of reduced forms of work.[38] Before 1941, most civilian invalids, many of them victims of industrial accidents, were already officially expected to continue working, and VTEK doctors were pressured to limit category 1 designations, which entailed a pension.[39]

VTEK commissions multiplied during the war and in 1944 alone conducted almost 1.7 million examinations of invalids. By 1948 there were 1,521,000 recognized war invalids in the USSR. The classification system dealt with war veterans harshly: only 29,000, or 1.9 percent, were category 1, pensioned invalids; 321,000 (22 percent) were category 2 and not getting support, although the most severe cases could be housed in residential institutions. These homes were so squalid and unpopular that the network was partly shut down in 1948–1952, with the shifting of homeless war invalids ever farther from public space and visibility.[40] The state treated its most deserving civilian invalids, both workers and war veterans, with striking harshness, a fact worth bearing in mind when examining the particular circumstances of invalid prisoners.

In the Gulag, invalidism quickly became statistically significant, because punishingly hard labor in extreme conditions and on deficient rations led to malnutrition, emaciation, and starvation disease, which the Soviet medical system came to label "alimentary dystrophy" during the Second World War.[41] This condition also left prisoners vulnerable to tuberculosis, wastage of the heart and circulatory system, and other degenerative diseases.[42] Staggeringly large cohorts developed preventable vitamin deficiencies (especially scurvy and pellagra) due to the monotonous diet. The degree of malnutrition and starvation ebbed and flowed over the lifetime of the Gulag; there were good years and several bad ones (particularly during national famines and the war). Large numbers of prisoners grew too ill to work and had to be released from general labor—that is, the main economic activity of any given camp (chiefly mining, forestry work, and construction). Disability also followed from industrial accidents, from self-inflicted wounds to escape general labor, and from violent conflict.[43]

From the Gulag economic managers' perspective, the disabled prisoner was a costly burden, and from the 1930s on camp bosses and doctors sought to measure the extent of disability among prisoners and find ways of lowering the associated costs. To ensure the smooth running of the Gulag's economy, managers needed inventories of prisoner labor. Plans were then set with production targets for each camp complex. The Moscow Gulag directorate constantly monitored the system's labor use (*trudispol´zovanie*) via routine statistical reports. These routines evolved from systems devised on the Solovetskii Islands in the 1920s. Originally, prisoners on Solovki had been assessed not by doctors but by work-assignment foremen (*nariadchiki*); from January 1927 on a decree established a Permanent Medical Commission to assess prisoners' fitness for labor, headed by the chief of the *sanchast´*.[44] For a brief interval, until 1931, it appears that doctors alone sorted prisoners by their capacity to work. If this physician-led sorting was indeed the case, such fully medicalized labor selection could not withstand the pressures of expansion once major construction projects were underway. In any case it is unsound to presume that medicalized labor assignments would necessarily be more beneficial to individual prisoners, given the collectivist and mobilized ethos that officially prevailed in Soviet medicine after 1929, whether for civilian, military, or penal populations.[45]

In 1931 medical-labor commissions were formally established at each camp, composed of doctors—some of them prisoners—placed explicitly under the supervision of the camp director and production managers. Sovereign, disciplinary, and biopower sat side-by-side on these commissions, a vivid expression of the intertwined imperatives of punishment and productivity that determined Gulag operations.[46] Twice a year they inspected all prisoners and classified them by labor capacity.[47] As in the civilian VTEK, clinical decisions were subject to the final approval of bureaucrats with an eye on the financial and legal implications.[48] Prisoners deemed fit for work were said to be in the labor balance or inventory or categorized (*kategoriinye*) prisoners. The disabled were identified (or had permanent disabilities confirmed) during these commissions. The prisoner discharged from labor duty permanently or for a long period of convalescence was said to be "off the labor balance" or inventory (*zabalansovyi*). Periodic classification of prisoners by their labor capacity operated throughout the lifetime of the Gulag, enabling managers to gauge the physical condition of prisoners and allocate them accordingly. The commissions became major public events, with Gulag bosses and *sanchast'* doctors typically presiding at a cloth-covered table, piled with inmates' personal files; prisoners bitterly recall their perfunctory examinations by free and prisoner doctors alike.[49] Prisoners capable of heavy physical labor (*tiazhelyi fizicheskii trud*, TFT) were assigned demanding general production tasks in forests, mines, and construction sites; moderate labor (*srednii*, SFT) often meant performance of the same tasks, but with a "discounted" norm; light labor (*legkii*, LFT) was often in ancillary roles.[50] Standing medical commissions assessed newly arriving prisoners and the newly injured and monitored prisoner-patients in camp infirmaries. Medical surveillance of the individual prisoner body as an input in Gulag economic processes was a routine and dynamic part of the multiple classification regimes that governed camp life.[51]

REGIMES OF INVALID MANAGEMENT AND THEIR EVOLUTION

During the 1930s three important institutions appeared in the camps to manage the disabled prisoner: first, the weak-prisoner teams (*slabosil'nye komandy*) and recovery teams (*ozdorovitel'nye komandy*) and, later, separate invalid camps attached to major camp complexes. These institutions went through periods of convulsion that buffeted the Gulag, and officials at national and local levels regularly redefined and reformed them. Nevertheless, despite significant pressures, Gulag directors never withdrew support for these special structures.

Weak-Prisoner and Recovery Teams

In November 1930 Deputy Director of the Gulag Matvei Davydovich Berman issued the first decree establishing weak-prisoner teams in the Gulag.[52] From 1 January 1931 on camps across the rapidly growing system were to establish these teams to house weakened and incapacitated prisoners for periods of one to two months, on a greatly reduced work regime and with a special ration intended to feed the prisoners up and restore their health. Prisoners "who had grown weak as a result of heavy labor" and the recently hospitalized incapable of being sent straight back to work were identified as the main clients for the weak-prisoner teams. Another key group highlights a major hazard of Gulag life: transport to camps (*etap*) was long and poorly supplied and left prisoners malnourished and sick; thus such candidates from prisoner transports were also listed. No camp was to assign more than 1.5 percent of its prisoners to these teams. In all cases, for an inmate to gain a place on the weak-prisoner team, Gulag authorities—probably the internal security organs and/or Cultural-Enlightenment Department agitators—had to vouch for the candidate's "good behavior and conscientious attitude toward labor." Explicitly excluded from the weak-prisoner teams were those whose health had so degenerated that "their full restoration of labor capacity cannot be counted on." The weak-prisoner teams were thus designed to feed up those who could be restored to general work, while specifically excluding work resisters and those unfortunates nearest to death, often from labor exhaustion. In February 1931 a decree from the Gulag's director, Lazar´ Iosifovich Kogan, made the purpose of the weak-prisoner team even more explicit: anyone assigned to these teams was to be sent back to heavy labor once they recovered. Periodic medical commissions were tasked with identifying the most suitable candidates who could be restored to the fittest labor category.[53]

The evolution of the weak-prisoner team in the Gulag medical surveillance system of the early 1930s shows that its early management was less centrally standardized than Moscow wanted. Such confusion arose against the backdrop of early efforts to divest the Gulag of tens of thousands of incapacitated prisoners via amnesties. A May 1933 Gulag report to the OGPU leadership called for the release of sixty-four thousand "invalids and those incapable of working."[54] By this time, in a report for Stalin the secret police estimated that of the half-million prisoners in the camps, 3.2 percent (12,700) were fully invalids, and a further 25 percent (ca. 100,000) were incapacitated due to illness and wastage from recent transportation.[55] Despite amnesties Gulag conditions continued to produce weakened prisoners, and doctors were called on to identify candidates sooner, before wastage demanding long treatment and convalescence set in. Decrees from Deputy Gulag Director Semen Grigor´evich Firin in 1933 tried to limit stays in the weak-prisoner teams to a maximum of fourteen days, but Berman (by now the Gulag's director) intervened to extend this tough limit by an additional two weeks, albeit with a quota of not more than 10 percent of the weak-prisoner team being allowed an extension.[56]

How the weak-prisoner team was taken up in individual camps can be gauged by a 1934 decree from one Fleishmaker, the director of the Sanitation Department at Dmitlag, the camp building the Moscow-Volga River Canal. The tone of this decree is aspirational, and there is scant likelihood that its directions could always be met in the local camp subdivisions, where free and prisoner doctors ran medical services. Candidates for the weak teams were to be selected from the "emaciated and sick" just coming off transports;

from those unable to fulfill the norm in general labor without a "discount" (*protsentniki*); from those recently discharged from hospital; and last, from those in good condition who were fulfilling or even overfulfilling the work norm, where doctors prescribed rest for strictly medical reasons. Weak-team prisoners were to be housed separately in well-furnished and well-supplied barracks and to be fed a very good hospital ration of 900 grams of bread per day plus various other foodstuffs. They also were due antiscurvy supplements and coupons to spend in the camp commissary shop. Under strict medical observation, they would be subject to a semihospital daily schedule set by medical personnel, who decided which prisoners were fit enough to perform very light tasks for short hours: housework and maintenance. Weak-team prisoners were to be tallied separately on the labor balance as weak-emaciated prisoners and not confused with hospitalized ones. No quota for the weak teams was given in the printed version of this decree, but limited resources and pressure from construction managers would have constrained numbers just as eloquently as an explicit quota.[57] Weak-prisoner and recovery teams were evidently reserved for the temporarily incapacitated and, on paper at least, were intended to refeed prisoners most readily recoverable for heavy labor duty.

The actual effect of these teams as remembered by inmates was at best mixed. Konstantin Petrovich Gurskii, a *zek*, recalled a 1936 weak-prisoner team in Ukhta being led into the forest by a medical orderly (*lekpom*) to collect mushrooms and berries according to a quota; these products were apparently intended for other prisoners. The foraging parties included prisoners deemed *dokhodiagi* (goners) by their peers. Yet Gurskii also found that the weak-prisoner team was a threshold to further medical care, where it was possible to attract the orderly's sympathy and receive treatment, perhaps leading to recovery.[58]

These teams proliferated dramatically as the camp system ballooned during the mid- and late 1930s. The numbers of nonworking prisoners soared as a result of the Terror, and a significant proportion of these inmates were temporarily or permanently disabled. As the Gulag matured in the 1930s, despite its "revolving door," it accumulated more invalids with increasingly dangerous "crimes" in their pasts, making it impossible—in the official view—to release them.[59] Reports by Gulag chiefs to Stalin emphasized that an intractable contingent of unreleasable, nonworking chronic patients and invalids, plus those not at work for other reasons, numbered about 100,000 prisoners by 1935 and 179,000 by mid-1938.[60] The Terror dispatched hundreds of thousands of prisoners to the camps in late 1937 and throughout 1938; the sudden rise in disabled and sick prisoners could not be accommodated in weak-prisoner/recovery teams—or in the invalid camps, discussed shortly—and from reports criticizing the practice, it appears that many invalids were hospitalized, undoubtedly in improvised and primitive conditions.[61] A significant proportion probably perished in desperate conditions; in 1938, 108,654 prisoners died officially registered deaths, a spike in recorded mortality not exceeded until the war.[62]

Late in December 1938, a central Sanotdel decree reformed the weak-prisoner team structure, dividing it into two groups.[63] Candidates for both groups were those weakened by general labor, transports, or recent illness; as before, they required a doctor's recommendation and references for productivity and attitude from workplace managers and cultural-enlightenment officials. This decree explicitly excluded chronic invalids with no hope of restoration of labor capacity, as well as "deliberate work-refusers, escape attempters, prisoners under punishment regime, or those who gamble away their rations." As in the past, there was no stated exclusion on the candidate's type of conviction; it was still formally possible after the Terror for "politicals" to join weak teams. Weak prisoners in the first group were to remain in their previous place of production, to be housed in specially provisioned barracks, and given rest days four times a month, medical examinations every ten days, and supplementary rations. Second-group team inmates were to live in hospital conditions and receive corresponding rations; supposedly they worked only if medical advice permitted, and no more than six hours per day at light housekeeping or workshop duties making consumer goods. They were to be subject to daily medical surveillance with doctors' examinations every five days. "Depending on the physical condition of the camp contingent," no more than 1–2 percent of the annual average camp population could be assigned to group 2 weak-prisoner teams; and no more than 2–5 percent to group 1 teams. These quotas, totaling 3–7 percent of the camp population, were a relaxation of the 1.5 percent limit set in 1931, a veiled admission of the seriously deteriorated condition of the prisoner population.[64] Group 1 prisoners were to remain allocated to the labor balance; "nonworking" team 2 prisoners were taken off the inventory. Recordkeeping and reporting to Moscow about these teams were to be overhauled, too.[65] The reconfiguration of the weak-prisoner teams, confirmed by the newly appointed Gulag director Gleb Vasil'evich Filaretov, was an early example of Beria's "reforms" intended to stabilize the Gulag economy after the chaos of the Terror.[66]

Separate Camps for Invalids

Significant numbers of camps were established for the permanently disabled in the Gulag in the 1930s. The spatial separation of disabled from able-bodied prisoners evidently gave bosses better control over the morale and labor discipline of both groups, rendering the most seriously work-incapable less visible. The invalid camps took different forms in the varied regions colonized by the secret police. By the late 1930s, they were a well-established part of the Gulag network of facilities operated by the Sanotdel, and all had some form of economic activity that justified if not supported their operation.

An early example again comes from Dmitlag. In a 1934 decree Dmitlag Sanotdel Director Fleishmaker laid out a detailed regime for an invalid settlement (*invalidnyi gorodok*) for the long-term disabled.[67] Those eligible were: (1) those who were totally incapacitated and who needed others to look after them (hospitalized chronically ill); (2) those who were totally incapacitated but did not require care; and (3) the emaciated and weakened whose recovery would take more than two months, the "temporarily invalid." The invalid settlement thus was to have a hospitalized, absolutely nonworking contingent and groups who could perform limited forms of labor. All inmates would be under the surveillance of a medical team and assigned work only with a "visa" from the doctor specifying the type of labor of which they were capable and the maximum time they could work. Work-capable invalids would make consumer goods in workshops for camp use. Hospitalized invalids were to get medical rations; workshop invalids, a base ration supplemented by production incentives. All were to receive antiscurvy supplements. The settlement was instructed to plant crops on its own allotments, too. These prisoners were to be removed from the labor inventory and recorded separately as invalids.

Grigorii Vlasovich Kniazev remembered how in 1938 an invalid camp was set up from scratch at Adak near Vorkuta, 20 kilometers from the nearest inhabited point. Able-bodied brigades were sent to clear the forest for tents, and in Kniazev's camp there was rising anxiety among the weakest prisoners, who feared transport to this empty quarter. He heard that the first invalid prisoners "were living in tents; there was no bathhouse, no kitchen, the food was prepared in a massive kettle in the open air. And regardless of the unfinished construction, one group after another of weak prisoners or crippled [*nepolnotsennye*] prisoners arrived there."[68] The elderly were discarded there too. Later in 1938 he was himself sent to Adak. There was little work organized for the inmates, and the weakest simply lay on bunks dreaming of food. The invalid-camp's doctor, also a zek, had few supplies and could do little to prevent death from starvation.[69] Kniazev, however, recovered sufficiently to be transferred to another camp, and he eventually found a job as an orderly (*sanitar*) in a camp infirmary.

Separate invalid-camp workshops probably made most of the consumer goods used in the Gulag. In 1933 the Gulag leadership could already boast a wide range of goods made in 1932 to a value of 11 million rubles, including furniture, toys, domestic products, hardware, leather goods, and musical instruments. The destination of these goods was unstated, but this report noted that future production was largely earmarked for consumption within the camps. The intended consumers were likely camp commandants, administrators, and their dependents.[70] Zinaida Danilovna Usova learnt to make furniture in a carpentry workshop at Talagi Invalids' Camp near Arkhangel'sk in the late 1930s. She eagerly mastered this trade and took pride in her stools, tables, and cabinets. Yet the ration in this camp was only 700 grams of bread per day, and the working day was far longer than those for the weak-prisoner teams: ten hours starting at 7 a.m.[71] At the same time, 23 kilometers from Magadan, at the other end of the USSR, Lev Lazarevich Khurges worked in a well-provisioned invalid camp, in a carpentry workshop and then a toy-making studio, receiving 800 grams of bread for an unspecified workday. Making toys, he wrote, "gave my heart a bit of joy. I would be decorating a doll, a toy rabbit or bear, and every time I took the next one in my hands and imagined some little kiddy's grin, I forgot about my hunger and all the humiliation of my life at that time."[72] These cases, contrasted with Kniazev's in a new camp for the disabled, highlight how assignment to an established invalid camp offered the chance of a degree of dignity gained through useful occupations, an aspiration shared by the disabled inside and beyond the Gulag.

The organization of separate invalid camps received additional impetus from the Terror, when the numbers of disabled swelled. A March 1938 instruction from Deputy People's Commissar of the NKVD Semen Borisovich Zhukovskii ordered all Gulag camps to organize invalids' subdivisions with workshops for consumer production, where the inmates would be held separately from the able-bodied and counted off the labor inventory.[73] The instruction came as part of a longer series of frantic directives trying to give order to the movement of prisoners out of urban prisons and onward to the remote camp complexes; disabled prisoners evidently confounded managers tasked with organizing this transportation. By one incomplete survey of twenty-eight camps, in May 1938 there were approximately thirty-three thousand invalids and weak prisoners in a total of just under nine hundred thousand prisoners (3.7 percent of this total). The situation was no better by the end of the year. In the first quarter of 1939 Gulag financial planners noted a population of sixty-three thousand invalids (3.11 percent of just over two million prisoners) including between thirty-five thousand and forty thousand who were absolutely incapable of work and had to be supported from the Gulag's state-subsidized coffers.[74] These, of course, were numbers of *designated* invalids, recognized as such by the administration. Certain camp complexes such as Noril´sk and Kolyma, because of extreme remoteness, refused to take weak and invalid prisoners from the mainland (although, of course, they produced and housed disabled prisoners like Khurges and Shalamov), and the pressure on all local Gulag commandants to meet production targets made them unwilling to accept such prisoners anyway.[75] Only by systematically excluding the disabled from the labor inventory and by subsidies could the invalid-prisoner be accommodated in the Gulag's economic model.

THE WAR'S IMPACT ON THE TREATMENT OF WEAK AND DISABLED PRISONERS

With the outbreak of war in June 1941 Gulag officials called on invalids to make a contribution to victory, and even the hospitalized and those normally considered incapacitated were mobilized. The wartime Gulag suffered historic peak rates of mortality, with 1942 the most lethal year and 1943 almost as bad.[76] Even productive, able-bodied Gulag prisoners received 800–1,500 calories per day less than required by the work they were supposed to perform. Gulag authorities presided over reduced rations and squeezed work rates that doomed huge numbers of prisoners to gradual death by starvation disease. As in civilian society, with few exceptions, malnutrition and associated disease, especially tuberculosis, were ubiquitous. Prisoners shared a common fate with free Soviet citizens, whose diets worsened severely during the war and remained remarkably deficient well after it. Donald Filtzer has demonstrated that Soviet civilian mortality in the urban rear reached two significant peaks at this time. First, in 1941–1942 the sudden shock of declining food stocks, evacuation, and worsening living conditions produced a spike in deaths among the elderly and infant populations. Second, a peak in deaths in 1943 among working-age males in the rear was the result of long-term starvation coupled with "nutrition-sensitive diseases," particularly tuberculosis.[77] Following Filtzer's analysis for civilian malnutrition-related mortality, it is unsurprising that the peak of Gulag deaths should have been reached somewhat earlier, in 1942, given the already prevailing poor nutrition, and that it should have continued into the following year. Just as refeeding programs began to arrest mortality in civilian Soviet cities in 1944, when the government secured better control over food stocks, similar programs operated, to a much more limited extent, inside barbed wire.[78] Gulag prisoners were not isolated from Soviet society when it came to the biopolitics of food distribution but suffered an extreme form of the same policies.[79] Even in these desperate circumstances the invalid in the Gulag was not regarded as "life unworthy of life." In late 1941, when the war was going badly for the Soviets, Gulag financial planners projected expenditures for 1942 of almost 86 million rubles on the upkeep of an estimated fifty-seven thousand recognized invalids. These projections represented a surprisingly marginal drop (of roughly 8 percent) on per capita expenses over the previous year, when there were fewer recognized invalids (53,528) and 87.6 million rubles spent on their maintenance.[80]

The realities of 1941–1942, and the brutality of life in some of the camps under the pressure of war, effectively meant that invalids were often put to work in general labor as though they were able-bodied. The futility and cruelty of such exercises is evident from investigations by legal officials. One prosecutor's report for the forestry camp Usol´lag in Perm´ oblast described three cases where commandants were punished for using invalids in general labor. Disabled prisoners were put to work fashioning felled logs into rafts to send downstream for refining.[81] At Iuzhlag in eastern Siberia, a similar case of the abuse of legless invalids—setting them work norms without a discount—was challenged successfully by a prosecutor inspecting a barrel-making factory in the spring of 1942.[82] The fact was that by 1942–1943 a huge proportion of the Gulag prisoner population was officially classed as invalids or sick and not available for general labor. In 1942 a staggering 801,350 of 1,777,043 prisoners fell into these categories—just over 40 percent of the prisoner population. The numbers fell to 411,921 of 1,286,294 prisoners in 1943, but it was still a huge increase from the rates of 20–25 percent of nonworking prisoners that so exercised Gulag officials in the 1930s.[83] One invalids' camp, Chernoistochniki, organized in 1942 for the Tagil´ camp complex, was said to have just one-third of its inmates at work in consumer-goods workshops; the rest were listed as weak and sick.[84] For the first two years of the war, the Talagi Invalid Camp inmate Zinaida Usova, having previously worked in a furniture workshop, was transferred to a boot-making shop. The workday was lengthened to twelve hours and rations diminished; the workshop received shipments of dead soldiers' blood-stained felt boots (*valenki*) which they repaired for reuse.[85] Memoir sources testify to experience in the invalid camps that taxed all endurance: invalid camps that were set up in a panic and shut down as quickly; a prisoner's struggle, as manager of an invalid house, to haul food across snow-blasted steppes to save her charges; the ghastly ritual of distributing basket-weaving materials to bedridden tubercular patients near death.[86]

As work capacity plummeted and sickness rates rocketed, Moscow tried to steer camp medical facilities toward priorities mirroring those in military medicine. In January 1943 Beria reminded all Gulag medical personnel that their principal task was to focus on the restoration of prisoners to production.[87] This decree adapted for the Gulag the basic principles of military triage in wartime: Red Army surgeons accorded top priority in battlefield medical care to soldiers who could be returned to the front.[88] Central Sanotdel authorities conducted a campaign in late 1943 to relieve overcrowded camp hospitals of the long-term sick and disabled, who were to be accommodated in "semihospital-like facilities."[89] Hospitalization was for the prisoner whose health was within reach, not for hopeless or chronic cases. Meanwhile, camp administrators addressed themselves to using invalid labor in more systematic ways.

As the war neared its conclusion and reconstruction loomed, disabled prisoner labor became the subject of closer scrutiny and schemes for productivity squeezing. Central camp authorities promoted the concept of "individual labor" (*individual´nyi trud*) calibrated to the capacity of each weakened, convalescing, or chronically ill prisoner. In December 1944 an instruction from Gulag Director Viktor Grigor´evich Nasedkin explained to camp bosses how to organize individual labor for consumer-goods production within infirmaries; the work was to be viewed as labor therapy, severely discounted from previously enunciated norms, and incentivized with food rewards for overfulfillment of quotas. One report issued simultaneously detailed how several forestry camps had established new subdivisions for the weakest working and incapacitated prisoners. There authorities assigned each prisoner individual labor tasks in agriculture or the usual consumer-goods workshops.[90] During and after the war officially sanctioned experiments in labor therapy (*lechenie trudom; trudoterapiia*) gained currency in certain camp sanitation departments in the Ukhta-Pechora region of the Komi Republic and elsewhere, with arguments that if labor assignments were brought under the control of physicians, weaker prisoners could be restored to full work capacity.[91] Gulag experiments in labor therapy mirrored long-standing and widespread civilian application of similar regimes with war veterans and convalescent tubercular or psychiatric patients.[92]

A striking biopolitical feature of Gulag experiments in invalid work therapy was the medicalization of virtually all norms and criteria enveloping the disabled prisoner. Doctors selected cohorts for these experiments according to familiar criteria: the weakened or disabled candidate who had not yet deteriorated irretrievably (by starvation or tuberculosis) was sought, and the psychological profile of candidates was assessed before and monitored during the experiments.[93] Doctors labeled their work prescriptions "dosages" (*dozirovki*).[94] Output norms were sometimes tied to incentive rations; in other experiments weakened prisoners got hospital rations regardless of output.[95] Doctors regulated prisoner housing, ensured supplies of soap and bed linen, and devised daily schedules. They monitored the subjects' physical condition using physiological, anthropometric, and weight-gain criteria.[96] Behind the language of "individual labor" and "labor dosages" was an increasing competition on the part of Gulag managers for able-bodied labor of all kinds, and a rising sense that, like all managers in the postwar Soviet economy, they would have to deploy more physically diminished labor power.[97] If before 1941 incapacitated zeks worked in locally improvised settings, now they were potentially subject to attempts designed by doctors to insert their damaged bodies into the production process. Such demands mirrored expectations placed on civilians; most of both the industrial and battlefield disabled might get official certification but were not exempt from the duty to toil.

The Gulag Sanotdel circulated the results of individualized labor therapy experiments across the system, but their intense use of resources could not be widely imitated.[98] Yet in the 1940s medical camp bosses using similar principles sought to rationalize existing structures aimed at the recoverable and invalid prisoner. In wartime the weak-prisoner and recovery teams of the 1930s were relaunched as recovery stations and recovery teams (*ozdorovitel'nye punkty/komandy*); as before they focused on reanimating the temporarily incapacitated prisoner while excluding the chronic invalid.[99] Recovery stations were reserved for relatively able workers in need of two weeks' rest (fig. 4.1). The recovery stations were the apparent mirror of refeeding programs targeting organized worker populations described by Filtzer.[100] The Sanotdel explained that recovery teams were for prisoners only able to perform general labor with a discounted norm and were intended to feed them back to health.[101] Memoirists recall the abuse of recovery teams and recovery stations by the criminal "aristocracy" of prisoners who had influence with gatekeepers or intimidated doctors to sign them in, but doctors also used them to save favored prisoners.[102] At Talagi, near Arkhangel'sk, in late 1942 Usova was admitted to a recovery-prophylactic station (*ozdorovitel'nyi-profilakticheskii punkt*, OPP) for a ten-day period, probably after a medical commission examined her. She thought she was chosen because she had learned boot making and was therefore "worth saving." She recalled that her friends "jokingly called the OPP our rest home" (*dom otdykha*), adding:

> In the OPP we did not work; they fed us better than usual and our mood improved somewhat. What really helped was that they gave us the chance to wash ourselves thoroughly, and we got fresh underwear, albeit men's. Our "holiday" [*putevka*] was for ten days and we decided to use the time as effectively as possible. We forced ourselves to toss all the dark thoughts out of our heads; we told each other funny stories, played checkers, chess,

Figure 4.1. "Patients in recovery-prophylactic stations make use of every sunny day. In April alone the OPP and infirmaries returned 2,886 persons to labor" (Tagil Corrective Labor Camp, 1943). *Source:* GARF f. 9414, op. 6, d. 6, Fotoal´bom Tagil´skogo ITL, 1: 1943.

dominoes. It was a moment to stop and catch our breath that we remembered for a long time. It did not do that much to improve our health, but we did step back from the edge of the grave just a little.[103]

In 1946 full-blown "recovery camps" were mandated, to be set up in existing agricultural camps, with the purpose of feeding up weakened prisoners; as before, medical commissions selected candidates according to their prospects for recovery of work capacity. Doctors were supposed to assign work corresponding to the individual's physical condition. Recovery camps were allowed to keep prisoners for up to five months.[104] In June 1947 a list of medical conditions entitling the prisoner to assignment to a recovery camp was produced; new was a list of proscriptions barring admission. As so often in the past, hopeless cases were formally excluded. The malnourished and those with tuberculosis and heart disease were only admitted if their condition could be improved. Others on the list of excluded prisoners were meant to be handled elsewhere in the Sanotdel network: those with mental and neurological illnesses (epilepsy, traumatic neuroses, severe mental illness); pregnant women; sufferers of sexually transmitted diseases.[105]

Meanwhile, the Gulag set up a growing network of discrete camps for the disabled in the late war and postwar years, spatially and financially separate from the general camps. In November 1946 a decree designated camps across the system as special invalid camps for the long-term incapacitated, to be supported by specially earmarked funds from the MVD budget. These camps were excluded from the general accounts that supposedly furnished the MVD with arguments for the profitability of forced labor.[106] The effect was self-deceiving. At this time the camps' central directors realized that local commandants hid many invalids in the weakest labor inventory categories. In part, this practice arose because managers lost many able-bodied workers during the postwar era, as the Gulag "contracted out" tens of thousands of work-ready prisoners to civilian economic ministries for postwar reconstruction. The camps were left with a larger proportion of weaker and nonworking prisoners.[107] The consequences again mirrored conditions in Soviet civilian life: invalids performed work normally done by able-bodied laborers. In 1952 in the Taishet camp system, Ivan Mikhailovich Evseev was certified an invalid by a medical commission and transferred to a special camp, where "they harnessed us, invalids, in teams of four to sledges and drove us into the forest to collect firewood. In a day we went there and back, it was about 7 or 8 kilometers."[108] Another mass phenomenon was perhaps driven by the expansion of Gulag clinics, infirmaries, and hospitals after 1945: self-inflicted injuries appear to have skyrocketed in the postwar years, contributing another stream of disabled prisoners.[109]

The Biopolitics of Disability in the Gulag

On the eve of Stalin's death, the infrastructure for housing weak and disabled prisoners had grown to proportions that challenged even MVD claims of the profitability of prisoner labor. Several camp complexes had large numbers of hospital, weakened-prisoner, and invalid camp subdivisions, sometimes comprising as much as one-third of the overall population of a complex.[110] On 1 January 1953, across the system 11.3 percent of inmates were officially classified as invalids.[111] Despite amnesties and labor-camp reform during the 1950s, disabled prisoners remained a major subgroup of the inmate population, and penal medical officers continued to debate how to improve their treatment.[112]

In the Gulag biopower was normally subordinate to the dictates of Foucault's sovereign and disciplinary power, represented at the center by NKVD commissars and Gulag directors, and at the local camp by its commandant and his administrative and security apparatus. The decrees defining the shifting regimes for disabled prisoners were not issued autonomously by the Sanotdel apparatus in Moscow but by the Gulag's director and his deputies. The Sanotdel was handed a problem created by sovereign and disciplinary powers: the prisoners' ever-deteriorating health. The dilemma was virtually

Figure 4.2. Participants in the doctors' conference of the Mariinskii raion health commit-tee and NKVD Siblag, 1935. *Source:* Narym Museum of Political Exile via the Memorial Society.

impossible to solve, given the limits to the Sanotdel's authority and the scarce resources at its disposal. One can infer that Sanotdel chiefs in Moscow pro-posed solutions and drafted these decrees for the approval of their superiors who ran the Gulag. Sanotdel leaders, who from the outset in 1930 personally inspected camps and received a vast quantity of reports from them, and who in later years presided over conferences (fig. 4.2) of their regional subordi-nates in the Gulag medical service, were well aware of the constraints to their expertise imposed by the specific position of their prisoner-patients.[113]

When confronting some of its most endangered charges—prisoners in-capable of labor and nearing death—the Sanotdel tried to marshal resources following the rationales imposed by its masters; this was the same logic found in civilian industrial and military medicine. Refeeding of the exhausted was to be reserved for the recoverable prisoner-worker body and, if possible, on a prophylactic basis to avoid long-term convalescence; quotas ring-fenced access to these programs; the prisoner's attitude toward labor mattered; and only in extremis was the disabled prisoner excused from some form of pro-ductive toil, no matter how symbolic. Where concentrations of disabled pris-oners accumulated, it apparently became necessary to separate them spatially from able-bodied zeks, no doubt to uphold the labor discipline of the major-ity of prisoners. Gulag bookkeepers also tried to render disabled prisoners invisible by keeping them off the balance sheet of the workforce. Within this rarified domain, in the later Gulag Sanotdel doctors might be granted the freedom to medicalize every aspect of the prisoner-invalid's existence in labor therapy and individualized labor regimes. Even here the gatekeeper was sovereign power, limiting the range of biopower to showcase experiments for a limited audience of medical and administrative officials.

The biopolitics of disability in the Gulag were cruel, but they reflected the bleakness of official policies applied to the disabled in civilian Soviet society, which in turn were a function of the larger biopolitics practiced by the Stalinist leadership to optimize resources and populations for industrial production and, from 1941 to 1945, for winning the war. Soviet biopolitical decisions mobilized scarce resources in a developing economy for the benefit of targeted populations; membership in a collective determined one's grade of access to provision, be it of medical care, sanitary supplies, and other life-sustaining goods. Allocation followed a complex logic dictated by strategic priorities in peace and war and, of course, ideology. As Donald Filtzer has pointed out for the late Stalin period, the regime consciously elected not to invest in urban infrastructure that assured optimal public health in the classic, West European biopolitical sense (water purification and sewerage, modern housing with indoor plumbing, health and safety equipment in the workplace). Soviet planners had other priorities. Epidemics and massive premature mortality among civilians were prevented only by sanitary measures such as quarantines, disinfection cordons, public baths where scarce soap could be rationed, frequent medical inspections of target populations, and "sanitary enlightenment."[114] This minimalist medico-sanitary regime prevailed outside the Gulag. Within it, the Gulag's biopolitical regime constituted a criminally reduced version. The treatment of disabled prisoners reflected this remorseless logic.

SCIENTISTS AND SPECIALISTS IN THE GULAG
Life and Death in Stalin's *Sharashka*

ASIF SIDDIQI

By THE EARLY 1970s the culture of underground or *samizdat* literature in the Soviet Union had evolved into a highly risky but established system for disseminating information among the dissident community. Banned literature—poems, fiction, accounts of current events—vied for space in poor-quality publications circulated through a clandestine network.[1] One such typewritten manuscript of less than two hundred pages struck a chord among many samizdat readers despite its unusual subject matter: it described the work of an aircraft design organization from three decades before. Known as *Tupolevskaia sharaga*, the manuscript, as one historian has noted, "attracted a large readership, becoming . . . a classic in the literature of dissent."[2] In vivid language its anonymous author recalled his experiences as an engineer in a special prison workshop headed by the giant of Soviet aviation Andrei Tupolev (fig. 5.1). The prison camp, organized sometime in the late 1930s as part of the Gulag, housed hundreds of leading Soviet aviation designers who, cut off from the outside world, labored through physical and psychological hardships to produce new airplanes for the cause of Soviet aviation. By coincidence, Tupolev died soon after this manuscript began circulating. In Moscow he was given a state funeral and his contributions were eulogized by Leonid Brezhnev, but unsurprisingly there was no mention of his arrest, incarceration, and work in a labor camp during the Stalin era.[3] The anonymously authored memoir, smuggled out to the West and published in English, remained a peculiar anomaly in the historical record, suggesting tantalizing lacunae in Tupolev's official biography.[4]

Although *Tupolevskaia sharaga* was the only substantive record of Tupolev's time in prison, it was not the first publication to describe the phenomenon of prison camps for scientific and technical work: in Alexander Solzhenitsyn's *The First Circle*, readers found a morally complex tale about

Figure 5.1. Andrei Tupolev in Omsk (1942). *Source:* S. P. Korolev Archive via Wikimedia Commons.

a dozen or so scientists and engineers—"specialists," in the parlance of the time—imprisoned in a penal colony who struggled to reconcile the frequently clashing requisites of conscience and ideology.[5] Solzhenitsyn's acerbic and ironic style brought to life a lost episode—albeit through fiction—of the Soviet intelligentsia. Both of these works, one fiction and one nonfiction, opened up a largely unknown dimension of the Stalinist system—the organization and maintenance of prisons established specifically to hold scientists, engineers, and technicians. The glasnost years brought more details.[6] The anonymous memoir, now much expanded, was finally published as *Stalin's Aviation Gulag* under the real name of its author, Leonid Kerber, a respected Soviet aviation designer.[7] A number of other scientists and intellectuals published memoirs of their own experiences in these camps, which the prisoners themselves called *sharaga* (*sharashka* in its diminutive form, pl. *sharashki*), a word derived from a Soviet-era slang expression meaning a shady organization based on fraud or deceit.[8] Partly because of the proliferation of testimonies about its history, and partly because memory of it confirms received wisdom about the Soviet state's damaging and ideological intervention into Soviet science, the sharashka remains one iconic example of the vicissitudes of Soviet science. Yet it has been a distinctly understudied topic in contrast to that other iconic exemplar of Soviet science, Lysenkoism, the memory of which has also embodied the triangulation of state, ideology, and science.

For many contemporary historians of Soviet science and technology, especially those based in Russia, the sharashka phenomenon represents only biographical history, an episode emblematic of the "tragic fates" of Soviet scientists and specialists.[9] The few scholars who have revisited the history of this unique system of incarceration have focused their questions either on how ideological concerns distorted the normal trajectory of Soviet science or on correcting the historical record by portraying the lives of those Soviet scientists and engineers who passed through the system in heroic terms.[10] The first assumes the existence of a normative science, and the latter lapses into hagiography. Both frame the history of the prison system as a great disruption—a Soviet rendering of "science interrupted." Here the scientists and experts are passive and subordinate to some larger levers of power emanating from an all-powerful, monolithic, central, and superstatist structure. State and science are frequently seen as two distinct categories with clashing motivations. Finally, although there has been a fundamental methodological shift within the literature on Soviet science, scholars have generally shied away from revisiting—this time with the benefit of open archives—the most coercive phenomena in the history of Soviet science, such as the Terror. Perhaps this has been because the horror of the Terror invites a narrative of perpetrators and victims, thus valorizing older unidirectional totalitarian models, where an omnipotent state, hand-in-hand with communist ideology, attacks helpless but noble scientists lacking in any agency.

While a biography of the sharashka network might be logically articulated in relation to the vicissitudes of Soviet science and technology, it also offers an excellent vantage point to revisit the relationship between the Soviet intelligentsia and Stalinist repression. My goal here is not to reconstitute a complete history of the prison network for specialists but to take a first step in wresting the history of the sharashka from the hagiographies of famous scientists and designers (such as Tupolev) and relocate it within the broader history of the Soviet Gulag. In the past decade work on the Gulag has expanded and deepened at an unprecedented pace. Making use of new archival sources and methodologies, historians and social scientists have investigated the Gulag at both the case study and the macro levels. Instead of seeing the Gulag as simply an outcome of state terror directed against the populace, scholars have variously analyzed it as a constituent part of the Stalinist economy, as a means to enforce strict control over public space and mobility, as a penal institution, or as a system for rehabilitation and redemption.[11] Despite this flowering of scholarship, there has been little study of the role of intellectual work as a constituent of the Gulag. Historians of the Gulag, while conceding the importance of the sharashka, have not engaged in any sustained study of the phenomenon.[12] Situating the history of intellectual labor within the history of the Gulag allows us to uncover how the activities of the Soviet intelligentsia—either by coercion or by its own initiative—reinforced and expanded the reach of the Gulag into the civilian economy.

The extent to which the Gulag and Soviet society writ large can be understood as coterminous or discrete objects of study has drawn the scholarly attention of many. Oleg Khlevniuk's notion of Gulag and non-Gulag, Golfo Alexopoulos's claim that the "gulag and non-gulag worlds regularly came into contact," and Galina Ivanova's summation that the geography of the Gulag "essentially coincided with the territory of the Soviet Union," all speak to the central issue of how best to conceive of the Gulag in Soviet history.[13] If, as Kate Brown has noted, the Gulag was "located along a continuum of incarcerated space," manifested in "a puzzling pattern of increasingly exclusive spatial practices," where does that leave the sharashka system, especially in comparison to other spaces of exclusion where knowledge was produced, such as the notorious "closed cities" (ZATOs) of the Soviet era?[14] What does the experience of the sharashka say about our understanding of the history of the Gulag, particularly about the tension between planned and ad hoc operation of the Gulag, institutional learning over its lifetime, and the overall economic effectiveness of the camp system? These are the questions that animate the current study.

A note on terminology: whereas historians have used a wide variety of terms to describe the inmate population of the sharashki, Gulag administrators almost always used *spetsialisty* (loosely translated as "experts" or "specialists"). This term came into widespread use in the aftermath of 1917 as the

Bolsheviks debated whether to recruit "bourgeois specialists" in the work of socialist reconstruction—Lenin himself having conceded that "to increase [the forces of production] without bourgeois specialists is impossible."[15] At the time, the label was most closely associated with the emerging technical intelligentsia, which included engineers and technicians but also applied scientists—that is, scientists whose work was linked with material production.[16] Yet, as became more common in the 1930s, many scientists involved in fundamental research in the basic sciences also redirected their priorities toward "practical" ends. Reflecting this shift, by the Second World War the specialists who crowded into the sharashka camps were a mix of scientists trained in basic research, applied scientists, engineers, and technicians, with the majority coming from applied science fields such as aeronautics, ballistics, metallurgy, mechanical engineering, and applied chemistry. Here I use a generic "specialist" or "expert" to denote this larger demographic, with specific attributions where more specificity is warranted.

Origins of the System

Despite the complexities and contradictions inherent in the history of the sharashka system, chronology provides a useful organizing framework to explore the phenomenon, with its endpoints coinciding with the beginning (1929) and end (1953) of Stalin's rule. The peak points of the system therefore parallel to some degree the traumas of Stalinism—the Great Break, the Terror and subsequent war, and late Stalinism after the Second World War. Although each era had its own dynamic, there were key continuities that ran through them. In all cases scientists and engineers were never arrested and incarcerated for the express purpose of intellectual work; in fact, the decision to use scientific expertise in prison-like conditions always followed short but intense waves of arrests among the Soviet intelligentsia. A necessary condition for the decision to put imprisoned specialists to work was thus an excess of penal labor generated by bursts of repression. But why were scientists and engineers arrested in the first place?

From the beginning of the Bolshevik era, the relationship between the political elite (in both the party and state hierarchies) and the scientific and technical elite was fraught with tension. On one hand, party leaders such as Vladimir Lenin, Nikolai Bukharin, and Lev Trotskii recognized that scientists and engineers would be indispensable in modernizing Russia. On the other hand, there was deep suspicion of the scientific and technical intelligentsia, because they represented all that the revolution promised to destroy: bourgeois culture, elitism, and a proclivity for academic concerns removed from the practicalities of the day. Such tension also produced in Bolsheviks a feeling of vulnerability as more and more scientists and engineers became entrenched in key positions in the Soviet economy. As Kendall E. Bailes has underscored in his classic works, the Soviet leadership used two strategies to resolve this tension: first, they threw the "old" specialists into jail; and second, they trained a new generation of so-called red specialists, younger men and women who would be more loyal to the demands of the Bolshevik era.[17] In the former case the attack on the old scientific and technical intelligentsia was embodied most famously in the Shakhty and Industrial Party trials of 1928 and 1930, respectively. Thousands were accused of wrecking the tempo of industrial production; many were sentenced, a few to death.[18] Simultaneously, the technical vocational schools in Moscow overflowed with young recruits, with large numbers from the peasantry.[19] The two options of repression and recruitment were effective, at least at first, but raised a secondary set of problems: it would take time to train the new intelligentsia; at least in the short term, the country lacked capable scientists and engineers to contribute to the First Five-Year Plan of industrialization. The solution to the problem thus created a new problem, demanding yet another solution.

Here the OGPU, the primary state security organ, played a key role. At this time, the OGPU was implementing a significant expansion of the Soviet penal colony system and using that network to feed labor to meet the pressures of massive building and construction projects. It is probably not a coincidence that the OGPU established the first prison facilities for specialists at approximately the same time that the Gulag and its network of corrective labor camps formally came into existence. Using skilled labor *under guard* for new projects, especially ones that required design supervision, offered a highly effective solution to the problem of what to do with the old specialists —seen as both indispensable and untrustworthy. The language of a circular prepared on 15 May 1930 by Valerian Kuibyshev and Genrikh Iagoda formalizing this arrangement suggested a contradiction that would mark the existence of these prisons through their lifetime.[20] The authors noted that "for the past two to three years, organs of the OGPU have revealed counterrevolutionary wrecking organizations in a number of branches of our economy" —specialists guilty of ideological untrustworthiness. Using this opportunity, the OGPU had sought "to use wreckers . . . in such a fashion that the work they carry out is primarily on the premises of OGPU organs. For this it has been necessary to select suitably trustworthy specialists [and] render them assistance in the matters of setting up experimental work."[21] This unstated but obvious tension between trustworthiness and untrustworthiness could be eliminated only within the OGPU, Iagoda argued, where "the conditions of work in a militarized environment will be able to ensure effective activities of the specialists, in contrast to the demoralizing situation in civilian establishments."[22] The OGPU began to implement its strategy with the Soviet aviation industry, which was undergoing significant expansion at the time, but the practice and the precedents established with the aviation specialists spread quickly to most other sectors of the Soviet industrial economy.

In 1928 and 1929, about thirty men, including the famous aviation designers Dmitrii Grigorovich and Nikolai Polikarpov, were arrested as part of the investigation into the Industrial Party conspiracy.[23] Initially, Polikarpov—the son of a priest—was sentenced to death (albeit without an actual trial), but while awaiting execution at the end of 1929, he was abruptly moved to the infamous Butyrka Prison, where he was escorted to the second floor of the compound to a large brightly lit room and shown a series of tables for drawing and a small technical library. Grigorovich, who was already there as a prisoner, announced to all who had just walked in—many of whom knew one another professionally—that he was in charge of this special design bureau, where they would be designing aircraft. Within a month, they were moved to an actual aviation factory, also in Moscow, where the men formed the core of the very first sharashka, a prison where all the inmates belonged to the scientific and technical intelligentsia.[24]

From the beginning, the OGPU established one of the most unique attributes of the system: under the watchful eye of OGPU officers, workers both incarcerated and free worked *together* in the laboratories. This peculiar arrangement, whereby free men and women labored with their fellow prisoners—at the end of the workday, the free specialists went home and the imprisoned went back to their barracks—was an organizational innovation that was passed down through the history of the sharashka system. It was a source of obvious social tension, exacerbated by the fact that typically, the ones incarcerated were elite and older scientists and engineers while those free, usually called "civilian" (*vol´nye*), specialists were the younger rank and file. This divide was as much symbolic as it was real: the arrangement was, after all, a metaphor for the clash between old and new, imperial and Bolshevik, oppressed and free. At the same time, the relationship between freedom and power was complicated by the OGPU's insistence on who should be in charge of the work. As one young and free engineer, B. V. Shavrov, later remembered: "We, the civilians, were subordinate to the [imprisoned engineers], although they lived under guard and could not even leave the factory. The arrested were our bosses, and over them were the [OGPU], who constantly interfered in everything."[25] The OGPU, it seems, did not trust the old specialists because they were too smart and did not trust the new red specialists because they were not smart enough.

Under extreme pressure to produce quickly, the imprisoned aviation design bureau worked in a rush. Red Air Force Commander in Chief Iakov Alksnis visited and ordered them to design a fighter aircraft with an air-cooled engine comparable in quality to those in Europe. Dozens of free technicians and designers were detailed to their projects, sometimes in a rather chaotic manner. Aleksandr Iakovlev, the prominent designer who would later be Stalin's personal adviser on aviation matters, recalled that the sharashka was "crowded and confused, the expense was great, and the returns were poor. Only Polikarpov worked brilliantly."[26] Yet the initial results made a big impression on their OGPU handlers. In May 1931, a year and a half after the sharashka had been organized, in a report addressed to the Presidium of the Central Executive Committee, Kliment Voroshilov and Sergo Ordzhonikidze were able to detail the "unprecedented acceleration of experimental construction" and "the exceptional work of Aircraft Construction Factory no. 39."[27] Among the seven different aircraft that the prison team designed and built in about six months, six were effectively dead-end projects, but one, a single-seat biplane fighter later named the I-5, remained on duty with the Red Air Force for nearly a decade (in fact, some were used for training in the Second World War). Principally designed by Polikarpov, Soviet industry produced more than eight hundred models of this aircraft, whose first prototype was wryly named VT-11 (from *vnutrenniaia tiur´ma*, internal prison]).[28]

Whereas the practice of maintaining specialists working in prisons was clearly begun and implemented without any systematic plan, in 1931 the OGPU's subdivision responsible for both auditing and investigating industrial activity, its Economic Administration (EKU), eventually assumed responsibility for managing and monitoring the work done at the various sharashki.[29] At the same time, the perceived success of the Grigorovich/Polikarpov prison design bureau in the aviation industry prompted the OGPU to organize similar projects in other industries and locales. By September 1931 the OGPU had comparable scientific and technical penal institutions in Moscow, Leningrad, Rostov-on-Don, and western Siberia, employing over four hundred scientists and engineers who had been arrested under laws applying to several different categories such as spies, terrorists, saboteurs, leaders of organizations, and Industrial Party members. The largest group of prisoners was accused of being "activists against the revolution."[30] Prisoners at these camps were initially tasked to military work—aviation, tanks, artillery, diesels and motors, submarines, conveyers, artillery targeting sights, chemical substances for military and industrial purposes, and protection against chemical warfare. Soon the profile of camps for specialists expanded to include nonmilitary matters, particularly to support large-scale industrial construction projects needing gas generators, coolers, high-pressure boilers, electrical motors, various electrification projects across the country, textiles, and the coal industry.[31]

As the OGPU began to assert its authority over the emerging sharashka system, it came into conflict with top industrial managers, a quarrel that appears to have remained constant throughout the existence of the specialist prison system. In May 1931, when Voroshilov and Ordzhonikidze wrote to Stalin "to grant full amnesty to . . . designer-wreckers [who had been] sentenced by the OGPU Collegium to various terms of social isolation," the OGPU resisted calls for their release.[32] This is evident in a series of exchanges in 1931 and 1932 over the issue between industrial managers such as Ordzhonikidze and OGPU leaders. In August 1931 Ordzhonikidze informed the Central Committee secretary in charge of industry, Lazar´ Kaganovich: "I think that at the current time the use of such [arrested] engineers is not appropriate. We have freed a significant number of specialists, [and] we need to free the remaining ones, excepting, of course, the especially serious [cases], and liquidate all existing planning and design bureaus from the OGPU, [and] transfer them to industry."[33] In response, OGPU Deputy Director Ivan Akulov wrote directly to Stalin to protect the sharashki, attaching a lengthy report about the many seemingly amazing achievements of the OGPU's 432 remaining imprisoned specialists.[34] Stalin was apparently unmoved, and Ordzhonikidze won. On 16 March 1932 the Politburo decreed that the prison specialist design bureaus should be "temporarily maintained" so that specialists could "finish their work," then liquidated. The plan was to quickly transfer specialists to the Commissariat of Heavy Industry (Narkomtiazhprom).[35] By 1933 almost all the specialist prison camps—even ones that produced little that they set out to do—were dissolved, with some surviving until 1935. While most transitioned into gainful civilian employment, a few unfortunate prisoners were given new papers and simply moved to regular prisons in the Soviet penal system.

Why was the system disbanded when it was? First, the political leadership —in particular, Stalin—had begun to express a more conciliatory attitude toward the prerevolutionary scientific and technical intelligentsia. In light of the perceived excesses of the Cultural Revolution, he and other industrial leaders such as Voroshilov and Ordzhonikidze articulated a broad rapprochement with "bourgeois" specialists in the early 1930s, in response to the demands of the massive takeoff of Soviet heavy industry as the country transitioned into the Second Five-Year Plan.[36] Stalin himself weighed in on the fate of specialists, noting in a major speech, "if in the period of defeating wrecking, our relationship to the old intelligentsia was expressed mainly in

Figure 5.2. Members of the TsKB-39 sharashka, including Kerber and Grigorovich, in 1931. *Source:* Wikimedia Commons.

the politics of defeat, now, during the turn of the intelligentsia to the side of Soviet power, our attitude to them should be expressed mainly in the policy of attracting and taking care of them."[37] That this was an explicit rationale for freeing imprisoned specialists was underscored when *Pravda* actually published, in July 1931, the decree releasing all the aviation engineers from the TsKB-39 sharashka (fig. 5.2).[38]

A second and more prosaic factor was the project-driven nature of many of these prison camps; almost all these installations were established to work on projects, and to work on them *fast*. For example, once the group of aviation designers completed their assignment to produce an effective interceptor aircraft, they were collectively freed by August 1931, since they had completed their assignments. Similarly, Leonid Ramzin had been put in an OGPU camp to supervise production of a new boiler system for industrial purposes; once the boiler was introduced into operation for Mosenergo, the Moscow energy authority, the design bureau was freed of its OGPU guards and subsequently operated as a standard industrial research organization at the same location.

Finally, and perhaps most important, the seed of the system's temporary demise stemmed from the conflict between the OGPU and industry over control of these design organizations. The evidence clearly suggests that the

OGPU leadership sought to extend their existence for as long as possible and keep them under its control. Yet neither happened, a symptom of the OGPU's weakened role in policing Soviet industry in the mid-1930s. In January 1932, in a major reorganization of Soviet industry, Ordzhonikidze engineered the creation of Narkomtiazhprom, the "super" ministry in charge of heavy industry, to lead the Second Five-Year Plan. An enormous number of industrial enterprises was brought under the ministry. One rationale behind this consolidation was to bring scientific research closer to factory production.[39] Despite the exaggerated claims of OGPU officials that extraordinarily impressive work was being carried out in the sharashka system, Ordzhonikidze and other industrial leaders were rightly suspicious of these claims. Barring a few major success stories such as the I-5 airplane, the first iteration of the sharashka system produced little that contributed to either Soviet industry or the military. In the mad rush to produce valuable research results, the outcomes were chaotic. As Vadim Shavrov, the Soviet aviation historian who worked in a sharashka, later lamented: "the system invented by the GPU was not justified. It was completely fruitless. It turned out that no matter how many people you throw at something, you can't make it go faster."[40]

THE SECOND WAVE

The second wave of prison camps followed rather than coincided with the Terror of 1937–1938. This is not so surprising when one considers that during the turbulence of the Terror, the NKVD was engaged in facilitating mass purges rather than managing economic growth, a duty it had increasingly taken on with the expansion of forced labor in the Gulag. At the height of the Terror, the repressions spread to almost every branch of science and technology, in institutions both within the Academy of Sciences and in the industrial commissariats, hitting especially hard in research institutes and factories associated with defense. In the aviation industry alone, almost every major aviation designer—including Robert Bartini, Konstantin Kalinin, Vladimir Miasishchev, Aleksandr Nadashkevich, Vladimir Petliakov, and Andrei Tupolev—ended up in prison (fig. 5.3). Factory managers were hit especially hard. In one major aviation factory specializing in engines, at least fifty people were arrested, including the director, the deputy director, and the chief mechanic.[41]

Most historical and popular accounts assume that NKVD Chairman Lavrentii Beria instigated and pushed the idea of a prison science system in the post-purge era.[42] But the resurgence of the system is more complicated and predates Beria's rise to chairmanship of the NKVD in December 1938. Remarkably, one source for a rejuvenated prison science network was the

Figure 5.3. The engineer Sergei Korolev not long after his arrest in 1938. *Source:* Wikimedia Commons.

imprisoned specialists themselves. Sometime in early 1938, as they awaited sentencing, a group of aviation designers who were languishing in the drudgery of the Lubianka put together two short proposals, one on airplanes and one on airplane engines. Fearing that they would inevitably be sent to forced manual labor camps in Siberia, the authors enumerated a list of specific military innovations that they could develop if given resources and sent their requests directly to Lazar´ Kaganovich, Ordzhonikidze's eventual successor as head of Narkomtiazhprom and a veteran of the aviation industry. Intrigued, Kaganovich passed the proposal onto then NKVD Chairman Nikolai Ezhov, with his own evaluation of the various technical aspects of the proposals—he liked some ideas, disliked others. He noted, "Having familiarized [myself] with the proposals of the arrested aviation designers, I consider it advisable to form them into a group."[43] Ezhov was clearly receptive to the suggestion and moved to implement Kaganovich's recommendations on airplanes and engines.

Kaganovich may not have known, but by the time he received the suggestion from aviation industry prisoners, a penal institution for scientists and designers had been operating in Leningrad since 1 December 1937. About 150 senior designers from the massive Bolshevik Factory—all independently arrested in the months and years before—had been sent to the infamous Kresty, one of the largest prisons in Europe, to work on naval artillery projects. Kaganovich's letter appears to have compelled Ezhov to put this work on a higher footing, and on 20 April 1938 Ezhov's deputy signed an order officially establishing a Special Design Bureau (OKB) of the NKVD Administration in Leningrad oblast.[44] At the Kresty the bureau initially included prisoners who had worked at the Bolshevik Factory but later grew to include scientists, engineers, and designers from a variety of factories involved in artillery design and production. The lead designer at the OKB was one Sergei Lodkin, a talented engineer specializing in turbine production who had originally been arrested in 1933 and worked for many years as a manual laborer on the White Sea–Baltic Canal, where he nearly died from tuberculosis. Having arrived at the Kresty in 1937, he was put in charge of developing a 130mm twin-gun naval artillery turret.[45]

As summer turned to fall in 1938, Ezhov's career was in trouble, and his first deputy, Beria, increasingly took over the day-to-day tasks of running the NKVD. On 25 November Beria formally succeeded Ezhov.[46] While he plunged with zeal into the task of undoing his predecessor's excesses—which included, of course, purging the NKVD of Ezhov's circle—Beria retained one innovation from the Ezhov era, the sharashka system. One of his first official duties as people's commissar of internal affairs was to consolidate and formally institutionalize the sharashka system directly under his command. In early January Beria wrote to Stalin about the various shortcomings of the work under Ezhov of the renewed sharashka system and suggested a number of improvements ("improve living conditions of the prisoners," "supplement the work staff with young specialists," etc.). Most critically, he noted that "to give more priority to the work of using imprisoned specialists . . . [the system] needs to be headed by the people's commissar [himself]."[47] The next day, 10 January 1939, the Politburo approved Beria's request and signed off on a charter for the "new" organization, now known as the Special Technical Bureau (OTB) of the NKVD. The goal of this institution was the "design and introduction of new weapons into the army and navy."[48]

What was the motivation for again committing to the practice of putting scientists, engineers, and specialists to work under guard? Undoubtedly, in the late 1930s the NKVD (especially under Beria), sought a stronger institutional role in the general rearmament in anticipation of war with Germany. As the historian Nikolai Simonov has shown, Beria dramatically increased the NKVD's share in defense industrial work by constructing, maintaining, and repairing strategic roads, investing in industrial development in remote areas with rich mineral deposits, and commandeering numerous factories producing metals.[49] Second, the control of leading scientists and engineers reinforced the NKVD's expansion of its own vast economic infrastructure based in the Gulag penal system—an obvious area for Beria to expand given its draconian control over vast human resources; and third and perhaps most important, the Terror that the NKVD had facilitated had so profoundly disrupted the functioning of scientific and technical organizations that some corrective work was required to bring the situation under control. In large measure the NKVD created a new phase of sharashki to limit damage of its own doing.

In formally institutionalizing and bringing under his direct command the renewed sharashka system, Beria classified work in this bureau into eight (later reduced to seven) different areas of science and technology. Each field would correspond to an independent team of specialists working at a given factory.[50] He also resurrected the old practice of attaching "groups of civilian specialists, [especially] young specialists" to work with the prisoners. In determining the content of the organization's work, the NKVD would take into account "proposals from the prisoners" but also initiate its own orders; final approval of any project was deferred directly to the GKO, the main defense policy organ under Stalin.

By mid-1939 Beria's Special Technical Bureau had at least three major locations where imprisoned scientists and engineers were working: a group working on naval artillery at the Kresty in Leningrad, two independent teams working on various airplane engines at a factory in Tushino in northwestern Moscow, and the newest addition—a team of prominent aviation designers under the "patriarch" of Soviet aviation, Andrei Tupolev—working in the Moscow suburb of Bolshevo.[51] Beria's intervention ensured that this network had the best resources available, including a staggering 35,870,000 rubles as its initial fixed-cost investment.[52] Although expenses in support of the sharashka soon descended to less stratospheric levels, one obvious financial perk was that there were fewer people to pay.[53]

All scientists and engineers who ended up working in the new sharashka network followed a general pattern of arrival. The experience of one engineer communicates the curious combination of trauma and relief experienced by inmates. Mikhail Khrapko had worked in Cheliabinsk, at one of the great Soviet factories of the First Five-Year Plan, where he helped produce the first mass-produced diesel tractor in the Soviet Union.[54] Known as the S-65 (Stalinets-65), it was extolled in speeches by leading party members as the ideal replacement for the horse-drawn carts (or if lucky, the Fordson tractors) that proliferated in collective farms across the nation. In the early 1930s Khrapko had visited the United States with his boss, Eliazar Gurevich, one of the most talented engineers at Cheliabinsk, a trip that came back to haunt both of them during the Terror. Gurevich disappeared from work in September 1937, and Khrapko was arrested two months later, among at least three hundred people from the factory. Khrapko was "lucky," since many of his compatriots, including Gurevich, were shot.

After a few terrible months at a prison in Cheliabinsk, Khrapko was sent to the Lubianka, beaten mercilessly, then moved to the Butyrka, the usual "sorting center" where specialist prisoners were selected for assignment to a particular sharashka. Many had just been returned from labor camps in Kolyma or Noril´sk, but some, like Khrapko, came directly from the Lubianka. Khrapko was finally assigned to Factory no. 82 in Tushino to help in the production of diesel engines for airplanes. He was thirty-five years old at the time. At Tushino, the conditions were spartan: he slept in the damp and dark prison barracks, in a large room with thirty-two beds. Like many, he felt a flush of relief for many of the "small" benefits of the sharashka of which he had been deprived after his arrest. Khrapko mentions one of his small joys: that inmates could use the toilet anytime during the day instead of the two allotted ten-minute periods at the Butyrka.[55]

Recruitment of specialists for the sharashka network took different forms. Initially, it was the responsibility of Valentin Kravchenko, who in November 1939 succeeded Beria as the operational head of the Special Technical Bureau.[56] Educated at the Odessa Institute of Communication Engineers, Kravchenko had a quiet ruthlessness about his activities. He would visit the Lubianka Prison, select specialists from its files, transfer them to Bolshevo, and assign them to the various different design bureaus in the sharashka network. As the practice expanded, Kravchenko depended on NKVD deputies such as Grigorii Kutepov, a barely educated man in charge of the aviation sharashki who had worked as an electrician at an airfield in his youth. Kutepov, perhaps lacking confidence in his ability to identify potential recruits, passed on this all-important responsibility to the prisoners—in particular, Andrei Tupolev, the de facto father of interwar Soviet aviation, who was thrown into the sharashka network in 1939.[57]

By mid-1939 over three hundred men (and these were only men) constituted the seed of the NKVD's specialist prison system, including the cream of the crop of the fields of aviation, shipbuilding, artillery, and firearms.[58] Although they had been arrested on the usual charges of wrecking, spying, and counterrevolutionary activities, most had been moved to the prison network *before* they could be brought to trial and sentenced; thus they were, in effect, in a state of legal limbo. On the matter of their jail sentences Beria displayed a marked coldness. He wrote to Stalin: "To resume investigation of [the confined engineers] and transfer them to trial in the usual order is inadvisable, since first, this will distract the arrested specialists for extended periods of time from work on designing important objects . . . and second, the investigations will not yield . . . positive results because the arrested, having been mutually associated [with one another] for a long time during their work, [may] have agreed among themselves on the nature of their testimonies for [any future] investigations."[59] Instead, without the usual formalities of a trial, Beria divided the prisoners into three categories of confinement, with ten-, fifteen-, and twenty-year sentences.[60] He proposed that the promise of a trial —and potentially shorter sentences—should be used to "encourage" prisoners to work harder.

The conditions in the prison design bureaus were far better than Siberian labor camps or indeed normal prisons of the NKVD, such as the Lubianka or Butyrka. When new prisoners arrived, they could hardly believe their eyes. Rumor has it that Tupolev, arrested in 1937 for being the "head of an anti-Soviet wrecking organization and an agent of French intelligence," arrived at the prison camp carrying a ragged empty bag, a piece of bread, and a few cubes of sugar, all of which he adamantly refused to give up even when told that there would be well-rounded meals.[61] Leonid Kerber, the author of the famous *Tupolevskaia sharaga*, remembered that "after the [hard labor] camp, such feeding . . . was like a sumptuous feast."[62] Beria responded quickly to inmate complaints about the poor quality of meals and once instructed the prison staff to improve rations.[63] For Tupolev's team of aviation designers, workdays usually began at 9:00 a.m. and lasted until 7:00 p.m., with one hour for lunch. Work conditions deteriorated with the onset of war. Khrapko, who worked at a sharashka prison in Kazan, remembers the lack of fuel for heat, fourteen-hour workdays, and food that was utterly inedible.[64]

Tupolev's group worked at Bolshevo for a while but moved to a larger facility, Factory no. 156 in Moscow. They worked on the top three floors of a building on Radio Street that capped three large dormitory rooms where the two hundred prisoners slept. Inmates were allowed to go for walks on the building's enclosed roof, which they called the "monkey cage." The specialists remained under armed guard at all times, had their conversations monitored, and were never left alone except for sleep at night. All the windows and doors were barred. For many, the most difficult aspect of the incarceration was the state of isolation; information about outside events was fully controlled, while prisoners' families had no idea where their relatives were—or if they were alive. This changed after 1940, when relatives were allowed a ten-minute visit to the Butyrka Prison every few months. The social structure was complicated to a large degree by the presence of civilian or free specialists who were junior to the prisoners but able to go home at the end of the day. Some former prisoners remember the relationship between the populations as being mostly cordial, whereas others felt more strained and saw the free specialists as aligned *against* the prisoners, working on behalf of the NKVD.[65] In Tupolev's aviation design bureau, TsKB-29 (fig. 5.4), about

Figure 5.4. The KOSOS building, home of TsKB-29, as it appears today. Photograph © 2015 Kirill Glebov.

five hundred free engineers reported to their prisoner chiefs during the day before heading home at night.[66]

Small groups of sharashka inmates were freed through the war, but most remained imprisoned until the outcome of the war was a foregone conclusion. A number of prison design bureaus were closed beginning in 1944, with prisoner specialists being freed in a slow trickle that continued until 1948, when the ten-year sentences from the time of the Terror expired. A typical round of releases came in July 1944, when thirty-five men at Factory no. 16 in Kazan were freed.[67] In a letter to Stalin Beria justified the seemingly abrupt release of these men, not because the system had failed to produce anything but because, apparently, the system had succeeded so well that there was no longer any need to maintain it. He noted, "given the importance of the work carried out, the USSR NKVD considers it appropriate to release, with the removal of criminal records . . . the eminent incarcerated specialists and direct them to work in the aviation industry."[68] Beria listed justifications for the release of each of the thirty-five men with specifics about their contributions to weapons and processes that helped the war effort.[69]

Was the Gulag's wartime prison science system productive? For the most part the answer would be yes. Extremely tight control, narrowly focused goals, and high levels of funding led engineers to achieve their targets. Judging by a summary of the entire sharashka system—officially known as the NKVD's Fourth Special Department—issued in 1944, the NKVD believed that the results were overwhelmingly positive. In the report the authors listed twenty major weapons systems or processes—including bombers, engines, propellant production techniques, radio systems, a host of artillery guns and cannons, and new chemicals—developed by prisoners. Of these at least twelve were introduced into mass production, a relatively high percentage in comparison to the prewar record of military research and development. Nearly all the projects reached the certification-testing stage.[70] Beria noted, "as a result of having introduced the many measures proposed by specialists and realized at various factories, [we have achieved] savings of state resources on the order of many millions [of rubles]."[71] Whether this was true, or even measurable, is perhaps less important than the fact that Beria tried to convince Stalin that it was so. At least on paper, the sharashka system was seen as a triumph of the NKVD's organizational innovation. No one considered the possibility that these prisoners might have achieved as much or more had they been kept out of prison.

THE LAST WAVE

The end of the Second World War raised the hopes of millions of Soviet citizens. After the traumas of terror and war, many hoped for a reprieve of the repressive Stalinist state. And for many there *was* a brief ray of hope. By 1948 almost the entire sharashka system—the Fourth Special Department of the NKVD—was disbanded and hundreds of specialists freed after serving their original sentences.[72] Yet this interregnum lasted a brief time. Most of those released after the war were rearrested. Less than two years after his release, for example, Mikhail Khrapko was abruptly arrested again and sentenced to lifelong exile in eastern Siberia, where he worked effectively (although not officially) as a prisoner in Igarka, a town more than 150 kilometers north of the Arctic Circle. Many of his colleagues suffered a similar trauma of rearrest in the late 1940s. Pavel Zhukov, who worked in Tushino during the war and was rearrested in 1948, believed that there were informers who tracked his opinions ("defeatist moods") during his brief period of freedom.[73]

Such stories of rearrest were common, especially in the third and last resurgence of the sharashka system, which coincided with renewed repression in both the scientific and engineering communities in the late 1940s and early 1950s. Because of Solzhenitsyn's semiautobiographical *The First Circle*, it is the best-known example of Soviet prison science. *The First Circle*'s mix of quasi-historical narrative, lyrical prose, and moral quandaries resonated deeply with a Western audience in the late 1960s and 1970s, and for many, the Marfino sharashka—based in a suburb northeast of Moscow where inmates developed spy equipment for the state security agency—remains the point of reference for popular conceptions, especially within Russia, of the specialist prison phenomenon.[74] Ironically, the postwar sharashka system has also been the least cited by historians; the bulk of scholarly work has favored the Tupolev sharashka, in part because several famous Soviet scientists or engineers were incarcerated there. The specialist prison system in the late Stalin period, in contrast, held few prominent members of the Soviet intelligentsia. It emerged from renewed mass repression in the postwar era but benefited from significant growth of the Gulag (and its economy) and concomitant pressures of rapid reconstruction in the light of widespread wartime destruction. Such factors, absent in the interwar sharashka system, filled the specialist prisons of the late Stalinist era with rank-and-file specialists from the Soviet scientific and engineering community.

The surge in repressions after the Second World War did not happen in a vacuum. The Gulag economy expanded at an unprecedented level during this period, so that by 1950 it held approximately 2.5 million prisoners in its various camps and colonies. About half of them worked in the Gulag's infamous Third Department, dedicated to gold mining and extreme hard labor. Another third worked in postwar reconstruction sectors such as forestry, railroad construction, military production, hydroelectric power, and capital construction.[75] All these activities required scientists, engineers, and technical specialists to supervise design and construction; many worked in the MVD structure as salaried employees, but others, already in prison, were forced into "employment" for the Gulag economy. From the Gulag administrator's perspective, the creation of a new phase of sharashki was a rational response to the broader social pressures of mass repression, growth of the Gulag economy, and the genuine needs of postwar reconstruction.

Conveniently and not coincidentally, many members of the scientific and technical intelligentsia arrested in the late Stalin years came from professions useful for Gulag activities on the periphery. In 1949, for example, as part of the Krasnoiarsk Affair, the MVD began a campaign of repression against Soviet geologists—many of them Jews—ostensibly because of the lack of uranium deposits in the Krasnoiarsk region. The arrests eventually spread to major cities across the country as dozens of geologists were given long prison sentences for the standard accusations of "wrecking" and "sabotage." Tellingly, the accusations included claims that the principal professional association of geologists privileged old specialists rather than newer and young Soviet-trained specialists, the exact allegations that had led off the first wave of repression against scientists and engineers in the late 1920s.[76] Almost all these geologists—and many hundreds more from a variety of other disciplines such as metallurgy—ended up in prison design bureaus in remote areas of the Soviet Union supporting mining or industrial operations.

The sharashka system in the late Stalin years was the largest incarnation of the specialist prison system. The scale of the postwar network was largely a result of the MVD's reformulation of the system as a fundamental part of the Gulag's *production* economy, which included mining in the eastern Soviet Union and massive construction projects. In fact, the amount of capital construction implemented by the MVD nearly doubled from 1949 to 1952, roughly the time period when the third phase of the sharashka system peaked.[77] One of the most important nodes of the new iteration was Special Technical Bureau no. 1 (OTB-1), created by the MVD in 1949 for geologists and metallurgists to conduct research on various aspects of mining. Their activities included the study of ore samples of mineral deposits, the search for deposits, the purification of ores and minerals (especially antimony, used in batteries), research on conversion of ores and metallic concentrates into industrial products, and the development of new equipment for mining, industrial work, and enrichment.[78] The design bureau, which had satellite facilities spread across eastern Siberia, operated under the dual control of Eniseistroi, a major Gulag directorate of ten camps, and the old Fourth Special Department of the MVD, once again headed by Valentin Kravchenko, the "veteran" of the wartime sharashka system who had been detailed back to the system.[79] Further expansion followed. In November 1949 the MVD's Fourth Special Department and the Gulag administration jointly organized five more bureaus that were to be staffed with "deportees . . . with a higher technical education." The importance of the work of these prisoners was stated unequivocally. They were to undertake "scientific-research and planning-design work" to ensure the "maximal use of economic resources in newly developed enterprises and construction sites in the remote areas of the USSR."[80]

Memoirs paint a surreal picture of the postwar sharashka system. Valentina Georgievna Perelomova, a civilian who worked at OTB-1, recalls a motley crew of prisoners working in a remote corner of Siberia: former professors, geologists, metallurgy experts, specialists in petroglyphs, photographers, even artists (assigned to lay out and design official reports for the MVD). There were occasional scientific expeditions into the wilderness to survey remote regions, and in some cases prisoners died in captivity from illnesses acquired during their incarceration. Of the nearly two hundred people imprisoned there, almost all were politicals, sentenced as a result of the infamous article 58. Perelomova met her future husband, Iurii Pogonia-Stefanovich, at the camp where, against all odds, they tried to maintain a romantic relationship.[81] Such relations were clearly exceptions, as dealings between prisoners and civilians at OTB-1 were generally fraught with tension. Characterizing this interaction as hostile, in contrast to the friendly relations between free and imprisoned specialists in the 1930s, M. I. Levichek, the first director of OTB-1, reflected that "this can probably be explained by the fact that in the 1930s there was still a . . . perception of the prisoners as victims, and the moral decay of society inherent in the Stalinist regime had not yet reached its depths, as in the 1950s."[82]

What motivated so many scientists and engineers to work diligently or at least somewhat productively in the sharashka system? During the war, patriotism was undoubtedly a factor, as many testimonials attest. Yet we cannot discount coercion, imposed using a variety of methods, including threats to be returned to manual labor camps. But MVD bureaucrats quickly learned that coercion alone was often ineffective and usually costly—especially given the relatively high wages necessary to maintain the tens of thousands of guards and the enormous logistical costs of supporting camps in remote locations to ensure secrecy. Work productivity was a huge problem for inmates, and MVD managers even adopted material incentives to improve work output. In 1948 the Gulag administration introduced wages into its economy. Through various periods the MVD also offered workday credits to selected prisoners; these credits essentially promised to reduce an individual's sentence by two days or more for every day that he overfulfilled a production norm.[83] For specialists producing patents the MVD even tried to offer some remuneration; in 1952 Beria signed a decree offering 25 percent of the normal "civilian" rate for patents filed by prisoners.[84] Despite these relatively radical measures, overall labor productivity continued its slow decline into the early 1950s. Although coercion and incentive motivated prisoners to work, they had no substantive effect on productivity or creativity.

By the time Stalin died in 1953, the gross economic inefficiencies of the Gulag system—especially its horrific system of forced manual labor—could no longer be ignored. The sharashka system, too, was subjected to scrutiny. Just three weeks after Stalin's death, on 30 March 1953, the MVD, under Beria's instructions, dismantled its Fourth Special Department governing prison camps for specialists. A few sharashka establishments continued to operate until 1955, but the system as a formalized institutional phenomenon ceased to exist.[85] Like the larger Gulag, the sharashka system proved unprofitable. The hidden costs of the system—particularly the need for guards and the concomitant requirement to maintain absolute secrecy surrounding its existence—mitigated any hope of productivity as compared to the free scientific and engineering community. Yet the seeming belief that the system was an effective solution to economic disruptions was sustained for over two decades, despite evidence to the contrary, especially in the later Stalin years. In referring to how it was possible for the state to maintain the Gulag based on economic rationales, the historian Valery Lazarev has noted that "a rational dictator . . . could institute and maintain such a 'surplus-extracting' enterprise" despite the obvious economic costs of the Gulag because of "the principal miscalculation . . . that Gulag labor was somehow 'free,' coming at no cost to society."[86] In the final accounting the social invisibility—of people, place, and knowledge—proved to be a central feature of the sharashka network, not only of its existence but also its demise.

In the last years of his life, Viacheslav Molotov, Soviet minister and diplomat, was asked about the rationale for imprisoning the best Soviet scientists and engineers. He responded

> at the time the intelligentsia was opposed to Soviet power! And they needed to be brought under control. The [scientists] were put behind bars, and the Chekists [political police] were instructed to do everything they could to create ideal conditions for them, serve them the finest food, better than what anyone else got, but not to release them. They were to work and design things for the country's military. The Chekists were told, "These are absolutely essential people; it is not the potential for open propaganda that makes them dangerous but their personal authority and influence; at a crucial moment they can become extremely dangerous."[87]

Molotov's coldhearted soliloquy is astute in one sense—in the eyes of the Bolsheviks (and later the Stalinists), what made members of the scientific and technical intelligentsia most dangerous was not their ideas but their authority and influence. Yet the Bolsheviks conceded that their mission to remake Russia as a modern socialist utopia would require the specialists' expertise. The sharashka system was in many ways an obvious solution to this conundrum.

This tension was a necessary but not a sufficient condition for the creation and maintenance of the prison science system. We must look for other contextual explanations for the foundation of this phenomenon. All three phases of the sharashka system were preceded by immense social upheaval in Soviet society—the Cultural Revolution, the Terror, and the resurgence of repression in the late Stalinist period. In each case the Soviet security services, often aided by leading party and government functionaries, instituted widescale campaigns of mass coercion in the form of purges, one of whose targets was the Soviet scientific and technical intelligentsia. Mass incarceration resulting from these purges undoubtedly disrupted important economic activities—the very activity that the Gulag was supposed to strengthen. As a short-term solution to the problems that the NKVD itself had created, it put scientists and engineers to work. The goal was to stabilize sectors of the economy that had been rendered unsteady.

These three massive traumas—each followed by heightened sharashki activity—mirrored and paralleled the peaks and troughs of the history of the Gulag. They underscore the inherently ad hoc quality of institution building within the Gulag and the way in which planning was rather muddled, accidental, and rarely reliant on institutional memory, each phase of the sharashki almost reinventing itself and learning its culture anew. More and more, we are finding that the birth, maintenance, and ultimate demise of the Gulag were all deeply contingent episodes characterized by pervasive confusion about the very purpose of the system, its goals being constantly redefined to fit the changing shortcomings that economic planners and security service administrators seemed to find in every nook and cranny of Soviet society.

Industrial managers and Beria's minions (and Gulag administrators) frequently disagreed on how to make proper use of the sharashki. For much of the Stalin era agents of state security enthusiastically supported the idea of having specialists work in prison, while industrial managers in charge of economic and scientific development resisted it. This is most evident in budget requests. In 1941, for example, Beria wanted 9.6 million rubles for one of the prisons, but Voroshilov agreed to only 4.8 million.[88] The ebbs and flows of the system in many ways mirrored the vicissitudes of this relationship, as claims for more security and faster development clashed with each other.

The sharashka camp network was successful as a coercive phenomenon, but was it successful as an economic one? Beria's claim in 1944 that the system achieved "savings of state resources on the order of many millions [of rubles]" cannot be accurately measured, since it represents essentially a counterfactual claim. Yet there are those today who see the sharashka idea as a valuable organizational innovation, a kind of progenitor to Silicon Valley or the proposed Skolkovo complex in Russia.[89] Mikhail Morukov, a young Russian historian, writes in *The Truth about the First Circle of the Gulag* that the "truth of the Gulag . . . lies in the fact that the isolation of scientists, designers, and workers in prison for defense work was necessary, and [it was] the only true condition for their personal survival and our common victory [in the war]."[90] Glaringly, his argument glosses over the fact that the four years of the war constituted only a *tiny* portion of the existence of the system, which spanned almost a quarter-century.

The obvious weakness of Morukov's claim still leaves us with the larger question of the economic productivity of the system as a whole. As recent scholarship has looked at the productive capacity of the Gulag—and its constituent role in the Soviet economy—a more accurate accounting seems possible. The overall inefficiency of the Gulag is not in question; based simply on human losses, the Gulag represents both a grossly inhuman and an inefficient enterprise.[91] Judged on economic indices, by the early 1950s it was clear to both Gulag managers and party officials that labor productivity was 50–60 percent *lower* within the camps than outside them. In the end a fundamental contradiction broke the system: a system designed to punish and a system designed to exploit the victims' labor proved successful at the former but not the latter.

Although the sharashka was left behind in the detritus of history, it cast a long shadow over the Soviet economy, particularly the Soviet defense sector. One of its legacies was the transmission of a kind of organizational *mentalité*. Because recruitment into the specialist prison network worked through the personal intervention of prisoners who remembered friends from their civilian lives, the system as a whole produced a generation of Soviet scientists and engineers who not only knew one another before their prison sentences but shared an enormous trauma that deeply affected their later lives. An entire cohort of elite scientists and engineers who were arrested during the second wave in the late 1930s went on to head their own design and engineering firms in the post-Stalin era. As a group they dominated research and development, especially within the Soviet military-industrial complex, thus propping up Soviet state power through much of the Cold War. Their adoption and occasional enthusiasm for certain traits of the organizational culture of the Soviet scientific and engineering system—extreme secrecy, strict hierarchies, coercive practices, rigid reporting protocols—owed much to their shared experiences with similar peculiarities characteristic of the sharashka system. For them the sharashka experience represented not only a shared rite of passage but also a deep enculturation into the values of coercion, incentive, and especially secrecy in institutional culture.

Knowledge of the history and work of the sharashki also invites us to consider its relationship to the regulation of space, information, and people in the late Soviet Union. Like the larger Gulag, the sharashki were occluded from public view. These camps were never shown on maps, and the knowledge that they produced was never discussed in public fora. The Gulag maintained its secrecy regime in creative ways. For example, administrators took great pains to create a unique and dehumanizing language of numbers, acronyms, and fake names. By the late 1930s the Soviet landscape was dotted with Gulag camps and colonies known only as "post office boxes," "special facilities," "units," and so forth. Not coincidentally, by the 1950s one could find the exact same conventions used by hundreds of thousands of men and women who worked in the Soviet scientific and defense industry—also a litany of post office boxes, special facilities, fake names, and fictitious towns.[92] For the many scientists and engineers with experience in the Gulag's sharashki, such an organizational nomenclature was undoubtedly familiar, a mode of identification legible and meaningful to those in the know, specialists who had spent time in the Gulag's islands of knowledge production.

The spatial dimension of the sharashki invites an obvious comparison with the "closed cities" of the Soviet scientific and military industry, known in official parlance as ZATO (*zakrytye administrativno-territorial'nye obrazovaniia*, closed administrative-territorial formations). These urban sites— about forty of them—were towns artificially created during the early Cold War to produce scientific and engineering work, largely for the military. The cities never appeared on any Soviet map, becoming visible en masse only in 1991, when forty-four "new" dots appeared on Russian maps.[93] During the Soviet period, the scientists, engineers, and specialists who worked in these places had special passes to live and leave and were themselves occluded from public view, unable to reveal their place or purpose of employment to relatives and friends who lived in "open" cities.

Besides secrecy—expressed in the language and cartography of omission—the sharashka network and the ZATOs shared three other key attributes: they were both designed as experiments to bring together experts to produce knowledge; they were highly exclusionary, employing for the most part elite and accomplished experts; and state-sponsored regulatory regimes made it extremely difficult for people or knowledge to cross the boundary that separated these sites from the outside. Living and working in ZATOs or sharashki was a commitment to exclusion, the former voluntary and the latter forced. This exclusion operated in different registers in each space: for members of the Soviet intelligentsia—particularly scientists, engineers, and technicians—the closed cities represented exclusion based on *aspiration*, where the day-to-day amenities of life were seemingly abundant and plentiful. The sharashka was also aspirational (a step up from the labor camp) but simultaneously dehumanizing (still within the Gulag).

The sharashki and the ZATOs were originally formed as sites for knowledge production, yet in practice they became sites where knowledge disappeared, like absent dots on a map. Everything about them was an official secret: the identities of those who worked there, the kind of work they did, the institutions involved, their population, even the precise contours of their borders. The work at these sites, as at Tupolev's sharashka or Solzhenitsyn's camp at Marfino or ZATOs such as Krasnoiarsk-26 or Cheliabinsk-65, was military in nature. Driven especially by the demands of Soviet modernization, these sites—both the sharashki and the ZATOs—became citadels where information disappeared, like black holes in the Soviet landscape. In their absence, both in maps and in discourse, they represented a particular intersection of the regulation of space and information. Of course, the regulation was rather imperfect—often deliberately so, as in the mix of free and imprisoned workers in the sharashki, and often accidentally, as in the rumors that proliferated about the sharashki and ZATOs in Soviet life.

All these concerns resonated at a practical level. Consider the transition from the sharashka to the post-Gulag world after 1953, made all the easier by the lack of a physical move. In many cases specialist prison camps that had operated under guard became free enterprises the next day just by allowing the specialists to go home at the end of the day. For example, in 1955, the prison laboratory where Solzhenitsyn worked (Special Prison no. 16) was renamed the Scientific-Research Institute of Automatics. It still exists today and develops secure communications systems for the Soviet government.[94] The mining sharashka at Krasnoiarsk is now the Siberian State Planning Institute of Ferrous Metallurgy.[95] Many prisoners from the last iteration of the sharashka system simply remained at their place of exile and adopted these alien cities as their new hometowns, where they raised their children. Pavel Zhukov, the Leningrader who was arrested a second time after the war and exiled to a sharashka in Karaganda in 1949, remained in Kazakhstan after his release. After his rehabilitation in 1956, he had the right to return to Leningrad, but after so many traumas he gave up and found a job at a local research institute, founded at the same site as the former specialist prison. He married and raised a family and continues to live in Karaganda, now no longer as a Russian citizen. Despite nearly twenty years in the Gulag, he feels lucky to have escaped hard labor for the most part, "but," he writes, "in any case, a youth spent in captivity with the stigma of being an inveterate enemy, even if you're doing something meaningful and spend time with famous people, cannot be called complete. It cripples the soul forever."[96]

Zhukov's fellow prisoner, the famous Sergei Korolev, founder of the Soviet space program, followed a different path in his later life but also struggled to come to terms with the sharashka's legacy. After he became the chief designer of the Soviet space program, Korolev was said to have joked that the guards who protected him in his high position were probably the same ones who watched over him in the sharashka. In both periods the guards had the same job, to serve as an immutable wall between the scientist and the outside world. In that sense at least, the sharashka—like its parent, the Gulag—created walls within Soviet civil society that remained standing long after the Gulag itself was consigned to the scrap heap of history.

FORCED LABOR ON THE HOME FRONT

The Gulag and Total War in Western Siberia, 1940–1945

WILSON T. BELL

IN THE *GULAG ARCHIPELAGO* Alexander Solzhenitsyn writes that prisoners found out about the German invasion of the Soviet Union only through rumor.[1] Although this may have been the case for the Gulag's more remote "islands," and rumor was certainly an important form of communication in the camps, much of the Gulag was fully integrated into the local, regional, and national planned economy, and prisoners were well aware of what was going on and of their role. One Gulag memoirist recalled how the outbreak of war affected a small workshop in Tomsk, western Siberia:

> Until this time, there was a children's labor colony here. They sent them someplace and surrounded the territory with a high fence with barbed wire on top with towers on the corners for guards, fully in order. The zone itself was divided into two parts: one part with barracks for living, and the second part [for] production with workshops. When the colonists lived here, they had a mus[ical instrument] factory, making guitars, balalaikas, and mandolins.
>
> But for us *zeks* came something entirely different. . . . In these very workshops only, in the place of the joiners' benches, [they] added lathes, and, well, we prepared all for the front, all for the war![2] What we produced were called readymade mortar shells [*gatovye* (sic) *miny*].[3] But really what appeared were mortar shells prepared with our hands.[4]

A study of the Gulag in western Siberia during the Second World War combines two stories that have usually been told in isolation, if they are told at all. The first is the story of the Gulag at war, and the second is that of total war in the Soviet Union from the perspective of the home front. Essentially the present chapter asks what light a case study of a fairly typical Gulag camp can shed on these stories.

Roger Chickering argues that total war is an "ideal type" in the Weberian sense, never reaching full totality. Yet the Gulag during the Second World War approached that totality in its comprehensive support of the armed forces, even to the detriment of the prisoners' health and lives. While cautioning against overuse of the term "total war," Chickering defines the phrase, in a practical sense, as including "increasing size of armies, the broadening scope of operations, the growing comprehensiveness of the effort to support armed forces, and the systematic, calculated incorporation of civilians into the category of participants."[5] The Second World War was without doubt the harshest period of the Gulag's existence, and prisoners died in incredibly large numbers at the same time as they manufactured artillery shells, built airfields, sewed Red Army uniforms, and produced foodstuffs for the front, to name just a few of the myriad war-related economic activities of Soviet forced labor. These activities clearly fall under Chickering's definition.

The western Siberian camps were more or less "typical" Gulag camps. They were never prioritized as those of Noril´sk were, for example. They were not a synecdoche, as were the camps of Kolyma. They were in neither the harshest climate nor the most forgiving. More important, however, the camps of western Siberia included a wide range of economic activity and types. Many of the largest subdivisions were located within the limits of major cities, including Novosibirsk and Tomsk. Unlike some of the Gulag's more remote camp systems, the urban areas of western Siberia were already well established and did not owe their existence primarily to the forced labor network. The case study thus provides a fascinating look at how Gulag and Soviet society interacted. Western Siberia, moreover, was crucial for the Soviet home front, as one of two main regions for evacuated factories and one of the most important receiving areas for evacuated personnel. Unlike most European areas of the Soviet Union, western Siberia actually grew economically over the course of the Second World War. While the USSR's industrial output for 1945 was only 91 percent of what it was in 1940, western Siberia's industrial output was 279 percent of its level in 1940.[6]

Gulag wartime operations in western Siberia certainly give pause to the idea that the Gulag's central function was to help purify society by removing undesirable individuals and groups. Far from being removed from society, the region's camps and colonies were fully integrated into the local wartime economy, and prisoners regularly interacted with nonprisoners. By and large, moreover, the local focus was more on wartime production than on the isolation of enemies, although certainly we cannot completely separate economic and political motivations. Thus this case study questions both Amir Weiner's characterization of the Great Patriotic War as the key "purification" event of the Soviet gardening state, and Steven Barnes's related argument concerning the Gulag's role in determining who belonged (and who did not belong) in Soviet society.[7]

The question of the Gulag's central function during wartime also allows for a preliminary discussion of the Gulag in comparative perspective. In terms of penal function, the mass mobilization of forced labor and the integrated nature of the Gulag mark the Gulag as at least a partial anomaly in modern criminal justice systems, where the stated role of the prison is related, in varying degrees, to deterrence, isolation, retribution, and rehabilitation. Certainly all four are present in the Soviet camp system, but the added emphasis on mass mobilization to aid the economy, plus a deemphasis on isolation (in practice) point to important differences in the Gulag. Moreover, as a wartime system of concentration camps the Gulag actually appears to have been *less* important to issues of state power and control than other camp systems in wartime, including those of Nazi Germany and the British during the South African War of 1899–1903. Unlike other concentration camps, it is not clear that the Gulag during the Second World War functioned as part of the "state of exception," in Giorgio Agamben's sense of the phrase.

The present chapter, then, offers an analysis of the wartime mobilization of forced labor in western Siberia, while including a preliminary discussion of how this aspect of the home front fits into both the Soviet system and a broader comparative framework.

THE GULAG IN WESTERN SIBERIA: AN OVERVIEW

Western Siberia's camp system was well established by the outbreak of the Second World War.[8] Encouraged by the perceived success of the Solovetskii camps, authorities created SibULON (the Siberian Administration of Camps of Special Significance) in 1929, even before GULag—the Main Administration of Camps—came into existence in April 1930. Initially charged with overseeing camps stretching all the way from Omsk to Krasnoiarsk, Siblag, as it became known, saw its jurisdiction shrink in size as western Siberia was divided administratively over the course of the 1930s. By 1937 Siblag was in charge of corrective labor camps, corrective labor colonies, and special settlements only in Novosibirsk oblast, which at the time comprised present-day Kemerovo, Novosibirsk, and Tomsk oblasts. Two separate camp systems—Gornoshorlag and Tomasinlag—existed in the region in the late 1930s and early 1940s, but both had been decommissioned, with many prisoners reabsorbed into Siblag, before the German invasion of the Soviet Union in June 1941. At the outbreak of Soviet involvement in the Second World War, the western Siberian camp system thus appears roughly as pictured in Figure 6.1.

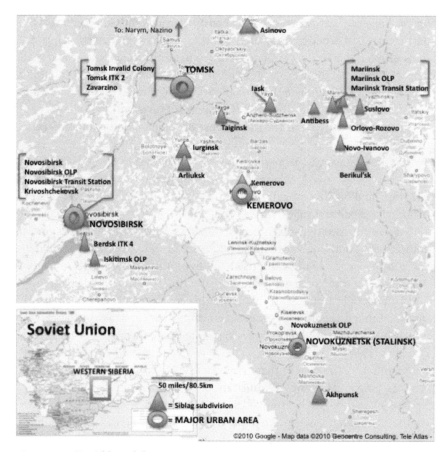

Figure 6.1. Key Siblag subdivisions, circa May 1941.

The author created this map using Google Maps, the map of the Soviet Union (1989) at http://theneosr.egloos.com/1109595, and Microsoft PowerPoint. The size of the triangle does not correspond to the size of the subdivision.

Note, however, that many of the camp subdivisions labeled on this map also had several stations (*punkty*), which were often a few kilometers apart from one another. As we can see from this map, camp subdivisions dotted the region, but all major urban areas had at least one subdivision, and many of the other subdivisions could be found in close proximity to the Trans-Siberian Railway. It was the special settlements, many of which were located in Narym, that tended to be far removed from the region's main cities and towns.

The region's camps were economically diversified, although agriculture predominated. Indeed Siblag, along with Karlag in Kazakhstan, was tasked with sending foodstuffs to camps throughout the Soviet Union. Many prisoners, however, also worked under contract from non-Gulag enterprises, particularly construction and defense enterprises, and there were camp stations devoted to mining, garment production, forestry, and railway and road construction. As I discuss below, following the outbreak of the war all these subdivisions and stations shifted to military production (if they had not done so already), including the agricultural camp subdivisions, which now provided food to the Red Army at the expense of sending food to other parts of the Gulag.

Administratively, there were several key changes during the war, too. In 1942 the Gulag moved Siblag's central administration from Novosibirsk to Mariinsk, and divided the camp system into two separate camps.[9] Siblag now included agricultural subdivisions, while the Novosibirsk Oblast Camp and Colony Administration—technically under the jurisdiction of provincial authorities—continued to be headquartered in Novosibirsk as a separate camp system and mainly comprised subdivisions that contracted out prisoner labor, focusing on defense and construction industries.[10] Many of these Novosibirsk oblast camp and colony subdivisions were corrective labor colonies, although the differences between camps and colonies in the case of Novosibirsk oblast were not always clear. Later, the formation of Kemerovo oblast (1943) and Tomsk oblast (1944) out of the larger Novosibirsk oblast led to an OITK for each of these regions, divided from the old Novosibirsk Oblast Camp and Colony Administration.

This changing administrative landscape complicates compiled statistics for the area's camps. According to published figures, Siblag's 1 January population from 1940 to 1945 is shown in Table 6.1.

Clearly, there are major discrepancies between Siblag and the Gulag in prisoner population changes from 1941–1942 and 1942–1943. The disproportionate increase in Siblag prisoners in 1941 was mostly due to the outbreak of the war. The NKVD evacuated close to 750,000 prisoners from corrective labor camps and colonies under threat from the Nazi invasion, and some of these prisoners ended up in Siblag or in one of Siblag's two transit stations, Novosibirsk and Mariinsk.[11] After the liquidation of Gornoshorlag in early 1941, moreover, the NKVD transferred many of the camp's eight thousand prisoners to Siblag.

The most striking change in Siblag's wartime population occurred over the course of 1942. The 1 January 1943 prisoner population was only 39.1 percent of the 1 January 1942 population, at first glance an astounding drop. For the Gulag as a whole, the 1 January 1943 population was 83.5 percent of the previous year's population, making the Siblag data stand out even more.

TABLE 6.1.1 January prisoner population, Siblag and Gulag

Year	Siblag (1 January population)	Gulag (1 January population)	Siblag population (percent of total)
1940	40,275	1,659,992	2.43
1941	43,857	1,929,729	2.20
1942	77,919	1,777,043	4.38
1943	30,463	1,484,182	2.05
1944	29,627	1,179,819	2.51
1945	39,455	1,460,677	2.70

Source: N. G. Okhotin and A. B. Roginskii, eds., *Sistema ispravitel´no-trudovykh lagerei v SSSR, 1923–1960: Spravochnik*, comp. M. B. Smirnov (Moscow: Zven´ia, 1998), 392. For Gulag statistics, see Aleksandr Bezborodov et al., eds., *Istoriia stalinskogo GULAGa: Konets 1920-kh–pervaia polovina 1950-kh godov. Sobranie dokumentov*, 7 vols. (Moscow: Rosspen, 2004–5), 4:129–30, Doc. no. 49.

What compiled Siblag statistics do not make explicit, however, is that the Novosibirsk Oblast Camp and Colony Administration functioned as a large camp system after the division of Siblag.[12] In the spring of 1942, just after the division, Siblag reported a population of 33,737 prisoners, while the Novosibirsk Oblast Camp and Colony Administration housed 50,453 prisoners, the majority working in so-called contract camps.[13] The Novosibirsk Oblast Camp and Colony Administration remained a large system.[14] Adding together the figures for these two camp systems, then, the actual population for the camps in the area probably increased from 1 January 1942 to 1 January 1943, in contrast to the decrease seen across the Gulag, revealing the importance of the Gulag in the region to the wartime Gulag as whole.[15]

THE GULAG AT WAR

The Gulag at war has not been the subject of much in-depth analysis in the small but burgeoning subfield of Gulag studies. One of the first monographs about the Gulag based on declassified documents was Edwin Bacon's *The Gulag at War*. Overall, Bacon's account gives the impression of an economic rationale for Gulag operations. Yet Bacon's main purpose was to reveal what sort of information one can find on the Gulag in the archives, and he used the wartime framework mostly to limit the chronological scope of his analysis.[16]

Hence much remains to be said on the Gulag's role in wartime mobilization, especially considering the voluminous amount of scholarship on both the Gulag and the wartime Soviet Union that has appeared since Bacon's work.

In their study of Noril´sk during the war, Leonid Borodkin and Simon Ertz note that unfit prisoners were often turned away from this camp, which had a relatively low mortality rate and remained relatively productive.[17] For Noril´sk at least, it seems that economic concerns trumped penal ones.[18] Alan Barenberg's recent work on the Gulag in Vorkuta underscores the economic rationale behind Vorkuta's wartime expansion. It was the closest coal supply to the blockaded city of Leningrad, and the largest supply of coal in European Russia after the Nazi invasion and occupation of key coal-producing regions.[19] The Gulag administration, moreover, had divided in 1941 into various *glavki* (main administrations), based on *economic* function (e.g., GULDZhS, the Main Administration for Camps of Railway Construction) rather than political considerations.[20] Yet economics—that is, a ready supply of forced labor for crucial production activities—does not tell the whole story.[21] Gulag labor was very inefficient and, despite a stated goal of self-sufficiency, generally cost the state more than it gave back.[22]

The politics of release during the war also clearly indicate that penal and political concerns were crucial. Many thousands of prisoners—often relatively healthy young men—were released to fight on the front; this without question hindered the Gulag's economic production. Although the Gulag remained a "revolving door" for those with lighter sentences, the regime barred the release of counterrevolutionaries who had completed their sentences.[23] Article 58ers (political prisoners) tended to receive harsher treatment than other prisoner populations and were thus more likely to be unfit for work. They were, moreover, by definition politically unreliable and thus hardly the most likely candidates to help the camp system in the Soviet Union's war effort. As Steven Barnes describes, "at a time when it was mobilized for a total war, the Gulag consisted of a smaller, less healthy, less politically reliable, older, and more feminine detained population with a smaller . . . staff."[24] Golfo Alexopoulos has argued that this sort of evidence, along with the frequent release and arrests, shows that "penal practices fundamentally undermined economic production."[25] Barnes even takes this a step farther, pointing to the continued efforts at reeducation as evidence of the Gulag's role as a "transformer of man," part of the modern gardening state.[26] Alexopoulos's most recent work complicates the question of the rationale behind Gulag operations, as she argues that, by design, a fundamental aspect of the Gulag was the destruction of the health and lives of the prisoners. She shows that labor categories for prisoners, based on physical health and capabilities, were designed to work the prisoners to the point of death or near-death. Although an economic rationale may be apparent in this analysis, fundamentally Alexopoulos agrees with Solzhenitsyn's contention that the camps were "destructive labor" camps.[27]

These emphases (economic, penal, ideological) are, of course, not mutually exclusive. If camp authorities at Noril´sk received only the able-bodied prisoners, Siblag's administrators frequently complained about the poor physical condition of the arriving inmates. In a 1943 report on conditions at Camp Station no. 3 (in Novosibirsk) authorities blamed poor production results on the worsening food supply and the "huge" number of arriving prisoners who were physically able to perform only light tasks.[28] Taken as a whole, then, the motivation for camp operations may have varied from camp to camp, and even subdivision to subdivision.

Despite the poor condition of prisoners entering western Siberian camps, on balance the case study points to an economic rationale for Gulag operations, at least at the local level. On one hand, there was an immediate shift to wartime production, in some cases even in support of the Winter War with Finland; suspect groups and individuals were given positions of responsibility because of their economic contributions; prisoners in crucial industries had to remain in the camps even after the end of their sentences; and camp propaganda was geared mainly toward increasing economic production. The shift to wartime production itself is not surprising. Similar shifts happened in many non-Gulag enterprises, and a crucial aspect of Soviet defense planning for most of the 1930s was an emphasis on the convertibility of industry to military production.[29] On the other hand, these economic factors intertwined and often conflicted with political and other factors, as the release of healthy prisoners to the front suggests.

As evidenced by Mikhail Grigor´evich Gorbachev, quoted near the outset of this chapter, the shift to military production had a profound effect on the region's camp system. The Tomsk Corrective Labor Colony, which Gorbachev describes, became an important part of the NKVD's munitions production. A plan for November 1941, for example, called for the production of ten thousand 50mm shells at the Tomsk plant, out of a total of sixty-five thousand for the Gulag as a whole.[30] Pre-June 1941 munitions plans for the NKVD had not even included the Tomsk Corrective Labor Colony, revealing the rapid shift to military production in the region.[31]

Alongside the Tomsk Corrective Labor Colony, the Iask subdivision had been sewing Red Army uniforms since the second half of 1940.[32] Another corrective labor colony near Tomsk ceased manufacturing furniture and began to produce skis for the Red Army. According to one Novosibirsk party committee (*obkom*) document, Siblag engineers even devised a way to attach a machine-gun system to skis, an invention that was tested and approved by the administration of the Siberian Military District.[33] In Novosibirsk prisoners at the large Krivoshchekovsk subdivision worked on the construction of the enormous munitions factory People's Commissariat of Munitions Combine no. 179, and under contract in the combine's various workshops, producing artillery and other munitions.[34] Prisoners stepped up construction on Chkalov Aviation Factory no. 153—another key defense enterprise—and on a local airfield.[35] Even the agricultural subdivisions played an important role for the front by sending food and horses to the Red Army. In early 1943, as camp mortality rates reached their highest recorded levels, one of Siblag's wartime slogans was, "Give the country and the front more vegetables, more foodstuffs."[36]

Central authorities clearly recognized the usefulness of prisoner labor for the war effort. On 30 July 1941 the NKVD in Moscow noted that a significant proportion of Gulag prisoners working on airfields and airports were nearing the end of their terms. The NKVD ordered freed prisoners to remain until the completion of the work, even if their sentences had technically ended.[37] Local camp authorities also recognized this economic imperative. At the Tomsk Corrective Labor Colony mentioned above, authorities granted permission to a convicted Trotskyist to live outside the camp zone, without guard, because he was a trained engineer and held a crucial position as the foundry shop's acting chief.[38] The practice of placing so-called counterrevolutionaries in key camp economic positions and giving them considerable privileges was common throughout the wartime Gulag and went against regulations.[39] In November 1941 the Novosibirsk party committee specifically called on Siblag's director, G. N. Kopaev, to send "qualified engineers and workers, sentenced for daily life *and* counterrevolutionary crimes," to the region's defense enterprises.[40] In these cases the economic rationale for camp operations, as opposed to political imperatives, is readily apparent.

Even camp propaganda, where one might expect a political rationale to be most visible, emphasized economic production. Of course, the economic and political are difficult to separate in the Soviet context, as proving oneself politically often meant performing competently in economic production roles, while the opposite was also true: authorities often viewed poor economic performance as evidence of political unreliability. Wartime camp propaganda focused on inspiring or shaming prisoners to work harder. In particular, camp authorities attempted to inspire prisoners by revealing the exploits of ex-prisoners on the front. As in Steven Barnes's description of Karlag at war, ex-Siblag prisoners supposedly sent letters back to Siblag, recounting their experiences and telling their former campmates that "idlers or saboteurs" were "direct helpers of the enemy." The prisoners who read and/or heard the letters were then reportedly inspired to work "selflessly on the home front for the rout of the enemy."[41]

While we should no doubt be skeptical about the truth of these reports—after all, conditions were terrible in most subdivisions, especially in 1942 and 1943—there are, indeed, numerous examples of ex-prisoners who received awards for their exploits at the front. Several even attained recognition as heroes of the Soviet Union.[42]

Another direct incentive was the practice of early release as a reward for productive labor. Even though the formal practice of reducing a prisoner's sentence by giving credit for days worked had ended in 1939, prisoners continued to receive early release for fulfilling and overfulfilling their work norms. In 1939 the Politburo had explicitly stated that prisoners must serve their full terms, with incentives in the form of rewards (higher rations, better barracks, etc.), rather than early release.[43] Local authorities, however, recognized the need for strong positive incentives. Although this practice in some ways reinforces Barnes's argument that the Gulag was not only about death but also about redemption, we should be somewhat cautious about such a clear-cut binary. First, many of these released prisoners worked in the camps, in the same position, after their release. Second, we will see later that the reasons for wartime release were quite complex. In any case, however, camp propaganda attempted to show prisoners that early release was a possibility if they overfulfilled their work norms. Many camp cultural reports include a section on "early release and reduced sentences."[44] In the second half of 1943 the Novosibirsk Oblast Camp and Colony Administration allowed the early release of 161 prisoners and reduced the sentences of another 262. Part of the work of the Cultural-Educational Department was to inform prisoners that only through "selfless labor and excellent behavior in daily life [v bytu] can they receive conditional early release."[45]

If Gulag propaganda in western Siberia as evidence for an economic or political rationale for Gulag operations is somewhat contradictory, there are some compelling reasons to view the Gulag primarily through a political lens. Perhaps most important, the extremely high mortality rates in the region during the Second World War attest to the lack of emphasis authorities placed on productive labor, while the upkeep of Gulag prisoners and personnel was also quite expensive. From January 1942 through August 1943 the Novosibirsk Oblast Camp and Colony Administration lost no less than 1.87 percent of its prisoners per month, with a high of 3.52 percent in May 1942.[46] In 1943 the Novosibirsk party committee formed an inspection brigade to examine the conditions of prisoners working in defense industries.[47] The brigade's report notes huge increases in mortality and invalid rates, particularly at the third Krivoshchekovsk division, in charge of construction at Combine no. 179. In January 1943, 2.2 percent of prisoners in the region's defense industries died; in February the figure was 2.9 percent; and in March 2.6 percent. At the third Krivoshchekovsk division, in March alone 5.4 percent of prisoners died. These percentages reflect monthly, rather than annualized, death rates and would translate into huge yearly mortality figures, well in excess of the average for the Gulag as a whole.

Wartime shortages and overwork meant that the struggle for survival in the camps entered a harsher stage, and prisoners often fought one another for the scarce food available. One prisoner, D. E. Alin, who worked at Chkalov Aviation Factory no. 153, remembered that although rations were drastically reduced after the beginning of the war, at first it was possible to live on the miniscule 260–460 grams of bread per day, plus a small amount of kasha, and that many prisoners supplemented this ration with food sent in packages from relatives.[48] As the war dragged on, however, the situation became dire. By the beginning of 1942 the prisoners in Alin's camp split a regular ration five ways. The prisoners began to smuggle and hide crowbars and other items (even axes) that could be used as weapons, not to try to escape but to defend their own rations and intimidate other prisoners into giving their rations away. Alin recalls an incident when he found a new arrival at the camp, who happened to be a distant cousin, with his head bashed in, murdered for his small bowl of kasha. Alin himself became so ill and malnourished by the fall of 1942 that he lost consciousness one day at work and considered himself lucky to survive the camp hospital, where patients were "dying like flies."[49]

Many prisoners became invalids and simply could not work, and some prisoners in this category received early release. The Novosibirsk Oblast Camp and Colony Administration's 1943 inspection brigade, when discussing invalids, noted, "This contingent, on the basis of the instruction of the NKVD of the USSR, the NKIu of the USSR, and the procurator of the [Soviet] Union from 23 October 1942, no. 467/18-71/117s, is released from camp ahead of schedule, as it is a large burden for the camp. By 1 April of t[his] y[ear], the medical commissions under the ITL, as a result of physical examination, had recognized as invalids 7,491 persons. Of these, 2,917 were released ahead of schedule, and 875 have died."[50]

In a 1944 report based on 1943 inspections of the area's camps and colonies, the procurator overseeing camp operations, A. Kondrashev, actually *encouraged early release for invalids as a way to help improve the camp's mortality statistics.* His statement provides a local example that supports Alexopoulos's contention that large numbers of prisoners were released to die and under-scores the utter disregard for the human misery of the camps—which, while not surprising, is especially galling considering his role as an inspector.[51] As Kondrashev wrote, "it is worth noting that the Camp Administration as well as the procurator in the first half of 1943 paid insufficient attention to ful-filling the directives of the NKVD and procurator of the USSR, [and] as a consequence in August there was a high mortality rate in the camp, whereas people could have been released in a timely way [*svoevremenno*], thereby considerably reducing the death rate."[52] Kondrashev went on, however, to suggest that the political reliability of those released must be considered and cited with disapproval two cases of release—one an Article 58er and one sen-tenced under article 162.d (theft of state property)—where "state security has not been observed."[53]

We see here that wartime release was not only about rewards for pro-ductive labor or about providing more soldiers for the front but was often related to relieving local camps of the need to care for dying and severely ill prisoners.[54] On one hand, that authorities frequently released dying prison-ers conceivably swings the pendulum back toward an economic explanation for Gulag operations—these prisoners, after all, were a burden economically and could not help production quotas. On the other hand, if Gulag economic production had been a top priority, one might expect authorities to place more emphasis on maintaining the prisoners' health. Although the central NKVD early in 1942 ordered the creation of "preventive health" camp sta-tions for every camp, designed to be well lit, spacious, and with access to in-creased rations, ostensibly to nurse unhealthy prisoners back to the position of productive laborers, it is clear that local authorities lacked the resources to create such stations.[55]

The upkeep of prisoners required expenses—including medical infra-structure and living quarters as well as the upkeep of personnel and guards, who were often demobilized soldiers. Camp Commander Kopaev com-plained in 1941, for example, that Siblag spent 11 million rubles/year main-taining the nine thousand invalid prisoners in the camp.[56] Siblag's budget for that same year allotted 25 million rubles for the upkeep of the camp's approx-imately four thousand guards, which, as Kopaev pointed out, was enough "to build a decent-sized factory [*nemalen′kii zavod*]."[57] The discrepancy in fund-ing between guards and invalid prisoners is telling, especially considering that invalids would have required considerable medical expenses.

The issue of prisoners' ill health is central to the discussion but once again complex. From late 1941 through at least the first half of 1943 the Soviet Union was fighting for its very existence, and resources were scarce for everyone. The peak year for mortality in western Siberia's non-Gulag population was 1942, the same year that the Gulag also reached its highest recorded mortality rates (2.69 and 24.9 percent, respectively).[58] Even outside the camps evacuees to Novosibirsk oblast received less bread than the amount the Gulag prisoner technically should have received before the war began.[59] Oleg Khlevniuk has demonstrated that, in certain times and places, rations in the Gulag were even better than in surrounding towns and villages for certain types of food.[60] So the lack of emphasis on prisoner health is not surprising given the general circumstances in the country. Nevertheless, it appears that priority camps—such as Noril'sk, Vorkuta, and even those in the Kolyma region—may have fared better than more typical camps like Siblag and others in western Siberia, precisely due to perceived economic necessity. Noril'sk received only able-bodied prisoners, for example, and its mortality rate peaked at 7.2 percent in 1943, compared with an overall Gulag mortality rate of 22.4 percent during that year. The mortality rate in the Kolyma region in 1943 was 12.4 percent, which was similar to that of Vorkuta.[61] As discussed above, the western Siberian camps experienced mortality rates that well exceeded the Gulag average.

The western Siberian camps thus show us that, at least as far as the evidence on mortality is concerned, both economic and political factors motivated camp operations, and this motivation varied from camp to camp. The rapid shift to military production, as well as the flexibility in labor use of prisoners and the incentives provided to exhort prisoners to work harder, tips the balance in favor of an economic motivation in the region. In contrast, the inefficiencies point to more political concerns, as inefficiency in labor and upkeep is not a problem if isolation is the key goal. Yet the close interaction between free and forced labor suggest that one of the main political concerns—isolation of those deemed dangerous to society, a common component of most prison systems—was not the most crucial element of Gulag operations. We see this interaction most clearly when considering issues surrounding the Gulag and total war.

TOTAL WAR

If most modern penal systems are designed with some degree of emphasis on deterrence, isolation, retribution, and rehabilitation, the total war experience of the Soviet Gulag points to peculiarities of the Soviet system.[62] Certainly, the Gulag contained within it all four of these justifications for imprisonment. Yet although many modern penal systems use some form of forced labor, the Gulag's focus on prisoner labor in key economic sectors is unusual.

As the penitentiary developed in Europe during the nineteenth century, labor became an integral part of daily life, but it was usually meant as part of the punitive or rehabilitative process. At most, economically speaking, authorities hoped the products of prisoner labor could offset the costs of running the penitentiary or give convicts necessary skills for future reintegration.[63] For Foucault forced labor was not economic at all but part of the disciplinary mechanism carried out on and through the prisoners' bodies. As he writes, "the prison is not a workshop; it is, it must be of itself, a machine whose convict-workers are both the cogs and the products."[64] The Gulag, however, was different in its application of forced labor, and this difference is especially evident in wartime. It *was* a workshop, and its specific products (artillery shells, uniforms, and so on) were intended to be useful to the state—perhaps even more useful than the convicts themselves, who died in large numbers.

Gulag prisoners sacrificed their health, and in many cases their lives, to support the Soviet war effort. In western Siberia, where agricultural camps predominated, prisoners even produced foodstuffs for the front while they themselves were malnourished and lived on the brink of starvation. If we understand the "totality" of total war in the Weberian sense, as a pure state not actually possible in reality, Gulag wartime production came close to reaching that state. There was almost nothing left over.

Certainly the shift to wartime production in the region, outlined above, points to the role the local Gulag played in the Soviet total war effort. The widespread use of forced laborers in defense industries seems to have helped production, at least from the regime's point of view. For the Gulag as a whole, from mid-1941 to the end of 1944 prisoners produced over twenty-five million shells, thirty-five million hand grenades and fuses, nine million mines, and a hundred thousand bombs, not to mention other military material such as telephone cable, skis, rafts, gas masks, and uniforms. As one scholar writes, "it was prison labor that filled many of the gaps created by the vast expansion of the Red Army during World War II."[65] Novosibirsk Oblast Camp and Colony Administration documents proudly report the awarding of the Order of Lenin to Combine no. 179 in November 1943 and give credit to prisoners for helping to make this happen.[66]

Combine no. 179 and Chkalov Aviation Factory no. 153 were two of the most important defense enterprises located within the city limits of Novosibirsk. Combine no. 179, situated on the left bank of the enormous Ob´ River, was a sprawling complex of factories and barracks and home to the largest camp subdivision in the region (fig. 6.2). On the eve of the war in May 1941 Krivoshchekovsk, with its various camp stations, held 7,807 prisoners.[67]

Figure 6.2. In the foundry of Combine no. 179 (1943). *Source:* The Museum of the City of Novosibirsk (Muzei goroda Novosibirska).

The degree to which forced and free labor overlapped in Combine no. 179 is striking, lending weight to Kate Brown's assertion that we should understand forced and free labor in the Soviet Union not as a binary but as a continuum, with various degrees of coercion and incentives provided in almost all contexts.[68]

Most striking is that provincial authorities, when organizing the workforce for military production, do not appear to have viewed Gulag labor much differently from labor from non-Gulag sources. All were simply a resource. Already before the war, in constructing Combine no. 179, the Novosibirsk party committee in December 1940 called for the transfer of five thousand Siblag prisoners as well as six thousand workers from the Soviet Union's central provinces to complete the project.[69] The Winter War against Finland necessitated the increased production of war materials, and local authorities sought to step up the production of this key industrial complex. The resolution's listing of these numbers one after another emphasizes the authorities' wide-ranging ability to draw on human resources for specific projects and blurs the distinction between free and forced labor.

Even central party authorities drew on a combination of Gulag and non-Gulag sources to help build Combine no. 179. In late December 1940 the Politburo itself discussed the amount of funding to supply for capital investment in Combine no. 179, and central plans called for production of eight hundred thousand shell casings (*korpusy snariadov*) of various types, as well as numerous other munitions, to be produced in 1941. The Politburo charged L. P. Beria, head of the NKVD, with increasing the number of Gulag prisoners working at the combine to ten thousand. The Politburo also ordered squared beams and saw timber (*brusa i pilomaterialy*) to be removed from the recently decommissioned Tomasinlag and shipped to the combine to aid in construction. Authorities in Novosibirsk and Kirov oblasts, Altai krai, and the Bashkir ASSR had to send eleven thousand free workers in the first half of 1941.[70] The Politburo ended this particular discussion by calling for the inclusion of Combine no. 179 as one of the "country's especially important construction projects."[71] Wartime orders continued to redirect human resources in a similar manner.[72] The key issue was having enough hands to complete the task, not whether that labor was free or forced. And if free laborers could be forced to relocate for specific projects, this was not free labor in the technical sense of the term, even if it was far preferable to the horrors of Gulag life.[73]

The oblast party committee also placed a considerable burden on Siblag to supply laborers as quickly as possible. At a 10 September 1941 meeting, the committee directed Kopaev to send an additional three thousand prisoners to Combine no. 179: a thousand by 13 September, a thousand by 20 September, and the final thousand by 1 October. Not surprisingly but again attesting to poor planning, a month later the party committee criticized Kopaev for not having done enough to build proper barracks for the incoming contingents.[74] Given the extremely short time he had in which to transfer the prisoners, the Party's demands must have seemed completely unrealistic. The story does not end there, however. In December the party committee then ordered Kopaev to clear most of these prisoners from the barracks to make room for demobilized Red Army soldiers.[75]

Evidently there was much opportunity for interaction between prisoners and nonprisoners in these contract camps. Central and local authorities dealt with numerous issues involving deconvoyed prisoners during the war, including many who took advantage of their unescorted status and smuggled correspondence and black market items or even escaped.[76] On 18 January 1943 the Gulag in Moscow issued an order to all camp and colony directors, asking them to take measures to prevent interaction at contract camps, as many prisoners were stealing items and foodstuffs from the civilian populations, both at the production sites and while on transfer or moving through settlement points.[77] D. E. Alin recalls that, on the way to the worksite, the

prisoners at Chkalov Aviation Factory no. 153 stopped and waved to mobilized soldiers heading to the front by train. The soldiers talked to them sometimes and even occasionally threw them food.[78] Thus the evidence suggests
that while there may have been some attempts at isolation, there was room
for considerable interaction and overlap between prisoners and nonprisoners. Isolation was less important than production in the total war effort.

Although conditions were certainly much worse for prisoners, free workers also experienced horrendous living conditions in the region. In Siberia's
urban areas the mortality rate for regular citizens increased by over 25 percent in the first year of the war, and Novosibirsk oblast saw huge increases
in diseases such as typhoid fever, dysentery, typhus, and whooping cough.[79]
Due to these conditions, Combine no. 179 suffered from shockingly high
turnover of its free workers, despite extremely harsh wartime labor laws, especially in defense industries.[80] In 1942, 11,497 persons arrived to work at
the factory, whereas 9,324 left. In 1943, 7,703 arrived and 7,600 left, approximately 5,000 of whom deserted.[81]

Many free workers in the region also left key industries to join the ranks of
the Red Army. Indeed, some five hundred thousand persons left Novosibirsk
oblast for the front during the war. Kuzbass Coal lost eleven thousand miners
to the Red Army in the second half of 1941 alone.[82] By January 1943 in Novosibirsk oblast there were only thirty-five men for every hundred women.[83]

Due to the high turnover, the party committee's turn to forced labor as a
partial solution is not surprising. Indeed, not only prisoners worked at Combine no. 179 but also exiles. Volga Germans—now called on to help the very
war effort against which they had supposedly collaborated—as well as exiled
Kalmyks, special settlers from Narym, and even prisoners of war (POWs)
worked at Combine no. 179. By the second half of 1942 over 20 percent of
the workforce in munitions (*boepripasy*) in Novosibirsk oblast was made up
of prisoners.[84] By the end of the war this percentage had fallen somewhat but
was still significant. On 1 May 1945 Combine no. 179's 25,117 workers included 3,120 prisoners (12.4 percent), 1,100 exiled Volga Germans (4.4 percent), 822 POWs, 106 former "kulaks" from Narym, and 98 exiled Kalmyks.[85]

The use of forced labor created its own problems, as authorities worried
about possible counterrevolutionary activity among prisoners and exile
groups. In November 1941 Comrade I. V. Ivanov, head of the Special Settlement Department of the NKVD, instructed NKVD officials in western
Siberia and neighboring regions to use exiled Volga Germans in their areas
of expertise. At the same time, Ivanov reported instances of roaming groups
of Volga Germans who, without permission, went to various organizations
and establishments looking for work. No doubt these Volga Germans were

merely trying to survive, to make the best of a bad situation, but from the authorities' point of view this posed problems: "At times this vagrancy [*bro-diazhnichestvo*] by fascist elements is used to establish connections with counterrevolutionary goals."[86] Novosibirsk oblast saw an increase in death sentences for counterrevolutionary activity in the first six months of the war, but starting in 1942 there was a sharp decline in the number of such sentences (especially death sentences) in the region, suggesting a relaxation of repressive measures.[87]

The regime also saw the Volga Germans as potentially useful. In January 1942 the GKO called for the mobilization of 120,000 exiled Volga German males, fit for physical labor, into "work columns" for the duration of the war. Later in 1942 the GKO expanded this mobilization order to include a greater age range of Volga German males (from fifteen to fifty-five), as well as females aged sixteen to forty-five, excluding pregnant women and mothers with children under three. These Volga Germans were placed in so-called special zones in Gulag camps, not as prisoners but as labor soldiers (*trudarmeitsy*). In western Siberia the labor soldiers worked mainly in forestry and in railroad construction.[88]

In these examples, then, we see that forced labor was an important aspect of Soviet total war, although just how much emphasis should be placed on forced labor in the context of the home front deserves further examination. According to Mark Harrison's data, forced labor accounted for roughly 2 percent of the Soviet Union's total (including agricultural) workforce before the war and held steady at 2 percent during the war, despite a decline in absolute numbers.[89]

In western Siberia authorities were able to make use of forced labor in military production and certainly saw it as an important component of available human resources. Yet in terms of sheer numbers we must view the Gulag as of only marginal importance to the region's economy and, therefore, to the Soviet home front. Evacuees and evacuated factories had a larger economic impact. Whereas the area's camps held seventy thousand to eighty thousand prisoners at any one time, the almost half-million evacuees, even if they included many children and elderly, helped compensate for the loss of workers to the front in much greater numbers. Of the evacuees many worked in agriculture, which was crucially important considering German advances into Ukraine.[90] The city of Novosibirsk itself received 150,000 evacuees in the first year and a half of the war, significantly more than better-known evacuee locations such as Tashkent.[91] The huge state investment required to relocate factories to the region also stimulated the economy and forced the state to recognize the centrality of the region to the Soviet Union's economy as a whole. In August 1943, by a decree of the Presidium of the Supreme Soviet of the RSFSR, Novosibirsk joined a select group of cities as a republican city (even as one evacuee noted, "only the very center of Novosibirsk resembled an actual city").[92]

The mass mobilization of the region's women and elderly into the workforce played an enormous role, too. As Isupov writes of the workforce in western Siberia, "the labor soldiers of work columns, prisoners, and POWs played an important but secondary role. The main labor resource of the Soviet Union was its own civilian [grazhdanskoe] population." In 1939 in western Siberia alone there had been almost eight hundred thousand women who were not in the workforce, as well as six hundred thousand persons over the age of sixty. Many of these people were put to work during the war.[93] Thus there was a large pool of "free" labor mobilized for the war effort.

Even if one focuses only on forced labor, however, the numbers are misleading. By 1 April 1943 the Novosibirsk Oblast Camp and Colony Administration was reporting that 51 percent of its prisoner contingent was unable to work due to poor physical condition.[94] A 1944 inspection of Corrective Labor Colony no. 8 in Tomsk, to cite another example, found that 437 of the 1,028 prisoners in the colony were unfit for physical labor, and this was not even during the harshest time of the war.[95] These figures are significantly higher than Gulag wartime averages, which saw 25–30 percent of prisoner contingents in this category.[96] Gulag labor was incredibly inefficient. Given Alexopoulos's work showing that even those deemed fit for physical labor often suffered from serious diseases and were in extremely poor physical shape, much of the prisoner contingent in western Siberia clearly was on the verge of death.[97]

The Gulag was one piece in the puzzle of a country-wide and regional total war effort. Comparatively speaking, however, the somewhat muted role of the Gulag highlights the Soviet camp system as significantly different from other wartime camp systems. Although it is beyond the scope of this chapter to consider the comparative aspect in detail, a few words are in order. Soviet authorities appear to have placed less significance on the concentration camp than many other twentieth-century wartime belligerents. In this sense the Gulag fits only marginally into Giorgio Agamben's currently fashionable argument surrounding the concentration camp and war.[98] For Agamben, the concentration camp occurs as modern states use the pretext of war and/or emergency to place certain unwanted citizen-subjects and/or groups into a "state of exception," where they are confined in a liminal legal state in the sense that they are defined by their extralegal status, thus existing outside the law but only in relation to the law. Agamben bases much of his argument on the work of the interwar German political theorist Carl Schmitt, who argued in his 1922 *Politische Theologie* (Political Theology) that the sovereign is "he who decides the exception," and therefore that the exception is central to the operation of the modern state.[99]

Soviet authorities, however, did not present the Stalin-era Gulag as something exceptional, at least not at first; indeed, it was supposedly a model of humane penal reform. Gulag inmates, moreover, were charged and convicted (however harsh the laws and/or the interrogation methods) of crimes that violated Soviet law. They were not extralegal; they had, in the eyes of the state in any case, committed illegal acts. In this sense no doubt the special settlements come closer to the "state of exception" in Agamben's meaning. Here were groups of people—first peasants, later ethnic groups—forced to resettle in remote areas, restricted in their rights, but not formally charged with anything. But perhaps most important for our purposes, unlike other twentieth-century wartime belligerents, such as the British during the South African War or the Nazis during the Second World War, the Soviet Union appears to have placed less emphasis on repressive measures like the Gulag *during* the war than it had beforehand (or afterward).

Even in the cases of the British camps and the Nazi camps, moreover, Agamben's theories have encountered difficulties when applied to aspects of these systems. Jonathan Hyslop, for example, finds fault with Agamben's emphasis on biopolitics. In the South African case Hyslop demonstrates that the moment when the British government actually became interested in monitoring the health of camp populations was precisely when the situation improved, not when those interned were reduced to bare life.[100] In the Nazi case, to cite one example, Mark Mazower critiques Agamben's work for not acknowledging the vast changes over time, and even from place to place, within the Nazis' network of camps, among other issues.[101] Nevertheless, Hyslop agrees with Agamben's focus on wartime and/or emergency measures as being key to the creation of the camps, and Mazower discusses Agamben in the context of "wartime paradigms" of power. What the case of the Gulag shows, curiously in the comparative context, is that wartime emergency in the Soviet Union did not necessarily play a crucial role in the formation and expansion of the exception.

Thus we can question the extent to which the Second World War in the Soviet Union actually represented the "pursuit of purity," as Weiner argues, or whether the Soviet state used the war as a pretext to define and exclude "the exception," as Agamben's arguments concerning the concentration camp suggest.[102] The Gulag actually decreased in population during the war, dropping from approximately 1.9 million prisoners on 1 January 1941 to a low of 1.2 million prisoners on 1 January 1944.[103] At the very least it would be hard to argue that the Soviet state relied *more* on the Gulag during the war than it had during peacetime. As mentioned, the Gulag's economic contribution during the war was similar, proportionately, to its prewar contribution.[104] In western Siberia specifically the prisoner contingents increased during the war, but the mobilization of other human resources was more important than Gulag labor, and local authorities exhibited a pragmatic approach to forced labor contingents.

Thus the Soviet state did not use the war as a pretext to expand a repressive camp system except, once again, if we focus on the special settlements. Even here, however, the situation is far from clear-cut. During the war, authorities reinstated most citizenship rights of the original special settlers, the so-called kulaks who had been exiled in the 1930s.[105] Many thousands of special settlers from Novosibirsk oblast and elsewhere were mobilized to fight in the Red Army, too.[106] So while the wholesale exile of certain suspect ethnic groups during the war—such as the Volga Germans, Chechens, and Kalmyks—appears to confirm Agamben's hypothesis and to support Weiner's argument, the special settlements were arguably less repressive than they had been in the 1930s. The Volga Germans, in particular, became relatively integrated into the local economies of places like western Siberia and Kazakhstan, in part because their labor was in high demand. They were not completely excluded.[107]

One could argue that the harsh labor laws of the war created another state of exception. These laws, however, were clumsily enforced: many workers sentenced for absenteeism, for example, were sentenced in absentia and never sent to the camps. These laws also existed alongside policies toward religion and even the cultural elite that suggest a partial relaxation of repressive measures.[108]

That prisoners worked in such close proximity to nonprisoners, and local authorities saw prisoner labor as just one piece in the human resource puzzle, also provides evidence that the wartime Gulag was not particularly about the removal of undesirable elements from Soviet society or about using the pretext of war to gain more control. Local authorities were even willing to use so-called enemies (counterrevolutionaries, exiled populations) to help support the war. At least as far as our case study is concerned, the total war effort as it included the Gulag appears to have been quite straightforward: an effort to mobilize all available resources to support the military, with little care for the actual cost in human lives.

The case study of the western Siberian camps during the Second World War ultimately highlights the tragedy of the Gulag. Prisoners had little choice but to give their health and frequently their lives to the war effort, but in the end human resources such as evacuees and underutilized groups were more important to the regional home front, especially considering the inefficiencies of forced labor. Although the camps proved marginally useful in terms of numbers of shells, uniforms, and so on that were produced, the human cost was staggering. Even so, the interaction between free and forced labor in the region, the quick and total shift to military production, and the pragmatic labor use of those labeled ideological enemies of the regime all suggest that economic motivations for Gulag operations were more important than political motivations during the Second World War.

Indeed, although the Gulag reached a turning point during the war, it did not, ultimately, turn. The more pragmatic approach to forced labor and the concentration camp system—comparatively unusual in twentieth-century wartime history—gave way, in the postwar years, to increased repression and greater levels of isolation, as the Gulag reached its peak population and created a series of special camps with incredibly harsh regimens. Even so, as has been argued elsewhere, central camp authorities became increasingly aware of the Gulag's inefficiencies and took immediate steps to reduce the size and scope of the Gulag after the death of Stalin.[109]

(UN)RETURNED FROM THE GULAG

Life Trajectories and Integration of Postwar Special Settlers

EMILIA KOUSTOVA

TRANSLATED BY ERINA MEGOWAN

A BRIEF EXCERPT from an interview with Antanas Kybartas, who was exiled from Lithuania in 1947 and spent ten years in a special settlement in Tiumen´ oblast, reveals a number of issues important for understanding the experience of Soviet postwar victims of deportation: "Working in the kolkhoz, studying in school, not knowing exactly where my father was and for what [he had been arrested], I arrived from Siberia raised as a Soviet person. . . . Raised on Ostrovsky's *How the Steel Was Tempered*, Korchagin, *Timur and His Squad*, Meres´ev's *Story about a Real Man*—as one would say now, I was 'red' or 'left.' I remember this with a smile, because with time I have discovered a very simple thing: whoever was not a leftist in youth will never become a true right-winger."[1] First, we see the contradictory combination of the violence that came with deportation and aspects of special settlement life that facilitated not only adaptation but also the integration and even Sovietization of some special settlers, first and foremost young people. This excerpt, moreover, shows the key mechanisms of such an integration— collective work and education. These factors eased adaptation, at times opening the doors to social mobility within the special settlement and especially after emancipation. Note that these two seemingly separate periods frequently turn out to be connected in the tales of former deportees—both in terms of continuity in social, professional, or family trajectories and in light of the fact that the sword of Damocles of potential stigmatization did not disappear with the end of exile. Last, the excerpt alludes to the long process by which some former deportees reconsidered their convictions and (re)conceptualized the individual and collective experience of deportation.

Kybartas is, in fact, entirely unexceptional. His and many other interviews with former deportees, were collected as part of the project "Sound Archives: European Memory of the Gulag."[2] These conversations reveal the necessity of revisiting a number of widespread ideas in the historiography and examining life in special settlements as something more than an exclusively traumatic experience that doomed an individual to marginalization and served as a sort of school for *Homo antisovieticus*.[3] Among more than two hundred interviews with victims of Soviet deportations from Eastern Europe, we focus here on those with natives of the Baltic states (above all, Lithuania) and western Ukraine who were deported to special settlements in Siberia immediately after the war, many of whom remained in Siberia after their emancipation. The majority of cases involve people born in the 1930s who wound up in special settlements as children or adolescents. Despite considerable deprivations, their experience of deportation included efforts to build a life for themselves; these were people who made plans and attempted to realize them by availing themselves of opportunities that arose.[4]

To understand the full spectrum of these opportunities, this chapter uses archival materials at different levels: holdings from the State Archive of the Russian Federation (GARF), which illustrate the administration of deportations at a macro level; regional archives, which enable us to view the special settlers through the eyes of local party leaders and administrative organs; and the archives of the MVD and the KGB of Lithuania, where some deportees' personal files allow us to capture their life trajectories as seen through the eyes of the police.[5]

This chapter analyzes both the adaptation of special settlers to the conditions of their exile and their incorporation into post-Stalinist society. It considers first the role of work in the life of special settlers. In contrast to the situation in camps and probably peasant exile in the 1930s, even involuntary work could feature positive motivation and facilitate deportees' physical survival while helping them overcome stigmatization, attain social mobility, and integrate them more broadly, up to the point of Sovietization.[6] By the last term, I have in mind not only the assimilation of officially sanctioned practices and values but also the inclusion of the individual in informal networks and exchanges, as well as his or her mastery of the tactics of avoidance and the ability to manipulate the rules of Soviet society.[7]

The corresponding analysis requires me to address lengthy intervals of time beyond the period of exile. In contrast to most works devoted to deportation, I attempt to place this repressive experience in the context of the individual's entire life. This allows us to see the bridges thrown from exiled life into free life, as well as to construct a microhistory of deportation that can reflect the variation in individual life trajectories and their interaction with other contexts, including nonrepressive ones. More broadly, the concern here is with the understudied transition from Stalinism and attempts to integrate various categories of repressed populations back into Soviet society during the wavering between coercion and liberalization that characterized the 1950s. Although already noted in the research on returnees from the camps, such contradictions appear in the cases of deportees as well.[8] In the second half of the 1950s deportees were gradually emancipated from special settlements but in most cases not rehabilitated, which left obstacles along their path in life.

The chapter draws on several large groups of historiographical studies: the numerous works dedicated to the Gulag and its system of forced labor, special settlements and mass deportations, the dismantling of the Stalinist system, and the Sovietization of the USSR's western borderlands, including works on national memories of deportation.[9] Nevertheless, the central questions here, such as the mechanisms and limits of the integration of postwar deportation victims into Soviet society, have received little attention. The main reason is the predominance of macroscopic analyses and the tendency to look at the experience of special settlers as an isolated episode. Although works drawing on personal documents and interviews and combining multiple layers of analysis have appeared, the macrohistorical approach traditionally dominates the literature on special settlements, leading to a concentration on the political, economic, and legal aspects of this phenomenon.[10]

Two approaches often characterize research on deportees from western territories, and they rarely coexist within the same work: one approaches the topic from the standpoint of national history, the other from within the history of the Gulag and special settlements.[11] The first, sometimes appropriating the concept of genocide, studies the tragic experience of survival of a group of compatriots in an alien world; the other examines the world of special settlements and camps through examples of individual categories of repressed populations, defined geographically and/or ethnically.[12] In both cases life in a special settlement is treated as an isolated episode geographically, chronologically, and biographically; the subsequent life of deportees, if analyzed at all, is considered through the prism of memory and trauma.[13]

Moreover, special settlements are frequently studied on the basis of materials relating to the peasant exiles of the 1930s.[14] On questions of work, integration, and social mobility of special settlers, my conclusions depart from these previous studies. This is partly a consequence of the different nature of the sources and approaches I use, but it also grows out of the important distinctions in the experience of victims deported during different waves. The specifics of each wave reflect a number of factors—the character of a special settlement regime, the amount of time that deportees spent in exile, the timing of emancipation (before or after 1953), and the nature of the repression that led to deportation. Despite the chronological proximity of the deportations considered here with the forcible displacement of the "punished peoples," the experiences of the two groups thus differ substantially. The fact that in the Baltics and western Ukraine only part of the community was subject to repression significantly shaped life in exile and gave an entirely different configuration to the moment of return. From this standpoint, a more promising approach is to compare the experience of deportees from western territories with the experience of Gulag prisoners. The latter, too, found themselves face to face with the non-Gulag after emancipation and encountered major difficulties.[15] But the condition of the special settlers was distinctive from many points of view. Their return—understood widely as engagement with officially free elements in Soviet society and adjustment to the non-Gulag—began on the day of their arrival in exile; many began the difficult experience of adaptation with their families, not on their own. This difference forces us to ask what role the preceding resocialization played at the moment of return. How much did it ease adaptation in one's native land? Did the Soviet regime's view of families returned from exile differ from its relationship to former Gulag prisoners? An analysis of the experience of life in the special settlement offers much in terms of understanding life after emancipation and other largely unstudied questions.[16]

SPECIAL SETTLERS' STORIES AS THE HISTORY OF SOVIET LIFE

Here I analyze interviews with former special settlers as narrative, focusing primarily on the construction of an individual's life history during the interview and the ways in which respondents allocate meaning to their experience. This approach permits us to uncover a number of key themes, which we then develop further using archival materials.

My interest in the adaptation and integration of special settlers into Soviet society derives largely from meetings with former special settlers who were deported from Lithuania and western Ukraine and then remained permanently in Irkutsk oblast.[17] Their recollections reveal such integration with exceptional strength while being generally consistent with the modern Russian historical narrative of "reconciliation . . . with the Soviet past as 'one's own.'"[18] Precisely for this reason these interviews serve as our starting point. However, as we will see, interviews with those who returned to their homeland after the emancipation tell us many similar details about deportation and everyday life in the settlements even as they bear traces of integration into Soviet life that began during the years of exile. The differences among recollections consist less of the description of life in the special settlements than in the present-day evaluation of that experience.

"Well, What Can You Say, It Was a Difficult Time, the Years after the War"

The main features of the interviews in Irkutsk oblast are the absence of a constructed narrative of deportation, the blurring of the repressive episode's time boundaries, and the integration of life in the special settlement with the experience of the surrounding population.[19] In contrast to respondents living in Eastern Europe, most former special settlers in Irkutsk oblast, by their own recounting, were speaking about their deportations in such detail for the first time. Their answers to questions about life in deportation were mostly laconic. After short but emotional stories about the moment of deportation (including a description of the arrival of soldiers or members of the security organs and then the long, grueling trip in overcrowded wagons) come accounts of the extremely difficult early years in the settlements, then of the gradual improvement of their material condition. The emphasis, in terms of both emotion and the level of detail, is on the moment of actual deportation itself.

On the whole, stories of deportation are largely devoid of references to "the big picture"; instead the individual is alone with his or her tragic past. In contrast to dekulakization, deportations from the Baltics and western Ukraine are often seen in Russia as an illegitimate history with a multitude of sore spots ("forest brothers," collaborationism). The absence of collective narrative structures makes conceptualizing and constructing the memory of deportation at the individual level especially difficult. As a result, recollections come to the narrator with difficulty; they concentrate on a short episode whose ending blurred boundaries. If the episode began on the day of exile, its conclusion is rarely dated with accuracy, being lost among other events. The seemingly most important moment—the settler's change in official status, his/her removal from the special registry (*spetsuchet*)—often do not appear in interviews as life-altering. Instead changes in a special settler's situation are linked to other events having little to do with repression: marriage, a new job, a move to a city, the flooding of a village, and so on. Such events establish bridges to life after emancipation, thus partially dissolving the deportation experience amid the rest of the individual's biography.

Such dissolution also occurs as a result of the repressive experience's convergence with the experience of those around them. For example, on arriving in exile, deportees quickly realized that they were by no means the only ones to suffer from forced relocation and repression. The majority of interviews mention people from earlier or parallel waves of deportation: Volga Germans, Ukrainians, Tatars, Moldovans, and Balts. Moreover, some interviews suggest that the presence of these others could ease the deportees' living arrangements in the first months or play a role in their further adaptation. Irina Tarnavska remembers how a young German woman came out to meet the frightened, weeping Ukrainians deposited on the banks of the Ob´ River and tried to cheer them up: "Don't worry. You were brought here; we're already here; we've already built you barracks. But when they brought us here, there wasn't anyone; it was worse for us."[20]

Even locals whose rights were not formally restricted lived only marginally better than the settlers, and the freedom they enjoyed was highly conditional, particularly in the villages.[21] This, too, impressed on deportees the idea that their condition was perhaps not exceptional. The apparent proximity of Gulag and non-Gulag inside a single system of forced labor—an important theme for historians—is echoed in the deportees' testimony.[22] They recall not only common work but frequently also living under one roof with ostensibly free collective farmers and workers, and they emphasize the similarity of their situations in the face of destitution and arbitrariness. This is not to say that the repressive dimension disappears entirely but rather to note that it is concentrated on specific moments and figures: the physically and morally difficult weeks spent en route to exile, the figure of the commandant, the humiliating necessity of reporting to him on a regular basis, and the ban on leaving the settlement without permission.

Although traits such as the emphasis on broadly shared difficulties characterize many interviews, they appear with maximal force among those who remained in Siberia. In interpreting their experience, such interviewees appeal to the collective Russian historical narrative, which provides its own hierarchy of historical values, with the experience of war as the core that justifies all hardships and serves as a source of legitimation at an individual and collective level. War offers an explanation for hunger, for why children had to work, and for the absence of men. Recounting her first difficult years in a Siberian village, where she was exiled as an adolescent in 1949, Elena Paulauskaitė repeated several times: "Well, what can you say, it was a difficult time, the years after the war; one person's husband died at the front, for someone else it was their father."

In this manner, former special settlers recite stories that are Soviet in terms of general structure, subject matter, lexicon, silences, and shadow zones. One of the stories' characteristic features is the substantial depoliticization of the entire experience, including the repression and coercion that our respondents experienced as both victims and witnesses.[23] These are first and foremost stories about life woven from hard, unceasing work and from efforts and achievements both individual and collective. The result in the narratives is a gradual personal and collective normalization: material improvements, study or more skilled work, the acquisition of housing, and successful careers for one's children.

"I Arrived from Siberia Raised as a Soviet Person"

In interviews with respondents who now reside in East European countries outside Russia, one finds more than a few dissimilarities with the stories of those who remained in Russia.[24] Many of these informants have shared their experience of deportation more than once, sometimes publicly, and a few have even published their recollections. Unsurprisingly, the majority of such stories feature a more defined structure, more details, exact dates, and other specifics sometimes based on documents and historical research. The tendency in parts of the post-Soviet space, especially the Baltics, to interpret the deportations as a collective tragedy representing a core component of national identity produces an emphasis on distinct themes and enables the consolidation of certain evidence as authoritative.[25]

Yet far from all these stories integrate the "popular narrative of trauma as the decisive symbol of the Soviet experience."[26] They bear significant similarities to the Siberian cases and at times explicitly acknowledge the Sovietization of their authors. Recounting their childhoods and adolescence, then their complicated return to Lithuania or Latvia, Silva Linarte, Sandra Kalniete, Marytė Kontrimaitė, and Antanas Kybartas admit that they arrived in their homelands "absolutely Soviet" or "red," to use their own words. They speak of how slowly thereafter they came fully to comprehend the tragedy that had befallen their families and their nation, and how gradually they distanced themselves from the reality around them.[27] Indeed, the distancing from one's own Soviet experience constitutes one of the main features of these interviews and allows that experience to be identified and understood as something distinct from the present.

These themes of hard work and shared destitution, similarity in the condition of special settlers and their neighbors, and bridges between the period in deportation and subsequent life create a framework for studying the adaptation, survival, and later integration of the deportees.

LIFE IN THE SPECIAL SETTLEMENTS

The world in which the deportees found themselves in postwar Irkutsk oblast featured an economy under heavy pressure, a severe scarcity of labor, extremely difficult living conditions, and a certain weakening of the ideological and even general control over the local periphery—the kolkhoz villages and the forest and industrial settlements. By no means unique to Irkutsk oblast, these factors played an important role in the fate of deportees, first and foremost by imparting a fundamentally economic character to their role on arrival. The economic functions of special settlers as a workforce and part of a general system of forced labor are today well known.[28] Less studied is the influence of these functions on the life trajectories of special settlers and their role in the settlers' Sovietization.

"Due to an Absence of Labor We Are on the Verge of Failing the Plan"

Numerous documents in Irkutsk archives reveal the significant difficulties confronting the oblast's industry and agriculture as they sought to fulfill the Fourth Five-Year Plan.[29] Most industries cited labor shortages that sometimes took on catastrophic proportions. The situation in the Cheremkhovo coal mines was exceptionally problematic, as was that of the forest industry, called on to increase its production significantly.[30] The year 1949 saw the formation of two new logging trusts, Taishetles and Bratskles, which included numerous new logging enterprises (*lespromkhoz*). Their directors had simultaneously to fulfill the logging plan and to create the infrastructure for the expansion of production and the settlement of workers. Both required massive amounts of manpower. In February 1949 Taishetles calculated its needs at 6,200 people, a significant number of whom were intended for logging enterprises, which were then staffed at less than 50 percent.[31] The situation was no better on the collective farms. For example, in 1949 the oblast executive committee (*oblispolkom*) sent a request to the Council of Ministers for 5,800 special settlers to work in agriculture.[32] Collective farms struggled with the flight of peasants to the city, to construction sites, and to forest enterprises, the last of which were permitted to accept collective farmers and their families on a permanent work basis without hindrance.[33]

Turnover had, of course, long been a problem for the Soviet economy. Numerous accounts mention the flight of workers from the region's mines and logging enterprises, sometimes en masse.[34] In some cases authors blamed this on the "poor-quality workers" sent to them by recruitment. A large proportion of these workers consisted "of former convicts, alcoholics, the ill, and mainly women who lead an immoral lifestyle and arrive not with the goal of working but purely with the goal of receiving the advance sums, linens, and so on provided for by the contract in order to run away from the logging enterprise with everything they get."[35] Admittedly, the authors of most documents recognized that the abominable living conditions were the primary cause of flight from work.[36] Archival files contain no lack of eloquent examples of factory directors and representatives of local government acknowledging "unbearable conditions": unsanitary and overcrowded dormitories (in some the average living space was 1.5–2 square meters per person); settlement in buildings unsuitable for human residence (cowsheds or smithies); irregularities in the distribution of bread and a total absence of other groceries in stores.[37] An audit conducted at the Dobchurskii logging enterprise in 1950 showed that in stores "there are absolutely no dry goods (salt, matches, tobacco, and other food products). There was one pickled watermelon at 18 rubles a kilo, and even that was already spoiled and not fit for consumption. Otherwise, the store is empty (though there is a sufficient supply of vodka)."[38] Residents of forest settlements, in particular, suffered from such conditions, located as they were at great distance from other inhabited locations. Thus in the Taishet logging enterprise "workers have become ragamuffins, but in the stores . . . there are no supplies and nowhere to buy them, since it is comparatively far to the raion center, 100 km. The result is that at night, workers leave the logging enterprise and go home of their own accord."[39]

"A Special Contingent Offers an Escape from This Difficult Situation"

To judge by requests received by the oblast party committee (*obkom*), directors of many oblast factories who faced an acute shortage of labor drew precisely this conclusion.[40] Of course, they were familiar with the drawbacks of such manpower, in particular the high percentage of those incapable of work as well as women with children, and were aware of the necessity—at least theoretically—to create the necessary infrastructure such as housing and schools.[41] But apparently the mobilization potential of the economics of forced labor, its ability to quickly provide reserves of manpower that were geographically fixed and supervised by a commandant overpowered other considerations.[42]

As preparations for new large-scale deportations primarily from the Baltics (Operations Vesna and Priboi) got underway in 1948–1949, and Irkutsk oblast was selected as a "receiving" region, oblast and raion authorities and the industrial administrations, first and foremost the logging trusts, expressed their desire to receive a significant number of "special contingents."[43] It was assumed that their assessments took stock of both the needs of local industry and the capacity for accommodating settlers. In the winter of 1948–1949, in the lead-up to the repressive operations planned for the spring, inspections were conducted to determine such capacity. Afterwards, detailed plans were put together, with provision for everything down to the number of families that would depart from which station for which enterprise and with which special echelon. In 1948 Irkutsk oblast received more than 11,600 special settlers from Lithuania (3,331 families), the majority of which (around 2,500)

TABLE 7.1. Special settlers in Irkutsk Oblast, October 1949

Contingent	Families	People	Men	Women	Children	Percent
Lithuanian exiles (*vyselentsy*)	7,877	25,107	7,864	9,981	7,262	37.4
Lithuanian special settlers (*spetsposelentsy*)	3,406	11,163	3,378	4,626	3,159	16.6
OUN members	3,241	8,243	1,773	4,160	2,310	12.3
Vlasovites	—	7,725	7,716	9	—	11.5
Germans	1,522	5,213	1,901	1,790	1,522	7.8
Moldovans	1,072	3,347	921	1,264	1,162	4.9
Estonians	726	1,648	377	785	486	2.5
Ukazniks	—	4,664	2,150	2,514	—	7.0

were assigned to the logging enterprises.[44] A year later, during Operation Priboi in April 1949, another eight thousand families were exiled here. Of these, a large number went to work in agriculture and extraction industries, in particular the gold mines of the Lenzoloto Trust.[45] Simultaneously, other categories of special contingents arrived in the oblast, most notably from Moldova and western Ukraine. As a result of these operations, by 1 October 1949 the special registry in Irkutsk oblast numbered 67,110 people: 26,080 men, 25,129 women, and 15,901 children (table 7.1). More than half of them were Lithuanians.[46]

"Special Settlers and Recruits Were Lodged in Dugouts Not Prepared for Habitation"

Despite all the careful planning based on the authorities' previously accumulated experience, in the regions where special settlers were distributed in 1948–1949 theory clashed with reality.[47] The enterprises of Irkutsk oblast struggled to absorb the special contingents, whom they had first to deliver to locations sometimes hundreds of kilometers from the train station and then to house, to outfit with work, and to furnish with at least minimal provisions. Very quickly—sometimes even before the operation began—warnings about impending difficulties appeared, in some cases leading to changes in the original plans and the redirection of echelons to other stations and enterprises.[48] Subsequent inspections of special settlers' living conditions revealed numerous "shortcomings," which represented exceptionally difficult, sometimes catastrophic living conditions for the deportees: the absence of housing and any sort of provisioning (the inspections established cases of dystrophy), outbreaks of diseases caused by malnutrition, an absence of warm clothing, and abominable sanitary conditions, all coupled with the absence of medical assistance.[49]

Nonetheless, both the implementation of deportations from the USSR's western territories in the late 1940s and the subsequent administration of special settlers were distinct from similar operations in the previous decade, which featured "deportations to nowhere" for peasant exiles in the 1930s and a logic of "disposable" manpower for temporarily "plugging holes" in the local economy.[50] We may base this assertion on the role of economic and social logic in allocating deportees across the oblast's territories and the authorities' growing attention to social considerations in the use of special contingents as manpower in subsequent years, along with the progressive elimination of differences between them and other categories of manpower.[51]

Should we regard these tendencies as the consequence of the severe shortage of manpower caused by the war, which undermined the idea of humans as an inexhaustible resource? Did the decree of 26 November 1948 in part alter perceptions of special settlers at the level of the administration and perhaps even the individual? The decision to make exile permanent indubitably testifies to the toughening of repressive policies at the central level, while hundreds of thousands of individuals were stripped of the hope of returning to their homelands.[52] But at the regional level the fact that special settlers became forever a part of the local population compelled authorities to adopt a long-term perspective in policy making and may have brought the special settlers closer to the rest of the population in terms of their socioeconomic status. Indeed, in archival documents on the management of labor and socioeconomic and migration policies we see signs of such a convergence, as well as the occasional merging of special contingents into the local population. In the archive of the oblast Department of Resettlement documents relating to special contingents alternate with those concerning regular migrants, primarily "migrants from land-poor regions." Notably, one and the same measures were taken for both categories: a search for available housing and livestock to sell to those arriving, allotment of household plots, granting of tax concessions, and so on.[53]

Hereafter, except for documents pertaining to the MVD's supervision of special settlers, all local administrative documents related to production, the social sphere, schooling, and so on address special contingents alongside the remaining population, if special settlers are distinguished at all. Even when

Figure 7.1. Estonian special settler at the door of her house (*zemlianka*), Novosibirsk oblast, 1950. Photograph © Eela Löhmus and Sound Archives—European Memories of the Gulag.

special settlers constituted a majority in a given community, their presence is often not mentioned. In terms of living and work conditions, little distinguished them from those around them. Dozens of documents clearly articulate this. Consider, for example in the following address to the obkom by the administration of one logging enterprise: "In the summer of 1951, 142 exiled families (from western Belarus) and 69 families of planned migrants (from Tambov oblast) arrived at the Morgudeiskii logging enterprise as permanent workers. . . . None of the newly arrived workers has warm clothes or shoes. Additionally, of the 616 permanent workers in the logging enterprise 70 percent likewise stand in need of warm clothes and shoes."[54] From Cheremkhovo came the following report: "230 special settlers and recruits were lodged in dugouts not prepared for habitation; people sleep on bare boards, without bedclothes—men, women, and children are all mixed together" (fig. 7.1).[55] In these and many other archival documents from the time, a sort of commonality of fates between the special settlers and neighboring workers and collective farmers took shape: general destitution and powerlessness at first, followed by a gradual improvement in one's material condition. This convergence of fate and condition comes across clearly in interviews with former deportees, especially on issues of work and daily life.

"As for Me . . . I Had to Work"

The subject of work is key to all the interviews.[56] Work not only defined the experience of life in the special settlements but also set the tone for descriptions of subsequent events and the respondents' interpretation of their repressive experience today. In their stories work plays a complicated, ambiguous role: it appears as a heavy obligation—at times a backbreaking burden —and as a source of various opportunities to improve one's condition and rebuild one's life. Herein lies one of the most important distinctions between the special settlement regime and the conditions of prisoners living and working in the camps.

Work, however, should be understood in all its forms and dimensions: collective and domestic, forced and voluntary, undertaken out of necessity or for the sake of personal gain. Alongside mandatory participation in collective work, special settlers engaged in all kinds of other labor: on their household plots or plying trades, entering into informal exchanges with the local population, and so on. All these forms of work were necessary for survival (especially on collective farms); many of them were regarded by the regime with suspicion and more than once came under the threat of a ban (e.g., there were numerous inspections designed to limit the size of collective farmers' household plots). But here as well this labor can be viewed as one vector of Sovietization, if we understand that term as a model of behavior combining officially sanctioned practices with the exploitation of various loopholes that permitted one to survive.

If many deportees recall the lengthy journey into exile as one of the most physically and morally difficult moments ("we were so ashamed while being transported like criminals," recounts one former deportee), then to judge by many stories arrival and the beginning of work in the special settlement initiated a certain normalization.[57] As the deportation began, permission to bring along household effects and tools represented a source of hope—a sign that the deportees were "being sent to work" and not to their deaths.[58] Work subsequently justified one's presence in exile, allowing settlers to rationalize the deportations, to themselves and to others, as Russian residents of the receiving villages recall even today. When asked what they knew about the reason for the deportation, a resident of the village Kaltuk in Irkutsk oblast recalled of deported Lithuanians: "they never talked about themselves. They never said anything . . . but we asked . . . and they said only, 'they sent us here to work.'"[59] The letters of deportees, subject to opening and analysis by the MGB, echo these and other recollections, emphasizing the function of special settlers as labor. One of these letters, sent in 1949 from the Iakutsk ASSR to Lithuania, mentions both the stigma of being labeled a kulak and the paradoxical way in which exile and the similar conditions facing special settlers and their local neighbors minimized the stigma: "Mummy, here in our new location no one gets on your nerves. As far as I can see, life is the same everywhere, only here no one calls you a kulak or some other name, they just call you workers. . . . I'm not angry at life, I work the hours set me, then come home, eat, and calmly occupy myself as I please. When I look around, I don't live worse than the others, and perhaps even better."[60]

These and similar words from letters of those years and recent interviews testify to the intense pressure that the village population of the Baltic region faced in the course of forced bread deliveries, collectivization, and the regime's struggle with "forest brothers" and their "servants," real and imagined. This pressure compelled one of our respondents, Juozas Miliauskas, to comment in a seemingly paradoxical fashion on the relief that his family members experienced on finding themselves in exile in Irkutsk oblast. For several years in Lithuania, they had had to hide first from the "forest brothers," who demanded food, then from the exile that threatened "servants of the nationalists." In Siberia, by contrast, "nobody hit us. Here my father used to say, 'I rest here.' Because he would go to sleep, and no one would bother him. Back home if it wasn't one, it was the other barging in. . . . You fret all night. . . . You hear a shot, but where can you go? You toss about all night. In the morning you get up—the pig is gone, and the hay has been taken."[61]

Political stigma did not disappear instantly. Nor was it confined to the relationship between the individual and the authorities; it also left its traces on relations with locals. Many witnesses speak—often reluctantly and not right away—of how local residents at first called them "fascists," "bandits," or "Banderites."[62] In this context work and the respect afforded to labor were practically the only mechanisms that could improve conditions for deportees, allowing them to shed their status as criminals and to adapt and sometimes integrate into local communities. Collective work enabled the establishment of initial contacts with locals, after which their perception of special settlers often began to change. This topic appears in every interview. Local residents, deportees who returned to their homeland, and those who remained in Siberia all speak of the respect that special settlers achieved among local populations through their work.

At the same time, neither the forced nature of the work nor its intrinsic difficulty nor the squalid living conditions are absent from their memories. Respondents recount how they were led "like sheep" to work in the collective-farm fields and emphasize the compulsory nature of the work, along with the consequences of shirking. One recounted: "I had to work in order to receive a little plot of land, to plant potatoes. If you didn't work, they could even kick you out of your quarters. . . . At fourteen years, I worked not eight hours a day but sixteen. Both day and night they made you work."[63] Work was first and foremost a means of survival, though it was sometimes insufficient. Elena Paulauskaitė recounts how, despite the difficult work, her earnings were not enough to provide for herself and her mother. They owed their survival to help from relatives in Lithuania, who from the beginning had "sent everything from home": money, food, and clothing.[64] Items that deportees had managed to bring into exile could also play an important role. In the course of Operations Vesna and Priboi each family had the right to take up to 1,500 kilograms of baggage, though few actually realized this theoretical right given the time allotted for packing, the availability of transportation, and so on.[65] As a result, if some respondents had with them only some hastily gathered clothes and food, others recall a large number of objects, including heavy ones. The foodstuffs taken along—flour, potatoes, and occasionally pigs, hastily slaughtered or sometimes even shot by convoy soldiers and cooked along the way as circumstances permitted—in particular helped deportees survive the first months, while clothing and household goods could play an important role for much longer.[66] Under extreme conditions of daily life—during the journey and for the first few months of exile—the absence of necessary supplies and foodstuffs could threaten special settlers' lives.[67] Authors of one report on the settling of deportees in Irkutsk oblast's collective farms made special note of the dire straits of those exiled from the cities, who therefore did not have sufficient reserves of food.[68] Later, in the conditions of "standard" everyday life, individual items, especially tools, could become important resources for adaptation and improvement of one's material condition: sewing machines taken by a farsighted mother, who could then sew for her family and the neighbors; a father's carpentry tools, and so on.

"We've Recovered a Bit. . . . We're Already Used to This Life"

As Sergei Krasil´nikov and Lynne Viola have pointed out, for special settlers work amounted above all to a "means of survival, and only afterwards could it evolve into a means of existence, a way to satisfy one's needs, an instrument for raising social status, and so forth."[69] The interviews allow us to trace this evolution, and many of them force us to disagree with these authors' conclusion that special settlers lacked any source of positive motivation for work and regarded it first and foremost as an opportunity to leave the special settlement.[70] The recollections of respondents who experienced the

postwar permanent special settlements in fact show signs of positive motivation, if we take this to include a determination to reconstruct one's life anew,
whatever the conditions, and if we consider work in all its forms.

For Juozas Miliauskas, work appears as a means to establish and (re)con-
struct one's life, but frequently also as a source of pleasure and pride—for
example, when he mentions his first wheeled tractor or speaks of how he
drove a combine from Irkutsk, 500 kilometers away. Even sixty years later,
he describes in detail how much grain his family received per workday and
how that amount grew as the situation improved: "Later on, in two years we
received 70 kilograms of wheat. For a year! They were paying 10 kopecks per
workday then. But later, when I became a tractor operator and worked on a
combine, we started to receive 800, then 1,000 kilograms, then one ton, then
one and a half tons. We started to feed our livestock, our pig, cows, geese. We
had our own mill, ground our own flour. We began to live." Antanas Kaunas
repeats these sentiments. He recounts with evident pleasure his work on the
tractor and the hunting that first helped his family to survive the hungry
years, then became one of his lifelong hobbies (as well as an opportunity to
earn extra money).[71]

In contrast, in the interview cited above with Elena Paulauskaitė, work appears as an unendurable burden. The youngest daughter of prosperous peasants, she was exiled from Lithuania as an adolescent with her middle-aged
mother. In Siberia she had to work on a collective farm and had full responsibility for supporting her family. The theme of backbreaking labor permeates
her interview—for example, when she notes that some of her friends attended school "but I had to work"; when asked whether she gathered berries in
the woods with other children ("what berries, when we were working!?"); in
recounting her reaction to Stalin's death (whereas people generally listened
to the radio, "I came home from work and rested"). Even so, Paulauskaitė's
account portrays gradual improvement in the material conditions of both
special settlers and regular collective farmers, as well as pride in her reputa-
tion as a good worker. In her story exemplary work and the resulting social
recognition produce a sort of self-rehabilitation. When asked whether her
future husband, a member of the Komsomol, was apprehensive about mar-
rying a Lithuanian special settler, she replied: "I always worked flawlessly; I
was awarded presents."

Archival documents confirm that the regime sought to raise discipline
and production with the same simple mechanisms of encouragement for
special settlers and others alike. In the postwar years the names of special
settlers—Lithuanians, Moldovans, Ukrainians—can regularly be found
among the winners of socialist competitions, Stakhanovites, and brigades

Figure 7.2. Brigade of Lithuanian and Buriat loggers with electric saw, Buriat ASSR, 1952. Photograph © Rymgaudas Ruzgys and Sound Archives—European Memories of the Gulag.

that received the red challenge banner.[72] Mechanical expertise was in especially high demand (truck or tractor driving, experience in using electric saws, etc.) and opened the doors to more prestigious jobs. Such skills could also raise productivity, and thus special settlers' pay in logging enterprises (fig. 7.2).[73] Young people from the special contingents attended courses for farm machine operators and drivers, while adults sometimes joined these professions thanks to their practical experience, given the scarcity of skilled labor.[74] Special settlers likewise found that traditional crafts such as construction, carpentry, and joinery, often in demand in factories and collective farms, sometimes allowed one to receive more qualified and more remunerative work.[75]

Skills were also consequential in informal economic relations. Marytė Kontrimaitė's father not only was valued by the authorities as an excellent carpenter and jack of all trades (in Bodaibo his skills prevented his family from being sent to even more distant regions and later facilitated his return to his native village in Lithuania); he was also famed for his ability to slaughter pigs, a skill that provided him with fresh meat in return for the service.[76] The recollections curiously mix markers of respect and material improvement referring to different cultural practices and systems of values:

the vouchers that Elena Paulauskaitė received for good work allowing her to purchase boots after spending her first Siberian winter in galoshes; Juozas Miliauskas's honorary certificates; signs of respect from Russian neighbors and opportunities to enter into the complicated system of informal relationships that encompassed paid work, barter of goods and services, and manifestations of solidarity.

Thus the interviews reflect the variety of tactics used by special settlers in adapting to and improving their condition. They testify to the gradual mastery of Soviet society's wide spectrum of norms and strategies, traces of which can also be found in the archives. Inspections of Irkutsk oblast's forest industries in places reveal "Lithuanian domination of food services, trade, and children's institutions" and reprehensible ties between special settlers and local bosses, who forgot, as one party instructor complained, that one "has to know the time and place, consider the circumstances, and know whom to drink with."[77]

"Those Lithuanians Dance Fabulously!"

If collective work facilitated the expansion of contacts with the surrounding world, adult special settlers otherwise associated primarily within national networks, at least until a significant number of special settlers returned to their homelands in the late 1950s.[78] Religious practices played a special role. In many interviews one finds mention of family and communal prayers and religious ceremonies, celebrated at first without clergymen and then from the mid-1950s sometimes with their participation, as the clergy were emancipated from the camps.[79] National holidays and other traditional forms of recreation uniting special settlers of one origin are regularly mentioned as well. Precisely these moments—as well as weddings, funerals (fig. 7.3), and christenings—were frequently captured in photographs.[80]

Some special settlers managed to organize something akin to Sunday schools, where children learned to read and write in their native language. All these efforts facilitated not only the consolidation of national communities at the local level but also the preservation of symbolic ties to the homeland, the reproduction of identification with the homeland in the younger generation, and sustained hopes of return.[81] The elders' stories, letters and packages from the homeland, and the presence of photographs and objects from home played a similar role. The identification with an almost unknown homeland could be so strong that some children who grew up in exile experienced disappointment when they returned to their native lands. On the contrast between dreams of the homeland and first impressions on seeing it, Marytė Kontrimaitė vividly recounts: "I imagined my homeland to be very

Figure 7.3. Burial of a Lithuanian special settler, Irkutsk oblast, 1950s. Photograph ©
Bronius Zlatkus and Sound Archives—European Memories of the Gulag.

beautiful: blooming fields, beautiful houses of which I had seen pictures in
schoolbooks. I dreamed of blossoming gardens. In Siberia that could never
have happened. This even got a bit confused, and I dreamed of flowering pine
trees. . . . I was horribly disappointed when I returned to Lithuania. Since I
arrived in November, the trees were bare, there were no flowers anywhere,
and everything was gloomy and dirty."[82]

If religious ceremonies incurred unequivocal condemnation, the authorities' attitude toward other ethnically tinged social and cultural practices
wavered between prohibition and allowance. The exact boundaries of the
permissible depended on the time and local conditions. Some respondents
speak of only being able to sing songs in their native language inside their
homes, while others stress that no one kept a low profile when organizing national holidays, including public ones. As materials from the MVD archives
testify, such forms of socialization and the connections among the special
settlers aroused the MVD's lively interest and sometimes motivated arrests
for nationalist and anti-Soviet activity.[83]

At the same time, opportunities for including national cultural practices
existed in official Soviet culture, for example, in the form of young special
settlers' amateur talent shows. Marytė Kontrimaitė recalls how Lithuanian
children and adolescents, studying on Sundays with her mother as teacher,
were known in Bodaibo for their talents: "They studied singing and danc-

Figure 7.4. Lithuanian musicians, Buriat ASSR, mid-1950s. Photograph © Rimgaudas Ruzgys and Sound Archives—European Memories of the Gulag.

ing and even performed at some Russian holidays. People already knew about them and would say, 'Don't those Lithuanians dance fabulously!'"[84] Rimgaudas Ruzgys also recalls musical and theatrical performances by the Lithuanian ensemble in his village and even mentions trips to the regional convention of Lithuanian amateur talent groups (fig. 7.4). Their activities apparently took on this scope in the mid-1950s, since at first they were regarded with suspicion, and special permission was required to stage performances. Incidentally, if in this village young people had the opportunity to perform in their native language (translations of plays were checked), then in other places special settlers performed in Russian.[85]

One may suppose that such practices relieved some of the tension among young special settlers pulled between stigmatization based on ethnic identification and inclusion in a supranational Soviet society. Even recollections that devoted much attention to life within ethnic communities, such as the interviews with Rimgaudas Ruzgys and Marytė Kontrimaitė, contain numerous references to the connections between local residents and ethnically different special settlers. In some interviews relationships with local residents (primarily Russians) at times eclipse those within the ethnic community, suggesting a meaningful level of inclusion in local society.[86] Such ties were especially strong in the stories of the younger generation of special settlers: when they recall their relationships with their peers, the borders of ethnic and supranational communities are frequently erased.

(Former) Special Settlers—Just Like Everyone Else, or Forever "Other"?

Does such integration mean identification with the Soviet ideological project, with the official system of values and norms as articulated in pioneer, Komsomol, and party organizations? To what degree did attempts at such identification conflict with the (former) status of special settler? More broadly, to what degree and in what domains did deportees encounter stigmatization and discrimination, even after removal from the special registry?

"From Six Years Old He Was Raised in Soviet Society, in Soviet Schools, by Soviet Teachers"

School was a key space of socialization for the younger generation of special settlers.[87] It was primarily a space for associating with other children, a place where children forced to confront adult life too early could temporarily find a semblance of a normal childhood.[88] At school children also assimilated the codes, practices, and norms that enabled their further integration and rising social mobility.[89] Study of Russian had particular importance for defining an individual's fate: for example, as concerned further study and work. Alongside direct political education (e.g., in the Pioneers), school gave students access to the full set of Soviet cultural codes, echoes of which still reverberate in interviews. In the quotation given at the beginning of this chapter, Antanas Kybartas, wishing to characterize the notions with which he left the special settlement, fluently recited the authors and heroes of literary works occupying a central place in Soviet educational discourse. Recalling how her parents illegally sent her from Bodaibo to relatives in Lithuania, Marytė Kontrimaitė recounts that when she discovered that no one was meeting her at the station, she thought, "I had read about Uncle Stepa the policeman, who saves children, brings home lost people, and decided to look for the police. It was exactly the one thing that I shouldn't have done."[90] This example shows that even families like hers, whose parents devoted much attention to their children's decidedly non-Soviet upbringing, withstood the schools' influence only with difficulty. Neither archival evidence nor interviews reveal traces of the regime's intentional policy of splitting generations that researchers have identified for kulak exile. But even in the absence of such policies echoes of this tension and occasionally open conflict can be heard, sparked by the growing inclusion of younger special settlers in the surrounding Soviet milieu. More often than not, these conflicts occurred on crossing that highly conditional line dividing one's studies and interaction with children from participation in the social life of the school.

If joining the Party (after removal from the special registry) remained rare, membership in Pioneer or Komsomol organizations was widespread among special settler children. The Komsomol, in particular, was evidently perceived as an important step toward integration and thus could provoke conflicts with other family members. Today it constitutes a subject for reflection for our informants. They offer various explanations for joining, both ideological and other: youthful idealism (Nadezhda Tutik refers to herself as a romantic Young Communist), the desire to be part of the vanguard of Soviet youth, or recognition that recommendation from the Komsomol was critical to continue one's studies.[91] Marytė Kontrimaitė recounts that by the time her parents came back to Lithuania a few years after she herself had made the trip, "I was already a Pioneer. I went myself. I needed some sort of ideology, and [there was] that rosy thaw when my parents were rehabilitated. Although there were mistakes and excesses, now we were all going to be brothers and friends. I joined the Komsomol myself. When my parents found out, my mother was furious and my father wept. It was very painful for me, but I thought that they just didn't understand, that we were going to build a bright future, and that it would all be all right."[92] This and other interviews force us to contest the idea that deportation was first and foremost a school of anticommunism, creating "an entire generation of young people who harboured no illusions about life in the Soviet state."[93] The experience of life in the special settlement alone did not always suffice to strip young people of illusions or to prevent them from arising in the first place— although, of course, illusions could gradually be dispelled in later years. Such second thoughts frequently came from within, from a starting point of active involvement. Both Marytė Kontrimaitė and Antanas Kybartas recall how, having become secretaries of their school Komsomol organizations and rubbed shoulders with the local petty elite on their return to Lithuania, they were shocked by the falsehoods that reigned among them. This led both to distance themselves rapidly from the Komsomol and gradually to a wider reconsideration of their views. For other former special settlers the catalyst for such reconsideration came with recognition of the tragic experience of deportation, to which they came through a better understanding of the trials that had faced their parents and other adult victims of exile.[94]

"They Made It Clear That He Was Rejected Because He Was a Special Settler"

These words are taken from a letter addressed in September 1953 to Minister of Internal Affairs Sergei Kruglov by a Lithuanian special settler.[95] Imploring him to liberate her son from the special settlement, she described the consequences of this "tarnishing mark" that jeopardized the eighteen-year-old youth's entire future, from the impossibility of joining the Komsomol to exclusion from an institute, despite his passing of the entrance exams, to which he had to travel, in his mother's words, "in a convoy, like a criminal."

The combination of outright and indirect discrimination described in the letter was characteristic for special settlers. Under the regime established for special settlers, the main form of discrimination involved limitations on freedom of movement. This required them to report to the commandant every week (later every month) and in general made them strongly dependent on the commandant and higher-level organs of the MVD for permission to leave the settlement and for many other questions central to their lives and survival.[96] Convoys, to which special settlers were often subject beyond the settlement, were likewise perceived as a clear stigma, one that marked them as criminals.[97] There were various other forms of discrimination, which in large measure depended on local authorities, whether representatives of the MVD and MGB, the chairmen of collective farms, or the directors of local enterprises. Although some informants were barred from joining the Komsomol and Pioneers and with disappointment regarded this as a sign of their marginalization, other special settlers were invited to join the Party (though this was admittedly rare).[98]

Paradoxically, the theme of stigmatization emerges more distinctly in many interviews when the conversation turns to the period after removal from the special registry. The majority of deportees, especially those who returned to their homeland, note obstacles hampering access to higher education, the impossibility of registering in particular cities or villages, hindrances on one's career path, various forms of interference by the "organs," and fear of stigmatization by locals, which inclined many to maintain complete silence about their past. Notably, most special settlers were rehabilitated only at the end of the 1980s, and until that point their original exile was not recognized as a mistake.[99] The political and social stigmas that had motivated their inclusion in a special contingent (kulak, members of families assisting bandits, etc.) made them especially vulnerable, especially given that even official rehabilitation did not guarantee immunity from discrimination.[100]

If some restrictions on former settlers were open and explicit, in other cases discrimination remained unofficial and frequently only implicit. In certain cases archives indirectly confirm that an individual's past as a special settler could influence his or her fate throughout the Soviet period, affecting career possibilities in particular. Until the second half of the 1980s the files of former settlers—including those who were in a special settlement as children

—were used in the course of background checks when granting access to secret information, determining eligibility for a particular job, or receiving permission to travel abroad.[101]

All these examples suggest that discrimination could manifest itself in different forms and to varying degrees in particular socio-occupational groups. Former deportees who remained in Siberian villages seem rarely to have encountered open manifestations of discrimination, since their lives unfolded outside politically tinged spheres.[102] True, even here one could come up against a sort of "glass ceiling": Ksenia Makovetskaia was awarded multiple prizes as a top dairymaid and traveled in this capacity to the Exhibition of the Achievements of the National Economy (VDNKh) in Moscow. Her husband, also an exiled Ukrainian, was a brigadier and later supervised a farm. But when in the 1970s Ksenia was proposed as a deputy of the regional soviet, the higher-ups suddenly remembered her origins. Such glass ceilings increased the farther some former settlers and their children rose and the closer they came to politically tinged positions and professional spheres that were crucial to the regime.

The height of such ceilings and the spheres they encompassed apparently varied from region to region. Both interviews and archival documents testify to a more intense pressure on former special settlers in the Baltic republics and Ukraine than in Siberia. Documents of the Lithuanian KGB from the late 1940s to the mid-1950s suggest that the mere existence of relatives who were special settlers, never mind contact with them, was constantly mentioned as compromising, sufficient cause for firing someone. Such considerations concerned above all the new Soviet national elite at multiple levels (e.g., chairmen of collective farms, deputies of local soviets, university instructors, young people selected for trips to study in Moscow and Leningrad), but it could even affect a worker on a pig farm.[103] When former special settlers began returning to their homelands, they not only found themselves under special observation by the KGB but also faced rejection by the local population.[104] Stigmatization proved especially strong in western Ukraine, where everything reminiscent of nationalists and Banderites came under suspicion.[105] Yaroslav Pogarskiy, in particular, recalls this reaction, noting that in Siberia he noticed the stigma of the past less.[106]

It was for such reasons that some former deportees actually returned to their place of exile after an unsuccessful attempt to settle in their homeland. One former settler of Lithuanian descent went from Siberia to Lithuania in the 1960s to inquire as to the possibility of returning there at the start of his service in the MVD. A commanding officer of the Vilnius city branch of the MVD unequivocally informed him that with such a background he would have no chance at a career there. He thus returned to Russia, where despite a few hindrances he ended his career with the rank of colonel.

The experience of the aforementioned Yaroslav Pogarskiy, which features the absence of housing as a red thread, suggests that in some cases deportation was significant less as a cause for stigma in any direct sense than in terms of its socioeconomic consequences. Former deportees encountering such difficulties could either see them or ignore them as signs of discrimination, depending on the manner in which they interpreted their life experience. For this reason it is difficult not only to generalize at the level of an entire special contingent, which existed as a single unit only in the reports of the punitive organs, but to assess with any certainty the character and degree of discrimination that a repressed individual encountered as a specific result of his or her past.

It is clear, however, that even in the absence of open discrimination many former deportees sensed their potential vulnerability. This had psychological consequences and could influence their strategies and life trajectories. Some interviews show efforts to prevent the situations in which the potential for discrimination might become a reality. An inveterate traveler, Antanas Kybartas always avoided trips in closed zones, where entry required a special pass. He feared that while processing such permission the Lithuanian KGB would demand from Tiumen´ oblast the file of his repressed father, and his entire career would come under threat. "It wouldn't be clear whether I would stay employed at the adding machine factory."[107]

The fates of former deportees testify simultaneously to strong similarities in their experiences of deportation and important variations, which are particularly evident in the diversity of their socio-occupational and geographical trajectories. Such differentiation becomes even more noticeable as the moment of exile recedes into the past. If memories of deportation itself—the arrival of soldiers or the police, the long train journey, the initial difficulties encountered in exile—are repeated in all interviews with surprising consistency, then accounts of the months and years spent in the special settlement testify to the appearance of dissimilarities of experience and adaptation. The status of special settler and conditions of life in the special settlement established the harsh framework—forced labor, beggarly everyday conditions, limitations, and discrimination—in which the deportees were compelled to make do. Despite their overall lack of rights, however, not all special settlers existed in the same situation. Their original potential for adaptation varied, depending on age, family composition, health, and so on. These factors governed the fundamental differences between, for example, single mothers with small children and families with several adult members capable of work. External factors that influenced possibilities for survival and adaptation could also vary, starting with time of year and place of exile and ending with circumstances about which it is harder to generalize.[108] In contexts where mechanisms for adjusting and improving one's conditions were few, changing just one parameter could have substantial significance. One family member obtaining a slightly better paid job could not only ease everyday life for the entire family but also influence the further trajectory of younger children, just as the presence of a high school in one's place of exile could play a critical role for some deportees by permitting them to continue their studies. Finally, we cannot forget psychological factors, which increase the variation of individual reactions even within a repressive framework.

After emancipation differentiation in trajectories intensified: existing distinctions made themselves felt more acutely, while new distinctions were added. Removal from the special settlement itself contributed to this outcome, as some former deportees received permission to return to their homeland or had property returned to them, while others did not. Such disparities could even affect people within one family. Diverse forms of discrimination—and thus new strategies of coping—developed alongside the increasingly complex trajectories of social mobility and modes of interaction with the state.[109] Behind this variety, which merits further study, we can assume the existence of a range of general patterns, which may themselves suggest a significant degree of the deportees' inclusion in Soviet society and their mastery of its rules.

Some of these rules, however, were inherited from the Stalin era and were later merely softened, not fundamentally revised. As a result, the condition of former deportees remained contradictory and vulnerable, often forcing them to maneuver between their present as people "brought up in Soviet society," on one hand, and their past, which no one ever fully forgot, on the other. In their fates we see in a concentrated form the contradictions of the post-Stalinist regime, which strove to integrate some of the repressed populations inherited from the past into its sociopolitical project without rejecting the project's foundations—in particular, class logic—that had authorized repression in the first place.[110]

A VISUAL HISTORY OF THE GULAG

Nine Theses

AGLAYA K. GLEBOVA

SANITIZATION

We have no photographs of the Gulag as atrocity.[1] Because the camps were phased out slowly, and many became regularly functioning prisons, there was no outside witnessing and documenting of the Gulag (this lack, which could have only been filled during a moment of historical rupture, also points to the continuity of the state apparatus responsible for the Russian penitentiary system). The magnitude of the Gulag's brutality is entirely missing from this photographic record: the cramped train cars used to transfer prisoners are never shown; the barracks, when pictured, are neat and decently appointed; and the internees themselves are rarely tired or thin and are—always—alive.[2] If the GPU/NKVD did photograph executions, critically ill prisoners, dead bodies, or mass graves, these images have yet to be found (by contrast, official camp records—even if in greatly suppressed numbers—do register illness and mortality in the Gulag).

AN INCOMPLETE RECORD

The visual history of Stalinist repressions and the Gulag is hence made up of gaps, disappearances, and excisions. The repressed, if they were high-ranking enough to appear in official photographs, were cut out of prints and scratched out of negatives; faces and names of private citizens were blotted out from family archives; paintings, murals, photographs, and sculptures by the condemned were locked away in museum storage rooms for decades or destroyed wholesale. The Gulag itself, in Alexander Solzhenitsyn's formulation, was an "almost invisible, almost imperceptible country."[3]

VISUAL INNOVATION

Russia has a long history of repression and surveillance that predates the Gulag. *The systems of political control used in Russia were profoundly visual. Moreover, they did not simply reflect modern disciplinary practices but pioneered some of their defining elements.* The Panopticon, for instance, was first conceived as a factory by Samuel Bentham (Jeremy Bentham's brother) while he was working on one of Prince Grigorii Potemkin's estates in 1786.[4] After the assassination of Alexander II in 1881 the state developed a sophisticated visual infrastructure for tracking political dissidents, which included extensive photographic archives. The Okhrana (the Russian security police established in 1881 and dissolved in 1917) was a "technological and methodological innovator in the arts of political control and surveillance."[5] Publicly the government promoted its penal reforms as humane and progressive, much as the Stalinist state would during the Gulag's early history. In 1890, for example, St. Petersburg hosted the Fourth International Penitentiary Congress, with extensive exposition grounds that included life-size models of prison cells, displays of objects manufactured by inmates, and an ethnographic exhibition on Sakhalin Island.[6] This kind of curating of prison visuality would later be employed in Soviet propaganda.[7]

IMPERIAL PRECURSORS

The visual landscape of late imperial Russia was saturated with representations of prisons, exile, and policing. Some early photographic examples include postcard series of "types and views" of Sakhalin (1880s–1890s) by Innokentii Pavlovskii and of the Nerchinsk *katorga* (1891) by Aleksei Kuznetsov, himself a former inmate.[8] Vlas Doroshevich's descriptions of his trips to Sakhalin (1903, fig. 8.1) and George Kennan's *Siberia and the Exile System* (translated and printed in Russia in 1906), both extensively illustrated, were among the best-known accounts of katorga and exile. These, however, were most certainly not official or laudatory accounts, and they aimed to show the miserable state of Russia's penal system.

The Stalinist propaganda machine shrewdly used the images of tsarist penitentiaries to make the Gulag seem progressive by comparison. In some ways, the Gulag must have appeared humane indeed when contrasted to images of katorga, some of which showed the convicts branded and shackled. Yet at other times, it would be difficult to distinguish between images of Soviet camps and their predecessors—the armed guards and the primitive tools of labor appear in both.

Figure 8.1. An illustration from Vlas Doroshevich's book *Sakhalin (Katorga)*, 1903 edition.

The penal systems of late imperial Russia preoccupied the Soviets. Many films, memoirs, and paintings of the early Soviet period addressed the arrests, police searches, katorga, and exile experiences of revolutionaries. In 1921 the Society of Former Political Prisoners and Exiles (Obshchestvo politicheskikh katorzhan i ssyl´no-poselentsev) was founded. It ran a publishing house, archive, and museum until its disbandment in 1935 and the subsequent repression of many of its members. There is little scholarship on the society or, more broadly, on the Soviet interpretation of imperial disciplinary institutions. Yet a rich historiography and visual mythology of katorga and exile—culminating with Mikhail Gernet's mammoth five-volume *History of the Tsarist Prison*, published between 1951 and 1954—emerged under Stalinism.

SELECTIVITY BY RESEARCHERS

The opening of the Soviet archives has brought to light thousands of photographs of the Gulag. Yet many of these images, which range from documentation of construction to portraits of prisoners and their overseers, are little known and seldom reproduced.[9] *Visually, Soviet repressions and forced labor camps remain largely defined by the mug shots from the Lubianka files, as well as the infamous propaganda films and photographs of the Gulag*, primarily of

Solovki and the White Sea-Baltic Canal, produced in the late 1920s and early 1930s for both domestic and international audiences.[10] The Lubianka head shots—each prisoner photographed in his or her own clothing both in profile and looking directly at the camera—are endlessly shocking, for here we come face to face with the victims of Stalin's secret police. These photographs show, above all, individuals, laying bare the human toll of Stalin's purges.[11] This is the side of the Gulag concealed in official propaganda, which attempted to present the camps as a humane system and a productive collective enterprise through a multitude of omissions and a variety of photographic and cinematic techniques. The Lubianka images have long been understood as an antidote to the faceless (if shocking) statistics of the Gulag, as performing the function of witnessing and reckoning.

THE APPEARANCE OF ORDINARINESS

In contrast to the tragic singularity of the Lubianka mug shots or the careful assemblage of propaganda films and photo essays, the archival photographs of the Gulag, now kept at the State Archive of the Russian Federation (GARF) and regional archives and museums, at first appear almost ordinary. Although some of these prints are meticulously hand-colored and carefully mounted into albums embellished with drawings, many are small, grainy, and poorly preserved. They are usually collected into portfolios with succinct captions, adhering to a format that was used to document the accomplishments of Soviet factories and collective farms, a common practice from the 1920s onward. Most of the Gulag photo albums focus on the camps and special settlements' production and infrastructure (fig. 8.2): here felled trees or close-ups of rock strata; a new road cleared; a group of prisoners in a barebones but clean canteen. *These photographs have so far largely defied scholarship, or even interpretation. It is as if, in their combination of careful staging and almost everyday ordinariness, they have become yet another gap in the Gulag's visual history.*

UNRULY PHOTOGRAPHY

The photograph, even when staged, is unruly. It requires the cooperation of photographer, camera, and subject; its blurs, margins, and accidents (what Roland Barthes called its "punctum") constantly threaten to defy the maker's intentions. The Stalinist state understood this well, working hard to combat the photographs' slipperiness: the arrangement of prints into albums systematized them, suggesting a narrative and encouraging a particular reading (fig. 8.3). Text fills these photographic collections: it appears on the covers, in the captions, but also in the images themselves. Everything is labeled, and build-

Figure 8.2. Hand-painted photographs from the commemorative photo album "Soviet Narym: Opening of the West-Siberian North by Labor Settlers, 1930–1936." *Source:* Tomsk Memorial Museum, "Sledstvennaia tiurma NKVD."

ings are decorated with painted propaganda slogans inside and out. *It is up to us to recover and acknowledge the innate unruliness and contingencies of these photographs, to look not only at what the state wanted to communicate but also what it failed to communicate through them—to see, that is, what the images manage to suggest in excess of their authors' intentions. This means looking to the marginal, the peripheral, and the accidental* (for even propaganda has moments of fracture); to read Gulag photographs only as illustrations of the system is to perpetuate the state's quest to appear all-powerful, systematic, organic.

VIGILANCE INSIDE AND OUTSIDE THE CAMPS

The visuality of the Gulag depends on, and in turn informs, the visuality of Soviet society, mirroring the modes of representation that were circulating outside the camps. There is what we could call a small zone of images that directly depict the Gulag and were created in the Gulag during the time of its operation: propaganda photographs and films, photographic archival reports, artwork and publications produced in the camps.[12] These reflect the visuality of the big zone, from the countless commemorative photoalbums and illustrated publications to the debates about the ideologically correct ways of seeing and representing.

Vision, after all, was a deeply politicized sense under Stalinism. Vigilance (*bditelnost'*), a kind of visual acuity, was one form of ideologically correct looking, often depicted in posters as an all-seeing eye (sometimes disembodied and sometimes belonging to especially vigilant Soviets, such as Feliks

Figure 8.3. A page from the photo album "Stakhanovtsy of the Ninth Division of BBK-NKVD," ca. 1934–1936. *Source:* National Archive of the Republic of Karelia.

Dzerzhinskii). The deep distrust of surface appearances that defined Soviet vigilance—a way of seeing that framed everyone and everything as ideologically suspect and sought to unmask the "class enemies" who were allegedly hiding in plain sight—was codified at the January 1933 Party Plenum. Although the collectivization of agriculture was largely complete by then, in his speech Stalin focused on kulaks as the main example of the class naiveté and blindness of the Soviet population. Good socialist citizens, Stalin lamented, "look for the class enemy outside the collective farms, they look for him in the guise of someone with a villainous countenance, with enormous teeth, a thick neck, and holding a rifle. They look for a kulak as we know him from posters." Criticizing the caricatured portrayal of kulaks in earlier propaganda posters as outdated, Stalin concluded that "such kulaks have long ceased to exist on the surface."[13] Only vigilance and its companion form of vision, *prozorlivost'*, which could be described as penetrating vision or far-sightedness, could counteract this "class blindness" and guarantee the unmasking of the chameleon-like enemy.

STALINIST MODERNITY

Although such skeptical ways of looking were characteristic of Stalinism and deeply connected to its ideological underpinnings, they were not unique to it. Indeed, distrust of empirical vision is characteristic of both modernity and modernism.[14] Although Socialist Realism is commonly opposed to avant-garde practices, it appears that even after 1934 Stalinist policies in the visual arts were shaped in part with an eye to the West; as has been recently suggested, this might account for the appearance of Suprematist forms in Soviet exhibition pavilions abroad, including at the 1937 Paris International Exposition and the 1939 New York World's Fair.[15] The avant-garde artists Aleksandr Rodchenko and El Lissitzky were designing layouts for the propaganda journal *SSSR na stroike* (The USSR in Construction)—albeit layouts that struck a compromise between their earlier work and the demands of Socialist Realism—as late as 1940.

Although ideological critiques deeply affected, and irrevocably damaged the careers of, the artists who belong to today's modernist canon, most of them survived Stalinist repression. One exception was the photomontage artist Gustav Klutsis, who was swept up in the purges against the Latvian community in 1937. Many lesser-known artists were likewise repressed because of their alleged nationalism.[16] Such, for example, was the case of the Ukrainian painter Mykhailo Boichuk and his school, with most of their monumental works destroyed in the late 1930s (in this case, works in monumental media proved particularly short-lived, as they were easier to eradicate than images in mass circulation).[17] Appreciation of, or adherence to, "anti-socialist" aesthetics was also dangerous, although the most dangerous kind appears to have been, again, not the avant-garde production that preceded Socialist Realism but rather aesthetics that predated the October Revolution (such as icon painting and its study or Pictorialist photography).

The above is not meant to suggest that the Stalinist state asserted a clear aesthetic hierarchy in its judgments; rather, it is an attempt to open new lines of inquiry. The goal, as I see it, should not be to pin down an overarching logic to what kind of art was allowed to exist, and what kind was suppressed—such an approach risks buttressing the doctrinaire master narrative that the Stalinist regime imposed on its citizens, making the state seem rational rather than largely unpredictable in its violence. *To fill in the excisions of Stalinist repressions and the Gulag, a study of this visual history must embrace fracture in both subject and methodology.*

PART II

COMPARISON

PENAL DEPORTATION TO SIBERIA AND THE LIMITS OF STATE POWER, 1801–1881

DANIEL BEER

In February 1839, having been sentenced to twenty years of penal labor in the mines of Nerchinsk in eastern Siberia, the Polish revolutionary Justynian Ruciński found himself clapped in irons and tramping eastward in a marching convoy of exiles:

> A life began for us that is difficult to name, let alone adequately to describe. It seemed there can be no harsher existence on earth. It comprised daily marches of 18 to 25 versts in chains, overnighting in prisons on filthy wooden benches . . . , lacking undergarments, clothes and boots, a starvation diet, extreme hunger, icy slush, heat, frosts, and all the time we had to keep marching onward and onward. There was the unceasing surveillance of the convicts, whose lives were full of the most cynical kinds of depravity, usually encouraged by corrupt convoy commanders. . . . Our bodies were terribly exhausted through physical exertion and our minds through anxiety and homesickness. That is but a pale rendering of our bitter fate.[1]

Like many Siberian exiles before him and after him, Ruciński would look back on the thirteen-month-long journey as the most torturous aspect of his Siberian exile. Yet Ruciński's formal punishment—his term of penal servitude—began only when he finally reached Nerchinsk. As far as the authorities were concerned, the torments of the marching convoys were an incidental preamble to Ruciński's actual sentence. The yawning gulf between the state's own conception of deportation as a strictly logistical operation, on one hand, and the convicts' experience of it as a brutal ordeal, on the other, reflected the weaknesses and limitations of the autocracy.

By the beginning of the nineteenth century, exile to settlement and, for more serious crimes, exile to penal labor (*katorga*) in Siberia had come to represent different conceptions of penality. At its most fundamental, exile was an expression of sovereign power. The autocrat could move his subjects around the vast territories of his empire at will—as the 1649 Law Code stipulated, "to wherever the sovereign shall direct."[2] The journey into exile was thus a measure of autocratic power; each footstep eastward a homage to the dominance of the state. From the mid-eighteenth century on, the rituals of civil execution that presaged expulsion into the Siberian penal realm were a performance of the might of a patrimonial Russian statehood.[3] Penal labor replaced the gallows in an act of imperial clemency that underlined the power of the ruler. Exiles were deported beyond the frontiers of the metropole to sites at the periphery (or indeed beyond the imaginative frontiers) of the state.[4] From its earliest origins, however, Siberian exile also served an important economic function. The deployment of forced laborers to harvest raw materials at discrete labor sites under Peter the Great expanded over the course of the eighteenth century into a full-blown state-led project to colonize the Siberian landmass under Catherine the Great.[5]

The demands of colonization implied some measure of disciplining, even rehabilitating, exiles. The eventual release of penal laborers to settlement assumed some level of readjustment of their "role as state subjects."[6] Over the course of the reigns of Alexander I and Nicholas I concern with social discipline supplemented the established colonial priorities of population transfer and resource extraction across Siberia.[7] As Abby Schrader and Andrew Gentes have shown, the state encouraged women to follow their husbands into exile, believing their presence would exert a pacifying, reforming influence over the men. Through the establishment of stable and productive family units individual regeneration neatly dovetailed with the state's colonial agenda.[8] By the era of the Great Reforms rehabilitation was an explicit justification for the exile system as a whole.[9]

Exile embraced overlapping modes of penality: sovereign, economic, colonial, and disciplinary. Central to each one was deportation, in Gentes's phrase, "the transmission belt linking the sovereign's punitive vengeance to the state's utilitarian exploitation."[10] Writing about later waves of deportations in the twentieth century, Judith Pallot has argued that coerced mobility needs to be folded into our understanding of the Russian state's penal regimes. Deportations were not simply a temporal antechamber to punishment; they were central to it.[11] Yet across the nineteenth century it was precisely as a temporal antechamber that senior government officials and exile administrators viewed the deportation convoys. To be sure, the act of banishment was a punishment in itself, one that heralded a painful separation of the criminal from native lands, but the archives do not appear to contain any official endorsement of the deportation convoys themselves as appointed sites of a deliberate ordeal to be inflicted.

Of course, the ardors of the journey undoubtedly served as a deterrent to would-be offenders. Individual exile officials, convoy commanders, and soldiers may have believed that, and often certainly behaved as if, the exiles marching eastward deserved their treatment. Yet right from the end of the eighteenth century the authorities in St. Petersburg and in the senior echelons of the exile administration viewed deportation primarily not as a form of punishment in its own right but as a means to a punitive end of exile. Officials approached the *process* of deportation as a logistical challenge, shaped by the need for efficiency and security. The marching convoys of exiles were designed to ensure the delivery of healthy and robust laborers and settlers to specific locations throughout Siberia. Far from being deliberate and calculated, the ordeal of the journey was inadvertent and incidental to the state's formal punishment of offenders.

This official view scarcely corresponded with the experience of the exiles themselves. On the road for many months, sometimes years, they experienced deportation as a grim, sometimes fatal, ordeal that often inflicted more suffering on the convicts than the punishments that awaited them at the end of the Great Siberian Highway. Across the nineteenth century the weakness of the autocracy was laid bare in the chaos, corruption, and brutality of the marching convoys. The state wielded a fundamental, raw power to exile imperial subjects from their towns and villages but then lacked the resources effectively to respond to the logistical challenges that flowed from this policy.

Far from a mobile carceral space in which the disciplinary power of the state was concentrated on convicts, the marching convoys were chronically undergoverned. Deportation was thus an ordeal dominated by administrative failings, inadequate infrastructure, corruption, and the maneuvering of subaltern groups for advantage. As a consequence, the convicts' experiences in the marching convoys bore no relation to the formal punishments appointed in the laws of the empire.[12] Penal migration emerges as a specific instance of a socially dispersed state power, one that reflected under-resourced, improvised, and negotiable practices of governance across the empire.[13] From the perspective of St. Petersburg the deportation of convicts and their families was so chaotic and costly in both material and human terms as to severely compromise the state's stated economic, colonial, and rehabilitative ambitions. For the exiles themselves the deportation convoys were a semilawless world of privation, hunger, dangerous exposure to the elements, disease-infested waystations, and the ever-present threat of violence. Punishment understood as a formally conceived instrument of the state bore little relation to the informal ordeal inflicted by the deportation convoys. The disorderly crucible of human misery that Ruciński endured en route to Siberia was, though unacknowledged by the state, at the heart of his experience as an exile. To be deported to Siberia was to suffer not just the punitive power of the autocracy but (arguably far worse) its limitations.

Between the reigns of Alexander I and Alexander II there were two major attempts to modernize the deportation of exiles. First, the Siberian reforms of 1822 sought to rationalize and bring administrative order to the system of penal migration. Second, from the 1860s on the state introduced new means of transportation designed to speed up the transfer of exiles and their families from European Russia to Siberia. In both instances the efficacy of these improvements was radically undercut by the rapid expansion in the numbers of exiles in the 1820s and again in the 1870s. The result was a near-permanent lag between expanding numbers and penal infrastructure that ensured that deportation convoys remained at best an ordeal for the exiles and at worst proved lethal. This basic thread of continuity runs throughout the nineteenth century: the retributive appetites of the imperial state outstripped its punitive capacities.

BEFORE THE SIBERIAN REFORMS, 1801–1822

At the beginning of the century all exiles made the journey to Siberia on foot. They would set out from cities across the empire and be funneled through Moscow before marching eastward through the town of Vladimir that gave its name to the notorious road that wound its way through Kazan, Perm´, across the Urals to Tiumen´, Tobol´sk, and on toward Tomsk, Krasnoiarsk, and Irkutsk.[14] The Vladimirka, or the Great Siberian Highway, was in reality nothing more than a narrow dirt track. It wound its way across the open steppe of western Siberia before plunging into the thick swampy forests of the taiga in Enisei and Irkutsk provinces.

The convicts walked all year round. During the intense heat of the summer, those at the rear of the marching column choked on the great dust clouds raised by hundreds of tramping feet. On the open steppe, the treeless horizon and cloudless skies offered no respite from the burning sun. Dehydration and sunstroke saw many exiles collapse as they marched. The autumn rains brought only temporary respite from the heat before they transformed the roads into a churning quagmire through which the convicts squelched knee-deep. The Russian term for this period, each autumn and spring, is *rasputitsa*—literally, the time without roads. The horse-drawn carts frequently became stuck in bogs; wheels and axles broke as they were hoisted over rocks and logs. Siberia's dense birch and coniferous forests played host each summer to swarms of ferocious mosquitoes and gadflies who feasted on the exposed flesh of the exiles. Late September already brought the first scorching winter frosts. The temperatures in this most continental of climates plummeted from a roasting 30 degrees Celsius to a bone-chilling minus 20 between August and November. In a custom that had developed over the seventeenth and eighteenth centuries, marching convoys overnighted in the villages strung out along the route. Smaller groups could be accommodated in peasant huts and barns, but larger parties were sometimes forced to sleep in the open air.[15]

At the beginning of the nineteenth century the deportation of exiles to Siberia was chaotic. A senior state official charged with inspecting conditions in Siberia in 1802, State Councillor Nikolai Osipovich Laba (1766–1816), reported directly to Alexander I that many of the exiles were not sufficiently equipped with money or clothing before they set out from their provinces in European Russia; others had their funds stolen by officials en route. Still others, although adequately provided for by their local officials, "had, from carelessness and fecklessness, frittered away their allowance before completing half their journey." In the end a large number of the exiles in marching convoys were obliged to sell their coats, suffered shortages in both food and clothing, and became exhausted, reliant for food on the alms of Siberian villagers in whose cabins they were put up for the night. Laba observed that recordkeeping was in a desperate state, with different convict parties mingling, documents being lost and altered.[16] In 1806 Alexander I issued a decree acknowledging that the Siberian authorities "did not accurately know the sex or the number of the people sent to them for settlement." It proposed the establishment of officials at the first settlement inside the border of each province through which the exiles passed. It would be their job to draw accurate lists of the numbers of exiles arriving, their condition, and their destination.[17] Yet recordkeeping within the system remained haphazard and incomplete. The transportation of exiles was in such disarray that officials "lost count of the people in their charge and of the money spent on feeding and clothing them."[18] A combination of escapes, deaths, and exiles waylaid in the provinces through which they marched defied the compilation of accurate statistics on exiles' numbers and location.[19]

Senior figures in the tsarist government were concerned that the failure to deliver healthy exiles to their appointed destination was subverting the state's economic goals. In 1813 Minister of the Interior Osip Petrovich Kozodavlev (1753–1819) fired off an angry letter to Siberian Governor-General Ivan Pestel', complaining that of the 1,111 male souls destined for Irkutsk Province between 1809 and 1811, only 625 had arrived. Four hundred and eighty-six had remained in Tomsk Province: 178 to settle, 219 because they were apparently too sick to travel, and the rest to work in the local factories. While acknowledging that the sick should indeed to be allowed to remain in Tomsk Province to be cared for by local communities, the minister noted, "under this pretext perfectly capable people are being detained who should be sent on to Irkutsk Province, and the Tomsk provincial authorities have been instructed not to detain such people."[20]

Officials at the end of the Siberian Highway shared St. Petersburg's indignation. In 1818 the Irkutsk provincial authorities were still complaining to St. Petersburg that less than half the allocated number of exiles were reaching eastern Siberia. Investigations revealed that the "best people in terms of age and abilities" were remaining in Russia and in western Siberia to be used as laborers. They were being sent on to Irkutsk only when periods of up to ten years of hard labor had destroyed their health. The authorities were aware of the problem. Noting that the journey to Irkutsk was often taking between four and ten years, St. Petersburg issued instructions in 1817 to all regional governors that exiles were to be transported to their destination "without delay." The central government was also sharply critical of the practice of deliberately sending on to eastern Siberia the frail and the sick, incapable of settlement. These exiles, the State Senate observed, "constitute a class of parasites and beggars who are in need of assistance to feed themselves. They are a burden on the local peasant communities and . . . infect them with vices and diseases." Beyond the reach of central government, local authorities continued to harvest healthy exiles en route to Siberia. An individual exile's destination depended therefore as much on his or her economic utility as on a formally determined sentence.[21]

The deportation convoys were hemorrhaging exiles not simply as a result of local officials filtering out the useful en route. Escapes were also commonplace. Fugitive exiles sometimes formed themselves into marauding bands of vagabonds who subsequently attacked "entire merchant caravans" that journeyed along Siberia's isolated highways. Governor-General of Siberia Ivan Selifontov wrote to Alexander I in March 1805, calling for the establishment of military units with mounted Cossacks along the main Siberian roads "not only to put an end to such acts of banditry and brigandage but also to remove the danger for inhabitants and travelers." Selifontov calculated that 2,880 soldiers, based in post offices along the main routes, would be required to undertake the transportation of prisoners successfully. He understood, however, that it would be difficult to raise the required numbers without severely impinging on the army's duties elsewhere, so he settled for 1,825. Alexander approved his request, and the Internal Watch was established in 1816. Yet the Cossacks who manned it proved no more reliable than the peasants they replaced.[22] Officials lamented that they "frequently, sometimes even deliberately in return for payment, release the convicts they are accompanying." The result was that in the year ending in October 1816, ninety-eight convicts had fled from marching convoys, and this figure included only those reported to the civilian authorities.[23] The endemic nature of escapes and the crime wave unleashed by fugitives in the Siberian provinces of Tobol´sk and Tomsk were a mounting concern for the authorities.[24]

Overlying these administrative problems in the years prior to the Siberian reforms of 1822, the numbers of exiles being marched off to Siberia were expanding at rates that threatened to overwhelm the system. If, on average, 1,606 people per year were exiled from 1807 to 1813, the figure for the period from 1814 to 1818 jumped to 2,476; in the period from 1819 to 1823, it had reached an annual average of 4,570.[25] The increasing use of administrative exile by both landowners and peasant communities, compounded by mounting conflict between the peasants and their masters under the impact of the Napoleonic Wars, fueled this growth in numbers.[26] The result was that by the end of the second decade of the nineteenth century the system was teetering on the verge of collapse. Responsibility for stabilizing and overhauling it was entrusted to the outstanding Russian statesman of the first half of the nineteenth century, Mikhail Mikhailovich Speranskii (1772–1839).[27]

THE SIBERIAN REFORMS OF 1822

Speranskii's Siberian reforms nurtured a vision of Siberia's eventual integration into the Russian Empire. Speranskii believed that moral energy and administrative reform could tackle the problems of the exile system.[28] He approached the challenges of deporting convicts to Siberia as a purely logistical project. His Regulation on Exile Transfer with Siberian Provinces was part of the Regulations on Exiles published in 1822 and comprised 13 articles and 199 clauses. The construction of purpose-built waystations (*étapes, etapy*) along the Great Siberian Highway had already begun in 1819. Speranskii's Regulation accelerated and expanded the process, mapping a route—little changed from the existing highway—along a series of stages, each punctuated by a succession of waystations. Each was separated by a day's march from a semistation (*poluetap*), then another day's trek to the next waystation.[29] Semistations were designed to accommodate marching convoys for a single night; waystations for two nights and a rest day. Speranskii ordered the construction of forty such stages in western Siberia and another twenty-one in eastern Siberia. Each had its own command, drawn from the Internal Watch and answerable to the Ministry of War, responsible for relaying marching

Figure 9.1. A party of exiles crossing the Enisei River. *Source*: George Kennan, *Siberia and the Exile System* (London: John Osgood, McIlvaine), 1:398.

convoys under armed guard along the route. The marching convoys were usually led by an officer, a noncommissioned officer, and a drummer, flanked by armed soldiers on both sides and with Cossacks on horseback at the front and the rear.[30]

In Speranskii's technocratic vision, the design of the étape system would allow the orderly movement of exiles to their assigned destinations and enforce accountability for their transfer. He was meticulous in his detailing of the route and schedule of the marching convoys: exiles beginning their exile at the First Siberian Étape Command in Tyguloe marched two days via a semistation to the next full station at Perevlova where they were turned over to the Second Étape Command. At this station, they received a day's rest and were permitted to use the bathhouse. The convoy then marched them on to Tiumen´, where it transferred them to the Tiumen´ Invalid Command, responsible for delivering them the 262 versts to the medieval town of Tobol´sk.[31] It was here that Speranskii's reforms established the headquarters of the Exile Office, transforming the town into the nerve center of the exile administration and the gateway to the Siberian penal realm. Exiles arriving here in marching convoys from all over the empire learned of their ultimate destination. Incarcerated in the Tobol´sk Transit Prison, they were redistributed into stable marching convoys, then continued their journey eastward.[32]

Setting out from Tobol´sk, exiles marched a staggering 1,470 versts to the city of Tomsk, averaging 25 versts a day over a twelve-week period with never more than a full day of continuous rest. Another 550 versts stood between Tomsk and Krasnoiarsk on the Enisei River in eastern Siberia (fig. 9.1), where the prisoners rested up for a week. After a further 1,000 versts of marching with never more than a single day's continuous rest, the convoy finally reached the eastern Siberian capital city of Irkutsk and another few days of respite. From there, penal laborers destined for the silver mines of Nerchinsk had another 1,500 versts to march.[33] According to Speranskii's calculations, an exile would, on reaching Irkutsk, have walked 3,344 versts in 29.5 weeks at an average distance of 25 versts per day.[34] Such calculations were, in most cases, wildly optimistic.

Beyond their naïve expectations of the speed at which the marching convoys would proceed, Speranskii's granular plans for an efficient and orderly transfer of exiles across the Siberian continent foundered for two other reasons: the explosion in the numbers of exiles banished each year beyond the Urals and the endemic corruption of the exile administration. Speranskii appeared convinced that annual numbers would remain fairly static, but fueled by a government crackdown on deserters from the army and vagabondage, they more than doubled during the 1820s.[35] From an annual average of 4,570 between 1819 and 1823 they rose to an annual average of 11,116 over the next three years. One official noted ruefully in 1825 that whereas in the years before 1822 the state was exiling between sixty and seventy individuals each week, it was now deporting in excess of two hundred.[36] In the period between 1823 and 1831, 10,886 penal laborers and 68,620 exiles—a total of 79,506 individuals of whom 9,166 were women—passed through the Tobol´sk Exile Office.[37] Speranskii's carefully calibrated reforms were swamped by this sudden and unforeseen expansion in the numbers of exiles.

The Regulation on Exile Transfer noted that "many years of experience have shown that exiles in Siberia seek to escape during the summer."[38] It accordingly set a limit of sixty exiles in each marching convoy during the summer and a maximum of a hundred in winter, when the ferocious cold dissuaded almost all from attempting to escape. Penal laborers, considered more dangerous than exiles, were to number no more than ten in each party. Speranskii furthermore stipulated that no more than one party should set out each week from the collection point in the village of Tyguloe on Tobol´sk's western border. Yet as the number of exiles increased in the 1820s, officials were obliged to ignore these limits and thus compromise the security of the

Figure 9.2. A marching party of exiles passing a train of freight sledges. *Source:* George Kennan, *Siberia and the Exile System* (New York: Century, 1891), 2:frontispiece.

convoys. Marching convoys exceeded four hundred exiles from the very moment Speranskii's reforms were implemented. Subsequent attempts to limit the size of each marching convoy were defeated by the sheer weight of numbers flooding into the exile system. In 1835 senior figures in the government charged with inspecting the state of the exile system noted that the huge and unforeseen increase in exile numbers made it "extremely difficult, not say impossible, for local officials to carry out their duties in accordance with the rules laid out in the Regulation on Exiles." They noted that marching convoys regularly exceeded 250 souls.[39]

The convoys themselves were processions of misfortune (fig. 9.2). At the front marched the penal laborers. Those sentenced not simply to exile but to penal labor were considered to be more dangerous and more likely to attempt an escape. Their hands were manacled, and they wore heavy leg fetters connected by a chain that ran through a ring attached to a belt. They were then chained in pairs to a pole, later replaced by a chain, to prevent escapes. When one collapsed, all had to stop. When one had to defecate, all had to attend.[40] As one contemporary observer of the exile system described: "the heavy fetters, even though surrounded by leather, chafed legs exhausted from walking; but most unbearable of all for these unfortunates was being shackled in pairs: every convict suffered from each jerking movement of his partner through the manacles, especially if they were of different heights and builds."[41] If there were not enough fetters to go around, convicts were shackled together in a single set.[42] Following them tramped those exiled to settlement, wearing only leg fetters. Next came those exiled administratively and those exiled to residence, neither of whom were shackled. The final group comprised the family members voluntarily following their relatives into exile. Behind the column rumbled four *telegi* (springless carts), each drawn by a single horse. These bore the exiles' belongings (each was permitted a maximum of 12 kilograms) and, if space allowed, the old, the young, and the sick.[43]

The waystations beyond the Siberian frontier, constructed according to a set of prescriptions spelled out in Speranskii's Regulation, were usually low stockades enclosing a yard. They contained three one-story log buildings painted in regulation ocher, one housing the convoy commander and the other two the soldiers and exiles. Inside the exiles' barracks were three or four large cells, each of which contained a Russian stove and rows of upper and lower planking running along the walls, on which the convicts could sit, sleep, and keep their belongings. Exiles struggled for space on the benches, hardened and aggressive criminals occupying premium positions near the stove in winter and the windows in the summer. The weak and the sick were forced to sleep under the benches on the filth-encrusted floors. Semistations were even more primitive: a wooden stockade containing huts, one for the officer and convoy soldiers and another for the exiles. Their maintenance was the responsibility of a local population with nothing to gain from investing in the state's prison buildings.[44]

A mere decade or so after most were constructed, one official reported to St. Petersburg that almost all the prison buildings in Tobol´sk Province "were in an absolutely terrible state, both cramped and badly designed."[45] Instructions to improve the construction of the waystations by building with stone were flouted by local authorities. As late as 1848 the central forwarding prison in Tobol´sk, through which all exiles passed and in which many spent several months awaiting the next stage of their journey, was still built of wood. In many waystations the prisoners' cells were poorly heated and ventilated, characterized by forced intimacy and a desperate lack of sanitation, as one Decembrist exile, Vasilii Kolesnikov, recalled: "It was so crowded on the benches that it was scarcely possible to turn over; some made room for themselves at the feet of others, at the very edge of the benches; the rest on the floor and under the benches. One can imagine how fetid it is, especially in foul weather, when all arrive soaked through in their dirty rags. Then there are the so-called *parashi* [wooden tubs that met the nocturnal needs of prisoners]. The stench from these *parashi* was unbearable."[46]

These leaking vats of excrement and the terrible ventilation ensured that the waystations were incubators of typhus, dysentery, cholera, and tuberculosis. The Great Siberian Highway was, however, no place to fall ill. Each waystation boasted only a single medical room containing six beds, hopelessly inadequate for the numbers of sick exiles in the marching convoys. In 1845 the government decreed that the sick be immediately transported on the convoy carts to the medical facilities in each of the district towns along the route. Yet in western Siberia there were only six such towns across a distance of 1,800 versts. Those in need of hospital treatment had to endure up to 200 versts and more of jolting along Siberia's notoriously potted roads in order to receive medical care.[47] Those fortunate or hardy enough to survive the journey often discovered that the medical facilities in Siberia's towns offered little respite. Some would only admit the sick if they could pay; others had no qualified medical staff.[48] In 1844 St. Petersburg was obliged to clarify that the local authorities should make available funds for the burial of exiles who expired en route.[49]

MALFEASANCE AND INADEQUATE RESOURCES IN THE EXILE ADMINISTRATION

An unintended but entirely foreseeable consequence of official malfeasance and administrative underfunding was that the marching convoys could prove not simply torturous but also lethal.[50] The venality of the Siberian authorities repeatedly circumvented the efforts of the central authorities to enforce oversight and accountability throughout the deportation system. Convoy officers would make available a daily allowance or sometimes would simply hand over a given sum when the convoy set out from the waystation on a given stage along the route. These funds were almost always insufficient to purchase food from the local villages through which the convoy passed. The convoy soldiers and their families then charged extortionate prices for bread and supplies at the waystations and semistations in which they operated monopolies.[51]

Such venality could prove fatal. In June 1855 four convicts froze to death in a snowstorm en route to the Kara mines from the Klichkin mine in Nerchinsk. The head of the Nerchinsk Mining District, Ivan Evgrafovich Razgil´deev (1810–?), reported that the cause of death had not been simply that the prisoners had not been equipped with the necessary warm clothing but that they had been effectively starving when the snowstorm struck. They had been unable to purchase more supplies of bread from the Cossacks at the waystations because the price charged for the food exceeded their daily allowance.[52] A report by the Third Department to the Ministry of the Interior in 1863 detailed a party of 130 convicts who arrived in Krasnoiarsk in October dressed in nothing but their shirts. The convicts explained that they had been forced to sell their clothing to pay for food because of their financial exploitation by families of commanders of the transit prisons and their staff.[53] In February 1866 another eleven convicts froze to death en route from Krasnoiarsk to the prison in Irkutsk. Autopsies of the bodies revealed that "their stomachs were completely empty." Moreover, "almost none of the convicts had warm clothing," and one of them "arrived without a shirt, in someone else's caftan under which he had stuffed straw." The survivors testified that they had reported to the authorities in Nizheudinsk that they did not possess the necessary clothing for the journey, but that "this had been ignored." The convicts had again been forced to sell their clothing to purchase bread at extortionate prices from the waystation soldiers and their families.[54]

Although sharply critical of these abuses, the central government was unable to stamp them out. In response to the deaths reported in 1866 Minister of the Interior Aleksandr Egorovich Timashev (1818–1893) wrote to the governor-general of eastern Siberia in the wake of the affair pointing out, "if what has been described can happen under the noses of the Enisei provincial authorities, it can only be imagined what occurs in localities far removed from such supervision." Not for the first time, Timashev drew the attention of provincial governors to the risks attendant on allowing convoy soldiers and their families to run monopolies over the sale of provisions to the marching convoys. He demanded "the severest prosecution of those guilty of these abuses." Timashev's subordinates, the governors of Enisei and Irkutsk provinces, Pavel Nikolaevich Zamiatnin and Konstantin Nikolaevich Shelashnikov, scrambled to excuse and explain the incident. They acknowledged that the deaths were unacceptable but argued that the men had already been sent on from Tomsk to Krasnoiarsk without adequate clothing; the overcrowding in the Krasnoiarsk Transit Prison had already led to an outbreak of typhus such that the authorities there had no choice but to send the convict party on to Irkutsk (7,500 exiles and their families were passing along the route each year). The deaths could have been averted, Zamiatnin averred, if the junior officer in charge of the convoy, Kashin, had permitted the exiles to shelter from the frost and recover in the villages along the route. Shelashnikov again affirmed the need to improve oversight and accountability over the provisioning of exiles during their journey eastward. The central government was unable to impose its will on the convoy commanders in waystations thousands of versts distant from St. Petersburg. In the 1860s and 1870s exiles continued to perish in the marching convoys from cold, hunger, and disease in numbers so high that they elicited protests from the local peasantry who were charged with disposing of the corpses.[55]

Speranskii had envisaged the Tobol´sk Exile Office as the efficient administrative headquarters of the exile system. In fact, it was a pit of corruption. Report after report highlighted cases of embezzlement, the theft of exiles' possessions, and a brisk illicit trade in places of banishment.[56] In 1833 one inspector, Colonel Maslov, reported to Minister of the Interior Count Benkendorf that officials in the Exile Office were establishing which exiles bound for eastern Siberia had money and were then selling them permission to remain in Tobol´sk Province.[57] The ensuing six-year-long investigation uncovered a whole host of abuses. More than two thousand exiles had been granted illicit permission to remain in Tobol´sk; others had purchased permits to return to the provinces from which they had been exiled, and still others had their sentences arbitrarily reduced.[58] Yet two decades later, little had changed. In a rare exposé of corruption in 1862, the St. Petersburg journal *Zritel´* reported on the persistent venality of the Tobol´sk Exile Office: "Here officials sometimes appear before the convicts, and pretending to be charged with special responsibilities from the head of the Exile Office, they call the convicts to one side for negotiations and offer them their services: lobbying so that they may remain in Tobol´sk, or so that those destined for the factories of Irkutsk might be transferred to settlement in Tobol´sk Province."[59]

The article occasioned a string of investigations initiated by the Ministry of the Interior, but the closing of ranks and the shielding of official posteriors was something of an art form in the administration of Siberian exile.[60] The Tobol´sk Exile Office continued to embezzle funds intended for the provision of warm clothing, leaving the exiles desperately vulnerable to the ferocity of the Siberian winter. One official reported in 1864 that exiles were still setting out from Tobol´sk with clothes of such poor quality that "if they did not have their own clothing, they would be quite unable to make the journey." Some were arriving in Tomsk with severe cases of frostbite, having lost fingers and toes to the cold.[61]

Such malfeasance remained difficult to root out, in part because even the most senior officials were themselves heavily involved in embezzlement and bribery schemes. Between 1822 and 1852 five of the eleven governors of Tobol´sk were dismissed for corruption.[62] In 1847 Governor-General of Eastern Siberia Vil´gel´m Iakovlevich Rupert (1787–1849) was forced to resign after an inquiry found him guilty of a whole spectrum of abuses, including commandeering penal laborers to work at his own private residence.[63]

Yet flagrant abuses of power and the venality of individual officials only compounded what were deep-seated structural problems of inadequate resources and chaotic administration. When challenged by St. Petersburg over the parlous state of affairs within the Tobol´sk Exile Office, officials routinely pointed to "the shortages in secretarial resources needed to cope with the growth in the number of cases following the 1823 edicts on vagrants."[64] They had a case to make. In 1856 the staff of the Tobol´sk Exile Office—charged with equipping, processing, and distributing almost every exile entering the Siberian landmass—boasted a total of seven members: a director, two assessors, two bookkeepers, and two secretaries. By 1873 the numbers had leapt to a total of nine.[65]

This threadbare administration ensured that half a century after Speranskii's reforms of the deportation system, recordkeeping was still in chaos. Prisoners were arriving in Irkutsk from western Siberia without the requisite papers specifying their crimes and sentences.[66] A government inspection revealed that between 1872 and 1875 the Irkutsk Exile Office had kept no accurate records of the exiles passing through it: "in the absence of such records, the office in the majority of cases does not know whether it ever processed a given exile, where he is, and what rights of estate he does or does not continue to enjoy." The inspectors found some five hundred unprocessed files dating back to 1870, "lying around in piles." There were cases of penal laborers who had long since served out their terms of hard labor and should have been released to settlement but "had not been released because the Irkutsk Exile Office had never sent through their papers." There were cases in which the office's failure to process the relevant paperwork had left convicts sent onward to prisons and penal settlements in eastern Siberia with no linen. Exiles transiting through Irkutsk were held up by this bureaucratic sloth and chaos for "up to several months, and sometimes for more than a year." One exiled peasant had already spent two years in prison in Irkutsk because the authorities were unable to locate his paperwork.[67] Back in the capital, the situation was little better. One hapless exile languished in a Moscow prison for half a year in 1877 before even setting out for Siberia while the authorities clarified his sentence.[68]

SHARED SOVEREIGNTY IN THE DEPORTATION CONVOYS: THE CONVICT'S ARTEL

Convicts responded to the brutal and unpredictable environment of the deportation convoys by organizing themselves into an artel, or prisoners' association, for the duration of the journey into exile. Composed of representatives from groups of approximately ten prisoners in each convoy, this unofficial but powerful community was effectively a duplication of the communal traditions of the peasant village. It held sway over all aspects of the convicts' lives in the marching convoy. Its primary function was the collective protection of its members against the authorities. Headed by an elected figure, the *starosta*, the artel's operations were governed by traditions embracing commercial activity, a central exchequer, and draconian codes of discipline and punishment.[69] Although the artel was not an official institution, the exile administration did recognize its existence and, to some extent, the necessity of it. The authorities turned a blind eye to many of its illegal practices and relied on its good will to manage the operation of the convoys. The convicts, in turn, valued the trust of the convoy commanders and sought to simplify their duties by obeying instructions and sticking to commitments undertaken.

Setting out from European Russian cities, the marching convoy would elect its starosta for the duration of the journey to Tobol´sk. The convicts usually selected an individual familiar with Siberia from previous periods in exile, often vagabonds who had escaped only to be recaptured and those possessed of useful skills and trades. On reaching Tobol´sk, the artels dissolved and reformed within new and stable marching convoys organized by the Tobol´sk Exile Office. The Exile Office would confirm the election of the new starosta before the convoy's departure from Tobol´sk. Once the authorities had confirmed his election, the starosta could not be dismissed by any of the convoy officers or waystation guards without the consent of the entire convoy.[70]

At the outset of the journey, the artel oversaw the *maidan*, which provided a number of commercial services within the marching convoy—grocers' shop, tobacconist, liquor store, and gambling den.[71] The artel also operated a kitty used principally as a source of bribes to purchase various concessions from the convoy soldiers and waystation commanders. This form of collective bargaining could be used to secure permission to beg for alms in the villages through which the convoy passed. Extra horse-drawn carts could be hired from local villages to carry the infirm and the sick. The artel also struck bargains with the convoy officers that secured concessions but implicated the convicts themselves in forms of self-policing.[72]

Unable to enforce its own control over the exiles in the deportation convoys, the state did not merely co-opt a select number of convicts who received individual benefits in exchange for the enforcement of compliance among their fellow captives. Through the institution of the artel the convoy commanders dispersed disciplinary responsibilities throughout the marching convoy in exchange for the extension of concessions to all. In violation of Speranskii's Regulation on Exiles convoy soldiers agreed to the removal of the hated leg fetters outside towns and villages in return for a promise that no escapes would be attempted.[73] The artel collectively vouched for the conduct of its members. Should any of the convicts break the terms of this bargain, he would be hunted down not only by the convoy soldiers but also by other exiles in the marching convoy.[74] On one occasion the exiles even helped the convoy soldiers extinguish a blaze that had taken hold in one of the waystations. None tried to escape.[75] When, however, near the town of Tiumen´ three exiles did flee a three-hundred-strong marching convoy that had just negotiated an extra day's rest from the convoy commander, the other exiles were outraged by this violation of their collective agreement. Fearful lest it jeopardize the concessions they had secured, the artel dispatched a group of exiles in pursuit of the fugitives. By morning they had caught up with their quarry and dragged them back to the convoy commander, who ordered that each man receive a hundred strokes of the birch rod. Finding such leniency unsatisfactory, the artel went on to administer a further five hundred strokes of its own "with such vigor that their cruelty shocked even the convoy officer, himself no stranger to corporal punishment."[76] The enforcement of loyalty to the artel was a necessity for all Siberian exiles, as the implacable brutality of the artel, and thus its powers of deterrence to would-be violators of its code, was the only basis on which the artel could enter into negotiations with the authorities. Every convict in the marching convoy thus had a personal investment in ensuring that the authority of the artel was upheld.

Official and informal disciplinary regimes did not, however, always coincide. Another of the artel's primary responsibilities was the enforcement of contracts, from the strictly financial to the very personal, between its members. Backed by the threat of violence, the artel oversaw, and indeed made possible, the constant bartering of goods and services between convicts. From the repair of boots to the purchase of vodka, the artel ensured that undertakings of deferred payment would be honored. Some had only their names—and fates—to barter. Each convict sentenced to exile or penal labor was issued with a card that bore his name, his rank, his origins, his crime, his punishment, and a brief description of his appearance. This paperwork often contained clerical errors—names misspelled or exile destinations mixed up—resulting in individuals marching thousands of versts to the wrong destinations. It could take several months to rectify mistakes.[77] The exiles themselves were acutely aware that these papers determined their fate. Guards in the marching convoys were keen to ensure that they arrived with the full complement of exiles in their charge, but they were preoccupied with names rather than individuals. It was quite impossible for convoy commanders to remember each individual's face, and at the changeover from one stage command to another only the overall number of convicts was counted; there was no roll call. Such laxity in recordkeeping presented an opportunity to determined and unscrupulous exiles.

The months, sometimes years, spent in the marching convoys provided scope for the formation not only of new friendships but also of more sinister and exploitative bonds. Fedor Dostoevskii explained the practice of exchanging names in his 1862 memoir of Siberian exile, *Notes from the House of the Dead*. Wily, hardened criminals would trick naïve and destitute exiles into swapping names (and fates) in exchange for a few rubles or vodka.[78] Anyone attempting to renege on such agreements would incur the wrath of the artel and might be, in George Kennan's words, "condemned to death by this merciless Siberian *Vehmgericht*." Even those who escaped immediate punishment might subsequently be hunted down and found with their throats slit in some remote village or waystation. Over the head of such traitors, Kennan wrote, "hung an invisible sword of Damocles, and sooner or later, in one place or another, it was sure to fall."[79]

Under the state-sponsored auspices of the artel, the practice of name swapping, already an acknowledged problem at the beginning of the nineteenth century, flourished as the size of the marching convoys swelled in the 1820s.[80] Seeking to contain the illicit trade in identities, the government passed a new law in 1828 that punished each exile to settlement who exchanged names with a penal laborer with five years of *katorga*. Penal laborers caught trafficking in identities were to be punished with a hundred blows of the rod and a minimum of twenty-five years of penal labor in the place of their original sentence of exile.[81] More draconian laws followed, but the traffic in identities remained impossible to root out.[82] In subsequent decades officials continued to complain that the practice was subverting the exile system. Cases of individuals who had switched names, and so had been delivered to the wrong destinations to serve out the wrong sentences, were clogging up local courts.[83]

Changing names was perhaps the most flagrant subversion of the state's deportations. It revealed the weakness of the authorities' chaotic recordkeeping and tenuous grasp on the identities of the convicts in their charge. When undetected, the practice decoupled a prisoner's fate from his or her sentence. While the state might succeed in banishing offenders *from* European Russia, their deployment to specific sites where punishment, utility, and rehabilitation might all blend together fruitfully remained an unfulfilled aspiration. The artel offered an alternative, even rival, disciplinary regime within the official carceral space of the deportation. Sometimes working in concert with the state's wider goals of penal migration, the artel was also able to subvert them. The state's disciplinary weakness in the deportation convoys pushed it to recognize and approve the existence of an alternative source of authority, even sovereignty, in the form of the artel. The sovereign could banish exiles to Siberia, but his power diminished the further it extended eastward.

WOMEN AND CHILDREN IN THE DEPORTATION CONVOYS

The deportation convoys reserved special torments for women. Female convicts, and even the innocent wives and daughters voluntarily following husbands and fathers into exile, often found themselves destitute and vulnerable to sexual assault and exploitation in the marching convoys. It became almost impossible for women to maintain any dignity. Female convicts and frequently the innocent wives of exiled convicts were often obliged to use the *parashi* before gaggles of jeering and ogling convicts.[84] Despite the fact that most female convicts had no history of vice, officials assumed that all female convicts were prostitutes even before they entered the marching convoys.[85] Many took to selling themselves in exchange for protection and the most basic supplies.[86] The Polish exile Justynian Ruciński witnessed at first hand in 1839 how every female exile was obliged to take a lover in the marching convoys. The choice of partner was not her own but that of the convicts' artel, which auctioned the women off to the highest bidder among the suitors. If a woman rejected the proposed union, she "was subjected to terrible reprisals." On several occasions, Ruciński "witnessed horrible rapes in broad daylight."[87]

The effects of this traffic in bodies on the moral and physical health of the exiles had long troubled the authorities. The Tomsk Medical Council observed in 1817 that "most of the sick exiles of both sexes transiting through Tomsk were suffering from venereal disease, the cause of which . . . was the dissolute life the women lead with their fellow prisoners on their way to distant regions."[88] In 1825 Minister of Police Count Sergei Kuz'mich Vziamitinov (1744–1819) and the head of the Internal Watch, Count Evgraf Fedotovich Komarovskii (1769–1843), both recommended that women and children should follow the men after an interval of two days in separate convoys.[89] These proposals were put into law the next year, but convicts of both sexes continued to be transported together as officials on the ground had not the resources to separate them. In violation of the regulations the wives and children following exiles into Siberia were often locked up overnight together with hardened criminals.[90] In 1840 the authorities in St. Petersburg were still issuing directives to have the sexes separated at the waystations.[91]

Yet the practice persisted. Even in the 1870s women and children following their husbands voluntarily into exile continued to be locked up in the transit prisons and waystations, in violation of rules that the center had repeatedly reaffirmed.[92] Observers of the marching convoys in the 1870s and 1880s referred to them "as huge mobile brothels" that serviced convoy soldiers and exiles alike.[93] The failure to separate small numbers of women from large groups of men created a combustible swirl of passions, lusts, and jealousies. In 1879 the Polish exile Wacław Sieroszewski found himself in a marching convoy that numbered some three hundred men and only a few female convicts: "all kind of romantic affairs developed, and one beautiful young woman ended up with her stomach sliced open in one of the waystations."[94]

Women were especially vulnerable when they were pregnant or carrying newborns. In 1837 the State Senate had ruled that female exiles should not be sent to exile if they were pregnant or breastfeeding, but like many directives from the center, the Siberian authorities routinely ignored this instruction.[95] Indeed, given the length of the journey into exile and the pressures on women to have sex with the men in the marching convoys, many became pregnant en route. One female convict in a group of penal laborers being transported by steamship down the Amur River in 1870 gave birth on deck, shielded from the eyes of onlookers and from the bad weather by only a few convict smocks. The child died within an hour, "probably having caught a chill in the cold air."[96]

Women often followed their husbands with several young children in tow.[97] They suffered, as the ethnographer Sergei Maksimov observed, "the foul dank air of the cells, the unnourishing and disgusting convict food, stifling heat, cold, sickness, and so on." The crowded waystations, train carriages, and ships' holds proved especially dangerous to young children.[98] In 1875 alone some 1,030 children died en route to Siberia in the forwarding prisons of Moscow, Nizhnii Novgorod, Kazan, Perm´, and in the waystations beyond. Two years later 404 did not survive the journey. Indeed, Nikolai Iadrintsev estimated in 1882 that as a result of woefully inadequate medical facilities en route, half of all children did not survive the journey to Siberia.[99]

In addition to hunger, cold, and lack of adequate medical care, the children faced the predatory appetites of the convicts whom they accompanied. The Interior Ministry official Vasilii Vlasov reported in 1873 that the authorities' failure to ensure that children were separated from the convicts in the marching convoys and transport ships resulted in their exposure to "orgies and illegal acts." He documented the rape of a young girl in one of the waystations and, in another convoy, two penal laborers' daughters, aged twelve and fourteen, already infected with syphilis. The ethnographer Vasilii Semevskii accompanied a party of five hundred exiles and family members to the Lena goldfields in 1878: among them were eleven-year-old boys who drank, played cards, and were interested in women; there was also a twelve-year-old girl, "considered common property by the convict party."[100] By the time they reached their destination, women and children had been subjected for months on end to grinding poverty, a barrage of personal humiliations, and often-violent sexual assault and exploitation. Their bitter fate was proof that the ordeal of the deportation convoys bore no relation to crimes. It also undermined autocracy's much-vaunted paternalism, exposing its negligence, indifference, and brutality.[101]

MODERNIZING DEPORTATIONS IN THE REIGN OF ALEXANDER II

When the exiled lecturer from Kiev University Ivan Belokonskii made the journey to eastern Siberia in 1880, he experienced the full range of transportational means now at the state's disposal: marching convoys and waystations, river barges and railways.[102] The government turned to waterways and to railways to ensure a faster, smoother, and more orderly transfer of convicts eastward. Despite this modernization of the deportation process, the convoys remained dangerous, violent, and unpredictable spaces in which suffering and punishment bore little relation to each other.

From 1862 on trains transferred convicts from Moscow and other collection points such as Kursk via Vladimir to Nizhnii Novgorod. The converted trains into which the convicts were crammed comprised third-class carriages with bars on the windows. The overcrowding forced convicts not simply to sit on the benches but also beneath them and in the aisles: "the sealed doors and the absence of ventilation" took their toll. The 410 versts to Nizhnii Novgorod took a day and a night.[103]

By the 1860s the authorities were turning to Siberia's rivers to expedite the deportations. Private contractors supplied barges in 1867 to transport a total of 5,434 exiles north along the River Tobol′ from Tiumen′ to Tobol′sk. The human cargo of 4,651 adults, 566 children under the age of fifteen, and 126 infants was delivered into the charge of the Tobol′sk Exile Office, which set about dispersing them into marching convoys or transport barges depending on their final destination. Those bound for Tomsk and beyond were loaded into other barges, which carried them north along the Irtysh River and then inched their way south, against the current of the Ob′ River, on a fourteen-day journey as far as Tomsk. These were "hurriedly converted" freight barges, fitted with bars to prevent convicts from leaping overboard to freedom. It was not always possible, one official noted, to separate the single women from the men. He reported, with pronounced understatement, that the *parashi* were located inside the convicts' cabins and, "with large accumulations of convicts, the air in the cells is insufficiently cleansed."[104]

Not all of Siberia's rivers neatly intersected, however, leaving stretches of the route that needed to be navigated by land. One such leg of the journey lay between Perm′ and Tiumen′, a route along which 16,235 convicts marched in 1867. That year, an enterprising merchant, Aleksei Mikhailov, came to an arrangement with the Ministry of the Interior. Mikhailov agreed to provide horses and carts, each capable of carrying six individuals, to transport convicts and their families along the 710 kilometers of the Perm′-Tiumen′ Highway for 1.5 kopecks per convict per verst, a price that was marginally lower than the costs the state was incurring for itself. Mikhailov undertook to transport up to 120 convicts and their families every day during the summer months and, in the winter, "as frequently as possible." He began his convict transportation business in August 1868.[105] For all its technological and logistical innovations, however, the government was unable to cope with the surge in the number of exiles being deported to Siberia. In the 1860s an average of 11,200 exiles and their families entered Siberia; by the 1870s the average had increased to 16,600, an average annual increase from one decade to the next of 48 percent.[106]

By the 1870s the transfer of exiles to Siberia had become an industrial enterprise that was sucking in increasing quantities of manpower and resources. The costs of maintaining the operation were spiraling. By 1869 the deportation convoys operating between Nizhnii Novgorod and Achinsk on the border between western and eastern Siberia involved a total of 56 officers, 96 senior noncommissioned officers, 472 junior noncommissioned officers, 1,851 privates, and 56 scribes.[107] One government audit in 1876 estimated that the government spent 659,841 rubles on the transfer of exiles to Siberia: 94,527 rubles on feeding them, 46,379 rubles on clothing them, 429,324 on transportation costs, 69,644 on treating the sick, and so on.[108]

Seeking to "safeguard the health of the convicts and to cut the costs of the exile system," the authorities decided in 1867 to suspend deportations during the winter months. Interior Minister Timashev argued that the ensuing delays to the deportation of convicts was a price worth paying: "detaining convicts for six months [over the winter] seems to aggravate their punishment, but in wintertime many of the exiles suffer the torments of the harsh northern climate and often die en route. Many more are so weakened by the journey that they cease to be capable of work, and so are deprived of the possibility of making their own living and become a burden on the local population. Consequently, it is surely better to suspend the transfer of convicts in the winter."[109] The ministry calculated that by restricting the deportations to the summer months, when the use of river navigation enabled much larger numbers of convicts to be transported quickly, the state could save up to 300,000 rubles each year.[110]

The policy proved difficult to implement. The stumbling block to the suspension of wintertime transfers was the lack of capacity within the way-stations and transit prisons along the route. The authorities struggled to flush sufficient numbers of convicts through the system in the brief five-month window available to them between the beginning of May and the end of September. One bottleneck was the Tomsk-Achinsk Highway. In the absence of either waterways or railways, the convicts in Tomsk were once again assembled into marching convoys to set out on the remainder of their journey: 590 kilometers to Krasnoiarsk, then a further 1,080 kilometers to Irkutsk. By 1869 around 7,500 convicts were arriving in Tomsk each year (the first groups arrived in early June) on barges from Tiumen´. The penal infrastructure—buildings and convoy soldiers—was able to process only 3,250 convicts over the four available summer months. The accumulated backlog of nearly 4,250 prisoners each summer would simply overwhelm the prisons of Tomsk. The authorities therefore decided to continue with deportations from Tomsk eastward all year around, including marches in the freezing and often lethal winter temperatures.[111]

Even so, European Russian prisons remained heavily congested with convicts destined for Siberia who "spend the entire winter in prison and set off for Siberia only the summer of the following year" when the waterways thawed.[112] Between 1 May and 1 August 1876, 413 exiles died of disease awaiting deportation in Moscow, more than 150 of them children. A further 512 died in Nizhnii Novgorod, Kazan, and Perm´, and 104 died along the route between these major transit points.[113]

Throughout the reign of Alexander II Siberia's waystations and transit prisons remained decaying, disease-ridden structures in which exiles and their families fell sick in large numbers in overcrowded, drafty, and inadequately heated prisons and waystations.[114] Vlasov reported in 1871 that in eastern Siberia "the majority of the waystation buildings are not fit for the purpose, they are so cramped and dilapidated. There is no way that order can be maintained in them."[115] Basic sanitation in the transit prisons and waystations remained dreadful. In 1868, "as a result of the acute overcrowding in the prison," typhus tore through the prison in Krasnoiarsk, into which more than 1,500 convicts were crammed. Built for eighty beds, the prison hospital was struggling to cope with 250 patients.[116] In 1880 no fewer than 87 of the 290 prisoners held in the Tobol´sk transit prison were suffering from scurvy, a fact that the authorities attributed to the "dampness of the building and the poor quality of the food."[117] Persistent overcrowding, underfunding, and administrative incompetence ensured that the convicts' journey into exile might have speeded up, but it still proved grueling, and sometimes fatal.

From the reign of Alexander I to that of Alexander II the autocracy proved unable to properly finance and efficiently administer penal migration to Siberia. Attempts to rationalize and modernize the deportation remained inadequate to the growing administrative and logistical challenges of the process. The deportations remained chaotic, often dangerously so, overwhelmed by the burgeoning numbers of exiles and subverted by lack of resources and corruption. Yet for all its injustice and inefficiency, the system endured. Bureaucratic inertia, the lack of funds for an alternative (chiefly the construction of a network of modern prisons in European Russia with sufficient capacity), and the absence of coordinated opposition from the mass of convicts themselves all ensured that the state continued to exercise the raw power of banishment.[118] Resistance to the deportation regime came not from the convicts themselves but from within government and from without, in Russian civil society.

Toward the end of Alexander II's reign, however, both official and public opinion began to shift decisively against the exile system. Various government commissions were established in the 1870s and 1880s, charged with devising solutions to the state's reliance on Siberia as a dumping ground for criminals.[119] Each one proposed a series of reforms in legislation to reduce the numbers being exiled each year and to promote the construction of prisons. One commission was chaired by Konstantin Grot under the auspices of the State Council in 1877 and drew on senior officials from all the key ministries and legal experts. After two years of regular sittings it found that "it is perfectly obvious that the reason for the disarray in the exile system lies in the very legislation governing it; in the unfeasibility of the very goals it has pursued up to now; in the shortage of funds [and] the shortage of experienced administrators; in the shortcomings of Siberia's location for penal colonization; and in the vast scale on which exile was used."[120] Reflecting the changed legal culture of the empire in the wake of the Great Reforms, the commission acknowledged that Siberian exile was "harmful and lacked any juridical foundation." It would, however, be another two decades before the government embarked on meaningful reform.[121]

This lack of "juridical foundation" was laid bare in deportation convoys—crucibles of privation, misery, and violence in which suffering bore little or no relationship to crimes committed or sentences passed. In the final decades of the nineteenth century the widely perceived lack of coherent moral economy underpinning the ordeal of deportation came to bedevil the autocracy. What had been confined to discussions and criticisms of failings in the pages of official reports and memoranda erupted in the last two decades of the nineteenth century into the pages of the popular press in both Siberia and European Russia.[122] The so-called thick journals published a hefty quotient of fiction, memoirs, and factual accounts lamenting the brutal dysfunctionalities of the deportation convoys in particular and the injustices of the exile system as a whole.[123] The fate of women, children, administrative exiles, political prisoners, and the hapless Siberians themselves commanded page after page of reportage clamoring for reform. Anton Chekhov spoke for many when he fulminated to his editor in 1890, "we have let *millions* of people rot in gaol, and let them rot to no purpose, treating them with an indifference that is little short of barbaric. We have forced them to drag themselves in chains across tens of thousands of miles in freezing conditions, infected them with syphilis, debauched them, hugely increased the criminal population."[124]

The serialization of Chekhov's own *Sakhalin Island* in *Russkaia mysl'* in 1893–1894 delivered a devastating blow to the image of the exile system and the legitimacy of the state that administered it.[125] George Kennan had meanwhile made a name for himself even in Russia as a ferocious critic of the exile system, and his articles and books, although published only in the West before 1905, were picked up, summarized, and discussed in the pages of the Russian press.[126] Perhaps the most influential condemnation of Siberian exile came from the pen of Lev Tolstoi in 1899. His last great novel, *Resurrection*, offered an unflinching portrait of the degrading conditions in which men, women, and children were forced to make the grueling journey into exile.[127] By the end of the century most educated Russians considered Siberian exile in general, and the marching convoys in particular, to be the embarrassing vestiges of a barbaric past and evidence of Russia's backwardness among its European neighbors.

Torn from their towns and villages, their family and friends, exiles found themselves hurled into an unfamiliar and frightening world of exhausting forced marches, overcrowded waystations, disease, penury, and the ever-present threat of violence. Yet these privations and torments were less the measure of a deliberate and calibrated penal policy emanating from St. Petersburg and more a consequence of the state's failure to implement its own directives and pursue its own stated penal and colonial goals. In making the arduous journey eastward into exile, convicts and their families were subjected to an unpredictable ordeal fundamentally detached by the official system of laws and punishments. By the 1880s the deportations to Siberia had become a widely denounced symptom of the weakness, arbitrariness, and abuses of state power.

BRITAIN'S ARCHIPELAGO OF CAMPS

Labor and Detention in a Liberal Empire, 1871–1903

AIDAN FORTH

CAMPS SUGGEST AN Enlightenment project derailed. Associated most often and perhaps most appropriately with Hitler's Germany and the Soviet Gulag under Lenin, Stalin, and their successors, the barbed-wire aesthetic of the camp and the skeletal profile of overworked and undernourished inmates stand as stark reminders of the ideological excesses of an age of extremes. They are emblems of modern terror. Yet camps are by no means unique to the despotic powers of a short twentieth century. Indeed, Britain presided over a considerable empire of labor and detention camps in a long and ostensibly liberal nineteenth century.

Camps segregated and immobilized populations deemed vagrant, criminal, or otherwise socially or politically dangerous. In contrast to prisons and other disciplinary sites, camps were instruments of collective detention that operated outside normal judicial procedures, often in the context of a perceived emergency. As an integral tool of multiple polities in the nineteenth and twentieth centuries, they enforced heavy labor and penal rations under dire economic restraints, often in the name of controlling and rehabilitating "problem populations." In Britain camps concentrated an undesirable "dangerous class" in the metropole. But it was the British Empire that offered an especially ripe environment for the development of camps. Directed at a racial and cultural "other" and detached, at times, from public scrutiny, the authoritarian nature of imperial rule motivated officials to assemble many of the physical and psychological prerequisites for the coercive encampment of suspect groups. Although labor, concentration, and extermination camps became infamous in the twentieth century, Britain and other colonial powers in the nineteenth century assembled many of the cultural, material, and political preconditions of forced encampment.

Given their global profile at the turn of the nineteenth century, British camps may have suggested a direct and conscious model for the early camps of the Soviet Union or Nazi Germany. But more than this, British rule helped foster the structural and conceptual preconditions for the development and management of camps. Imperial administration generated a sophisticated logistical and bureaucratic apparatus aimed at the organization and control of unfamiliar and potentially dangerous populations. Furthermore, it incubated a mental framework (shared across the Western world) that at times demanded the exclusion and incarceration of groups deemed socially or racially suspect. As instruments of the modern "gardening state," moreover, camps embodied an Enlightenment impulse to classify and rationalize large populations on a macro scale, rooting out potential weeds in the name of order, prosperity, and social purity.[1] The products of coercion and suspicion, British camps were also justified by discourses of social welfare, humanitarian uplift, and sanitary reform—the justifying imperatives of European rule—that were always preached but only imperfectly practiced.

British camps were often the expedient products of emergencies: famine, disease, and war. Although contingent on circumstance, they help reveal the deeper structures of Western culture that gave rise to extrajudicial detention. As artifacts of social and political modernity assembled by the world's first "modern" state, British camps offer insight into an archaeology of violence shared by states across the ideological spectrum. By confining in a preemptive manner populations deemed "potentially dangerous" but not convicted of any crime, British camps conformed to a more general typology of concentration camps in the modern world.[2]

Checked by liberal ideology and an open public sphere, Britain never assembled anything so brutal as the Soviet Gulag, let alone the Nazi extermination camp. On the contrary, relief and rehabilitation often proved the dominant stated motive. But British camps stemmed nonetheless from new mind-sets and government rationalities that sought to organize potentially dangerous segments of the population on a mass scale. While attending to the specific characteristics of camp regimes in liberal and authoritarian states, an examination of Britain's "archipelago of camps" reveals that the coercive and extrajudicial use of camps was by no means the exclusive prerogative of "evil" and "illiberal" empires. Indeed, the term "concentration camp" was first coined to describe British practices in South Africa, even if this was not the first campaign to concentrate or resettle populations in fortified enclosures.[3] Connected by the genealogical sinews of social and political modernity, camps spanned the political spectrum from left to right, from liberal to totalitarian, and from moderate to fanatical; those erected by Britain bore a family resemblance (if only a distant one) to the more notorious enclosures of Germany and the Soviet Union. This chapter cautions against any false or facile equivalency between British and Soviet camps. Furthermore, I recognize the great variety of camps within the British and Soviet regimes across both space and time. But with these provisos, the chapter offers insight into the encampment practices of a liberal and capitalist polity in hopes that we may further refine our understanding of camps operating under the disparate ideological priorities and logistical possibilities of the Soviet empire and other regimes.

Britain's Universe of Camps

Erected during war or moments of perceived crisis, British camps served to concentrate, contain, and care for colonial populations according to the overlapping social, political, and epidemiological imperatives of segregation, quarantine, and rehabilitation. The term "camp" derives from the Roman *campus martius* or "field of Mars," and camps have long been associated with martial practices. With their serried rows of tents and huts, modern military camps emerged during the Napoleonic Wars to regulate and discipline mass armies under a unified and organized command. As material incarnations of a new political culture, army camps provided a logistical model (in terms of layout, sanitation, rationing, and water provision) for future camps concentrating civilian populations. This military pedigree was evident in Britain's network of concentration camps in South Africa during the Anglo-Boer War (1899–1902). Here officials adapted a military technology to the mass confinement of civilians in the context of martial law. A controversial measure that attracted international publicity, these camps stand as the most famous incarnation of civilian concentration in the British Empire, for they showcased the idea of mass internment to the world.

But South Africa's concentration camps were only one episode in a much longer history of British camps. In India, Britain's prized imperial possession, officials concentrated colonial populations in makeshift campsites for the purposes of social welfare, labor, punishment, and social/political reeducation. Famine relief camps provided labor and shelter for the destitute; plague segregation camps incarcerated the dirty and epidemiologically suspect; and camps for "criminal tribes" segregated those who could not be safely incorporated into the social body. Meanwhile, tented penal camps on the Andaman Islands harbored criminals and political dissidents after the 1857 "Mutiny" (or Anglo-Indian War). All these camps built on discourses and practices of detention and rehabilitation first pioneered in Britain's metropolitan prisons, workhouses, and other institutes of mass industrial society.

The specific policies that led to camps varied from context to context.

In general, however, camps concentrated populations collectively for the *potential* threat they posed, and according to emergency decrees and the suspension of law. Hard and fast boundaries between camps and other related technologies cannot always be drawn, for they existed on a continuum of modern discipline and punishment. Camps are nonetheless distinguished by their preemptive or preventive nature: camp inmates were "suspects" rather than criminals convicted of some statutory crime. At the level of culture and representation, British camps involved the segregation of a denigrated "other" perceived through metaphors of purity and pollution and defined as a collective threat by virtue of race, class, or communal membership. At the same time, Britain's archipelago of camps can be recognized by a characteristic combination of coercion and care redolent of the Janus-faced tendencies of British power, both at home and abroad.

Workhouses and Labor Camps

The nineteenth century in Britain was a period of rapid social and political transformation in which an urban and fully industrialized society replaced a rural, agricultural economy; a "revolution in government" established the mechanisms of universal education and modern administration; and mass democracy replaced an earlier system of aristocratic privilege, fortifying the rule of law and transforming subjects into rights-bearing citizens. According to Whiggish narratives, a series of legislative acts consolidated a constitutional system based on popular sovereignty and an ever-expanding franchise, and Britain's liberal constitutional monarchy further benefited from capitalist development and prosperous free trade. Meanwhile, Britain harbored refugees fleeing ethnic and political violence on the continent, whether the revolutionary émigrés of France or victims of Jewish pogroms in Russia and Eastern Europe.

When compared to the autocratic regimes of the eighteenth century and the totalitarian regimes of the twentieth century, the case for labeling Britain a liberal and democratic polity is undeniable. But if Britain stood out for its inclusive liberal sentiment, a history of modern Britain must also attend to those who were excluded. As Zygmunt Bauman argues, modern political societies are structured around the premise that outcast groups, whether colonial others or metropolitan deviants, must be either incorporated into the body politic or physically excluded. Building on metaphors of the body politic, Bauman argues that the logic of political modernity demands that deviant groups be either "devoured" through a process of "making the different similar" or else "vomited" from the social body.[4] The development of Britain in the nineteenth century is largely a narrative of reform in which rural peasants and the urban working classes were rendered respectable members of the political nation through the discipline of factories, prisons, and workhouses. Yet by the end of the century there remained a "dangerous residuum" thought to be beyond the pale of reform: a "degenerate" and "rootless" class of vagrants that seemingly defied efforts to include—or digest—them. Efforts to exclude, "amputate," or "fence off" these outcast groups, either temporarily or permanently, reflected the limits of liberal reform and opened space for the development of camps.

Metropolitan workhouses erected after the Poor Law of 1834 combined with the system of passes, permits, and police registration used to control the movement of Britain's "dangerous classes" in the wake of the 1869 Habitual Criminals Act and provided an important template for future camps in Britain and elsewhere. In theory workhouses aimed to reform and rehabilitate, excluding inmates temporarily in the name of (eventually) incorporating them as productive members of society. But despite the promise of reform, workhouses also existed as preemptive institutions designed to protect the productive classes by segregating a social category associated with criminality, excrement, and disease. Class often intersected with discourses of race to exemplify the danger. Targeting a "criminal class" as a social and biological rather than juridical category and confining populations against their will, workhouses curtailed liberty of movement and enforced harsh living conditions by conscious design. As enclosed spaces managed by superintendents, workhouses enforced a residence test that denied "outdoor" charitable relief and concentrated the needy in demarcated spaces, offering a prototype for future camps in India and southern Africa. Moreover, workhouses offered a template for forced labor and exacting discipline, highlighting the affinities between camp organization and industrial management.[5]

By the 1880s a climate of pessimism descended on British social reformers as they faced a "submerged residuum" of social "irreconcilables," whom they conceived as an insurgent threat to middle-class property owners. In 1886–1887, for example, the denizens of "darkest London"—at this time the East End was increasingly imagined in racial terms as a "colonial space"—"invaded" the invisible urban boundaries of middle-class respectability and occupied the "civilized" environs of Hyde Park and Trafalgar Square in the name of social protest.[6] Forsaking a program of inclusion and uplift, municipal authorities embraced the tactics of spatial exclusion and forced segregation as a new network of fenced labor colonies supplemented existing workhouses and prisons. These camps drew from the logic of the workhouse but reflected growing frustration with the domestic "civilizing mission" of the existing penal infrastructure.

Articulating a discourse of social danger, the pioneering social scientist and humanitarian reformer Charles Booth proposed a scheme for the mass removal of Britain's racially and biologically degenerate "residuum" to overseas labor camps, where some 345,000 "dangerous" social elements could be segregated from mainstream society.[7] With its combination of impracticality and stoic authoritarianism, Booth's system was never fully implemented. But amid currents of eugenicist thought, which recast the "criminal classes" as an abnormal human type, calls for the erection of overseas penal camps remained popular throughout the 1890s. These camps, according to one spokesman, would house a "peculiar" and "separate class" of the metropolitan poor, who were born lazy, immoral, and deficient in intellect. As advocates of overseas labor camps maintained, "not all men can be treated as equal." Rather, forced relocation was necessary to "prevent [the unfit] from bringing into the world children stamped with the character of their parents."[8] Although metropolitan work camps for the destitute emerged in a different political context from other camps in the empire, the logic of exclusion aimed to purify mainstream society from social or political contamination by removing populations—now conceived as a racial or biological category—for the *potential* threat they posed to the social and political order, rather than for any convicted crimes.

Although the mass exclusion of the poor never took place, a more modest network of semiofficial work camps emerged in the 1890s, administered by the Salvation Army and the London Central Committee for the Unemployed. Located at Hadleigh, Laindon, Hollesley Bay, and other sites outside London, these camps provided shelter and work—in the form of chopping down trees, breaking stones, digging ditches, and preparing rough roads—for the unemployed until the Second World War and the eventual institution of the welfare state (fig. 10.1). Modest in scale, each camp contained several hundred men housed in tents and huts for three months of training. Fences and security personnel regulated egress and ingress, and inmates were in some senses compelled into camp by the threat of denied benefits. In this way the "submerged residuum" was segregated at a safe distance where it could no longer contaminate the more respectable categories of British urban workers.

In addition to their preventive function, agricultural labor camps upheld the promise, however remote, of rehabilitation. Although the inmates of work camps constituted a "residuum of unhelpables," the camps did not constitute a permanent exile from the social body. The stated goal, according to the historian John Field, was to "harden young men through heavy manual labour" and "recondition them" for the regular workforce.[9] In a sterner tone, however, the Victorian economist Alfred Marshall maintained that the

Figure 10.1. Entrance to Hadleigh Work Camp. *Source:* http://www.workhouses
.org.uk/labourcolonies.

camps' primary purpose was to segregate "descendants of the dissolute" and
thus preserve "living room" for the more "legitimate" working classes.[10]

Penal Colonies, Managed Institutions, and Criminal Tribe Camps in the British Empire

In Britain labor camps operated on a relatively modest scale. In contrast,
the "dangerous classes" of the colonies offered much greater scope for forced
encampment, creating what Frantz Fanon called "a world divided into com-
partments."[11] Just as metropolitan workhouses offered a confined site to control populations cast as suspect—if never convicted of a crime—the earlier establishment of "managed institutions" for aboriginals in Australia and
North America added to Britain's record of concentrating colonial populations in enclosed compounds.

In the empire discourses of racial (in addition to class) supremacy combined with the priorities of imperial conquest and occupation to provide an
extra impetus for the use of camps. "Particularly in its settler form," the historian Cole Harris argues, colonialism was "about the displacement of people
from their land and its repossession by others."[12] Whether for the purposes
of extermination (as at the Wyabalenna Reserve, where the final members of
Tasmania's native population perished), or in the name of "containing, controlling, and segregating" native populations from "a civilization that they
[did] not understand and from which they need[ed] protection" (as at the

Kahlin Aboriginal Compound), British rule mandated spatial confinement.[13] In the process enclosed camps "arranged in a manner conducive to order and regularity of appearance" emerged as a means to carve up the colonial world and manage the inscrutable and potentially threatening masses that it contained.[14] Although these compounds were motivated in part by humanitarian care and Christian uplift, they exhibited an impersonal aesthetic of "barbed-wire fence[s] and . . . bark and iron huts" that was later replicated by camps in the twentieth century. Moreover, these settlements enabled constant supervision and efficacious punishment, though they were justified by a rehabilitative agenda that enshrined the triumvirate of "industry, cleanliness, and order" as the favored conduits of civilization.[15] Proponents recommended the "gathering together" of natives in confined camps because they "contained the spread of disease and provided supervision, so that Aboriginal people would not be disinclined to work."[16]

As racial attitudes hardened over the course of the nineteenth century, the British state took a more interventionist approach to the government of empire. This was especially the case after the 1857 "Mutiny," when a system of overseas penal colonies emerged to segregate at considerable distance those accused of sedition, civil disobedience, and other political crimes. In contrast to the permanent brick-and-mortar infrastructure of prisons in metropolitan Britain, which accommodated criminals convicted by standard juridical procedures, the contingent nature and fiscal stringency of colonial rule generated temporary al fresco camps. In the absence of a capitalist wage labor market, meanwhile, camps proved important instruments in the organization of forced labor. Accommodated in tents and huts, some twenty thousand inmates performed heavy labor on public works projects, providing officials with experience in administering this distinctive colonial mechanism of confinement. Relegated to the remote Andaman Islands, inmates endured a tropical version of the spatial exile later experienced by inmates of the "Gulag archipelago."[17] For officials, spatial distance served to purify the subcontinent of social and political disorder, while for prisoners, transportation across the "black waters" entailed a loss of caste and social connection that approximated the "civil death" of the Siberian Gulag.[18] In this way empire offered a space to reinstate old technologies of punishment that appeared outdated in Britain (penal transportation from Britain to Australia and the Americas had been phased out) while synthesizing new measures of exclusion.

The maritime nature of British power produced numerous island camps, but it was the subcontinent of India itself that emerged as the primary arena of encampment in the nineteenth century. Efforts to compel the nomadic tribes of South Asia into a sedentary and "civilized" existence generated a system of monitored settlements in the 1830s, and British officials concentrated tribal populations like the Bhils of upland Bombay Presidency—feared for their mobility and martial prowess—in "guarded villages."[19] Supplemented by a system of travel passes, this policy isolated an insurgent military threat and reorganized the colonial world according to the dictates of modern administration, in many ways paralleling efforts in Britain to combat vagrancy and control the itinerant "dangerous classes." Initially officials conceived the practice of removing tribal people to settled villages as a humanitarian policy that shed the light of civilization onto native populations. But like other ostensibly liberal elements of Britain's civilizing mission, it entailed substantial coercion and hardship for those so targeted.

Sporadic efforts to encamp South Asia's tribal populations intensified in 1871 with the passing of the Criminal Tribes Act by the British Government of India. Drawing from analogous practices of controlling the "criminal" segment of Britain's metropolitan poor, this legislation adapted the Habitual Criminals Act to a colonial context, empowering officials to confine outcast and vagrant groups in purpose-built camps. Exemplifying the "rule of colonial difference," the 1871 act provided for more sweeping powers of summary arrest and preventive detention than any British legislation. In contrast to England, where there was "some chance," according to one official, "of crime not being concealed [and] of criminals being informed against," colonial India presented a vast and dangerous arena of unknown and untrustworthy colonials who required special measures of discipline and surveillance.[20] Cast as deviant by virtue of heredity, registered "criminal tribes" like the Gypsies, Bawarias, Minas, and Sanorias were herded into enclosed compounds, guarded by armed sentries, and forced to perform heavy labor on canals, railways, and other public works projects under British supervision.

Criminal tribe camps emerged to protect a settled and respectable agricultural class from hereditary criminals that existed "in enmity with society."[21] Indian habitual criminals were "enemies of us all," according to P. H. Egerton, the commissioner of Amritsar, and required special treatment outside the existing penal code.[22] To impose mandatory labor and residency, British officials collected the scattered members of these castes and detained them at fixed sites. Using metaphors of contagion, the framers of the 1871 act likened criminal elements to the plague and demanded that they be quarantined "so that they would not infect the social body."[23] In this way the colonial state could "localise and concentrate their residence"[24] and thus place criminal tribes "under the supervision of an officer who will rule them firmly but wisely."[25] Police guards and passes regulated camp egress and ingress, and superintendents enforced nothing less than "open prison discipline."[26]

Meanwhile, rations reflected the assertion that "nothing short of starvation [would] induce [inmates] to undertake labor of an arduous nature."[27] With economy ever a top priority, moreover, the enforcement of heavy labor helped make these camps self-sufficient.

The concentration of criminal tribes rested on the familiar logic of extrajudicial exception and on cultural representations of camp inmates as innately dangerous nomads who required special handling. In contrast to other penal institutions, which operated against individuals convicted or suspected of a crime, the categories of colonial anthropology distinguished between "individuals becoming criminal" and "groups being criminal by birth." Colonial officials accordingly denied members of designated tribes the status of rights-bearing individuals, treating them collectively as a criminal class. Faced with the "peculiar or hereditary nature" of criminal tribes, ordinary laws proved "deficient," and criminal tribes were "dealt with as a whole, and under . . . special rules."[28] Like future camps in the twentieth century—whether Nazi concentration camps or the Soviet Gulag—criminal tribe camps in India confined a class of people designated a potential threat by virtue of their ethnicity or communal membership. Although they were justified by humanitarian language and the belief that settled labor was a civilizing force, criminal tribe camps segregated a population by administrative decree, targeting a category of people rather than individuals deemed guilty by any juridical procedure.

Famine and Plague Camps in British India

Criminal tribe camps offered an exceptional space for designated ethnic groups, while overseas penal camps accommodated political prisoners. But the social crises precipitated by famine and plague in the 1870s and 1890s extended forced labor and detention more widely, confining millions in public works camps or plague segregation camps under the aegis of various colonial health acts.[29] Relief camps for famine refugees reflected the underlying tensions of a colonial state operating in the contested space between "civilizing missions" and economic exploitation. Their bamboo huts and bramble and barbed-wire fences were the product of colonial crisis management and constituted a tentative humanitarian intervention into the welfare of destitute populations under the repressive conditions and fiscal constraints of a colonial emergency. Plague segregation and evacuation camps (fig. 10.2) likewise entailed a biopolitical intervention into the lives of colonial subjects, relegating a "dirty" and "uncivilized" segment of the native population to fenced barracks.

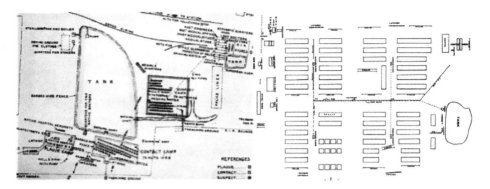

Figure 10.2. Layout of plague segregation and evacuation camps. *Left:* Khana Junction Plague Segregation Camp, 1897, MSA General Dept., "Plague, 1897," 69: "Railway Disinfectant and Detention Camps." *Right:* Baden Evacuation Camp, Bombay, 1890, from *Report of the Bombay Plague Committee* (Bombay: Times of India Steam Press, 1898), appendix.

On the surface, plague and famine camps suggest a rational response to the crises of starvation and disease. But encampment was also premised on cultural representations of colonial people as a social and sanitary danger. Although legitimized by the "objective" spokesmen of economics and medical science, British plague and famine camps were never simply a straightforward response to hunger and disease but were the ideological products of Victorian capitalism and racially inflected discourses of public health. In their pretensions to save life and their use of harsh discipline, famine and plague camps highlight the substantial overlap between the medical and penal technologies of segregation and social isolation. They therefore open an additional lens onto the genealogy of future camps in Nazi Germany, the Soviet Union, and elsewhere, which likewise incorporated the language of dirt, disease, parasites, and contagion.

Of primary concern to colonial administrators, the major famines of 1876–1877 and 1896–1897 disrupted existing mechanisms of social control, uprooting a potentially dangerous "criminal class" and portending social and political danger. Apart from a feared increase in crime, the political implications of hungry, wandering masses could not be ignored after the uprisings of 1857–1858.[30] Although migration to towns, cities, and irrigated tracts offered a rational strategy of survival for the Indian famine sufferer, British officials viewed "aimless wandering" as an irrational flight emerging from "the blind instincts of the wild animal."[31] At once the sympathetic objects of humanitarian concern, famine victims were alternately cast as "intolerable pests" and "utterly useless and worthless members of the community."[32] Such mind-sets

facilitated coercive measures to round up and detain emaciated and potentially dangerous wanderers as "the first object of famine administration."[33]
Once captured, itinerant groups were concentrated in enclosed detention
camps, where they could be made to work in return for rations.

The British Raj met earlier famines with the charitable distribution of
government grain. But policies of forced removal and summary detention
proved more popular in the 1890s, as urban cleansing campaigns swept up
famine refugees, "retain[ing them] by considerable persuasion and practically against their will."[34] Famine officials conceded that forced detention often
constituted "practically illegal confinement divorced from legal and democratic oversight."[35] In the militaristic words of Lieutenant-Colonel S. J. Thomson, the sanitary commissioner of the North-Western Provinces (and a figure
who later presided over wartime concentration camps in South Africa), all
consideration of "'rights' . . . disappear[ed] in a conflict [as] cataclysmic as a
great famine." Executive orders could not be questioned nor "brought before
a legal tribunal"; on the contrary, an effective "campaign" demanded "a leader—a Dictator," whose "summary words" would "sharply punish" offenses
against government orders.[36]

Apart from detaining famine wanderers, officials also used camps to accommodate settled and more "respectable" peasant cultivators who came
under increasing distress as scarcity intensified. Reflecting the government's
abiding ideological reluctance to remit revenue collection or intervene in the
market price of grain, the British Raj provided a bare subsistence wage in
exchange for labor and residence in large dormitory camps attached to public
works projects. Born of a similar set of attitudes that generated workhouses
and labor colonies in Britain, these camps enforced rigorous labor and residence tests as a condition of relief. Noting that Indians of the "better sort" felt
the same "repugnance for relief camps which the respectable poor in England
have for the Union Workhouse," the journalist William Digby observed that
the "degradation of living at a relief camp offered some test in preventing the
better classes from partaking of the charity of Government."[37] Considered to
be repressive and unpopular by inmates themselves and designed as such by
officials, the harsh conditions of camp life served as a deterrent against "de-
moralization" and the "sins of sloth." By dosing out a "just measure of pain,"
camps provided a minimal means of subsistence for those who had no other
choice, while weeding out relief applicants with other means of support.[38]
Dormitory labor camps reflected an uncompromising laissez-faire ideology
that reified Victorian attitudes to work and militated against the more generous distribution of "outdoor" charity in times of need.

The outbreak of plague in Bombay, Cape Town, and other British colonial ports in 1896 offered an additional context for the establishment of camps under the auspices of colonial welfare. As the history of leper colonies suggests, forced segregation has long featured as a component of medical policing and social exclusion. Medicine and sanitation have likewise served as lasting metaphors for the encampment projects of the twentieth century, though in the case of plague, fears of contagion were more than metaphorical.

Colonial medical officials cast detention and quarantine as objective measures of medical and sanitary science, but invasive home searches by military patrols and the summary detention of unsanitary "suspects" cannot be understood outside the social and racial categories of empire. Like the denizens of metropolitan slums, the colonial poor suggested danger and disorder to British observers, and the otherness of the "dirty native" was counterpoised to the cleanliness of the colonial officer, bedecked in white. Such symbolic ecologies intersected with racial discourses, as colonial dirt suggested more general and "sometimes hidden dangers, political and corporeal, moral and cultural."[39] The use of barbed-wire plague camps rested on layers of social, cultural, and political meaning external to the epidemic itself.

Like other episodes of encampment, the use of plague camps emerged from the discursive criminalization of suspect groups. Official correspondence exhibited a common slippage of language that cast target populations simultaneously as victims and offenders. Although a humanitarian appreciation of the human tragedy of the pandemic was never absent, the image of Indian and African plague carriers as suspects, fugitives, and fleeing pestifiers informed British efforts to trap and detain them behind barbed wire.[40] Reflecting visions of the metropolitan "dangerous classes" and the mindset of Victorian social reform, plague operations targeted "persons of the unsafe classes" while exempting Europeans and, to a lesser extent, upper-class natives from encampment and other coercive measures.[41] As such, plague camps were deployed as a preemptive measure against classes of people suspected of harboring disease, rather than individuals determined to be infected by scientific analysis.

In the words of Louis Chevalier, "epidemics do not create abnormal situations" but "betray deeply rooted and continuing social imbalances," thereby sharpening existing behavior patterns.[42] Plague provided a pretext for the forced removal of unwanted social and racial elements from the center of colonial cities. In Bombay military troops relocated impoverished Hindu and Muslim laborers from central urban areas, suggesting a template for suburban public housing complexes. Meanwhile, police in Cape Town cleansed the city of black Africans, forming in the process the nucleus of future "native locations" that would come to prominence in the apartheid era.[43]

Concentration Camps in South Africa

The plague and famine emergencies of the 1890s made possible the proliferation and standardization of camps across British India, offering colonial officials a toolkit of experience caring for and controlling indigent but suspect populations at concentrated sites. Whereas military camps offered early training in the logistical arrangement of concentrated bodies in temporary shelters, camps in India helped officials apply these practices to civilians. By the turn of the century camps had emerged in India as a discrete and recognizable instrument of colonial rule. With their own internal rules of conduct and codified procedures of management, camps could be used to concentrate and contain "dangerous" populations. But it was across the Indian Ocean in South Africa that the term "concentration camp" first entered the English language.

Over the course of the Anglo-Boer War British forces presided over a network of more than a hundred camps used to detain a quarter-million African and Afrikaner (or Boer) civilians.[44] In the face of devastating mortality rates—20 percent of inmates died, usually from epidemic diseases aggravated by exposure, malnutrition, and cramped and unsanitary conditions—it is tempting to equate British concentration camps with those of the Soviet or Nazi empires later in the century. There are compelling reasons to place South African camps at the beginning of a twentieth-century trajectory of political violence. Hannah Arendt noted, for example, that "Boer camps correspond[ed] in many respects to the concentration camps at the beginning of totalitarian rule, used for 'suspects' whose offenses could not be proved and who could not be sentenced by ordinary processes of law."[45] In the wake of the Second World War Afrikaner nationalists also equated British practices (cynically, perhaps) with Nazi death camps.[46] Nonetheless, British concentration camps differed substantially from Soviet or Nazi camps in their size, their duration, and the extent of their brutality. In the context of an active military conflict rather than a less tangible "war" against racial, class, and political enemies, the stated (if not the more underlying) motivations of encampment in South Africa must also be distinguished from the Soviet and Nazi cases. British concentration camps emerged as part of a counterinsurgency campaign to cleanse the battlefield of potential partisan fighters and sources of supply. Detaining civilian populations in harsh and unhealthy conditions according to an extrajudicial and preemptive logic, British concentration camps exhibited a repressive edge emblematic of twentieth-century state violence. But at the same time, they emerged out of an existing nineteenth-century tradition of colonial camps, and the dictates of rehabilitation and refugee relief remained central to camp management.

In contrast to earlier colonial enclosures, the concentration camps of South Africa emerged in the context of war, and martial law endowed British officials with greater powers of forced removal and detention than vagrancy laws and the emergency legislation of plague or famine. As a colonial "small war" that quickly assumed much larger dimensions, the conflict anticipated future "total wars" by blurring the distinction between civilians and combatants. In this respect the indiscriminate confinement of the South African population reflected the "politically modern" intensification and expansion of war, which transformed the entirety of a civilian population—including women and children—into the legitimate targets of violence.[47] Amid a bitter partisan engagement that rendered Boer civilians suspected insurgents by virtue of their ethnic or national identity, camps emerged as a means to control a dehumanized enemy population (and an unfamiliar colonial landscape) on a macro scale and to prevent civilians from providing moral and material provisions to guerrilla commandos.

After British forces captured Pretoria, Bloemfontein, and other cities of the former Boer Republics, the war transitioned into a guerrilla conflict dispersed across an amorphous terrain. Hunting guerrillas and punishing civilians who supplied them with shelter, food, and ammunition, British forces turned to a devastating policy of scorched earth warfare, rendering the landscape a sterile void every bit as barren as drought-stricken India. In his more manic phases the British commander Lord Kitchener even suggested that enemy civilians be transported to Madagascar, Fiji, or some other island in order to make South Africa "safe and available for white [that is, British] colonists."[48] But such proposals proved logistically unsound, and Kitchener turned instead to a policy of forced urbanization, compelling Afrikaner civilians into captured cities, and eventually to suburban concentration camps where they could be observed and controlled. In this way British tactics resembled Spanish General Valeriano Weyler's earlier "reconcentration" campaign to gather Cuba's rural population in fortified towns and isolate civilians from guerrilla insurgents.[49] The South African War also foreshadowed future episodes in colonial Kenya and Malaya, where departing British officials deployed camps—described by the historian Caroline Elkins as "Britain's Gulag in Kenya"—in an effort to sort civilians from suspected rebels.[50]

It is true that concentration camps performed a specific military function. But historians often overstate the extent to which the camps were the instrumental agents of a sober military strategy. As in India, the violence of forced encampment depended on a familiar set of cultural representations casting Afrikaners as a "dangerous class": a dirty and degenerate race of "savages with only a thin white veneer," General Kitchener proclaimed.[51] Coming from a culture that equated sanitation with civilization, British authorities routinely described "semicivilized" upcountry Boers as a "dirty, careless, lazy lot," who had lost the "instincts of their European forefathers" and whose habits would be "a disgrace to any European nation."[52] Even though the military context of South Africa generated a distinct set of strategic motivations for encampment, the discourses that justified wartime camps conformed to a familiar cultural framework of purity and pollution that underwrote earlier episodes of encampment.

Instruments of military control, South African camps also resembled earlier efforts to detain and rehabilitate social outcasts. Indeed, for the vast majority of their existence, concentration camps were administered not by military officials steeped in a cult of violence but by civilian authorities reared in an existing tradition of concentrating suspect colonial populations in makeshift camps. Indeed, the Colonial Office highlighted the similarities between wartime concentration camps and earlier episodes of civilian concentration when they recruited such figures as S. J. Thomson and other "camp experts" from India, who boasted "very analogous experience in plague and famine camps," to administer Britain's latest system of camps in South Africa.[53] The Colonial Office also mobilized an inspection committee experienced in health, sanitation, and social work, who visited the camps in the fashion of "guardians of the poor" in Britain; they compared their duties in South Africa to inspecting workhouses and the lodgings of the poor in Britain.[54] As such, familiar practices of controlling a socially suspect and racially degenerate population ultimately informed the development and administration of British concentration camps. If South African camps were precursors, as Arendt argues, to the more infamous concentration camps of the twentieth century, they were also products of a nineteenth-century brand of imperialism and social control, with its characteristic mix of dehumanizing rhetoric and humanitarian care. While anticipating a new century of political violence and total war, they had their roots in an existing tradition of forced encampment.

BRITISH AND SOVIET CAMPS—A COMPARATIVE AGENDA

Britain was the homeland of liberalism. Yet it, too, had camps. Such a reality demands further reflection—both by scholars of the British Empire, who have largely neglected Britain's own indigenous camp history, and by Soviet scholars, who might benefit from incorporating the Gulag into a more general spectrum. A transnational and comparative analysis should address two different research questions. First, how did nineteenth-century camps in the British Empire and elsewhere inform future practices in the more infamous camps of the Soviet Union and Nazi Germany? Were there any concrete genealogical connections in terms of policy and personnel? Second, what are the structural continuities that bind together different camp regimes? How did broadly shared ideas about social and political danger, criminality and rehabilitation, and labor, rations, and welfare develop in camps across different political regimes?

The task of comparison, still in a provisional state, must consider the very real differences between British and Soviet practices (as well as those of other camp regimes—German, Chinese, etc.), while recognizing the variety of camps over which each power presided. The diverse forms and functions of British famine, plague, and concentration camps are evident, even if they are connected by a more underlying set of concerns. Conditions in the Gulag varied over space and time: under Lenin or Stalin, and in the *katorga* camps of Siberia or the less brutal corrective labor colonies. Likewise, the Nazi concentration camps of 1933–1934 may offer richer material for transnational comparison than the extermination factory at Auschwitz-Birkenau II, which represented an extreme rather than a norm within the vast German system.[55] History demands that we be sensitive to diversity and change. But at the same time, historians place themselves at an interpretive disadvantage if they fail to recognize broad similarities shared across different political contexts and policy objectives. To this end it may prove instructive for historians of the Gulag to look beyond the "usual suspects"—the concentration camps of Nazi Germany—in their comparative analysis. Doing so may unsettle comfortable distinctions between "liberal" polities like Britain and autocratic states like the Soviet Union. Such analysis could also provide a lens onto the deeper cultural and material foundations that underlie the proliferating camps of the modern world.

Concrete Connections

Until the 1920s commentators and policy makers across Europe associated "concentration camps" primarily with the British Empire. As an international media event the Anglo-Boer War disseminated the idea of the camp to a global audience. At a more regional level the conflict spread new practices throughout the colonial regimes of southern Africa. While they remained rivals, relations among European colonial powers also depended on mutual cooperation.[56] German officials in Southwest Africa witnessed British camp policies at close hand before using their own camps during the Nama and

Herero genocide (1904–1905). These enclosures, in turn, may have inspired the Nazi camps of the 1930s, though more research is necessary to flesh out the connection.[57]

British camps later proved a common referent in Nazi speeches and propaganda.[58] A heated 1939 exchange between Herman Göring and the British ambassador Nevile Henderson was typical. Consulting a German encyclopedia, the Nazi leader read aloud: "*Konzentrationslager:* first used by Britain in the South African War."[59] A year later Hitler also referred to British precedent when he declared that Britain had "invented" the concentration camp. Germany, he continued, had merely "read up on [British practices] in the encyclopaedia and then later copied it."[60]

It is clear, then, that globalized media and colonial connections helped transmit British innovations to a world stage.[61] But work remains for historians to trace the concrete and tangible impact of colonial camps on later regimes. Hannah Arendt's insights concerning the connection between colonialism and future European violence are analytically compelling but require further empirical validation, especially for the Soviet case.[62] In this regard awareness and debate in tsarist Russia concerning the high-profile concentration camps of rival colonial powers suggest a potentially fruitful starting point in accounting for the global origins of the Gulag. The first reference to camps in the Soviet Union came, after all, from Lev Trotskii, who had followed events in South Africa closely and probably became familiar with concentration camps in their original British iteration.[63] But did an awareness of British and other transnational precedents actually inspire policy decisions? Historians have yet to seriously grapple with the question.

While exploring possible sources of connection and continuity, the degree to which future camps in the Soviet Union and elsewhere were "planned" or "modeled" on British precedents should not be overstated. The radicalization of World War I and the revolutionary context of the interwar decades remain essential to our understanding of the Gulag in its mature form. Apart from imperial rivalries in Afghanistan, Britain and Russia had little direct interaction in the colonial world. Exploring transnational continuities, then, is not to deny the very real variations between different national histories.

Structural Continuities

In addition to searching for concrete genealogical connections that may or may not materialize, a consideration of the deeper structures of a common social and political modernity offers further grounds for comparison. An investigation of British camps highlights cultural preconditions and aspects of camp management that were shared with the Soviet Gulag and other camp regimes. The provision of food and welfare, an emphasis on didactic and productive labor, debates about punishment and rehabilitation, and the isolation of political prisoners: analysis of such themes should top the comparative agenda.

British and Soviet officials acted on an ideology of labor that emerged out of the structural forces of industrialization and factory discipline common to the Western world. Inmate labor at large public works projects constituted a principal activity at British famine and criminal tribe camps in India. Work commenced at 7 a.m., paused for a meal and period of rest at midday, then resumed until sunset. Ideally camp labor was productive, aiding in the construction of canals, roads, and railways—the material markers of modern British administration—at a minimum possible cost. But work performed a didactic purpose as well, and it was enforced even when there was no means of employing inmates in a useful manner. Such was the case at Indian famine camps, where activities like shifting stones from one pile to the next were imposed "for the sake of the people employed."[64]

A discourse of rehabilitative labor also prevailed in South Africa, where concentration camps helped initiate inmates into a modern world of industrial production. As in India camp labor consisted of "a system of working squads" that prohibited inmates from "spend[ing] their time in idleness." Camps for black Africans enforced a heavy regime of unremunerated agricultural labor, though work conditions were less severe for white Afrikaners (especially women and children), who got paid for their work. Women performed sewing, laundry, sweeping, and light cleaning, while men and teenage boys were put to work "digging, trenching, camp cleaning, wood chopping . . . and a dozen other necessary duties."[65] The labor and discipline of camp life, according to one official, would enable inmates to "hold their own in an industrial community."[66] Given the unique racial and political climate of South Africa, the project of social engineering proved especially promising in Boer camps, which concentrated an ambiguous population—half-civilized and half-savage—that was in "special need of ordering."[67] More generally the production of governable, hard-working subjects emerged as an animating goal of camps in both Britain and the Soviet Union.

For the most part labor in Boer concentration camps was less burdensome or coercive than in the Soviet Gulag. Labor in other British camps, however, could be more destructive than productive. This was especially the case at Indian famine camps, where racial prejudice and an uncompromising capitalist ideology mitigated against "gratuitous" or "indiscriminate" charity. Limited by strict budgets and an exploitative approach to work, many famine-camp inmates suffered seriously from diminished health and vitality as a result of minimal rations and heavy labor. At a camp in Broach, for example, the district medical officer reported, "the condition of the workers has seriously deteriorated. The young and healthy . . . have become slack and skinny, the others have lost a considerable amount of flesh, and the number of emaciated gangs are on the increase."[68] Famine camps were ostensibly instruments of relief, but the impact of forced labor on inmate bodies is suggestive of the "destructive labor camps" described by Alexander Solzhenitsyn.[69]

According to Golfo Alexopoulos, food and rationing suggest a new subject area for Gulag research. To this end, penal rations at British camps offer an instructive point of comparison. Modeled explicitly on British workhouses, "feeding times" at Indian famine camps were an occasion for "great discipline," and rations were carefully calibrated according to the productive output of each inmate.[70] To spare expense, officials experimented with the minimal threshold "necessary for the preservation of human life."[71] This was a "bare life" that sustained basic biological functions but purposely denied comfort or health. Critics condemned famine-camp rations as a starvation diet that simply "prolong[ed] a man's death . . . instead of cutting his misery short."[72] Penal rations also prevailed at South African concentration camps, and the diet of political undesirables was "so entirely inadequate," the British nutritional expert J. S. Haldane observed, that "without extra supplements [which, in practice, could sometimes be purchased at camp stores], death from sheer starvation (uncomplicated by disease) would probably result within a few months."[73] By inviting merchants into camps and paying inmates a monetary wage, British authorities maintained a semblance of capitalist free enterprise. But despite surface differences in ideological content, British and Soviet attitudes regarding the disciplinary efficacy of labor and rations were at times remarkably similar.

The treatment of political prisoners and other problem inmates offers further scope for comparison. Embodying the aspirations for order characteristic of modern institutions, the internal organization of British and Soviet camps classified and sorted inmates according to such criteria as labor capacity, social class, and political affiliation. Plague camps refined the practices of classification to a medical science, though the classificatory impulse proved important at other camps as well. In light of recurring analogies between medical and military policing in the larger history of forced encampment, it was only fitting that officials in South Africa turned to the epidemiological techniques of segregation and isolation when combating political subversion within the enemy population. By segregating and, it was hoped, rehabilitating the deviant, the confinement of political "undesirables" in special

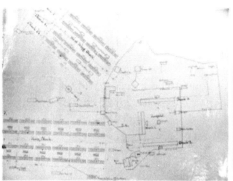 

Figure 10.3. Blueprint of a model concentration camp in South Africa and image of an "undesirable camp." *Left:* Amalinda Bluff Camp, East London, Cape Colony NASA Free State Archive Depot, SRC vol. 38. *Right:* TNA, CO 1069/215 South Africa 3, South African War: Views of Concentration Camps, 1901, no. 105, also reproduced in Thomas Pakenham, *The Boer War* (London: Weidenfeld and Nicholson, 1979), inside cover.

barbed-wire enclosures conformed to the "rational and scientific principles" of nineteenth-century penal practice (fig. 10.3).

Concentration camps in South Africa were depots of relief and rehabilitation, but they were also venues for political surveillance and control. Similar to the Soviet Gulag, British officials reserved the harshest measures for "political undesirables." Enclosed by barbed wire, segregation wards extracted punitive labor from those "who raise[d] rebellion" and "[could] not hold their tongues from speaking politics."[74] In Bloemfontein, for example, a "wired-in enclosure" known colloquially as "the Bird Cage" enforced "8 hours [of work] a day with pick and shovel" for "all singing birds."[75] At Winburg, meanwhile, "a fence of galvanized iron 7 to 8 feet high" segregated those who "foster[ed] resistance to rules and regulations."[76] The stated purpose was to prevent the infection of the general inmate population with subversive ideas. Such was an epidemiological language employed quite literally at Indian plague camps, and more metaphorically at camp regimes throughout the twentieth century.

Animated by a Victorian obsession with sanitation, moreover, British officials often conflated social and political danger, rendering the indolent and unhygienic liable to detention in undesirable camps alongside politically dangerous inmates. At Bloemfontein, for example, the superintendent punished "dirty and lazy" inmates by sending them to the Bird Cage.[77] A similar undesirable camp at Norvals' Pont was known as "Hog's Paradise" because it concentrated the "extremely dirty" and "verminous."[78] The degree to which Bolshevik officials conflated social and political danger (class enemies were both a social and a political threat, after all) and mobilized similar images of vermin, dirt, and disease is worth further exploration in relation to the underlying logic of British and other camps.[79]

At the same time, however, political motivations suggest a significant point of divergence. Ordinary criminals constituted a majority of Gulag inmates, thereby placing Soviet camps within a continuum of earlier forced labor systems in the British Empire and elsewhere. But Bolshevik officials evidently placed a greater emphasis on political traitors, internal enemies, and the fanatical maintenance of ideological purity than their counterparts in Britain. The isolation of political undesirables framed the development of British camps, and ideological commitments (capitalism and social/racial difference rather than Marxism-Leninism) informed British officials in powerful ways. But in general, politics and ideology were of only secondary importance at most British camps and featured only obliquely in famine and plague enclosures. As the instrument of a revolutionary polity in continual crisis, the Soviet Gulag incarcerated political enemies on a vastly greater scale, at least for the duration of Stalin's (perhaps unrepresentative) leadership.

Any comparative study should therefore identify demonstrable differences as well as suggestive likenesses. At a fundamental level British and Soviet camps materialized within the structural conditions of a shared Western modernity. They developed according to similar frameworks of purity and contagion and emphasized productive labor, fiscal restraint, and fears of social and political danger. But although British and Soviet camps share hitherto unrecognized and at times unsettling similarities, clear cultural and contextual differences exist in terms of the motives, duration, and conditions of encampment.

The period of Soviet rule has been characterized as an unending emergency lasting nearly the entirety of the twentieth century. But while British camps provided the foundation for more permanent geographies of social and racial exclusion, many functioned as genuinely temporary measures. Workhouses, penal colonies, and criminal tribe camps became permanent features of Britain's carceral landscape, but other British camps—famine, plague, and concentration camps—were disassembled on conclusion of the "state of exception" that first justified them. They should therefore be distinguished from the Gulag, which was arguably normalized (despite a substantial retrenchment following Stalin's death) as a standard apparatus of discipline and punishment central to Soviet society and the Soviet state.

In addition to the length of incarceration, the experience of many Gulag inmates was undoubtedly harsher than that of their British counterparts. Suffering and brutality, of course, are hard to quantify. But if camps, prisons, and other penal infrastructure can be located on a spectrum, the Soviet Gulag (like Russian prisons today, as Judith Pallot notes) should most realistically be placed at the repressive end of the continuum.[80] With the exception of undesirable wards, British concentration camps in South Africa were not always fenced, and authorities routinely granted inmates passes to visit town. As such, these camps more closely resemble Soviet corrective labor colonies (the Gulag's more gentle iteration) than the notorious *katorga* camps that dominate the collective memory of Soviet violence.[81]

Historians must resist the impulse to sensationalize suffering in the Gulag or conflate Soviet camps with the death and unrelenting terror of Nazi extermination camps. Indeed, sober revisionist exploration of the quotidian experiences of inmates and the putatively humanitarian and rehabilitative agenda articulated by Soviet officials might serve to complicate popular assumptions about the Gulag as a vehicle of political terror. Conversely, we must recognize the potential for brutality at British camps, which brought inmates into direct and unmediated contact with the coercive powers of an often-hostile colonial state. At the same time, Britain should be distinguished from the Soviet Union by its open and lively civil society. Floggings and corporal punishment did occur at some British camps, especially when power was delegated to the "man on the spot." But such practices were often at odds with the official humanitarian mandate of British camps. And significantly, the oversight of "London liberals" served at key moments as a brake on violence and abuse.[82] As a result, public pressure in Britain often forced officials to improve grim conditions according to humanitarian precepts. Controversy and resulting reforms therefore constitute a central chapter in the history of British camps, which largely escaped the Gulag's cycle of violence and brutality.

At first glance, then, liberalism did make a difference, not in preventing camps but in stemming their abuse. In the worst cases mortality rates at British camps approached a tragic 25 percent. But such figures ignited a press scandal that would have been unfeasible in the Soviet Union. Popular agitation over concentration camps in South Africa provoked vigorous efforts to reform camp conditions. Ultimately epidemics like cholera and measles proved the primary killers in British camps, but public pressure reduced camp mortality rates to near zero in their reformed and sanitary reincarnations. In this connection disease and resulting efforts at epidemiological policing within crowded camp confines suggest a more universal camp experience that deserves further comparative examination by British and Soviet historians.[83]

Finally, the vast majority of British camps were products of overseas imperial conquest rather than metropolitan politics—the existence of metropolitan workhouses and a modest network of labor camps (as well as wartime internment camps) notwithstanding.[84] More readily unleashed in the empire than in the metropole, blunt sovereign force and physical detention were often suited to the surveillance and control of foreign and largely illegible colonial masses. Moreover, camps proved particularly useful at arresting the movement of nomadic (and therefore menacing) colonial populations, fixing them in space in a process often informed by dehumanizing "hunting and trapping" metaphors. But in Britain, where state and society were more deeply integrated, social control depended on what Michel Foucault described as "liberal governmentality": an internalization of norms and a diffusion of power far more subtle and sophisticated than external restraints alone.[85] Prisons and workhouses were central to the building of modern British society, and they provided a conceptual template for the organization of camps overseas. But only in rare cases did power in the metropole rest on forced, collective, and extrajudicial encampment.

In this respect the British experience stands out, for Britain pursued overseas conquest rather than territorial expansion in Europe. With insular boundaries Britain retained a relatively clear distinction between metropole and empire, even if the experience of colonial rule inflected metropolitan culture in profound and sometimes covert ways. Presiding over the largest empire in world history, Britain could easily export its coercive practices overseas. But as marginal powers in Africa and Asia the Soviet Union and Germany after the First World War pursued colonial ambitions in Europe instead. Here the distinctions between metropole and colony rapidly broke down in Russia's Eurasian land empire and Germany's *Ostland*. Certainly Britain exhibited its own modern "heart of darkness," but it was largely confined to a distant empire.

By some accounts Britain stands out for its inclusive liberalism. But it was by no means immune from modern maladies. British camps were built on strident rhetoric—whether articulated in terms of racial difference, social danger, or metaphors of contagion—that dehumanized en masse the targets of encampment. Although the concept of individual rights emerged in the nineteenth century, it was tempered by "states of exception" and emergency legislation. In this context British camps detained potentially dangerous populations by administrative decree rather than juridical procedure. Meanwhile, the classifying impulses of the emerging social sciences facilitated the categorical demarcation of populations as a collective threat by virtue of group membership.

British camps, like their Soviet counterparts, did not spring out of thin air but were predicated on an existing set of practices and discursive frameworks. A comparative and transnational analysis helps identify the shared ingredients that gave rise to modern camps across a variety of polities. Whether the instruments of a revolutionary and authoritarian regime, or the agents of a "liberal" empire, camps relied on a sophisticated logistical and disciplinary machinery assembled over the course of the nineteenth century. Mass industrial armies provided expertise in rationing and billeting large numbers on a uniform basis. Factories, workhouses, and prisons served as laboratories for a new ideology of work central to camps in particular and the organization of a new mass society more generally. Factory labor, scientific racism, and an encounter with difference fostered a new degraded image of humankind and facilitated the development of new dehumanizing methods of controlling populations.

Camps inflicted untold suffering in both Britain and the Soviet Union. But in each case they emerged, ironically, from the shared impulses of the Enlightenment. As modern states built new political societies based on inclusive membership and aimed to govern populations in addition to territories, difference had either to be assimilated, exterminated, or spatially displaced. Although justified with the promise of rehabilitation, camps often existed to contain outcast groups. By offering "protective custody," they isolated danger and prevented infection of the wider social body while bringing inmates into unmediated contact with the state. These were the external motivations and cultural preconditions for the development of British camps. But these were foundations widely shared with the Soviet Gulag and other camp regimes.

II.   CAMP WORLDS AND FORCED LABOR

A Comparison of the National Socialist and Soviet Camp Systems

DIETRICH BEYRAU

TRANSLATED BY NICOLE EATON

PROBLEMS AND CRITERIA FOR THE COMPARISON

The nascence of the camp as an institution of the twentieth century is strongly connected to the invention of barracks, barbed wire, and modern modes of transportation in the nineteenth century but also to the development of organizational technologies that made it possible to enclose masses of people, who could be held in check by only a few armed guards. The British concentration camps in South Africa during the Boer War became a model recognized worldwide. Over the course of the twentieth century the camp, as an institution for the concentration of people, took on many different functions: as internment camps for refugees and resettled peoples, as (forced) labor and reeducation camps, as ersatz prisons, and, last but not least, as places of mass death through systematic deprivation, as was often the case in prisoner of war (POW) camps in the twentieth century. The Nazi sites of extermination —Belzec, Sobibor, and others—were, in a narrow sense, not camps but at best transport stations to industrial mass killing. Camps such as Auschwitz and Majdanek combined forced labor and extermination.

In this chapter camps, forced labor, and imprisonment are considered together. In Europe it was during the First World War that camps became long-term places of stay for over nine million prisoners of war (and refugees). The outcome already demonstrated in the British camps in South Africa—mass death, at least to a certain extent, due to malnourishment and epic disease—was repeated in the POW camps during the war, especially in those of the Central Powers and Russia. New in that situation was the more or less compulsory labor assignments for imprisoned groups. During the war, the untapped potential of imprisoned men was supposed to be used as a military resource, to address workforce labor shortages due to the mobilization of soldiers to the front. The prisoners were relatively inexpensive in that they were supposed to be housed and paid like the soldiers of the army detaining them. But with only a few exceptions, forced labor was not used for punishment or reeducation, as had been the case before in some of the colonies or later in totalitarian dictatorships.[1]

Camps and forced labor have attracted much attention in the recent historiography of twentieth-century totalitarian dictatorships.[2] Although camps can hardly be described as a "concealed paradigm in the political sphere of modernity," they nevertheless form the central building blocks—modules—of totalitarian dictatorships: the camp serves as their representative image.[3] This statement includes questions about predecessors and models, about variations, transformations, and changing functions of the concentrations of human beings in camps. The establishment of camps arose in particular historical contexts. Therefore, it is possible to note some knowledge transfer between cases, rather than historical continuities. The question of possible continuities or knowledge transfers in the case of individual countries is controversial in the German case and has so far not even been a topic of discussion in relation to Russia.[4] Wars and political conflicts were the main factors leading to the forced concentration of people into enclosed spaces. In the Second World War alone the number of people contained in camps is estimated at roughly fifty million: twenty million each in camps on German and Japanese territory, and about ten million in the Soviet Union.[5] The crowding of people in camps, the deprivation of their private sphere, and the subjection to punitive or humiliating discipline were usually accompanied by psychological pressure, threats of force, or violence.

The discussion here focuses on a comparison between Nazi Germany and the Stalinist Soviet Union, two systems that came close, in very different ways, to the model of the totalitarian state. With their changing forms and disparate functions, camps in these contexts were part of a sprawling system for the quasi-barracks-style molding of people—of the "masses," to use the language of the time. In criminal states camps constituted the hard core of rule. They were embedded in a differentiated system of many kinds of police and administrative coercion: for example, the obligation to work, the restriction of freedom of movement to the point of forced labor, imprisonment, and murder. The camps formed the dark sides of the emerging *Volksgemeinschaft* in Germany and of socialism in the Soviet Union under Stalin—that is, of dictatorships that were supported and propped up by the "enthusiastic" groups of society, as they were called in the Soviet Union, or by the "idealists," as they were known in Germany.[6] The formation of a militant community, imagined and real, bred violence alongside enthusiasm or idealism. Politics was in both cases defined exclusively, as in Carl Schmitt's understanding, as a struggle and as a friend-foe relationship.[7]

Both systems adopted the techniques of concentrating people in camps and using forced labor, as practiced during the First World War.[8] Both the chaotic establishment of torture centers and camps in Germany after 1933 and of camps and special settlements for deported kulaks in the USSR were embedded in revolutionary upheavals. The regime was thus permitted to use all available means of violence, especially the elimination—"liquidation," in Stalinist terminology—of real and imagined enemies. The camps became a central part of the broader project to transform society. In the German case the goal was the formation of a national community and, during the war, the establishment of a highly hierarchical system of apartheid, which would secure German rule and domination over the continent. In the Soviet case the goal was the construction of socialism and the formation of a new type of historical community.

The other "positive" side of camps came in the form of the "education," even the inculcation, of people, particularly youth, in the regime's goals. The camp became, in various incarnations, a way of life for large sectors of the population: children's camps, youth camps, and pioneer camps with a (political) educational mission; military sports and, not least, military service; competitions designed to foster toughness in oneself and vis-à-vis others. Labor mobilizations, *subbotniki*, and other "voluntary" work assignments were designed to foster the sense that labor was a communal responsibility. The camp-and-barracks-style formation of masses through demonstrations, at festivals and (for the National Socialists) party days, served as collective manifestations. They represented and symbolized the *Volksgeimeinschaft* or socialism and did have some effect on daily life.[9] In the Soviet case the effect was particularly noticeable for the urban population. The [German] Lecturer's Camp [*Dozentenlager*] praised by the philosopher Martin Heidegger had its Soviet analogue in the internally organized Bolshevik party meetings and meetings by individual industries and organizations. They functioned as resolution machines and as platforms for public criticism and self-criticism, and they practiced collective community and exclusionary proceedings.[10] Camps mobilized and conditioned the "enthusiastic" and "idealistic" sectors of the population and were at the same time institutions of coercion and violence for those excluded.[11]

I have selected three models of coercive institutions to form the basis for a comparative analysis of the Nazi and Soviet camp worlds. Camps may be defined as "total institutions," following Erving Goffman's *Asylums*.[12] They also show features described by Wolfgang Sofsky in institutions of "absolute power": for the old disciplinary power, space was a means for drilling and observation.[13] This classification corresponds in essence to Goffman's "total institution" or to Michel Foucault's model in *Discipline and Punish*.[14] For absolute power, however, space is an instrument for social discrimination and for death.[15] Sofsky developed his model from the example of the Nazi concentration camps and death camps. But most camps in Germany and in the USSR actually correspond more closely to the model of the "total institution" than to that of "absolute power," if only because the emphasis was on forced labor. Their goal was, in the context of the larger transformative project, to achieve total control and exploitation, the complete control over time, space, the body, and the psyche of the camp inmate—in the words of Maksim Gor'kii, of the "units" (*edinitsy*).[16] The typology of a particular camp depended largely on the degree of control over the freedom of movement for those detained there.

Power in its own right provoked all kinds of humiliations and violence, up to and including homicide. Coercion and violence from above were not limited to the relationship between the authorities and inmates and led, to a considerable degree, to the brutalization of relations among the inmate population. The permanent shortages of food, clothing, and space, as well as poor hygiene, caused conflicts with camp staff and among fellow prisoners. The starting point of the establishment of terror (according to Sofsky) is the enforcement of the absolute powerlessness of the subjugated. Absolute power begins where traditional despotism ends. Despotism is, in spite of its arbitrariness, interested in the productive labor capacity of the subjugated. With significant reservations, this model applies to the world of the Soviet camps and to the majority of Nazi forced labor camps. Absolute power, however, turned labor into a component of the economy of killing, as in the case of Auschwitz or Majdanek.

But even the most absolute power depended on delegation to executors.[17] This understanding is incorporated even more into Goffman's model of total institutions, in which power works only through delegation and the "collaboration" of the subjugated. Goffman describes the phenomenon of "underlife"—the internal dynamics that develop in the process of implementing demands from above. Richard Overy points out that orders by camp authorities existed alongside unwritten rules within the camp community.[18] It was not only in the case of Soviet camps that there was, in economic terms, a permanent discrepancy between official instructions and their realization.[19] This kind of discrepancy arose from contradictory instructions that attempted to combine "disciplining" (violence and threats of violence) with economic efficiency in the Gulag and, after 1942–1943, in the Nazi concentration camps. The combination of contradictory interests among the executors, which shaped official demands and existing local constraints, in their implementation resulted in the miserable condition of inmates: malnutrition, disease, complete lack of motivation to perform the labor, and the inmates' use of any opportunity to undermine labor goals or to escape performing them entirely. The violence between the camp management and the inmates, but also among the inmates themselves, could not be controlled from the center: total control remained elusive. Instead, camps developed into a specific "sphere of violence," enclosed by barbed wire and watch towers.[20] Incidence of violence and the persistent threat of violence among prisoners was determined by excessive and often arbitrarily executed power, on one hand, and by disenfranchisement, constriction, and struggle for survival, on the other. The situation developed to the point that by the late 1940s the local Soviet camp leadership could no longer be certain it maintained a monopoly on violence.[21]

NAZI GERMANY AND OCCUPIED EUROPE

The Development of the Apartheid Society

In 1935, when the number of inmates in the Soviet Union already exceeded half a million, Nazi Germany was holding only around four thousand prisoners in concentration camps. After a chaotic initial phase when the Nazis imprisoned their political opponents in improvised cellars, abandoned factories, and warehouses and tortured and sometimes murdered them, by the mid-1930s the SS and the Gestapo shifted toward using the already established concentration camps as a racial-biological and racial-hygienic "general preventative," the Nazi version of "cleansing" society.[22] On the eve of the war, the number of concentration camp inmates stood at about twenty-one thousand, which by November 1939 expanded to about thirty thousand.[23] The concentration camp system expanded during the war; the establishment of the Economic Administration Main Office (WVHA) in 1942 signaled the new desired combination of punishment and productivity. Given the routine violence already entrenched in the camps, this policy led to a practice of carrying out extermination through labor. Concentration camps, therefore, operated—in addition to the pure extermination camps of Chelmno, Sobibor, Treblinka, Majdanek, and Auschwitz-Birkenau—as places of mass murder, in part through executions and in part through the use of mobile gassing vans or stationary gas chambers. In January 1945 there were around 714,000 concentration camp prisoners (203,000 of whom were women), falling under the WVHA's purview.

Between 1935 and 1945 the total population passing through the twenty-four concentration camps (including the approximately one thousand satellite camps) in the Reich and in occupied Europe is estimated at 2.5–3.5 million people. The number of inmates who disappeared or were murdered is 2,000,000, 450,000 in the territory of the Reich.[24] After the failed Blitzkrieg against the Soviet Union, Adolf Hitler and Heinrich Himmler turned the murder of the Jews into one of their war aims, which explains the vast resources dedicated to this goal, to the point of hindering the war effort.[25] After the mass murder of the Jews in the Soviet Union and Poland, the survivors were at first put to work in the ghettos from 1941 to 1943. These ghettoes were then transformed into forced labor camps; in the General Government, the number of ghetto camps was estimated between three hundred and four hundred.[26]

In 1941–1942 the treatment of Soviet POWs by the Nazis was not much better than that of the Jews. In the main camps and transit camps on Soviet territory, in Poland, and in Germany, Soviet prisoners were allowed simply to starve until late 1941 or early 1942. There are divergent estimates concerning the proportion of those killed through "excision" (*Aussonderung*) and those who perished in the camps as POWs.[27] Current estimates suggest a total of approximately 5.3 million Soviet POWs, of whom 2.6 million died or were systematically murdered. Through December 1945 a total of more than 2 million Soviet POWs were registered by Soviet authorities in the liberated areas occupied by the Allies, 1.8 million of whom returned to the USSR.

In September 1941 there were 127 camps for Soviet POWS planned for the territory of the Reich, many in the form of simple enclosed camp areas without any proper infrastructure. In August 1944 more than 1.9 million prisoners of war were working as forced laborers in the Great German Reich, including around 632,000 Red Army soldiers, nearly 600,000 French prisoners of war, and 158,000 Italian "military internees" (the official name for Italian prisoners of war).[28] The majority of POWs were employed outside the camps in construction projects in industry and mines, as well as in agriculture. There were 142 so-called Main Camps (*Stammlager*) (more established, permanent camps) in the Reich for noncommissioned officers and other ranks, and 16 in the General Government.[29] In the White Ruthenian General Commissariat (Belorussia), there were more than two hundred camps for prisoners of war between 1941 and 1944, with constantly changing occupancy and duration of operation, including nearly ninety camps for the Mitte Railway Main Administration, each housing a hundred to six hundred prisoners of war.[30] There were hundreds of camps for prisoners of war in occupied Ukraine as well, many of them with thousands of inmates.[31]

As a consequence of the Führer Directive of 25 September 1944, prisoners of war were removed from oversight by the High Command of the Armed Forces, and Himmler was appointed commander of the Reserve Army (*Ersatzheeres*).[32] Although this development probably did not alter the POWs' material situation, it did indicate the growing power of Himmler. This measure was a further step in the development of an apartheid society, as it developed in greatly varying ways in the individual regions of Nazi rule.

Camp Worlds

Christian Gerlach has described the camp as an "essential feature of the Nazi regime."[33] After the war began, the region under Nazi control was covered with camps of various administrative designations and functions. The administrative designations included concentration camps, work camps, prisons/penitentiaries, prisoner of war camps, internment camps, forced labor camps, prison camps, justice camps, and camps for resettlers (from the territories occupied by the USSR in 1939 and from South Tyrol).[34] For the most part, the labor force of the camps fell under the aegis of the Organisation Todt, which was responsible, beginning in 1940, for construction projects and armaments—and the corresponding deployment of domestic and foreign labor, forced laborers, prisoners of war, and concentration camp inmates. Most foreign workers were housed in camps, and their wages were generally below those of German workers.[35]

The enforcement of a strong racial hierarchy among the inmates of all camps was demonstrated in the various allotments for food rations and wages. Soviet prisoners of war and *Ostarbeiter* always had to get by with less than their Allied fellow inmates. The Italian military internees were between them.[36] In one *Stammlager* the discrimination was so deeply institutionalized that dentures were produced "only for Western prisoners and Poles"; "Russians were not approved for dental treatment."[37]

In the Reich foreign workers in mid-1944 made up 10–40 percent of the workforce, depending on the industry.[38] As the labor shortage became more severe, however, discriminatory policies against Soviet POWs and *Ostarbeiter* were loosened.[39] As a rule, however, the policy of exterminating Jews through work remained in place until the unconditional surrender.

Hierarchies were enforced according to racial or ethnic ancestry among the foreign workers, volunteers, and forced laborers. On the lower rungs there were Jews, Gypsies, and members of the East Slavic peoples (labeled with the badge "Ost"), followed in ascending order by Italians, East Europeans, Poles, Westerners, and, on the highest rung, North Europeans. This hierarchy was especially apparent in food rations and wages, in bonuses, in the receipt of mail, and in the degree of (still limited) freedom of movement—

that is, the permission to leave the camp and be either permitted or denied access to restaurants, cinemas, and so on. The situation for prisoners of war who were employed in the mining industry was especially traumatic. Here morbidity and mortality rates were so high that even the Supreme Command of the Wehrmacht complained.[40] There were also differences regarding sexual contact with foreigners. Contact between French prisoners of war and German women carried relatively minor punishment, but if sexual relations were discovered between Soviet POWs and German women, the prisoners were threatened with death by hanging, and the German woman sent—due to their racial disgrace—to a concentration camp.[41] In brothels for foreign civilian laborers and camp inmates (including in concentration camps), only foreign women were allowed to be employed.[42]

The situation of *Ostarbeiter* was reflected in the letters that were carefully recorded by German censors: of the letters censored in March 1943, 98 percent contained "unfavorable remarks about Germany." They referred to "long workdays (up to eighteen hours), difficult and dirty work, and work without days off. Very often there were complaints that, despite the cold temperatures, they had to work in rags and without winter clothes, in tattered shoes or without shoes entirely." There were also complaints about bad food and insufficient rations, about dilapidated and often unheated barracks, about low wages, poor medical care, and verbal abuse and discrimination by the local population.[43]

The Dregs of the Apartheid Society: The Concentration Camp

The knowledge transmitted about the internal life of concentration camps is much greater than about civilian labor camps and POW camps.[44] Compared to these camps, the informal hierarchies, the rules, and the intensity of competition between groups were much more destructive and life-threatening in concentration camps. Concentration camps were, symbolically speaking, the Hell of the social hierarchy: in them, the characteristics of camp existence, as they could exist potentially in all camp systems, were expressed to the extreme, up to and including the death of the inmates.

Absolute power, in Sofsky's formulation, was already manifest through the depersonalization of the prisoners during their intake into the concentration camp: the stripping naked, the head shaving, the assignment of numbers, and the deindividualization caused by outfitting inmates in identical clothing. Total control was implemented in the open yard, in the barracks regulations, in the long identical rows of sleeping bunks, in the marching formations, in labor supervision, and in tedious roll call drills. "The personal sphere and the boundaries of bodily distance were largely eliminated, so that prisoner society, as atomized as it seemed, at the same time meant the prisoners' extreme proximity to one another."[45] They were objects of verbal attacks and physical violence. All procedures, from intake to labor deployment, humiliated them and degraded them physically and psychologically. In addition, they witnessed or were themselves victims of violence and torture. The executions that took place were also audible.

One feature of depersonalization was the total control over the prisoners' time. While there were various limited possibilities for spending time outside of work for those in civilian labor camps and in POW camps, those in concentration camps had no such opportunity.[46] Time was structured by hustling in the morning, often hours of tedious roll calls, raid-like operations, superfluous labor, and inadequate (and always rushed) food intake. Free, unregulated time was possible for only certain elite prisoners.

During the war, prisoners were chronically malnourished and suffered from hunger. In the Kaiserwald Concentration Camp near Riga, an aphorism went around that one's bread ration could be carried away by a louse.[47] All one's senses and all one's efforts revolved around food: the inmate was in this sense reduced to his or her bodily functions. The hygienic and sanitary conditions were as catastrophic as they were degrading. They led to periodic epidemics in the camps and total quarantines, to the point that even the SS supervisors no longer entered the camp grounds. Later in the war the average survival time in many concentration camps was only a few months. Industrial enterprises also accepted without protest the constant turnover of prison laborers—that is, high mortality rates.[48]

Muselmänner—the colloquial term for "goners," or prisoners so physically and mentally drained that they lost any ability to work or communicate—became emblematic figures in these circumstances. They were regarded as beings between death and life, capable only of ingestion and excretion.[49]

For the majority of camp inmates, atomization and dissociation—the physical and psychological destruction of the individual—were a characteristic experience. Therefore, it became virtually impossible to develop any sort of camp "society" or community built around some sense of solidarity in victimhood. The high fluctuation in camp populations, frequent transports, and high mortality rates, reinforced by the frequently changing populations of the satellite camps and subcamps (*Außenkommandos*), served to reinforce this atomization during the war. Another equally important factor was the practice of categorizing and identifying prisoners through colored wedge-shaped uniform patches—from the yellow Star of David marked with "J," to red (political), green (career criminal), pink (homosexual), and many others. During the war, foreign, sometimes hostile, and often linguistically unintelligible members of many other nations were added in, mostly with red (political) wedges and various national markings.

Prisoner Staff: "Himmler's Corporals"?

Using the example of Auschwitz, Anna Pawelczynska studies which groups in concentration camps had the best chances of survival.[50] Important for survival was the type of social capital with which a prisoner entered the camp—as a political convict, as a national resistance fighter, or as a random victim of some raiding squad. Some groups—such as the "politicals," some religious believers, and resistance fighters—found it easier to find like-minded people and support in the often life-or-death critical period of settling into the routine of the concentration camp.

There were segments in the concentration camps (and in other camps) that were able to escape individual and collective dissociation. These groups were those necessary for the SS and camp supervisors to enforce absolute power. The so-called prisoner functionaries or prisoner staff (*Funktionshäftlinge*) were inmates who worked in various capacities in the "blocks" (barracks), on police or office duty, as craftsmen, kitchen help, paramedics, or nurses—often having attained the position after a struggle against rival candidates. Some individuals and groups also managed to help out fellow prisoners, but the power structure of the SS meant that these acts of assistance also involved "burdening oneself with guilt," because "the opportunities to help fellow prisoners were rarer than the pressure to act against other prisoners."[51] The victory in securing a prisoner staff position, with the small privileges ever so important for survival, inevitably separated the prisoner from other individuals and groups. The battle for these positions and their use created what Goffman described as the "underlife" of total institutions.

In the battle for positions, solidary groups or coalitions also formed. Often rivalries emerged, encouraged by the camp management as a means of "divide and rule" by pitting criminals (with green wedges) and political prisoners (with red wedges) against one another. Before the war, when the primary emphasis was on the humiliation and degradation of the inmates, prisoner staff positions were often given to criminals. During the war, because the concentration camps were supposed to serve a useful purpose for construction projects and industrial production, political and national groups (those with red wedges) found greater opportunities for advancement. The conditions in the camps, satellite camps, and work commands varied significantly.[52] One observable trend, however, is that because of their long experience and linguistic proximity, German groups—be they political or criminal—had a strong chance of getting the coveted prisoner staff positions.

The same applied to members of other Central or West European nations—Czechs, Dutch, and others. The prejudices held by SS and other supervising staff against Sinti, Roma, Jews, and Slavs, as well as against asocials and homosexuals, were often also shared by other categories of prisoners. Those prejudices were exacerbated by the close spatial proximity of the prisoners and competition for ever scarcer resources.[53]

The situation of the prisoner staff may be compared with that of the Jewish councils and Jewish police in the ghettos. Wolfgang Kirstein speaks in this regard of the concept of "shared guilt" but emphasizes the asymmetry of responsibility.[54] The execution of commands and the implementation of "order" in the accordance with the demands of the camp leader were not carried out by the camp staff alone but only with the help of prisoner staff, beginning with the camp seniority to the foreman (*Kapo*). Along with the lowest SS-Personnel, the prisoner staff often had to do the "dirty work." Prisoner staff, through manipulation of the paperwork or statistical offices, or in the medical stations, could save a fellow prisoner by allocating that person to a lighter work command or by falsifying medical records. This intervention inevitably came at the expense of other prisoners who had no relations with the prisoner staff. The Labor Statistics Office (office for the allocation of labor) in Buchenwald was responsible for drawing up transport lists for work deployment, including to the lethal concentration camp Mittelbau-Dora, where the V1 and V2 rockets were supposed to be built. On one hand, the camp leadership in Buchenwald directed incoming transports straight on to the Mittelbau Concentration Camp; on the other hand, transport lists that were assembled with the names of inmates already in Buchenwald were manifestly filled with members of prisoner groups that had no connections to the prisoner staff (in this case, Communists of various nationalities), which meant that the list of people to be sent to the Harz region, where Mittelbau was located, included mainly criminals, asocials, homosexuals, and foreigners.[55] In the labor camp at Auschwitz, the Polish underground had established itself and had attained many of the prisoner staff positions. But it did not escape the same dilemma and abandoned the Jewish resistance to save itself.[56]

In Natzweiler and in certain subcamps of Mittelbau-Dora, French prisoners at times had the highest death rates. Many of them were the "night and fog" prisoners, members of the Résistance who had been deported to Germany on Keitel's orders on 7 December 1941. In work details they, often officials or members of intellectual professions, came under the oversight of criminals, resulting in higher death rates.[57]

Solidarity communities, which, in the battle for scarce resources always led, for one's own survival, to the necessary exclusion of other individuals or groups, formed mainly when prisoners worked together for a long time—that is, in camp offices, in infirmaries, and sometimes on work crews and in factories. In isolated cases, especially in medical infirmaries, prisoners and SS personnel could come into personal contact. Exchange and corruption rings sometimes overcame spatial and social distances. From the perspective of "normal," half-starved prisoners the foremen, block elders, and other prisoner staff were agents of the SS. Himmler is said to have referred to prisoner functionaries as his "corporals."[58] On one hand, the privileges they could be granted—such as the ability to engage in sexual activity, brothel visits, and participation in leisure activities—were especially repulsive manifestations of the sometimes blatantly conspicuous consumption.[59] On the other hand, as bearers of so-called self-government the prisoner staff formed the only milieu in which resistance, information exchange, and assistance could be organized.[60]

Camp Personnel

In both the Gulag and the universe of Nazi camps, the numerical discrepancy between the camp staff and guards and the prisoners is astonishing. In both cases criminal organizations, with their uninhibited violence, had inherent potential for significant control and mobilization. The "absolute power" realized in the camps was done above all through threatened and consummated violence and killing and through the delegation of power, in exchange for minimal privileges, to a minority among the potential victims. Limitless supply meant that camp inmates could be used to their deaths, depending on the political objective, through their "productivization," either in the sense of their extermination through labor, through labor exploitation, or through "improvement." For both systems the principle of organized, unrestrained violence was regarded as a power resource. The difference between them lay in their goals.

In the concentration camp headquarters in 1943 there were around 2,500 SS members employed for a prisoner population of more than 200,000 people. In January 1945 the Camp-SS guard units totaled nearly 38,000 people, including—depending on the source—3,500 to 4,000 women supervisors. Technically, only men were allowed to be SS members; women were instead referred to as part of the "female entourage of the Waffen SS." The prison population in the concentration camps was around 714,000 people at this time.[61] Through the start of the war guards units for the concentration camps were composed of units of the so-called SS-Totenkopf. During the war they were increasingly supplemented by members of the armed forces disabled on the front, by *Volksdeutsche*, Latvians, and Ukrainians.[62] The guards were not permitted to enter the camps themselves but were used to guard the mobile work brigades.

The camp staff, as well as other prominent perpetrators of Nazi violence, came from the "center" of society. They represented the Nazi (male) wartime youth generation. They had not accepted the postwar order and often had not been integrated into it. The camp staff came most likely from the lower-middle classes, often from precarious employment situations.[63] Hostility and aggressiveness characterized the Nazi elite as well as the rank and file and those ascending the ranks of the SS. This staff was used in prisons, camps, and concentration camps and in the occupied territories—especially in the East, where the "dirty work" was to be done. Indoctrination played mostly a subordinate role. An often-cited example is the use of women as supervisors in the Ravensbrück Women's Camp and elsewhere. The initially scared, shy young women were transformed in a short time into scolding, sometimes kicking, sadistic women who modeled themselves on their supervising authorities.[64] For the men, molding took place through the practice of compulsive comradeship (in youth organizations and often in the military) where one cultivated toughness in oneself and against others, discipline, competition, and the practice of the *Führerprinzip*. In the higher offices established during the war and responsible for "productivizing" the concentration camps, elements of professionalism, toughness, and role distancing came into play. Ultimately, the result was invariably the escalation of violence against enemies and especially against *Untermenschen*. Finally, violence instigated complicity.[65]

After visiting the remnants of Treblinka's Labor Camp no. 1, the Russian journalist and writer Vasilii Grossman speculated about whether there were specifically German roots of the crime.[66] What he identified as specifically German was the recourse to barracks drills, designed with the aim not of military training but of the physical and psychological breakdown of the individual. There was also the fanatical orderliness of the barracks, the hours-long parading, the barking of commands by supervisors, the punitive exercises, mad rushing work, forced jogging or column marches, uniforms, and the shaving of the head and of the entire body. Military rank insignia were replaced by color-coded wedges. Also reintroduced were barracks traditions that had not existed in Prussian Germany since the Napoleonic reforms, such as unrestrained beatings (as had been the case in the Prussian military in the eighteenth century) and equally unrestrained shouting. Newly enacted were long-forgotten German traditions of public hangings and punishments. They were staged as spectacles on the parade grounds, always with camp inmates in audience and, from 1942–1943 at the latest, with prisoners themselves as the hangmen and executioners. In addition, there was torture in the so-called bunkers, the arrest rooms. The sadistic imagination for humiliating prisoners knew no limits.[67]

Camp ordinances actually allowed only for "regulated" violence and prohibited arbitrary attacks. After 1942 "beasts" who had been compromised by committing excesses were supposed to be replaced by "decent" camp leaders. Even if the extent of the violence was curbed in some isolated cases, once again the internal dynamic of relationships of violence emerged, working in opposition to prisoner labor productivity. In diluted form this dynamic also applied to other types of camps.[68]

Power was established through spatial separation as well as through the sharply emphasized distance between camp staff and inmates. Depending on the position, staff lived outside the camps in bourgeois or petty bourgeois idyllic neighborhoods with private houses and gardens and with more or less varied possibilities for leisure activities. In the case of Labor Camp no. 1 at Treblinka, Grossman wondered about this coexistence of nightmarish atrocity and meticulous German order.[69] The movement between the idyll and orderliness outside the barbed wire and the violence, hunger, and disease inside the fence was, in many respects, paradigmatic for the extreme form of a split personality. Rudolf Höß, with his love for flowers and animals, represents in his capacity as head of the concentration and death camps a typical example of role distance, a moral schizophrenia and dissociation on the part of the perpetrators.[70] Eugen Kogon pointed to this phenomenon as the juxtaposition of completely incompatible "chambers of experience."[71]

In the occupied East the conditions for camp staff were a little less idyllic. Compared to the misery of the surrounding population, and even more so to the camp inmates, camp staff lived in islands of comfort. Here the vision of the Germans as the master race was most genuinely realized. Elements of apartheid were more pronounced here than in Germany—also through the spatial segregation of the local population, who encountered their new masters only as servants and subalterns. Along with physical distance, standards of living also diverged greatly. In reminiscences the contrast appears repeatedly between the wretched figures of the (concentration) camps and the well-fed, well-dressed guards (and often the prisoner staff).[72]

Distance was officially maintained by the fact that any private contact between camp personnel and prisoners was forbidden—as was, as a matter of course, the exchange of any gifts or favors and, above all, unauthorized infringements. Ideology was infused less through direct indoctrination than through official orders and practices: the prisoners were cast as enemies, as threats (including to individual health), and as scum. Given the dirt, the rampant epidemics, and lice infestations of prisoners, especially in the occupied territories of the East, fear of contagion reigned, and physical contact was made with prisoners only through boots and batons. Senior camp personnel wore gloves and in any case had little to do with the prisoners. They sat behind desks in orderly offices.[73]

At the same time, the camp employees lived in a "disciplinary sphere," which meant they were also subject to military discipline and supervision and to the strict regulation of their time and behavior. Control and sanctions came both from above and from colleagues. This environment offered a sense of safety and comfort: people celebrated the same parties and festivities, sometimes even the same orgies, and lived seemingly normal lives outside the camps, with the usual family and professional concerns. This sphere, the material security of being spared from serving on the frontlines, served in some ways as a "moral shock absorber."[74]

There was an element of uncertainty for the mostly young camp personnel: control over marriage. Members of the SS and female guards were allowed to marry only after examination of their Aryan certificate and official certificate of genetic health. In short, discipline in the private interior space of the camp personnel's world correlated with excessive violence in an environment perceived as hostile, be it in the camps or in the wider environment of the occupied territories, with the ubiquity of partisans and sabotage.

THE SOVIET UNION

Camps and Forced Labor in Soviet Society

The war was the main medium that Hitler and Himmler wanted to use to transform European peoples and societies. It made possible, facilitated, and legitimized the breakdown of barriers to violence and structured the dimension of forced labor, the camp, and the extermination camps. The Stalinist system owes its origin and militant expression, however, to the First World War and, especially, to the Russian Civil War. The system then evolved during peacetime, or at least in a state of nonwar and the expectation of war.

If the Gulag was understood during the 1950s and 1960s in the context of the totalitarian model and later (and in some respects, to this day) in the context of the rapid industrialization drive to overcome backwardness and the Great Terror, other contemporary historians focus on the concentration of power in Stalin's hands, the despotic designs of his rule, and the willingness of his executioners.[75] It is indisputable that all the major repressive operations were initiated by Stalin, that he unleashed them and could rein them in or allow them to continue. Still less clearly articulated, it seems to me, is the fact that Stalin, in all the violence, always acted in accordance with a political vision in line with socialist traditions. Bolshevik authorities' understanding of socialism assumed that the system could be imposed on a resistant population. Violence and coercive measures were therefore justified, as well as the accumulation of power to the point of despotism. Socialist elements such as a centralized state and planned economy combined with the party organization to create the necessary conditions for a new type of territorial *Machtstaat*. From the 1930s onward he also mobilized patriotism in its service. Thus alongside the category of "class enemies" appeared "enemies of the people" and "enemy nations." Stalinist despotism was similar to the *Führerstaat* in that both emerged from mass movements and imagined themselves as communities of combat.

In the Stalinist system, however—taking quantitative criteria into account—the submission, intimidation of the enemy, exploitation of labor, and sometimes reeducation took precedence over physical destruction. The "liquidation of the kulaks as a class" assumed that murder and the death of kulaks would be part of the package but did not aim for their total destruction. Some camps—especially in the Far North, as in the Kolyma region, on the Igarka-Salekhard Railway, or surrounding the uranium mines—in effect practiced the same destruction through labor as the Nazi concentration camps.[76] A significant proportion of the victims who died during transport, on arrival at the new camp or exile location, or inside the camps died as part of the system-specific culture of improvisation and organizational overload and incompetence that was the model of the "epileptic" First Five-Year Plan.[77]

The handbook for the camp system lists for the 1920s–1950s a total of 476 camp complexes of different sizes and durations. In 1949 there were 67 camp complexes and 1,734 colonies.[78] There were territories outside the jurisdiction of the Soviet government and subordinate only to the camp management, such as BelBaltLag (for the White Sea-Baltic Canal), a large part of Karelia or the SevVostLag (Northeast Camp), which controlled the region at Kolyma and Chukhotka. The size and extent of the camp population changed over the years. In 1936 there were 1.2 million people in the camps and colonies; in 1940, 1.7 million; in 1953, 2.3 million.[79] During the war, camp inmates reportedly accounted for 3–4 percent of the entire Soviet labor force.[80] A 1940 card catalogue contained eight million entries of former and current prisoners.[81] Between 1934 and 1953 approximately eighteen million to nineteen million people are estimated to have passed through the camps.[82] Deported kulaks were supervised by a special police regime of the NKVD. As long as they had not been designated as dangerous class enemies, they were deported into the so-called special settlements (*spetsposeleniia*). In 1938 the number of special settlers (former kulaks) was counted at just short of a million.[83] Entire peoples, such as the Russian Germans (1.2 million), Crimean

Tatars (ca. 165,000), and many other peoples from the North Caucasus were exiled "in perpetuity." After the war, they were joined by kulaks who were purported or actual enemies of the Soviet regime and resistance fighters from those western regions annexed first in 1939 and then again in 1944, a total of 351,000 combined.[84]

The Bolsheviks started out with the claim that they would liberate both workers and labor. But by the time of collectivization corrective labor camps, corrective labor colonies, and special settlements were already embedded into a system of societal coercion. This system included the issue (or withholding) of labor books and domestic passports starting in the early 1930s, the abolition of freedom of movement for collective farmers, the tying of laborers to their workplaces in industry and administration after 1940, compulsory labor at work (for reduced wages), exile and the constant requirement to register oneself with the police in the place of exile, and, in the worst case, admission into a camp.

In 1943, in a return to a practice of the prerevolutionary period, camps were created where prisoners were assigned to *katorga*—separated from the other inmates and forced to perform especially arduous work. The impetus for this labor was to punish collaborators.[85] In 1948 so-called special camps were created, designed to house political prisoners deemed most dangerous to the regime. In 1951 ten such camps existed, with a total of about two hundred thousand inmates.[86] In addition, in 1945 a separate justice camp was established, further intensifying pressure on prisoners.[87] During the war the various institutions used work armies, whose members were deported peoples or minorities, such as the Soviet Germans. After the war special contingents—that is, military formations of forced laborers—were used by the NKVD/MVD, the Red Army, and other institutions. The filtration camps, where all Soviet POWs and civil internees were vetted for suspicion of collaboration, sent more than nine hundred thousand people who were not considered fully rehabilitated into labor battalions or special contingents of the MVD.[88]

The world of the camps expanded after the war with POWs from Germany, its allies, and Japan, who were controlled by the Main Administration for Prisoners of War and Internees (GUPVI). It is estimated that, in the hunger and supply crises during and after the war, approximately 300,000 of the estimated 3.1–3.4 million German POWs died from hunger and malnourishment, either during transport or in the camps. In 1947 there were 1.75 million POWs deployed for labor in 200 camps and 192 so-called labor battalions. Added to those were around a hundred thousand civil internees, mostly ethnic Germans from Poland, Romania, and Hungary.[89] The forced labor of POWs and civil internees was, in the eyes of the regime, part of the postwar collective reparations agreement, not part of the individual punishment that was a feature of the Gulag. Therefore, officers were not required to work during the war; after the war, when necessity required their labor, it was cast, with official pressure, as voluntary labor. Members of the Wehrmacht, the SS, and the occupation governments were sentenced as war criminals and sent to Gulag camps or into special divisions with stricter controls within the POW camps. This population is estimated at thirty-five thousand people.[90]

The Status of the Camp Population in Society

A feature of both dictatorships was the fact that most camp inmates were arrested because they belonged to certain categories of the population, not because of their individual behavior. The main exceptions to this trend would be the inmates of German concentration camps before the mid-1930s and of the Soviet concentration camps during the Civil War, as well as the camps on the Solovetskii Islands (SLON). In 1938 "counterrevolutionaries" from the Civil War period, Trotskyists, and other "deviants" were still being detained.[91] In 1948 the spectrum of enemies, in the narrow sense of the word, had expanded, especially in terms of collaborators (around 122,000 people) and members of Baltic and Ukrainian resistance movements. In the camps, there were still individuals who had been associated with the old categories of *kaery* (counterrevolutionaries, deviants, and class enemies).[92] In the narrow sense enemies of the regime were neither the so-called bourgeois specialists, tried and sentenced from the late 1920s in court, nor the masses of kulaks and permanently exiled peoples, nor even the victims of the Great Terror of 1936–1938. In the words of Solzhenitsyn, "half of the archipelago consisted of the [Article] 58ers. But politicals—there weren't any of those."[93] In his crude language he described them instead as "rabbits."[94]

The Soviet camps were part of a society with hierarchical levels of rights, privileges, and discrimination that were initially determined according to socio-moral and political criteria. But beginning in the late 1920s the social hierarchy was determined largely according to the political-economic classifications of the workplace. The "dregs" were the camp inmates and special settlers, followed by collective farmers, and many status groups in urban and rural areas with higher levels of rights and privileges. Work and living spaces were ordered through many kinds of controls, restricted (or repealed) freedom of movement, and gradated access to material goods and perks. Beginning in the 1930s Soviet society developed into a system in which status was determined through the place and type of workplace and through membership in the Party. Accordingly, one's expulsion from the Party usually preceded arrest.[95]

The public stigmatization campaigns, criminal justice, and the camps (whose existence was no secret, given the cycling of millions of Soviet citizens through them and their spatial proximity to normal workplaces), should be understood as factors that produced constant anxiety and conditioned behavior. Such was also the case when one followed the standards of "speaking Bolshevik" in public as well as in private. This situation resembled in many ways that of hostages.[96] A quip at the time laid out the situation: Soviet society is divided into three categories—those who used to be prisoners, those who are prisoners, and those who will become prisoners.[97]

The status of hostage applied even for groups who actually belonged to the elite or even to those executing the terror. This situation differs in an important way from the Nazi regime. Despite constant rivalry and conflicts over competences—totalitarian anarchy—the lives of members of the German elite or camp personnel were never threatened. In the Soviet Union, however, around twenty-three thousand Chekists (agents of the political police) are said to have been arrested and killed during the Stalin period.[98]

In contrast to the classification of peoples under Nazi rule, the categorization of Soviet citizens was, as a whole, less rigid—if due to weakness in the administration's executive management. The Soviets also selectively chose to pursue the reeducation and potential for rehabilitation of class enemies.[99] The population of the camps was composed of the "dregs" of society, but given the high turnover among camps and between the camps and the outside world, prisoners could change their status—in exceptional cases, from inmate to Stalin Prize winners, marshals, or Heroes of Labor. German scientists deported into the Soviet Union described the situation of their Soviet colleagues: having lost their freedom, they received it back—piecemeal—as privileges.[100]

"Work in the USSR Is a Matter of Honor"

In Dachau and Auschwitz the slogan *Arbeit macht frei* graced the entrance gates. Likewise, in the Soviet Union, camps were referred to euphemistically as "corrective labor camps" or "corrective labor colonies" starting in the mid-1930s. From the time of the Civil War people had spoken openly about the existence of concentration camps.[101] The 1930s concept of "correction" (*ispravlenie*) contained some of the original, still recognizable components propagated in the 1920s by Soviet judicial officials on educating offenders through labor and on having penitentiaries finance themselves through prison labor. With the emergence of large camp complexes since the collectivization campaigns, reeducation (reforging [*perekovka*], in the language of the time) was propagated in the camps. Instead of the slogan "Workers of the World Unite," newspapers in the camps paraphrased Stalin's comment to the meeting of Stakhanovite Representatives (1935): "Work in the USSR is a matter of honor, a matter of glory, a matter of bravery and heroism."[102] There were considerable funds mobilized for reeducation propaganda, to make the educational character of forced labor seem believable to the prisoners and—especially—to the outside world. Here perverted remnants of the socialist utopia of liberated labor were on display. As had been the case during the Civil War, emphases on violence and enlightenment coexisted. The propaganda of reforging was especially strong in the case of the White Sea-Baltic (Belomor) Canal and escalated to bizarre heights with public visits by Gor´kii and other writers.[103]

Prisoners of war also could not leave the camps without exposure to propaganda. In the case of German POWs the antifascist movement (*Antifa* for short) was organized at the end of the war. Its task was to engage in the political reeducation of prisoners, especially concerning the Germans' responsibility to the Soviet Union, and—quite practically—the necessity and legitimacy of forced labor as atonement. POWs had to prove themselves in competitions on the forefront of reconstruction as a way of reparation through labor.[104]

On the White Sea-Baltic Canal, incentives for inmates were incorporated in the 1930s, with food norm rations continuing until the end of the 1940s and the potential for bonus days until 1939. That is, by overachieving the norm, one could earn more to eat or shorter detention periods. Before the late 1940s, when wages in rubles were introduced, receiving food depended directly on one's performance on the job. One hundred percent fulfillment, let alone overfulfillment, of the norm was generally tantamount to overexertion and emaciation for the already weakened prisoners. Former inmates repeatedly emphasized that one's survival chances increased by *not* working to fulfill the norms, even though underfulfillment meant lower food rations.[105] With brief respites, hunger and malnourishment were everyday experiences in the camps until the late 1940s. The hunger years in the USSR, with high death rates especially in the early 1930s and during and after the war, paralleled the general nutritional conjunctures in the camps.[106] As has often been noted, death in most camps, as in exile regions, was less part of a targeted intent to kill and more of a systemic overtaxing of local authorities and administrative indifference.[107] Hunger and malnutrition remained an all-controlling factor in the Soviet camps for a decade and a half: "Hunger never gets tired."[108] Hunger was also a permanent state of affairs for most German

POWs before 1947. The physical and psychological concomitant phenomena and their consequences appear in countless memories: the rituals of food distribution and consumption, the powerful role of bread—bread as a bargaining chip, fantasies of eating and the occasional (and as a rule, secret) food excesses, the constant search for food, pilfering of food and other kinds of theft, the slowed-down movements of the body—the "*plennyi* [prisoner] walk"—the skeleton-like figures of the *distrofiki*, the loss of sexual desire, "eunuchoid frugality," and the reduction of emotions and mental activity.[109] Until 1947–1948 the figure of the "goner" (*dokhodiaga*) in the Soviet camps became as emblematic as the concentration camps' *Muselmann*.[110]

The detainees' chances of survival remained precarious until the dissolution of the camp system. After the shock of arrest, interrogation, and trial, the future inmate's depersonalization proceeded through the transit prisons to the arrival at the camp. Depersonalization occurred through the stripping away of clothes, the robbery of one's few possessions, incessant controls, roll calls, and transports in always crowded train cars. In the camps the prisoners were allotted 1.5–2 square meters each, at least according to official specifications.[111] In fact, this standard was often not maintained. Especially in the 1930s inmates had no accommodations and had to sleep on boards, in dugout pits in the ground, or in similar spots. Even the most minimal furnishings, such as blankets or other basic items, were in general insufficient or unavailable.[112] In prisoners' recollections the struggle to carve out a space for oneself played an important role.[113] The regimentation of inmates' time more closely resembled the situation in Nazi camps for *Ostarbeiter* and POWs than in concentration camps.

In the Soviet camps the vast majority of prisoners without protective networks suffered from malnutrition, hard work, isolation, and—as was the case in German camps—often from psychic dissociation and "icing up" (*oblede-nie*).[114] Former kulak children who remembered the early days of exile recalled conditions similar to those descriptions of material deprivation, with the humiliating dependence on command headquarters and the mention of mass death surrounding them and the question about whether their suffering had any sense to it. Their recollections usually did not focus, thematically speaking, on their psychological state of mind.[115]

Although the conditions in the SLON camps until the end of the 1920s resembled those of Nazi concentration camps, these and other camps later shifted to become places of punishment as well as sites of economic exploitation.[116] Before and after the war the camp personnel—now and then, at least— were admonished in the interests of economic efficiency not to taunt the prisoners. In practice, however, acts of violence were part of the daily reality.[117] That included torture, beatings, insults, binding in straightjackets or shackles, dousing with water, food deprivation, and isolation in cold dwellings.[118]

Underlife in the Camps

In the Soviet case, too, there was a marked divergence between totalitarian aspirations to power and the underlife of total institutions. The camp personnel on site—from the leadership down to the guards, the prisoner staff (in camp jargon, the *pridurki*), and the criminals—all had specific unwritten codes governing their behavior that made up the underlife of the camp. The structure and selection of personnel were similar to that in the forced labor and concentration camps under German control (that is, after Stalingrad), when economic performance was emphasized without regard to the prisoners' physical capabilities. This practice seems to be an impossible scenario only when indifference to human life is perceived as offensive, which was not the case for either side. Violence, disorganization, improvisation, neglect, illness, and mortality rates were not allowed to interfere with accounting figures and with the fulfillment of the plan and were, when necessary, even manipulated. In striking uniformity camp reports would state that between 10 and 15 percent of inmates were considered unfit for work (*slabosil'nyi*). Only during the war did that number, according to Gulag statistics, rise to 35–40 percent. Taking into account prisoners flat-out refusing to work, sometimes almost half of the population was not being put to work during the war.[119] In the POW camps, too, the proportion of those incapable of working—those held "in recovery squads"—was also very high during the war.[120]

Given the shortage of skilled labor, prisoners were used to work in the administration, and released prisoners then worked in factories, with the status of exiles. This practice was forbidden again and again by Moscow. Eventually, however, they became ready to reach a compromise regarding the practice.[121] The large camp territories at Noril´sk or Magadan were surrounded by settlements where exiles or free workers lived. They worked partly within and partly outside the camps.[122] Even craftsmen and professionals among the POWs, as well as officials, moved frequently in the Russian environs outside the camp.[123] As such, connections to the outside lay beyond the full control of the camp leadership, which meant that fraud, trafficking, falsification of labor statistics, and standardizing job performance as a "plaything of chance" were daily occurrences according to the memoirs of the prisoners and POWs.[124] Coalitions formed in the camps in this manner, as did in the later period solidarity communities, corruption rings, and silence cartels, all collectively known as *tufta* or *tukhta*—"techniques of fictional accounting of work."[125] Hence Beria's accounting of the Gulag's contribution to victory in the war and postwar reconstruction was probably to a large extent fictitious, since he silenced the victims and the loss of materials.[126]

In the Gulag camps after the war non-Russian ethnic groups also competed for prisoner staff positions. This struggle was often quite brutal. Recollections by POWs make pejorative references to such "camp elites" and "camp bourgeoisie."[127] Most Gulag prisoners could hardly gain access to these privileges and remained subject to hunger or chronic malnourishment, at the mercy of criminals and supervisors.

The underlife of the camp became a growing problem, not by chance, as the material situation of the camps improved in the late 1940s. The battle over resources and control of the barracks and zones took on dramatic and violent forms. There were shifting coalitions (always at the expense of third parties). There were not only political (ethnic) groups battling criminals but also criminals—position holders and work shirkers—fighting one another. The camp personnel (with their spies as the preferred murder victims) sometimes lost control and themselves joined the battling parties. The documents portray these conflicts as battles with camp banditism (*banditizm*). One of the earliest highlights of this battle was the so-called dog war (*suchia voina*) around 1950. The large-scale camp riots of 1953–1954 arose from these disputes and were regarded in Moscow at the time as a political signal that it was necessary to change the camp system fundamentally and dissolve its existing form.[128]

The Camp Staff

Working at a camp was not a particularly attractive job, either for the onsite leadership or for the lower-level personnel or guards. Many of the camp leaders did not take these jobs entirely voluntarily. Work assignment in camp zones often came as a consequence of an explicit or implicit relocation as a form of punishment for any sort of offense in the OGPU or NKVD. Serving in inhospitable places was made bearable thanks to extended work leave, vacation time in the South, and other perks. Over the years camp leaders could create some comforts for themselves, according to their tastes and preferences. Gradually, even in the most inhospitable places, there were theaters, choirs, and other cultural institutions staffed by prisoners. Just as Russian aristocrats had once done, the camp administration had its "enserfed" artists.[129]

Lower-level personnel and guards had to take whatever job was available.

Particularly after the war former Red Army soldiers, reservists, or "filtered" peoples who had not been fully rehabilitated were sent to serve as guards. For the lower-level staff and guards work in and around the camp was not particularly appealing. Because they often did not live much better than the prisoners, the search for additional income and susceptibility to corruption were inevitable.[130] Only toward the end of the 1930s were schools and courses set up to train for service in the camps.[131] With the establishment of the branch administrations (*glavki*), a degree of professionalism, and a higher level of participation by both free and unfree technical workers, plan ful-fillment together with research and development offices became of growing importance in the Gulag.[132] In contrast to Stalin, who wanted inmates to be treated primarily as convicts, from the 1940s on economic insights gained influence: half-starved prisoners and labor-shirking criminals were not good for increasingly sophisticated technical work.[133]

It is striking that a party administration was set up in the Gulag only in 1937. Party membership was concentrated among the higher-up administrators—more than 90 percent membership—while the average staff barely exceeded 20 percent. The lower the position in the administration and among the guards, the lower the proportion of party membership. The indoctrination of party members appears not to have been intensive. Party meetings could serve as a platform for complaints. Incidentally, there was resentment against both prisoners and "those at the top" because of poor pay, accommodation, and care.[134]

The underlife of the camp was determined by its dual function as a place of punishment and as a site of economic production as well as by the insuf-ficient penetration of control from above. It was common from the 1930s on to hand over leadership positions to "socially familial" (*sotsial'no bliz-kie*) people, meaning criminals. At the same time, one could not complete-ly dispense with skilled workers and "politicals." In daily life more physical violence probably came from criminals than from supervisors.[135] Such was the case especially when they took over functions as guards, as brigadiers, or as *desiatniki* (charged with leading groups of ten). Shouting, beatings, and robbery were then part of everyday life, because—whether malicious or indifferent—those in command were under pressure to fulfill the plan under generally poor working conditions (in terms of equipment, food, and sanita-tion).[136] But their room for maneuver was relatively large. This was also true for the POW brigadiers and their Soviet foremen or construction managers (*prorab*, short for *proizvoditeli raboty*).[137] Prisoner staff were also subject to surveillance. In 1944 at least 72,455 spies were active in the Gulag camps, and among banned or exiled workers there were over 19,000 spies.[138] In addition to hunger and hard labor, the presence of the spies created the "the greatest emotional distress" among German POWs, too.[139]

The distance among guards, camp personnel, and prisoners was usually not as great as the distance in German camps. The lower-level personnel and guards had to rely on additional income. Thus corruption chains formed between criminals and prisoner staff, including exiles working in camp industries or camp personnel. Occasional interventions from Moscow, dismissals, and arrests suppressed the worst infractions. Given the general economy of shortages, these efforts were unlikely to have a significant effect.[140] In the early 1930s, when there were still not enough security guards, inmates in outlying regions were in charge of guarding themselves. The guards, often recruited from the criminal ranks, improved their own food rations by raiding their environs.[141] (Toward the end of the war the self-guarding of prisoners was practiced even on the German side.)[142]

The camp in the first half of the twentieth century was a transitory experience that large portions of the population (especially males) had to endure: from youth camps, summer camps, training camps, and barracks to POW and forced labor camps, detention camps, and finally extermination camps, often as component parts of camp territories. Camps were institutions of both socialization and punishment and features of total war and totalitarian dictatorships. Camps and forced labor formed the dark side of the *Volksgemeinschaft* and socialism, which were supported by enthusiasm and militancy by significant parts of the population. The camps were embedded in the transformation of society—the development of the apartheid society in Germany and in German-controlled Europe and in the formation of a society organized according to stratified rights in the USSR. The spectrum of camps ranged from institutions of comprehensive control and exploitation to places for extermination through labor. The camps combined economic "productivization" with punishment to the point of "using up" the prisoners. With this combination, the criminal state gained economic advantages without regard for human life.

The organizational strength of the punitive entities is noteworthy in both systems when one looks at the relations between the guards and the guarded. A striking difference is in the relationships with one another: in the German case, a great distance was maintained from the dirty, wretched figures, and even hostility on the basis of national belonging, whereas in the Soviet Union the differences and sociocultural distances between the lower ranks were not as pronounced. Special conditioning in the form of ideological indoctrination played no major role in either case. The manifest circumstance of the containment in a quasi-military disciplinary space conditioned cruelty and indifference to suffering and death of prisoners.

Even in the system of terror, camp authorities depended on delegating the meting out of punishment and exploitation, and thus on the cooperation (and corruption) of a part of the subjugated population. Set up with life-saving minimal privileges, a heterogeneous milieu formed and secured the functioning of the camps—including the occasional self-guarding of prisoners. In the terminology of Goffman, in total institutions, too, an underlife developed. Most notably, this resulted in the occasional veto power of criminals in the Soviet camps or in solidarity and rescue operations among the prisoners.

The differences between the Soviet and Nazi camp systems should not be flattened through their comparison. In the case of the German camps forced labor and extermination sites were part of the conduct of war, with the purpose of restructuring European populations around a "Germanic" overlordship. This included a stronger (relative to the Soviet Union) program and practice of mass murder. But the Soviet side was also not free from Social Darwinist and nationalist population politics. Constitutive parts of the Soviet system were the administered famines, deportations, and special settlements. The status of prisoners in the Soviet Union, however, was more fluid than in the Nazi system of rule. This surely had something to do with the longer duration of the Stalinist regime and with the fact that most of the inmates were Soviet citizens whose reeducation, at least in theory, was not deemed impossible. Such was also considered true for the "fascist" prisoners of war.

Both camp systems blossomed and ended under the dictatorship of the Führer (or *Vozhd'*). That is, there was a connection between the leadership cult and various forms, degrees, and goals of terror in both systems.

"REPAYING BLOOD DEBT"

The Chinese Labor Camp System during the 1950s

KLAUS MÜHLHAHN

WHEN MAO PROCLAIMED the founding of the People's Republic of China on 1 October 1949 at Tiananmen Square, his words conveyed the expectation that a new age was being ushered in. The rhetoric of a New China quickly gained popularity in China and among Western observers, reflecting the widespread feeling of being part of a truly revolutionary process that was about to turn the old backward Middle Kingdom into a renewed, invigorated, and progressive socialist society. Certainly the 1950s did in fact introduce a series of policies that changed China profoundly and propelled it in the direction of a socialist system. On one hand, there can be no doubt that the new government in the 1950s pursued an active reform agenda that affected many areas of politics, economics, and daily life, reaching from land reform and state building to collectivization and a new marriage law. Through these policies existing institutions, policies, and social relations were displaced, and new structures and social practices began to emerge. On the other hand, although Mao liked to compare China with a clean sheet of paper, on which the most beautiful characters could be written, there was no zero hour, and many links can be traced between pre-1949 China and China under socialism. Only since 2000 have historians begun to look into these continuities that bridge the 1949 divide. Up to now, they have mostly studied policy goals (development, modernization), political structures (the one-party state), and foreign policy as examples of the continuities that link the 1950s with the 1930s and 1940s.[1] One additional and important area that still needs to be studied more fully relates to the spasms of violence that connect the 1950s (and 1960s) with the war period in the 1940s. In 1949 and in the early 1950s fighting was still going on in many parts of China. Various insurgencies continued to threaten the new government far into the 1950s. The new government responded to these challenges with aggressive and violent political and military campaigns. As a matter of fact, public use of violence was an inseparable part of the experience of living in New China and under socialism in the 1950s. Whether in the villages or the cities, citizens of the new state were likely, at one time or another, to witness violent scenes, which were conducted and organized by the new state against real or perceived enemies. This calculated violence was seen as necessary to defend the socialist system and overcome resistance against specific socialist policies such as collectivization, nationalization, and state control over society.

This chapter focuses on the labor camp system in Mao's China as the site where policies characterized by a combination of violence and expulsion, deliberate acts of terror, and social humiliation were carried out to deal with the "enemies of the people." The 1950s witnessed mass violence on a large scale, although this is difficult, if not impossible, to quantify. But size is not the main concern of this chapter; rather, I want to reconstruct the historical factors and contexts that allowed such a massive wave of violence to happen, with the victimization of millions of people and the involvement of large numbers of perpetrators and bystanders. My interest is in the key components of those policies, *who* organized the violence, and how the policies of violence fit into the new political system, what they looked like, how they operated, and what some of their key strengths and weaknesses were in the eyes of those who operated them. What is captured by the notion of violence here? What is to be gained from historicizing the labor camps? My intention is not to portray the Chinese Communist Party (CCP) or its leaders as evil dictators or mass murderers and explain the camps as the result of murderous fury but rather to point out the inherently contradictory dynamic of Chinese socialism and its complicated legacy. For Hannah Arendt, the frequent resort to violence by revolutionary states displayed their inherent instability and (self-perceived) lack of legitimacy.[2] Based on this observation, it would seem that the use of labor camps was itself a reflection of the weakness and fragility of CCP rule.

Mass violence can be characterized by the destruction of large segments of a civilian population, often accompanied by atrocities, which at first sight seem to be random or without purpose. Yet beyond the murderous fury of men, which we often hold responsible for such crimes, mass violence and mass murder follow a particular "rationality." They do not simply flow out of "battlefield frenzy," a term used by Christopher Browning to describe the atrocities committed by soldiers against one another in the dynamics of war.[3] Rather, they result from a policy deliberately designed to remove and annihilate groups of civilian populations (men, women, and children).

The term "mass violence" does not imply a particular technology or specific murder weapons (knives, machine guns, lethal gas, etc.) but an act or a series of acts, collectively organized, aimed at eliminating entire groups of unarmed individuals. Demanding a high level of organization, mass crimes are often the responsibility of states. It is obvious that private groups, militias, and guerrilla movements could and can commit such atrocities in their efforts to gain power. However, this form of violence becomes more effective when its organizers have particularly efficient means at their disposal: with the help of an army, a police force, administrative capabilities, and various communication networks within the population, large-scale acts of murder can be carried out.[4] At the same time, concrete images, metaphors, and a political ideology are also important parts of the modern system of state violence. According to James C. Scott, high modernism in authoritarian form lies at the root of political programs aiming at the vast reordering of society needed to effect the elimination of future conflict.[5] This utopian goal led necessarily to denial of many individuals' basic rights, if not their existence. High modernism also undergirded the type of communist modernity that was developed in the wake of the Soviet model. Maoism as a variation of Stalinism was equally influenced by some elements of this approach toward creating a new man and a new society. This chapter situates the labor camp within larger historical developments and delineates transfers of concepts and practices between the Chinese and Soviet camp systems that resulted in similarities but also differences and modifications.

Toward this end, I discuss the discourse behind the leaders' inclination to resort to violence when dealing with real or perceived enemies. Mass crimes and mass violence were carried out in two modes and by two different sets of agencies. The first mode involved mass movements and mass campaigns, organized by local party cells with the support of local state agencies. The second used law enforcement agencies. I conclude that the labor camp system played an important and systemic role in the 1950s. In response to a lack of legitimacy and continued resistance, the leaders intended to build an effective system for dealing with opponents. But this aspect has been ignored or played down in most scholarship, so the question of mass violence still awaits comprehensive and critical reassessment.

There are few comprehensive studies on the Laogai camp system. Earlier work drew mainly on published documents and memoirs, in part because of the lack of reliable archival sources.[6] The most important holdings are in the archives of the central government and the central party organizations, which remain closed to researchers. Scholars have been more successful with local archives. A large amount of previously classified materials has become available, including secret police reports, camp files, unexpurgated drafts of speeches and instructions by cadres and leaders, individual prisoner files including confessions and work reports, memoirs, letters, and oral histories. These materials shed light on the everyday operation in the Laogai camps—especially violence, work conditions, and reeducation—while the central administration of the whole Laogai system, including detailed statistics, remains elusive.[7] One of the central questions discussed in the literature is the discrepancy between the benign official rhetoric and the harsh realities of the camps. Another issue concerns the overall political or social purpose of the camp system.

THE STATE AS A WEAPON

Behind the violence that regularly rippled though China in the 1950s was a particular politico-legal discourse that shaped and justified the use of force. The leaders of the CCP viewed the state and law as tools of government and power, not as values in themselves. As such, law or the state could never pertain to values or rights existing independently of society. In the CCP's view law was not tied to ideas of justice (or fairness); rather, it was a weapon for dealing with the enemies of socialism. In the words of Mao Zedong, "The state apparatus, including the army, the police and the courts, is the instrument by which one class oppresses another. It is an instrument for the oppression of antagonistic classes."[8] The Party also rejected the idea of equality before the law. On the contrary, since law was seen as the continuation of the class struggle and a tool for dealing with enemies, a fundamental distinction should always be made between "us" or "the people" and "them"—that is, "enemies of the people." The people was entitled to participate in public affairs, but the so-called enemies of the people or counterrevolutionaries were subject to the "democratic dictatorship" of the people. In Mao's texts as well as in later official or legal documents, it remained ambiguous who was an enemy or counterrevolutionary. Over time criteria such as "backward political attitude," "historical questions," or "class background" were introduced that nonetheless were always porous and flexible, depending on the time and policy. Whereas in the beginning designated enemies tended to be outside the Party, such as Guomindang remnants and other oppositional forces, by the mid-1950s the targets shifted to groups and individuals within work units or party cells. Over the course of the 1950s vagueness in defining enemies increased, widening the extent of targeting. "Democratic dictatorship" meant that enemies or counterrevolutionaries had to be dealt with strictly and severely—differently and more violently than offenders who came from the ranks of the people. Enemies had either to be annihilated or forced to remold themselves through hard labor and become "new persons" (*xin ren*). Mao also described the latter process as "turning rubbish into something useful."[9]

Although in general the Party focused on forced reeducation, depending on the circumstances, counterrevolutionaries needed to be killed, because they "were deeply hated by the masses and owed the masses heavy blood-debts."[10] The use of violence was thus justified by popular resentment and blood debts (*xie zhai*). The latter expression frequently occurred in Mao's speeches and writing. The concept of "blood debts" was used to argue that popular indignation legitimized the Party to seek retribution and retaliation when dealing with its worst enemies. Mao also made it clear that counter-revolutionaries would still exist in China, so that future campaigns would be necessary. The socialist state had to be vigilant and could not afford to renounce the use of violence: "We cannot promulgate [a policy] of no executions at all; we still cannot abolish the death penalty. Suppose there is a counter-revolutionary who has killed people or blown up a factory, what would you say, should that person be executed or not? Certainly such a person must be executed."[11]

Revolutionary justice in Mao's thinking inevitably encompassed "exceeding the limits, in order to righten the wrongs of the old order."[12] Justice would come through heavy-handed responses, through open and violent retaliation. The punishments had to be such that they could be understood as a symbolic expression of public indignation over heinous crimes. If applied with skill, public spectacles of retribution were a powerful tool. They could be used to suppress and eliminate opponents. At the same time, when staged as public theater, the drama of retributive justice could serve as a vehicle to rally popular sentiment behind the Party's course and direct indignation toward targeted opponents. Mao made no effort to hide his notion that this should take the form of terror. Terror was not only acceptable as a necessary evil but indispensable for the revolutionary project.

At the center of this discourse is a way of thinking that originates in the binary friend-enemy distinction or, in Mao's words, the distinction between the people and the enemies of the people.[13] As a result, not only in all legal affairs but also in political matters and daily life a fundamental distinction was made between friend and enemy. Carl Schmitt identified this distinction as one of the fundamental tenets of a dictatorship.[14] For almost fifty years after the mid-1930s the division between friend and enemy framed politics and law in China in a fundamental sense, so that the whole "nation operated almost entirely on the basis of this binary divide."[15] Political and legal matters became overdetermined and overwritten by the perceived need to police and guard the binary distinction between friend and foe. The state and its agencies were seen as weapons to fight enemies and to protect the people. The question of loyalty or betrayal overrode all other concerns, opening the way for violent excesses conducted and permitted by the state. The discourse of class struggle thus framed political life: it justified and encouraged the suppression and killing of those deemed recalcitrant or viewed as impeding the course of the revolution.

MASS CAMPAIGNS, TERROR, AND REGIME CONSOLIDATION

The new government's most important lever for wielding state power against enemies was the so-called People's Tribunal. Tribunals existed alongside the regular people's courts but were ad hoc in nature and lasted only through the duration of a given campaign.[16] The introduction of the tribunals first took place in the context of the Land Reform Movement in 1950. On 20 July 1950 the Organic Regulations of People's Tribunals were promulgated. The tribunals were formed by people's governments at the provincial level or above and dissolved on completion of their tasks. The main task was "the employment of judicial procedure for the punishment of local despots, bandits, special agents, counter-revolutionaries, and criminals who violate the laws and orders pertaining to agrarian reform."[17] The tribunals were allowed to make arrests, detain suspects, and pass sentences extending from imprisonment to the death penalty.[18] The members serving in the tribunals mostly came from local party organizations. Thereafter, many of them were appointed to the regular courts on the grounds that they had received judicial training through their work in the tribunals.

People's tribunals used "mass line" devices such as mass trials or accusation meetings to dispense justice. Three formats were widely used by the tribunals: "accusation meetings" (*kongsu hui*), "big meeting to announce the sentence" (*xuanpan dahui*), and "mass trial" (*gongshen*).[19] All three forms could involve up to tens of thousands of people. They were organized in ways that would best mobilize the population and educate it through negative examples and the deterrent of public punishment. Bypassing the formal court system, people's tribunals, in cooperation with public security organs and party organizations, often carried out massive purges implementing the government's policy. Between 1950 and 1953, in the context of nationwide campaigns and movements, several social groups were singled out and isolated from the rest of society: landlords (the Land Reform Campaign), counterrevolutionaries (the Campaign to Suppress Counterrevolutionaries), corrupt bureaucrats (the Three Antis Campaign: anticorruption, antiwaste, antibureaucratism), capitalists and private entrepreneurs (the Five Antis Campaign:

antibribery, antitax evasion, antifraud, antitheft of state property, antileakage of state economic secrets), and the educational sector and intellectuals more generally (the Thought Reform Campaign).

The following example demonstrates the course of an accusation meeting held during the Campaign to Suppress Counterrevolutionaries. The Peking Municipal People's Government held a huge public meeting to accuse counterrevolutionaries on 20 May 1951. Addressing the excited crowd, Luo Ruiqing, minister of public security, suggested that some 220 criminals of the 500 or so accused persons be sentenced to death. He was followed by Mayor Peng Zhen, who wrapped up the process by saying:

> People's Representatives! Comrades! We have all heard the report given by Minister Luo and the accusations of the aggrieved parties. What shall we do to these vicious and truculent despots, bandits, traitors, and special service agents? What shall we do to this pack of wild animals? ("Shoot them to death!" the people at the meeting shouted.) Right, they should be shot. If they were not to be shot, there would be no justice. . . . We shall exterminate all these despots, bandits, traitors, and special service agents. We shall shoot as many of them as can be found. (Loud applause and loud shouts of slogans: "We support the people's government! We support Mayor Peng.") The other day, the Public Security Bureau transferred the results of its investigation to the Municipal Consultation Committee for discussion. Today those results were further discussed by all of you. You have expressed your unanimous opinion on that matter. After the meeting, we shall hand over the cases to the Military Court of the Municipal Military Control Committee to be convicted. Tomorrow, conviction; day after tomorrow, execution. (Loud applause and loud shouts.)
>
> The present accused represent only a part of the counterrevolutionaries. There is still a group being kept in jail. Moreover, there are not a few who are concealing themselves in Beijing. All the people of the municipality should rise and cooperate with the public security organs to liquidate and exterminate them (loud applause).[20]

Carefully arranged and organized as they were, mass trials and accusation meetings were "designed to concentrate free-floating public hatred of counterrevolutionaries while galvanizing support behind the regime in a highly public manner."[21] Through the organization of campaigns, the government tried to deliberately rally popular support behind the regime, extend the coercive formal and informal instruments of the revolutionary state, and vertically integrate and enhance the rule of the bureaucracy. By conducting mass campaigns in the early 1950s, the government aimed at fighting potential opposition, pacifying the country, and winning compliance and support from the populace. Many policies such as land reform, collectivization, and nationalization of private enterprises in urban areas were highly unpopular and encountered resistance.[22] Given the lack of legitimacy, the Party needed to carry out campaigns to create support. Significant personal and financial resources were set aside for campaigns that therefore had a high priority for the regime.

During the movements of the early 1950s, according to official, incomplete statistics, an estimated four million arrests were made by the police, the army, or party organs without any real involvement of the regular courts.[23] Hundreds of thousands of "class enemies" or "enemies of the people" were sentenced to death and executed. In mass trials the death penalty was carried out immediately or the next day.[24] As a rule, executions were public. The convicts were forced to kneel and then shot from behind with a single bullet. The public display of excessive violence had a profound impact on society. It showed unequivocally what the "class struggle" ultimately entailed. Millions were sentenced to imprisonment by irregular ad hoc courts, the army, or the police.[25] Opponents and real or suspected enemies were subjected to a regime of violence and terror. The CCP proved ready to employ violence and terror against its own nationals and, if deemed necessary, to substantially alter or pass over key provisions of the fragile socialist law and regulations at any time of its own choosing.

However, the scope of arrests and executions and the willingness of local cadres to participate in the movement seem to have taken the leadership by surprise. The longer movements like the land reform and the suppression of counterrevolution lasted and the more blood was spilled on the execution grounds, the more urgent grew the appeals of the central leadership to local units to exercise restraint.[26] Apparently many local actors (cadres, militia) used these movements to settle old scores with neighbors and decide long-term local conflicts in their favor.

The masses should not only watch such events but also participate actively. They should be "stirred up" (*fadong qunzhong*) and were invited to play a vicarious part in the policy imposed by the state, thus collectively reaffirming its popular legitimacy. The close and direct participation of the masses in the criminal process was to be carefully rehearsed. The numerous trials and campaigns drew in people from all sectors of society, mobilizing the rank and file of cadres and rallying them behind the government-sponsored objectives. As Julia Strauss has argued in respect to the mass campaigns, the most important audiences were the "regional and local layers of the revolutionary state."[27] It was incumbent on the central state to win over the leading local and municipal cadres on whom the center relied to implement its directives. Campaigns, mass trials, and people's tribunals therefore played a vital role in the imposition and enforcement of norms set by the government. By bypassing the formal justice system, they provided the central state with a forceful set of ideological and moral incentives to elicit compliance and responsiveness from low-level cadres and officials as well as from the general population. While the judicial system continued to serve as the organizational core of the sanctioning process, mass trials and mass campaigns functioned as flexible and informal mechanisms for the effective, direct, and rapid transmission of sociopolitical norms and the mustering of broad popular support for these norms and their enforcement.

The campaign to suppress counterrevolutionaries established a more structured form for these mass organizations and, with official encouragement, enabled them to expand their powers. By the time this campaign ended in 1953, China had 170,000 resident or work unit security committees with a mass activist base numbering more than 2,000,000 people.[28] These formed a support force for the numerically weak public security units, solving a problem that had plagued that ministry since the time of liberation. Operating under the leadership of the local public security organs, work units, villages, or towns, their combined strength allowed them to stretch across all facets of social life and protect the social order right down to the street and work unit level.

REFORM THROUGH LABOR: THE LAOGAI CAMP SYSTEM

After the People's Liberation Army captured the cities, a military-based administration imposed a new order. The new power holders had first to deal with the civil unrest that followed the fighting in many areas, especially urban ones. Consolidation and the restoration of order through the above-mentioned campaigns was the first task. The military authorities started searches for alleged war criminals, secret service agents, and collaborators in order to mop up existing pockets of resistance and any remaining Guomindang forces. At the same time, the People's Liberation Army took action against criminals, prostitutes, street gangs, and vagrants. The combined attack on military opponents and social troublemakers enabled the new authorities to enlist the popular support that was seen as essential for upholding the new order. Campaigns, work and residential committees, and public security institutions carried out their duties with great success in the 1950s and 1960s. Millions of Chinese were rounded up by the various agencies or in campaigns. Some faced immediate execution, but most were deported to remote regions for forced labor. Although the new authorities made many arrests, they still lacked sufficient facilities to house the arrested. A few months after the promulgation of the People's Republic of China, prisons were already severely overcrowded. Soon after 1949 the regime confronted the question of how to handle the enormous number of people labeled as bad elements and suspected of being hostile to the socialist cause. The answer was to build an extensive labor camp system.

It was in May 1951 that the foundations of the labor camp system were laid down. The Third National Conference on Public Security was held then, and it intended for the first time to systematically discuss the treatment of sentenced offenders and to find solutions concerning the whereabouts of those arrested.[29] Many important members of the leadership attended the meeting—a fact that illustrates the importance attributed to its discussions. Among others Liu Shaoqi gave a keynote speech, Peng Zhen made comments, and Mao Zedong personally revised the final resolution of the conference.[30] This is not to say that the "reform through labor system" (laogai) has no precursive forms; these existed in both the Jiangxi and Yan'an periods.

In his address Liu Shaoqi pointed out the significance of the problem. He told the conference that a solution for accommodating the high numbers of prisoners was urgently needed. Ways had to be found for the prisoners to be guarded, organized, reformed, and, if necessary, punished.[31] He proposed that the public security apparatus should be in charge of the prison sector. Liu furthermore suggested organizing the camps in such a way that the prisoners were given incentives to comply with the rules and to engage earnestly in labor. Those who work should be rewarded: "If one works well, give him a little reward or give him a little pay. Give him small things like cigarettes, meat, or soap to heighten his activity." Another point he made was related to the benefits of prison labor for the national economy:

> If we handle this matter well, it has many benefits. This is a workforce numbering XXX people [number deleted in the text—KM], as much as the whole workforce of Bulgaria. [This workforce] does not need insurance or wages; it can do a lot of work, can build great things. In the Soviet Union prisoners were used to build several canals. If we do this well, it has economic and political benefits. Because we did not kill them, we can let them work, and possibly they will at some time in the future turn into good people (hao ren).[32]

As the quotation shows, the Soviet Gulag was an important reference point in the discussions within the Chinese leadership. Soviet advisers were providing the Chinese leaders with detailed blueprints.[33] In this field, during the first years of the existence of the People's Republic the Chinese relied not only on Soviet advisers but also on books and articles translated from Russian into Chinese. The labor camps themselves would be China's most advanced and most socialist form of penal treatment. They would reeducate offenders and produce bountiful surpluses. Beneath the propaganda, government documents of the time show that China's camps were set up as "turnkey operations," based on Russian blueprints to the degree possible given China's relatively small budget.

The resolution adopted on 15 May 1951 was a crucial document that determined the basic organization of the Laogai.[34] One of the important issues addressed was that of the supervision of the prison sector. The conference approved the ruling that the Ministry of Public Security should oversee the whole prison sector from then on. The resolution also contained detailed regulations that mapped out the internal structure of the Laogai.[35] Convicts sentenced to five years and more should be organized in detachments (*dadui*) that were administered by provincial Laogai organs. Major production and construction projects, which were drafted in accordance with the need for national reconstruction, were all to be assigned to Laogai detachments. The Laogai detachments were, in organizational terms, tantamount to large labor camps; they formed the backbone of the Laogai system.[36] One feature of the Laogai system (an analogy to the Soviet Gulag) was that it mostly relied on self-policing (through enforcing, for instance, the division between politicals and criminals in the camps) and used few guards. Convicts sentenced to more than one year but less than five years were to be sent to smaller Laogai units administered by special districts or the counties. They would therefore remain in the vicinity of their homes and under the control of local authorities. Convicts sentenced to a prison term of under a year should work under surveillance (*guanzhi*) and remain in their units and homes. Apart from labor and production, it was stressed that the camps should organize measures to reeducate the criminals. Education in the Laogai included political, ideological, and cultural education as well as hygienic education. Good performance in regard to thought reform and labor should be rewarded with privileges up to parole, while insurgent behavior was to be punished, the most severe available punishment being the extension of one's prison term.

Finally, the resolution called for the creation of an administrative apparatus responsible for the Laogai. The public security organs at all levels were called on to open special bureaus for the administration of the Laogai facilities. The provinces and large cities should assign twenty to thirty officials to the Laogai bureaus, the districts five to ten, and the counties two to three. The regulations concerning the administrative structure are quite remarkable, in particular when compared with those of the Soviet Union. The Chinese leadership obviously did not want the creation of a separate, central administration for the Laogai, which was the system used in the Soviet Union. Instead, the existing public security apparatus was used. All large Laogai divisions or Laogai camps were thus governed by the provincial public security organs, not by any central agency in Beijing. Whereas the central agency for corrective labor camps in Moscow (GULag) was in charge of all camps, the Ministry of Public Security in Beijing had no direct command over most Laogai institutions.[37] Apart from a few interprovincial infrastructure projects, the Eleventh Department (*shiyi ju*) of the ministry confined itself to loosely overseeing the provincial Public Security Bureaus, which in turn supervised the day to day operations of the camps.[38]

From May 1951 on the establishment of the Laogai took place on a large scale. To coordinate the Laogai policy, the central government organized joint administrative committees staffed from departments such as public security, finances, water works, public construction, heavy industry, and railways at various branches and levels of the administration. The committees were to implement concrete steps for setting up Laogai institutions. An important issue discussed at the meetings was related to the Laogai's contributions to the national economy. Central government directives demanded that the Laogai institutions take over important economic tasks within the national reconstruction. This mission, of course, was also a central part of the Soviet Gulag. As noted above, Chinese leaders borrowed from the Soviet Union when insisting on the economic contribution of the Laogao. The central government viewed the deployment of Laogai detachments in water control projects (Yellow River, Huai River), canal construction, and railway construction as particularly appropriate. The central party institutions also urged local authorities to find ways to quickly transfer large numbers of prisoners to the new Laogai institutions so that the Laogai could go into operation without further delay. A few months later, in September 1951, the Fourth National Congress on Public Security was held. Again the question of imprisonment was discussed in detail.[39] Minister Luo Ruiqing stressed in his report the task of reforming counterrevolutionaries. Labor and politics, punishment and education had to be combined in the processes of the Laogai. Despite Luo's emphasis on reeducation, the final resolution primarily focused on the organization of labor in the camps. From the very outset there was tension over whether to prioritize labor or reeducation within the Laogai system. Despite a lip-service commitment to reeducation, the leaders emphasized prison labor and prison production in the early 1950s. They talked almost exclusively about the economic role of the Laogai, rarely mentioning reeducation. Here, too, the situation in the Laogai mirrored similar problems in the Gulag. Ideas of rehabilitation were initially high on the agenda of Soviet penal policy but faded quickly after the 1920s.[40]

The central government initiatives soon produced tangible results. By June 1952, 62 percent of inmates were engaged in labor. Prison labor grew to become an essential economic factor. At large construction sites, the deployment of prison labor made it possible for the government to slash the civilian workforce by about eighty thousand workers. Apart from the use of Laogai in the infrastructure projects coordinated and managed by Beijing, many provincial Laogai facilities were agricultural farms. By 1952 there were 640 Laogai farms, 56 of them camps holding more than a thousand prisoners. On a slightly smaller scale there were also mining operations and kilns. The industrial sector included 217 Laogai units in 1952, 160 of which had more than 100 prisoners. Twenty-nine used more than five hundred prisoners each.[41] By 1952 the government was operating at least 857 Laogai facilities, not including the mobile camps used for the construction of railways and canals.

The implementation of the First Five-Year Plan, which formally covered the years 1953 to 1957, provided an opportunity to fully utilize prison labor for the task of national construction on a country-wide scale. The goal was to make maximum economic use of the Laogai system. By 1954 the number of Laogai places had grown exponentially; the central government could count altogether 4,671 Laogai units. Many of these were relatively small, run by county governments or local cadres. More than 83 percent of prisoners were engaged in forced labor. Forty percent of the Laogai inmates were working on farms, 34 percent in industrial operations such as mining and heavy industry, and 20 percent in construction sites for canals and railways.

The establishment phase of the Laogai was completed by the promulgation of the Statute on Laogai in the People's Republic of China, on 26 August 1954. The text of the statute was drafted with the help of Soviet advisers. The language of the statute also suggests that the drafters were primarily preoccupied with technical issues and organizational questions.[42] Only the first two articles of the statute deal with questions of principle. Article 1 articulates the purpose of the Laogai: to "punish counterrevolutionaries and other criminal offenders and reeducate them into new persons through labor."[43] As article 2 makes clear, all Laogai institutions were regarded as "one of the instruments of the people's democratic dictatorship." This explanation of Laogai as an instrument of the people's democratic dictatorship is crucial; it represents far more than a general phrase. It should be kept in mind that in his 1949 speech Mao explained democratic dictatorship as the rule of the people (that is the alliance of workers and peasants) over the counterrevolutionary classes.[44] To exercise dictatorship over internal enemies was, as he went on to say, a prerequisite for securing the victory of the revolution. It follows that the Laogai was regarded as the state's main instrument for dealing with socialist China's assumed or real enemies. The democratic dictatorship of the people was a weapon that would deal with the enemy to ensure that the people's government could not be overthrown. At stake was not justice or fairness but the victory of the revolution. This emphasis on dictatorship and class struggle as established in article 2 carries an open connotation of being at war and thus vindicates the use of blatant violence. In seeing politics as the continuation of war, the Chinese leaders clearly followed the path devised by Leninism and Stalinism. As Minister Luo Ruiqing explained, this strategy was an "effective way to eradicate counterrevolutionary activities and all criminal offenses."[45]

The most controversial paragraph in the statute was, perhaps, article 62.[46] This article ruled that after completing their sentences, prisoners wishing to remain in the camps, who had no home nor any prospect of finding work, or who were living in sparsely populated areas where their settlement was possible should continue to be employed by the labor camps. In short, the paragraph said that under certain conditions prisoners had to remain in the camp even after serving their sentences. The crucial question was: which of the prisoners still had a home or work and were not living in sparsely populated areas? Most prisoners lost their residential registration once they were sentenced, so most inmates no longer actually had a home or work. Although the article was vague, it provided the basis for the so-called job placement system (*jiu ye*) for prisoners who had completed their terms. Released convicts were placed in jobs and residential units in or near the labor camps where they had served their sentences.[47] Their official designation was "job placement personnel" (*jiu ye renyuan*), but colloquially they were called "free convicts" (*ziyou fan*). In fact, most prisoners who were officially released after the expiration of their terms were retained in the camp as free convicts for an indefinite period of time.[48] This was one of the main features of the Laogai before 1978: only a few inmates were ever able to come back from the camps, return to their homes, and resume their civilian lives. The number of free convicts grew steadily, and in some institutions the job placement personnel even formed the majority.

Although the job placement system formally existed alongside the Laogai system, it has to be seen as an extension of the Laogai. It is evident that political, economic, and security considerations led the authorities to adopt the general policy of "keeping more, releasing less" (*duoliu, shaofang*).[49] This policy was tantamount to deporting groups of the civilian population that were regarded as enemies. It also prioritized the general economic demands of the system over specific demands for reform and reeducation. The Laogai had a constantly growing workforce at its disposal; at the same time, it ensured that counterrevolutionaries and other enemies would never again represent a threat to socialist China. This reality, however, reveals another remarkable inconsistency within the official Laogai theory. The whole Laogai was officially praised for its ability to reform and reeducate offenders, yet only a few of those offenders were ever accepted as having been fully reformed. A similar dilemma occurred in the Soviet Union in the 1930s.[50] Despite the official rhetoric of reform and rehabilitation, prisoners were de facto treated as incorrigible and stigmatized, often together with their family members and relatives.

The rapid and often uncoordinated establishment of Laogai institutions in the early 1950s created a scattered system that was difficult and costly to manage.[51] After 1955, therefore, the central government encouraged provincial authorities to merge and concentrate existing smaller Laogai camps and units. Nearly all the institutions that were created after 1955 were large-scale operations with the capacity to hold tens of thousands of prisoners. In 1955 the 4,600 Laogai units were reduced to 2,700. In 1957 this number was again reduced, to two thousand. Of these units 1,323 were industrial enterprises, 619 farms, and 71 infrastructure projects.[52] Within a few years the center of gravity shifted from agriculture to industry.

Between 1955 and 1958 the leaders came to view the Laogai as an important economic asset. They justified this view by asserting that all offenders under socialism had an obligation to contribute to the construction of the nation. It was quite bluntly stated that prisoners had a duty to produce "material riches" in exchange for forgiveness from the collective.[53] Prison labor was theoretically regarded as a means of reeducation, but in fact labor was an economic resource that the state could not afford to waste. Moreover, the emphasis on labor and production supposedly had many benefits: by gradually turning prisons into self-sufficient farms and factories, the central government could reduce its expenditure on the prison sector. At the same time, Laogai labor became almost indispensable for the sustained implementation and consummation of large-scale, ambitious construction projects that were regarded as hallmarks of what a socialist society could achieve. Prison labor took over important functions for huge infrastructure projects; it was systematically used as a replacement for work that civilian workers considered to be too dangerous or too hard. The cultivation of wastelands, the basic construction work for railways and canals, the digging of shafts and galleries for mines was regularly assigned to the Laogai workforce. Only when the strenuous and hazardous preparatory work was completed were the vanguards of

Chinese communism, the workers, brought in by the state to complete the work.

The total number of prisoners increased from five million in 1951 to forty to fifty million by the eve of the Cultural Revolution.[54] Death rates were high: Jean Luc Domenach estimated that the death rates in the camps rose by up to 10 percent annually from 1959 to 1962. The total number of deaths in these four years was probably around four million people.[55] Also according to Domenach, approximately two million people died between 1949 and 1952. At least six million victims must have died in the 1950s in Chinese camps and prisons as a result of execution, starvation, abuse, or disease. This number does not include the millions who were executed or killed outside the camps: for instance, during campaigns. These figures may be inaccurate, but we cannot ignore the fact that these estimates clearly point to mass deportations, mass violence, and mass deaths occurring in China in the 1950s.

In this chapter I have explored and addressed an aspect of the interaction between politics and society—and between the individual and the new socialist state—in the first years of the People's Republic of China that has not yet not been widely researched. It is clear that socialist China was fundamentally marked/characterized by a pervasive spread of violence. However, the modes and forms of the violence changed. The open and public use of violence in the early 1950s in the course of mass campaigns was superseded from 1953 on by a less public system that deported, exploited, and exhausted enemies in camps, mostly in remote regions. Violence continued and, of course, remained visible, yet it was somehow obscured from view. What Carl Schmitt once called the state's "monstrous capacity" to exercise the power of life and death over human beings began to fundamentally shape Chinese political culture in the 1950s. The emerging binary divide between friend and enemy led to growing polarization and politicization, which severely affected and, in fact, radicalized life in the 1950s.

How can we explain this development? The People's Republic of China had inherited indisputably difficult circumstances from previous regimes: bombed cities, broken dikes, impoverished villages, and refugee movements across the country. It had to expend an enormous amount of energy, with varying degrees of success, to reeducate, reconstruct, or eradicate, through means of coercion and persuasion, an existing world of capital and global connections. The prerevolutionary world held on in bits and pieces and resisted radical tranformation. The socialist world struggled to be born. In retrospect the early People's Republic is an era of contestation that required the invasive and even violent use of governing technologies such as thought reform and rectification campaigns. The CCP then did have to contend with the China that existed, despite growing party power or the expanding reach of the state. Above all, under these conditions of fear, uncertainty, and anxiety the Party resorted to a "state of exception" to impose its power, won on the battlefield. For Giorgio Agamben, writing about concentration camps in general, the lawlessness of the camps mirrored a more general "state of emergency." "In the camp," Agamben writes, "the state of exception, which was essentially a temporary suspension of the rule of law on the basis of a factual state of danger, is now given a permanent spatial arrangement, which as such nevertheless remains outside the normal order."[56] This statement points to the fundamentally unstable form of revolutionary dictatorship, which gathers beneath it those emergency categories while emphasizing that the state has as its defining characteristic that it transcends the borders of the strictly constitutional.

The camp regime that was established in China in the 1950s imposed forced labor and programs for reeducation. However, release from the camps was uncertain and depended on the will of the local staff. Since the prisoners rarely received specific sentences, none of them could know the length of their terms of imprisonment. The pressure to increase production and the stigmatization of prisoners led to increasing violence in the camps. Deprivation and horrendous mass deaths were the consequences. In this space outside society all human rights, civilized standards, norms, and morals were suspended. Those interned were stripped of their human attributes and, according to Agamben, reduced to their "bare lives." With this operation, then, the state power established a space where it no longer faced any limits or restrictions. In the camps the state proclaimed itself on a war footing against its internal enemies and could relentlessly wage an assault against those presumed to be hostile or dangerous. While the establishment of a regular state apparatus and system of government was accompanied by the promulgation of legal rules and procedures, the socialist regime also, clandestinely or openly, set up mechanisms allowing the Party to bypass criminal justice operations. This state of exception made possible the mass deportations of civilians and the mass crimes that occurred in the 1950s and 1960s in the People's Republic of China.

In many ways this development in socialist China followed the trajectory of the Gulag in the Soviet Union. In both camp systems there was a strong, even dominant emphasis on the economic functions of the camps, with the goal of using prison production as a factor in industrialization. High modernist thinking gave priority to economic development that was to be achieved at all costs and led to what Christian Gerlach termed "developmental violence" in the camps.[57] Common to both systems was the initial ideological prerogative of rehabilitation and a belief in the social roots of crime. Hence the intention to reforge "new people" was present in both systems. In practice, however, assumptions of incorrigibility and social stigma undermined efforts at rehabilitation. As a result, there were very high mortality rates in both systems, due to extreme exploitation of human physical labor and the ideology of class struggle.[58] The latter had an enormous effect, making the camps punitive vehicles for punishing and isolating enemies.

However, there were also at least three key differences related to specific historical circumstances that set China and the Soviet Union apart. First, unlike in the Soviet Union, there was no central Chinese administration of the camps. In the 1950s the central state remained relatively weak and was still struggling to gain control over the regions. In China the central state depended on the provinces and localities to carry out and implement initiatives. Second, techniques of reeducation and ideological remolding were very important in camp governance. This emphasis can be dated back to the Republican period, when prisoner reformation already dominated practices of incarceration. Third, whereas frenzied mass mobilization from below does in fact find analogues in Stalinism and Soviet history, it was qualitatively different in China.[59] The reason lies in the peculiar structure of authority and social control in China.[60] It did not resemble Stalinist totalitarianism, because the dynamics, though initiated by directives from above, were fueled by enthusiastic mobilization and mass participation from below. Chinese "mass line" socialism was characterized by a highly decentralized method of coercion and pervasive voluntarism among both victims and victimizers. Such mechanisms drew everyone in; no person was allowed to be a mere bystander. It systematically blurred the categorical differences between victim and perpetrator. Together these measures and technologies pushed state power in directions not seen in the periods before the revolution. In its continuing assault on the structure of feudal-capitalist authority, the revolutionary leadership was thus able to score an enormous success. The prerevolutionary class structure dwindled, and most opponents of and dissidents to the Party's policy initiatives were interned and eliminated within the first few years.

THE ORIGINS AND EVOLUTION OF THE NORTH KOREAN PRISON CAMPS

A Comparison with the Soviet Gulag

SUNGMIN CHO

WHEN NORTH KOREA collapses, its concentration camps, commonly called Kwan-li-so, will gain recognition for their massive violations of human rights, on the order of the Nazi concentration camps and the Soviet Gulag.[1] These prison camps have existed since 1945, when North Korea's state building began under the trusteeship of the Soviet Union and Kim Il-sung established them based on the Soviet model. Every event in North Korean history, from the Korean War to the dynastic power succession of the Kim family, seems to increase the scale of the camps. Today estimates put the number of prisoners in camps across North Korea between 150,000 and 200,000.[2] As the number of North Korean defectors has dramatically increased following the severe famines in the mid-1990s, testimonies of former detainees have revealed the scale and level of human rights violations within the camp system.[3] The United Nations Human Rights Council (UNHRC) passed the North Korea Human Rights Resolution in 2003 to condemn these violations. Since then, the international community has paid increasing attention to the widespread and systemic human rights violations within the North Korean camps. In February 2014, the Commission of Inquiry (COI), established by the UNHCR, published a devastating report that concluded that the North Korean government has committed crimes against humanity at a scale without parallel in the contemporary world—including extermination, murder, enslavement, torture, imprisonment, rape, forced abortions, and other forms of sexual violence.[4]

While most reports on North Korean prison camps have focused on investigating the intensity of human rights violations, relatively few studies have addressed what caused the evolution of the North Korean camp system in the first place. Why have the camps persisted through the six decades of North Korean history from state building to the recent power succession of

Kim Jong-un? How have the functions of the North Korean camps changed? What are the relationships between North Korea's political repression or economic crisis and the evolution of the camp system? What impact do North Korea's cultural factors have on the formation of camps? This chapter addresses these questions by identifying a set of factors that can explain the origins of and functional changes in North Korean camps.

The most straightforward explanation for the origin of the North Korean prison camps is that the Kim family regime has utilized the camp system as a political tool to maintain a reign of terror. But North Korean camps could fulfill this repressive role without such human rights abuses as "guilt by association" and "racially motivated infanticide," which do not characterize other labor camps like the Gulag. The former is the practice also known as *yeon-jwa-je*, which imposes punishment for political opposition or deviance on three generations. The latter refers to the practice of forcefully aborting the pregnancies of North Korean women deported from China in prison camps or killing their babies when they are born.[5] As this chapter argues, the specific context of North Korea's historical background, cultures, and traditional values explain these distinctions.

Systematic and contextualized comparison enables us to identify the distinctive nature of the North Korean case more clearly. The method of comparative historical analysis is useful in generalizing across multiple instances of a phenomenon under investigation, but it also helps us understand how unique a specific case is by analyzing the extent of similarities and differences between cases.[6] In this context, the accumulated knowledge of the Gulag, which until the end of the Cold War was as dark a "black box" as North Korea's camps now are, will allow us to extrapolate from existing knowledge about the North Korean camps. Comparison with the Gulag is a crucial tool given the lack of primary information available for a researcher outside North Korea. Most information currently available on the North Korean camps has been gathered from the testimonies of North Korean defectors. Without obtaining firsthand materials like official documents published by the North Korean government or memoirs of top officials, however, we cannot confirm why and how the Kim regime has developed the camp system in North Korea. We can attempt to fill this gap by carefully comparing the similarities and differences between the Soviet Union and North Korea and referring to the history of the Gulag in particular. Although the findings drawn from this method remain in need of confirmation, the exercise will help researchers focus their investigation when they gain access to archives in North Korea in the future.

North Korea and the Soviet Union shared similarities at the initial stage of state building but later diverged. Despite a time difference of thirty years, North Korea under the Kim family resembled the Soviet Union under Stalin in terms of its political structure: a totalitarian state under a one-man dictatorship. Like Stalin, Kim Il-sung purged many real and imagined enemies to consolidate his power, which led to the significant expansion of North Korea's concentration camps in the 1950s. However, a decade after their creation, the trajectory of the North Korean camp system clearly diverged from that of the Gulag. Whereas internal uprisings occurred in the Soviet case and the state diminished its use of camps after Stalin's death, the North Korean camps continue to spread, and human rights violations seem to worsen with each decade that passes. Soviet historians may dispute the balance among penal, economic, and political functions in the Gulag, but most would agree that those functions were present. In North Korea, I argue, cultural factors such as the Confucian concept of family ties and the idiosyncratic *juche* ideology have influenced the development of the North Korean camps more than political or economic motives.

In the pages that follow, I review the literature on North Korean camps published in both English and Korean and discuss what we know so far. Next I examine the formative stage of the North Korean camps during the state-building phase in the 1950s and its similarities to the Gulag in Stalin's era. I trace the expansion and increasing brutality of the North Korean camps in the 1960s, in contrast to the diminishment of the Gulag under Khrushchev's rule, and close by comparing the political and economic functions of the North Korean camp system with those of the Gulag and analyzing cultural and ideological factors that shape the North Korean camps in ways that are distinct from the Soviet case.

What Do We Know about the North Korean Camps?

Factual information regarding the North Korean camps appeared first in the personal memoirs of North Korean defectors in the 1990s. For example, Kang Chul-hwan had been detained in Camp 16 for ten years before escaping to South Korea in 1992, and he published a memoir in 2003. It was the first book that disclosed a detainee's daily routine and the brutal reality of the North Korean camps. Ahn Myung-chul was a former prison guard at the Hoeryong-Area Prison and had previously worked at four different camps. Ahn's memoir, published in 2007, deserves special attention because it was the first account on the operation of North Korea's prison camps from the perspective of those who control the camps.[7]

Kang's book was translated into English in 2001.[8] It successfully drew international attention to the human rights violations within North Korea's prison camps, and the US Congress passed the North Korean Human Rights Act in 2004.[9] International organizations like the United Nations Human Rights Council and human rights-related nongovernmental organizations (NGOs) also started to investigate North Korean human rights issues. Of these, David Hawk's *Hidden Gulag*, published by the Committee for Human Rights in North Korea in 2003, provides a comprehensive analysis of the operation of North Korea's prison camps based on interviews with more than sixty North Korean defectors.[10]

With increased interest in the situation inside the North Korean camps, more personal memoirs have been published in English. Shin Dong-hyuk, raised in North Korea's prison camps, escaped to South Korea in 2006. Shin's story is exceptional in the sense that he was born to inmates within the "total control zone" of Camp 14. It is currently known that the prison camps in North Korea have two separate sections: the "revolutionary zone" and the "total control zone." Prisoners in the first zone are detained for relatively less serious crimes, such as illegally listening to South Korean broadcasts. They may be released, depending on the evaluation of their progress in "re-revolutionization" or reindoctrination in North Korea's orthodox ideology. The total control zone, in contrast, is designed for lifetime confinement. The North Korean authorities regard the inmates there as politically unreliable, thus not worthy of reintegration into society.[11] From the moment of his birth, Shin was automatically regarded as an "incurable enemy" of the country and destined to be detained for life. With the help of an American journalist, Shin's *Escape from Camp 14* was first published in English in 2012 and later translated into Korean.[12] A controversy arose when Shin later admitted to the inaccuracy of his account: he was not only detained in Camp 14, as described in the book, but was moved around among different camps.[13] However, it remains true that he escaped from North Korea's prison camp system and was brutally tortured while detained there.

Based on these memoirs and a collection of testimonies from North Korean defectors, the South Korean government and NGOs involved in human rights advocacy have published a number of reports concerning the camp system in North Korea. The Korean Institute of National Unification, affiliated with the Ministry of Unification, has published the White Paper on North Korean Human Rights annually since 1996.[14] The Archives of North Korean Human Rights Record, an NGO based in Seoul, published *North Korean Prison Camps' Operational System and Human Rights Situations* in 2011.[15] This report provides perhaps the most comprehensive examination of the procedure of arrest and detention, the institutional position of the camp system, detainees' daily routines, the operational system, and human rights violations in the North Korean camps. The main focus of such reports has been to reveal North Korea's widespread and systemic human rights violations.

Concerning the reliability of information provided by North Korean defectors, the experience with the study of the Gulag before and after the opening of the archives indicates a need for extreme caution regarding certain types of information, such as the size of the prisoner population or the relative weight of different types of prisoners within that population. Although the bulk of Alexander Solzhenitsyn's reporting on the Gulag has proved accurate, it has been least reliable for quantitative issues, such as the size of inmate populations, the number of inmates released annually, and so forth.[16] Nearly all the information we hear about the North Korean camps is more similar to Solzhenitsyn's account than to the official archival materials that underpin recent scholarship on the history of the Gulag.

Despite uncertainty caused by the unavailability of primary sources from North Korea, we have accumulated a great deal of knowledge about the North Korean camps, ranging from their locations to how they are operated. First, the locations of the prison camps are confirmed by cross-referencing multiple sources of information. Many reports supplement specific locations of prison camps on the map with satellite images of individual camps.[17] North Korean defectors can then identify the guard posts, barracks, and various buildings from the pictures.

Second, the hierarchy among detention facilities has been identified. Depending on the length of the sentence and the nature of the crime, prisoners are detained at different levels of the custody system.[18] For example, Kwan-li-so is a type of concentration camp where the vast majority of prisoners and their families are detained for life. It is close to the Gulag in terms of its size and magnitude of forced labor. A Kyo-hwa-so is a prison camp where political criminals and their families serve out long periods of detention, but not a lifetime. A Kyo-hwa-so is different from a Kwan-li-so because families and friends know of the fate and whereabouts of the detained, unlike the inmates of a Kwan-li-so, whom the authorities force to disappear. A Kyo-yang-so detains political prisoners, together with felons, but the sentences are shorter than those of a Kyo-hwa-so.

Third, the institutional structure of the camps' management has been uncovered. The Bo-wi bu, North Korea's State Security Department (SSD), plays a role similar to the Cheka or Gestapo in terms of organizing and operating the camp system. Due to the Bo-wi bu's lack of manpower, the An-jun-bu, North Korea's Ministry of People's Security (MPS), provides military-trained personnel to physically guard the prison camps. Fourth, information about the daily routine of prisoners' lives inside the prison camps can be collected from North Korean defectors' testimonies.[19]

Nevertheless, there has been a striking lack of attention paid to the origins and evolution of the camp system in North Korea from a historical perspective. As North Korea has maintained a totalitarian system under one-man dictatorship, observers tend to take it for granted that the Kim regime is bound to develop its own version of prison camps to terrorize the people. The main reason for the adoption of this commonsense explanation lies in the lack of scholarly efforts to elucidate motives other than the inculcation of terror for the expansion of the camp system in North Korea. Similarly, the widespread "presentism" in research on North Korean camps, prevailing as a result of moral obligation to criticize North Korea's ongoing and systemic human rights violations, diverts attention from the need to understand the evolution of North Korea's camp system from a historical perspective.[20]

To identify the critical factors that influence the evolution of the North Korean camps, one has to trace what the primary function of the camp system has been in North Korea and how it changed over time. In the field of Gulag studies, scholarly debate has centered on the balance between political repression and economic exploitation in explaining the rise and evolution of the camp system. A similar debate can hardly be found in the case of North Korea. There have been some attempts among South Korean scholars to compare the North Korean camps with the Gulag, but they merely lay out the histories of the two cases in parallel without an analysis of similarities and differences.[21] How do North Korean camps differ from the Gulag, and how does the comparison help our understanding of the North Korean camp system's distinctiveness?

To answer these questions, we need to trace the historical evolution of North Korea's camp system and analyze its connection with political events and economic situations in the country over time. While doing this, we can compare the political and economic functions of the North Korean camps with those of the Gulag.

THE ORIGINS OF THE CAMP SYSTEM IN NORTH KOREA

In 1945, at the end of the Second World War, Moscow set up a communist regime in Pyongyang, placing North Korea under the trusteeship of the Soviet Union, which deployed massive aid and dispatched an advisory group to North Korea. Soviet support allowed the North Korean leadership to gain international recognition and to receive material support to overwhelm its capitalist rivals in South Korea. Soviet advisers in North Korea played a major role in drafting the 1948 constitution, along with numerous reform laws and ordinances.[22] The advisory group also provided Kim Il-sung with knowledge of the Gulag as a prototype of a communist regime's prison system.[23] This information came in part from Soviet security advisers dispatched by Moscow, who directly participated in the establishment of the North Korean police system—including a Soviet-born head of North Korean security, Pang Hak-se. According to archival research conducted by Andrei Lankov, an authority on North Korean history, Pang was known to have worked in police investigation and intelligence in Central Asia, possibly in Kzyrl-orda, before he was sent to Korea by a Soviet Politburo decision of 10 September 1946.[24] Drawing on his police operational experience in the Soviet Union, Pang became the leading figure in the installation of North Korea's repressive security apparatus, including the camp system.[25] Pang's case illustrates how deeply the USSR influenced state building in North Korea by transferring its political system.

In establishing a communist state, North Korea actively replicated the initial communist program of the Soviet Union after the Bolshevik revolution. The Soviets launched the dekulakization campaign in 1929 to repress better-off peasants, or kulaks, labeling them a class enemy of the proletariat. Stalin announced the "liquidation of the kulaks as a class" and executed or deported to "special settlements" two million peasants in 1930 and 1931.[26] North Korea followed suit with a nationwide land reform according to the principle of "free acquisition and free distribution" in 1946. Although execution was uncommon, the North Korean program followed and combined policies from the Bolshevik revolution of 1918–1920 and Stalin-era collectivization (as well as Sovietization policies in the USSR's western borderlands after 1939) by labeling the landlord class as the enemy, dispossessing landlords, collectivizing the land, and detaining many in new, special camps as "enemies of the revolution." The North Korean documents obtained by US forces during the Korean War identify seventeen special camps for forced labor workers established by 1950.[27] Like Soviet colonies and special settlements in remote places like Siberia, North Korea's new prisons played an instrumental role in repressing domestic resistance against the communist program to establish the dictatorship of the proletariat class at the initial stage of socialist state building.

Kim Il-sung displayed a similar leadership style to Stalin's. Both leaders utilized state repressive mechanisms, which they initially developed to ensure political transition to a socialist state, as a political weapon to purge their rivals in the struggle for power. Stalin launched the Great Terror from 1937 to 1939 to eliminate potential opposition groups, deporting or executing about a million military leaders, party members, government officials, national minorities, peasants, "social aliens," and all those identified as "enemies of the people." Likewise, Kim Il-sung began to purge his political enemies within the Korean Workers' Party in the early 1950s. He removed members of sects like the pro-China Yeon-an group, represented by Choi Chang-ik, and the "Soviet group" led by Pak Chang-wook, sending them to the camps.[28] Like Stalin, Kim Il-sung privatized the camp system as his personal instrument of terror and repression on the way to consolidating his power base.

The size of North Korea's prison camps expanded significantly during the Korean War of 1950–1953. Kim Il-sung detained large numbers of North Koreans for collaborating with US and South Korean forces in wartime. Similarly, during the Nazi invasion of the Second World War, Stalin was driven by real as well as imagined worries that counterrevolutionaries would collaborate with advancing German armies during the war. Populations living under German occupation and Red Army soldiers captured by the German military soon swelled the ranks of Gulag prisoners. In the first two years after the Nazi invasion, the combination of massive releases of prisoners to join the Red Army and extraordinarily high prisoner death rates dramatically decreased the Gulag population, but the loss of these prisoners was replaced by new detainees from the war with Germany.[29] On the very day of the German attack, the NKVD issued an order to create special camp zones tightening security over counterrevolutionaries and other especially dangerous criminals. Likewise, Pyongyang set up more concentration camps during the Korean War as the regime attempted to imprison everyone suspected of opposition, no matter how minor.

A significant divergence between the Gulag and the North Korean camps emerges in comparing their trajectory after the wars that swelled their ranks. That is, the demographic composition of inmates within the Gulag changed significantly in the immediate postwar period, with Polish and Ukrainian detainees arriving from the newly annexed western territories. Foreign prisoners, who had no semblance of loyalty to the Soviet Union, fomented fierce resistance in the later years of Gulag history. In contrast, the ethnic diversity of prisoners in the North Korean camps did not shift significantly after the Korean War, because most of the foreign and South Korean captives were released in exchange for North Korean prisoners of war.

Another factor contributing to increased resistance in the Gulag was that the Soviet Union also set up special camps in the aftermath of the Second World War to isolate and concentrate political prisoners.[30] As a result, political prisoners no longer had to struggle to survive in prisons dominated by violent felons.[31] They could coordinate a revolt against the guards in the segregated environment of political prisons, a situation that planted the seeds of the Gulag's decline.[32] North Korea also isolated political criminals in special camps, but unlike the political prisoners of the Gulag, North Korean political prisoners did not launch any organized activities, because their numbers were kept small during the war. In the years after the Korean War, however, the repressive mechanism continued to expand as Kim Il-sung continued to consolidate his dictatorship through a power struggle. Kim Il-sung effectively used the war as a pretext to purge many of his opponents and sent them to special camps for political criminals. Before consolidating absolute power, Kim Il-sung had to compete with the Soviet and Yanan factions—backed by the USSR and China, respectively—as well as a faction drawn from the Workers Party of South Korea (WPSK). In August 1953, during the Sixth Plenum of the Korean Workers' Party Central Committee, Kim Il-sung first moved against the WPSK and arrested Pak Hon-yong, then the foreign minister in charge of planning a coup. Pak's trial was accompanied by the arrest of other members and activists of the former WPSK, with defendants being executed or sent to prison camps.[33]

The contrast in the two camp systems' postwar trajectories does not belie the similarity in their political origins. Both were part of grandiose programs to restructure society by purging counterrevolutionary forces on a national scale. Both became political tools to imprison the dictators' personal enemies as they struggled for power. And war was an exogenous factor that changed them both, largely in similar ways. These similarities reflect strong Soviet influence and North Korea's conscious efforts to replicate the Soviet system.

THE GULAG SYSTEMS DIVERGE

Even before Stalin's death, it can be argued, the groundwork for the demise of the system of mass incarceration in forced labor camps in the Soviet Union had begun. A series of prisoner riots, including the forty-day uprising at Kengir, raised questions about the long-term viability of the Gulag.[34] Furthermore, the Gulag camps were clearly turning into economic burdens rather than economic assets. The declining productivity of forced labor, coupled with shortages of food and other necessities in the country and the financial costs of running the camps, forced political elites to question the economic viability of the Gulag.[35]

Stalin's death in March 1953 and his successor's decision to move beyond Stalin's legacy allowed the Soviet state to resolve the explosive burden of the Gulag system by closing many prison camps. Nonpolitical prisoners received amnesty right away, and most of the political prisoners were released in the mid- and late 1950s. The largest releases of political prisoners occurred in the lead-up to and aftermath of Khrushchev's 1956 "secret speech" denouncing Stalin's policies.[36] Some traits of the Gulag system survive in the Russian penal system today, but it no longer functions as a dictator's personal tool of political repression and massive labor exploitation.[37]

By contrast, North Korea's camp system continues in its seventh decade. Although the riots in the Gulag, which had no North Korean counterpart, had a strong impact on the different fates of the two camp systems, the nature of the succession to power in each country also affected their divergence. Kim Il-sung's cult of personality intensified in North Korea under his rule and that of his son, Kim Jong-il, through the 1980s. Although the Second World War gave rise to a major period of expansion of the Gulag and its population reached its greatest extent in the early 1950s, North Korea's camps grew as Kim Il-sung required new and more detailed checks of people's loyalty. Pyongyang launched a political campaign to reclassify the entire North Korean population according to a new social classification system, *songbun*.[38] The regime undertook a three-year period of examination in 1967 and subsequently classified the entire population into three political groups: a loyal "core class," a suspect "wavering class," and a politically unreliable "hostile class." According to one account, it assigned some seventy thousand people to this "hostile class" and sent them to prison camps in remote mountains.[39]

Kim Il-sung also launched another large-scale purge targeting the elite of the Gapsan faction at a meeting of the Central Political Committee of the Korean Worker's Party in March 1967. Beginning in the mid-1960s, when North Korea faced security challenges as its relationship with China deteriorated during the Chinese Cultural Revolution, several Central Committee members criticized Kim Il-sung's policy calling for the simultaneous development of heavy industry and national defense and the expansion of Kim's cult of personality.[40] Since many of those arrested had served as county officials across the country, the purge left vacant two-thirds of government positions below the provincial level. North Korean defectors have testified that the camp system expanded suddenly in the 1960s, with more prison camps being established and more detainees pouring into the camp regions. Specifically, Camp 18 opened in Buk-chang in 1961 and Camp 13 in Jong-song in April 1964. Camp 13 had some five thousand detainees, but as the number quadrupled, it was divided into Camp 12 and Camp 13.[41]

Having eliminated every shadow of threat to his power with the camp system and put the majority of citizens on high alert, Kim Il-sung reorganized the internal security apparatus. With the adoption of a new constitution in 1972, Kim Il-sung ordered the creation of a separate secret police organization and named Kim Pyong-ha to head the State Political Security Department. The new organization created new prison camps in the Kae-chun and Chung-jin regions. Most suspected political prisoners were relocated to these camps, and human rights abuses increased.[42]

Kim Il-sung's consolidation of power in the 1970s provided political stability for Kim Jong-il to launch a similar campaign in the 1980s and early 1990s. At his first public appearance at the Sixth Party Congress in October 1980, he was elected a standing member of the Politburo, secretary of the Secretariat, and member of the Central Military Committee, signaling his rise to the status of heir apparent.[43] Establishing a second cult of personality, Kim Jong-il also began to control the security apparatus. As the dynastic succession proceeded, some elites showed signs of protest or dissatisfaction, and Kim Jong-il expanded the camp system again. According to a North Korean defector who escaped in April 1982, some fifteen thousand people were sent to political prisons in 1980–1982, charged with opposing the plan for the succession, and Kim Jong-il opened four more prison camps.[44]

The pattern of challenge, suppression by the regime, and large-scale purges repeated throughout the early 1990s. In 1992, for example, the State Security Department uncovered a plot by a group of disaffected North Korean military officers to carry out a coup on 25 April during the parade commemorating the sixtieth anniversary of the founding of the Korean People's Army (KPA).[45] According to Choe Chul-hwal, a former colonel in the KPA who defected in 1995, after the attempted coup Kim Jong-il issued instructions for a massive purge of the officer corps. Between October 1992 and June 1994, North Korean authorities arrested or executed nearly 300 of 370 high-ranking military officers and sent the officers' families to Political Criminal Detention Center 16.[46]

From the mid-1990s to the early 2000s, a dramatically changing security environment posed serious challenges to the North Korean regime. The collapse of the communist bloc and China's "betrayal" when it established diplomatic relations with South Korea in 1992 created a sense of isolation in North Korea. The end of the Cold War prompted Pyongyang to keep a closer watch on North Koreans abroad, such as students and diplomats, whom it suspected might question the legitimacy of the Kim regime after observing people's loss of confidence in their governments in Eastern Europe and the Soviet Union. Indeed, detainees from these groups in prison camps increased in this period, most of them charged with "ideological crimes."[47] There is no clear definition of what constitutes ideological crime. The term represents the arbitrariness of North Korea's legal system, the sole purpose of which is to remove potential opponents of the Kim regime.

Although Kim Il-sung's death on 8 July 1994 did not destabilize the camps, the camp system appears to have stopped expanding in the 2000s in response to increasing attention paid by the international community to human rights violations. Pyongyang officially denies the concentration camps' existence. Some prison camps near the border area were closed and the prisoners relocated to other camps.[48] However, no evidence indicates that these measures have led to the freeing of prisoners or to a decline in human rights violations. On the contrary, the government takes these measures to conceal its rampant violation of human rights. The ideological contest with democratized South Korea continues to challenge North Korea, and the Kim regime needs to retain a hold on people's loyalty. The third generational succession of power from Kim Jong-il to Kim Jong-un in 2011 motivated Pyongyang to sustain the camp system. Consequently, the regime has strengthened the authority of North Korea's security and surveillance apparatus, and the latest estimates suggest some 150,000 people are in the remaining five political prison camps controlled by the SSD.[49]

The Political and Economic Functions of the Soviet and North Korean Camps

The origins of the Soviet and North Korean camp systems share common features in that they were used as political tools by Stalin and Kim Il-sung to maintain their reigns of terror. The camp systems diverged when Khrushchev's denunciation of Stalin led to the demise of the Gulag, whereas the dynastic transfer of power within the Kim family supported the camp system's continued existence. In economic terms, fierce debates have raged over whether the Gulag played an important role in driving expansion. Evidence of whether the North Korean camps played the same role as the Gulag in mobilizing a large-scale labor force for the purpose of national industrialization, however, is scant.

There is no doubt that the Gulag economy made significant contributions to national projects like the construction of the White Sea Canal during the early phase of Soviet industrialization, and significant numbers of Gulag prisoners participated in railroad construction, extraction of coal, and hydroelectric projects.[50] During the Second World War, the Soviet Union intensified the exploitation of the Gulag labor force to meet an increasing demand for military supplies.[51] Therefore, one can argue that the Gulag economy's involvement in labor-intensive national projects confirms that economic motivations played a primary role in the expansion of the Gulag.

However, some scholars argue these projects may not have been decisive.[52] Anne Applebaum, for example, suggests that the shipping route from the Baltic to the White Sea did not prove to be so urgent after all.[53] Oleg

Khlevniuk, a leading authority on the history of the Gulag, also argues that it is not always clear how important these projects, built by prisoners at great sacrifice, were: it is impossible to evaluate the economic contribution of the prison camps in terms of capital investment.[54] Certainly, the Gulag burdened the economy more than it contributed in the years leading up to the dissolution of the system of mass incarceration.[55] Major politically motivated episodes like the 1937–1938 mass shootings also call into question the notion that the Soviet regime aimed first and foremost at the simple utilization of forced labor for economic purposes, since a large portion of the hundreds of thousands executed were able-bodied men, many of them qualified specialists.[56] Applebaum concludes that the Gulag's purposes were to suppress the smallest manifestations of opposition and strengthen the personal power of the supreme leader.[57]

Ultimately, the debate as to whether political function or economic performance explains the Gulag is a chicken-and-egg problem. Analysts who believe that political repression drove the establishment of the system argue that Soviet leaders only later recognized the economic utility of labor forces extracted from the prison camps. Those who stress the role of economics argue that, from the start, Soviet leaders intended to mobilize massive labor forces to develop remote areas that had adverse weather and tough terrain. They argue that economic needs exacerbated the political purges. Resolving the issue of which intention came first and which second is beyond the scope of this chapter.[58] Both sides acknowledge that the Gulag mobilized its labor forces for national industrialization projects and thus played a significant economic role.

The data suggest that the North Korean camps have not contributed to the industrialization of North Korea in the same way as the Gulag did to the USSR. The expansion of prison camps in North Korea correlates positively with the power consolidation and succession of the Kim regime. But the North Korean economy declined from the early 1970s to the mid-1990s, then collapsed even as the camp system expanded, which suggests either a negative or an insignificant relationship between that expansion and North Korea's economic development. While North Korean defectors' testimonies often indicate that prison labor forces have produced a variety of small commodities like groceries, garments, and furniture, the evidence suggests that Pyongyang has not mobilized prisoners for grand construction projects comparable to the White Sea Canal in the Soviet Union.[59] Instead, the location of each prison camp chiefly determines its industry. For example, in mineral-rich areas prisoners mine. In other places they work in agriculture or with livestock.[60] The camp economies in North Korea appear to concentrate on producing a variety of commodities for the country, then on meeting their own needs.[61] The scale of North Korean camps' contribution to the national economy appears to be far from comparable to that of the Gulag.[62]

Given the size of North Korea's territory compared to that of Soviet Union, the need for grand construction projects such as the White Sea Canal or the development of a vast area like Siberia do not exist in North Korea. Although some North Korean defectors have cited rumors of prisoners being used to construct facilities such as dams, underground tunnels, or nuclear and other military sites, the economic impact of these projects probably does not match that of the Gulag on national industrialization in the USSR.[63] Instead, North Korea could mobilize a large-scale labor force among the masses in the same way as China did during its Great Leap Forward. North Korea launched the *Cheon-li-ma* campaign in 1957, signaling the start of rapid industrialization using mass mobilization.[64] It mobilized all available labor from every industrial sector under the slogan of "One for All, All for One." Given the scale of mass mobilization, the country's small size, and its high population density, it seems likely that the North Korean government has not mixed political prisoners with North Korean citizens whose contributions the regime terms "heroic" or "revolutionary." Although archival data may one day shed light on this question, the chances that North Korean camps have matched the Gulag in their economic contribution to national industrialization seem slim.

In short, compared to the Gulag, the expansion of North Korean camps does not appear to be driven by economics. Despite the similar political motivations that led to the creation of a camp system, the prison economy has less significance for North Korea than it did for the Soviet Union. Although the development of one-man dictatorship coincides with the expansion of prison camps in North Korea, it remains unclear what factors other than economic function have sustained the camp system and led to more brutal human right abuses. To explain these distinctive features of the North Korean camps, we have to take into account the effects of traditional culture and locally developed ideology on the evolution of prison camps.

CULTURAL AND IDEOLOGICAL FACTORS IN THE NORTH KOREAN CAMP SYSTEM

Korean culture accords particular importance to blood ties. In fact, North Korean politics expresses Korean social tradition in almost every respect, which distinguishes it from the political culture of the Soviet Union. For example, Kim Il-sung referenced Confucian concepts like filial piety (*hyo*) to parents and absolute loyalty (*chung*) to the fatherland rather than the communist concepts of class antagonism and class struggle, which Soviet leaders invoked together with socialist patriotism and loyalty to the state.[65] By elevating the Confucian values of the orderly family to the national level, Kim Il-sung conceptually transformed the whole North Korean society into a single united family, with himself as the father and the Korean Workers' Party as the mother.[66] This approach directs the people's filial piety and absolute loyalty toward the supreme leader and the party-state apparatus. Human rights are regarded as a reward bestowed by the fatherly leader.[67] Stalin's cult of personality also ratified the notion of the leader as a fatherly figure, formulating the economic and social connections through which citizens received ordinary goods and services as gifts from a generous leadership.[68] But in North Korea, the relationship between the supreme leader and his subjects appears to be more closely tied in the imagined connection of bloodline within one family. Such Confucian emphasis on family values has facilitated the expansion of the camp system and the brutalization of human right abuses in North Korea.

The distinct features of *Yeon-jwa-je* (guilt by association) and racially motivated forced abortions demonstrate the influence of the emphasis on family values. *Yeon-jwa-je* is based on the ancient belief that descendants of political dissidents are likely to inherit subversive ideas and to avenge their parents if not eliminated. Although there was a stigma attached to relatives of the repressed in the Soviet Union, Stalin famously pronounced in 1935 that "a son does not answer for his father," in reference to the children of the disfranchised.[69] In contrast, Kim Il-sung directed the elimination of the seeds of dissidents through three generations in 1972.[70] North Korea therefore sends extended families to prison camps along with convicted political criminals. The recent purge of Jang Song-taek in 2014 extended to associates and relatives, thus confirming that the *Yeon-jwa-je* system is still applied in Kim Jong-un's North Korea.[71] This practice sheds light on the institutional dimension of the North Korean camps' dramatic expansion at every conjuncture of North Korea's history.

North Korea's cultural obsession with purity of blood within the family has also facilitated the systemic practice of forced abortions and infanticide.[72] Since the disastrous famine of the mid-1990s, the human trafficking of North Korean women for forced marriage with Chinese farmers has dramatically increased.[73] When the Chinese police discover these trafficked women's illegal status, they are repatriated to North Korea, where the government consigns them to the camps. Several North Korean defectors have indicated that forced abortions terminate any pregnancies among such women to remove "Chinese seeds" on North Korean soil.[74] No evidence clearly points to similar crimes in the Gulag in a systemic fashion and on the same scale as North Korea.[75]

North Korea's cultural emphasis on family and blood has contributed to society's dehumanization of camp prisoners as "nonfamily members." Convicted traitors to the fatherly supreme leader and motherly party suffer a fate worse than convicted murderers: complete expulsion, with no hope of a return to society. The North Korean class system may have been another determining factor in this difference, which also reveals a sharp distinction between North Korea and Soviet society under Stalin.[76] As noted above, North Korea classified fully 30 percent of the population as a loyal "core," while registering 40 percent as a suspect "wavering" and 30 percent as a politically unreliable "hostile class." In contrast, in the Soviet Union, only 3.5–3.9 percent of all potential voters were *lishentsy* (disenfranchised) in the 1920s and early 1930s.[77] As a result, the vast majority of North Koreans have to live with the fear that their loyalty is closely monitored by the regime at all times. In this kind of social structure, the position of the camp prisoners is the worst. At least the "hostile classes" are still considered part of normal North Korean society, but the prisoners are not even included in the social pyramid. Their alienation and powerlessness thus exceed that of "counterrevolutionaries" within the Gulag. Simply put, North Korea does not perceive camp prisoners as fully human. The guards of prison camps are deliberately trained by the North Korean authorities to view the detainees in such a way. In the sense that detainees are deemed completely unworthy of living as human beings, North Korean prisons are more like Nazi concentration camps than the Gulag. The sole criterion of discrimination among a single ethnicity is not communist ideology, as in Cambodia's killing fields, but perceived loyalty to the Kim family.[78]

North Korea's *juche* ideology can also be identified as a cause of extreme human right violations in the prison camps. *Juche*, literally "self-reliance," is a crucial part of the North Korean mentality and its development. In the aftermath of the Soviet-China conflict and North Korea's frictions with these two countries through the 1960s, Kim Il-sung decided to abandon Marxism-Lenism and adopt *juche* as the official ideology of the party at the Fifth Party Convention in November 1970.[79] The three pillars of *juche* are maintaining independence in ideology, self-reliance in the economy, and self-defense in national security. Under its influence, North Korea has become increasingly nationalistic. The regime expands the *juche* ideology with the concept of an "organic society," portraying North Korea as a unified sociopolitical life form in which the supreme leader, party, and the masses are connected by blood ties. The supreme leader plays the role of the brain, and the masses constitute the body and limbs. The masses have to obey the leader/brain; the body and limbs cannot survive without him. Camp prisoners are thus perceived as disconnected from the unified body of the organic society, not worthy of life. This logic normalizes their death in prison camps and permits great brutality in human rights violations.

Under Soviet-style communism, the class struggle defines the working people and their enemies. Only the proletariat is fully entitled to human rights, and the government can legitimately deprive the bourgeoisie and imperialists of their rights.[80] However, North Korea has departed from this Marxist view and turned its back on class rights. The practice of worshipping Kim Il-sung as a benevolent ruler contradicts what Marxism preaches and instead favors the Confucian concept of benevolent government.[81] *Juche* is a loyalty-based form of social stratification that has replaced class consciousness; North Korea officially abandoned communism when it amended its socialist constitution in 2009. Loyalty to Kim Il-sung has become the sole criterion entitling a person to human rights. It is the indigenously developed *juche* ideology, mixed with the elements of Confucian culture, that has had the greatest influence on the evolution of the camp system in North Korea.

The North Korean camps have survived for more than sixty years, twice as long as the Gulag and fifteen times as long as Auschwitz. This chapter explains the historical evolution of the camp system in North Korea by comparing it to its model, the Gulag. Following Stalin, Kim Il-sung used the camp system as a political tool to intensify his reign of terror. Stalin's death and Khrushchev's subsequent rise to the top soon led to the demise of the Gulag. In North Korea, in contrast, the scale of North Korean camps expanded during the hereditary transfer of power. This chapter finds that while political and economic functions can largely explain the Gulag, cultural factors have influenced the evolution of North Korean camps in a way not evident in the USSR. The Confucian emphasis on hierarchical order within the family and filial piety, combined with the idiosyncratic *juche* ideology, has shaped North Korea's distinctive camp system. Absolute loyalty to the Kim family is the sole protection against arrest, and cultural notions also facilitate the arrest of three generations within families. Culture and ideology have thus given the camp system a life of its own beyond the role of a repressive mechanism.

The case study of North Korean camps raises profound questions about the relationship between totalitarianism and concentration camps. In her seminal book on the origins of totalitarianism, Hannah Arendt argued that the concentration camp was the "true central institution of totalitarian organizational power, in which propaganda has become as superfluous as humanity itself, and the extermination camp the monument to the totalitarian regime's ideological consistency."[82] In addition to what Arendt identified as the general imperative of spreading terror, concentration camps in Nazi Germany and the Soviet Union in practice were oriented to other, overriding purposes. Nazi extermination camps, most obviously, were designed to implement the genocide of European Jewry, and the Soviet leadership greatly expanded the Gulag when it embarked on forced industrialization and monumental construction projects. By contrast, the North Korean camps seem to have no practical function other than isolating potential dissidents and spreading terror within society. Instead, cultural factors have shaped a distinctive logic: as supreme leadership is passed down through three generations, political criminals should also be punished for three generations. The cultural emphasis on lineage and purity of blood, reinterpreted as political ideology in the name of *juche*, has facilitated the practice of forced abortion and infanticide within the North Korean camps. These features of the North Korean camps are not designed to serve any functional purpose. The continuation of such practices implies that the expansion of prison camps itself probably reflects the traditional culture and specific traits of a locally developed ideology. As such, the system may continue far longer than any other of its kind.

The comparison between North Korean camps and the Gulag not only illuminates the particularity of the former but also offers new implications for the study of the latter. While this chapter finds that Confucianism has influenced the evolution of the North Korean camp system, cultural factors influencing the treatment of prisoners remain largely unstudied in the case of the Gulag and penal systems more generally. The relative weight of political and economic factors in shaping Gulag history has been a subject of scholarly debate. No scholar of the Gulag would dismiss cultural factors as wholly insignificant, but culture can be analyzed more causally, not merely assessed for its meaning.[83] In general, cultural factors deserve equal attention when investigating the repressive institutions of authoritarian regimes as the cause of their development.[84] In particular, the impact of Confucian culture on the treatment of detainees within the Chinese variation on the Gulag, the Laogai, could be another subject for future study, especially in comparison with the North Korean case. A better understanding of the historical origins and evolution of prison systems is essential for those attempting to address human rights violations in general, and in the case of North Korea in particular.

JUDITH PALLOT

I BEGIN BY comparing two women's descriptions of their transportation to prison.

Sometime later they rudely woke us at night and ordered us to ready ourselves for departure. They put us in vans with the logo "bread," literally jammed us in, so we could hardly breathe. The van began to move. The air became so stifling that several women fainted. . . . The van stopped, and we were put on cattle carts outfitted with plank beds. On the floor, in front of the doors was a small hole—our toilet. The plank beds were made for two people. For those who were thin, it was not that bad, but for the bigger women there was very little space. Soon the train started. We were given herring and bread, and a bucket of water. The trip was exhausting and we lost count of the passing days. Nobody knew where we were being taken. At last on dawn of one day the train stopped and we were taken out. The station sign said Pot´ma, so it was in the Mordovian republic. . . . What a picture it was! A line of women of various ages surrounded by a convoy of young soldiers, walking along a forest road. Behind them several carts with their belongings. The line seemed endless. It was a whole train. We walked for a long time. There were rest stops, when we ate some bread. We were very thirsty. If one had to go to the toilet, it was done without any shame, right there, in the crowd of women. (Liudmila, 1937)[1]

We didn't know where we were going. We were herded into these cells to wait for the convoy to arrive and collect the *matrioshki*. They took us to the station; it was cold, winter, and we were left in these *voronki* in the freezing cold for one and half hours waiting for the train. Then the train came; first they took one load, then another—men, and then the women. There was a four-person compartment, but they put ten of us in, along with our cases. Ten people there, all with bags in the compartment . . . we traveled like that on top of one another the whole way. Some young girls were traveling with us; they went further; we were all together even though they were juveniles . . . HIV- and tuberculosis-infected should have traveled separately, but we were all in together . . . we were only allowed to go to the toilet every twelve hours. They gave us prison rations—a jar of dried potatoes and a jar of oats but no hot water . . . it was a nightmare. . . . And the guard was some young man, and he told us we had to entertain him, tell him jokes. It was just awful . . . so demeaning. . . . There was one girl who had a very high temperature, but the convoy said she was putting it on. She was dripping wet with sweat all the way there, and they wouldn't let her go to the toilet alone—you had to be accompanied. But she took two steps and fell, so they just pushed her back in. (Sonia, 2007)[2]

The first quotation is taken from the memoir of Liudmila Ivanovna Granovskaia, arrested in 1937 and transported from Leningrad to Mordovia to serve a five-year sentence; the second is from a women prisoner whom I interviewed in 2007—transported more recently from Moscow, also to Mordovia, to serve an eight-year sentence. The circumstances of these two women were different: Liudmila was a political prisoner, arrested as a wife of an enemy of the people, while Sonia was sentenced for drug dealing. The context of their punishment also differed. Liudmila Ivanovna was not protected by Russia's signature on the European Convention on Human Rights, and after her release she was exiled in northern Russia. Sonia, in contrast, benefiting from an amnesty introduced to relieve prison overcrowding in the early 2000s, was allowed to return home in 2008, there to await her partner's release from his twelve-and-a-half year sentence, also for drug dealing.

There is a compelling similarity to these women's stories of penal transportation; they both experienced it as humiliating, demeaning, and as a denial of their individual personhood, the markers, as we shall see below, of "harsh punishment." The reason why prisoners in the Russian Federation today, like their predecessors, have to endure lengthy transports is the inheritance of a penal estate designed to disperse offenders to peripheral "spaces of punishment." The Russian penal system has a distinctive geographical division of labor that was laid down during the years of the Gulag and carried forward to the present day by the choices made in the decade after Stalin's death about which "islands of the archipelago" to retain. It consists of pretrial facilities located in metropolitan centers and "correctional colonies" in

Figure 14.1. Sentry point at a Mordovian camp. Photograph © 2016 Judith Pallot.

which convicted prisoners serve their sentences, distributed in predominant-ly extraurban, remote locations, many clustering in discrete zones in periph-eral regions.[3] The facilities in which prisoners are held have been rebuilt since the 1930s–1950s; barracks containing dormitory blocks are generally now brick rather than wood, washrooms have been brought inside and concert and sports halls and churches added, but the basic plan is much the same as in the Soviet era. Internal colony space is divided into administrative, pro-duction, and domestic zones, and the whole area is enclosed within perime-ter fences, topped by barbed wire and watchtowers (fig. 14.1).

Sonia's sufferings during her transportation to the correctional colony hint at a much deeper and problematic Gulag inheritance. It turns out that principles of prisoner management have also been handed down to the pres-ent time. These include a collectivist approach to living arrangements and to rehabilitative interventions, the compulsory use of prison labor, reliance on prisoners' self-organization for a variety of housekeeping tasks, and dis-ciplinary practices such as mutual responsibility, competition, and prisoner-on-prisoner informing. These are underpinned by a pervasive militarism and notoriously harsh "penal backup." If the Gulag inheritance is obvious in as-pects of how people are punished in Putin's Russia, there are echoes linking both Liudmila's and Sonia's experiences to more distant penal practices originating in the self-regulatory peasant commune and *volost'* (township) court, and in the punitive powers of the gentry (*pomeshchiki*) and imperial Russian state. The principle of joint responsibility (*krugovaia poruka*) used to ensure the payment of taxes by the peasant commune, for example, has been used in the penal context by imperial, Soviet, and post-Soviet states to punish the collective of prisoners for the shortfalls of the individual, whether the issue has been fulfilling a work target or keeping a bedside cabinet tidy. Despite shifts in penal policy after the revolution, in the immediate post-Stalin period, and between 1984 and 1993, the pillars on which the current Russian system of punishment is constructed have remained remarkably constant over time.[4] As I argue here, one result is that the Russian Federation has entered the twenty-first century with institutions and practices that keep it at the harsh end of the punishment spectrum.

Modernity and Russian Penality

In this chapter, I discuss how continuities in punishment forms in Russia can be understood by asking why particular institutions that were used in the past have been preserved, even though their original rationale may have long since passed. The answer favored by the Russian authorities is the familiar *perezhitki* (remnants) argument. Negative legacies of the Soviet system of punishment, so this argument goes, will be removed as Russia continues along a path toward global best practice; the reason why, twenty years after communism's collapse, this convergence has not yet taken place is the cost of reform, a rise in crime associated with the "transition," and institutional obstacles. Critics analyze the situation differently. Insisting that continuities reflect the incomplete democratization of post-Soviet Russia, they maintain that remnants of the Gulag will not be excised until Russia is properly democratized. The extreme version of this argument is that of the human rights activist Lev Ponomarev, who labels today's penal system a neo-Gulag.[5]

Both arguments are consistent with modernization theory. Applied to the history of punishment, modernization theory holds that punishment is an adjunct of some form of legal or rational domination within the broader totality that is modernity, its showpiece the prison. In the classic formulations of Weber, Durkheim, and Montesquieu, modernity is marked by a tendency toward ever milder and welfare-based systems of punishment. This is because restitutive approaches and civil remedies are better suited to market-oriented and contract-like relationships than penal regulation and criminal punishment; in the modern state the goal is the reformation of the offender, not the destruction of the body. It follows from such reasoning that the more despotic and less democratic the state, the more harshly it will punish its citizens. We know that late imperial Russia saw the beginnings of a modern penal system, including its essential features of the individualization of punishment (punishment fitting the person, not the crime), prisonization, a retreat from exile, a centralized penal bureaucracy, and reformation through work and individual reflection. In the agricultural colony on Sakhalin Island, the Russian Empire had its equivalent of the Pénitentiare de Mettray; in the Kresty, built according to panoptic design by the architect Antony Tomishko and run according to the Philadelphia system, it had its version of Pentonville. The urban-based prison had established its foothold in Russia in the half-century before the revolution, and as Michael Jakobson has shown, progressive ideas about individualization and rehabilitation informed early Bolshevik thinking about punishment, even as practice was taking the Soviet penal system in more sinister directions.[6] In terms of classic modernization theory, what happened thereafter was an interruption of normal progression toward a modern welfare-oriented system of punishment. Official historiographies accept this argument with the qualifier that, notwithstanding the "excesses" of the Gulag, the underlying trajectory in the Soviet period was progressive.

Poststructuralism provides an alternative teleology, with the prison, in this case, the carrier of modernity's aspiration for order and a methodical appropriation of space. Best known are the ideas of Michel Foucault. I will not rehearse Foucault's arguments about the rise of disciplinary power or how it is critiqued. For Foucault, prison is not about retribution, deterrence, or the imposition of legal sanctions but, rather, is the exemplar of the prioritization of order in all industrial societies. The purpose of the penal technologies that Foucault describes in his influential *Discipline and Punish: The Birth of the Prison* is to destroy the autonomous self, control the dangerous classes, and provide models of ever more subtle and pervasive modes of regulation to diffuse through society.[7] Although in this work Foucault was primarily commenting on the nature of power in the whole social body, few historians of penal systems can ignore his observations about the rise of the prison. His borrowing of the archipelago metaphor would suggest the Soviet experience as integral to Foucault's theoretical schema, but his treatment of the Soviet Union was inconsistent.[8] In Foucault the Gulag appears both as a pre-enlightenment mechanism of punishment and as bourgeois penal practice, though in respect of the latter he insisted that terror and tough punishment were evidence of the failure, not the zenith, of the modern disciplinary order.

Foucault's ambivalence about the USSR notwithstanding, his excavation of the capillaries of modern power has provided historians of Russia with suggestive insights about how order was maintained in the Russian Empire and the Soviet Union. Among historians of imperial Russia, Andrew Gentes is the most overt Foucauldian, attempting to fit the tsarist system of exile into the "punishing the body" and "disciplining the soul" binary, and using Foucault's theory of governmentality to describe the self-regulatory "counter-communities" of convicts, Decembrists, brigands, and bureaucrats that the exile system created in Siberia.[9] Exile does not, in fact, figure prominently in Foucault, yet in various forms and labeled in different ways, it has been a defining feature of Russia's punishment culture from the earliest times up to the present.

The centrality of "regulation by exclusion"—or what has variously been described as "excisionary violence," "expulsion," "gardening episodes," "deportations," banishment, and exile—in achieving disciplinary order surfaces in recent analyses of the Soviet period. The kulak and ethnic deportations are obvious cases, but recent research uncovering the "mass operations" has shown how pervasive was this form of social control.[10] More generally, the enumeration, categorization, and statistical description of the Soviet population and the state's elaborate system of surveillance speak to the emergence of biopolitics in the USSR. There are elements of Foucault's analysis that resonate strongly with what we know about power in the Gulag. Ideas about panoptic surveillance have informed some analyses, such as Maria Los's suggestion, strongly influenced by her reading of Hannah Arendt, that conditions in Stalin's camps allowed the emergence of "enhanced panopticism"—a form of "totalitarian surveillance-orientated bio-politics."[11] The labor camp was not panoptic in the classic sense but was based on comprehensive mutual surveillance made possible by communal living and labor. Los labels this form of panopticism "enhanced" because it goes beyond "the internalization of the all-seeing eye and the habit of self-policing" by making each prisoner also aware of being "potentially viewed by others as a secret eye of the system."[12]

Foucauldian perspectives challenge, but are not incompatible with, the more familiar political economy explanations for the rise of the Gulag and the punishment modalities with which it was associated. In political economy explanations, following Georg Rusche and Otto Kirchheimer's Marxian analysis, punishment has the purpose of meeting the pressing needs of the state.[13] The nineteenth-century exile system was, accordingly, a response to imperial Russia's pressing need to settle the peripheries and secure borders and the Gulag to the Soviet state's need to mobilize resources. The point about such explanations is that the penological content of a given punishment form is subordinated to another function.[14]

Modernization theory as the frame for understanding the historical diversity of punishment forms has been widely criticized by sociologists and historians of penality. The critique is relevant to my task here of understanding continuities in Russian punishment to the present time. First, although they may explain in general terms shifts in punishment modalities over time (such as from public execution and torture to prisonization), theories of modernity fail adequately to account for differences in punishment forms among modern societies. As measured quantitatively and qualitatively (that is, by the number of offenders incarcerated and how well they are treated), prison regimes in modern societies exist along a mild to harsh spectrum, with Nordic "exceptionalism" at one end and Anglophone "excess" at the other.[15] Second, differences among countries do not map onto a more-to-less democratic spectrum, as modernization theory would predict. The greatest anomaly is the United States, which possesses the harshest of punishment regimes yet is a well-developed democracy. Third, rather than following a trajectory toward ever milder and restitutive punishment forms since the 1970s, punishment in many Western democracies has become more punitive.[16] Foucault's theorization of diffuse modes of penal control, ironically, coincided with the punitive turn in Western societies, marked by an explosion in prison populations and the abandonment of many of the postwar welfare principles.

In relation to all three criticisms of modernity's account of punishment, it is worth noting that the initial emptying of prisons that accompanied the collapse of the USSR and Russia's political transition to a form of democracy, was followed by such an expansion in the prison population that in the mid-1990s Russia displaced the United States in the top spot globally for the rate of imprisonment. With 475 prisoners per 100,000 population at the end of 2013, Russia remains among the top ten, together with a clutch of more overtly authoritarian regimes.[17]

The "Cultural Turn" in Penology and Its Relevance to Russia's History of Punishment

The contradictions between theories of modernity and punishment practices noted above have focused penologists' attention on the ways in which punishment is mediated by culture. Rather than searching for utilitarian explanations for punishment forms, a new generation of penal sociologists views punishment as an irrational act founded in ritual. Attention is focused on its emotional and affective aspects. The cultural turn in penology is associated, in particular, with the prison sociologist David Garland, who has drawn attention to the ways in which punishment is shaped by "penal sensibilities" reflecting a broader societal ethos and concerns. These sensibilities are deeply embedded in national cultures and transmitted from one generation to the next, even though social, political, and economic contexts can change.[18] Garland pays particular attention to penal agents—the people responsible for administering punishments—whose "commonsense practices" are constitutive of distinctive "penal cultures." Prison officers operate within frames of reference that normalize and rationalize particular beliefs about their work. The domination of group norms over the individual's own perceptions and behaviors—the hallmark of total institutions—was reinforced in the Soviet Union by the concentration of prison institutions in enclosed "zones," which created a social environment made up predominantly of other prison officers and their families. In these spaces "commonsense practices" about how to do the job of being a prison officer have been passed down from the Soviet period, in some cases, from one generation to the next in a single family.[19]

The scope of today's penological scholarship is extremely broad. In addition to understanding punishment forms as grounded in cultural values and specific sensibilities, analysts have studied penal institutions as sites of ritual performance and cultural production that have diffuse cultural consequences above and beyond any crime control effects they may produce. The principal exponent of this more hermeneutic approach is Philip Smith, who rejects outright functional theories of punishment and of modernity as the driver of penal change.[20] Smith insists that punishment is as much about poetics as about power; his is a dramaturgic, semiotic, and religious theory of punishment in which its material architecture is simultaneously the domain of mythology. He illustrates his ideas with detailed analyses of the principal icons of "Western" punishment—the guillotine, the chain gang, the electric chair and lethal injection, the prison and panopticon. The equivalents for Russia would be the windowless Stolypin carriage attached to the end of railway trains that transports prisoners between penal institutions; the wooden fences, watch towers, and barracks of the labor camp; and the iron bars and slamming doors of the metropolitan isolator (as in the atmospheric opening sequence of the television serial *Zona*). The task of the historian of punishment is to excavate these punishment forms for the protean cultural categories running through and under them. Following Émile Durkheim, Mary Douglas, and Mikhail Bakhtin, Smith identifies these as the codes underpinning all social life: the binaries of order and disorder, purity and pollution, and the sacred and evil.

Contra Foucault, in Smith's schema, the experts who invent punishments are not engaged in a process of producing ever more rational and detached means of reforming criminals (or, in the USSR's case, the more efficient use of their labor) but in responding to public fears about disorder, pollution, and indignity. Central to his argument, therefore, is societal reflexivity over the criminal justice process: penal practices are shaped by the to and fro of statement and counterstatement between center and Bakhtinian periphery about the appropriate treatment of offenders. The pivotal role of dialogue in Smith's penology makes it difficult to apply his ideas to the shifts in punishment forms in Russia, where penalties associated with "incorrect" readings of the messages in official discourses have been high and the state's power to close down debate almost unlimited. Even so, punishment forms in Russia have been the subject of discursive battles; the official image of the Sakhalin penitentiary colony as a paradise where "corn and watermelons grow" was destroyed by Chekhov's powerful counterimages of the colony as a joyless, living grave.[21] At the height of the Stalinist repression, laughter, jokes, and carnivalesque inversions deconstructed hierarchies and challenged official discourses.[22] Soviet society in the 1950s was able to make its feelings known about penal policy in an "epistolatory outcry" prompted by the tattoos, verbal outbursts, criminality, and contagion of returning prisoners.[23] Other players on the periphery—the varied ranks of people involved at all levels in administering punishments, for example—also could let their views be known about the state of affairs in the Soviet Union's prisons through institutional channels. The input of the periphery into shifts in punishment forms in the Soviet period cannot, therefore, be discounted.

Following the collapse of the USSR, there has been a sea change in the dialogue between the center and the periphery about the state of Russia's prisons. Public awareness of conditions in penal institutions is high, as crime and punishment are discussed in print and broadcast media and on the Internet. Former prisoners and their relatives make frequent appearances on television discussing the criminal justice system, prison-based soap operas attract large audiences, and "true crime" books and journals have wide circulations. In the popular representations prisons appear as repressive, barbaric, and anachronistic or as houses of fun. Familiar tropes—that prisoners live better than people on the outside and that "the thief belongs in jail"—exist side by side with YouTube videos of guards beating juvenile offenders, critical reporting of the deaths of high-profile prisoners, and memoirs that "tell the truth" about incarceration in Russia today.

Few penal sociologists today would disagree that punishment is a communicative process that has to be decoded by situated actors, but they would hesitate to discount the role of contingent economic and political factors or the impact of new surveillance technologies on the development of penal policy and practice. It is easy to agree with Garland that an analytical framework for understanding modern punishment forms is one that embraces *both* culture and power, *mythos* and *techne,* meaning and machinery, and that allows for cultural meanings to be shaped in local usage, as well as transcendental cultural imperatives.[24] Such a multifaceted approach is particularly relevant to Russia, where the institutions of the criminal justice system have been called on to fulfill functions and attain goals beyond the penal realm. Indeed, historians have tended to emphasize the nonpenal functions of Russia's systems of punishment, so that the penal—understood in the twentieth century as having the triple purpose of retribution, incapacitation, and rehabilitation—has tended to be relegated to the background. Since the turn of the twenty-first century, histories have gone a long way to redress this balance by probing the everyday practices of incarceration and engaging with the Gulag's puzzling contradictions.[25]

Reading these histories, I see scholars grappling with the consequences of understanding the Gulag as, first and foremost, a prison. All punishments inflict suffering; that, after all, is their purpose, but penal sociology tells us that they do this in different ways, with different purposes in mind and different consequences. Historians of punishment in Russia have yet to address questions of why specific punishments were chosen above others, and what explains the longevity of some and the only temporary appearance of others. It is here that cultural penology's focus on the link between punishment and the social can help overcome the gaps and inconsistencies in the account that modernization theory gives of the shifts in punishment forms over the long term. It does this by drawing attention to the learned practices of the people responsible for administering punishments, the relationship between "penal sensibilities" (of elites, experts, and society at large) and penal policy, and the deep cultural rootedness of the meanings vested in punishments.

HARSH AND MILD PUNISHMENT FORMS

Here I need to digress to explain what I mean when I refer to "harsh punishment," because I argue that one of the enduring features of penality in Russia is that it inflicts a high degree of suffering on prisoners. Since Gresham Sykes wrote his pathbreaking work on the society of captives, penologists have attempted to classify punishment forms according to their inherent harms or pains.[26] Prison regimes that permit inmates to work, allow visits on a regular basis, satisfy prisoners' basic needs, provide comfortable and safe living quarters, give access to education and job training, supply opportunities for recreation and entertainment, and allow them to exercise their civil rights can be said to be mild. By contrast, enforced idleness, exposure to violence from other prisoners, arbitrary treatment by guards, loss of civil rights, restrictions on free speech, low levels of amenity, lack of physical and mental care, solitary confinement, and sensory deprivation are all features of harsh penal systems that intensify imprisonment's pains. Fundamental to harsh punishment is degradation—the treatment of prisoners in ways that make them feel diminished, lessened, or lowered and deny their individual personhood. There are many forms of degradation; extralegal punishments such as torture are obviously degrading, but so too are more symbolic forms like forcing prisoners to wear uniforms, placing them in cages for their court appearances, depriving them of privacy including for the performance of intimate personal tasks, shackling them, and making them walk in a stressed position. These are among the everyday practices of the criminal justice system in Russia today.

It is axiomatic that conditions of detention in the Gulag were harsh and that many punishments meted out were extralegal. But not all were, and it is these that bear examination for what they might reveal about society's broader ethos and moral concerns in relation to punishment. Historians of Germany have pointed to the continuities in the use of probation and amnesties during the Third Reich that formed the building blocks of the moderate penal system that emerged after the war.[27] In Russia it is difficult to find equivalents, even if the most extreme forms of extralegal punishments are bracketed off. The progressive proposals discussed by penologists in the first decade of Soviet rule were mostly stillborn, and it was the concentration camps, forced labor, and executions of the Red Terror that provided the models for the Stalinist labor camp.[28] But harsh punishment did not begin with the Bolshevik revolution; exiles to Siberia were subjected to humiliations, deprivations, and torments that were out of proportion to what was necessary to cleanse metropolitan society of deviancy and populate Siberia. Bad treatment evidently did not offend the masses' sensibilities, as peasants turned out to mock and ridicule their compatriots en route to transport (*etap*) stations.[29]

In a recent comparison of the United States and Continental Europe, James Whitman locates differences in the harshness with which the systems treat their offenders today in the historical relationship between punishments and social hierarchy.[30] Whereas from the eighteenth century in Continental Europe, punishments were "leveled up" so that common criminals came to share the same nondegrading and dignified punishments traditionally enjoyed by high-status offenders, in the United States egalitarianism was achieved by "leveling down." Over the course of the nineteenth century, Whitman argues, the Anglo-American world attacked high-status punishments in a process that was associated in complicated ways with slavery and has left the United States today lagging behind other developed countries in the way it treats prisoners. This thesis is suggestive when it comes to Russia, where in contrast to its predecessors, the Stalinist state's pursuit of penal egalitarianism was ultimately achieved, as in Anglo-America, by leveling down punishments to the lowest common denominator, with the result that degradation, humiliation, and lack of respect for offenders was generalized to all prisoners. Now, when the Russian Federation has to administer punishments that are consistent with international conventions for the humane treatment of prisoners, the tendency is for the system to seek the maximum conditions of confinement permissible under these norms.

Already we have seen in the narratives of Sonia and Liudmila Granovskaia that the experience of transportation was/is degrading. The similarity of the two women's narratives is remarkable not just because of the fifty years separating them and the fact that today's Russian Federation does not remotely resemble Stalin's USSR, but because the two women came from very different social classes. I am not arguing that there is a direct comparison between the Gulag and Russian prisons today, or with prerevolutionary exile. The point I am making, rather, is that particular carceral arrangements inflict harms that may transcend historical settings. Listening to prisoners' talk today can draw attention to punitive aspects of the everyday in the Gulag that have hitherto been overlooked. It can also point to received wisdoms about the degree of inhumanity associated with different punishments that bear reexamination. In what follows I discuss penal exile and penal collectivism—two institutions that have historically defined Russian punishment—excavating them for their cultural meanings and examining current prisoners' talk for the clues they contain about how they were experienced in the past. I draw on interviews conducted for two research projects, the first in 2007–2010 focused on women prisoners and the second, ongoing, on prisoners' relatives.[31]

"Transportation Was, in Itself, Punishment: The Punishment of Exile"

Penal historians understand exile and prisonization as separate punishment modalities, perpetuating a binary that originated with Jeremy Bentham, for whom the transportation of offenders to the colonies was the prison's antithesis.[32] The idea of exile (and its alternative forms and or synonyms, expulsion and banishment) as a distinctive disciplinary form was extended by Foucault in his metaphorical portrait of exile and madness—"the ship of fools"—where he describes the victim suspended in a barren wasteland between lands that can never be his own.[33] Today, penology understands exile and prison as compatible opposites rather than alternatives, but the analytical distinction is, nevertheless, maintained in contrasting concepts of mobile and fixed exclusion, each with its own characteristics.[34] But exile is more than merely removing people from the metropole—the excision of the mutilated or civilly dead body from the larger social body. It is always critically about what happens to people at their destination. Convicts transported to the New World became indentured laborers and worked their way to freedom, but they also were confined in barracks, put to public works, or incarcerated in penitentiaries.

The distinction between exile and other punishment forms runs also through the history of Russian penality, even though exile was associated with hard labor under conditions of fixed exclusion.[35] In the minds of legislators, the distinction between the various categories of penal labor and exile in Siberia to which offenders could be sentenced may well have been clear, but villagers referred interchangeably to compatriots sentenced to jail or penal battalions by *volost´* courts as exiles and prisoners. In a modern parallel, Russians receiving custodial sentences today understand this as involving being sent a long distance from home and having to endure a painful journey to reach the destination colony. The struggle of successive penal reform commissions in the second half of the nineteenth century to maintain the legal and conceptual distinctions between exile and hard labor is reflected in the scholarship on penality in imperial Russia; *katorga* has been described by one historian as a system *including* prisons but not as prisonization per se, for example.[36] Solzhenitsyn similarly is informed by a vision of exile as a "pure" punishment form, bemoaning its degradation by katorga when, in reality, it was always constitutive of it. It is these sorts of confusion that may have led Foucault to suggest that the French *relégation* was the inspiration for the Soviet labor camp; as Plamper observes, he had failed to understand the carceral nature of katorga.[37]

For all the new Bolshevik state's claim to be developing a socialist penal system, the concentration camps set up during the Civil War and Red Terror to isolate and use the labor of political opponents provide a link between the tsarist exile system and the Gulag, carrying forward the idea that society could be cleansed by the physical removal to places outside the city of undesirable elements (Lenin's "harmful insects, swindler-fleas, and wealthy bugs").[38] In the 1930s the criminologist F. P. Miliutin built on this practice in articulating the principle that serious offenders should not be confined in the "home provinces" or those with a clement climate but should be shipped east where the climate itself "will assist in hastening re-education."[39] As the Gulag expanded into the geographical margins, any prisoner, regardless of status, stood a high chance of being transported long distances to serve sentences, followed by a period of exile, in hostile environments.[40] The principle was reasserted in 1961, when strict-regime colonies were statutorily required to be located far from population centers. Today the criminal correction code exempts convicts sentenced to special- and strict-regime colonies from the provision that prisoners should be held in their own oblast.

The best of the empirical scholarship on the Gulag has gone a long way toward deconstructing the boundary between exile and imprisonment. We now understand that camp inmates who earned "nonconvoy" status could spend long periods outside the confines of the camp, while exiles and deportees shared many of the experiences of prisoners.[41] In his analysis of the Gulag in Kazakhstan, Steven Barnes treats camps, colonies, prisons, and internal exile as a single punishment system, and evidence of the merging of camps and special settlements reinforces Kate Brown's view of the USSR as composed of a spectrum of carceral spaces.[42] As these works make clear, the treatment of people expelled to the peripheries did not necessarily map neatly onto their legal status.

Collapsing the boundary between exile and imprisonment for the 1930s–1950s has implications for understanding Russia's subsequent penal history. Rather than administering a "long overdue" death blow to the system of exile, the dismantling of the Gulag after 1953 witnessed the merging of mobile and fixed exclusion into a single punishment form that we may label "in exile imprisonment."[43] The past half-century has revealed the practice of sending people away *as* and *for* punishment as a deeply sedimented response to criminality, social deviancy, and political opposition in Russia, notwithstanding the ending of mass deportations after 1953 and the removal of exile from the repertoire of punishments available to the courts after 1991. Cultural radicals like Philip Smith would understand "in exile imprisonment" as a powerful signifier of the Russian state's attempt to purify society of evil, pollution, and disorder. The very public sending of Mikhail Khodorkovskii, Platon Lebedev, and Pussy Riot to distant colonies reveals punishment in Russia to be a highly communicative process, intently transmitting the message that social disorder can take malevolent forms that require the symbolic penal response of exile.

THE "TERRORS OF THE TRANSPORT"

Transportation, understood in the penological sense as a system of expulsion or exile, necessarily involves prisoners in long journeys. Benthamite penal reformers understood that even short journeys to the penitentiary created a space for prisoners to reflect on and regret their actions, so that they emerged from "the terrible torture" of physical transportation transformed. For Foucault also, the "cell-carriage" was a site of panoptic processes.[44] Historically, prisoner transportation has also been accompanied by the standard degradation rituals of confinement—including poor food rations, barking dogs, surveillance, flow control, and loss of self and autonomy—which are integral to punishment, regardless of whether the destination is a prison, a penal colony, indentured labor, or a special settlement.[45]

In her popular history of the Gulag, Anne Applebaum puzzles about the Stalinist prison transport: it was, she declares, "the most inexplicable aspect of life in the Gulag" and a "puzzle almost as hard to understand as the camps themselves."[46] It is possible to explain the cruelty of camp commanders or interrogators but "far more difficult to explain why an ordinary convoy guard would refuse to give water to prisoners dying of thirst, to give aspirin to a child with fever, or to protect women from being gang-raped to death."[47] Solzhenitsyn is similarly puzzled, although he provides an explanation in the convoy guards' boredom and injured pride.[48] The observation I have is that the cruelty of the transport is puzzling only if transportation is viewed functionally, as a means of moving prisoners from A to B. If, rather, it is understood as integral to the punishment of offenders, its cruelty is less puzzling. Mark Finnaine argues in relation to the eighteenth- and nineteenth-century transportations from Britain to Australia that the deterrent effect of the "terrors of the transport"—the uncertainty of the voyage and indeterminate fate—was the factor that made transportation such an attractive penal option for the British authorities as an alternative to the death penalty.[49] The cruelty of the transport had been a feature of prerevolutionary exile, when convicts wore iron fetters, were subjected to long marches, rested in poorly constructed transit prisons, had a restricted diet, and were denied medical services.[50] By the dawn of the twentieth century, the "commonsense practices" associated with the job of convoy guard were well established; these evidently did not include treating prisoners with dignity. Subsequently, it is unlikely that there were more than small shifting baselines in the guards' established rules of behavior, routines, habits, and certainties. The Convoy is among the least visible of the departments in the Federal Prison Service today and has remained on the margins of reform initiatives.

In response to a question I put to a former prisoner in the spring of 2013 about why in the twenty-first century the transport has to be such an ordeal, I received the unequivocal answer that it is because that is its purpose. He went on to list the familiar terrors: "You are absolutely unsettled; you do not have any stability; you are in motion—and—you have these searches . . . always these searches . . . on the transport you can't access any of your own food . . . you have to eat what they do or don't provide—that's all suffering. At the same time, you are surrounded by people you don't know. So it's a very nerve-racking environment. After all, you never know where you'll end up—so that's why it's punishment."

Another interviewee, also a former prisoner, was convinced that prison transports are designed to break prisoners before they arrive at the colony:

> You see, they are already victims, broken and therefore compliant with the regime they find there [in the colony]. This contemptible system means that the person who is humiliated just wants to escape, for it to stop. She comes, shall we say, like fresh meat; those who have been through it once know what's going on, and they hate it but do nothing, they do nothing. Why? Because it's a vicious circle, you understand? That is, when she arrives in the colony she is already done for. Her personality is already broken, she's lost her reason. (Marina, interviewed 2009)

We have no evidence that convoy guards are under instructions to make the transport an ordeal, but there are established rituals that appear to be designed to demean. I would include the requirement that prisoners run from prison van (*avtozak*) to Stolypin carriage, which may involve dodging the convoy guards' batons, and the withholding from prisoners of information about destinations: "In the first place, they don't tell you where they are sending you. . . . We were in the dark about it, and when they fetched us for the transport, they didn't mention it. It's not talked about. I was told that it's a secret. You get ready, and you go on transport, and that's it" (Liuda, interviewed 2009).

In defense of practice in the United States, Russia's comparator, the transport of prisoners to penitentiaries generally takes place swiftly and prisoners know where they are going. The process of moving prisoners long distances does not have to be punitive. In Russia it is and always has been.

"In Exile Imprisonment" as Harsh Punishment

There is a striking similarity between the descriptions current prisoners and ex-prisoners in Russia give of their feelings about transportation and the anxieties expressed by refugees, asylum seekers, and other displaced people who are expelled from their homes or sent into exile. It is a feeling that, as described by Solzhenitsyn, previsions the "living death" of Giorgio Agamben's *Homo Sacer*: "Here we see that the threat of exile—of mere displacement, of being set down with your feet tied—has a sombre power of its own, the power which the ancient potentates understood, and which Ovid long ago experienced. Emptiness . . . Helplessness. A life that is no life at all."[51]

Prisoners' talk today contains many unconscious references to exile. This is from a woman serving a twelve-year sentence, responding to a question about distance:

> It's just that it's emotionally easier if you are in prison in a familiar place. You know, they bring transports with women who don't even know where [this town] is. We have women here from all over. They can't even imagine where they are and what sort of place this is. They know it's somewhere in the North, but they have no idea of where precisely. Yes, for them, it is very difficult, they don't understand anything, it's as if they've arrived in a foreign country . . . they think they are in a strange land. (Marina, interviewed 2009)

The words of prisoners today confirm that it is correct to consider being sent "out of region" as transportation in the historical, penological sense. The time taken, circuitous routes, and the suspension of all communication with home create in prisoners a sense of estrangement that underlines their physical separation from all that is familiar. It also creates an impaired sense of geography. For juvenile women, the prison transport is often the first long journey they have taken. As an example, one sixteen-year-old in the L´govo Colony, Riazan´ oblast, interviewed in 2007, had been brought from Ukhta in the Komi Republic—a distance of well over 1,000 kilometers. The two-month-long journey had intensified her sense of being "far away" several-fold, though she could not express how this made her feel as eloquently as Solzhenitsyn. It is for good reason that the seventeenth-century name for the miserable, overcrowded waystations in which Russian convicts spent their nights en route to exile was in time generalized to embrace the whole process of transportation. Despite attempts by the current penal service to expunge the vocabulary of exile from discourses about the penal system—by replacing *etap, etapirovanie,* and *ssyl´nye punkty* with *konvoi, konvoirovanie,* and *tranzitnye tiur´my,* the old formulations remain in popular usage among penal personnel, prisoners, and the wider population.

Further evidence of the normalization of the idea of "in exile imprisonment" is in the way that the Decembrist uprising has shaped a distinctive cultural and symbolic narrative that has been employed to describe the experience of penality in the twentieth and twenty-first centuries. Today it surfaces in self- and societal representations of prisoners' relatives as *dekabristki.* Quintessentially the symbol of a devoted wife, in the twenty-first century the Decembrist trope has crossed the class and family-status divide, so that it is used as an appellation by anyone who has a relative in prison.[52] These examples are from interviews with prisoners' relatives at the present time:

> It seems to me there is no difference. . . . It's possible to say that because the Decembrist wives followed their husbands to Siberia, into the cold wastes.

And we, in essence, are tied by the same chains . . . we can be compared, yes. (Prisoner's wife, interviewed 2010)

I will do what I want. Let them say what they want. . . . We are indeed wives—dekabristki—where the husband goes, so does the wife.[53]

There is some truth in it [the Decembrist appellation]. Yes, many leave everything behind, but I will say of myself, I won't go. (Ol´ga, interviewed 2010)

I know something about Decembrist wives, but I dislike them. I don't know why, but probably because they are in the same situation as us . . . but it was easier for them. . . . There are a lot of poems about them that every schoolchild knows . . . they know about Trubetskaia: every history teacher tells her pupils about them, but nobody knows about the wives, sisters, and daughters of prisoners in the Soviet Union and Russia today, and nobody wants to help, and there is no honor in it. . . . Now in our circle, in our society, there is more condemnation. It's a different situation. We [her mother and sister] wouldn't have moved for sure. We didn't have enough money or the time, and there wouldn't have been any benefit. (Daughter of a prisoner, interviewed 2011)

The last comment echoes Evgeniia Ginzburg's unfavorable comparison of the sufferings endured by Decembrists and Gulag prisoners: "I always thought the Decembrists endured the most frightful sufferings, but listen to this: 'of the wondrous built, so firm, so fast the carriage' . . . they ought to have tried one of Stolypin's coaches."

In all these extracts, the point is not how the historical stereotype is being used but that it is used at all to describe twenty-first-century prisonization. Ol´ga Romanova, the wife of a financier held in the Butyrka, affirms that the need to travel great distances defines the modern-day Decembrist wife:

And when you without thinking fill bags with food and trudge through the snow field to prison or camp—is that not a dekabristka, and is it not a heroic feat? And here I think; for me to get to the prison is ten minutes on the Metro, but women come from the auls, leave children at stations, almost don't speak Russian, know nothing and don't understand but make their way to this devil's prison and try there, by hook or by crook, to find out anything about husbands, but all of them are interrogated, humiliated—go and talk to them about extraordinary love and a high sense of duty.[54]

The disciplining power of exile and banishment expands punishment, taking the capillaries of power into the arena of transportation through space. The giant Soviet penal monolith expanded excessively and grotesquely beyond conventional incarceration and embedded itself into the physical landscape of the USSR where, albeit in shrunken form, it persists to the present time. When prisoners talk about being sent "to another country" or to katorga, or say that women from the Far North are "in exile" in colonies in the South, or when prisoners' relatives compare their experiences with those of the dekabristki they are positioning themselves within a historical stereotype about Russian "in exile imprisonment."

COLLECTIVISM AS HARSH PUNISHMENT

Like transportation, collectivism has been one of the most enduring building blocks of punishment in Russia. Historically, it has appeared in different ways: determinate sentencing; the exile of whole social and ethnic groups; amnesties applied by criminal code; paroling, evaluating, and rewarding inmates in teams; and the group management of prisoners within detention facilities for the purposes of domestic living, work, reeducation, and rehabilitation. In Russia collectivism has always been in a dialogue with individualism, even during the Gulag, but the former has invariably got the upper hand.[55] On the punishment spectrum, collectivism is at the harsh end when it denies the individual personhood of the prisoners and, as a result of inadequate supervision, subjects them to additional harms by allowing prisoner-on-prisoner bullying.

One of the many ways that collectivism has been embodied in Russian colonies is the communal dormitory (fig. 14.2). There were prerevolutionary precursors—in the barrack-like accommodation and cells assigned to artels in transit prisons and penal colonies in Siberia—and in the Gulag, when the living arrangements were supposed to imitate workers' dormitories and to provide a context for prisoners' psychological enrichment and reeducation. In the 1950s the detachment (otriad) was inserted between brigade and administration.[56] The use of prisoners to perform a variety of domestic and administrative jobs around the camp was closely associated with communal living and functional in maintaining disciplinary order. Kseniia Medvedskaia, incarcerated in Siblag as the wife of an enemy of the people, described the system: "The regimen corrupted people, and that was terrible. Denouncing each other was not only demanded but praised. If someone saw somebody break the rules and did not report it, they would be reported along with the person who committed the infraction."[57] It is a small step from this situation

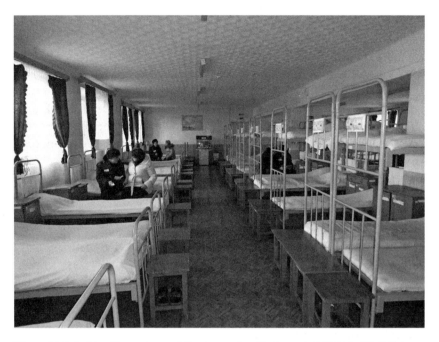

Figure 14.2. Inside of barracks on visitors' open day. Photograph © 2016 Judith Pallot.

to everyone being afraid that they, too, were under suspicion as a potential informant—which Maria Los theorizes as "enhanced panopticism."

The practice of using prisoners for housekeeping tasks is a feature of prisons in many jurisdictions, but it was the institutionalization of authority positions among prisoners in the USSR that ensured that communal living in the detachment would always fall short of the democratic models of the collective. Here is Anatoly Marchenko's description of a meeting in his detachment in a Mordovian colony in the 1960s: "The hut is chock full of people, they've rounded up as many as can be found. Behind the table sits the presidium, the chairman is conducting a general meeting of the company. The presidium is made up of prisoners—beside them sit the company officers. Democracy! On the agenda elections to the Council of the Collective. Does anyone have any proposals? . . . why do we do it? The answer is simple. For in fact the candidates are not chosen by the prisoners but by the administration through its previously prepared stooges, etc."[58]

The triad of communal living and labor, self-organization, and the system of administratively chosen "prefects" that took shape in the Gulag are the pillars of prisoner management in correctional colonies today. Prisoners are housed in multistory dormitory blocks, occupied by several detachments, each with a prisoner in charge (*zavkhoz* or *starshaia dneval'naia*), who is appointed by the administration. The prisoner in charge is supported by deputies and self-organization committees concerned with a variety of housekeeping and other functions—fire safety, education, energy saving, health and safety, social support, cleanliness and tidiness, counseling, and, until abolished in 2009, discipline and order. Approximately 30 percent of prisoners are members of self-organization committees, although the proportion of activists is smaller. The council of the collective to which Marchenko refers (today the detachment collective) is made up of the prisoner in charge and chairs of the self-organization committees. It sends representatives to the colony-level Committee of Collectives.

Communal living deprives prisoners of privacy, a problem that is exacerbated by the overcrowding in dormitories, the absence of doors in bathrooms, and the strict spatio-temporal control of groups of prisoners. In addition to privacy issues, penal collectivism enhances feelings of insecurity and fear among prisoners. In the words of one prisoner who served his sentence in a series of strict-regime colonies, "the Russian colony is the place where fear rules and, to some extent, that fear is deliberately encouraged by the administration." Describing living in the detachment, he continued, "It is constant fear that is habitual, so eventually you stop thinking about it. It is a very dangerous place; it is like walking on thin ice."

Prison subcultures, consisting of overlapping power hierarchies, are the principal source of insecurity among the rank and file. Criminal groups in colonies are popularly supposed to be descended from the thieves in law of the Gulag, but research on current prison subcultures indicates various tendencies, including those that reject the original "thieves' law."[59] But whatever their position in relation to historical stereotypes, career criminals determine the quality of every prisoner's life in the detachment. The criminals' aim is to make life comfortable for themselves, and to this end other prisoners have to meet their demands, whether these involve handing over the contents of a parcel or taking part in an action to wring a concession from the administration. My male informant again: "It's a fearful experience to say no—they might ask you not to go to work; to go on a hunger strike and refuse to eat, and it's the criminals who make everyone conform to this."

Activists and informers recruited by the operations officer also contribute to high levels of stress among prisoners. The prisoners in charge are generally unpopular among the rank and file. They normally are experienced prisoners, not infrequently career criminals, who have crossed over to the administration's side to earn some years off their sentence. Self-organization committees can be benign, but they are also one of the capillaries through which penal power is exercised. Here is one prisoner's account of the otherwise innocent-sounding sanitary committee in her colony:

> The sanitary committee has invented a system of interdetachment competition for cleanliness and tidiness. They thought up this nonsense themselves. So today we can have a raid by one committee and tomorrow by another which are essentially the same, but just different people doing it. They need to promote their own detachment, and so they think these things up. . . . They go through every detachment and section making everyone lie on their bunks while they do an inspection, making sure there are no personal belongings about, no clothes, in other words it's a complete marasmus. If you take it into your head to go to the toilet at that time, you'll be held responsible for the loss of a point from your detachment's score because you're meant to be lying on your bunk. And the prisoners thought this up themselves, all the nuances are theirs. (Ex-prisoner, interviewed 2009)

Particularly notorious were the sections for discipline and order that functioned to ensure compliance with detachment house rules (these are numerous, covering timekeeping, dress, places to smoke, silence after lights out, etc.) but became a vehicle for bullying and violence. When these sections were dissolved in 2009, the minister of justice admitted that they were being used by "corrupt prison administrations" and "violated legal norms." A year later he was pessimistic that the practices with which they were associated would disappear: "Referring to the unfortunate Sections of Discipline and Enforcement (SDiP). More than a year ago we abolished them. I have no illusions and I do not think that all the phenomena connected with the existence of that institution have been eliminated."[60] These words are testimony to just how difficult to dislodge are some of the everyday practices that have been incubated in the collectivist ethos of Russian penal facilities.

Unlike in Western-type cellular prisons, prisoners have nowhere to retreat for security and safety at night. Guards patrol internal colony spaces 24/7, but at five o'clock when the detachment officer (*nachal´nik otriada*) goes home, groups of 100–120 prisoners—who include career criminals, recidivists, and first-time offenders, the educated and the uneducated, the previously employed and the unemployed, Muslims and Russian Orthodox, and citizens of any of the countries of the former Soviet Union—are left to their own devices. It would be remarkable if this did not create what penologists refer to as a "low-trust environment."

THE POLYVALENCE OF PENAL COLLECTIVISM

The Soviet penal inheritance has not been without its problems for the penal service, especially since the conditions of its facilities became subject to external monitoring. As the political conjuncture has changed, so the structures and management principles of the administration of punishment have had to acquire new justifications, with the result that they entered the twenty-first century with multiple meanings attached to them. I recall the spirited defense of the communal dormitory made by a general at a Prison Service conference I attended in 2005 who, in response to a critical observation by a Norwegian delegate, insisted that Russians are culturally disposed to live together and would be unhappy given single cells. In the nineteenth century barracks were justified on the grounds that peasants were too uneducated to pass their time in reflection in single cells.[61] As observed above, the barrack of the Soviet labor camp, in contrast, was justified by reference to the socialist principle of communal living. When not justified by references to Russian culture, the communal dormitory is most often put forward today as an example of the liberal, welfarist "principle of approximation" (that living arrangements in prison should approximate as closely as possible what prisoners would experience were they free). Here is one officer in 2007: "They [the prisoners] should get used to living in society. We are preparing them for life in freedom. They cannot live as if they are on a desert island. They will be exposed to people, and they will need to be able to communicate. They must learn to respect those around them. They must learn to understand people and understand relationships. So they have to learn to live in the detachment." Competition (no longer socialist) between detachments and colonies, remains the order of the day, but *KVN*, beauty contests, football, and energy efficiency have been added to the more traditional roster of production and "dormitory tidiness."

Self-organization is similarly polyvalent. Before the revolution, institutions of peasant communal life were imported into the setting of the exile transport and penal labor colony to perform the same tasks as they did in civilian life—to adjudicate disputes, distribute food, and maintain order—and were understood as such. In the twentieth and twenty-first centuries these institutions have been variously recoded by the authorities as vehicles for prisoner democracy, as means for keeping barracks clean, and as instruments for neoliberal responsibilization interventions. Penal labor has been represented over time as a vehicle for punishing transgression; for the socialist reforging (*perekovka*), correction (*ispravlenie*), and reeducation (*perevospit-*

anie) of the criminal; and as a site of resocialization (*resotsializatsiia*) interventions.

These recodings draw on a variety of traditional discourses about the national character and gender. In women's colonies, for example, the argument is made today that the detachment is "one large family," a representation that both infantilizes prisoners and reproduces gender stereotypes. In this myth the role of mother is sometimes fulfilled by the prisoner in charge: "There is something useful, maternal, about it [giving prisoners authority positions over one another]; it's like having to take responsibility for your children. . . . Yes, for women it seems there is something to be gained from this. It doesn't work like this for men. Men's colonies don't have anything like it; they wouldn't even understand the principle" (prison officer, interviewed 2007).

In conversations with personnel in women's colonies, the detachment officer was also represented as a mother figure or, alternatively, a teacher, as in the explanation given in one interview about personnel's use of military uniforms: "The detachment officer is an educator, but she cannot let prisoners relax in her presence, because she is demanding of them that they fulfill their duties to the collective—that they work, that they clean up after themselves. . . . It's like being a teacher; we learn as teachers that we must be dressed appropriately, so the children see us and pay attention. If you are not dressed correctly, the lesson won't go well" (prison officer, interviewed 2007).

The messages contained in penal practices are not necessarily decoded as their authors intend, but so long as alternative readings, such as those of the prisoners themselves, can be contained within the penal monolith, this is not necessarily troubling to the exercise of power and control. In the last two decades, however, the penal center has experienced difficulties in controlling meanings, with the result that it has been forced into action both to keep its own practitioners "on message" and to convince the public that Russia's prisons remain fit for their purpose—that they are not creating more disorder, evil, and pollution than they are eliminating.

THE BIRTH OF THE RUSSIAN PRISON?

Prison reform in the Russian Federation has taken place in the context of the counterdiscourses about the administration of punishment and, at least in part, in response to them. The first steps toward reforming the system were made in the early 1990s and shaped by the Russian Federation's application to join the Council of Europe. Part of broader changes in the criminal justice system, the early penal reforms outlawed extralegal practices, improved prisoners' living conditions (by establishing new norms for the provision of

Figure 14.3. Courtyard of barracks on visitors' open day. Photograph © 2016 Judith Pallot.

space, visiting regimes [fig. 14.3], food, and hygiene), and introduced symbolic changes, such as addressing prisoners by name, not number, dropping the word "labor" from the title of penal institutions, and renaming industrial plants where prisoners still put in eight- to twelve-hour days in "centers for labor adaptation." The reformation of the offender had been a stated goal of carceral politics of the Soviet state, but after 1991 this role was further emphasized. In reality, though significant in some areas, improvements in the first decade were modest, as penal institutions were overwhelmed by numbers. More important, the reforms did not challenge the established penal culture or question the foundation myths of the system, including my two concerns here—that punishment takes place in the peripheries and involves the submersion of the individual in the collective. This was, finally, set to change in 2010 when the Russian Federation announced a radical policy shift with the publication of the Conception for the Development of the Penal System to 2020.[62]

The new reform was closely associated with President Dmitri Medvedev and reflected his genuine interest in modernizing the criminal justice system. Calling the reform a "conception" signaled the fundamental nature of the changes now proposed. There was much in the Conception about the humanization of punishment, alternatives to incarceration, and the modernization of surveillance technologies, which had been proposed before, but its eye-catching feature was the proposal to abolish the correctional colony and to replace it with high-security prisons—*tiur´my*—with cells for two to eight prisoners and small-scale workshops—and open prisons, modeled on existing colony settlements (*koloniia-poselenii*). The Conception mentioned the need to rationalize the length of the journey to prison, but it did not propose a geographical restructuring of the prison estate.

Although the provisions in the Conception were in part designed for an international audience as evidence of the Russian Federation's penal modernization, it is the message it contained for home consumption—that the Gulag inheritance was the source of current problems in the penal system—that is of more interest here. Medvedev, in a speech subsequently criticized, "confessed" in 2011 that the Russian penal system was failing to rehabilitate prisoners because it was "95 percent Soviet."[63] Aleksandr Reimer, who as the head of the Prison Service until the summer of 2012 was appointed to see through the changes, introduced the Conception: "The principal task that stands before us is the fundamental change of the correctional system. It is necessary to remove the prison camp archipelago with all its attendant traditions and principles of collectivism and labor."[64]

Minister of Justice Aleksandr Konovalov confirmed the analysis, observing that "[We] still have a lot of Gulag heredity." In September 2011 he addressed a Duma committee, noting that the current penal system "carries many features reminiscent of Gulag days and perhaps even of the prerevolutionary *katorga*."[65] The Conception's preamble explains why, from the current Prison Service's point of view, this is a problem: "Among the historical inheritances of the current penal system is the peculiar mode of life of the accused and convicts. It has perpetuated the activities of criminal leaders who try to spread the so-called thieves' law. The widespread nature of criminal culture and the domination among the special contingent of a criminal orientation is clearly a product of the collective system of holding prisoners."[66] In an interesting echo from the late 1950s, Konovalov reassured a conference of prison officers assembled to discuss the Conception that "prisons are not holiday resorts."

Returning to Philip Smith's suggestion that shifts in punishment modalities take place when the center can no longer control unruly meanings in the periphery, the current reform can be understood as a discursive assault on negative perceptions of the penal service's performance, rather than evidence of a commitment to refining the technologies of power-knowledge (Foucault), the pursuit of humanitarian forms of punishment (Durkheim), or a response to a change in the functional needs of the state (Rusche and Kirch-heimer). From the cultural radical's perspective, the aim to eliminate collec-tivism indicates that the penal center has received the message of society's revulsion at the disorderliness of its institutions. These include the percep-tion that Russia's correctional colonies are a source of crime, not the solution to it, and are supremely polluted and unhealthy places (prison transports, communal dormitories, and bathrooms are all implicated in the spread of antibiotic-resistant tuberculosis and other infectious diseases in Russia). The Prison Service's courtship of the Russian Orthodox Church speaks to Smith's insistence on the religious roots of much punishment.[67]

The announcement of "the birth of the prison" in Russia was prema-ture. In June 2012 Reimer was dismissed, and plans to replace colonies with Western-style penitentiaries were abandoned. The reason for the retreat is a combination of corruption scandals, prison riots, and lack of the funds need-ed to reprofile colonies. No doubt, the sidelining of Medvedev and the res-toration of Putin's muscular presidency are also factors. Recent commentary on the Conception has reasserted the value of traditional practices: a volume on the correctional system from a leading law faculty, for example, contained the surprising assertion that the colony system has won the admiration of European penal reformers.[68] The State Duma has set up a new commission, which sat for the first time in January 2014, to correct the Conception.[69]

The rejection of the Conception is evidence of the resilience in Russia of a penal culture with deep historical roots, whether this is explained by con-tinuities in the frame of reference within which the Prison Service interprets its role and goals or a product of deeper cultural imperatives. In this chapter I have argued that there is a commitment in Russia to certain punishment forms whose longevity cannot be satisfactorily explained by reference solely to "rational" economic or political factors. This does not mean, however, that explanations for the use and persistence of these punishment forms cannot be found outside the cultural realm. By the same token, even though I have drawn attention to the punitive aspects of the punishment forms I have de-scribed, this should not be taken to imply that they invariably *are* punitive. Whether dormitory accommodation causes problems of lack of privacy or insecurity, for example, depends on the particular supervisory arrangements put in place and the organization of living space. It is difficult to put a positive construction on sending prisoners long distances to serve their sentences, but there are more humane ways than those used in Russia to effect transfers. The concrete constellations of social, economic, and political events within which punishment is administered are important in how different punishment forms are experienced. For this reason, and notwithstanding the disturbingly similar experiences of Liudmila Granovskaia and Sonia with which I began this essay, I am not suggesting that dynamism does not exist in the Russian penal system or that the center will always manage to contain the effects of discordant prison discourses. As of 2015, however, with radical restructuring off the agenda, incremental change in Russia's penal culture and in the institutions with which it is associated seems to be the best that can be hoped for.

THE GULAG

An Incarnation of the State That Created It

BETTINA GREINER

TRANSLATED BY NICOLAS KUMANOFF

WHAT, PRECISELY, WAS the Gulag? As each article in the present volume clearly demonstrates, this seemingly simple question repeatedly eludes any clear answer. The problem begins with the ambiguous term "Gulag." Strictly speaking, it was the administration within the Soviet secret police that was responsible for coordinating forced labor. This central function points to the term's second meaning, with Gulag having become a synonym for the Soviet penal system in general. Moreover, instead of referring just to camps, the term also encompasses prisons, penal colonies, and special settlements. There was even a Gulag without a place, as the Stalinist regime condemned millions of people to forced labor not in camps but at their regular workplaces. As Felix Schnell has pointed out, this diverse morphology is probably part of the reason that "the Gulag has no textbook location and, in a higher sense, no 'face' as the Holocaust does. The Gulag has no 'Auschwitz,' no iconic images like the entrance gate with its slogan *Arbeit macht frei*, no revealing buzzwords like 'gas chambers.'"[1]

The Gulag was lethal for millions of people. From 1923 onward this gigantic network, at times comprising more than thirty thousand concentration camp units and innumerable penal colonies, held roughly twenty million prisoners and forced laborers. Precisely how many people were imprisoned in the Gulag or how many died there will never be determined accurately; most existing estimates, which are generally for certain periods only, remain disputed. There is consensus on one point, however—the enormous loss of life in the Stalinist camps, which, as Norman Davies has written, "accounted for far more human victims than Ypres, the Somme, Verdun, Auschwitz, Majdanek, Dachau, and Buchenwald put together."[2] Yet these millions, as has also been established, did not, even at the height of Stalinist repression, fall victim to a deliberate extermination policy of the kind pursued by the

Germans in Treblinka, Sobibor, Belzec, and the other extermination camps. The prisoners were, as is well documented, victims of misanthropy and indifference—of an attitude that reduced the value of a human life to the labor that could be extracted from it.

Therefore, the fact that millions of lives were snuffed out in the camps, penal colonies, and special settlements does not in and of itself permit any conclusions regarding the function of the Gulag. Certainly, Golfo Alexopoulos's convincing interpretation of the List of Illnesses that she presents in this volume looms large. Using this source, she firmly establishes that the "goners" (*dokhodiagi*)—that is, those prisoners deliberately condemned and utterly exhausted through harsh work—were routinely released to die outside the camps. The ramifications for our understanding of Gulag mortality rates are clear, which is also why there is much to be said for her argument that the Gulag was not only an institution of "mass death," as is commonly accepted, but also of "mass murder." Whether the function of the Gulag meshes with this conclusion is, however, a completely different issue. One fact suggesting otherwise, for example, would be that the Bolshevik regime hardly destroyed fewer lives outside the Gulag. Starvation, violence, and death reigned on both sides of the barbed wire fence, with equally devastating consequences.

Indeed, these fences did not demarcate any real frontier between freedom and captivity. They should instead be understood as porous membranes, permeable in both directions. Above all, the world beyond the barbed wire was anything but free. The strict residence and travel laws and passportization enacted in the 1930s made the distinction between "inside" and "outside" relatively marginal. Collectivized farmers became de facto modern serfs. Workers fared little better. Almost all the state's citizens were subjected to this strict disciplinary regime that enslaved them in the name of ambitious modernization programs. Seen in this light, the Gulag was the most extreme variant of captivity in a continuum of incarcerated geographies within the Soviet Union as a whole. It represented the dramatic pinnacle of an increasingly complex hierarchy of privileges and exclusion. Hence we would also be mistaken to view the Gulag as an excess or a phenomenon with its own logic within the Soviet regime.[3]

David R. Shearer has argued along similar lines: "The Gulag system reproduced, in the purest unmitigated forms, the fundamentally coercive ways in which the Soviet state interacted with Soviet citizens."[4] Nearly all the chapters in this book affirm this reading of the Gulag system as the quintessential incarnation of the system that created it. This reading also owes much to Oleg Khlevniuk's evocative observations (likewise in this volume) on the Gulag and the non-Gulag and Kate Brown's no less stimulating proposal from 2007 to regard the Gulag not as an isolated phenomenon but against the backdrop of the larger history of the Soviet Union.[5] Within less than a decade these impulses have opened up new perspectives for Gulag research. Issues that were so urgent following the demise of the Soviet Union, concerning the dimensions of the Gulag or interpretations of it as an insular or monolithic institution, seem less relevant now. Interest is increasingly focusing on the Gulag's connections, interactions, and parallels with the Soviet Union's broader culture. The chapters collected here vividly demonstrate how productive this shift in perspective has been for our comprehension of the Gulag.

Reading these essays is so enormously stimulating because the new lines of investigation they follow often yield findings that are surprising and disturbing in equal measure. Emilia Koustova's exploration of special settlers from Lithuania and western Ukraine, showing that forced labor could have socially integrative effects—indeed, that it enabled some deportees to self-define positively both collectively and individually through their performance—stands in utter contradiction to commonplace (and often nationally tinged) narratives of trauma and victimization. This reversed perspective will also supply a suitable and durable irritant to politicized interpretations.

The contribution by Asif Siddiqi provides another example. His investigation of the *sharashki*, or camps for scientists, offers fascinating glimpses into a largely unexplored chapter of the Gulag that witnessed a singular collaboration between captive and free scientists. Especially intriguing is, however, that this forcible cooperation set up in the early 1930s was dissolved from above and then reestablished during the Great Terror and again in the late 1940s, without regard for scientific or economic successes. This tumultuous chapter draws the reader's interest in multiple ways. It shows that the history of penal practice in the Soviet Union can in no way be separated from the country's political history. The Gulag was not only dependent on the system's political cycles; it reflected them as well. The actual problem, however, lies in the circumstance that the function of the Gulag cannot be fully explained in economic terms either.

It is not my intention to discuss all the chapters here. I think it important to emphasize, however, that the editor has demonstrated a thoroughly deft touch in selecting the topics at hand. This is not only because many of the essays draw on previously undiscovered sources or take viewpoints that have received little attention in the past. What thrills me equally is that all these texts are like mosaic tiles, each of which adds its own color and detail to our understanding of the Gulag. Their felicitous arrangement in this volume yields a greater image reflecting how contradictory, erratic, and—above all—dynamic the history of the Gulag was. The individual elements of the mosaic do not combine into a clearly composed or unified whole. Instead they produce an uneven, pointillist composition made of many spotlighted moments in time.

This presentation, of course, has consequences for issues of Gulag research that remain hotly debated anyway. What function did the Gulag have? Can it be explained better in economic terms or as a tool of political repression? What role did reeducation play? How relevant was efficiency in the penal colony economy? The authors in this volume offer differing answers within the framework of their case studies. Yet this result, too, underscores the strength of the book, making clear as it does that these issues surrounding the Gulag's vigorous development can be answered only provisionally, if ever. Wilson Bell's chapter on the Gulag and war in western Siberia is a case in point. He focuses on certain corrective labor camps that were quickly retooled for military production in a region where more people lost their lives during the war than in the entire Gulag system during the same period. Bell's detailed and balanced discussion of economic and penal concerns—also and especially at the local level—against the background of the Soviet war effort makes for compelling reading. In the end we cannot be surprised that, in the singular context of total war, the balance tipped in the direction of economic necessity. We also know that with the end of the war the repressive element again gained strength. What makes the discussion so engrossing, however, is that Bell does not regard the camps he investigates in isolation. Instead he places them in the context of mass mobilization on the home front. This approach also makes clear that the Gulag "was one piece in the puzzle of a country-wide and regional total war effort"—an additional, important indication that inquiries into the function of the Gulag cannot be separated from its always evolving political context.

With this collection the editor also invigorates Gulag research in another respect. Several articles take a comparative approach. In this way they do not only open readers' eyes to a (not only in the Soviet case) sparsely researched field.[6] They themselves provide the best proof of how productive this approach can be. Whether the focus is on inhuman traditions and routines—such as the transports to the camp sites in the nineteenth century or the present day, or national and transnational processes of teaching and transfer—comparisons add nuance to our knowledge of the Gulag. The same applies equally to comparative investigations into the relationships among the periphery, metropolitan centers, and imperial claims to power. Equally instructive are inquiries into the radicalization and mobilization of the astonishingly adaptable institution of (concentration) camps and their adoption and application by regimes both democratic and dictatorial. Yet another stimulating question asks what relationships camps had to other forms of incarceration, the practice of resettlement, exile, and execution sites. And, with a special view toward contemporary focal points of Gulag research, how did they distinguish themselves from these other forms?

The Nazi-Soviet comparison is probably the archetypal classic in the comparative history of camps and is found here as well. For the task, the editor has secured Dietrich Beyrau, one of Germany's most distinguished historians of Eastern Europe. Strikingly, he avoids any discussion (practically compulsory in German research literature) of the legitimacy of comparing the two camp systems. Generally, the avowal that any such comparison cannot reduce the singularity of the Holocaust has become a matter of good form in Germany. In this sense the debate in this country is not completely free of the political adjustment that had its justified roots in Germany's avoidance of blame in the years following 1945. One might well ask whether such reflexes still reflect today's political culture in Germany. Beyrau's comparative analysis stands out because, instead of focusing on the most extreme forms of camps and execution sites, he takes a much wider perspective. In doing so, he implicitly takes up a relatively recent issue of research that has become increasingly scrutinized in Germany with reference to Nazi camps. The central keywords are "exclusion" and "inclusion," which target the ambiguity of camps in Germany as instruments for establishing a "national community" (*Volksgemeinschaft*). Beyrau's recommendation to think in this direction in the Soviet case as well is something I thoroughly endorse.

Equally fascinating are his treatments of other Russian/Soviet camp systems that also illuminate the history of the Gulag: the prisoner of war (POW) camps of the two world wars. There can be no question that the first concentration camps emerged around the beginning of the twentieth century along the fringes of empires and as an instrument of what would today be called counterinsurgency. Moreover, the fact that multiple colonial powers harnessed the idea of population concentration nearly simultaneously also points to a then-novel media discourse and the significance of the military as an adaptable institution with a lively international information transfer. In his discussion of the British concentration camps in the Boer War, Aidan Forth is in no way wrong to point out a "family resemblance" that remains recognizable into the Gulag era. Yet it should be borne in mind that only the expansion of modern state power through the integration of technology, science, and ideology in the First World War would enable the modern camp system to emerge. That which the imperial powers had rehearsed on the experimental spaces along the imperial periphery or, in Russia's case, the equally peripheral state frontiers would now be applied on a greatly expanded scale in the cities and, crucially, with the resources and mentality of the modern state.[7] It was not just the previously unimaginable figure of eight to nine million prisoners of war, the extensive infrastructure, or the militarized transnational culture of the camps that was historically new. So was the fact that the POW camps had become reserve labor pools or administration centers for forced labor squads, often in operational zones behind the front.

POW estimates in Russia range between 1.6 and 2.3 million enemy troops. Studies also indicate about 250 POW camps country-wide that, instead of being dismantled at war's end, were absorbed into the Gulag shortly thereafter. According to some interpretations, about 80 percent of these prisoners were forced to work. After 1915 the nominally free civilian population was also pressed into labor in the Russian army's frontline and staging areas, meaning that one of the central functions of the Gulag was already being practiced during the First World War. Whether this seeming continuity can be called a "Gulag before the Gulag" is something we must put aside for now.[8] At the very least, however, it would be worthwhile to inquire into knowledge transfers, institutional memory, and mobilization in times of war and crisis.

Dietrich Beyrau's reference to the Soviet POW camps in the Second World War appears equally instructive in clarifying our view of the Gulag. Some thirty-five million soldiers were taken prisoner during the Second World War. No other camp system in the twentieth century had to cope with numbers that came close to those in POW camps. POW captivity was a mass phenomenon on an unparalleled scale. Depending on the authority in charge of the POWs and on the date of their capture, death in captivity was also a mass phenomenon, especially in the German and Soviet cases: almost 60 percent of Soviet POWs in German captivity died. Death also occurred on a massive scale in the Soviet POW camps of the Main Administration for Prisoners of War and Internees (GUPVI) within the NKVD/MVD. Roughly one-third of the approximately 3.2 million members of the Wehrmacht who were taken prisoner did not survive, even though the labor force in the GUPVI camps was of great importance to Moscow. Stalin instructed that he was to be informed regularly on the prisoners' state of health, on their rations and medical care. Even though the food situation in the war-ravaged country was precarious at best and a state of emergency repeatedly had to be declared in the camps, the GUPVI inmates were better fed on average than Gulag prisoners, sometimes even better than their respective regions' civilian populations. Stalin was even prepared to allow releases on grounds of ill health, to the extent that these were compatible with his notions of economic utility. The possibilities for comparison with other national camp systems are thus plentiful.

Klaus Mühlhahn's chapter on the Chinese Laogai in the decade before the Cultural Revolution demonstrates just how enriching the comparative perspective can be. In a little more than a decade, the number of prisoners rose tenfold, from about five million to an estimated fifty million. In the brief span between 1959 and 1962 alone, some four million prisoners were either killed or died from starvation, abuse, or disease. Again, the question of the labor camps' function—ideological remolding, punishment, economic exploitation, colonization of remote areas—figures prominently in Mühlhahn's account. He discusses it and the definition of counterrevolutionaries against the backdrop of much broader mass violence, which was gripping the entirety of Chinese society yet was also supported from below by enthusiastic mobilization and mass participation. This statement identifies but one of the differences laid bare by the comparison with Stalinism. Another has to do with the decentralized organization or, more precisely, the deliberate avoidance of a central authority that, in any case, would not (yet) have been powerful enough to implement its objectives across China. Despite these differences, one must keep in mind that the Chinese leadership demonstrably depended on Soviet expertise. Scientific works on the Gulag were translated into Mandarin and studied in the Politburo. Soviet advisers were also consulted. This example of a transnational knowledge transfer is striking, not least because the Chinese side actively made adjustments, at least in matters of administration. Also, the expertise was sought at a time when the first voices critical of the Gulag began to be heard within the Soviet leadership. The North Korean case described by Sungmin Cho reveals similar overlaps and influences.

Even the comparative approach does not provide conclusive answers to the question of what the Gulag was. Yet it offers important insights into the historical place of this institution, and it hones our sense of the contexts and mass phenomena that gave the Gulag its shifting and contradictory form as the quintessential incarnation of the state that created it.

FOREWORD

1. A. Solzhenitsyn, *Arkhipelag Gulag*, 3 vols. (Paris: YMCA Press, 1973–75).

2. "The Soviet Gulag: New Research and New Interpretations," *Kritika: Explorations in Russian and Eurasian History* 16, no. 3 (2015).

1. INTRODUCTION: FROM BOUNDED TO JUXTAPOSITIONAL

1. For a systemic approach clearly inspired by Solzhenitsyn, see Galina Mikhailovna Ivanova, *Labor Camp Socialism: The Gulag in the Soviet Totalitarian System*, trans. Carol Flath (Armonk, NY: M. E. Sharpe, 2000, orig. 1997); and Ivanova, *Istoriia GULAGa 1918–1958: Sotsial' no-ekonomicheskii i politiko-pravovoi aspekty* (Moscow: Nauka, 2006). For a landmark study of a single camp complex, see Viktor Berdinskikh, *Istoriia odnogo lageria (Viatlag)* (Moscow: AGRAF, 2001). To get a sense of the state of the field in the wake of intense Western "focus on numerical issues," see Stephen Barnes, "Researching Daily Life in the Gulag," *Kritika: Explorations in Russian and Eurasian History* 1, no. 2 (2000): 377–90.

2. Although clearly its origins must also be sought in the era of the First World War and the history of the Soviet camp system between 1917 and 1930. See Michael Jakobson, *Origins of the GULAG: The Soviet Prison Camp System, 1917–1934* (Lexington: University Press of Kentucky 1993).

3. Dmitrii Likhachev, "Mesto pod narami: Solovki, 1928–1931 gody," *Pervoe sentiabria*, 6 November 1999, 5.

4. Aleksandr Bezborodov et al., eds., *Istoriia stalinskogo GULAGa: Konets 1920-kh–pervaia polovina 1950-kh godov. Sobranie dokumentov*, 7 vols. (Moscow: Rosspen, 2004–2005).

5. Lynne Viola, *The Unknown Gulag: The Lost World of Stalin's Special Settlements* (New York: Oxford University Press, 2007); the Russian translation was aptly entitled *Krest' ianskii GULAG: Mir stalinskikh spetsposelenii* (Moscow: Rosspen, 2011).

6. Oksana Kornilova, *Kak stroili pervuiu sovetskuiu avtomagistral' 1936–1941* (Smolensk: Svitok, 2014); Kornilova, "Gulag ot Moskvy do Minska: Stroitel'stvo pervoi sovetskoi avtomagistrali Moskva-Minsk (1936–1941)," paper presented at the Russian History Seminar of Washington, DC, Georgetown University, 2015.

7. For example, Wilson T. Bell, "Was the Gulag an Archipelago? De-Convoyed Prisoners and Porous Borders in the Camps of Western Siberia," *Russian Review* 72, no. 1 (2013): 116–41; Alan Barenberg, "Prisoners without Borders: Zakonniki and the Transformation of Vorkuta after Stalin," *Jahrbücher für Geschichte Osteuropas* 57, no. 4 (2009): 513–34.

8. Kate Brown, "Out of Solitary Confinement: The History of the Gulag," *Kritika: Explorations in Russian and Eurasian History* 8, no. 1 (2007): 67–104.

9. Miriam Dobson, *Khrushchev's Cold Summer: Gulag Returnees, Crime, and the Fate of Reform after Stalin* (Ithaca, NY: Cornell University Press, 2009); Alan Barenberg, *Gulag Town, Company Town: Forced Labor and Its Legacy in Vorkuta* (New Haven: Yale University Press, 2014).

10. Bettina Greiner and Alan Kramer, eds., *Die Welt der Lager: Zur "Erfolgsgeschichte" einer Institution* (Hamburg: Hamburger Edition, 2013). See also Christoph Jahr and Jens Thiel, eds., *Lager vor Auschwitz: Gewalt und Integration im 20. Jahrhundert* (Berlin: Metropol, 2013), as well as the literature cited in this volume by Greiner and Dietrich Beyrau.

11. Kim Wünschmann, *Before Auschwitz: Jewish Prisoners in the Prewar Concentration Camps* (Cambridge, MA: Harvard University Press, 2015).

12. Here see Michael David-Fox, Peter Holquist, and Alexander M. Martin, eds., *The Holocaust in the East: Local Perpetrators and Soviet Responses* (Pittsburgh: University of Pittsburgh Press, 2014).

13. Mark Levene, *The Crisis of Genocide, 2: Annihilation: The European Rimlands, 1939–1953* (Oxford: Oxford University Press, 2013), 316.

14. Viktor Berdinskikh, "GULAG: Ekonomika i ideologiia ponevol'nogo truda v 20-m veke," paper delivered at the conference "The Soviet Gulag: New Research and New Interpretations," Georgetown University, 25–27 April 2013; Alexander Etkind, "Soviet Subjectivity: Torture for the Sake of Salvation?" *Kritika: Explorations in Russian and Eurasian History* 6, no. 1 (2005): 172, 175n8.

15. Wilson T. Bell, "The Gulag and Soviet Society in Western Siberia" (PhD diss., University of Toronto, 2011), 114–25.

16. Christian Gerlach and Nicholas Werth, "State Violence—Violent Societies," in *Beyond Totalitarianism: Stalinism and Nazism Compared*, ed. Michael Geyer and Sheila Fitzpatrick (Cambridge: Cambridge University Press, 2010), 151.

17. Barenberg, *Gulag Town, Company Town*, 9.

18. Prominent and provocative among them is Alessandro Stanziani, "Free Labor —Forced Labor: An Uncertain Boundary? The Circulation of Economic Ideas be-

tween Russia and Europe from the 18th to the Mid-19th Century," *Kritika: Explorations in Russian and Eurasian History* 9, no. 1 (2008): 27–52; Stanziani, *Bondage: Labor and Rights in Eurasia from the Sixteenth to the Early Twentieth Centuries* (New York: Berghahn, 2014). See also Brown, "Out of Solitary Confinement"; and the new research by Willard Sunderland on the broad variety of serfs and serfdoms within the Russian Empire ("The Imperial Emancipations: Abolition and Empire in Tsarist Russia," lecture presented at the Russian History Seminar of Washington, DC, Georgetown University, 5 November 2015).

19. The debates over Stalinism are far too numerous to cite here, but for my own take on the conceptual issues involved, see "Razmyshleniia o stalinizme, voine i nasilii," in *SSSR vo Vtoroi mirovoi voine: Okkupatsiia. Kholokost. Stalinizm*, ed. Oleg Budnitskii and Liudmila Novikova (Moscow: Rosspen, 2014), 176–95.

20. Paul R. Gregory and Valery Lazarev, eds., *The Economics of Forced Labor: The Soviet Gulag* (Stanford, CA: Hoover Institution Press, 2003); on administrators "grossly" underestimating the numbers of prisoners, see Gregory, "Introduction to the Economics of the Gulag," 4. On the "Gulagization" of the Soviet economy, see V. A. Berdinskikh, "Gulag v Sovetskom Soiuze: Ideologiia i ekonomika podnevol´nogo truda," http://illhkomisc.ru/wp-content/uploads/2014/11/berdinskih.pdf, and his forthcoming one-volume history of the Gulag.

21. On Stalin's own outlook on political and economic enemies as "enveloped within the regime's vocabulary and worldview," see Stephen Kotkin, *Stalin, 1: Paradoxes of Power, 1878–1928* (New York: Penguin, 2014), 530, 658 (quotation), 676. Over time, the realization that material and other incentives as well as coercion were necessary in the Gulag served further to blur the line between prisoner and civilian labor (Gregory, "Introduction to the Economics of the Gulag," 6).

22. On crises in the 1930s and unexpected consequences, see David R. Shearer, "Stalinist Repression, Modernity, and the Social Engineering Argument," in *The Anatomy of Terror: Political Violence under Stalin*, ed. James Harris (Oxford: Oxford University Press, 2013), 105–22.

23. For my understanding of "shared" versus "alternative" modernity, see Michael David-Fox, *Crossing Borders: Modernity, Ideology, and Culture in Russia and the Soviet Union* (Pittsburgh: Pittsburgh University Press, 2015), chaps. 1–2.

24. Peter Holquist, "Violent Russia, Deadly Marxism? Russia in the Epoch of Violence, 1905–21," *Kritika: Explorations in Russian and Eurasian History* 4, no. 3 (2003): 635–36; Holquist, *Making War, Forging Revolution: Russia's Continuum of Crisis, 1914–1921* (Cambridge, MA: Harvard University Press, 2002), 201.

25. Klaus Mühlhahn, "The Dark Side of Globalization: The Concentration Camps in Republican China in Global Perspective," *World History Connected* 6, no. 1 (2009), http://worldhistoryconnected.press.illinois.edu/6.1/muhlhahn.html#_ftnref47.

26. Dariusz Tolczyk, *See No Evil: Literary Cover-Ups and Discoveries of the Camp*

Experience (New Haven: Yale University Press, 1999); Michael David-Fox, "Gorky's Gulag," chap. 4 of *Showcasing the Great Experiment: Cultural Diplomacy and Western Visitors to the Soviet Union, 1921–1941* (New York: Oxford University Press, 2012).

27. For one prominent intervention here, see Steven A. Barnes, *Death and Redemption: The Gulag and the Shaping of Soviet Society* (Princeton, NJ: Princeton University Press, 2011).

28. Barenberg, *Gulag Town, Company Town*, 61.

29. Here see esp. Lynne Viola, "The Aesthetic of Stalinist Planning and the World of the Special Villages," *Kritika: Explorations in Russian and Eurasian History* 4, no. 1 (2003): 101–28.

30. Donald Filtzer, "Starvation Mortality in Soviet Home-Front Industrial Regions during World War II," in *Hunger and War: Food Provisioning in the Soviet Union during World War II*, ed. Wendy Z. Goldman and Donald Filtzer (Bloomington: Indiana University Press, 2015), 307–8.

31. Loren Graham, *The Ghost of the Executed Engineer: Technology and the Fall of the Soviet Union* (Cambridge, MA: Harvard University Press, 1996).

32. For an early study, see Edwin Bacon, *The Gulag at War: Stalin's Forced Labour System in the Light of the Archives* (New York: Macmillan, 1994); for a recent contribution, see Fyodor Vasilyevich Mochulsky, *Gulag Boss: A Soviet Memoir*, ed. and trans. Deborah Kaple (New York: Oxford University Press, 2013).

33. David-Fox, "Razmyshleniia o stalinizme, voine i nasilii."

34. Judith Pallot, "The Topography of Incarceration: The Spatial Continuity of Penality and the Legacy of the Gulag in Twentieth and Twenty-First Century Russia," *Laboratorium: Russian Review of Social Research* 7, no. 1 (2015): 80–105; and the maps available at http://www.gulagmaps.org/.

35. For more depth on how enemies were identified in both cases, see Christopher Browning and Lewis Siegelbaum, "Frameworks for Social Engineering: Stalinist Schema of Identification and the Nazi Volksgemeinschaft," chap. 6 of *Beyond Totalitarianism* (Cambridge: Cambridge University Press, 2008).

36. Klaus Mühlhahn, *Criminal Justice in China: A History* (Cambridge, MA: Harvard University Press, 2009), 148, 159.

37. Mühlhahn, *Criminal Justice in China*, 160.

38. Mühlhahn, "Dark Side of Globalization."

CHAPTER 2. THE GULAG AND THE NON-GULAG AS ONE INTERRELATED WHOLE

I am grateful to *Kritika*'s anonymous readers and to Stephen Lovell for his valuable comments, which pressed me to reconsider and revise several of this chapter's contentions. The chapter was prepared within the framework of a subsidy granted to the National Research University Higher School of Economics (HSE) by the government of the Russian Federation for the implementation of the Global Competitiveness Program. I also thank Simon Belokowsky for his skillful translation.

1. Contemporary historiography employs the term "Gulag" in reference to both the camp system itself and a wider array of penal zones (prisons, labor colonies, special settlements, etc.).

2. The literature on Stalin's camps and other elements of the Stalinist penal system is voluminous to the extent that a single footnote could not possibly account for even its most significant works. I reference relevant studies below, including works of general focus and utility in addition to more specialized studies.

3. By way of example, a source as significant as the materials of the camp security apparatus (*operativnye otdely lagerei*) is presently inaccessible. Suffice it to say, these documents are a precious, irreplaceable source: they include agents' reports on topics relevant to the state of the Gulag on such questions as morale and uncovered plots, real and imagined. However, the secrecy surrounding these documents does not allow historians even to assess the state of their preservation. Certain documents relevant to the intelligence structure of the Gulag (largely directives) are available in the sixth volume of Aleksandr Bezborodov et al., eds., *Istoriia stalinskogo GULAGa: Konets 1920-kh–pervaia polovina 1950-kh godov. Sobranie dokumentov*, 7 vols. (Moscow: Rosspen, 2004–2005).

4. A. I. Solzhenitsyn, *The Gulag Archipelago, 1918–1956: An Experiment in Literary Investigation* (New York: Harper and Row, 1974).

5. A. I. Kokurin and Iu. N. Morukov, "GULAG: Struktura i kadry," *Svobodnaia mysl'-XXI*, no. 12 (2001), 100–101. The authors give a figure of eighteen million imprisoned but do not explain their methodology. It appears, though, that they have arrived at this number by aggregating figures found in reports of the OGPU/NKVD/MVD/MGB (as a rule, extrajudicial sentences) with judicial records. The data for 1930–1936 are almost certainly incomplete, although this is also not made explicit (judicial records before 1937 were poorly kept and have been poorly preserved). This figure is also invoked by Anne Applebaum, whom Kokurin aided with archival work: see her *Gulag: A History* (New York: Doubleday, 2003), appendix. We should add to this figure up to one million who were shot or tortured to death under interrogation and never reached the camps.

6. V. N. Zemskov, *Spetsposelentsy v SSSR, 1930–1960 gg.* (Moscow: Nauka, 2003); Lynne Viola, *The Unknown Gulag: The Lost World of Stalin's Special Settlements* (New York: Oxford University Press, 2007).

7. Frederico Varese, "The Society of the *vory-v-zakone*, 1930s–1950s," *Cahiers du monde russe* 39, no. 4 (1998): 515–38.

8. This figure is derived from arrest and judicial records associated with the work

of the state security apparatus, particularly OGPU/NKVD/MGB reports. See Gosu-darstvennyi arkhiv Rossiiskoi Federatsii (GARF) f. R-9401, op. 1, d. 4157, ll. 202–5.

9. Peter H. Solomon, Jr., *Soviet Criminal Justice under Stalin* (Cambridge: Cambridge University Press, 1996), 443; Eugenia Belova and Paul Gregory, "Political Economy of Crime and Punishment under Stalin," *Public Choice* 140, nos. 3–4 (2009): 463–78.

10. N. Vert [Nicolas Werth], *Terror i besporiadok: Stalinizm kak sistema* (Moscow: Rosspen, 2010), 427–28.

11. G. [Jacques] Rossi, *Spravochnik po GULAGu*, ed. N. E. Gorbanevskaia (Moscow: Prosvet, 1991), 1:59.

12. G. Rossi, "Real'nyi sotsializm," *Volia: Zhurnal uznikov totalitarnykh sistem*, nos. 2–3 (1994): 178.

13. Bezborodov et al., *Istoriia stalinskogo GULAGa*, 1:616–19; Oleg Khlevniuk, *The History of the Gulag: From Collectivization to the Great Terror* (New Haven: Yale University Press, 2004), 303–5. This makes a total of fifty million who received sentences, including, as mentioned above, twenty million sentenced to loss of life or freedom.

14. Bezborodov et al., *Istoriia stalinskogo GULAGa*, 1:609.

15. Bezborodov et al., *Istoriia stalinskogo GULAGa*, 1:221.

16. Golfo Alexopoulos, "Stalin and the Politics of Kinship: Practices of Collective Punishment, 1920s–1940s," *Comparative Studies in Society and History* 50, no. 1 (2008): 91–117.

17. GARF f. R-9479, op. 1, d. 60, ll. 136–40; Khlevniuk, *History of the Gulag*, 267–69.

18. S. A. Nefedov, "Prodovol'stvennoe potreblenie sovetskikh trudiashchikhsia v 1930-e gg.," *Voprosy istorii*, no. 12 (2012): 73–75; A. I. Kokurin and N. V. Petrov, *GULAG: Glavnoe upravlenie lagerei, 1917–1960* (Moscow: Mezhdunarodnyi fond "Demokratiia," 2000), 477. These data cannot be said to fully reflect reality, as available resources were often insufficient to meet published rations for prisoners. However, it is true that budgeted quantities for the non-Gulag were also prone to being inflated. It should be emphasized that the *minimal* prisoner ration is included here; that is, Ration no. 1, intended for prisoners unable to meet production targets as well as nonworking invalids.

19. Donald Filtzer, *Soviet Workers and Late Stalinism: Labour and the Restoration of the Stalinist System after World War II* (Cambridge: Cambridge University Press, 2009), 117–57.

20. Nancy Adler, *The Gulag Survivor* (New Brunswick, NJ: Transaction Publishers, 2002); Amir Weiner, "The Empires Pay a Visit: Gulag Returnees, East European Rebellions, and Soviet Frontier Politics," *Journal of Modern History* 78, no. 2 (2006): 333–76; Marc Elie, "Les politiques à l'égard des libérés du Goulag: Amnistiés et réhabilités dans la région de Novosibirsk, 1953–1960," *Cahiers du monde russe* 47,

nos. 1–2 (2006): 327–48; Miriam Dobson, *Khrushchev's Cold Summer: Gulag Returnees, Crime, and the Fate of Reform after Stalin* (Ithaca, NY: Cornell University Press, 2010).

21. Golfo Alexopoulos, "Amnesty 1945: The Revolving Door of Stalin's Gulag," *Slavic Review* 64, no. 2 (2005): 274–306. The conception of the Gulag as an open system that served millions of prisoners' "reeducation" is an important element of Steven A. Barnes, *Death and Redemption: The Gulag and the Shaping of Soviet Society* (Princeton, NJ: Princeton University Press, 2011).

22. Bezborodov et al., *Istoriia stalinskogo GULAGa*, 4:111, 135–36 (data for 1948 are missing). Golfo Alexopoulos ("Amnesty 1945," 275) concludes that the figures provided for freed prisoners do not include those freed as a result of mass amnesties. I must also mention that chronically and/or terminally ill prisoners were often "released to die" so as not to reflect badly on camp statistics. See Michael Ellman, "Soviet Repression Statistics: Some Comments," *Europe-Asia Studies* 54, no. 7 (2002): 1152.

23. Alexopoulos, "Amnesty 1945," 306.

24. Alan Barenberg, "Prisoners without Borders: Zazonniki and the Transformation of Vorkuta after Stalin," *Jahrbücher für Geschichte Osteuropas* 57, no. 4 (2009): 513–34. Steven Barnes (*Death and Redemption*, 44) notes an analogous practice at Karlag.

25. Wilson T. Bell, "Was the Gulag an Archipelago? De-Convoyed Prisoners and Porous Borders in the Camps of Western Siberia," *Russian Review* 72, no. 1 (2013): 116–41.

26. GARF f. R-9414, op. 1, d. 326, ll. 25, 31.

27. Bezborodov et al., *Istoriia Stalinskogo GULAGa*, 3:36.

28. Applebaum, *Gulag*, chap. 13; D. Kheintsen [James Heinzen], "Korruptsiia v GULAGe: Dilemmy chinovnikov i uznikov," in *Gulag: Ekonomika prinuditel'nogo truda*, ed. L. I. Borodkin, P. Gregori [Paul Gregory], and O. V. Khlevniuk (Moscow: Rosspen, 2005), 157–76; A. V. Zakharchenko, *NKVD i formirovanie aviapromyshlennogo kompleksa v Povolzh'e, 1940–1943 gg.* (Samara: Institut rossiiskoi istorii Rossiiskoi akademii nauk [IRI RAN], 2013), 451–61. See also Cynthia V. Hooper, "Bosses in Captivity? On the Limitations of Gulag Memoir," *Kritika: Explorations in Russian and Eurasian History* 14, no. 1 (2013): 117–42.

29. Bezborodov et al., *Istoriia stalinskogo GULAGa*, 3:41–45.

30. Klaus Gestwa, *Die Stalinschen Großbauten des Kommunismus: Sowjetische Technik- und Umweltgeschichte, 1948–1967* (Munich: Oldenbourg, 2010); Florian Mildenberger, "Die Polarmagistrale: Zur Geschichte strategischer Eisenbahnprojekte in Rußlands Norden und Sibirien (1943 bis 1954)," *Jahrbücher für Geschichte Osteuropas* 48, no. 3 (2000): 407–19; M. B. Rogachev, "USEVLON i istoriia 'Mertvoi dorogi,'" in *Pokaianie: Martirolog*, ed. Rogachev (Syktyvkar: Komi knizhnoe izdatel'stvo, 2000), 3:345–73.

31. The concept of internal colonization has recently gained popularity thanks to works of cultural studies. See, e.g., Alexander Etkind, *Internal Colonization: Russia's Imperial Experience* (Cambridge: Polity, 2011). Historians of the Soviet period are similarly seeking approaches to this important problem. See Judith Pallot, "Forced Labour for Forestry: The Twentieth-Century History of Colonisation and Settlement in the North of Perm´ Oblast´," *Europe-Asia Studies* 54, no. 7 (2002): 1055–83; A. I. Shirokov, "Prinuditel´nyi trud i vtoraia volna kolonizatsii Rossiiskogo Severa," in *Istoriia Stalinizma: Prinuditel´nyi trud v SSSR. Ekonomika, politika, pamiat´*, ed. L. I. Borodkin (Moscow: Rosspen, 2013), 55–64; Lynne Viola, "Stalin's Empire: The Gulag and Police Colonization in the Soviet Union in the 1930s," in *Stalin and Europe: Imitation and Domination, 1928–1953*, ed. Timothy Snyder and Ray Brandon (New York: Oxford University Press, 2014), 18–43; and Den Khili [Dan Healey], "Nasledie GULAGa: Prinuditel´nyi trud sovetskoi epokhi kak vnutrenniaia kolonizatsiia," in *Tam vnutri: Praktiki vnutrennei kolonizatsii v kul´turnoi istorii Rossii*, ed. A. Etkind, D. Uffellmann, and I. Kukulin (Moscow: Novoe literaturnoe obozrenie, 2012), 684–728.

32. Iu. A. Poliakov, ed., *Vsesoiuznaia perepis´ naseleniia 1939 goda: Osnovnye itogi* (Moscow: Nauka, 1992), 23–25, 229, 233.

33. Alan Barenberg, "From Prisoners to Citizens? The Experience of Ex-Prisoners in Vorkuta during the Thaw," in *The Thaw: Soviet Society and Culture during the 1950s and 1960s*, ed. Denis Kozlov and Eleonory Gilburd (Toronto: University of Toronto Press, 2013), 143–75.

34. Iu. A. Iurkov, ed., *Naselenie Rossii za 100 let (1897–1997): Statisticheskii sbornik* (Moscow: Goskomstat, 1998), 114–15, 136.

35. Disparate work on Soviet crime and crime fighting based on closed MVD archival materials suggests that these sources seem likely to be fruitful. See, e.g., I. V. Govorov, "Razgul prestupnosti v poslevoennom Leningrade," *Voprosy istorii*, no. 4 (2003): 139–43; and Govorov, "Neglasnaia agentura sovetskoi militsii v 1940-kh gg.," *Voprosy istorii*, no. 4 (2004): 109–19.

36. On the connection between the Great Purge and the fight against crime, see David R. Shearer, *Policing Stalin's Socialism: Repression and Social Order in the Soviet Union, 1924–1953* (New Haven: Yale University Press, 2009). On the return of exiled kulaks to the village, see Sheila Fitzpatrick, *Stalin's Peasants: Resistance and Survival in the Russian Village after Collectivization* (New York: Oxford University Press, 1994).

37. Rossiiskii gosudarstvennyi arkhiv sotsial´no-politicheskoi istorii (RGASPI) f. 558, op. 11, d. 901, ll. 10–13. This letter was included among a summary delivered to Stalin and forwarded to Malenkov for review (RGASPI f. 558, op. 11, d. 901, l. 2).

38. A. Ia. Livshin et al., eds., *Pis´ma vo vlast´, 1928–1939: Zaiavleniia, zhaloby, donosy, pis´ma v gosudarstvennye struktury i sovetskim vozhdiam* (Moscow: Rosspen, 2002), 236.

39. E. Iu. Zubkova, *Poslevoennoe sovetskoe obshchestvo: Politika i povsednevnost'* *1945-1953* (Moscow: Rosspen, 1999), 93-94.

40. John Round, "Marginalized for a Lifetime: The Everyday Experiences of Gulag Prisoners in Post-Soviet Magadan," *Geografiska Annaler*, Series B: *Human Geography* 88, no. 1 (2006): 22.

41. Ronald Grigor Suny, *The Revenge of the Past: Nationalism, Revolution, and the Collapse of the Soviet Union* (Stanford, CA: Stanford University Press, 1993). On the study of internal deportation, see Yaacov Ro'i, "The Transformation of Historiography on the 'Punished Peoples,'" in "Historical Scholarship in Post-Soviet Russia," ed. Gabriel Gorodetsky, special issue of *History and Memory* 21, no. 2 (2009): 150-76.

42. L. P. Kosheleva et al., eds., *Sovetskaia natsional'naia politika: Ideologiia i praktiki 1945-1953* (Moscow: Rosspen, 2013).

43. On the complex topic of witnessing (as relevant to prisoners of Nazi concentration camps), see Giorgio Agamben, *Homo sacer: Chto ostaetsia posle Osventsima. Arkhiv i svidetel'*, trans. I. Levina, O. Dubitskaia, and P. Sokolov (Moscow: Evropa, 2012).

44. Michael Kaznelson, "Remembering the Soviet State: Kulak Children and Dekulakisation," *Europe-Asia Studies* 59, no. 7 (2007): 1164.

45. On politically loyal former prisoners, see Nanci Adler, *Keeping Faith with the Party: Communist Believers Return from the Gulag* (Bloomington: Indiana University Press, 2012). On the pressure to remember through an optimistic lens, see Polly Jones, "Memories of Terror or Terrorizing Memories? Terror, Trauma, and Survival in the Soviet Culture of the Thaw," *Slavonic and East European Review* 86, no. 2 (2008): 346-71.

46. On the conflicting vectors of de-Stalinization, including a "conservative shift" in the organization of the camp system at the beginning of the 1960s, see Marc Elie, "Khrushchev's Gulag: The Soviet Penitentiary System after Stalin's Death, 1954-1964," in *The Thaw*, 125-32; and Jeffrey S. Hardy, "'The Camp Is Not a Resort': The Campaign against Privileges in the Soviet Gulag, 1957-61," *Kritika: Explorations in Russian and Eurasian History* 13, no. 1 (2012): 89-122.

47. See a similar chronology in R. W. Davies, *Soviet History in the Gorbachev Revolution* (Bloomington: Indiana University Press, 1989); and Davies, *Soviet History in the Yeltsin Era* (New York: St. Martin's, 1997).

48. Nanci Adler, "The Future of the Soviet Past Remains Unpredictable: The Resurrection of Stalinist Symbols amidst the Exhumation of Mass Graves," *Europe-Asia Studies* 57, no. 8 (2005): 1093-99; A. B. Roginskii, "Pamiat' o stalinizme," in *Istoriia stalinizma: Itogi i problemy izucheniia*, ed. E. Iu. Kandrashina (Moscow: Rosspen, 2011), 21-27; B. V. Dubin, *Rossiia nulevykh: Politicheskaia kul'tura, istoricheskaia pamiat', povsednevnaia zhizn'* (Moscow: Rosspen, 2011).

49. On such parochial literature on the Gulag, see G. M. Ivanova, *Istoriia GULAGa,*

1918–1958: Sotsial′no-ekonomicheskii i politiko-pravovoi aspekty (Moscow: Nauka, 2006), 9. A relatively recent example of parochial apologia is M. Iu. Morukov, *Pravda GULAGa iz kruga pervogo* (Moscow: Algoritm, 2006).

50. M. Nakonechnyi, "Prazdnik liudoedov," *Pskovskaia guberniia*, 6 February 2013.

51. Nakonechnyi, "Prazdnik liudoedov." The inclination toward a particular rehabilitation of the Gulag also has a significant economic foundation. In several regions within the Russian Federation, camp complexes remain the main source of employment for the local population. See Judith Pallot, "Russia's Penal Peripheries: Space, Place, and Penalty in Soviet and Post-Soviet Russia," *Transactions of the Institute of British Geographers*, n.s., 30, no. 1 (2005): 109–10.

CHAPTER 3. DESTRUCTIVE LABOR CAMPS: RETHINKING SOLZHENITSYN'S PLAY ON WORDS

I am grateful to Wilson Bell, Alain Blum, Michael David-Fox, Sam Diener, Paul R. Gregory, Dan Healey, Peter Holquist, Deborah Kaple, Judith Pallot, Valerie Sperling, and *Kritika: Explorations in Russian and Eurasian History*'s anonymous reviewers for their comments on earlier drafts of this piece. This research was supported by a Campbell National Fellowship at the Hoover Institution, and the archival documents cited herein largely derive from the Hoover's microfilm collection of the Soviet Communist Party and Soviet state archives.

1. David Remnick, "Putin's Pique," *The New Yorker* (17 March 2014): 19; Lidiia Chukovskaia, "Breakthrough," in *Aleksandr Solzhenitsyn: Critical Essays and Documentary Materials*, ed. John B. Dunlop, Richard Haugh, and Alexis Klimoff (New York: Collier Books, 1975), 457.

2. Jacques Rossi, *The Gulag Handbook: An Encyclopedia Dictionary of Soviet Penitentiary Institutions and Terms Related to the Forced Labor Camps* (New York: Paragon House, 1989).

3. Aleksandr Solzhenitsyn, *Arkhipelag Gulag* (Moscow: Al′fa-Kniga, 2009), 385.

4. Solzhenitsyn, *Arkhipelag Gulag*, 386.

5. See, e.g., Anne Applebaum, *Gulag: A History* (New York: Doubleday, 2003); Steven A. Barnes, *Death and Redemption: The Gulag and the Shaping of Soviet Society* (Princeton, NJ: Princeton University Press, 2011); Viktor Berdinskikh, *Viatlag* (Kirov: V. Berdinskikh, 1998); Galina Mikhailovna Ivanova, *Labor Camp Socialism: The Gulag in the Soviet Totalitarian System* (Armonk, NY: M. E. Sharpe, 2000); Oleg V. Khlevniuk, *History of the Gulag: From Collectivization to the Great Terror* (New Haven: Yale University Press, 2004); Lynne Viola, *The Unknown Gulag: The Lost World of Stalin's Special Settlements* (Oxford: Oxford University Press, 2007); and Nicolas

Werth, *Cannibal Island: Death in a Siberian Gulag* (Princeton, NJ: Princeton University Press, 2007).

6. The exception here would be Robert Conquest, *Kolyma: The Arctic Death Camps* (New York: Viking, 1978).

7. On the distinctions between Nazi and Soviet state violence, see Michael Geyer and Sheila Fitzpatrick, eds., *Beyond Totalitarianism: Stalinism and Nazism Compared* (Cambridge: Cambridge University Press, 2008); Peter Holquist, "State Violence as Technique: The Logic of Violence in Soviet Totalitarianism," in *Landscaping the Human Garden: Twentieth-Century Population Management in a Comparative Framework*, ed. Amir Weiner (Stanford, CA: Stanford University Press, 2003), 19–45; Norman M. Naimark, *Stalin's Genocides* (Princeton, NJ: Princeton University Press, 2011); Timothy Snyder, *Bloodlands: Europe between Hitler and Stalin* (New York: Basic Books, 2012); and Weiner, *Making Sense of War: The Second World War and the Fate of the Bolshevik Revolution* (Princeton, NJ: Princeton University Press, 2002).

8. Yet Eugenia Ginzburg famously asserted, "No prisoner ever lived to old age" (*Within the Whirlwind* [New York: Harvest Books, 1982], 207).

9. See, e.g., Robert Jay Lifton, *The Nazi Doctors: Medical Killing and the Psychology of Genocide* (New York: Basic Books, 1988); and Robert N. Proctor, *Racial Hygiene: Medicine under the Nazis* (Cambridge, MA: Harvard University Press, 1988).

10. On Gulag doctors and medical practices, see Dan Healey, "'Dramatological' Trauma in the Gulag: Malingering and Self-Inflicted Injuries and the Prisoner-Patient," in *Geschichte(n) des Gulag—Realität und Fiktion*, ed. Felicitas Fischer von Weikersthal and Karoline Thaidigsmann (Heidelberg: Winter-Verlag, forthcoming); Healey, "'Send Me as Far Away as Possible!' The Gulag Doctor's Notebook as Heroic Genre" (unpublished paper); Healey, "Gulag Spas: Healing Technologies behind Barbed Wire, 1930–1953" (unpublished paper); Boris Nakhapetov, *Ocherki istorii sanitarnoi sluzhby Gulaga* (Moscow: Rosspen, 2009); A. I. Kaufman, *Lagernyi vrach* (Tel Aviv: AM OVED, 1973); V. A. Samsonov, *Zhizn´ prodolzhitsia: Zapiski lagernogo lekpoma* (Petrozavodsk: Kareliia, 1990); S. F. Sapolnova, T. A. Vekshina, and F. G. Kanev, eds., *Liudi v belykh khalatakh* (Syktyvkar: Komi respublikanskaia tipografiia, 2009).

11. The Gulag's ideological-cultural project is explored in Barnes, *Death and Redemption;* and Maxim Gorky, L. Auerbach, and S. G. Firin, eds., *Belomor: An Account of the Construction of the New Canal between the White Sea and the Baltic Sea* (New York: Harrison Smith and Robert Haas, 1935). See also Michael David-Fox, *Showcasing the Great Experiment: Cultural Diplomacy and Western Visitors to the Soviet Union, 1921–1941* (Oxford: Oxford University Press, 2012); Stephen Kotkin, *Magnetic Mountain: Stalinism as a Civilization* (Berkeley: University of California Press, 1995); and Cristina Vatulescu, *Police Aesthetics: Literature, Film, and the Secret Police in Soviet Times* (Stanford, CA: Stanford University Press, 2010).

12. See, e.g., Paul R. Gregory and Valery Lazarev, eds., *The Economics of Forced Labor: The Soviet Gulag* (Stanford, CA: Hoover Institution Press, 2003); Oleg Khlevniuk, "The Economy of the Gulag," in *Behind the Façade of Stalin's Command Economy: Evidence from the Soviet State and Party Archives*, ed. Gregory (Stanford, CA: Hoover Institution Press, 2001), 111–29; and Simon Ertz, *Zwangsarbeit im stalinistischen Lagersystem: Eine Untersuchung der Methoden, Strategien und Ziele ihrer Ausnutzung am Beispiel Norilsk, 1935–1953* (Berlin: Duncker & Humblot, 2006).

13. Slavoj Žižek, *Violence: Six Sideways Reflections* (New York: Picador, 2008), 2, 12–13.

14. On the experiences of women and children in the camps, see Cathy A. Frierson and Semyon Vilensky, *Children of the Gulag* (New Haven: Yale University Press, 2010); Paul R. Gregory, ed., *Women of the Gulag: Portraits of Five Remarkable Lives* (Stanford, CA: Hoover Institution Press, 2013); and Simeon Vilensky, ed., *Till My Tale Is Told: Women's Memoirs of the Gulag* (Bloomington: Indiana University Press, 1999).

15. Christian Gerlach and Nicolas Werth, "State Violence—Violent Societies," in *Beyond Totalitarianism*; Paul Hagenloh, *Stalin's Police: Public Order and Mass Repression in the USSR, 1926–1941* (Baltimore: Johns Hopkins University Press, 2009); David R. Shearer, *Policing Stalin's Socialism: Repression and Social Order in the Soviet Union, 1924–1953* (New Haven: Yale University Press, 2009); Peter H. Solomon, Jr., *Soviet Criminal Justice under Stalin* (Cambridge: Cambridge University Press, 1996).

16. David Brion Davis, *Inhuman Bondage: The Rise and Fall of Slavery in the New World* (Oxford: Oxford University Press, 2006); Orlando Patterson, *Slavery and Social Death: A Comparative Study* (Cambridge, MA: Harvard University Press, 1982).

17. Khlevniuk, *History of the Gulag*, 337.

18. Alexander Etkind, *Warped Mourning: Stories of the Undead in the Land of the Unburied* (Stanford, CA: Stanford University Press, 2013), 26.

19. Paul R. Gregory, "An Introduction to the Economics of Forced Labor," in *Economics of Forced Labor*, 8, 19–20.

20. Solzhenitsyn, *Arkhipelag Gulag*, 355, 436, 450. In particular, the writer drew attention to the dehumanizing term "human raw material," which Maksim Gor´kii used to describe penal laborers on the White Sea Canal project (M. Gor´kii, L. Averbakh, and S. Firin, eds., *Belomorsko-Baltiiskii kanal imeni Stalina: Istoriia stroitel´stva, 1931–1934* [Moscow: Gosudarstvennoe izdatel´stvo "Istoriia fabrik i zavodov," 1934], 609). The analogous term "human material" (*chelovecheskii material*) also appears in a similar context (Gor´kii et al., *Belomorsko-Baltiiskii kanal*, 248).

21. Gustaw Herling, *A World Apart* (New York: Penguin, 1986), 41.

22. Gosudarstvennyi arkhiv Rossiiskoi Federatsii (GARF) f. 9414, op. 1, d. 2737, l. 2.

23. An April 1930 investigation of the Solovetskii camps stated that prisoners were assigned to their category of labor capability by "a special commission" composed of

camp administrators and doctors and that "until this year, this determination had been the sole responsibility of the doctor." See Aleksandr Bezborodov et al., eds., *Istoriia stalinskogo GULAGa: Konets 1920-kh–pervaia polovina 1950-kh godov. Sobranie dokumentov*, 7 vols. (Moscow: Rosspen, 2004–2005), 4:139.

24. GARF f. 9414, op. 1, d. 2737, l. 1.

25. Leona Toker, *Return from the Archipelago: Narratives of Gulag Survivors* (Bloomington: Indiana University Press, 2000), 88–90. On Gulag narratives, see also Anne Applebaum, *Gulag Voices: An Anthology* (New Haven: Yale University Press, 2011); Jehanne M. Gheith and Katherine R. Jolluck, *Gulag Voices: Oral Histories of Soviet Incarceration and Exile* (New York: Palgrave Macmillan, 2011); Gheith, "'I Never Talked': Enforced Silence, Non-Narrative Memory, and the Gulag," in "Memoria, Memory, and Commemoration," special issue of *Mortality* 12, no. 2 (2007): 159–75; and Catherine Merridale, *Night of Stone: Death and Memory in Twentieth-Century Russia* (New York: Viking, 2001).

26. G. I. Kasabova, ed., *O vremeni, o Noril'ske, o sebe . . .* (Moscow: PoliMedia, 2005), 6:550–51.

27. Mark Mazower, *Hitler's Empire: How the Nazis Ruled Europe* (New York: Penguin, 2008), 306–7.

28. Bezborodov et al., *Istoriia stalinskogo GULAGa*, 4:352–53.

29. GARF f. 9414, op. 1, d. 2756, l. 219.

30. Arkhiv Mezhdunarodnogo obshchestva "Memorial" (Memorial Society), Moscow f. 2, op. 1, d. 5, l. 135.

31. Fyodor Michulsky, *Gulag Boss: A Soviet Memoir*, ed. and trans. Deborah Kaple (New York: Oxford University Press, 2011), 83.

32. Aleksandr I. Solzhenitsyn, *The Gulag Archipelago, 1918–1956: An Experiment in Literary Investigation III–IV*, trans. Thomas P. Whitney (New York: Harper and Row, 1975), 49.

33. Prior to that, in 1930, new arrivals in the Solovetskii labor camps were assigned to one of the following categories: (4) capable of all forms of labor; (3) capable of labor, except especially heavy labor; (2) capable of light labor; (1) invalid. See Bezborodov et al., *Istoriia stalinskogo GULAGa*, 4:139–40.

34. GARF f. 9414, op. 1, d. 2737, ll. 3–11.

35. GARF f. 9414, op. 1, d. 2737, l. 1.

36. The special settlers were divided into five labor groupings: (A) able to perform any kind of physical work; (B) able to perform light physical work; (C) incapable of physical work but able to work in and around the special settlement in various seasonal activities (gathering mushrooms, berries, etc.) and in handicrafts; (D) incapable of work; and (E) children under 16 (Viola, *Unknown Gulag*, 98).

37. The earliest reference that I have seen to the List of Illnesses is from April 1930, and it suggests that the Solovetskii camps had just begun to use the list on orders of

the administration of the northern camps (USLON). See Bezborodov et al., *Istoriia stalinskogo GULAGa*, 4:139.

38. GARF f. 9414, op. 1, d. 2747, ll. 1, 11.

39. GARF f. 9414, op. 1, d. 2747, ll. 3–10.

40. GARF f. 9414, op. 1, d. 2747, l. 4.

41. GARF f. 9414, op. 1, d. 2747, l. 11.

42. Barnes, *Death and Redemption*, 36–38.

43. GARF f. 9414, op. 1, d. 352, l. 264. In a 1939 report, the Smolensk oblast NKVD placed inmates in its colonies into these four categories.

44. Rebecca Manley, "Nutritional Dystrophy: The Science and Semantics of Starvation in World War II," in *Hunger and War: Food Provisioning in the Soviet Union during World War II*, ed. Wendy Z. Goldman and Donald Filtzer (Bloomington: Indiana University Press, 2015), 206–64.

45. A. I. Kokurin and N. V. Petrov, *GULAG (Glavnoe upravlenie lagerei), 1918–1960* (Moscow: Materik, 2000), 866.

46. GARF f. 9414, op. 1 (dop.), d. 366, l. 80 (1942).

47. Kokurin and Petrov, *GULAG*, 278.

48. GARF f. 9414, op. 2, d. 165, ll. 39–45.

49. Sick prisoners would be subject to reexamination to determine whether they had recovered enough strength to be fit for manual labor once again (GARF f. 9414, op. 1, d. 2737, l. 2).

50. Donald Filtzer, *Soviet Workers and Late Stalinism: Labour and the Restoration of the Stalinist System after World War II* (Cambridge: Cambridge University Press, 2002), 101.

51. Solzhenitsyn, *Gulag Archipelago III–IV*, 216.

52. GARF f. 9414, op. 2, d. 169, l. 126.

53. GARF f. 9414, op. 1, d. 374, l. 47.

54. In the stenogram, the assigned category is given as 4, which must be a misprint.

55. GARF f. 9414, op. 2, d. 165, ll. 39–45.

56. GARF f. 9414, op. 2, d. 169, l. 22.

57. GARF f. 9414, op. 2, d. 165, ll. 39–45.

58. GARF f. 9414, op. 2, d. 169, l. 22.

59. Solzhenitsyn, *Gulag Archipelago III–IV*, 556.

60. GARF f. 9414, op. 2, d. 169, l. 113. Loidin referenced the forestry camps because they were generally known as among the most harsh.

61. Solzhenitsyn, *Arkhipelag Gulag*, 769.

62. Bezborodov et al., *Istoriia stalinskogo GULAGa*, 4:139–40.

63. GARF f. 9414, op. 1, d. 459 (dop.), ll. 59–62; d. 469 (dop.), l. 4. These reports are largely handwritten, and it appears that they were meant for internal Gulag use only.

64. Kokurin and Petrov, *GULAG*, 433–34; Solomon, *Soviet Criminal Justice*, 405–44.

65. *Ugolovnyi kodeks RSFSR: Ofitsial'nyi tekst s izmeneniiami na 1 iiulia 1950 g. i s prilozheniem postateino-sistematizirovannykh materialov* (Moscow: Gosudarstvennoe izdatel'stvo iuridicheskoi literatury, 1950), 142–43. On Stalin's draconian 1947 theft decrees, see Filtzer, *Soviet Workers;* Yoram Gorlizki, "Rules, Incentives, and Soviet Campaign Justice after World War II," *Europe-Asia Studies* 51, no. 7 (1999): 1245–65; Paul R. Gregory, *Lenin's Brain and Other Tales from the Secret Soviet Archives* (Stanford, CA: Hoover Institution Press, 2008); James Heinzen, "Corruption in the Gulag: Dilemmas of Officials and Prisoners," *Comparative Economic Systems* 47 (June 2005): 456–75; and Solomon, *Soviet Criminal Justice*.

66. Yoram Gorlizki and Oleg Khlevniuk, *Cold Peace: Stalin and the Soviet Ruling Circle, 1945–1953* (Oxford: Oxford University Press, 2004), 125.

67. The words of Ol'ga Vasileeva, an engineer and inspector for the Gulag, quoted in Applebaum, *Gulag*, 114.

68. See, e.g., Mark Kramer, "Stalin, the Split with Yugoslavia, and Soviet–East European Efforts to Reassert Control, 1948–1953," in *Stalin and Europe: Imitation and Domination, 1928–1953*, ed. Timothy Snyder and Ray Brandon (New York: Oxford University Press, 2014), 295–315.

69. GARF f. 9401, op. 1a, d. 313, l. 7.

70. GARF f. 9401, op. 1a, d. 313, l. 7.

71. GARF f. 9401, op. 1a, d. 313, l. 8. The three-tiered system was supposed to take effect on 1 August 1949. In a November 1950 letter from G. P. Dobrynin to S. N. Kruglov, the Gulag director mentions the contents of MVD Order no. 0418, and reminds Kruglov of the categories, as if the MVD director did not have this information readily available. The categories were largely for internal Gulag use (GARF f. 9414, op. 1, d. 2854, ll. 82–83).

72. GARF f. 9401, op. 1a, d. 313, l. 8. The introduction of this practice appears to have been a 1947 MVD order that approved the use of category 3 light labor prisoners in medium labor with a 25 percent reduction in their work quota. These weakened individuals still had to meet their production targets, for their food rations depended on it. See Bezborodov et al., *Istoriia stalinskogo GULAGa*, 4:426.

73. On the one hand, the Gulag Sanitation Department director stated in 1945 that the sanitation department directors had in their possession a listing of prisoners' jobs and their corresponding level of physical difficulty (*nomenklatura vsekh vidov rabot po tiazhesti truda*). He said, "Medical workers who have control over labor utilization must know this document and use it daily in their work" (GARF f. 9414, op. 2, d. 169, l. 144). On the other hand, several sanitation department directors indicated that they lacked guidelines concerning what jobs constituted heavy, medium, and light labor.

74. GARF f. 9414, op. 1 (dop.), d. 372, l. 110. A report on the physical profile of prisoners in the Borskii Camp for 1949 reflected this abrupt change from five categories to three between August and September. In September, category 2 prisoners were moved to category 1, and category 3 and category 3 individualized labor were moved to category 2.

75. The MVD ruled that category 2 and invalid prisoners were supposed to undergo a medical reexamination on a quarterly basis, while prisoners in category 1 were supposed to be reexamined only twice a year, in January and July (GARF f. 9401, op. 1a, d. 313, l. 10).

76. GARF f. 9401, op. 1a, d. 313, l. 8.

77. GARF f. 9401, op. 1a, d. 313, ll. 14–18.

78. GARF f. 9414, op. 1, d. 2854, ll. 82–83.

79. GARF f. 9414, op. 1, d. 621, ll. 46–47.

80. GARF f. 9414, op. 1 (dop.), d. 378, l. 322.

81. The Khabarovsk krai labor camps and colonies recorded 44.8 percent category 1 prisoners, 43.9 percent category 2 prisoners, and 11.2 percent invalids (GARF f. 9414, op. 1, op. 1, d. 2854, l. 33).

82. An NKVD order of 20 August 1940 included an elaborate listing of code words that had to be used in all telegraphic communications concerning prisoners. See Kokurin and Petrov, *GULAG*, 866.

83. Mark Harrison, "Secrecy, Fear, and Transaction Costs: The Business of Soviet Forced Labour in the Early Cold War," *Europe-Asia Studies* 65, no. 6 (2013): 1115.

84. Vladimir Voinovich, *Moscow 2042* (New York: Harcourt Brace Jovanovich, 1987), 220.

85. Marta Craveri and Oleg Khlevniuk, "Krizis ekonomiki MVD (konets 1940-kh–1950-e gody)," *Cahiers du monde russe*, 36, nos. 1–2 (1995): 179–90.

86. Kokurin and Petrov, *GULAG*, 441–42; Applebaum, *Gulag*, 582–83; Barnes, *Death and Redemption*, 76, 116.

87. GARF f. 9414, op. 2, d. 169, l. 26.

88. J. Arch Getty, Gabor T. Rittersporn, and Viktor N. Zemskov, "Victims of the Soviet Penal System in the Pre-War Years: A First Approach on the Basis of Archival Evidence," *American Historical Review* 98, no. 4 (1993): 1017–49.

89. Barnes, *Death and Redemption;* Leonid Borodkin and Simon Ertz, "Coercion versus Motivation: Forced Labor in Norilsk," in *Economics of Forced Labor*, 85–89.

90. Golfo Alexopoulos, "Amnesty 1945: The Revolving Door of Stalin's Gulag," *Slavic Review* 64, no. 2 (2005): 274–306; Alexopoulos, "Exiting the Gulag after War: Women, Invalids, and the Family," *Jahrbücher für Geschichte Osteuropas* 57, no. 4 (2009): 563–79.

91. Applebaum, *Gulag*, 583.

92. M. Iu. Nakonechnyi, "Sazlag OGPU–NKVD kak lager' permanentnoi katas-

trofy so smertnost´iu zakliuchennykh: Sravnenie s Bukhenval´dom SS," in *Trudy III Mezhdunarodnykh istoricheskikh chtenii, posviashchennykh pamiati professora, General´nogo shtaba general-leitenanta Nikolaia Nikolaevicha Golovina (1875–1944), Sankt-Peterburg, 18–20 oktiabria 2012 goda*, ed. K. M. Aleksandrov and S. V. Sheshunova (St. Petersburg: Skriptorium, 2013), 337–80.

93. *Ugolovno-protsessual´nyi kodeks, s izmeneniiami na 1 dekabria 1938 g.: Ofitsial´nyi tekst s prilozheniem postateino-sistematizirovannykh materialov* (Moscow: Iuridicheskoe izdatel´stvo Narodnogo komissariata iustitsii SSSR, 1938), 108 (article 457-8).

94. Khlevniuk, *History of the Gulag*, 78.

95. V. A. Isupov, *Demograficheskie katastrofy i krizisy v Rossii v pervoi polovine XX veka: Istoriko-demograficheskie ocherki* (Novosibirsk: Sibirskii khronograf, 2000), 164.

96. GARF f. 9414, op. 1, d. 2743, l. 6.

97. GARF f. 8131, op. 12, d. 38, l. 2.

98. GARF f. 8131, op. 12, d. 38, l. 4. In fact, these cases were reviewed by different organs. Dal´lag in the Far North reported on 20 October 1935 that it had over a thousand cases for the early release of invalids being reviewed by the camp's own court or commission or by military tribunals or the Gulag (GARF f. 8131, op. 12, d. 38, l. 9).

99. Oleg Volkov, *Pogruzhenie vo t´mu: Iz perezhitogo* (Moscow: Sovetskaia Rossiia, 2000), 366.

100. Michael Ellman, "Soviet Repression Statistics: Some Comments," *Europe-Asia Studies* 54, no. 7 (2002): 1153. See also Khlevniuk, *History of the Gulag*, 108.

101. GARF f. 9414, op. 2, d. 169, l. 93.

102. GARF f. 9414, op. 2, d. 169, l. 13.

103. Kasabova, *O vremeni, o Noril´ske*, 6:553.

104. Memorial Society, St. Petersburg f. B-1, op. 1, d. Gol´ts, Ekaterina Pavlovna, interview with Niki Georgievna Gol´ts in Moscow on 13 October 2010, conducted by Irina Suslova of Memorial in St. Petersburg. This citation comes from 3–4 of the transcribed interview or item 10 in the file.

105. Solzhenitsyn, *Gulag Archipelago III–IV*, 220.

106. GARF f. 9414, op. 1 (dop.), d. 492, l. 111.

107. GARF f. 9414, op. 1 (dop.), d. 493, l. 54.

108. Varlam Shalamov, *Kolymskie rasskazy* (Moscow: Sovetskaia Rossiia, 1992), 1:115.

CHAPTER 4. LIVES IN THE BALANCE: WEAK AND DISABLED PRISONERS AND THE BIOPOLITICS OF THE GULAG

1. Michel Foucault, *The History of Sexuality*, 1: *An Introduction*, trans. Robert Hurley (London: Penguin, 1978), 135–44; see also his lecture of 17 March 1976 in Foucault, *Society Must Be Defended: Lectures at the Collège de France, 1975–1976*,

trans. David Macey, ed. Mauro Bertani and Alessandro Fontana (London: Penguin, 2004), 238–64.

2. See, e.g., J. Arch Getty, Gabor T. Rittersporn, and Viktor N. Zemskov, "Victims of the Soviet Penal System in the Pre-War Years: A First Approach on the Basis of Archival Evidence," *American Historical Review* 98, no. 4 (1993): 1017–49; Otto J. Pohl, *The Stalinist Penal System: A Statistical History of Soviet Repression and Terror, 1930–1953* (Jefferson, NC: McFarland, 1997); John Keep, "Recent Writing on Stalin's Gulag: An Overview," *Crime, histoire, et sociétés/Crime, History, and Societies* 1, no. 2 (1997): 91–112; Anne Applebaum, *Gulag: A History of the Soviet Camps* (London: Allen Lane, 2003), 518–21; and the extended conversation among Stephen Rosefielde, Steven Wheatcroft, John Keep, Robert Conquest, et al. in *Europe-Asia Studies*, esp. from 1996 to 2000.

3. Twenty years ago, Keep dismissed official Gulag records as fragmentary and mendacious ("Recent Writing on Stalin's Gulag"), but the editors of *The History of Stalin's Gulag*, a major document collection, have demonstrated in their introductory articles the utility of these records. See Aleksandr Bezborodov et al., eds., *Istoriia stalinskogo GULAGa: Konets 1920-kh–pervaia polovina 1950-kh godov. Sobranie dokumentov*, 7 vols. (Moscow: Rosspen, 2004–2005). On this collection, see Kate Brown, "Out of Solitary Confinement: The History of the Gulag," *Kritika: Explorations in Russian and Eurasian History* 8, no. 1 (2007): 67–103.

4. This chapter is part of a wider project, "Medicine in the Gulag Archipelago," supported by the Wellcome Trust (grant no. 085948). I am indebted to Dr. Kirill Rossiianov, Russian Academy of Sciences, for his assistance in the archives and for our fruitful discussions. The views expressed in this chapter are mine alone.

5. The department's name varied slightly between 1930 and 1953. For factual introductions to the Sanotdel, see Boris A. Nakhapetov, "K istorii sanitarnoi sluzhby Gulaga," *Voprosy istorii*, no. 6 (2001): 126–36; and Nakhapetov, *Ocherki istorii sanitarnoi sluzhby Gulaga* (Moscow: Rosspen, 2009). For a local history using the archives of the Muzei istorii zdravookhraneniia g. Ukhty (Ukhta Museum of the History of Public Health), see Charlotte Sophie Kühlbrandt, "Rereading the Gulag through Medicine: Ukhta 1929–1955" (MPhil diss., University of Cambridge, 2011).

6. In May 1941, the Gulag Sanotdel apparatus had 45 out of 526 central Gulag posts; see Gosudarstvennyi arkhiv Rossiiskoi Federatsii (GARF) f. 9414, op. 1, d. 847, ll. 19–21, "Utverzhdenie shtaty tsentral'nogo apparata GULaga 1941 g."

7. For 1939, see Oleg Khlevniuk, *The History of the Gulag: From Collectivization to the Great Terror* (New Haven: Yale University Press, 2004), 210; for wartime (1943), see GARF f. 9414, op. 1, d. 68, l. 23; for 1 January 1953, see GARF f. 9414, op. 1a, d. 627, l. 62.

8. GARF f. 9414, op. 1, d. 2750, ll. 1–4, published in *Istoriia stalinskogo GULAGa*, 4:485–89.

9. A 1939 statute on the camp regime explicitly permitted the employment of doctors with article 58 convictions in their professional capacity: "Vremennaia instriuktsiia o rezhime soderzhaniia zakliuchennykh v ITL NKVD SSSR," in *GULAG (Glavnoe upravlenie lagerei), 1918–1960*, ed. A. I. Kokurin and N. V. Petrov (Moscow: Materik, 2000), 467. Three-quarters of all skilled professionals were being used in their professional specializations in 1947, while 88.2 percent of medical specialists were so employed; see Viktor N. Zemskov, "GULAG (Istoriko-sotsiologicheskii aspekt)," *Sotsiologicheskie issledovaniia*, no. 6 (1991): 10–27, and no. 7 (1991): 3–16, data on 7:11.

10. Graduate assignments to various *vedomstvennye* medical services and to the civilian network are detailed in GARF f. 8009, op. 14, "Otdel kadrov, Sektor raspredeleniia okanchivaiushchikh VUZy NKZ SSSR."

11. Apparently the first courses were devised locally by individual camps—e.g., in the Karaganda Camp as early as 1931 (GARF f. 9414, op. 2, d. 108, ll. 220–35); and in Dmitlag as early as 1933 (GARF f. 9489, op. 2, d. 25, l. 254). In 1936 a central directive from Moscow ordered camps to set up six-month training courses for nurses and paramedics; see Nakhapetov, *Ocherki istorii*, 88. Shalamov was trained as a paramedic in Magadan in 1946; see Varlam Shalamov, *Neskol'ko moikh zhiznei: Vospominaniia, zapisnye knizhki, perepiska, sledstvennye dela* (Moscow: Eksmo, 2009), 230. He described the courses in two stories, "Kursy" and "Veismanist."

12. See, e.g., Janusz Bardach and Kate Gleeson. *Man Is Wolf to Man: Surviving Stalin's Gulag* (London: Simon and Schuster, 1998); Eugenia Ginzburg, *Within the Whirlwind*, trans. Ian Boland (London: Collins and Harvill, 1989); and Efrosiniia Antonovna Kersnovskaia, *Skol'ko stoit chelovek* (Moscow: Rosspen, 2006).

13. Alexander Solzhenitsyn, *The Gulag Archipelago, 1918–1956: An Experiment in Literary Investigation*, trans. Thomas P. Whitney and H. T. Willetts, 3 vols. (London: Collins and Harvill, 1974–1978), 2:218.

14. Solzhenitsyn, *Gulag Archipelago*, 2:214, 218.

15. Shalamov, *Neskol'ko moikh zhiznei*; Varlam Shalamov, "Perchatka," *Preodolenie zla* (Moscow: Eksmo, 2011), 727–56. For short descriptions of Kolyma medical services drawing on Shalamov, see Robert Conquest, *Kolyma: The Arctic Death Camps* (London: Macmillan, 1978), 136–39. On Shalamov's complex literary output, see Leona Toker, *Return from the Archipelago: Narratives of Gulag Survivors* (Bloomington: Indiana University Press, 2000), 141–87.

16. Ginzburg's second volume of her *Krutoi marshrut* details her medical career in the camps (*Within the Whirlwind*, 10, 37, 39, 49, 56, 71). For further fragmented reflections on camp medicine, see Kersnovskaia, *Skol'ko stoit chelovek*; and Zhak [Jacques] Rossi, *Spravochnik po GULAGu*, 2 vols. (Moscow: Prosvet, 1991), 1:36 (*bol'nitsa*), 2:347–49 (*sanchast'*).

17. Applebaum, *Gulag*, 337–46, quotations 337, 339.

18. Steven A. Barnes, *Death and Redemption: The Gulag and the Shaping of Soviet Society* (Princeton, NJ: Princeton University Press, 2011); for an argument that medicine should be considered as one of the incentives offered to prisoners, see Kühlbrandt, "Rereading the Gulag through Medicine," 12–13.

19. There is little historiography of penal medicine with which to compare the Gulag Sanotdel. Aside from the infamous, and radically distinctive, case of Nazi medical abuse of camp inmates, there is little historical writing on medicine in prisons, and social scientists find modern penal medical systems in liberal democracies remarkably resistant to scholarly investigation. From 1877 to 2006 England's Prison Medical Service was an entirely "embedded" medical institution; only after 2006 did British prisoners gain access to the civilian National Health Service (established in 1948). See Stephen Ginn, "Prison Environment and Health," *BMJ* 345 (2012), http://www.bmj .com/content/345/bmj.e5921; Joe Sim, *Medical Power in Prisons: The Prison Medical Service in England, 1774–1989* (Milton Keynes: Open University Press, 1990). For a detailed study of women's prisons in Russia today, see Judith Pallot, Laura Piacentini, and Dominique Moran, *Gender, Geography, and Punishment: The Experience of Women in Carceral Russia* (Oxford: Oxford University Press, 2012).

20. Foucault did not publish a conclusive statement on "biopower," and in his lectures at the Collège de France in the 1970s, he modified the concept enunciated in the first volume of *History of Sexuality*. A helpful guide to the evolution of the idea is Sven-Olov Wallenstein, "Introduction: Foucault, Biopolitics, and Governmentality," in *Foucault, Biopolitics, and Governmentality*, ed. Jakob Nilsson and Wallenstein (Stockholm: Södertörn Philosophical Studies, 2013).

21. Foucault, *History of Sexuality*, 1:140.

22. Michel Foucault, *Discipline and Punish: The Birth of the* Prison, trans. Alan Sheridan (New York: Vintage, 1979), first published in 1975; Foucault, *History of Sexuality*, 1:139.

23. Foucault, *Society Must Be Defended,* 249–50.

24. Foucault, *History of Sexuality*, 1:144. On norms as common to both disciplinary and biopower, see *Society Must Be Defended,* 253. Even in his later lectures Foucault began to subsume biopolitics into a larger model of governmentality that focused on liberal and neoliberal political systems; see Wallenstein, "Introduction." Foucault saw these forms of power (which succeeded but did not supplant "sovereign" power—"the right to take life or let live") evolving in historical succession but not eclipsing each other. Rather, they interacted productively in specific contexts: see Thomas Lemke, "Foucault, Politics, and Failure: A Critical Review of Studies of Governmentality," in *Foucault, Biopolitics, and Governmentality*, 38–40.

25. For critiques from Russian historians, see Laura Engelstein, "Combined Underdevelopment: Discipline and the Law in Imperial and Soviet Russia," *American*

Historical Review 98, no. 2 (1993): 338–53; and Jan Plamper, "Foucault's Gulag," *Kritika: Explorations in Russian and Eurasian History* 3, no. 2 (2002): 255–80.

26. Engelstein, "Combined Underdevelopment," 342–44; for a more pessimistic view of liberal projects, see Daniel Beer, *Renovating Russia: The Human Sciences and the Fate of Liberal Modernity, 1880–1930* (Ithaca, NY: Cornell University Press, 2008).

27. Plamper, "Foucault's Gulag," 261–68.

28. The story of the judicial supervision of the Gulag is unwritten. A department of the USSR Procuracy "for monitoring places of confinement" (Otdel po nadzoru za mestami zakliucheniia) supervised legality in the Gulag. See GARF f. 8131, op. 37. Note also the considerable volume of Gulag-relevant Procuracy files listed in Bezborodov et al., *Istoriia stalinskogo GULAGa*, 7:191–276.

29. See, e.g., Solzhenitsyn, *The Gulag Archipelago*, 2:86–92, 142–67; S. Swianiewicz, *Forced Labour and Economic Development: An Enquiry into the Experience of Soviet Industrialization* (London: Oxford University Press, 1965); G. M. Ivanova, *Gulag v sisteme totalitarnogo gosudarstva* (Moscow: Moskovskii obshchestvennyi nauchnyi fond, 1997), 82–147; and Oleg Khlevniuk, "Vvedenie," in *Istoriia stalinskogo GULAGa*, 3:21–52.

30. Paul R. Gregory and Valery Lazarev, eds., *The Economics of Forced Labor: The Soviet Gulag* (Stanford, CA: Hoover Institution Press, 2003). For a survey of Russian views of Gulag productivity, see Nikita Belykh, *Ekonomika Gulaga kak sistema podnevol'nogo truda (na materialakh Viatlaga 1938–1953 gg.)* (Moscow: Rosspen, 2011), 171–87.

31. In June 1953 Beria proposed closing penal enterprises as "inefficient" and "without a future"; see Ivanova, *Gulag v sisteme totalitarnogo gosudarstva*, 145. On decisions to keep the coal mines of Vorkuta operating after 1953, see Alan Barenberg, *Gulag Town, Company Town: Forced Labor and Its Legacy in Vorkuta* (New Haven: Yale University Press, 2014); for similar decisions in Magadan oblast, see Pavel Grebeniuk, *Kolymskii led: Sistema upravleniia na severo-vostoke Rossii 1953–1964* (Moscow: Rosspen, 2007).

32. For a useful comparison of Gulag/non-Gulag economics, see O. V. Khlevniuk, "Zony sovetskoi ekonomiki: Razdelenie i vzaimodeistvie," in *Istoriia stalinizma: Prinuditel'nyi trud v SSSR. Ekonomika, politika, pamiat'*, ed. L. I. Borodkin, S. A. Krasil'nikov, and Khlevniuk (Moscow: Rosspen, 2013); on the porousness of the Gulag camps, see Wilson T. Bell, "Was the Gulag an Archipelago? De-Convoyed Prisoners and Porous Borders in the Camps of Western Siberia," *Russian Review* 72, no. 1 (2013): 116–41.

33. A Central Committee decree of 18 December 1929, "About the Medical Service of Workers and Peasants," and the replacement of the Old Bolshevik Nikolai Aleksandrovich Semashko by Mikhail Fedorovich Vladimirskii in February 1930

marked this turn; see Christopher M. Davis, "Economics of Soviet Public Health, 1928–1932: Development Strategy, Resource Constraints, and Health Plans," in *Health and Society in Revolutionary Russia*, ed. Susan Gross Solomon and John F. Hutchinson (Bloomington: Indiana University Press, 1990), 156.

34. For the argument that there is value in setting inquiry into government rationalities apart from "social history" because they "are different kinds of inquiry, requiring specific tools of analysis," see Lemke, "Foucault, Politics, and Failure," 47.

35. "Invalidnost'," in *Bol'shaia sovetskaia entsiklopediia*, ed. B. A. Vvedenskii (Moscow: Bol'shaia sovetskaia entsiklopediia, 1952), 17:611–12. No critical history of civilian disability in Russia has been written, but sociological and anthropological studies of contemporary disability are emerging. See William O. McCagg and Lewis H. Siegelbaum, eds., *The Disabled in the Soviet Union: Past and Present, Theory and Practice* (Pittsburgh: University of Pittsburgh Press, 1989); P. V. Romanov and Elena Iarskaia-Smirnova, *Politika invalidnosti: Sotsial'noe grazhdanstvo invalidov v sovremennoi Rossii* (Saratov: Nauchnaia kniga, 2006); and the special issue on disability edited by Marianna Murav'eva for *Zhurnal issledovanii sotsial'noi politiki* 10, no. 2 (2012). This article uses "invalid" and "disabled" interchangeably while recognizing that further research needs to be conducted to problematize uses of these terms in the Russian and Soviet context.

36. Sarah D. Phillips, "'There Are No Invalids in the USSR!' A Missing Soviet Chapter in the New Disability History," *Disability Studies Quarterly* 29, no. 3 (2009), http://dsq-sds.org/article/view/936/1111#endnoteref00.

37. On forced-pace industrialization and its pressures on those who studied labor processes, see Lewis H. Siegelbaum, "Industrial Accidents and Their Prevention in the Interwar Period," in *The Disabled in the Soviet Union*, 85–118; and Siegelbaum, "Soviet Norm Determination in Theory and Practice, 1917–1941," *Soviet Studies* 36, no. 1 (1984): 45–68.

38. M. V. Korobov, I. A. Dubinina, and L. N. Karpov, *Mediko-sotsial'naia ekspertiza v Rossii: Etapy stanovleniia i razvitiia* (Moscow: Federal'noe agentstvo po zdravookhraneniiu i sotsial'nomu razvitiiu, Sankt-Peterburgskii institut usovershenstvovaniia vrachei-ekspertov, 2008), 5–11.

39. On approaches to the invalid in Soviet industry of the 1930s–1940s, see Mark G. Field, *Doctor and Patient in Soviet Russia* (Cambridge, MA: Harvard University Press, 1957), 170–72.

40. Korobov et al., *Mediko-sotsial'naia ekspertiza v Rossii*, 11–12; Beate Fieseler, "'La protection sociale totale': Les hospices pour grands mutilés de guerre dans l'Union soviétique des années 1940," *Cahiers du monde russe* 49, nos. 2–3 (2008): 419–40; Robert Dale, "The Valaam Myth and the Fate of Leningrad's Disabled Veterans," *Russian Review* 72, no. 2 (2013): 260–84.

41. Rebecca Manley, "Nutritional Dystrophy: The Science and Semantics of Star-

vation," in *Hunger and War: Food Provisioning in the Soviet Union during World War II*, ed. Wendy Z. Goldman and Donald Filtzer (Bloomington: Indiana University Press, 2015), 206–64.

42. Donald Filtzer, "Starvation Mortality in Home-Front Industrial Regions during World War II," in *Hunger and War*, 265–338.

43. On self-inflicted wounds (*chlenovreditel'stvo*) and faked illness (*simuliatsiia*), see Dan Healey, "'Dramatological' Trauma in the Gulag: Malingering and Self-Inflicted Injuries and the Prisoner-Patient," in *Geschichte(n) des Gulag—Realität und Fiktion*, ed. Felicitas Fischer von Weikersthal and Karoline Thaidigsmann (Heidelberg: Winter-Verlag, forthcoming).

44. GARF f. 9414, op. 1, d. 2918, l. 41, "Doklad nachal'nika USLONa o deiatel'nosti Upravleniia Solovetskikh lagerei osobogo naznacheniia OGPU za 1926–1927."

45. The Shanin Commission that inspected Solovki in April 1930 after widespread criticism claimed that doctors alone controlled labor selection (Bezborodov et al., *Istoriia stalinskogo GULAGa*, 4:139–46 [Doc. no. 55]). This document and the 1927 report cited in the preceding footnote were both intended to persuade readers that the Solovki camp was well managed. On the mobilized nature of Soviet medicine, see Field, *Doctor and Patient*, 146–80, 221–24. Despite aspirations to make clinical decisions "Soviet-minded," such consistency of outlook in the medical profession was evidently not widespread, as postwar reviews of qualifications demonstrated: Christopher Burton, "Soviet Medical Attestation and the Problem of Professionalisation under Late Stalinism, 1945–1953," *Europe-Asia Studies* 57, no. 8 (2005): 1211–30.

46. On the mixed purposes of the Gulag and their mutual reinforcement, see Khlevniuk, "Zony sovetskoi ekonomiki."

47. For the 1931 decree on medical commissions to classify labor capacity, see GARF f. 9414, op. 1, d. 2737, ll. 1–1 ob., 2–3, 11. Portions of this decree, "Ob ustanovlenii trekh kategorii trudosposobnosti zakliuchennykh v ispravitel'no-trudovykh lageriakh OGPU," were published in *Istoriia stalinskogo GULAGa*, 3:72–74 (Doc. no. 7).

48. For civilian commission practice of the 1930s, see Field, *Doctor and Patient*, 166–70. Such pressures operated in capitalist countries: Steve Sturdy, "The Industrial Body," in *Medicine in the Twentieth Century*, ed. Roger Cooter and John Pickstone (Amsterdam: Harwood Academic Publishers, 2000), 217–34.

49. One prisoner arrested in 1948 described the ritual: "the commission would arrive, and they were from higher ranks—okay, not generals, but *kapitany* of the medical service or lieutenants with silver stripes, and these commissions were often held in the open air on the territory of the zone. They'd cover a table with a green or red cloth, sit down, and write in their 'Talmud' their concealed observations on every prisoner, and . . . you were made to approach the table, they told you, 'Drop your trousers!' You dropped them. 'Turn around!' You turned around. They pinched you

around your buttocks and said, 'Go.' If, so to say, they found 'meat' there, if they didn't feel any bone there, that meant that you were more or less healthy and you could go on working" (interview by the author with Iurii L'vovich Fidel'golts, 23 March 2009, Moscow). For a prisoner paramedic's account of how medical commissions were organized in the late 1940s, see Viktor A. Samsonov, *K tebe, Onego, vse puti: Zapiski lagernogo lekpoma, studenta, vracha, prepodavatelia* (Petrozavodsk: Izdatel'stvo Petrozavodskogo universiteta, 2000), 145–49.

50. The actual names and criteria of categories used varied considerably over the lifetime of the Gulag, and long-term comparison of the statistical size of invalid prisoner numbers is hazardous; the shifting categories enabled camp bosses to conceal weaker prisoners.

51. Officials classified Gulag prisoners by numerous criteria (class origin, type of crime, gender, nationality, labor productivity, political attitudes) to keep order, and manage individual punishment and rehabilitation. See Barnes, *Death and Redemption*, 79–106.

52. "O slabosil'nykh komandakh," GARF f. 9414, op. 1, d. 2736, ll. 4–4 ob., published in *Istoriia stalinskogo GULAGa*, 3:71–72 (Doc. no. 6).

53. Bezborodov et al., *Istoriia stalinskogo GULAGa*, 3:72–74. This decree mentioned "convalescent" (*vyzdoravlivaiushchie*) prisoner teams as well; apparently they were intended for prisoners recently discharged from crowded Gulag hospitals who were in need of further medical attention.

54. "Zapiska nachal'nika GULAG M. D. Bermana, nachal'nika finansovogo otdela GULAG L. I. Berenzona i nachal'nika stroitel'stva kanala Moskva–Volga L. I. Kogana zamestiteliam predsedatelia OGPU G. G. Iagode i G. E. Prokof'evu ob uluchshenii ispol'zovaniia zakliuchennykh lagerei na proizvodstve. 17.05.1933," in *Istoriia stalinskogo GULAGa*, 3:106–11 (Doc. no. 14).

55. "Dokladnaia zapiska zamestitelia predsedatelia OGPU G. G. Iagody I. V. Stalinu ob itogakh khoziaistvennoi deiatel'nosti lagerei za 1932 i pervyi kvartal 1933 g." (not earlier than 26 April 1933), in *Istoriia stalinskogo GULAGa*, 3:95–106 (Doc. no. 13).

56. "Tsirkuliar GULAG no. 669600 ob ozdorovlenii slabosil'nykh zakliuchennykh i uluchshenii ispol'zovaniia rabochei sily v lageriakh" (31 August 1933), GARF f. 9414, op. 1, d. 2741, ll. 47–47 ob., published in *Istoriia stalinskogo GULAGa*, 3:111–12 (Doc. no. 15); see also GARF f. 9414, op. 1, d. 2741, l. 57 (decree of 5 November 1933, extending stays up to a further fourteen days).

57. "Polozhenie o slabosil'nykh v DMITLAGe OGPU," 28 February 1934, GARF f. 9489, op. 2, d. 46, ll. 90–93.

58. Konstantin Petrovich Gurskii, "Po dorogam GULAGa" [vospominaniia], kn. 3-ia, "Ukhtpechlag," Arkhiv Mezhdunarodnogo obshchestva "Memorial" (Memorial Society), Moscow f. 2, op. 3, d. 17, ll. 19–20, 27. Note similar experiences in Shalamov, *Neskol'ko moikh zhiznei*, 204–7.

59. For the amnesties, see Golfo Alexopoulos, "Amnesty 1945: The Revolving Door of Stalin's Gulag," *Slavic Review* 64, no. 2 (2005): 274–306.

60. For 1935, see "Spravka GULAG ob ispol′zovanii kontingentov ITL NKVD na 11.01.1935," 23 January 1935, in *Istoriia stalinskogo GULAGa*, 3:116–17 (Doc. no. 19); for 1938, "Ob″iasnitel′naia zapiska nachal′nika GULAG I. I. Plinera k svodke o trudovom ispol′zovanii zakliuchennykh v lageriakh NKVD za mai 1938 g." (June 1938), in *Istoriia stalinskogo GULAGa*, 3:144–45 (Doc. no. 27). In 1938 about half of the nonworking were either held in penal barracks, deemed recidivist work refusers, or incapable of working because they were unclothed or unshod.

61. GARF f. 9414, op. 1, d. 2753, ll. 134–35 (5 April 1938), ll. 234–35 (6 June 1938). "Hospitalization" in the early Gulag might mean simply permission to remain in one's own barracks, with or without medical attention, particularly in new camps without infirmaries and with few medics. The mobility of the Gulag penal economy, with transports to empty places to establish new camps, meant that many prisoners experienced hospitalization in primitive circumstances. Established camps had infirmaries with beds for hospitalized cases, but these were in constant use; a hierarchy developed of local camp and central hospitals with specialized wards, laboratories, and other medical facilities. An October 1944 Gulag decree indicates that a network of central and local modern, scientific hospitals with specialist wards and laboratories was the stated goal of the Sanotdel management and the Gulag director, although these facilities began to emerge only after 1945 (GARF f. 9414, op. 2, d. 165, ll. 85–87, in *Istoriia stalinskogo GULAGa*, 4:519–22 [Doc. no. 287]).

62. GARF f. 9414, op. 1, d. 2740, ll. 52–53 (combined camp, colony, and prison deaths).

63. "Polozhenie o komandakh slabosil′nykh v lageriakh i koloniiakh NKVD SSSR," 21 December 1938, GARF f. 9414, op. 1, d. 2753, ll. 372–79. The decree was signed by the deputy director of Sanotdel, one Sokolov.

64. Local statistics present a far grimmer picture than central ones. On 1 June 1938, e.g., out of 19,974 prisoners in Sevzheldorlag only 8,483 were capable of labor; the rest were weakened, invalids, hospitalized, or suffering from vitamin deficiencies. See O. I. Azarov, "Zheleznodorozhnye lageria NKVD (MVD) na territorii Komi ASSR (1938–1959 gg.)" (Candidate's diss., Syktyvkarskii gosudarstvennyi universitet, 2005), 130 (table 6).

65. GARF f. 9414, op. 1, d. 2753, ll. 377–78.

66. Khlevniuk, *History of the Gulag*, 186–235.

67. GARF f. 9489, op. 2, d. 46, ll. 89–90 ob.

68. Grigorii Vlasovich Kniazev, "Vospominaniia," 3 vols., Memorial Society, St. Petersburg (no fond/opis′numbers assigned), 2:281.

69. Kniazev, "Vospominaniia," 2:318–23.

70. Bezborodov et al., *Istoriia stalinskogo GULAGa*, 3:105.

71. Zinaida Danilovna Usova, "ChSIR: Vospominaniia. Moskva, 1988," Memorial Society, Moscow f. 2, op. 1, d. 118, ll. 53–55.

72. Lev Khurges, *Moskva–Ispaniia–Kolyma* (Moscow: Vremia, 2012), 602.

73. GARF f. 9414, op. 1, d. 1138, l. 39 (March 1938).

74. GARF f. 9414, op. 1, d. 1140, ll. 176–77. These totals include camps and colonies; for the total population, see Getty et al., "Victims of the Soviet Penal System," 1023.

75. GARF f. 9414, op. 1, d. 1140, ll. 38–41, for protests against limiting transports to Kolyma to the fittest. For a survivor-invalid recalling the deportation of disabled prisoners from Kolyma to mainland camps in eastern Siberia in 1940, see Grigorii Moiseevich Muravin, "Iz mraka kul´ta lichnosti," Vospominaniia, n.d., Memorial Society, St. Petersburg (no fond, opis´, delo nos. assigned), ll. 130–31.

76. Applebaum furnishes recorded mortality figures of 115,484 (6.1 percent) for 1941; 352,560 (24.9 percent) for 1942; 267,826 (22.4 percent) for 1943; 114,481 (9.2 percent) for 1944; and 81,917 (5.95 percent) for 1945 (*Gulag*, 519).

77. Filtzer, "Starvation Mortality." On postwar undernourishment among workers, see Donald Filtzer, *The Hazards of Urban Life in Late Stalinist Russia: Health, Hygiene, and Living Standards, 1943–1953* (Cambridge: Cambridge University Press, 2010), 163–253.

78. Civilian refeeding programs targeted key industrial workers (Filtzer, "Starvation Mortality," 323, 327–28).

79. The state's food distribution policies are described in Wendy Z. Goldman, "Not by Bread Alone: Food, Workers, and the State," in *Hunger and War*, 44–97.

80. GARF f. 9414, op. 1, d. 2006, ll. 4, 14, "Ob″iasnitel´naia zapiska k finansovomu planu UITK GULAGa na 1942 god" (3 November 1941).

81. GARF f. 8131, op. 37, d. 1253, ll. 154–56.

82. GARF f. 8131, op. 37, d. 1253, l. 209.

83. GARF f. 9414, op. 1, d. 1181, l. 35.

84. GARF f. 9414, op. 1, d. 1181, l. 49.

85. Memorial Society, Moscow f. 2, op. 1, d. 118, ll. 73–77.

86. Anna Filippovna Rabinovich (Vospominaniia), Memorial Society, Moscow f. 2, op. 1, d. 99, ll. 40 (camps set up and shut down quickly near Pot´ma ITL); Raisa L´vovna Volynskaia (Vospominaniia), Memorial Society, Moscow f. 2, op. 2, d. 13, ll. 14–15 (hauling food across the steppes near Akmolinsk ITL); Muravin, "Iz mraka kul´ta lichnosti," ll. 158–59 (distributing work to prisoners near death, Tynda ITL).

87. GARF f. 9414, op. 1, d. 2785, l. 16.

88. On medical priorities at the front see, e.g., N. G. Ivanov, A. S. Georgievskii, and O. S. Lobastov, *Sovetskoe zdravookhranenie i voennaia meditsina v Velikoi Otechestvennoi voine 1941–1945* (Leningrad: Meditsina, 1985), 24–26; P. F. Gladkikh and A.

E. Loktev, *Sluzhba zdorov´ia v Velikoi Otechestvennoi voine 1941–1945 gg.: Ocherki istorii otechestvennoi voennoi meditsiny* (St. Petersburg: Dmitrii Bulanin, 2005), 45, 48.

89. GARF f. 9414, op. 1, d. 2785, ll. 49, 100–100 ob. (June and November 1943 decrees signed by Sanotdel leaders).

90. See Gulag instruction "Ob ispol´zovaniia vyzdoravlivaiushchikh i khronicheski bol´nykh zakliuchennykh na rabotakh po izgotovleniiu predmetov shirpotreba" (1 December 1944), published in *Istoriia stalinskogo GULAGa*, 4:523 (Doc. no. 288); for the report, see GARF f. 9414, op. 1, d. 325, l. 13, "Spravka o vypolnenii . . . prikaza NKVD SSSR no. 0202 'Ob organizatsii spets. lagpodrazdelenii i kolonii dlia soderzhaniia zakliuchennykh III-kategorii individual´nyi trud.'"

91. See the following studies in labor therapy, all conducted in the Northern Railway Camp (Sevzheldorlag) in Ukhta-Pechora and now in GARF f. 9414, op. 2: S. A. Solodovnikov, "Metody ozdorovleniia kategoriinykh bol´nykh," and N. N. Ravich, "Opyt raboty s nepolnotsennymi kategoriiami v usloviiakh lageria," d. 168, ll. 36–45, 176; "Trudoterapiia (dozirovannyi trud i ego rol´ v dele vosstanovleniia rabochei sily)" (conducted by Drs. Dubrovskii and Solodovnikov), d. 172, l. 3; and O. A. Meburnutov, "'Lechenie trudom' (po materialam Tsentral´noi bol´nitsy Ukhtokombinata MVD)," dd. 178–79.

92. Korobov et al., *Mediko-sotsial´naia ekspertiza v Rossii*, 5–11; Solomon Grigor´evich Gellershtein, *Vosstanovitel´naia trudovaia terapiia v sisteme raboty evakogospitalei* (Moscow: Medgiz, 1943); "Trudoterapiia," in *Bol´shaia sovetskaia entsiklopediia*, ed. B. A. Vvedenskii (Moscow: Bol´shaia sovetskaia entsiklopediia, 1956), 43:333–34.

93. Subjects apparently had little education but some experience in light construction and handicrafts, i.e., skills typical of the peasantry (GARF f. 9414, op. 2, d. 172, ll. 11 ob., 24–25; d. 178, ll. 6–9, esp. l. 7).

94. GARF f. 9414, op. 2, d. 178, l. 9; d. 171, l. 15 ob. This file records a "labor therapy" experiment in Unzhlag on prisoner-patients recovering from tuberculosis.

95. GARF f. 9414, op. 2, d. 172, ll. 15–18 ob. (experiment assigning output norms); d. 178, ll. 1–2 (output not subject to quotas).

96. GARF f. 9414, op. 2, d. 178, l. 11. Weight gain was a key measure of success in these experiments, and optimal prisoner bodies demonstrating such improvement might be photographed for the Sanotdel's internal use; see GARF f. 9414, op. 6, d. 40, l. 4 ob., Fotoal´bom "2-I mesiachnyi dopolnitel´nyi ozdorovitel´nyi punkt Solikamskogo ITL," 1946.

97. See the comments by managers attending conferences about contracts with civilian ministries for Gulag prisoner-labor in GARF f. 9414, op. 1, d. 1208 (1944).

98. Gulag Director Nasedkin praised the experiments and ordered all camps to emulate them on 6 March 1945; see GARF f. 9414, op. 1, d. 2801, ll. 35–36 ob. On

plans for a conference in Pechorlag to discuss nutrition research and to publish results within the Sanotdel system during 1946, see GARF f. 9414, op. 1a, d. 619b, l. 8 ob.

99. GARF f. 9414, op. 1, d. 77, ll. 38 (Lektsii nachal´nika GULAGa Nasedkina dlia Vysshei shkoly NKVD SSSR, 1945).

100. Filtzer, "Starvation Mortality."

101. GARF f. 9414, op. 1, 2790, l. 2 (January 1944).

102. Solzhenitsyn, *Gulag Archipelago*, 2:218–20. For a Kolyma doctor's assignment of a favored priest to a recovery team in this period, see Boris Lesniak, "Voitsek Dazhitskii (Otets Martyn´ian)," in *Dodnes´ tiagoteet,* 2: *Kolyma,* ed. Semen Vilenskii (Moscow: Vozvrashchenie, 2004), 310–18.

103. Memorial Society, Moscow f. 2, op. 1, d. 118, ll. 83–84. Usova referred to her weakened physical condition as the reason she had recently been rejected for a transfer out of the camp.

104. MVD SSSR Order no. 0154 "Ob organizatsii spetsial´nykh podrazdelenii dlia ozdorovleniia fizicheskogo sostoianiia zakliuchennykh. . . ," 27 May 1946, published in *Istoriia stalinskogo GULAGa,* 4:529–31 (Doc. no. 293).

105. "Raspisanie boleznei dlia otbora zakliuchennykh v ozdorovitel´nye podrazdeleniia. . . ," 30 June 1947, in *Istoriia stalinskogo GULAGa,* 4:541–42 (Doc. no. 303). The mentally ill and pregnant women were subject to periodic amnesties or, if they could not be released, were meant to be held respectively in psychiatric wards of Gulag hospitals or camp maternity homes. Patients with sexually transmitted diseases were isolated in "venereal disease camps" (*venzony*), where containment and treatment was thought to be easier.

106. MVD SSSR Order no. 0390, "O spetsial´nykh invalidnykh lageriakh MVD," 19 November 1946, in *Istoriia stalinskogo GULAGa,* 4:535–36 (Doc. no. 297). See also a 7 March 1948 letter to Stalin from Gulag officials admitting that invalids were supported from the state budget, not camp income (GARF f. 9414, op. 1, d. 1312, l. 189).

107. GARF f. 9414, op. 1, d. 1347, l. 23 (invalid prisoners hidden in weakest labor categories); ll. 5–6 (contract labor draining the Gulag of its fittest prisoners).

108. Ivan Mikhailovich Evseev, "Vid na zhitel´stvo" (Vospominaniia), Memorial Society, Moscow f. 2, op. 1, d. 60, l. 71.

109. In a survey of 3,336 camp inmates transferred to central Russian prisons in 1951, one-third were sick or disabled, and of these 294 (26 percent) were deemed invalids because they lacked one or more hands or feet, largely evidence of self-harm to avoid work (GARF f. 9413, op. 1, d. 129, l. 131; see also Healey, "'Dramatological' Trauma in the Gulag").

110. In early 1952 Mineral´nyi Camp had 33 subdivisions, of which 8 were hospital/weak prisoner facilities, while Pechora Camp had 105 subdivisions, of which 14 had similar functions (N. V. Upadyshev, *Gulag na evropeiskom severe Rossii: Genezis, evoliutsiia, raspad* [Arkhangel´sk: Pomorskii universitet, 2007], 286–88, 294–302).

111. Georgii Valentinovich Ustinchenko, "O sostoianii mediko-sanitarnogo ob-sluzhivaniia zakliuchennykh i volnonaemnogo sostava v ITL-UITLK-OITK i merakh po ego uluchshcheniiu" (not later than 11 March 1956), GARF f. 9414, op. 1, d. 2888, l. 79.

112. In April 1957 there were 78,815 invalids in all camps and colonies; civilian disability classification was now applied to prisoners, and 1.27 percent were category 1, 23.7 percent category 2, and 75.03 percent category 3 (GARF f. 9414, op. 1a, d. 627, l. 123). Improving services to disabled nonworking prisoners was on the agenda at conferences of Gulag medical staff (GARF f. 9414, op. 1, d. 2886, ll. 33–43, 46 [1955 conference]; GARF f. 9414, op. 1, d. 2888, l. 174 [1956]).

113. The first Sanotdel director, I. G. Ginzburg, traveled to Kem, Kotlas, Arkhangel´sk, Kungur near Sverdlovsk, Novosibirsk, and elsewhere to inspect camps and issue instructions (GARF f. 9414, op. 1, d. 1, ll. 10, 26 ob.; d. 2736, ll. 2–3 ob.). A conference in Novosibirsk in September 1945 appears to have been the first to bring local Sanotdel directors together (GARF f. 9414, op. 2, d. 169).

114. Filtzer, *Hazards of Urban Life in Late Stalinist Russia*, 127–62.

CHAPTER 5. SCIENTISTS AND SPECIALISTS IN THE GULAG: LIFE AND DEATH IN STALIN'S *SHARASHKA*

1. On samizdat culture, see Ann Komaromi, "The Material Existence of Soviet Samizdat," *Slavic Review* 63, no. 3 (2004): 597–618; and Gordon Johnston, "What Is the History of Samizdat?" *Social History* 24, no. 3 (1999): 115–33.

2. Von Hardesty, "Introduction," to L. L. Kerber, *Stalin's Aviation Gulag: A Memoir of Andrei Tupolev and the Purge Era* (Washington, DC: Smithsonian Institution Press, 1996), 2.

3. "Andrei Nikolaevich Tupolev," *Izvestiia*, 24 December 1972.

4. A. Sharagin [L. L. Kerber], *Tupolevskaia sharaga* (Frankfurt: Possev-Verlag, 1971). A French translation was published in 1973.

5. A. I. Solzhenitsyn, *V kruge pervom* (Frankfurt am main: Fischer, 1968); Solzhenitsyn, *The First Circle*, trans. Thomas P. Whitney (New York: Harper and Row, 1968).

6. Unexpurgated excerpts from the Tupolev manuscript were first published in seven parts in *Izobretatel´ i ratsionalizator* in 1988 (nos. 3, 4, 5, 6, 7, 8, 9) and titled "A delo shlo k voine." A follow-up series appeared in five issues of the same journal in 1990 (nos. 5, 6, 7, 8, 9) under the title "Epopeia bombardirovshchika Tu-4."

7. The full manuscript appeared first in English in 1996 (Kerber, *Stalin's Aviation Gulag*). It was published in Russian as L. L. Kerber, *Tupolev* (St. Petersburg: Politekhnika izdatel´stvo, 1999).

8. For a small sampling of memoirs on the sharashki, see "Istorii Timofeeva-Resovskogo, rasskazannye im samim," *Chelovek*, no. 2 (1993): 148–62; Aleksandr

Emel´ianenkov, "Vyshli my vse iz sharashek . . .," *Soiuz: Belarus'–Rossiia*, 2 February 2006; A. A. Berzin, "Parovozy za koliuchei provolokoi," *Voprosy istorii estestvoznaniia i tekhniki*, no. 4 (1991): 35–37; M. M. Mordukovich, "Nakazanie bez prestupleniia," *Nauka i zhizn´*, no. 3 (1990): 96–105, and no. 4 (1990): 88–94; P. I. Zhukov, "Moia 'sharashka,'" *Nauka i zhizn´*, no. 9 (2006): 86–92, and no. 10 (2006): 74–79. See also Lev Kopelev, "With Solzhenitsyn in the *Sharashka*," *Michigan Quarterly Review* 20, no. 4 (1981): 444–56. Dictionaries of Russian slang typically note that *sharaga* means a "group or company of thieves." See, e.g., V. M. Mokienko and T. G. Nikitina, eds., *Bol´shoi slovar´ russkogo zhargona* (St. Petersburg: Norint, 2000).

9. The phrase is from V. A. Kumanev, ed., *Tragicheskie sud´by: Repressirovannye uchenye Akademii nauk SSSR* (Moscow: Nauka, 1995).

10. See, e.g., D. A. Sobolev, "Repressii v sovetskoi aviapromyshlennosti," *Voprosy istorii estestvoznaniia i tekhniki*, no. 4 (2000): 44–58; A. Pomogaibo, *Oruzhie pobedy i NKVD: Sovetskie konstruktory v tiskakh repressii* (Moscow: Veche, 2004); O. N. Soldatova, *Izobretateli v GULAGe: Istoricheskii ocherk* (Samara: NTTs, 2004); and Soldatova, ed., *Politicheskie repressii pervoi poloviny XX veka v sud´bakh tekhnicheskoi intelligentsii Rossii: Materialy vserossiiskoi nauchnoi konferentsii* (Samara: NTTs, 2009).

11. For a small sampling of recent scholarship on the Gulag, see Steven A. Barnes, *Death and Redemption: The Gulag and the Shaping of Soviet Society* (Princeton, NJ: Princeton University Press, 2011); Oleg V. Khlevniuk, *The History of the Gulag: From Collectivization to the Great Terror* (New Haven: Yale University Press, 2004); G. M. Ivanova, *Istoriia Gulaga, 1918–1958* (Moscow: Nauka, 2006); Paul R. Gregory and Valery Lazarev, eds., *The Economics of Forced Labor: The Soviet Gulag* (Stanford, CA: Hoover Institution Press, 2003); and Lynne Viola, *The Unknown Gulag: The Lost World of Stalin's Special Settlements* (Oxford: Oxford University Press, 2007). In this category, one must also include memoir literature: Fedor V. Mochulsky, *Gulag Boss: A Soviet Memoir*, trans. and ed. Deborah Kaple (Oxford: Oxford University Press, 2011); and Jehanne M. Gheith, ed., *Gulag Voices: Oral Histories of Soviet Incarceration and Exile* (New York: Palgrave Macmillan, 2011).

12. Most works on the Gulag have brief paragraphs on the sharashki, often noting that further research needs to be done. See Khlevniuk, *History of the Gulag*, 32–34, 196–98, 385; Anne Applebaum, *Gulag: A History* (New York: Doubleday, 2003), 110–11, 193, 521; and Ivanova, *Istoriia Gulaga, 1918–1958*, 370–73.

13. O. V. Khlevniuk, "Gulag—ne gulag: Vzaimodeistvie edinogo," paper presented at "The Soviet Gulag: New Research and New Interpretations," conference at Georgetown University, 26–27 April 2013 and published in this volume; Golfo Alexopoulos, "Amnesty 1945: The Revolving Door of Stalin's Gulag," *Slavic Review* 64, no. 2 (2005): 274–306; Galina Mikhailovna Ivanova, *Labor Camp Socialism: The Gulag in the Soviet Totalitarian System* (Armonk, NY: M. E. Sharpe, 2000), 188.

14. Kate Brown, "Out of Solitary Confinement: The History of the Gulag," *Kritika: Explorations in Russian and Eurasian History* 8, no. 1 (2007): 67–103.

15. V. I. Lenin, *Polnoe sobranie sochinenii*, 5th ed., 55 vols. (Moscow: Institut marksizma-leninizma, 1967), 38:166.

16. Kendall E. Bailes, in his classic *Technology and Society under Lenin and Stalin: Origins of the Soviet Technical Intelligentsia, 1917–1941* (Princeton, NJ: Princeton University Press, 1978), has a similar definition for the technical intelligentsia, including "engineers, agronomists, technicians, and applied scientists," although his study focused primarily on "engineers with higher education."

17. Bailes, *Technology and Society under Lenin and Stalin;* Nicholas Lampert, *The Technical Intelligentsia and the Soviet State: A Study of Soviet Managers and Technicians, 1928–1935* (New York: Holmes and Meier, 1980). See also Susanne Schattenberg, *Stalins Ingenieure: Lebenswelten zwischen Technik und Terror in den 1930er Jahren* (Munich: Oldenbourg, 2002), translated into Russian as *Inzhenery Stalina: Zhizn´ mezhdu tekhnikoi i terrorom v 1930-e gody* (Moscow: Rosspen, 2011).

18. Bailes, *Technology and Society under Lenin and Stalin*, 69–158; S. A. Krasil´nikov, ed., *Shakhtinskii protsess 1928 g.: Podgotovka, provedenie, itogi*, 2 vols. (Moscow: Rosspen, 2011–12); L. P. Beliakov, "Shakhtinskoe delo," in *Repressirovannye geologi*, 3rd ed., ed. Beliakov and E. M. Zablotskii (Moscow: MOR RF, 1999), 395–98; "Dela 'prompartii' i 'trudovoi krest´ianskoi partii (TKP)' (1930–1932)," in *Prosim osvobodit´ iz tiuremnogo zakliucheniia: Pis´ma v zashchitu repressirovannykh*, ed. V. Goncharov and V. Nekhotin (Moscow: Sovremennyi pisatel´, 1998), 173–77.

19. Sheila Fitzpatrick, *Education and Social Mobility in the Soviet Union, 1921–1934* (Cambridge: Cambridge University Press, 1979); Michael David-Fox, *Revolution of the Mind: Higher Learning among the Bolsheviks, 1918–1929* (Ithaca, NY: Cornell University Press, 1997).

20. At the time, Kuibyshev was chairman of the USSR Supreme Council of the National Economy (VSNKh), while Iagoda was the first deputy chairman of the OGPU.

21. Document cited in Iu. I. Stetsovskii, *Istoriia sovetskikh repressii* (Moscow: Znak-SP, 1997), 2:166–67.

22. Iagoda to V. M. Molotov, quoted in Sobolev, "Repressii v sovetskoi aviapromyshlennosti."

23. D. P. Grigorovich was arrested on 1 October 1928, and N. N. Polikarpov a year later, on 24 October 1929. For a list of other prominent aviation industry designers and managers arrested, see V. Ivanov, *Neizvestnyi Polikarpov* (Moscow: EKSMO Iauza, 2009), 314–15.

24. The original name for the organization was the Internal Prison Design Bureau (Konstruktorskoe biuro vnutrenniaia tiur´ma, KB VT). After it moved to V. P. Menzhinskii Factory no. 39, it was renamed Central Design Bureau-39 (TsKB-39).

25. Shavrov quoted in A. B. Grigor´ev, *Mezh dvukh stikhii: Ocherki o konstruktorakh* (Moscow: Mashinostroenie, 1992), 125. At the OGPU level, the two men effectively in charge were A. G. Gor´ianov (head of the Technical Department of the OGPU) and N. E. Paufler (director of Factory no. 39).

26. A. S. Iakovlev, *Tsel´ zhizni* (Moscow: Politizdat, 1973), 73.

27. Voroshilov and Ordzhonikidze to the Presidium of TsIK SSSR (May 1931), Gosudarstvennyi arkhiv Rossiiskoi Federatsii (GARF) f. R-3316, op. 64, d. 1130, ll. 1–4. At the time, Voroshilov was people's commissar of military and naval affairs, while Ordzhonikidze was chairman of VSNKh.

28. John T. Greenwood, "The Designers: Their Design Bureaux and Aircraft," in *Russian Aviation and Air Power in the Twentieth Century*, ed. Robin Higham, Greenwood, and Von Hardesty (London: Frank Cass, 1998), 164–66.

29. On 1 April 1931 the OGPU's chief of the EKU, G. E. Prokof´ev, signed Order no. 160/96 naming L. G. Mironov as his new deputy responsible for the Fifth Special-Technical Department in charge of imprisoned specialists, thus formally taking over the sharashka network.

30. I. A. Akulov to L. M. Kaganovich (7 September 1931), Arkhiv Prezidenta Rossiiskoi Federatsii (APRF) f. 3, op. 58, d. 142, l. 2.

31. "O rabotakh zakliuchennykh spetsialistov, rabotaiushchikh v tekhnicheskom otdelenii EKU OGPU" (7 September 1931), APRF f. 3, op. 58, d. 142, ll. 3–12.

32. Voroshilov and Ordzhonikidze to the Presidium of TsIK SSSR, ll. 1–4.

33. Ordzhonikidze to Kaganovich (28 August 1931), APRF f. 3, op. 58, d. 142, l. 23.

34. Akulov to Stalin (23 February 1932), APRF f. 58, op. 142, ll. 24, 25–46. The actual report, authored by EKU Chief L. G. Mironov, divided the work of the imprisoned specialists into twenty separate sections, devoted to the following themes: automobile, tank, and tractor construction; diesel construction; various chemical substances; various explosive substances; nitrogen; resins; alcohol; projectiles and explosives; power networks and installations; electrical locomotives; major electrical engineering projects; boilers; armor; beryllium; ship building; conveyers; cable-laying expeditions; microbiology; textiles; combines; and underwater equipment for the Black Sea-Caspian Sea Canal. See Mironov, "Spravka o rabotakh osuzhdennykh spetsialistov ispol´zuemykh tekh. otd. EKU P.G.P.U.," APRF f. 3, op. 58, d. 142, ll. 25–46.

35. "Vypiska iz protokola no. 92 zasedaniia Politbiuro TsK ot 16 marta 1932 g.," APRF f. 3, op. 58, d. 142, l. 47.

36. David R. Shearer, *Industry, State, and Society in Stalin's Russia, 1926–1934* (Ithaca, NY: Cornell University Press, 1996); Robert A. Lewis, *Science and Industrialization in the USSR: Industrial Research and Development, 1917–1940* (London: Macmillan, 1979).

37. Stalin spoke on 23 June 1931 at a meeting of the Central Committee attended by representatives of various national and regional economic organizations. See

"Novaia obstanovka—novye zadachi khoziaistvennogo stroitel´stva," *Pravda*, 5 July 1931.

38. "O nagrazhdenii aviazavoda no. 39 za iskliuchitel´nye dostizheniia po samoletostroeniiu grazhdanskoi aviatsii," *Pravda*, 10 July 1931.

39. See Voroshilov's note to the military urging them to focus research within Narkomtiazhprom because the ministry could afford them significant manufacturing support: Voroshilov to Tukhachevskii (28 April 1934), Rossiiskii gosudarstvennyi voennyi arkhiv (RGVA) f. 4, op. 14, d. 1171, ll. 54–59.

40. Shavrov quoted in Ivanov, *Neizvestnyi Polikarpov*, 330.

41. This was Aviation Factory no. 24 (also known as the M. V. Frunze Factory) in Moscow. See Rossiiskii gosudarstvennyi arkhiv ekonomiki (RGAE) f. 7515, op. 1, d. 153, ll. 417–18; and N. S. Simonov, *Voenno-promyshlennyi kompleks SSSR v 1920–1950-e gody* (Moscow: Rosspen, 1996), 110–11.

42. N. S. Simonov attributes it to Beria (*Voenno-promyshlennyi kompleks SSSR v 1920–1950-e gody*, 113).

43. Kaganovich to Ezhov (13 March 1938), RGAE f. 7515, op. 1, d. 408, ll. 83–84. See also l. 78 for Kaganovich's assessment of proposals from imprisoned aviation engine designers A. D. Charomskii, B. S. Stechkin, and A. M. Kolosov.

44. "Prikaz Narodnogo komissara vnutrennikh del Soiuza SSR za 1938 god, no. 00240," GARF f. 9401, op. 1a, d. 20, l. 160.

45. N. S. Kruk, "Istoriia OKB-172," in *Vestnik Memoriala* (St. Petersburg: Memorial, 2001), 6:46–54.

46. Marc Jansen and Nikita Petrov, *Stalin's Loyal Executioner: People's Commissar Nikolai Ezhov, 1895–1940* (Stanford, CA: Hoover Institution Press, 2002).

47. Beria to Stalin (9 January 1939), APRF f. 3, op. 58, d. 142, ll. 72–73.

48. For the OTB charter, see "Polozhenie ob osobom tekhnicheskom biuro pri narodnom komissare vnutrennikh del SSSR," APRF f. 3, op. 58, d. 142, ll. 70–71. The document is also stored in GARF f. 9401, op. 1, d. 513, ll. 58–64. For the NKVD order, see APRF f. 3, op. 58, d. 142, l. 77. Prior to the OTB designation, the sharashka was known as the Department of Special Design Bureaus of the NKVD (29 September–21 October 1938), the Fourth Special Department of the NKVD (21 October 1938–9 January 1939), and then the Special Technical Bureau of the NKVD. See A. I. Kokurin and N. V. Petrov, eds., *Lubianka: VChK-OGPU-NKVD-NKGB-MGB-MVD-KGB, 1917–1960. Spravochnik* (Moscow: Memorial, 1997), 129.

49. Simonov, *Voenno-promyshlennyi kompleks SSSR v 1920–1950-e gody*, 113.

50. The original eight themes were aircraft design and propellers; aircraft engines and diesel engines; shipbuilding; (gun)powder; artillery shells and fuses; steel armor; chemical warfare agents and chemical protection; and a group to put into production the AN-1 diesel engine at Factory no. 82 ("Polozhenie ob osobom tekhnicheskom biuro").

51. These were Factory no. 172 (Leningrad); Factory no. 82 (Tushino) where there were two teams; and the NKVD camp in Bolshevo, respectively. In February 1940 the Tupolev team moved from Bolshevo to Factory no. 156 in Moscow.

52. "Reshenie ot 31.3.39 g.: 127. Ob assignovaniiakh NKVD SSSR," APRF f. 3, op. 58, d. 142, l. 83. By comparison, the amount matched the *total* allocated to the leading Soviet rocket research institute, NII-3, between 1934 and 1940. See Asif Siddiqi, "The Rockets' Red Glare: Technology, Conflict, and Terror in the Soviet Union," *Technology and Culture* 44, no. 3 (2003): 470–501.

53. Although the total figures are missing, the amount spent on the sharashka in 1940 and 1941 was 4.1 million and 4.8 million rubles, respectively (Voroshilov to Molotov [20 January 1941], GARF f. 8418, op. 25, d. 635, l. 32).

54. This was the Cheliabinsk Tractor Factory (ChTZ).

55. V. Gurevich, "Zhizn' inzhenera Gurevich," *Zametki evreiskoi istorii*, no. 2 (2008), http://berkovich-zametki.com/2008/Zametki/Nomer2/Gurevich1.htm; Gurevich, "Dizel'nye sharagi," *Zametki po evreiskoi istorii*, no. 6 (2009), http://berkovich-zametki .com/2009/Zametki/Nomer6/Gurevich1.php.

56. Officially, the sharashka network was headed by an NKVD man, M. A. Davydov (21 October 1938–15 January 1939), then L. P. Beria (15 January 1939–4 September 1939), then Davydov again (4 September–8 October 1939), then V. A Kravchenko (from 8 October 1939 on). Actual day-to-day operational activities of the system were overseen by Davydov from October 1938 to October 1939 until his arrest on 8 October 1939. Purged by Beria as part of a general "cleansing" of personnel identified with Ezhov, Davydov was sentenced to death on 7 July 1941 and executed on 27 August 1941. See his biography in A. I. Kokurin and N. V. Petrov, eds., *GULAG (Glavnoe upravlenie lagerei), 1918–1960* (Moscow: Materik, 2000), 812.

57. Nikolai Iamskoi, "NII 'Sharashka,'" *Sovershenno sekretno*, 1 September 2006.

58. Beria mentions 316 specialists working in the sharashka system as of 4 July 1939 (Beria to Stalin [4 July 1939], APRF f. 3, op. 58, d. 142, ll. 84–86).

59. APRF f. 3, op. 58, d. 142, ll. 84–86.

60. These sentences were all issued in absentia on 28 May 1940 on the cases of 307 scientists, designers, engineers, and specialists (A. L. Dedov, P. V. Baranov, and I. A. Serov to N. S. Khrushchev [23 February 1955], APRF f. 3, op. 24, d. 440, ll. 56–58).

61. Tupolev was arrested on 21 October 1937 (Sobolev, "Repressii v sovetskoi aviapromyshlennosti").

62. Kerber, *Tupolev*, 134.

63. Zhukov, "Moia 'sharashka'" (part 1).

64. Gurevich, "Dizel'nye sharagi."

65. Khrapko and Zhukov have differing views on this relationship, for example (Gurevich, "Dizel'nye sharagi"; Zhukov, "Moia 'sharashka'" [part 1]).

66. Sobolev, "Repressii v sovetskoi aviapromyshlennosti," 52.

67. "Protokol no. 18, 27 iiulia 1944 goda" (27 July 1944), Arkhiv Rossiiskoi akademii nauk (ARAN) f. 1546, op. 1, d. 28, l. 1.

68. Beria to Stalin (16 May 1944), GARF f. 9401, op. 2, d. 65, ll. 385–86.

69. [List of Prisoners], GARF f. 9401, op. 2, d. 65, ll. 386–92.

70. "Kratkii otchet o rabotakh 4-go spetsotdela NKVD SSSR s 1939 po 1944 g." (14 August 1944), GARF f. 9401, op. 2, d. 88, ll. 155–61. This lengthy account was prepared as part of a proposed but never published book on the activities of the NKVD during the war.

71. GARF f. 9401, op. 2, d. 88, esp. l. 159.

72. In September 1945 some in the NKVD tabled a proposal to liquidate the Fourth Special Department of the NKVD, but the suggestion remained only that. Only one new sharashka prison design bureau was organized after the war, OKB-86 at Factory no. 86 in Taganrog, headed by the Italian airplane designer R. L. Bartini. It was disbanded in 1948. Another design bureau, OKB-172 at Kresty, appears to have been the only major sharashka that existed through the war and into the mid-1950s.

73. Zhukov, "Moia 'sharashka'" (part 2).

74. Russian television broadcast an immensely popular ten-episode serialization of *The First Circle* in 2006, directed by Gleb Anatol'evich Panfilov.

75. Paul R. Gregory, "An Introduction to the Economics of the Gulag," in *Economics of Forced Labor*, 13.

76. Document from the Ministry of Geology cited in L. P. Beliakov, "Krasnoiarskoe delo," in *Repressirovannye geologi*, 422–27. See also N. Iu. Godlevskaia and I. V. Kreiter, "'Krasnoiarskoe delo' geologov," in *Repressirovannaia nauka*, ed. M. G. Iaroshevskii (Moscow: Nauka, 1994), 2:158–66.

77. Oleg Khlevniuk, "The Economy of the OGPU, NKVD, and MVD of the USSR, 1930–1953: The Scale, Structure, and Trends of Development," in *Economics of Forced Labor*, 53.

78. "Prikaz ministra vnutrennikh del Soiuza SSR no. 0080: Ob organizatsii osobogo tekhnicheskogo biuro no. 1" (22 August 1949), http://www.memorial.krsk.ru/LAGER /Eniisroy/490822.htm.

79. From 14 March 1947 to 3 May 1949 Kravchenko served in other positions within the MVD (Kokurin and Petrov, *GULAG*, 827).

80. "Ob organizatsii v sostave 4 Spetsotdela MVD SSSR 8-go otdeleniia i osobykh biuro 4-go Spetsotdela MVD SSSR v sisteme glavkov i stroke MVD SSSR" (9 November 1949), http://www.memorial.krsk.ru/DOKUMENT/USSR/491109.htm. The new sharashki were designated OKB-2, OPKB-3, OPB-4, OTB-5, and OTB-6.

81. "Soobshchenie Valentiny Georgievny Perelomovi," http://www.memorial.krsk .ru/svidet/mperel.htm.

82. "OTB-1: Stranitsy pamiati," http://www.memorial.krsk.ru/Work/Konkurs/6 /Korj/OTB.htm.

83. Andrey Sokolov, "Forced Labor in Soviet Industry: The End of the 1930s to the Mid-1950s," in *Economics of Forced Labor*, 40; Leonid Borodkin and Simon Ertz, "Forced Labour and the Need for Motivation: Wages and Bonuses in the Stalinist Camp System," *Comparative Economic Studies* 47, no. 2 (2005): 418–36.

84. GARF f. R-5446, op. 86a, d. 7799, ll. 18–25.

85. Kokurin and Petrov, *Lubianka*, 129.

86. Valery Lazarev, "Conclusions," in *Economics of Forced Labor*, 190–91.

87. F. I. Chuev, *Sto sorok besed s Molotovym: Iz dnevnika F. Chueva* (Moscow: Terra, 1991), 458–59, cited in Ivanova, *Labor Camp Socialism*, 113.

88. Voroshilov to Molotov (20 January 1941), GARF f. 8418, op. 25, d. 635, l. 32.

89. See, e.g., Valentin Simonenkov, *"Sharashki": Innovatsionnyi proekt Stalina* (Moscow: Algoritm, 2011).

90. Mikhail Morukov, *Pravda GULAGa iz kruga pervogo* (Moscow: Algoritm, 2006), 175.

91. See esp. chaps. 1, 2, and 3 of Gregory and Lazarev, *Economics of Forced Labor*.

92. An incomplete list of leading specialists (chief designers) who spent time in sharashki, viewed alongside the names of the institutions they headed in the 1960s after their release, conveys a sense of the esoteric, clinical, and numerical nomenclature that was part of their daily lives: A. I. Berg (radar specialist who headed TsNII-108), N. A. Dollezhal´ (nuclear reactors, NII-8), V. P. Glushko (rocket engines, OKB-456), S. P. Korolev (missiles and spacecraft, OKB-1), S. N. Kovalev (submarines, TsKB-18), V. M. Miasishchev (bombers, OKB-23), D. D. Sevruk (rocket engines, OKB-3), M. Iu. Tsirul´nikov (artillery, OKB-172), and A. N. Tupolev (airplanes, OKB-156).

93. Much of the academic literature on ZATOs is driven by the concerns of security studies scholars rather than humanists. For some history and social science literature that touches on ZATOs, see Richard H. Rowland, "Russia's Secret Cities," *Post-Soviet Geography and Economics* 37, no. 7 (1996): 426–62; Ira N. Gang and Robert C. Stuart, "Where Mobility Is Illegal: Internal Migration and City Growth in the Soviet Union," *Journal of Population Economics* 12, no. 1 (1999): 117–34; Cynthia Buckley, "The Myth of Managed Migration: Migration Control and Market in the Soviet Period," *Slavic Review* 54, no. 4 (1995): 896–916; and David R. Shearer, "Elements Near and Alien: Passportization, Policing, and Identity in the Stalinist State, 1932–1953," *Journal of Modern History* 76, no. 4 (2004): 835–81.

94. The website of this institution is OAO "Kontsern Avtomatika," http://niia.ru.

95. The organization is known by its abbreviation, SibtsvetmetNIIproekt. In 1954 OTB-1 was moved from the MVD's jurisdiction to the Ministry of Ferrous Metallurgy. On 24 January 1956 it became Sibtsvetmetproekt and on 13 June 1958, SibtsvetmetNIIproekt, http://sibmetproekt.ru/about/history.

96. Zhukov, "Moia 'sharashka'" (part 2), quotation on 79.

CHAPTER 6. FORCED LABOR ON THE HOME FRONT: THE GULAG AND TOTAL WAR IN WESTERN SIBERIA, 1940–1945

I am very grateful to the editors and outside readers of *Kritika* as well as to Golfo Alexopoulos, Alan Barenberg, Michael David-Fox, Robert Johnson, Dan Healey, Judith Pallot, Martha Solomon, and Lynne Viola for helpful comments and suggestions on aspects of this work.

1. Aleksandr Isaevich Solzhenitsyn, *The GULAG Archipelago, 1918–1956: An Experiment in Literary Investigation III–IV*, trans. Thomas P. Whitney (New York: Harper and Row, 1975), 131.

2. Note that the wartime slogan "All for the Front, All for Victory!" was common in the Gulag.

3. *Miny* can mean mines or mortar shells, and the misspelling in the first word is somewhat confusing, although it is clear from documents about the camp that it refers to shells.

4. Mikhail Grigor´evich Gorbachev, unpublished memoir, Tomsk Memorial Society archives, pages not numbered. This excerpt is from the third notebook in the file and is riddled with spelling errors, which have not been included in the translation.

5. Roger Chickering, "Total War: The Use and Abuse of a Concept," in *Anticipating Total War: The German and American Experiences*, ed. Manfred Boerneke, Roger Chickering, and Stig Forster (Cambridge: Cambridge University Press, 1999), 26. For a discussion of the concept in the Soviet context, see Chris Bellamy, *Absolute War: Soviet Russia in the Second World War* (New York: Knopf, 2007), 16–38. Bellamy uses "total war" to mean the total mobilization of industry and society for the war effort, distinguishing it from "absolute war," which includes the targeting of civilians and a goal of the complete destruction of the other side. See also Mark von Hagen, "New Directions in Military History, 1900–1950: Questions of Total War and Colonial War," *Kritika: Explorations in Russian and Eurasian History* 12, no. 4 (2011): 867–84.

6. V. V. Alekseev and Z. G. Karpenko, "Razvitie narodnogo khoziastva," in *Rabochii klass Sibiri v period uprocheniia i razvitiia sotsializma*, ed. V. V. Alekseev et al. (Novosibirsk: Nauka, 1984), 148.

7. Amir Weiner, *Making Sense of War: The Second World War and the Fate of the Bolshevik Revolution* (Princeton, NJ: Princeton University Press, 2001); Steven A. Barnes, *Death and Redemption: The Gulag and the Shaping of Soviet Society* (Princeton, NJ: Princeton University Press, 2011).

8. For more on the regional camp system, see Wilson T. Bell, "The Gulag and Soviet Society in Western Siberia, 1929–1953" (PhD diss., University of Toronto, 2011); and Bell, "Was the Gulag an Archipelago? De-Convoyed Prisoners and Porous Borders in the Camps of Western Siberia," *Russian Review* 72, no. 1 (2013): 116–41.

9. The NKVD order creating this division (Order no. 0116, 7 April 1942) can be found at Gosudarstvennyi arkhiv Rossiiskoi Federatsii (GARF) f. 9401, op. 1a, d. 117, ll. 26–27.

10. UITLK UNKVD po NSO (Upravlenie ispravitel′no-trudovykh lagerei i kolonii upravleniia narodnogo komissariata vnutrennikh del po Novosibirskoi oblasti) is the cumbersome acronym for the Novosibirsk Oblast Camp and Colony Administration.

11. The 750,000 prisoners came from 27 corrective labor camps and 210 corrective labor colonies. See J. Otto Pohl, *The Stalinist Penal System: A Statistical History of Soviet Repression and Terror, 1930–1953* (London: McFarland and Co., 1997), 16.

12. N. G. Okhotin and A. B. Roginskii, eds., *Sistema ispravitel′no-trudovykh lagerei v SSSR, 1923–1960: Spravochnik*, comp. M. B. Smirnov (Moscow: Zven′ia, 1998), 391. Although this book is otherwise an excellent source of information on the camps, it lacks detailed information about locally administered camps and colonies—which, for the last ten years of the Stalin era, held huge numbers of prisoners.

13. Danila S. Krasil′nikov, "Lageria i kolonii na territorii Novosibirskoi oblasti v gody Velikoi Otechestvennoi voiny (1941–1945)" (Diploma thesis, Novosibirsk State University, 1999), 44.

14. See I. S. Kuznetsov et al., eds., *Novonikolaevskaia guberniia—Novosibirskaia oblast′: 1921–2000. Khronika, dokumenty* (Novosibirsk: Sibirskoe otdelenie Rossiiskoi akademii nauk [RAN], 2001), 146.

15. Note that 1 January figures are not available for UITLiK NSO.

16. Edwin Bacon, *The Gulag at War: Stalin's Forced Labor System in the Light of the Archives* (New York: New York University Press, 1994), 39, 123–44.

17. Leonid Borodkin and Simon Ertz, "Coercion vs. Motivation: Forced Labor in Noril′sk," in *The Economics of Forced Labor: The Soviet Gulag*, ed. Paul R. Gregory and Valery Lazarev (Stanford, CA: Hoover Institution Press, 2003), 79–80.

18. Simon Ertz also argues that by the mid-to-late 1930s "the Gulag administration had evolved in the minds of top Soviet leaders from an organization that supplied prisoner labour to an administration that could, on its own, carry out complex construction projects of the highest priority"("Building Noril′sk," in *Economics of Forced Labor*, 133). David Nordlander has come to a similar conclusion for the camps of Kolyma, where "economic rather than political needs were paramount" ("Magadan and the Economic History of Dalstroi in the 1930s," in *Economics of Forced Labor*, 107).

19. Alan Barenberg, *Gulag Town, Company Town: Forced Labor and Its Legacy in Vorkuta* (New Haven: Yale University Press, 2014), 44.

20. A good overview can be found in Bacon, *Gulag at War*, 72–77.

21. After all, scholars such as Ivanova and Khlevniuk have shown that resources spent on the camps drained resources from the front and, potentially, from other projects. See, e.g., Oleg Khlevniuk, "The Economy of the OGPU, NKVD, and MVD

of the USSR, 1930–1953: The Scale, Structure, and Trends of Development," in *Economics of Forced Labor*, 63–65; and Galina Ivanova, *Labor Camp Socialism: The Gulag in the Soviet Totalitarian System*, trans. Carol Flath (Armonk, NY: M. E. Sharpe, 2000), 69–125, esp. 86, 104.

22. Ivanova, *Labor Camp Socialism*, 76, 86, 96.

23. Golfo Alexopoulos, "Amnesty 1945: The Revolving Door of Stalin's Gulag," *Slavic Review* 64, no. 2 (2005): 274–306. The NKVD and the USSR Procurator Directive no. 185 from April 1942 ordered Article 58ers to remain in the camps, even after their terms had ended, for the duration of the war. For an example, see the prisoner file in Gosudarstvennyi arkhiv Tomskoi oblasti (GATO) f. R-1151, op. 1, d. 319, esp. l. 119.

24. Steven A. Barnes, "All for the Front, All for Victory! The Mobilization of Forced Labor in the Soviet Union during World War Two," *International Labor and Working-Class History* 58 (October 2000): 242.

25. Alexopoulos, "Amnesty 1945," 303.

26. See Barnes, "All for the Front," 252; and Barnes, *Death and Redemption*.

27. Alexopoulos, "Destructive Labor Camps: Rethinking Solzhenitsyn's Play on Words," in this volume.

28. See Gosudarstvennyi arkhiv Novosibirskoi Oblasti (GANO) f. P-260, op. 1, d. 24, ll. 40–41 ob. By 1 April 1943, 51 percent of the camp contingent was unable to work due to poor physical condition. Given Alexopoulos's argument ("Destructive Labor Camps") concerning labor categories—that even those deemed physically fit for heavy labor were generally in poor physical condition—a majority of the prisoner contingent in western Siberia was likely on the verge of death at this time.

29. Lennart Samuelson, *Plans for Stalin's War Machine: Tukhachevskii and Military-Economic Planning, 1925–1941* (New York: St. Martin's, 2000).

30. GARF f. 9414, op. 1, d. 1978, l. 35.

31. See the 13 June 1941 ammunition plan for the NKVD (GARF f. 9414, op. 1, d. 1978, ll. 1–2).

32. GANO f. P-260, op. 1, d. 1, l. 58.

33. Kuznetsov et al., *Novonikolaevskaia guberniia—Novosibirskaia oblast'*, 138. The Siberian Military District was administered from Novosibirsk, and in 1941 it included Novosibirsk oblast (including present-day Tomsk and Kemerovo oblasts), Omsk oblast, Altai krai, and Krasnoiarsk krai.

34. For more on Combine no. 179, see I. M. Savitskii, "Sozdanie v Novosibirske krupneishego v Sibiri tsentra oboronnoi promyshlennosti v gody Velikoi Otechestvennoi voiny," in *Ural i Sibir' v stalinskoi politike*, ed. S. A. Papkov and K. Teraiama (Novosibirsk: Sibirskii khronograf, 2002), 192–204.

35. S. A. Papkov, *Stalinskii terror v Sibiri, 1928–1941* (Novosibirsk: Izdatel'stvo Sibirskogo otdeleniia RAN, 1997), 133–34.

36. This comes from a report on the work of Siblag's Cultural-Educational Department for the first half of 1943 (GARF f. 9414, op. 1, d. 1452, l. 155).

37. GARF f. 9401, op. 1a, d. 107, l. 192.

38. Bell, "Was the Gulag an Archipelago?," 127.

39. For another example, see the case of Georgii Strelkov, an Article 58er in Pechora, who before his arrest had headed the Minusazoloto Gold-Mining Trust in Krasnoiarsk. During the war he led a research lab at the Pechora camp and was allowed to live in that lab and wear a suit rather than prison garb. See Orlando Figes, *Just Send Me Word: A True Story of Love and Survival in the Gulag* (London: Allen Lane, 2012), 57.

40. GANO f. P-4, op. 33, d. 503g, l. 161. Emphasis added.

41. GARF f. 9414, op. 1, d. 1461, l. 196. See also Barnes, "All for the Front!"

42. Bacon, *Gulag at War*, 106.

43. Aleksandr Bezborodov et al., eds., *Istoriia stalinskogo GULAGa: Konets 1920-kh–pervaia polovina 1950-kh godov. Sobranie dokumentov*, 7 vols. (Moscow: Rosspen, 2004–2005), 2:158, Doc. no. 76, "Reshenie Politburo VKP(b): 'O lageriakh NKVD,' 10 September 1939." For more on workday credits, see Simon Ertz, "Trading Effort for Freedom: Workday Credits in the Stalinist Camp System," *Comparative Economic Studies* 47, no. 2 (2005): 476–91.

44. See, e.g., GARF f. 9414, op. 1, d. 1463, l. 145. The following discussion and quotation come from the same report.

45. GARF f. 9414, op. 1, d. 1463, l. 145.

46. D. S. Krasil'nikov, "Lageria i kolonii na territorii Novosibirskoi," 89–90.

47. For this report, see S. A. Krasil'nikov, ed., *Nasha malaia rodina: Khrestomatiia po istorii Novosibirskoi oblasti, 1921–1991* (Novosibirsk: Ekor, 1997), 282–85.

48. For Alin's account of work and life at Chkalov Aviation Factory no. 153, see D. E. Alin, *Malo slov, a goria rechen'ka. . .: Nevydumannye rasskazy* (Tomsk: Volodei, 1997) esp. 127–38.

49. Alin, *Malo slov*, 135–38, quotation 137.

50. S. A. Krasil'nikov, *Nasha malaia rodina*, 282–83. For another discussion of the release of invalids in the region during the war, see V. A. Isupov, *Glavnyi resurs Pobedy: Liudskoi potentsial Zapadnoi Sibiri v gody Vtoroi mirovoi voiny (1939–1945 gg.)* (Novosibirsk: Sova, 2008), 168–69.

51. See Alexopoulos, "Destructive Labor Camps." Kondrashev's statement is reminiscent of Zygmunt Bauman's contention that the drive toward bureaucratic efficiency has no inherent moral boundaries (Bauman, *Modernity and the Holocaust* [New York: Columbia University Press, 1989]).

52. GANO f. R-20, op. 4, d. 12 (Doklad o rabote prokuratury ITL ITK UNKVD [NSO] za 1943 god i 1-i kvartal 1944 god), l. 14.

53. GANO f. R-20, op. 4, d. 12, l. 15. The reluctance to release Article 58ers who

were near death complicates Alexopoulos's argument ("Destructive Labor Camps"). Article 58ers tended to have the longest sentences (particularly in the postwar period) and were treated worse than most other prisoners. It seems likely that a greater percentage of Article 58ers, compared to other prisoner contingents, would have found themselves at the point of near death. Yet if they were not being released early, one would expect to see an increase in the Gulag mortality rate in the postwar years, rather than the reported decrease. Clearly more investigation is needed on this crucial question.

54. See also Alexopoulos, "Destructive Labor Camps."

55. See NKVD Order no. 067 from 2 March 1942, GARF f. 9401, op. 1a, d. 116, ll. 66–69.

56. GANO f. P-260, op. 1, d. 1, l. 21.

57. GANO f. P-260, op. 1, d. 1, l. 33.

58. For mortality rates during the war, see Anne Applebaum, *Gulag: A History* (New York: Doubleday, 2003), 594; and Isupov, *Glavnyi resurs Pobedy*, 76, 113.

59. Ninel′ Severiukhina, *Proshchanie s detstvom: Fragmenti semeinoi khroniki 1941–1944* (St. Petersburg: Izdatel′stvo imeni N. I. Novikova, 2004), 42. Here she notes that wartime rations for *izhdiventsy* were 400 grams of bread per day, for *sluzhashchie* 500 grams, and for *rabochie* 800 grams. The 1939 Order on Gulag Rations had called for 1,100 grams of bread per day. The official rations can be found in A. I. Kokurin and N. V. Petrov, eds., *GULAG (Glavnoe upravlenie lagerei) 1918–1960* (Moscow: Materik, 2002), 476–89, Doc. no. 113.

60. Oleg Khlevniuk, "The Gulag and the Non-Gulag as One Interrelated Whole," in this volume.

61. See Barnes, *Death and Redemption*, 116; and Barenberg, *Gulag Town, Company Town*, 61–62. For the Noril′sk figures, see Leonid Borodkin and Simon Ertz, "Nikel′ v zapoliar′e: Trud zakliuchennykh Noril′laga," in *Gulag: Ekonomika prinuditel′nogo truda*, ed. L. I. Borodkin, P. Gregori [Paul Gregory], and O. V. Khlevniuk (Moscow: Rosspen, 2005), 203–7.

62. For more on modern justification for punishment, see Philip L. Reichel, *Comparative Criminal Justice Systems: A Topical Approach*, 3rd ed. (Upper Saddle River, NJ: Prentice Hall, 2002), esp. 238–41. For more on the development of the modern prison, see Norval Morris and David J. Rothman, eds., *The Oxford History of the Prison: The Practice of Punishment in Western Society* (New York: Oxford University Press, 1995); and Michel Foucault, *Discipline and Punish: The Birth of the Prison*, trans. Alan Sheridan (New York: Vintage Books, 1995). Foucault discusses justifications for punishment most clearly on 236–48.

63. Patricia O'Brien, "The Prison on the Continent: Europe, 1865–1965," in *Oxford History of the Prison*, 203–5.

64. Foucault, *Discipline and Punish*, 242.

65. Pohl, *Stalinist Penal System*, 40.

66. See the report of the KVO UITLK NSO for the second half of 1943 (GARF f. 9414, op. 1, d. 1463, l. 137).

67. Papkov, *Stalinskii terror v Sibiri*, 134–35. Siblag at the time consisted of twenty-seven subdivisions housing 63,646 prisoners.

68. Kate Brown, "Out of Solitary Confinement: The History of the Gulag," *Kritika: Explorations in Russian and Eurasian History* 8, no. 1 (2007), 67–103, esp. 77. See also Khlevniuk, "Gulag and the Non-Gulag."

69. GANO f. P-4, op. 33, d. 238a, l. 43.

70. Two thousand were to come from Novosibirsk oblast, three thousand from Altai krai, four thousand from the Bashkir ASSR, and two thousand from Kirov oblast.

71. Rossiiskii gosudarstvennyi arkhiv sotsial'no-politicheskoi istorii (RGASPI) f. 17, op. 162, d. 31, ll. 73–74.

72. See, e.g., Protocol no. 216, point 4, of the Novosibirsk obkom resolutions, 25 September 1941 (GANO f. P-4, op. 33, d. 503v, ll. 70–78).

73. For more on the gray areas between free and forced labor, see Khlevniuk, "Gulag and the Non-Gulag"; and Barenberg, *Gulag Town, Company Town*.

74. For the 10 September resolution, see GANO f. P-4, op. 33, d. 503v, ll. 1–31, esp. l. 3. For the 14 October resolution, see GANO f. P-4, op. 33, d. 503v, ll. 83–96, esp. ll. 83–85.

75. GANO f. P-4, op. 33, d. 503d, ll. 112–14.

76. Bell, "Was the Gulag an Archipelago?," 131–32.

77. GARF f. 9414, op. 1, d. 2513, l. 14.

78. Alin, *Malo slov*, 130.

79. V. A. Isupov, "Na izlome: Smertnost' naseleniia Sibiri v nachale Velikoi Otechestvennoi voiny," in *Istoricheskaia demografiia Sibiri: Sbornik nauchnykh trudov*, ed. R. S. Vasil'evskii and N. I. Gushchin (Novosibirsk: Nauka, 1992), 186, 193.

80. For a good discussion of the effects of these laws, see Donald Filtzer, *Soviet Workers and Late Stalinism: Labour and the Restoration of the Stalinist System after World War II* (Cambridge: Cambridge University Press, 2002), esp. 27, 162. The harsh labor laws of June 1940, whereby one could be punished for showing up late to work or for illegally changing jobs, were made even harsher under wartime conditions. With a December 1941 decree workers in war industries (broadly defined as the war progressed) could be sentenced to the camps for five to eight years for leaving their jobs without authorization, although many were sentenced in absentia and never actually sent to the Gulag (see Martin Kragh, "Stalinist Labour Coercion during World War II: An Economic Approach," *Europe-Asia Studies* 63, no. 7 [2011]: 1253–73). Transport workers also could receive severe sentences for labor infractions. By 1942–1943 "war industries" included the coal, textile, chemical, and gasoline industries. This decree, moreover, stayed in effect until 1948. From 1942 to 1945 over nine hun-

dred thousand persons were sentenced under this decree, and another two hundred thousand between the end of the war and 1948. See N. Vert [Nicolas Werth], "Vvedenie," in *Istoriia stalinskogo Gulaga,* 1:79.

81. According to I. M. Savitskii, this turnover was directly related to poor living conditions. See I. M. Savitskii, "Formirovanie kadrov oboronnoi promyshlennosti Novosibirskoi oblasti v gody Velikoi Otechestvennoi voiny," in *Zapadnaia Sibir' v Velikoi Otechestvennoi voine (1941–1945 gg.): Sbornik nauchnykh trudov,* ed. V. A. Isupov, S. A. Papkov, and I. M. Savitskii (Novosibirsk: Nauka-Tsentr, 2004), 17–19.

82. Alekseev et al., *Rabochii klass Sibiri,* 81.

83. Isupov, "Sotsial'no-demograficheskaia politika Stalinskogo pravitel'stva v gody Velikoi Otechestvennoi voiny (na materialakh Sibiri)," in *Zapadnaia Sibir' v Velikoi Otechestvennoi voine,* 115–43, esp. 120.

84. Savitskii, "Formirovanie kadrov," 20–21.

85. Kuznetsov et al., eds., *Novonikolaevskaia guberniia—Novosibirskaia oblast',* 157. For an interesting work on German POWs in the Soviet Union, see Andreas Hilger, *Deutsche Kriegsgefangene in der Sowjetunion, 1941–1956: Kriegsgefangenenpolitik, Lageralltag und Erinnerung* (Essen: Klartext, 2000). Hilger argues that from central directives, the *intention* was to treat the German POWs humanely, but often inefficiencies on the ground undermined this effort.

86. See the November 1941 instruction in GARF f. 9479, op. 1, d. 71, ll. 202–3.

87. S. A. Papkov, "'Kontrrevoliutsionnaia prestupnost'' i osobennosti ee podavleniia v Sibiri v gody Velikoi Otechestvennoi voiny (1941–1945)," in *Ural i Sibir' v Stalinskoi politike,* 205–23, esp. 208–11.

88. V. N. Zemskov, *Spetsposelentsy v SSSR, 1930–1960* (Moscow: Nauka, 2005), 84–85.

89. Mark Harrison, *Accounting for War: Soviet Production, Employment, and the Defence Burden, 1940–1945* (Cambridge: Cambridge University Press, 1996), 98. Khlevniuk, in "Gulag and the Non-Gulag," argues that there was a significant gray area of semiforced labor, so we should be cautious about making clear-cut distinctions between free and forced labor in the Stalinist system.

90. K. M. Shchegolev, "Uchastie evakuirovannogo naseleniia v kolkhoznom proizvodstve Zapadnoi Sibiri v gody Velikoi Otechestvennoi voiny," *Istoriia SSSR,* no. 2 (1959): 139–45.

91. For these population figures and more information about wartime evacuations, see Kristen Edwards, "Fleeing to Siberia: The Wartime Relocation of Evacuees to Novosibirsk, 1941–1943" (PhD diss., Stanford University, 1996), esp. 3–8. Note that I. M. Savitskii lists the 1939 population of Novosibirsk oblast at just over four million ("Formirovanie kadrov," 5). For more on wartime evacuations to the region, see Isupov, "Na izlome," 186–98. On the evacuations more generally, see Rebecca Manley, *To the Tashkent Station: Evacuation and Survival in the Soviet Union at War*

(Ithaca, NY: Cornell University Press, 2009). Note that Tashkent was one of the most famous evacuation destinations, as many prominent intellectuals spent the war there (including Anna Akhmatova), but Tashkent received fewer evacuees overall (100,000) than Novosibirsk (150,000). See Manley, *To the Tashkent Station*, 2, 6.

92. Kuznetsov et al., eds., *Novonikolaevskaia guberniia—Novosibirskaia oblast'*, 148. See also Edwards, "Fleeing to Siberia," 5–6. Republican status meant that Novosibirsk officials now answered directly to the Russian Soviet Republic, bypassing provincial authorities; this status was granted to cities deemed especially important for the war effort. For the quotation from the evacuee, see Severiukhina, *Proshchanie s detstvom*, 39.

93. Isupov, *Glavnyi resurs Pobedy*, 311.

94. GANO f. P-260, op. 1, d. 24, ll. 40–41 ob.

95. GANO f. R-20, op. 4, d. 12, l. 10.

96. Bacon, *Gulag at War*, 132.

97. Alexopoulos, "Destructive Labor Camps."

98. See Richard Ek, "Giorgio Agamben and the Spatialities of the Camp: An Introduction," *Geografiska Annaler*, Series B: *Human Geography* 88, no. 4 (2006): 363–86; Giorgio Agamben, *Homo Sacer: Sovereign Power and Bare Life*, trans. Daniel Heller-Roazen (Stanford, CA: Stanford University Press, 1995); and Agamben, *State of Exception*, trans. Kevin Artell (Chicago: University of Chicago Press, 2005).

99. Carl Schmitt, *Political Theology: Four Chapters on the Concept of Sovereignty*, trans. Charles Schwab (Chicago: University of Chicago Press, 2005), 5.

100. Jonathan Hyslop, "The Invention of the Concentration Camp: Cuba, Southern Africa, and the Philippines, 1896–1907," *South African Historical Journal* 63, no. 2 (2011): 251–76.

101. Mark Mazower, "Foucault, Agamben: Theory and Nazis," *boundary 2* 35, no. 1 (2008): 23–34.

102. Weiner, *Making Sense of War*, 87.

103. Applebaum, *Gulag*, 591.

104. Harrison, *Accounting for War*, 98.

105. Lynne Viola, *The Unknown Gulag: The Lost World of Stalin's Special Settlements* (New York: Oxford University Press, 2007), 178–79.

106. For a file on the mobilization of special settlers for the Red Army, see GARF f. 9479, op. 1, d. 113. Novosibirsk oblast is discussed in numerous documents in this file, including ll. 13, 78–80, 99–100, 202–3. As of 12 May 1942, Novosibirsk oblast had mobilized 9,500 special settlers, more than every region except Central Asia.

107. Michael H. Westren, "Nations in Exile: 'The Punished Peoples' in Soviet Kazakhstan, 1941–1961" (PhD diss., University of Chicago, 2012).

108. For some of the trouble the regime had enforcing its harsh labor laws, see Kragh, "Stalinist Labour Coercion during World War II." For more on the partial

relaxation of measures affecting religion and the cultural elite, see Bernd Bonwetsch, "War as a 'Breathing Space': Soviet Intellectuals and the 'Great Patriotic War,'" in *The People's War: Responses to World War II in the Soviet Union*, ed. Robert W. Thurston and Bernd Bonwetsch (Urbana: University of Illinois Press, 2000), 146.

109. See, e.g., Oleg Khlevniuk and Yoram Gorlizki, *Cold Peace: Stalin and the Soviet Ruling Circle, 1945–1953* (New York: Oxford University Press, 1997).

CHAPTER 7. (UN)RETURNED FROM THE GULAG: LIFE TRAJECTORIES AND INTEGRATION OF POSTWAR SPECIAL SETTLERS

A preliminary version of this chapter was presented at the seminar "The Soviet Gulag: New Research and New Interpretations," held on 25–27 April 2013 at Georgetown University. I am grateful to its organizers and participants for the fascinating discussions and good-natured atmosphere. The advice and critical remarks of anonymous reviewers and *Kritika: Explorations in Russian and Eurasian History*'s editor Paul Werth were very useful in the final revisions of the article. I am likewise deeply grateful to Alain Blum and Marta Craveri, scientific directors of the project "Archives sonores: Mémoires européennes du Goulag," without which this research would have been impossible. Alain Blum gave a number of valuable suggestions on this article and graciously permitted me to use materials collected in the course of our joint project on the return of special settlers.

1. Interview with Antanas Kybartas, recorded by Jurgita Mačiulytė, Vilnius, October 2009, Archives sonores: Mémoires européennes du Goulag, CERCEC/RFI, Paris. All interviews cited here come from this collection. Here and elsewhere, the names of all informants who agreed to this in writing in accordance with the rules of CNIL and international law in the realm of defense of personal information, are given in full. All cited interviews were recorded in Russian by Alain Blum, Larisa Salakhova, and myself unless otherwise noted.

2. Detailed information on the project and the methodology of collecting interviews is at http://museum.gulagmemories.eu and in A. Blium [Alain Blum] and Emiliia Kustova, "Zvukovye arkhivy: Evropeiskaia pamiat' o Gulage," in *Migratsionnye posledstviia Vtoroi mirovoi voiny: Etnicheskie deportatsii v SSSR i stranakh Vostochnoi Evropy*, ed. N. N. Ablazhei and Blium (Novosibirsk: Nauka, 2012), 124–68. On the project's results, see Alain Blum, Marta Craveri, and Valerie Nivelon, eds., *Déportés en URSS: Récits d'européens au Goulag* (Paris: Autrement, 2012).

3. Compare, e.g., the simultaneous distancing from this outlook and its reproduction in Tomas Balkelis, "Ethnicity and Identity in the Memoirs of Lithuanian Children Deported to the Gulag," in *Maps of Memory: Trauma, Identity, and Exile in Deportation Memoirs from the Baltic States*, ed. Balkelis and Violeta Davoliūtė (Vilnius: Institute of Lithuanian Literature and Folklore, 2012), 49, 62.

4. On the specificities of children's views of deportation, see M. Kraveri [Craveri] and A.-M. Lozanski [Losonczy], "Traektorii detstva v GULAGe: Pozdnie vospominaniia o deportatsii v SSSR," in *Migratsionnye posledstviia Vtoroi mirovoi voiny*, 168–85. Consider also the observations of Irina Shcherbakova on the specific recollections of former prisoners sent to the postwar Gulag in their youth ("Opyt issledovaniia memuaristiki i ustnykh svidetel'stv byvshikh uznikov," *Uroki istorii*, http://www.urokiistorii.ru/memory/oral/2009/05/pamyat-gulaga).

5. Some of the GARF documents have been published by N. F. Bugai, V. N. Zemskov, N. L. Pobol', P. M. Polian, and T. V. Tsarevskaia-Diakina. The regional archive in question is Gosudarstvennyi arkhiv noveishei istorii Irkutskoi oblasti (GANIIO). Police records come from the Lithuanian Special Archives (LYA) and Lithuanian Central State Archives (LCVA).

6. On the situation of peasants in the camps, see S. A. Krasil'nikov and L. A. Viola, "Vvedenie," in *Politbiuro i krest'ianstvo: Vysylka, spetsposelenie, 1930–1940*, ed. N. N. Pokrovskii et al. (Moscow: Rosspen, 2006), 2:46–47.

7. Iu. A. Levada, "Chelovek lukavyi: Dvoemyslie po-rossiiski," *Monitoring obshchestvennogo mneniia: Ekonomicheskie i sotsial'nye peremeny* 45, no. 1 (2000): 20. For an interesting attempt to summarize the discussion of tactics compatible with "accommodation and even enthusiasm regarding the authorities' decisions and actions," see Elena Osokina, "O sotsial'nom immunitete, ili Kriticheskii vzgliad na kontseptsiiu passivnogo (povsednevnogo) soprotivleniia," *Sotsial'naia istoriia: Ezhegodnik* (St. Petersburg: Aleteiia, 2010), 284–300.

8. Nanci Adler, *The Gulag Survivor: Beyond the Soviet System* (New Brunswick, NJ: Transaction Publishers, 2001); Adler, "Life in the 'Big Zone': The Fate of Returnees in the Aftermath of Stalinist Repression," *Europe-Asia Studies* 51, no. 1 (1999): 5–19; Adler, "Enduring Repression: Narratives of Loyalty to the Party before, during, and after the Gulag," *Europe-Asia Studies* 62, no. 2 (2010): 211–34; Stephen Cohen, *The Victims Return: Survivors of the Gulag after Stalin* (New York: Publishing Works, 2010); Miriam Dobson, *Khrushchev's Cold Summer: Gulag Returnees, Crime, and the Fate of Reform after Stalin* (Ithaca, NY: Cornell University Press, 2009); Marc Elie, "Les anciens détenus du Goulag: Libérations massives, réinsertion et réhabilitation dans l'URSS poststalinienne, 1953–1964" (PhD diss., Paris, EHESS, 2007).

9. Oleg Khlevniuk, *The History of the Gulag: From Collectivization to the Great Terror* (London: Yale University Press, 2004); G. M. Ivanova, *Istoriia GULAGa, 1918–1959: Sotsial'no-ekonomicheskii i politichesko-pravovoi aspekty* (Moscow: Nauka, 2006); V. N. Zemskov, *Spetsposelentsy v SSSR, 1930–1960* (Moscow: Nauka, 2005); P. M. Polian, "*Ne po svoei vole. . .*" *Istoriia i geografiia prinuditel'nykh migratsii v SSSR* (Moscow: OGI-Memorial, 2001); J. Otto Pohl, *Ethnic Cleansing in the USSR, 1937–1949* (Westport, CT: Greenwood, 1999); Amir Weiner, *Making Sense of War: The Second World War and the Fate of the Bolshevik Revolution* (Princeton, NJ: Prince-

ton University Press, 2002); Weiner, "Nature, Nurture, and Memory in a Socialist Utopia: Delineating the Soviet Socio-Ethnic Body in the Age of Socialism," *American Historical Review* 104, no. 4 (1999): 1114–55; Kevin McDermott and Matthew Stibbe, eds., *Stalinist Terror in Eastern Europe: Elite Purges and Mass Repression* (Manchester: Manchester University Press, 2010); Olaf Mertelsmann, ed., *The Sovietization of the Baltic States, 1940–1956* (Tartu: KLEIO, 2003); Elena Zubkova, *Pribaltika i Kreml'*, *1940–1953* (Moscow: Rosspen, 2008); Tonu Tannberg, *Politika Moskvy v respublikakh Baltii v poslevoennye gody, 1944–1956* (Moscow: Rosspen, 2010); Balkelis and Davoliūtė, *Maps of Memory*.

10. Jehanne M. Gheith and Katherine R. Jolluck, *Gulag Voices: Oral Histories of Soviet Incarceration and Exile* (New York: Palgrave Macmillan, 2011); Blum, Craveri, and Nivelon, *Déportés en URSS*; V. A. Berdinskikh, *Spetspereselentsy: Politicheskaia ssylka narodov Sovetskoi Rossii* (Moscow: Novoe literaturnoe obozrenie, 2005); S. A. Krasil'nikov, M. S. Salamatova, and S. N. Ushakova, *Korni ili shchepki: Krest'ianskaia sem'ia na spetsposelenii v Zapadnoi Sibiri v 1930kh–nachale 1950kh gg.* (Moscow: Rosspen, 2010).

11. Aldis Purs, "Soviet in Form, Local in Content: Elite Repression and Mass Terror in the Baltic States, 1940–1953," in *Stalinist Terror in Eastern Europe*, 19, 20, 26–28, 32.

12. Berdinskikh, *Spetspereselentsy*; A. B. Suslov, *Spetskontingent v Permskoi oblasti, 1929–1953* (Moscow: Rosspen, 2010). Note here a number of interesting publications by V. Iu. Bashkuev, dedicated to Lithuanian special settlers, e.g., "Po obe storony rezhima: Nabliudatel'nye dela otdela spetsposelenii MVD BMASSR kak istochnik po istorii litovskoi ssylki v Buriat-Mongoliiu," in *Migratsionnye posledstviia Vtoroi mirovoi voiny*, 24–39.

13. V. Skultans, *The Testimony of Lives: Narrative and Memory in Post-Soviet Latvia* (New York: Routledge, 1997); Balkelis and Davoliūtė, *Maps of Memory*.

14. S. A. Krasil'nikov, *Serp i molot: Krest'ianskaia ssylka v Zapadnoi Sibiri v 30e gody* (Moscow: Rosspen, 2003); Krasil'nikov et al., *Korni ili shchepki*; Lynne Viola, *The Unknown Gulag: The Lost World of Stalin's Special Settlements* (New York: Oxford University Press, 2007).

15. Dobson, *Khrushchev's Cold Summer*; Adler, "Life in the Big Zone"; Elie, "Les anciens détenus du Goulag," 287, 363–68.

16. A rare exception is Amir Weiner, "The Empires Pay a Visit: Gulag Returnees, East European Rebellions, and Soviet Frontier Politics," *Journal of Modern History* 78, no. 2 (2006): 333–76.

17. Our team of interviewers recorded more than thirty interviews with former deportees from these areas who today live in Irkutsk oblast.

18. Boris Dubin, "Pamiat', voina, pamiat' o voine: Konstruirovanie proshlogo v sotsial'noi praktike poslednikh desiatiletii," *Otechestvennye zapiski* 43, no. 4 (2008): 21.

19. The title of this section comes from the interview with Elena Paulauskaitė, Bratsk (Irkutsk oblast), August 2009.

20. Interview with Irina Tarnavska, recorded by Marc Elie and Marta Craveri, Lviv, October 2009.

21. On the similarity of collective-farm villages to the Gulag in terms of coercion, see A. K. Sokolov, "Prinuzhdenie k trudu v sovetskoi ekonomike, 1930-e–ser. 1950-kh gg.," in *Gulag: Ekonomika prinuditel'nogo truda*, ed. L. I. Borodkin, P. Gregori [Paul R. Gregory], and O. V. Khlevniuk (Moscow: Rosspen, 2008), 30.

22. Oleg Khlevniuk, "Zony sovetskoi ekonomiki: Razdelenie i vzaimodeistvie," in *Istoriia stalinizma: Prinuditel'nyi trud v SSSR. Ekonomika, politika, pamiat'. Materialy mezhdunarodnoi nauchnoi konferentsii* (Moscow: Rosspen, 2013), 8–18; Borodkin et al., *Gulag*.

23. The depoliticization of recollections about repression is noted in Elena Iarskaia-Smirnova and Pavel Romanov, "At the Margins of Memory: Provincial Identity and Soviet Power in Oral Histories, 1940–53," in *Provincial Landscapes: Local Dimensions of Soviet Power, 1917–1953*, ed. Donald J. Raleigh (Pittsburgh: University of Pittsburgh Press, 2001), 314. On the gradual depoliticization of Soviet society as a whole, see I. V. Glushchenko, "Shest' tezisov ob izuchenii 'sovetskogo,'" in *SSSR: Zhizn' posle smerti*, ed. Glushchenko, B. Iu. Kagarlitskii, and V. A. Kurennyi (Moscow: Izdatel'skii dom Vysshei shkoly ekonomiki, 2012).

24. The title of this section comes from the interview with A. Kybartas.

25. Violeta Davoliūtė, "'We Are All Deportees': The Trauma of Displacement and the Consolidation of National Identity during the Popular Movement in Lithuania," in *Maps of Memory*, 109, 132–35.

26. Purs, "Official and Individual Perceptions," 35.

27. Interview with Sandra Kalniete, recorded by Alain Blum and Juliette Denis, Riga, January 2009 (in French); interview with Marytė Kontrimaitė, Vilnius, June 2011; conference held by Silva Linarte, Paris, 28 March 2012; interview with A. Kybartas.

28. See the aforementioned works by Lynne Viola, S. A. Krasil'nikov, and A. B. Suslov.

29. The title to this section comes from GANIIO f. 127, op. 30, d. 546, ll. 147–51.

30. GANIIO f. 127, op. 17, d. 316, ll. 156–65.

31. GANIIO f. 127, op. 30, d. 548, ll. 31–34.

32. GANIIO f. 127, op. 14, d. 692, ll. 15–16.

33. GANIIO f. 127, op. 30, d. 376, ll. 24–28 ob.

34. GANIIO f. 127, op. 17, d. 367, l. 17; op. 30, d. 376, l. 1 ob.; op. 17, d. 365, l. 20.

35. GANIIO f. 127, op. 30, d. 546, l. 36.

36. GANIIO f. 127, op. 17, d. 165, l. 89; op. 30, d. 376, l. 1.

37. GANIIO f. 127, op. 30, d. 354, l. 42; d. 546, ll. 208–9; d. 548, ll. 135–44.

38. GANIIO f. 127, op. 30, d. 546, l. 90 ob.

39. GANIIO f. 127, op. 30, d. 354, l. 39.

40. The section title comes from GANIIO f. 127, op. 30, d. 546, l. 36.

41. Complaining of the insufficiency of manpower (and a large percentage of adolescents and adults unfit for work among the workers they did have), in 1951 the administration of Bol'sherechenskii logging enterprise noted with disappointment that the special contingent "for the fulfillment of regular tasks is not real manpower, since first, it is unknown when they will arrive, and second, even if they arrive, we will have to put them to work constructing the amenities that they themselves will use" (GANIIO f. 127, op. 30, d. 546, ll. 23–24; see also op. 30, d. 354, l. 28; and op. 26, d. 6, l. 383). Many deportees recount how directors of local enterprises, when selecting special settlers, did their best to avoid receiving single women with children.

42. On the role of forced labor in the logging sector, see Judith Pallot, "Forced Labor for Forestry: The Twentieth-Century History of Colonization and Settlement in the North of Perm Oblast," *Europe-Asia Studies* 54, no. 7 (2002): 1055–83.

43. Alain Blum, "Déportés en Union soviétique (1930–1953): Décision politique, articulation bureaucratique, diversité des conditions," *Revue d'histoire moderne et contemporaine*, forthcoming; Heinrihs Strods and Matthew Kott, "The File on Operation 'Priboi': A Re-Assessment of the Mass Deportations of 1949," *Journal of Baltic Studies* 33, no. 1 (2002): 1–36; Strods, "Deportatsiia naseleniia Pribaltiiskikh stran," *Voprosy istorii*, no. 9 (1999): 130–36; Vanda Kašauskiene, "Deportations from Lithuania under Stalin, 1940–1953," *Lithuanian Historical Studies* 80, no. 3 (1998): 73–82.

44. Gosudarstvennyi arkhiv Rossiiskoi Federatsii (GARF) f. 9479, op. 1, d. 427, l. 101.

45. GARF f. 9479, op. 1, d. 471, ll. 75–84 ob., 71.

46. Report on the fulfillment of the MVD's instructions of 19 August 1949 no. 3825/k on work among exiled special settlers (GARF f. 9479, op. 1, d. 471, ll. 220–31).

47. The title of this section comes from GANIIO f. 127, op. 14, d. 692, l. 47. On the planning, see Blum, "Déportés en Union soviétique (1930–1953)." On the discrepancies between the "aesthetics" of bureaucratic planning and the reality of Stalinist repressions based on examples of "kulak" exile, see Lynne Viola, "The Aesthetic of Stalinist Planning and the World of Special Villages," *Kritika: Explorations in Russian and Eurasian History* 4, no. 1 (2003): 102–3; and Viola, *Unknown Gulag*, 96, 113.

48. For cases of such redirection, see GARF f. 9479, op. 1, d. 427, ll. 99–100; and Fond A. N. Iakovleva, Al'manakh "Rossiia: XX vek" (electronic resource), Docs. no. 4.50, http://www.alexanderyakovlev.org/fond/issues-doc/1023156, and 4.68, http://www.alexanderyakovlev.org/fond/issues-doc/1023213.

49. 1948: GARF f. 9479, op. 1, d. 427, ll. 102–5; GANIIO f. 127, op. 17, d. 368, l. 103. 1949: GARF f. 9479, op. 1, d. 471, ll. 66–68, 91–96, and d. 475, ll. 75–85; GANIIO f. 127, op. 14, d. 692, ll. 48–53.

50. On "déportations-abandons," see Nicolas Werth, "'Déplacés spéciaux' et 'colons de travail' dans la société stalinienne," *Vingtième siècle: Revue d'histoire*, no. 54 (1997): 34–50. On temporary, disposable manpower, see Viola, *Unknown Gulag*, 102.

51. On allocations, see, e.g., the decision of the Irkutsk oblast ispolkom of 23 February 1949 "O meropriiatiiakh po khoziaistvennomu ustroistvu i rasseleniiu vyselentsev v kolkhozakh i sovkhozakh Irkutskoi oblasti," GANIIO f. 127, op. 14, d. 692, ll. 20–22. As an example of attention to the social aspect (at least at the level of rhetoric), see the arguments used by directors of logging enterprises designed to obtain special settlers attached to other enterprises (ibid., op. 30, d. 545, ll. 124–25).

52. Werth, "'Déplacés spéciaux' et 'colons de travail.'"

53. GARF f. 9479, op. 1, d. 475, ll. 82, 83; GANIIO f. 127, op. 14, d. 692, ll. 22, 48–53.

54. GANIIO f. 127, op. 30, d. 545, l. 68.

55. GANIIO f. 127, op. 14, d. 692, l. 47.

56. The quotation in the section heading comes from the interview with E. Paulauskaitė.

57. Quotation from interview with E. Paulauskaitė. Echoes of the perception of the journey as one of the most frightening moments of deportation can be found in fragments from letters and conversations reported to the heads of echelons by informants in the wagons. The head of Echelon no. 97927 reported to his superiors on the low spirits of his deportees, who considered themselves arrested and were preparing for women and children to be sent to the Far North and for the men to be executed (the experience of deportation in 1941 may have influenced these expectations). If we believe these reports, deportees cheered up when they received permission to open the windows and were told that they were "only" being moved to other regions of the USSR (GARF f. R9479, op. 1, d. 427, ll. 189–97).

58. Interview with A. Kybartas.

59. Interview with Aleksandra Belomestnykh, Kaltuk (Irkutsk oblast), August 2009.

60. Special message to the head of the Second Chief Administration of the MGB USSR (LYA f. K-1, op. 10, d. 69, l. 319). Another author in a separate letter repeats this: "We are calm now; no one calls us kulaks, monsters, or bastards. It was announced that here we had equal rights along with all citizens and however much we worked, that's how much we would earn" (LYA f. K-1, op. 10, d. 69, l. 315).

61. Interview with Juozas Miliauskas, Bratsk (Irkutsk oblast), August 2009.

62. Interview with Antanas Kaunas, Tangui (Irkutsk oblast), January 2010; interview with E. Paulauskaitė; interview with M. Kontrimaitė; interview with Kseniia Makovetskaia, Bada (Irkutsk oblast), January 2010.

63. Interview with E. Paulauskaitė.

64. Interview with E. Paulauskaitė. See the statistics on the distribution of bread per workday in the collective farms of Kachugskii raion (Irkutsk oblast): in 1948, forty

of forty-six collective farms gave out 100–500 grams of bread per workday (GANIIO f. 127, op. 14, d. 692, l. 47). Meanwhile, "dependents" lived only on groceries obtained from stores purchased with money they brought with them (GANIIO f. 127, op. 14, d. 692, ll. 48–53).

65. Order of the Minister of Internal Affairs of the USSR no. 00225 "O vyselenii s territorii Litvy, Latvii i Estonii kulakov s sem´iami, semei banditov i natsionalistov, 12 marta 1949," in *Istoriia stalinskogo GULAGa: Konets 1920-kh–pervaia polovina 1950-kh godov. Sobranie dokumentov*, ed. Aleksandr Bezborodov et al., 7 vols. (Moscow: Rosspen, 2004–5), 1:519–22.

66. Interview with A. Kybartas; GARF f. 9479, op. 1, d. 427, l. 193. See likewise on the frequent thefts of exiles' property by convoy soldiers (reports by heads of echelons, etc.).

67. I draw on the concept offered in Viola and Krasil´nikov, "Vvedenie," 53.

68. GARF f. R9479, op. 1, d. 475, l. 80 (30 April 1949).

69. Krasil´nikov and Viola, "Vvedenie," 50. The section title comes from the interview with J. Miliauskas.

70. Krasil´nikov and Viola, "Vvedenie," 50.

71. Interview with A. Kaunas.

72. GANIIO f. 127, op. 30, d. 545, l. 28; d. 546, ll. 38, 225.

73. Interview with J. Miliauskas; interview with A. Kaunas; interview with Rimgaudas Ruzgys, recorded by Jurgita Mačiulytė, Vilnius, October 2009 (in Lithuanian).

74. GANIIO f. 127, op. 30, d. 548, ll. 94–96.

75. Interview with A. Kaunas; interview with M. Kontrimaitė.

76. Interview with A. Kaunas; interview with M. Kontrimaitė.

77. The reason for one of these inspections was, apparently, a complaint by one of the other workers that Lithuanians received easier work by taking advantage of the protection of the commandant and the director of that mechanized forestry station (GANIIO f. 127, op. 17, d. 368, ll. 18–20, 52–55).

78. The title of this section comes from the interview with M. Kontrimaitė.

79. Interview with Nadezhda Tutik, recorded by Marc Elie and Marta Craveri, Lviv, October 2009; interview with E. Paulauskaitė; interview with R. Ruzgys.

80. See photographs from personal archives of former deportees at http://museum .gulagmemories.eu.

81. See the song lyrics from the MVD archives analyzed in Bashkuev, "Po obe storony rezhima," 33–37; and V. Iu. Bashkuev, "Songs from Siberia: The Folklore of Deported Lithuanians," *Baltic Worlds*, no. 2 (2012): 15–18.

82. Interview with M. Kontrimaitė.

83. See Bashkuev, "Po obe storony rezhima."

84. Interview with M. Kontrimaitė.

85. GANIIO f. 127, op. 30, d. 546, ll. 105–11.

86. Interview with J. Miliauskas; interview with A. Kybartas.

87. The section title comes from the letter of a mother petitioning for her son's release from the special settlement (LYA f. V5, op. 1, d. 38493/5, l. 59).

88. Kraveri and Lozanskii, "Traektorii detstva v GULAGe," 182.

89. On the role of school as a "space for hope and possibility," offering at least some chance for leaving the "archipelago" of peasant special settlements, see Viola, *Unknown Gulag*, 171–73.

90. Uncle Stepa the policeman was a character in a well-known poem by Sergei Mikhalkov.

91. Interview with N. Tutik; interview with M. Kontrimaitė.

92. Interview with M. Kontrimaitė.

93. Balkelis, "Ethnicity and Identity," 62.

94. Purs, "Official and Individual Perceptions," 37; Kraveri and Lozanskii, "Traektorii detstva v GULAGe," 177.

95. Letter of a mother petitioning for the release of her son from the special settlement (LYA f. V5, op. 1, d. 38493/5, l. 58).

96. GARF f. R-5446, op. 47a, d. 3205, ll. 13–14, Decree of the Council of People's Commissars of the USSR no. 34-14s "Ob utverzhdenii polozheniia o spetskomendaturakh"; Decree of the Council of People's Commissars of the USSR no. 35 "O pravovom polozhenii spetspereselentsev," 8 January 1945, published in *Deportatsii narodov SSSR (1930–1950e gody)*, ed. O. L. Milova (Moscow: Institut etnologii i etnicheskoi antropologii Rossiiskoi akademii nauk, 1992), 1:76–80. For a detailed consideration of the legal status of special settlers, see L. P. Belkovets, *Administrativno-pravovoe polozhenie rossiiskikh nemtsev na spetsposelenii, 1941–1955: Istoriko-pravovoe issledovanie* (Moscow: Rosspen, 2008).

97. Compare with R. Ruzgys's views on the initially suspicious attitude of local residents, which he attributes to the Lithuanian special settlers' arrival in a Buriat village in a convoy.

98. On those banned from joining youth organizations, see the interview with Yaroslav Pogarskiy, recorded by Alain Blum, Pereiaslav-Khmelnytskyi, April 2009. For more detail, see Alain Blum, "Difficile retour," in *Déportés en URSS*, 212–27; and http://museum.gulagmemories.eu/en/salle/yaroslav-pogarskiy. On those invited to join, see the interview with M. Kontrimaitė. The status of special settlers was not incompatible with party membership, and in May 1953 the special contingents included eight thousand party and candidate party members (letter of S. N. Kruglov to the Central Committee, July 1953, GARF f. 9479, op. 1, d. 725, l. 182). We can assume that most of them belonged to "punished peoples," who preserved their Komsomol and party cells in exile, according to V. N. Zemskov.

99. In Lithuania on 1 May 1988 little more than 10 percent of the 37,362 deported

families had been declared rehabilitated or "exiled without grounds" (LYA f. V-135, op. 7, d. 549, l. 91).

100. Adler, "Life in the Big Zone," 13. For a detailed description of the various types of problems faced by former Gulag prisoners, see Adler, *Gulag Survivor*, chap. 5.

101. See, e.g., LYA f. V5, op. 1, dd. 23398/5, 38493/5, 11986/5.

102. Compare with Oxana Klimkova's hypothesis about peasant families' insufficient comprehension of the limitations connected with their status of (former) special settlers ("Special Settlements in Soviet Russia in the 1930s–50s," *Kritika: Explorations in Russian and Eurasian History* 8, no. 1 [2007]: 125).

103. Memorandum on the Impurity of Primary and Secondary Educational Institutions in the LLSR, LYA f. K-1, op. 10, d. 99, ll. 85, 336; Special Message to First Secretary of the Central Committee of the Lithuanian Communist Party (TsK KPL) Antanas Sniečkus from the Minister for State Security of the LSSR P. P. Kondakov, 27 March 1953, LYA f. K-1, op. 10, d. 152, ll. 85–86; Memorandum to Antanas Sniečkus on the Result of Additional Checks of Students sent to Moscow for study, March 1953, LYA f. K-1, op. 10, d. 155, ll. 108–11. On the pig farm, see the Memorandum of the MVD LSSR to theTsK KPL on Anti-Soviet Moods, 1951, LYA f. K-1, op. 10, d. 131, l. 42.

104. See various reports of local units of Lithuanian KGB in LYA f. K-1, op. 10, dd. 253, 255; and f. K-18, op. 1, dd. 131, 135, 325. See also Amir Weiner and Aigi Rahi-Tamm, "Getting to Know You: The Soviet Surveillance System, 1939–1957," *Kritika: Explorations in Russian and Eurasian History* 13, no. 1 (2012): 5–45. On rejection, see the interviews with M. Kontrimaitė, J. Miliauskas, A. Kaunas, and K. Makovetskaia.

105. On this, see esp. Weiner, "Empires Pay A Visit."

106. For details, see Blum, "Difficile retour," 212–27.

107. Interview with A. Kybartas. Compare with Rimgaudas Ruzgys, who in his interview underscores that he always felt pressure and for that reason tried to behave as quietly as possible, never moving beyond the framework of his professional activity as an engineer.

108. Others have noted these effects. See, e.g., Purs, "Official and Individual Perceptions," 42.

109. On the variety of forms of discrimination and strategies for overcoming them by former prisoners, see Elie, "Les anciens détenus du Goulag," 367.

110. For more detail, see Weiner, "Empires Pay a Visit," esp. 335–36.

CHAPTER 8. A VISUAL HISTORY OF THE GULAG: NINE THESES

1. This chapter is a revised and expanded version of "Picturing the Gulag," *Kritika: Explorations in Russian and Eurasian History* 16, no. 3 (2015): 476–78.

2. I am aware of only one set of photographs of the Gulag that shows dead prison-

ers: the archive of Vladimir Ablamski, now at the Musée d'histoire contemporaine in Paris, which contains photographs of two internees killed during an escape attempt. Ablamski, a skating champion and professional photographer until his arrest by the Soviet army in Harbin in 1946, was ordered by the Ozerlag camp administration to photograph freed convicts from 1953 to 1956, when he himself was freed.

3. A. I. Solzhenitsyn, *The Gulag Archipelago, 1918–1956: An Experiment in Literary Investigation I–II*, trans. Thomas P. Whitney (New York: Harper and Row, 1974), x.

4. Simon Werrett, "The Panopticon in the Garden: Samuel Bentham's Inspection House and Noble Theatricality in Eighteenth-Century Russia," *Ab Imperio*, no. 3 (2008): 47–70.

5. Iain Lauchlan, "The Okhrana: Security Policing in Late Imperial Russia," in *Late Imperial Russia: Problems and Prospects,* ed. Ian D. Thatcher (Manchester: Manchester University Press, 2005), 44.

6. Aleksandr Belianovskii, "Poslednee slovo tiurmovedeniia: Mezhdunarodnaia tiuremnaia vystavka i kongress 1890 goda," *Ekspo vedomosti*, no. 5–6 (2009): 34–39. No fewer than four catalogues of the exhibition were published at the time.

7. Cristina Vatulescu briefly discusses the history of criminology museums in Russia, as well as the Gulag as a site of display in the 1928 film *Solovki*, in "The Camp as Soviet Exotica: *Solovki*," *Police Aesthetics: Literature, Film, and the Secret Police in Soviet Times* (Stanford, CA: Stanford University Press, 2010), 124–35. See also Julie Draskoczy, *Belomor: Criminality and Creativity in Stalin's Gulag* (Brighton, MA: Academic Studies Press, 2014). Some camps, most notably Solovki and the White Sea-Baltic Canal, had museums that were run by inmates.

8. Aleksei Kirillovich Kuznetsov was himself a *katorzhanin*, sentenced to ten years of katorga and permanent internal exile in Siberia in 1871 for his involvement in the murder of a member of Narodnaia Rasprava (The People's Reprisal), to which Kuznetsov himself belonged. On being released, he went on to found an ethnographic museum and the first photographic studio in Nerchinsk. *Views and Types of the Nerchinsk Katorga* was published as a series of postcards, and a copy of the album was acquired by Vladimir Stasov for the Imperial Public Library in St. Petersburg (now the Russian National Library), where it is still held. Kuznetsov would be sentenced to katorga again in 1906 for his participation in the revolutionary movement.

9. The most extensive collection of these archival photographs is Tomasz Kizny's *Gulag* (Buffalo, NY: Firefly Books, 2004). Anne Applebaum describes some of the Gulag photo albums she encountered in the Russian archives in her review of Kizny's book. See Anne Applebaum, "Album From Hell," *New York Review of Books*, 24 March 2005.

10. Many of the Lubianka head shots are reproduced in David King's *Ordinary Citizens: The Victims of Stalin* (London: Francis Boutle, 2003). For the representation of forced labor camps in Soviet films of the 1920s and early 1930s, see, e.g., Vatulescu,

Police Aesthetics. On Aleksandr Rodchenko's 1933 *USSR in Construction* photo essay on the White Sea-Baltic Canal, see Leah Dickerman, "The Propagandizing of Things," in *Aleksandr Rodchenko*, ed. Magdalena Dabrowski, Leah Dickerman, and Peter Galassi (New York: Museum of Modern Art, 1998), 63–99; and Erika Wolf, "The Visual Economy of Forced Labor: Alexander Rodchenko and the White Sea-Baltic Canal," in *Picturing Russia: Explorations in Visual Culture*, ed. Valerie A. Kivelson and Joan Neuberger (New Haven: Yale University Press, 2008), 168–74.

11. Susie Linfield has described the effect of these photographs as "sabotaging their own intent" and speaking on behalf of the victims. See her *The Cruel Radiance: Photography and Political Violence* (Chicago: University of Chicago Press, 2010), 52–54.

12. For the connection between the Gulag and the non-Gulag (the small and big zones, in Solzhenitsyn's formulation and common parlance), see Oleg Khlevniuk's chapter in this volume.

13. I. V. Stalin, "O rabote v derevne: Rech´ 11 ianvaria 1933 g.," *Sochineniia* (Moscow: Gosudarstvennoe izdatel´stvo politicheskoi literatury, 1952), 13:229.

14. See, for example, Martin Jay, *Downcast Eyes: The Denigration of Vision in Twentieth-Century French Thought* (Berkeley: University of California Press, 1993); Michael Leja, *Looking Askance: Skepticism and American Art from Eakins to Duchamp* (Berkeley: University of California Press, 2004); and Malcolm Turvey, *Doubting Vision: Film and the Revelationist Tradition* (New York: Oxford University Press, 2008).

15. Il´ia Kukulin, *Mashiny zashumevshego vremeni: Kak sovetskii montazh stal metodom neoffitsial´noi kul´tury* (Moscow: Novoe literaturnoe obozrenie, 2015), n.p.

16. The most extensive database of repressed artists and art historians is maintained by the Sakharov Center at http://www.sakharov-center.ru/asfcd/khudozhniki/.

17. See, e.g., John E. Bowlt, "National in Form, International in Content: Modernism in Ukraine," Daria Zelska Darewych, "Ukrainian Art and Culture through the Ages," and Liudmila Koval´skaia, "Mykhailo Boichuk and the Ukrainian School of Monumental Art," all in *Ukrainian Modernism, 1910–1930* (Kyiv: National Art Museum of Ukraine, 2006).

CHAPTER 9. PENAL DEPORTATION TO SIBERIA AND THE LIMITS OF STATE POWER, 1801–1881

The research for this article was funded by a Leverhulme Trust Research Fellowship. I am grateful to Ilya Magin, Jonathan Waterlow, Gavin Jacobson, Rebecca Reich, and the editors and anonymous readers of *Kritika: Explorations in Russian and Eurasian History* for their comments on earlier drafts.

1. Iustynian Ruchin´skii [Justynian Ruciński], "Konarshchik, 1838–1878: Vospominaniia o sibirskoi ssylke," in *Vospominaniia iz Sibiri: Memuary, ocherki, dnevnikovye*

zapisi pol´skikh politicheskikh ssyl´nykh v vostochnuiu Sibir´ pervoi poloviny XIX stoletiia, ed. B. S. Shostakovich (Irkutsk: Artizdat, 2009), 331.

2. Cited in Andrew A. Gentes, *Exile to Siberia, 1590–1822* (Basingstoke: Palgrave, 2008), 48.

3. John P. LeDonne, *Absolutism and Ruling Class: The Formation of the Russian Political Order, 1700–1825* (Oxford: Oxford University Press, 1991), 216–17; Evgenii Anisimov, *Dyba i knut: Politicheskii sysk i russkoe obshchestvo v XVIII veke* (Moscow: Novoe literaturnoe obozrenie, 1999), 498–500; Cyril Bryner, "The Issue of Capital Punishment in the Reign of Elizabeth Petrovna," *Russian Review* 49, no. 4 (1990): 389–416.

4. Abby M. Schrader, *Languages of the Lash: Corporal Punishment and Identity in Imperial Russia* (DeKalb: Northern Illinois University Press, 2002), 80–83; Mark Bassin, "Expansion and Colonialism on the Eastern Frontier: Views of Siberia and the Far East in Pre-Petrine Russia," *Journal of Historical Geography* 14, no. 1 (1988): 3–21.

5. Gentes, *Exile to Siberia*, 5–6; Marc Raeff, *The Well-Ordered Police State: Social and Institutional Change through Law in the Germanies and Russia, 1600–1800* (New Haven: Yale University Press, 1983), 204–50.

6. Gentes, *Exile to Siberia*, 94.

7. On the evolving practice and meanings of this colonial project, see "Forum: Colonialism and Technocracy at the End of the Tsarist Era," *Slavic Review* 69, no. 1 (2010): 120–88; and Alberto Masoero, "Territorial Colonization in Late Imperial Russia: Stages in the Development of a Concept," *Kritika: Explorations in Russian and Eurasian History* 14, no. 1 (2013): 59–91.

8. Andrew A. Gentes, "'Licentious Girls' and Frontier Domesticators: Women and Siberian Exile from the Late 16th to the Early 19th Centuries," *Sibirica* 3, no. 1 (2003): 3–20; Gentes, "Sakhalin's Women: The Convergence of Sexuality and Penology in Late Imperial Russia," *Ab Imperio*, no. 2 (2003): 115–37; Abby M. Schrader, "Unruly Felons and Civilizing Wives: Cultivating Marriage in the Siberian Exile System, 1822–1860," *Slavic Review* 66, no. 2 (2007): 230–56.

9. Schrader, *Languages of the Lash*, 83.

10. Gentes, *Exile to Siberia*, 57.

11. Dominique Moran, Laura Piacentini, and Judith Pallot, "Disciplined Mobility and Carceral Geography: Prisoner Transport in Russia," *Transactions of the Institute of British Geographers* 37, no. 3 (2012): 455–57. See also Pallot's chapter in this volume. On the Stalin period, see Anne Applebaum, *Gulag: A History* (London: Penguin, 2003), chap. 9.

12. These are, of course, arguments that can be applied to the exile system more generally. See the discussion of the chaotic conditions in Nerchinsk in the late 1820s in Daniel Beer, "Decembrists, Rebels, and Martyrs in Siberian Exile: The 'Zerentui

Conspiracy' of 1828 and the Fashioning of a Revolutionary Genealogy," *Slavic Review* 72, no. 3 (2013): 528–51.

13. Daniel R. Brower and Edward J. Lazzerini, eds., *Russia's Orient: Imperial Borderlands and Peoples, 1700–1917* (Bloomington: Indiana University Press, 1997); Willard Sunderland, *Taming the Wild Field: Colonization and Empire on the Russian Steppe* (Ithaca, NY: Cornell University Press, 1996); Jane Burbank, Mark von Hagen, and Anatolyi Remnev, eds., *Russian Empire: Space, People, Power, 1700–1930* (Bloomington: Indiana University Press, 2007); Nicholas Breyfogle, *Heretics and Colonizers: Forging Russia's Empire in the South Caucasus* (Ithaca, NY: Cornell University Press, 2005); Jane Burbank, "An Imperial Rights Regime: Law and Citizenship in the Russian Empire," *Kritika: Explorations in Russian and Eurasian History* 7, no. 3 (2006): 397–431.

14. N. Rumiantsov, *Istoricheskii ocherk peresylki arestantov v Rossii* (St. Petersburg: n.p., 1876), 10.

15. O. N. Bortnikova, *Sibir' tiuremnaia: Penitentsiarnaia sistema Zapadnoi Sibiri v 1801–1917 gg.* (Tiumen': Ministerstvo vnutrennikh del, 1999), 45.

16. Rossiiskii gosudarstvennyi istoricheskii arkhiv (RGIA) f. 383, op. 29, d. 924 (1806), l. 27; G. G. Peizen, "Istoricheskii ocherk kolonizatsii Sibiri," *Sovremennik*, no. 9 (1859): 29–30.

17. RGIA f. 383, op. 29, d. 953 (1818), l. 24.

18. RGIA f. 383, op. 29, d. 924 (1806), l. 29.

19. RGIA f. 383, op. 29, d. 953 (1818), l. 2.

20. RGIA f. 383, op. 29, d. 938 (1811), ll. 88–89.

21. RGIA f. 383, op. 29, d. 953 (1818), ll. 1, 12–14. On the wider problem of the incapacitated exiles reaching Siberia, see Andew A. Gentes, "'Completely Useless': Exiling the Disabled to Tsarist Siberia," *Sibirica* 10, no. 2 (2011): 26–49.

22. S. M. Shtutman, *Na strazhe tishiny i spokoistviia: Iz istorii vnutrennikh voisk Rossii (1811–1917 gg.)* (Moscow: Gazoil, 2000), 107–9.

23. RGIA f. 1286, op. 1, d. 195 (1804), ll. 51, 53, 64; op. 2, d. 245 (1817), l. 1.

24. "O prestupleniiakh po vsei Sibiri, v koikh uchastvovali ssyl'nye s 1823 po 1831 god," *Zhurnal Ministerstva vnutrennikh del*, no. 8 (1833): 224–33.

25. *Ssylka v Sibir': Ocherk ee istorii i sovremennogo polozheniia* (St. Petersburg: Tipografiia S.-Peterburgskoi tiur'my, 1900), appendix no. 1. For further examples of the effects of the increase, see L. M. Damashek and A. V. Remnev, eds., *Sibir' v sostave Rossiiskoi Imperii* (Moscow: Novoe literaturnoe obozrenie, 2007), 274–77.

26. Gentes, *Exile to Siberia*, 137.

27. Marc Raeff, *Michael Speransky: Statesman of Imperial Russia, 1772–1839* (The Hague: Martinus Nijhoff, 1957).

28. Marc Raeff, *Siberia and the Reforms of 1822* (Seattle: University of Washington Press, 1956), 44.

29. Bortnikova, *Sibir´ tiuremnaia*, 47.

30. "Ustav ob etapakh v sibirskikh guberniiakh," *Uchrezhdenie dlia upravleniia sibirskikh gubernii* (St. Petersburg: Senatskaia tipografiia, 1822), 4–5; Ippolit Zavalishin, *Opisanie Zapadnoi Sibiri*, 2 vols. (Moscow: Grachev, 1862), 1:355–56.

31. "Ustav ob etapakh v sibirskikh guberniiakh," 26.

32. "Ustav o ssyl´nykh," 24, articles 210–13.

33. RGIA f. 1286, op. 21, d. 1118 (1860) l. 1.

34. Gentes, *Exile to Siberia*, 198–99.

35. Gentes discusses the various reasons for the surge in exile numbers in Andrew Gentes, *Exile, Murder, and Madness in Siberia, 1823–61* (Basingstoke: Palgrave Macmillan, 2010), chap. 1.

36. RGIA f. 1264, op. 1, d. 414 (1825), l. 6.

37. RGIA f. 1264, op. 1, d. 71 (1835), l. 138.

38. "Ustav ob etapakh v sibirskikh guberniiakh," no. 22.

39. RGIA f. 1264, op. 1, d. 71 (1835), ll. 136 ob.–37.

40. S. V. Maksimov, *Sibir´ i katorga*, 3rd ed. (St. Petersburg: V. I. Gubinskii, 1900), 14.

41. Rumiantsov, *Istoricheskii ocherk peresylki*, 12.

42. N. M. Iadrintsev, *Russkaia obshchina v tiur´me i ssylke* (St. Petersburg: A. Morigerovskii, 1872), 320.

43. Aleksandr Vlasenko, "Ugolovnaia ssylka v Zapadnuiu Sibir´ v politike samoderzhaviia XIX veka" (Candidate's diss., Omsk State University, 2008), 63.

44. Rumiantsov, *Istoricheskii ocherk peresylki*, 10–11.

45. Gosudarstvennyi arkhiv Rossiiskoi Federatsii (GARF) f. 109, op. 8, 1 eksp., d. 357 (1833), l. 10.

46. Gosudarstvennyi arkhiv Tiumen´skoi oblasti v gorode Tobol´sk (GATOvgT) f. 152, op. 31, d. 127 (1849), l. 18; RGIA f. 1286, op. 29, d. 836 (1868), l. 8; Vasilii Kolesnikov, "Zapiski neschastnogo," *Zaria*, no. 5 (1869): 25–26.

47. Vlasenko, "Ugolovnaia ssylka," 66–67.

48. RGIA f. 1286, op. 22, d. 925 (1857), l. 8 ob.; Grytsko [G. Z. Eliseev], "Ugolovnye prestupniki," *Sovremennik*, no. 74 (1860): 286.

49. RGIA f. 1286, op. 9, d. 719 (1844), ll. 1–2, 17–18.

50. The British government took swift and decisive action in response to lethal excesses in the British deportation of convicts to Australia in the late eighteenth century because the organized and efficient transfers of healthy convicts were understood to be necessary to the wider project of penal colonization. See Robert Hughes, *The Fatal Shore: A History of the Transportation of Convicts to Australia, 1787–1868* (London: Vintage, 2003), 129–57; and J. McDonald and R. Shlomowitz, "Mortality on Convict Voyages to Australia, 1788–1868," *Social Science History* 13, no. 3 (1989): 285–313.

51. "Arestanty v Sibiri," *Sovremennik*, no. 11 (1863): 139–40, 149.

52. RGIA f. 468, op. 20, d. 1198 (1855), ll. 1–6.

53. RGIA f. 1286, op. 24, d. 941 (1863), ll. 1–2.

54. RGIA f. 1286, op. 29, d. 771 (1868), l. 10.

55. RGIA f. 1286, op. 29, d. 771 (1868), ll. 4–5, 19–23 ob., 32–34; op. 36, d. 686 (1875), l. 14.

56. The tradition of *kormlenie*, of using one's office as a source of bribes and embezzlement, stretched back to the Muscovite state (Richard Pipes, *Russia under the Old Regime*, 2nd ed. [New York: Penguin, 1997], 96).

57. GARF f. 109, 1-aia eksp, op. 8, d. 357 (1833), l. 15.

58. RGIA f. 1286, op. 7, d. 377 (1840), l. 38.

59. "Po etapu ot Peterburga do Tobol′ska," *Zritel′*, no. 52 (1862): 790–91.

60. RGIA f. 1286, op. 24, d. 231 (1863), ll. 14, 20–21.

61. GATOvgT f. 152, op. 39, d. 114 (1864), l. 4.

62. Gentes, *Exile, Murder, and Madness*, 52.

63. RGIA f. 1286, op. 10, d. 1428 (1846) ll. 15–22.

64. RGIA f. 1286, op. 7, d. 377 (1840), l. 71.

65. Vlasenko, "Ugolovnaia ssylka," 299.

66. RGIA f. 1286, op. 36, d. 698 (1875), ll. 1–2.

67. RGIA f. 1286, op. 36, d. 793 (1875), ll. 7, 12–17, 49.

68. RGIA f. 1286, op. 38, d. 407 (1877), ll. 103–3 ob.

69. Iadrintsev, *Russkaia obshchina*, 151–52.

70. Alan Wood, "Administrative Exile and the Criminals' Commune in Siberia," in *Land Commune and Peasant Community in Russia: Communal Forms in Imperial and Early Soviet Russia*, ed. Roger Barlett (London: Macmillan, 1990), 403–4.

71. Andrew A. Gentes, "'Beat the Devil!' Prison Society and Anarchy in Tsarist Siberia," *Ab Imperio*, no. 2 (2009): 209–10.

72. Wood, "Adminstrative Exile," 404–5.

73. "Ustav ob etapakh v sibirskikh guberniiakh," no. 61.

74. Iadrintsev, *Russkaia obshchina*, 176; George Kennan, *Siberia and the Exile System*, 2 vols. (New York: Century, 1891), 1:393.

75. Iadrintsev, *Russkaia obshchina*, 179.

76. Maksimov, *Sibir′ i katorga*, 17–18.

77. Iadrintsev, *Russkaia obshchina*, 276.

78. Fyodor Dostoevsky, *The House of the Dead*, trans. David McDuff (London: Penguin, 2003), 101–2 (translation modified—DB).

79. Kennan, *Siberia and the Exile System*, 1:391–92.

80. RGIA f. 383, op. 29, d. 924 (1806), l. 28; Gosudarstvennyi arkhiv Irkutskoi oblasti (GAIO) f. 24, op. 3, k. 2, d. 23 (1827), l. 9; GAIO f. 24, op. 3, d. 69, k. 4 (1829), ll. 33, 65; V. Kubalov, "Zabytyi dekabrist (A. N. Lutskii)," in *Dekabristy v Vostochnoi Sibiri: Ocherki* (Irkutsk: Izdatel′stvo Gubernskogo arkhivbiuro, 1925), 157–58.

81. *Polnoe sobranie zakonov Rossiiskoi Imperii: Sobranie vtoroe* (hereafter *PSZ* 2), 55 vols. (St. Petersburg: Tipografiia Vtorogo otdeleniia Sobstvennogo Ego Imperator-skogo Velichestva Kantseliarii, 1830–85), 3: no. 2286; 4: no. 3377; RGIA f. 1264, op. 1, d. 51 (1828), ll. 187–88 ob.; A. D. Margolis, "Soldaty-dekabristy v Petropavlovskoi kreposti i sibirskoi ssylke," in *Tiur'ma i ssylka v imperatorskoi Rossii: Issledovaniia i arkhivnye nakhodki*, ed. Margolis (Vita: Lanterna, 1995), 73.

82. *PSZ* 2, vol. 28, sect. 1, no. 27736.

83. RGIA f. 1149, op. 2, d. 99 (1838), l. 6; f. 1286, op. 7, d. 341 (1840), l. 112 ob.; f. 1286, op. 8, d. 1086 (1843), l. 6; Maksimov, *Katorga i ssylka*, 17.

84. I. Mel'shin [P. Ia. Iakubovich], *V mire otverzhennykh: Zapiski byvshego kator-zhnika* (St. Petersburg: V. M. Vol'f, 1896), 17.

85. Stephen P. Frank, "Narratives within Numbers: Women, Crime, and Judicial Statistics in Imperial Russia, 1834–1913," *Russian Review* 55, no. 4 (1996): 541–66.

86. See the literary representations of this practice in Nikolai Leskov's *Lady Mac-beth of Mtsensk District* (1865).

87. Ruchin'skii, "Konarshchik, 1838–1878," 374.

88. RGIA f. 1263, op. 1, d. 415 (1825), l. 296.

89. RGIA f. 1263, op. 1, d. 415 (1825), ll. 296, 298; f. 1264, op. 1, d. 414 (1825), l. 1. See also Gentes, "'Licentious Girls' and Frontier Domesticators"; and Schrader, "Unruly Felons and Civilizing Wives," 243.

90. RGIA f. 1286, op. 4, d. 413 (1828), l. 12; f. 1264, op. 1, d. 414 (1825), ll. 4–5; V. I. Efimov, *V zhizni katorzhnykh ilginskogo i aleksandrovskogo togda kazennykh, vinokurennykh zavodov, 1848–1853 g.* (St. Petersburg: Universitetskaia tipografiia, 1899), 51.

91. RGIA f. 1286, op. 7, d. 341 (1840), l. 30; Vlasenko, "Ugolovnaia ssylka," 66.

92. RGIA f. 1286, op. 36, d. 686 (1875), ll. 13–14; GAIO f. 32, op. 1, d. 199 (1877), l. 1.

93. V. Moskvich, "Pogibshie i pogibaiushchie: Otbrosy Rossii na sibirskoi pochve," *Russkoe bogatstvo*, no. 7 (1895): 73.

94. V. L. Seroshevskii, "Ssylka i katorga v Sibiri," in *Sibir': Ee sovremennoe sostoian-ie i ee nuzhdy. Sbornik statei*, ed. I. S. Mel'nik (St. Petersburg: A. F. Devrien, 1908), 209.

95. RGIA f. 1149, op. 2, d. 97 (1837), l. 14 ob.

96. V. I. Vlasov, *Kratkii ocherk neustroistv, sushchestvuiushchikh na katorge* (St. Petersburg: n.p., 1873), 39.

97. RGIA f. 1263, op. 1, d. 1067 (1836), ll. 134–35.

98. I. P. Belokonskii (Petrovich), *Po tiur'mam i etapam: Ocherki tiuremnoi zhizni i putevye zametki ot Moskvy do Krasnoiarska* (Orel: N. A. Semenova, 1887), 57; Sergei Maksimov, *Sibir' i katorga* (St. Petersburg: V. I. Guninskii, 1870), 24.

99. Kennan, *Siberia and the Exile System*, 1:108; RGIA f. 1286, op. 36, d. 686 (1875), l. 20; RGIA f. 1286, op. 38, d. 467 (1877), l. 41 ob.; Nikolai Iadrintsev, *Sibir' kak koloniia* (St. Petersburg: M. M. Stasiulevich, 1882), 175.

100. Vlasov, *Kratkii ocherk neustroistv*, 33, 36–38; V. I. Semevskii, *Rabochie na sibirskikh zolotykh promyslakh: Istoricheskoe issledovanie*, 2 vols. (St. Petersburg: M. M. Stasiulevich, 1898), 1:xvii–xviii.

101. Pavla Miller, *Transformations of Patriarchy in the West, 1500–1900* (Bloomington: Indiana University Press, 1998); Susan K. Morrissey, *Suicide and the Body Politic in Imperial Russia* (Cambridge: Cambridge University Press, 2006), 11–12; Richard S. Wortman, *Scenarios of Power: Myth and Ceremony in Russian Monarchy*, 1 (Princeton, NJ: Princeton University Press, 1995), chap. 9.

102. Belokonskii, *Po tiur´mam i etapam*, 167–80.

103. Belokonskii, *Po tiur´mam i etapam*, 80; RGIA f. 1286, op. 38, d. 467 (1877), l. 34.

104. RGIA f. 1286, op. 28, d. 917 (1867), l. 80.

105. RGIA f. 1286, op. 28, d. 921 (1872), ll. 1–3, 115, 298–300.

106. *Ssylka v Sibir´*, appendix, table 1.

107. RGIA f. 1286, op. 28, d. 920 (1869), l. 122.

108. RGIA f. 1286, op. 38, d. 380 (1877), l. 5.

109. RGIA f. 1286, op. 28, d. 290 (1869), ll. 125–26.

110. RGIA f. 1286, op. 28, d. 290 (1869), l. 74.

111. RGIA f. 1286, op. 28, d. 290 (1869), ll. 77–79.

112. RGIA f. 1286, op. 38, d. 407 (1877), l. 103.

113. RGIA f. 1286, op. 36, d. 686 (1875), l. 20.

114. RGIA f. 1286, op. 29, d. 836 (1868), ll. 8–8 ob.

115. Vlasov, *Kratkii ocherk neustroistv*, 37.

116. RGIA f. 1286, op. 29, d. 771 (1868), l. 2; GAIO f. 32, op. 1, d. 199 (1877), l. 1.

117. GARF f. 122, op. 5, d. 619 (1880), ll. 1–2.

118. One notable exception was the acts of collective resistance organized by Polish exiles following the repression of the Polish rebellion of 1863 (Andrew A. Gentes, "Siberian Exile and the 1863 Polish Insurrectionists according to Russian Sources," *Jahrbücher für Geschichte Osteuropas* 51, no. 2 [2003]: 197–217).

119. RGIA f. 1149, op. 9, d. 3 (1877), l. 337.

120. RGIA f. 1149, op. 9, d. 3 (1877), l. 777; *Ssylka v Sibir´*, 78–80; Bruce Adams, *The Politics of Punishment: Prison Reform in Russia, 1863–1917* (DeKalb: Northern Illinois University Press, 1996), 97–120.

121. Margolis, "Sistema sibirskoi ssylki i zakon ot 12 iiunia 1900 goda," in *Tiur´ma i ssylka*, 19; Richard S. Wortman, *The Development of a Russian Legal Consciousness* (Chicago: University of Chicago Press, 1976), chap. 9.

122. *Sibir´*, no. 15 (5 October 1875): 5; *Sibir´*, no. 37 (11 September 1877): 1; "Gonimye," *Vostochnoe obozrenie*, no. 3 (15 April 1882): 12.

123. E. Andreev, "Obiazatel´naia rabota katorzhnykh i arestantov v Rossii," *Zhurnal grazhdanskogo i ugolovnogo prava*, nos. 1–2 (1877): 82–107; S. Chudnovskii,

"Kolonizatsionnoe znachenie sibirskoi ssylki," *Russkaia mysl'*, no. 10 (1886): 40–66; Moskvich, "Pogibshie i pogibaiushchie"; L. Mel'shin [P. Ia. Iakubovich], "Kobylka v puti," *Russkoe bogatstvo*, no. 8 (1896): 5–37; N. Belozerskii, "Ot Peterburga do Nerchinska," *Russkaia mysl'*, no. 12 (1902): 53–71; Harriet Murav, "'Vo Glubine Sibirskikh Rud': Siberia and the Myth of Exile," in *Between Heaven and Hell: The Myth of Siberia in Russian Culture*, ed. Galya Diment and Yuri Slezkine (New York: St. Martin's, 1993), 95–111.

124. Anton Chekhov, *A Life in Letters*, ed. Rosamund Bartlett, trans. Bartlett and Anthony Philips (New York: Penguin, 2004), 204–5.

125. A. P. Chekhov, "Ostrov Sakhalin," *Russkaia mysl'*, no. 10 (1893): 1–33; no. 11: 149–70; no. 12: 77–114; no. 2 (1894): 26–60; no. 3: 1–28; no. 5: 1–30; no. 6: 1–27; no. 7: 1–30.

126. *Vostochnoe obozrenie*, no. 4 (1 October 1889): 9.

127. Leo Tolstoy, *Resurrection*, trans. Anthony Briggs (London: Penguin, 2009).

CHAPTER 10. BRITAIN'S ARCHIPELAGO OF CAMPS: LABOR AND DETENTION IN A LIBERAL EMPIRE, 1871–1903

1. According to Zygmunt Bauman, gardening and medicine form the two primary activities of the modern state (*Modernity and the Holocaust* [Ithaca, NY: Cornell University Press, 1989], 70–73). For attempts by modern states to "landscape the human garden" according to Enlightenment visions of perfectibility, see Amir Weiner, ed., *Landscaping the Human Garden: Twentieth-Century Population Management in a Comparative Framework* (Stanford, CA: Stanford University Press, 2003).

2. For a general consideration of modern camps and their defining features, see Joel Kotek and Pierre Rigoulot, *Le siècle des camps: Détention, concentration, extermination. Cent ans de mal radical* (Paris: Lattes, 2000).

3. British commentators during the South Africa War, for example, commented frequently on Spanish "reconcentration" in Cuba (1896–1898), whereby General Valeriano Weyler detained the island's civilian population in fortified villages, if not purpose-built camps.

4. Zygmunt Bauman, quoted in Dirk Moses, ed., *Genocide and Settler Society: Frontier Violence and Stolen Indigenous Children in Australian History* (New York: Berghahn, 2004), 32.

5. For the foundational role of such disciplinary institutions as the British workhouse and factory to the development of twentieth-century state violence, see Enzo Traverso, *Origins of Nazi Violence* (New York: New Press, 2003).

6. Gareth Stedman Jones, *Outcast London: A Study in the Relationship between Classes in Victorian Society* (Baltimore: Penguin, 1976).

7. John Brown, "Charles Booth and Labour Colonies, 1889–1905," *Economic History Review* 21, no. 2 (1968): 349–61. For languages of "degeneration" at the fin-de-

siècle, see Daniel Pick, *Faces of Degeneration: A European Disorder, 1848–1918* (New York: Cambridge University Press, 1989).

8. "To Check the Survival of the Unfit: A New Scheme by the Rev. Osborn Jay, a Militant Bethnal Green Parson, for Sending the Submerged to a Penal Settlement," *The London* (12 March 1896), http://www.mernick.org.uk//thhol/survunfi.html.

9. John Field, "Able Bodies: Work Camps and the Training of the Unemployed in Britain before 1939," in *The Significance of the Historical Perspective in Adult Education Research* (Cambridge: University of Cambridge, Institute of Continuing Education, 2009).

10. David A. Reisman, *Alfred Marshall: Progress and Politics* (New York: St. Martin's, 1987), 439.

11. Frantz Fanon, *The Wretched of the Earth* (New York: Grove, 1963), 27.

12. N. Cole Harris, *Making Native Space: Colonialism, Resistance, and Reserves in British Columbia* (Vancouver: University of British Columbia Press, 2002), xxiv.

13. Benjamin Madley, "From Terror to Genocide: Britain's Tasmanian Penal Colony and Australia's History Wars," *Journal of British Studies* 47, no. 1 (2008): 77–106; A. Dirk Moses, "Genocide and Settler Society in Australian History," in *Genocide and Settler Society*, 3–48; Samantha Wells, "Labour, Control, and Protection: The Kahlin Aboriginal Compound, Darwin, 1911–38," in *Settlement: A History of Australian Indigenous Housing*, ed. Peter Read (Canberra: Aboriginal Studies Press, 2000), 64.

14. Bain Attwood, "Space and Time at Ramahyuck, Victoria, 1863–85," in *Settlement*, 44.

15. Wells, "Labour, Control, and Protection," 67.

16. Ibid., 69.

17. Clare Anderson, "Sepoys, Servants, and Settlers: Convict Transportation in the Indian Ocean, 1787–1945," in *Cultures of Confinement: A History of the Prison in Africa, Asia, and Latin America*, ed. Frank Dikotter and Ian Brown (Ithaca, NY: Cornell University Press, 2007), 185–220.

18. Clare Anderson, "The Politics of Convict Space: Indian Penal Settlements and the Andaman Islands," in *Isolation: Places and Practices of Exclusion*, ed. Alison Bashford and Carolyn Strange (New York: Routledge, 2003), 40–55. For the role of exile in the Soviet Gulag, see the chapters by Daniel Beer and Judith Pallot in this volume.

19. N. Benjamin and B. B. Mohanty, "Imperial Solution of a Colonial Problem: Bhils of Khandesh up to c. 1850," *Modern Asian Studies* 41, no. 2 (2007): 363.

20. National Archives of India (NAI), Home Department (Judicial), January 1876, nos. 139–50: Adoption of the Necessary Measures in Order to Render Part I of the Criminal Tribes Act XXVII of 1871 Applicable to the Lower Provinces of Bengal.

21. C. P. Carmichael, inspector general of police to secretary to government, North-Western Provinces (NWP), 6 July 1870, NAI, Legislative Department, November 1871, nos. 44–127, Part A: The Criminal Tribes Act, 1871.

22. P. H. Egerton, commissioner and supt., Amritsar Division, 20 February 1869, NAI Legislative Department, November 1871, nos. 44–127, Part A: The Criminal Tribes Act, 1871.

23. Sanjay Nigam, "Disciplining and Policing the 'Criminals by Birth,' Part 2: The Development of a Disciplinary System, 1871–1900," *Indian Economic and Society History Review* 27, no. 3 (1990): 266.

24. NAI Home Department (Judicial), January 1879, nos. 59–64: Workings of the Criminal Tribes Act in the North-Western Provinces during 1877.

25. J. F. K. Hewitt, magistrate, Chumparun, NAI Home Department (Judicial), January 1876, nos. 139–50.

26. C. A. Elliott, esq., offg. secy. to govt. NWP, 21 April 1871, NAI Legislative Department, November 1871, nos. 44–127, Part A: The Criminal Tribes Act, 1871.

27. NAI Legislative Department, November 1871, nos. 44–127, Part A: The Criminal Tribes Act, 1871, description of the Mughya Domes by Lieut.-Col. A. H. Paterson, insp. gen. of police, Lower Provinces.

28. NAI Legislative Department, December 1873, nos. 27–30, Part A: North-Western Provinces Rules under Criminal Tribes Act, 1871: Note from Officiating Inspector-General of Police, NWP, no. 28, 29 August 1873.

29. Statistics on camp populations are spread throughout the archival records, not centralized in any accessible manner. Official figures indicate 1.111 million inmates at Bombay Presidency camps during the 1876–1877 famine. A total inmate population of over ten million across India during the famines of the 1870s and 1890s is likely. See David Hall-Matthews, "Famine Process and Famine Policy: A Case Study of Ahmednagar District, Bombay Presidency, India, 1870–84" (DPhil thesis, University of Oxford, 2002), 231.

30. For the perceived political danger of wandering masses, see David Hall-Matthews, "Historical Roots of Famine Relief Paradigms," *Disasters* 20, no. 3 (1996): 228; and Jim Masselos, "Migration and Urban Identity: Bombay's Famine Refugees in the Nineteenth Century," in *Bombay: Mosaic of Modern Culture,* ed. Sujata Patel and Alice Thorner (Oxford: Oxford University Press, 1995), 25–58.

31. David Arnold, *Famine: Social Crisis and Historical Change* (New York: Basil Blackwell, 1988), 91–92; quotations from C 3086, Report of the Indian Famine Commission, Part IV: Evidence in Reply to Inquiries of the Commission (1885), 181.

32. C 3086, 67.

33. British Library (BL), Temple Papers, MSS EUR F86/208(a): Minutes of Evidence, 49.

34. BL, Bombay Famine Proceedings, IOR/P/6257.

35. What Giorgio Agamben terms a "state of exception" in reference to his stimulating but empirically problematic depiction of Nazi concentration and extermination camps. See Agamben, *States of Exception* (Chicago: University of Chicago Press,

2005); and Agamben, *Homo Sacer: Sovereign Power and Bare Life* (Stanford, CA: Stanford University Press, 1998).

36. S. J. Thomson, *The Real Indian People: Being More Tales and Sketches of the Masses* (London: William Blackwood and Sons, 1914), 115–16.

37. William Digby, *Famine Campaign in Southern India: Madras and Bombay Presidencies and Province of Mysore, 1876–1878* (London: Longmans, Green, 1878), 2:351, 295.

38. Michael Ignatieff, *A Just Measure of Pain: The Penitentiary in the Industrial Revolution, 1750–1850* (London: Peregrine, 1989).

39. Rajnarayan Chandavarkar, "Plague, Panic, and Epidemic Politics in India, 1896–1914," in *Epidemics and Idea: Essays on the Historical Perception of Pestilence*, ed. Terence Ranger and Paul Slack (Cambridge: Cambridge University Press, 1992), 211.

40. Maharashtra State Archives (MSA) General Department (Plague) 1899, volume 617: Views of the Various Officers regarding the Establishment of Detention Camps; MSA General Department (Plague), vol. 366: Detention and Disinfection Measures.

41. MSA General Department (Plague) 1898, vol. 366: Detention and Disinfection Measures, Bombay.

42. Quoted in Maynard Swanson, "The Sanitation Syndrome: Bubonic Plague and Urban Native Policy in the Cape Colony, 1900–1909," *Journal of African History* 18, no. 3 (1977): 389.

43. Swanson, "Sanitation Syndrome."

44. For a straightforward policy account, see S. B. Spies, *Methods of Barbarism? Roberts and Kitchener and Civilians in the Boer War, January 1900–May 1902* (Cape Town: Human and Rousseau, 1976). For a recent social history of the camps, see Elizabeth van Heyningen, *The Concentration Camps of the Anglo-Boer War: A Social History* (Auckland Park: Jacana Media, 2013).

45. Hannah Arendt, *The Origins of Totalitarianism* (New York: Harcourt, 1968), 440.

46. For the politics and contested memory of the camps within South Africa, see Liz Stanley, *Mourning Becomes . . .: Post/Memory and Commemoration of the Concentration Camps of the South African War* (New York: Manchester University Press, 2006).

47. David Bell, *The First Total War: Napoleon's Europe and the Birth of Warfare as We Know It* (Boston: Houghton Mifflin, 2007). Bell's argument is a substantial reworking of Carl Schmitt, *Theory of the Partisan: Intermediate Commentary on the Concept of the Political* (New York: Telos, 2007).

48. The National Archives of Great Britain (TNA) PRO 30/57/22, Correspondence of Lord Kitchener, Kitchener to Brodrick, 21 June 1901, Y62.

49. Iain Smith and Andreas Stucki, "The Colonial Development of Concentration Camps," *Journal of Imperial and Commonwealth History* 39, no. 3 (2011): 417–37; A. M. Davey, "The Reconcentrados of Cuba," *Historia* 5, no. 3 (1960).

50. Caroline Elkins, *Imperial Reckoning: The Untold Story of Britain's Gulag in Kenya* (New York: Henry Holt, 2005); Laleh Khalili, *Time in the Shadows: Confinement in Counterinsurgencies* (Stanford, CA: Stanford University Press, 2013).

51. TNA PRO 30/57/22, Middleton Papers. Kitchener to Brodrick, 21 June 1901, Y62.

52. TNA CO 879/75/3: African no. 687, Correspondence Relating to Refugee Camps in South Africa, no. 165.

53. TNA CO 879/75/3, no. 54, Mr. Chamberlain to Administrator Lord Milner, 16 November 1901.

54. London School of Economics (LSE), Deane/Streatfield Papers, Streatfield 2/11, Transcripts of Letters from Lucy Streatfield to Her Sister.

55. Recent scholarship has explored Nazi camps as an element of a wider set of disciplinary practices. See, e.g., Jane Caplan and Nikolaus Wachsmann, eds., *Concentration Camps in Nazi Germany: The New Histories* (New York: Routledge, 2010).

56. Ulrike Lindner, "Imperialism and Globalization: Entanglements and Interactions between the British and German Colonial Empires in Africa before the First World War," *German Historical Institute London Bulletin* 32, no. 1 (2010): 4–28.

57. Isabel V. Hull, *Absolute Destruction: Military Culture and the Practices of War in Imperial Germany* (Ithaca, NY: Cornell University Press, 2005); Casper Erichsen and David Olusoga, *The Kaiser's Holocaust: Germany's Forgotten Genocide and the Colonial Roots of Nazism* (London: Faber and Faber, 2011).

58. In 1941 Joseph Goebbels produced and directed the film *Ohm Krüger*, which focused entirely on British concentration camps in South Africa, depicting them as instruments of massacre and genocide.

59. Nevile Henderson, *Failure of a Mission: Berlin 1937–1939* (New York: G. P. Putnam's Sons, 1940), 21.

60. Paul Moore, "'And What Concentration Camps Those Were!' Foreign Concentration Camps in Nazi Propaganda, 1933–9," *Journal of Contemporary History* 45, no. 3 (2010): 672.

61. For an instructive example of how transnational connections among British, Soviet, and Chinese camps might be explored—in terms of both policy and personnel—see Klaus Mühlhahn, "The Dark Side of Globalization: The Concentration Camps in Republican China in Global Perspective," *World History Connected* 6, no. 1 (2009), http://worldhistoryconnected.press.illinois.edu/6.1/muhlhahn.html.

62. For the empirical limits of what remains an analytically promising connection between European imperialism and Soviet and Nazi violence, see Robert Gerwarth and Stephan Malinowski, "Hannah Arendt's Ghosts: Reflections on the Disputable Path from Windhoek to Auschwitz," *Central European History* 42, no. 2 (2009): 279–300.

63. Jonathan Hyslop, "The Invention of the Concentration Camp: Cuba, Southern

Africa, and the Philippines, 1896–1907," *South African Historical Journal* 63, no. 2 (2011): 251–76. For Russian media coverage of the South African camps, see Peter Holquist, "Violent Russia, Deadly Marxism? Russia in the Epoch of Violence, 1905–21," *Kritika: Explorations in Russian and Eurasian History* 4, no. 3 (2003): 635–36.

64. Report of the Bombay Famine Commission (1880), 42.

65. National Archives of South Africa (NASA) Free State Depot (FSD) SRC 6060: Compulsory Labour in Refugee Camp Vredefort Rd.

66. NASA FSD SRC, vol. 138: Report by Lewis Mansergh on Burgher Refugee Camp—Amalinda Bluff, East London, 18 July 1902.

67. In a passage that describes perfectly the British view of Boers, the sociologist Philip Smith notes "that which is ambivalent, belonging to no category or sitting on the fence between them, has a high probability of being perceived as dangerous, magical, illegitimate, or in need of ordering" (*Punishment and Culture* [Chicago: University of Chicago Press, 2008], 28).

68. BL, IOR/P/5986, no. 2285, Fortnightly Inspection Reports of Officers of the Sanitary Department for the Fortnight Ending 13 April 1900.

69. A useful comparison is suggested by reference to Golfo Alexopoulos, "Destructive Labor Camps: Rethinking Solzhenitsyn's Play on Words," in this volume.

70. C 3086, 234.

71. MSA Revenue Department (Famine), 1900 no. 71, vol. 49: Orders Regarding the Restriction of Famine Relief to What Is Necessary for the Preservation of Health and Strength.

72. Mr. Knight, letter to the *Statesman and Friend of India*, 15 February 1878, quoted in *George Couper and the Famine in the North-West Provinces, 1878* (Statesman Office, 1878), 3.

73. TNA CO 879/75/3: African no. 687. Correspondence Relating to Refugee Camps in South Africa, no. 79, memorandum by Dr. J. S. Haldane on the rations in the concentration camps.

74. NASA Transvaal Depot (TD) SOPOW 41 PR/A3828/02.

75. NASA FSD SRC 3966: Discipline in Bloemfontein Refugee Camp.

76. NASA FSD SRC 5998: Report on the Showyard Refugee Camp.

77. NASA FSD SRC 3966, Discipline in Bloemfontein Refugee Camp.

78. Women's Library, London, 7MGF/E/2, Millicent Fawcett's diary.

79. In terms of the treatment of political prisoners, other connections across time and space are also possible. Highlighting common cultural representations and mind-sets about social and political contagion, a comparative and transnational analysis might explore France's *camps de regroupement* in Algeria and America's "strategic hamlets" in wartime Indochina. Britain's "pipeline" of rehabilitative centers for Mau Mau suspects in colonial Kenya offers further comparative material in the Cold War era. For camps in Algeria, the United States, and elsewhere, see Colman Hogan and

Marta Marin-Domine, eds., *The Camp: Narratives of Internment and Exclusion* (Newcastle: Cambridge Scholars Publishing, 2007).

80. Judith Pallot, "The Gulag as the Crucible of Russia's Twenty-First-Century System of Punishment," in this volume.

81. Steven A. Barnes, *Death and Redemption: The Gulag and the Shaping of Soviet Society* (Princeton, NJ: Princeton University Press, 2011), 20–27.

82. Certainly this was the case vis-à-vis the genocidal practices in German Southwest Africa, at least according to Hull, *Absolute Destruction*, 183–94.

83. See, e.g., Dan Healey, "Lives in the Balance: Weak and Disabled Prisoners and the Biopolitics of the Gulag," in this volume.

84. The large literature on internment camps in Britain has not been incorporated into Britain's larger history of civilian encampment. See Tony Kushner and David Cesarani, eds., *The Internment of Aliens in Twentieth-Century Britain* (Portland, OR: Frank Cass, 1993); and Richard Dove, ed., *"Totally Un-English"? Britain's Internment of "Enemy Aliens" in Two World Wars* (Amsterdam: Rodopi, 2006).

85. Michel Foucault, "On Governmentality," in *The Foucault Effect: Studies in Governmentality*, ed. Graham Burchell et al. (Chicago: University of Chicago Press, 1991).

CHAPTER 11. CAMP WORLDS AND FORCED LABOR: A COMPARISON OF THE NATIONAL SOCIALIST AND SOVIET CAMP SYSTEMS

1. Reinhard Nachtigal, *Die Murmanbahn: Die Verkehrsanbindung eines kriegswichtigen Hafens und das Arbeitspotential der Kriegsgefangenen (1915–1918)* (Grunbach: Greiner, 2001); Jochen Oltmer, ed., *Kriegsgefangene im Europa des Ersten Weltkriegs* (Paderborn: F. Schöningh, 2006); O. S. Nagornaia, *Drugoi voennyi opyt: Rossiiskie voennoplennye Pervoi mirovoi voiny v Germanii (1914–1922)* (Moscow: Novyi khronograf, 2010).

2. Dittmar Dahlmann and Gerhard Hirschfeld, eds., *Lager, Zwangsarbeit, Vertreibung und Deportation: Dimensionen der Massenverbrechen in der Sowjetunion und in Deutschland 1933 bis 1945* (Essen: Klartext, 1999); Joël Kotek and Pierre Rigoulot, eds., *Das Jahrhundert der Lager: Gefangenschaft, Zwangsarbeit, Vernichtung* (Berlin: Propyläen, 2001); Richard Overy, *Die Diktatoren: Hitlers Deutschland, Stalins Russland* (Munich: Dt. Verl-Anst, 2005), 785–839, which focuses on a comparison of the Nazi concentration camps and the Soviet camp system; Christoph Jahr and Jens Thiel, eds., *Lager vor Auschwitz: Gewalt und Integration im 20. Jahrhundert* (Berlin: Metropol, 2013); Bettina Greiner and Alan Kramer, eds., *Die Welt der Lager: Zur "Erfolgsgeschichte" einer Institution* (Hamburg: Hamburger Edition, 2013); Kerstin von Lingen and Klaus Gestwa, eds., *Zwangsarbeit als Kriegsressource in Europa und Asien* (Paderborn: F. Schöningh, 2014).

3. Quotation from Giorgio Agamben, *Homo sacer: Die souveräne Macht und das nackte Leben* (Frankfurt am Main: Suhrkamp, 2002), 130; Kiran Klaus Patel,

"Volksgenossen und Gemeinschaftsfremde: Über den Doppelcharakter der nationalsozialistischen Lager," in *Lager vor Auschwitz*, 311–34.

4. Jürgen Zimmerer, "Lager und Genozid: Die Konzentrationslager in Südwestafrika zwischen Windhuk und Auschwitz," in *Lager vor Auschwitz*, 54–67; Overy, *Diktatoren*, 789.

5. Von Lingen and Gestwa, eds., *Zwangsarbeit*, 16, 18.

6. Hannah Arendt, *Eichmann in Jerusalem: Ein Bericht von der Banalität des Bösen* (Munich: Piper, 1986), 70–71.

7. Ellen Kennedy, "Carl Schmitt und die 'Frankfurter Schule': Deutsche Liberalismuskritik im 20. Jahrhundert," *Geschichte und Gesellschaft* 12, no. 3 (1986): 380–419.

8. Vejas Gabriel Liulevicius, *War Land on the Eastern Front: Culture, National Identity, and German Occupation in World War I* (Cambridge: Cambridge University Press, 2000); M. B. Smirnov et al., eds., *Sistema ispravitel′no-trudovykh lagerei v SSSR, 1923–1960: Spravochnik* (Moscow: Zvenia, 1998), 10–15; A. L. Litvin, *Krasnyi i belyi terror v Rossii 1918–1922 gg.* (Kazan: Tatarskoe gazetno-zhurnal′noe izdatel′stvo, 1995), 76, 114–15; Michael Jakobson, *Origins of the Gulag: The Soviet Prison Camp System, 1917–1934* (Lexington: University Press of Kentucky, 1993).

9. Yvonne Karow, *Deutsches Opfer: Kultische Selbstauslöschung auf den Reichsparteitagen der NSDAP* (Berlin: Akademie, 1997); Malte Rolf, *Das sowjetische Massenfest* (Hamburg: Hamburger Edition, 2006); Sheila Fitzpatrick and Alf Lüdtke, "Energizing the Everyday: On the Breaking and Making of Social Bonds in Nazism and Stalinism," in *Beyond Totalitarianism: Stalinism and Nazism Compared*, ed. Michael Geyer and Sheila Fitzpatrick (Cambridge: Cambridge University Press, 2009), 266–301.

10. Lorenz Erren, "Zum Ursprung einiger Besonderheiten der sowjetischen Parteiöffentlichkeit: Der stalinistische Untertan und die 'Selbstkritik' in den dreißiger Jahren," in *Sphären von Öffentlichkeit in Gesellschaften sowjetischen Typs: Zwischen partei-staatlicher Selbstinszenierung und kirchlichen Gegenwelten*, ed. Gábor T. Rittersporn et al. (Frankfurt am Main: Peter Lang, 2003), 131–63.

11. Stefan Plaggenborg, "Staatlichkeit als Gewaltroutine: Sowjetische Geschichte und das Problem des Ausnahmezustandes," in *Staats-Gewalt: Ausnahmezustand und Sicherheitsregimes. Historische Perspektiven*, ed. Alf Lüdtke and Michael Wildt (Göttingen: Wallstein, 2008) 117–44.

12. Erving Goffman, *Asylums: Essays on the Social Situation of Mental Patients and Other Inmates* (New York: Anchor, 1961). Without much consideration some historians have rejected Goffman's, Foucault's, and Sofsky's models as unhistorical, without fully understanding the meaning and function of these sociological models. See Alan Kramer, "Einleitung," in *Welt der Lager*, 7–42, 20.

13. Wolfgang Sofsky, *Die Ordnung des Terrors: Die Konzentrationslager* (Frankfurt am Main: S. Fischer, 1993).

14. Michel Foucault, *Überwachen und Strafen: Die Geburt des Gefängnisses* (Frankfurt am Main: Suhrkamp, 1976).

15. Sofsky, *Ordnung des Terrors*, 69.

16. Quoted in V. G. Makurov et al., eds., *GULag v Karelii: Sbornik dokumentov i materialov 1930–1941* (Petrozavodsk: Karel'skii nauchnyi tsentr RAN, 1992), 79.

17. Sofsky, *Ordnung des Terrors*, 27–40.

18. Overy, *Diktatoren*, 828.

19. L. I. Borodkin, "Vertikal' upravleniia GULAGom: Problema prinsipal-agent," in *Istoriia stalinizma: Prinuditel'nyi trud v SSSR. Ekonomika, politika, pamiat'*, ed. Borodkin et al. (Moscow: Rosspen, 2013), 16–13; Mark Spoerer, "Profitierten Unternehmen von der KZ-Arbeit? Eine kritische Analyse der Literatur," *Historische Zeitschrift* 268, no. 1 (1999): 61–95.

20. Wolfgang Sofsky, *Traktat über die Gewalt* (Frankfurt am Main: Fischer, 1996); Jörg Baberowski, "Gewalt verstehen," *Zeithistorische Forschungen* 5, no. 1 (2008): 5–17; Randall Collins, *Dynamik der Gewalt: Eine mikrosoziologische Theorie* (Hamburg: Hamburger Edition, 2011).

21. Aleksandr Bezborodov et al., eds., *Istoriia stalinskogo GULAGa: Konets 1920-kh–pervaia polovina 1950-kh godov. Sobranie dokumentov*, 7 vols. (Moscow: Rosspen, 2004–2005), 6:65–77.

22. Karin Orth, *Das System der nationalsozialistischen Konzentrationslager: Eine politische Organisationsgeschichte* (Hamburg: Hamburger Edition, 1999), 338.

23. Ulrich Herbert, Karin Orth, and Christoph Dieckmann, eds., *Die nationalsozialistischen Konzentrationslager: Entwicklung und Struktur* (Göttingen: Wallstein, 1998), 25–29, 56.

24. Herbert et al., *Nationalsozialistischen Konzentrationslager*, 31.

25. Raul Hilberg, *Die Vernichtung der europäischen Juden*, vol. 1–3 (Frankfurt am Main: Fischer Taschenbuch, 1990).

26. Herbert et al., *Nationalsozialistischen Konzentrationslager*, 419.

27. *Aussonderung* was the technical term for the execution of Soviet political commissars and other "intolerable" people. See Alfred Streim, *Die Behandlung sowjetischer Kriegsgefangener im "Fall Barbarossa": Eine Dokumentation unter Berücksichtigung der Unterlagen deutscher Strafverfolgungsbehörden und der Materialien der Zentralen Stelle der Landesjustizverwaltungen zur Aufklärung von NS-Verbrechen* (Heidelberg: C. F. Müller Juristischer Verlag, 1981); Reinhard Otto, *Wehrmacht, Gestapo und die sowjetischen Kriegsgefangenen im deutschen Reichsgebiet 1941/42* (Munich: R. Oldenbourg, 1998); and Felix Römer, *Der Kommissarbefehl: Wehrmacht und NS-Verbrechen an der Ostfront 1941/42* (Paderborn: F. Schöningh, 2008).

28. Ulrich Herbert, *Fremdarbeiter: Politik und Praxis des "Ausländer-Einsatzes" in der Kriegswirtschaft des Dritten Reiches* (Berlin: J. H. W. Dietz Nachf, 1985), 271. Different bases for calculation are in Mark Spoerer, *Zwangsarbeit unter dem Hakenkreuz:*

Ausländische Zivilarbeiter, Kriegsgefangene und Häftlinge im Deutschen Reich und im besetzten Europa 1939–1945 (Stuttgart: DVA, 2001), 221; and Jörg Osterloh, *Ein ganz normales Lager: Das Kriegsgefangenen-Mannschaftsstammlager 304 (IV H) Zeithain bei Riesa/Sa. 1941 bis 1945* (Leipzig: Gustav Kiepenheuer, 1997), 8.

29. Gerhard Schreiber, *Die italienischen Militärinternierten im deutschen Machtbereich, 1943–1945: Verraten, verachtet, vergessen* (Munich: R. Oldenbourg, 1990), 20, 313–16; Gianfranco Matiello and Wolfgang Vogt, eds., *Die Kriegsgefangenen- und Internierteneinrichtungen 1939–1945: Handbuch und Katalog. Lagergeschichte und Lagerzensurstempel* (Koblenz: Selbstverlag, 1986), vol. 1.

30. V. I. Adamushko et al., eds., *Lageria sovetskikh voennoplennykh v Belarusi 1941–1944: Spravochnik* (Minsk: NARB, 2004), 70–167.

31. G. V. Boriak et al., eds., *Dovidnyk pro tabory, tiurmy ta hetta na okupovanyi terytorii Ukrainy (1941–1944)/Handbuch der Lager, Gefängnisse und Ghettos auf dem besetzten Territorium der Ukraine (1941–1944)* (Kyiv: Derzhavnyi komitet arkhiviv Ukrainy, 2000), 205–65.

32. Streim, *Behandlung*, 16.

33. Christian Gerlach, *Kalkulierte Morde: Die deutsche Wirtschafts- und Vernichtungspolitik in Weißrussland 1941–1944* (Hamburg: Hamburger Edition, 1999), 495.

34. Martin Weinmann, ed., *Das nationalsozialistische Lagersystem* (Frankfurt am Main: Zweitausendundeins, 1990), lxxxix–cxxxiii, cxiv–cxlv; Gudrun Schwarz, *Die nationalsozialistischen Lager* (Frankfurt am Main: Campus, 1990), 72.

35. Herbert, *Fremdarbeiter*, 181, 270–71; Spoerer, *Zwangsarbeit*, 89–167, 222; Wolfgang Benz and Barbara Distel, eds., *Der Ort des Terrors: Geschichte der nationalsozialistischen Konzentrationslager*, 2nd ed. (Munich: C. H. Beck, 2008), 1:1, 344.

36. Schreiber, *Italien Militärinternierten*, 450, 454, 456; Spoerer, *Zwangsarbeit*, 80–84, 122–35, 228; Rüdiger Overmans, Andreas Hilger, and Pavel Polian, eds., *Rotarmisten in deutscher Hand: Dokumente zur Gefangenschaft, Repatrierung und Rehabilitierung sowjetischer Soldaten des Zweiten Weltkrieges* (Paderborn: Ferdinand Schöningh, 2012), 23, tables 9–11, 880–82.

37. Hans-Hermann Stopsack and Eberhard Thomas, eds., *Stalag VI A Hemer: Kriegsgefangenenlager 1939–1945: Eine Dokumentation im Auftrag der Stadt Hemer und der Volkshochschule Menden-Hemer-Balve* (Hemer: Stadt Hemer, 1995), 37.

38. Herbert, *Fremdarbeiter*, 221, 270–72, 425.

39. Herbert *Fremdarbeiter*, 263–69; Spoerer, *Zwangsarbeiter*, 158–60.

40. Stopsack and Thomas, *Stalag VI A Hemer*, 124–29.

41. Karl Hüser and Reinhard Otto, *Das Stammlager 326 (VI K) Senne 1941–1945: Sowjetische Kriegsgefangene als Opfer des Nationalsozialistischen Weltanschauungskrieges* (Bielefeld: Verlag für Regionalgeschichte, 1992), 158, 326; Spoerer, *Zwangsarbeit*, 204–5.

42. Martin Weinmann, ed., *Das nationalsozialistische Lagersystem*, cxi; Jens-

Christian Wagner, *Produktion des Todes: Das KZ Mittelbau-Dora* (Göttingen: Wallstein, 2004), 415–18.

43. Herbert, *Fremdarbeiter*, 287–88; Spoerer, *Zwangsarbeit*, 200–202.

44. See Stopsack and Thomas, *Stalag VI A Hemer*, and Hüser and Otto, *Das Stammlager 326*. Spoerer deals with the subject cursorily (*Zwangsarbeit*, 168–73, 190–99).

45. Gerhard Botz, "Binnenstrukturen, Alltagsverhalten und Überlebenschancen in Nazi-Konzentrationslagern," in *Strategie des Überlebens: Häftlingsgesellschaften in KZ und Gulag*, ed. Robert Streibel and Hans Schafranek (Vienna: Picus, 1996), 45–71, 55.

46. Spoerer, *Zwangsarbeit*, 196–99.

47. Herbert et al., *Die nationalsozialistischen Konzentrationslager*, 489.

48. Peer Zumbansen, ed., *Zwangsarbeit im Dritten Reich: Erinnerung und Verantwortung. Juristische und zeithistorische Betrachtung/NS-Forced Labor: Remembrance and Responsibility. Legal and Historical Observations* (Baden-Baden: Nomos Verlagsgesellschaft, 2002); Andreas Heusler et al., eds., *Rüstung, Kriegswirtschaft und Zwangsarbeit im Dritten Reich* (Munich: R. Oldenbourg 2010).

49. Anna Pawelczynska, *Values and Violence: A Sociological Analysis* (Berkeley: University of California Press, 1979), 125–26; Sofsky, *Ordnung des Terrors*, 229–36.

50. Pawelczynska, *Values and Violence*, 52–57.

51. Benz and Distel, *Ort des Terrors*, 1:121, 242–57; 208–12; Jens-Christian Wagner, *Produktion des Todes: Das KZ Mittelbau-Dora* (Göttingen: Wallstein, 2004), 345–56, 445–51.

52. Osterloh, *Ein ganz normales Lager*, 106, 130-137; Tomas Stopsack, ed., *Stalag VI A Hemer*, 49; Hüser and Otto, *Das Stammlager 326 (VI K)*, 127-128.

53. Wagner, *Produktion des Todes*, 399.

54. Wolfgang Kirstein, *Das Konzentrationslager als Institution totalen Terrors: Das Beispiel des KL Natzweiler* (Pfaffenweiler: Centaurus Verlagsgesellschaft, 1992), 57.

55. Lutz Niethammer, ed., *Der "gesäuberte" Antifaschismus: Die SED und die roten Kapos von Buchenwald. Dokumente* (Berlin: Akademie, 1994); Herbert et al., *Nationalsozialistischen Konzentrationslager*, 939–58; Orth, *Konzentrationslager-SS*, 49–52; Wagner, *Produktion des Todes*, 402.

56. Herbert et al., *Nationalsozialistischen Konzentrationslager*, 959–82; Benz and Distel, *Ort des Terrors*, 1:242–57.

57. Kirstein, *Konzentrationslager*, 77; Wagner, *Produktion des Todes*, 404.

58. Benz and Distel, *Ort des Terrors*, 1:120.

59. Wagner, *Produktion des Todes*, 440–41.

60. Herbert et al., *Nationalsozialistischen Konzentrationslager*, 208–12; 959–82; Benz and Distel, *Ort des Terrors*, 1:242–57.

61. Orth, *Konzentrationslager-SS*, 59–60; Benz and Distel, *Ort des Terrors*, 1:33–39, 195; Elissa Mailänder Koslov, *Gewalt im Dienstalltag: Die SS-Aufseherinnen des*

Konzentrations- und Vernichtungslagers Majdanek (Hamburg: Hamburger Edition, 2009), 18, 20, 99.

62. Orth, *Konzentrationslager-SS*, 53–55; Mailänder Koslov, *Gewalt im Dienstalltag*, 85–86.

63. Orth, *Konzentrationslager-SS*; Mailänder Koslov, *Gewal im Dienstalltagt*, 92–136.

64. Mailänder Koslov, *Gewalt im Dienstalltag*, 136–39.

65. Gerhard Paul and Klaus-Michael Mallmann, eds., *Karrieren der Gewalt: Nationalsozialistische Täterbiographien* (Darmstadt: Wissenschaftliche Buchgesellschaft, 2004); Harald Welzer, *Täter: Wie aus ganz normalen Männern Massenmörder werden* (Frankfurt am Main: Fischer, 2005).

66. Vasilii Grossman, *Die Hölle von Treblinka* (Moscow: Verlag für Fremdsprachige Literatur, 1946), 51–52.

67. Orth, *Konzentrationslager-SS*, 126–35; Kirstein, *Konzentrationslager*, 51–61; Mailänder Koslov, *Gewalt im Dienstalltag*, 410–50.

68. See Herbert et al., *Nationalsozialistischen Konzentrationslager*, 922–25; and Jens-Christian Wagner, "Apotheose des Lagerterrors: Die Boelcke-Kaserne in Nordhausen (1944/45)," *Sozialwissenschaftliche Informationen* 29, no. 3 (2000): 152–58.

69. Grossman, *Hölle von Treblinka*, 6–7.

70. Harald Welzer, "'Härte und Rollendistanz': Zur Sozialpsychologie des Verwaltungsmassenmordes," *Leviathan* 21, no. 3 (1993): 358–73; Yves Ternon, *Der verbrecherische Staat: Völkermord im 20. Jahrhundert* (Hamburg: Hamburger Edition, 1996), 99–101; Mailänder Koslov, *Gewalt im Dienstalltag*, 169–72.

71. Eugen Kogon, *Der SS-Staat: Das System der deutschen Konzentrationslager* (Frankfurt am Main: Verlag der Frankfurter Hefte, 1948), 353.

72. Mailänder Koslov, *Gewalt im Dienstalltag*, 195–256.

73. Mailänder Koslov, *Gewalt im Dienstalltag*, 152–57, quotation on 222.

74. Kirstein, *Konzentrationslager*, 59.

75. Lynne A. Viola, "The Question of the Perpetrator in Soviet History," *Slavic Review* 72, no. 1 (2013): 20–21; Nicolas Werth, "Ein Staat gegen sein Volk," in *Le livre noir du communisme*, ed. Stéphane Courtois et al. (Paris: Laffont, 1997); Rolf Binner, Bernd Bonwetsch, and Marc Junge, *Massenmord und Lagerhaft: Die andere Geschichte des Großen Terrors* (Berlin: Akademie, 2009); Jörg Baberowski, *Verbrannte Erde: Stalins Herrschaft der Gewalt* (Munich: C. H. Beck, 2012); Oleg Khlevniuk, *Stalin: New Biography of a Dictator*, trans. Nora Seligman Favorov (New Haven: Yale University Press, 2015).

76. On the history of the Gulag, see Anne Applebaum, *Gulag: A History* (New York: Doubleday, 2003), of which I used the German edition, *Der Gulag* (Berlin: Siedler, 2003); Paul R. Gregory and Valery Lazarev, eds., *The Economics of Forced Labor: The Soviet Gulag* (Stanford, CA.: Hoover Institution Press, 2003); Oleg Khlevni-

uk, *The History of the Gulag: From Collectivization to the Great Terror* (New Haven: Yale University Press, 2004); Zh. A. Medvedev, "Atomnyi GULAG," *Voprosy istorii*, no. 1 (2001): 44–60; Borodkin et al., *Istoriia stalinizma*; Alan Barenberg, *Gulag Town, Company Town: Forced Labor and Its Legacy in Vorkuta* (New Haven: Yale University Press, 2014); and Bezborodov et al., *Istoriia stalinskogo GULAGa*.

77. A. I. Solzhenitsyn, *Arkhipelag Gulag*, 3 vols. (Paris: YMCA Press, 1973–1974), 1:386; Moshe Lewin, "The Disappearance of Planning in the Plan," *Slavic Review* 32, no. 2 (1973): 271–87.

78. M. B. Smirnov et al., eds., *Sistema ispravitel´no-trudovykh lagerei v SSSR 1923–1960: Spravochnik* (Moscow: Zvenia, 1998); G. M. Ivanova, *GULAG v sisteme totalitarnogo gosudarstva* (Moscow: Gosudarstvennyi obshchestvennyi nauchnyi fond, 1997), 97, 111, 115.

79. V. N. Zemskov, "Zakliuchennye, spetsposelentsy, ssyl´noposelentsy, ssyl´nye i vyslannye (Statististichesko-geograficheskii aspekt)," *Istoriia SSSR*, no. 5 (1991): 151–65; J. Arch Getty, Gábor T. Rittersporn, and Viktor Zemskov, "Victims of the Soviet Penal System in the Pre-War Years: A First Approach on the Basis of Archival Evidence," *American Historical Review* 98, no. 4 (1993): 1017–49; Stephan Merl, "Das System der Zwangsarbeit und der Opferzahl im Stalinismus," *Geschichte in Wissenschaft und Unterricht* 46, nos. 5–6 (1995): 277–305.

80. Edwin Bacon, *Gulag at War: Stalin's Forced Labor System in the Light of the Archives* (Basingstoke: Macmillan 1994), 125.

81. Bezborodov et al., *Istoriia stalinskogo GULAGa*, 4:80.

82. Michael Ellman, "Soviet Repression Statistics: Some Comments," *Europe-Asia Studies* 54, no. 7 (2002): 1161.

83. V. N. Zemskov, *Spetsposelentsy v SSSR, 1930–1960* (Moscow: Nauka, 2005), 33.

84. Zemskov, "Zakliuchennye, spetsposelentsy, ssyl´noposelentsy," 155.

85. Bezborodov et al., *Istoriia stalinskogo GULAGa*, 2: Doc. no. 197; 4: Doc. no. 149.

86. Bezborodov et al., *Istoriia stalinskogo GULAGa*, 2:40–41.

87. Galina Ivanova, "Eine unbekannte Seite des GULag: Lagersondergerichte in der UdSSR (1945–1954)," *Jahrbücher für Geschichte Osteuropas* 53, no. 1 (2005): 25–41.

88. Pavel Polian, *Zhertvy dvukh diktatur: Ostarbaitery i voennoplennye v Tret´em Reikhe i ikh repatriatsiia* (Moscow: Vash Vybor CIRZ, 1996), 294.

89. See selected volumes of *Zur Geschichte der deutschen Kriegsgefangenen des Zweiten Weltkrieges: Die deutschen Kriegsgefangenen in der Sowjetunion* (Munich: Ernst und Werner Gieseking, 1965): 2—Diether Cartellieri, *Die Lagergesellschaft: Eine Untersuchung der zwischenmenschlichen Beziehungen in den Kriegsgefangenenlagern* (1967); 3—Hedwig Fleischhacker, *Die deutschen Kriegsgefangenen in der Sowjetunion: Der Faktor Hunger* (1965); 4—Werner Ratza, *Die deutschen Kriegsgefangenen*

in der Sowjetunion: Der Faktor Arbeit (1973); 7—Kurt W. Böhme, *Die deutschen Kriegsgefangenen in sowjetischer Hand: Eine Bilanz* (1966); and 8—Gert Robel, *Die deutschen Kriegsgefangenen in der Sowjetunion: Antifa* (1974). See also M. M. Zagorul´ko, ed., *Voennoplennye v SSSR 1939–1956: Dokumenty i materialy* (Moscow: Logos, 2000), 1038, 1041; and Rüdiger Overmans, *Deutsche militärische Verluste im Zweiten Weltkrieg* (Munich: R. Oldenbourg, 1999), 286.

90. Stefan Karner, *Im Archipel GUPVI: Kriegsgefangenschaft und Internierung in der Sowjetunion 1941–1956* (Munich: R. Oldenbourg, 1995); Andreas Hilger, *Deutsche Kriegsgefangene in der Sowjetunion, 1941–1956: Kriegsgefangenenpolitik, Lageralltag und Erinnerung* (Essen: Klartext, 2000), 259–83, 332–67. In light of the arbitrariness of Soviet justice, it is estimated that more than half of those convicted were actually responsible for war crimes. Contemporaries spoke—without much awareness of responsibility—about the Soviet "interrogation mill" or "sentencing machine" (Cartellieri, *Lagergesellschaft*, 321, 324).

91. Bezborodov et al., *Istoriia stalinskogo GULAGa*, 4:70.

92. Bezborodov et al., *Istoriia stalinskogo GULAGa*, 4: Doc. no. 37.

93. Solzhenitsyn, *Arkhipelag Gulag*, 2:297.

94. Solzhenitsyn, *Arkhipelag Gulag*, 1:20; Nadezhda Mandelstam, *Jahrhundert der Wölfe: Eine Autobiographie* (Frankfurt am Main: Fischer, 1971), 82.

95. E. A. Osokina, *Ierarkhiia potrebleniia: O zhizni liudei v usloviiakh stalinskogo snabzheniia 1928–1935* (Moscow: Izdatel´stvo Moskovskogo gosudarstvennogo universiteta, 1993); Nathalie Moine, "Passportisation, statistique des migrations et controle de l'identité sociale," *Cahiers du monde russe* 38, no. 4 (1997): 587–600; V. P. Popov, "Pasportnaia sistema v SSSR (1932–1976 gg.)," *Sotsiologicheskie issledovaniia*, no. 8 (1995): 3–14.

96. This view is critical to Jochen Hellbeck, *Revolution on My Mind: Writing a Diary under Stalin* (Cambridge, MA: Harvard University Press, 2006). See also Dietrich Beyrau, "Geiseln und Gefangene eines visionären Projekts: Die russischen Bildungsschichten im Sowjetstaat," in *Stalinismus vor dem Zweiten Weltkrieg: Neue Wege der Forschung*, ed. Manfred Hildermeier (Munich: R. Oldenbourg, 1998), 55–77.

97. Andrzej Józef Kaminski, *Konzentrationslager 1896 bis heute: Geschichte, Funktion, Typologie* (Munich: Piper, 1990), 167.

98. Evgeniia Albaz, *Geheimimperium KGB: Totengräber der Sowjetunion* (Munich: dtv, 1992), 84; G. M. Ivanova, "Poslevoennye repressii i Gulag," in *Stalin i kholodnaia voina*, ed. I. V. Gaiduk, N. I. Egorova, and A. O. Chubarian (Moscow: Institut vseobshchei istorii Rossiiskoi akademii nauk, 1997), 254–73, 259.

99. The aspect of reeducation is emphasized in Steven A. Barnes, *Death and Redemption: The Gulag and the Shaping of Soviet Society* (Princeton, NJ: Princeton University Press, 2011); Felicitas Fischer von Weikersthal, *Die "inhaftierte" Presse: Das Pressewesen sowjetischer Zwangsarbeitslager, 1923–1937* (Wiesbaden: Harrassowitz, 2011).

100. Heinz Barwich and Elfi Barwich, *Das rote Atom* (Munich: Scherz, 1967), 46.

101. Bezborodov et al., *Istoriia stalinskogo GULAGa,* 2: Doc. no. 30.

102. Iosif Stalin, *Sochineniia* (Stanford, CA: Hoover Institution on War, Revolution, and Peace, 1967), 1:90; A. Iu. Gorcheva, *Pressa GULAGa: 1918–1955* (Moscow: Izdatel'stvo Moskovskogo universiteta, 1996), 51.

103. Jakobson, *Origins of the Gulag,* 48–50, 119–27, 133; Joachim Klein, "Belomorkanal: Literatur und Propaganda in der Stalinzeit," *Zeitschrift für Slavische Philologie* 55, no. 1 (1995): 53–98; Barnes, *Death and Redemption*; Fischer von Weikersthal, *"Inhaftierte" Presse.*

104. For example, there is a photograph of a gathering of POWs in an Estonian camp where the German slogan is not quite correct: "Unsere Lager 286 arbeiten in der ersten Front der Wiedergutmachung." See also Ratza, *Deutschen Kriegsgefangenen in der Sowjetunion,* 112–13; Robel, *Deutschen Kriegsgefangenen in der Sowjetunion*; and Hilger, *Deutsche Kriegsgefangene,* 220–55.

105. Aleksandr Solzhenitsyn, *Arkhipelag Gulag* (Paris: YMCA Press, 1974), 3–4:199, 205; Paul Barton, *L'institution concentrationnaire en Russie, 1930–1957* (Paris: Librairie Plon, 1959), 224; V. I. Iukshinskii, *Sovetskie kontsentratsionnye lageri v 1945–1955 g.,* (Munich: Institut po izucheniiu SSSR , 1958), 16; Ratza, *Die deutschen Kriegsgefangenen in der Sowjetunion,* 65.

106. V. N. Zemskov, "Sud'ba kulatskoi ssylki (1930–1955 gg.)," *Otechestvennaia istoriia,* no. 1 (1994): 121–23; Getty, Rittersporn, and Zemskov, "Victims of the Soviet Penal System," 1042; Lynne A. Viola, *The Unknown Gulag: The Lost World of Stalin's Special Settlements* (Oxford: Oxford University Press, 2007), 132–49.

107. Böhme, *Deutschen Kriegsgefangenen,* 49, 151; Hilger, *Deutsche Kriegsgefangene,* 402–7; Applebaum, *Gulag,* 618–19; Stephen G. Wheatcroft, "The Scale and Nature of German and Soviet Repression and Mass Killings, 1930–1945," *Europe-Asia Studies* 48, no. 8 (1996): 1319–53.

108. Herta Müller, *Atemschaukel: Roman* (Munich: Carl Hanser, 2009), 89.

109. Fleischhacker, *Die deutschen Kriegsgefangenen in der Sowjetunion*; Albrecht Lehmann, *Gefangenschaft und Heimkehr: Deutsche Kriegsgefangene in der Sowjetunion* (Munich: C. H. Beck, 1986), 58–90, quotation on 88.

110. Solzhenitsyn, *Arkhipelag Gulag* 3–4:205–7.

111. Bezborodov et al., *Istoriia stalinskogo GULAGa,* 4:228–32, 254, 260, 271.

112. Werth, "Ein Staat gegen sein Volk," 250; Khlevniuk, *History of the Gulag,* 209–10, 231–32, 275–76.

113. Solzhenitsyn, *Arkhipelag Gulag,* 2:204.

114. Pawelczynska, *Values and Violence,* 131–32; Wolfgang Sofsky, "An der Grenze des Sozialen: Perspektiven der KZ-Forschung" in *Nationalsozialistischen Konzentrationslager,* 1159; Makurov et al., *Gulag v Karelii,* 36–37, 146.

115. V. N. Maksheev, ed., *Narymskaia khronika 1930–1945: Tragediia spetspere-*

selentsev. Dokumenty i vospominaniia (Moscow: Russkii put´, 1997), 36–37, 43–44, 133–34, 149–50.

116. Bezborodov et al., *Istoriia stalinskogo GULAGa*, 2:31–44.

117. Alfred Eisfeld and Viktor Herdt, eds., *Deportation, Sondersiedlung, Arbeitsarmee: Deutsche in der Sowjetunion 1941 bis 1956* (Cologne: Verlag Wissenschaft und Politik, 1996), 269; Viola, *Unknown Gulag*, 91, 110–11; Bezborodov et al., *Istoriia stalinskogo GULAGa*, 4: Doc. no. 63.

118. V. A. Kozlov, "Vvedenie," *Istoriia stalinskogo GULAGa*, 6:87.

119. A. I. Kokurin, ed., "GULAG v gody voiny: Doklad nachal´nika GULAGa NKVD SSSR V. G. Nasedkina, August 1944," *Istoricheskii arkhiv*, no. 3 (1994): 67; Werth, "Ein Staat gegen sein Volk," 250; Borodkin et al., *GULAG*, 209, 259; Bezborodov et al., *Istoriia stalinskogo GULAGa*, 3:503; 4: Doc. no. 23.

120. Ratza, *Deutschen Kriegsgefangenen in der Sowjetunion*, 126, 128, 131, 137; Hilger, *Deutsche Kriegsgefangene*, 165–72.

121. Bezborodov et al., *Istoriia stalinskogo GULAGa*, 2: Doc. no. 163.

122. Alan Barenberg, "From Prison Camp to Mining Town: The Gulag and Its Legacy in Vorkuta, 1938–1965" (PhD diss., University of Chicago, 2007), 7–10, 70–71, 202–8.

123. Ratza, *Deutschen Kriegsgefangenen in der Sowjetunion*, 1–61; Lehmann, *Gefangenschaft und Heimkehr*, 96–97; Hilger, *Deutsche Kriegsgefangene*, 198–206, 211–19.

124. Ratza, *Deutschen Kriegsgefangenen in der Sowjetunion*, 141.

125. Solzhenitsyn, *Arkhipelag Gulag*, 2:156; Khlevniuk, *History of the Gulag*, 110–22; Bezborodov et al., *Istoriia stalinskogo GULAGa*, 2: Docs. 27, 30, 127, 150, 161.

126. R. W. Davies et al., eds., *The Economic Transformation of the Soviet Union, 1913–1945* (Cambridge: Cambridge University Press, 1994), 24–37, 292; Ivanova, *GULAG*, 97–98, 136; Bezborodov et al., *Istoriia stalinskogo GULAGa*, 4:94–95.

127. Cartellieri, *Die Lagergesellschaft*, 89–95; Lehmann, *Gefangenschaft und Heimkehr*, 52; Hilger, *Deutsche Kriegsgefangene*, 156–59.

128. Solzhenitsyn, *Arkhipelag Gulag*, 5–7:262–348; Applebaum, *Der GULAG*, 429–34, 511–31; Kozlov, "Vvedenie," 60–102.

129. Bezborodov et al., *Istoriia stalinskogo GULAGa*, 2:42–48 and Docs. no. 12, 15, 44, 130, 131, 135; Tomasz Kizny, *Gulag* (Hamburg: Hamburger Edition, 2004), 258–96.

130. Bezborodov et al., *Istoriia stalinskogo GULAGa*, 2: Docs. 38, 61, 104, 125, 132, 153, 169, 259.

131. Bezborodov et al., *Istoriia stalinskogo GULAGa*, 2:46 and Docs. no. 12, 15, 109–24, 154–71, 176.

132. Bezborodov et al., *Istoriia stalinskogo GULAGa*, 2: Doc. no. 17; 3: Docs. no. 167–79.

133. Bezborodov et al., *Istoriia stalinskogo GULAGa*, 3:47; Klaus Gestwa, *Die Stalinschen Großbauten des Kommunismus: Sowjetische Technik- und Umweltgeschichte, 1948–1967* (Munich: R. Oldenbourg, 2010), 390–440.

134. Ivanova, *Gulag*, 48, 158–60, 172–73, 188–91; Bezborodov et al., *Istoriia stalinskogo GULAGa*, 2: Docs. no. 49, 126, 127, 130.

135. Ivanova, *Gulag*, 70–74.

136. Solzhenitsyn, *Arkhipelag Gulag*, 2:155–57.

137. Ratza, *Deutschen Kriegsgefangenen in der Sowjetunion*, 129.

138. Bezborodov et al., *Istoriia stalinskogo GULAGa*, 4:96.

139. Quotation from Cartellieri, *Die Lagergesellschaft*, 116. See also Lehmann, *Gefangenschaft und Heimkehr*, 50–51; and Hilger, *Deutsche Kriegsgefangene*, 256, 284.

140. Iukshinskii, *Sovetskie kontsentratsionnye lageri*, 72; David J. Nordlander, "Origins of a Gulag Capital: Magadan and Stalinist Control in the Early 1930s," *Slavic Review* 57, no. 4 (1998): 791–812.

141. Jakobson, *Origins of the Gulag*, 43, 99; Ralf Stettner, *"Archipel Gulag": Stalins Zwangslager—Terrorinstrument und Wirtschaftsgigant. Entstehung, Organisation und Funktion des sowjetischen Lagersystems, 1928–1956* (Paderborn: F. Schöningh, 1996), 256–59; Wladislaw Hedeler, "Das Beispiel KARLag," in *Stalinscher Terror 1934-41: Eine Forschungsbilanz*, ed. Wladislaw Hedeler (Berlin: BasisDruck, 2002), 109–31, 110, 116, 120; Makurov et al., *Gulag v Karelii*, 38–39.

142. Orth, *Konzentrationslager-SS*, 54; Wagner, *Produktion des Todes*, 440.

CHAPTER 12. "REPAYING BLOOD DEBT": THE CHINESE LABOR CAMP SYSTEM DURING THE 1950S

A much earlier version of portions of this chapter, without the comparision to the Soviet Gulag, appeared in *Rethinking China in the 1950s*, ed. Mechthild Leutner (Münster: LIT, 2007), 35–48.

1. On the continuities, see William C. Kirby, "The Chinese Party-State under Dictatorship and Democracy on the Mainland and on Taiwan," in *Realms of Freedom in Modern China*, ed. Kirby (Stanford, CA: Stanford University Press, 2004), 113–38.

2. Hannah Arendt, *The Origins of Totalitarianism* (New York: Harcourt, Brace, 1951), xv, 477.

3. Christopher R. Browning, *Ordinary Men: Reserve Police Battalion 101 and the Final Solution in Poland* (New York: HarperCollins, 1992), 160.

4. Benjamin A. Valentino, *Final Solutions: Mass Killings and Genocide in the Twentieth Century* (Ithaca, NY: Cornell University Press, 2004).

5. James C. Scott, *Seeing Like a State: How Certain Schemes to Improve the Human Condition Have Failed* (New Haven: Yale University Press, 1998).

6. Jean-Luc Domenach, *Chine, l'archipel oublié* (Paris: Fayard, 1992); Michael Dutton, *Policing and Punishment in China: From Patriarchy to "the People"* (Cambridge: Cambridge University Press, 1992); Harry Wu, *Laogai: The Chinese Gulag* (Boulder, CO: Westview, 1992); Philip F. Williams and Yenna Wu, *The Great Wall of Confinement: The Chinese Prison Camp through Contemporary Fiction and Reportage* (Berkeley: University of California Press, 2004).

7. See, among others, Aminda M. Smith, *Thought Reform and China's Dangerous Classes: Reeducation, Resistance, and the People* (Lanham, MD: Rowman and Littlefield, 2013); Jan Kiely, *The Compelling Ideal: Thought Reform and the Prison in China, 1901–1956* (New Haven: Yale University Press, 2014); Frank Dikötter, *The Tragedy of Liberation: A History of the Chinese Revolution, 1945–57* (London: Bloomsbury, 2013); Klaus Mühlhahn, *Criminal Justice in China: A History* (Cambridge, MA: Harvard University Press, 2009); and Michael Schoenhals, *Spying for the People: Mao's Secret Agents, 1949–1967* (Cambridge: Cambridge University Press, 2013).

8. Mao Tse-tung, *Selected Works*, 5 vols. (Beijing: Foreign Languages Press, 1967), 4:445. I use here the official, redacted version of Mao's text, because it is in this form that the text was circulated in China.

9. Mao Zedong, *The Writings of Mao Zedong, 1949–1976*, ed. Michael Y. M. Kau et al., 2 vols. (Armonk, NY: M. E. Sharpe, 1986–1992), 2:57.

10. Mao, *Writings of Mao Zedong, 1949–1976*, 2:57.

11. Mao, *Writings of Mao Zedong, 1949–1976*, 2:57.

12. Mao, *Selected Works*, 1:29.

13. See Michael Dutton, *Policing Chinese Politics: A History* (Durham, NC: Duke University Press, 2005), 3.

14. Carl Schmitt, "The Concept of the Political" (New Brunswick, NJ: Rutgers University Press, 1976), reference in Dutton, *Policing Chinese Politics*, 3.

15. Dutton, *Policing Chinese Politics*, 4.

16. There were several types of campaigns, distinguished by the extent of their reach into society and the target groups. See Julia Strauss, "Morality, Coercion, and State Building by Campaign in the Early PRC: Regime Consolidation and After, 1949–1956," *China Quarterly* 188 (December 2006): 891–912. In this chapter, I focus on two types: the great mass campaigns (*qunzhong yundong*) that took place in 1950–1953 and the frequent, more limited campaigns implemented through the bureaucracy against restricted social or occupational groups. Both types deployed tribunals.

17. Quoted from Dutton, *Policing Chinese Politics*, 36.

18. Prison sentences over five years needed ratification from the provincial government.

19. Mühlhahn, *Criminal Justice in China*, 181.

20. *Renmin Zhoubao* (Beijing), 3 June 1951.

21. Julia C. Strauss, "Paternalist Terror: The Campaign to Suppress Counterrevo-

lutionaries and Regime Consolidation in the People's Republic of China, 1950–1953," *Comparative Studies in Society and History* 44, no. 1 (2002): 97.

22. Gao Hua, *Hong taiyang shi zenyang shengqi de* (How the Red Sun Rose over China) (Hong Kong: Chinese University Press, 2000); Yang Kuisong, *Zhonghua remin gongheguo jianguoshe yanjiu* (Studies on the Establishment of the People's Republic of China) (Nanchang: Jiangxi Remin chubanshe, 2009); Frank Dikötter, *The Tragedy of Liberation: A History of the Chinese Revolution, 1945–57* (London: Bloomsbury, 2013).

23. Dutton, *Policing Chinese Politics*, 167.

24. An example of a mass trial and mass execution of around fifty landlords during the Land Reform Movement is described in Gregory Ruf, *Cadres and Kin: Making a Socialist Village in West China, 1921–1991* (Stanford, CA: Stanford University Press, 1998), 86–87.

25. The total of eight hundred thousand executed counterrevolutionaries is often mentioned. In 1957 Mao Zedong himself explained that during the campaign to eliminate counterrevolutionaries in 1950–1953, seven hundred thousand people were killed. In the period from 1954 to 1957 an additional seventy thousand were executed as counterrevolutionaries. He also admitted that mistakes were made and innocent people killed. See Mao Tse-tung, *The Secret Speeches of Chairman Mao: From the Hundred Flowers to the Great Leap Forward*, ed. Roderick MacFarquhar et al. (Cambridge, MA: Council on East Asian Studies, Harvard University, 1989), 142. If, on average, a third to a quarter of all accused counterrevolutionaries were executed, one can estimate that the number of accused counterrevolutionaries totaled between 2.1 and 2.8 million people. This is only the minimum; the true figure is probably much higher. See also Yang Kuisong, "Reconsidering the Campaign to Suppress Counter-Revolutionaries," *China Quarterly* 193 (March 2008): 102–21.

26. In 1950 and 1951 Mao Zedong wrote several comments on the Movement to Suppress and Liquidate Counterrevolutionaries (Mao, *Writings of Mao Zedong, 1949–1976*, 1:189, 112). He expressed increasing unease that the movement would get beyond control. On 8 May 1951 (Mao, *Writings of Mao Zedong, 1949–1976*, 1:189) he argued that only perpetrators who have committed the most severe crimes (murder, rape) should be executed immediately; all others should receive a two-year delay. On 15 June 1951 (Mao, *Writings of Mao Zedong, 1949–1976*, 1:202), he argued that his earlier policy should not be mistaken as too lenient. In any case, Mao's frequent comments demonstrate how difficult it was to control the movement.

27. Strauss, "Paternalist Terror," 85.

28. See Tao Siju, *Luo Ruiqing: Xin Zhongguo di yi ren gong'an buzhang* (Luo Ruiqing: New China's First Minister of Public Security) (Beijing: Qunzhong chubanshe, 1996), 104.

29. See Yang Xianguang, ed., *Laogai faxue cidian* (Juristic Dictionary on Labor Reform) (Chengdu: Sichuan cishu, 1989), 25.

30. See Yang Diansheng and Zhang Jinsang, eds., *Zhongguo tese jianyu zhidu yanjiu* (Studies on the Prison System with Chinese Characteristics) (Beijing: Falü, 1998), 30.

31. See Cai Yanshu, *Laodong gaizao gongzuo gailun* (Concise History of the Laogai Work) (Guangdong: Guangdong gao deng jiao yu, 1988), 9. Part of this speech is reprinted in Wang Gengxin, *Mao Zedong laodong gaizao sixiang yanjiu* (Mao Zedong's Thoughts on Reform through Labor) (Xi'an: Shehui kexue, 1992), 163–64. In this speech Liu Shaoqi mentioned the total number of prisoners, but in the reprint this information was omitted.

32. See Liu Shaoqi, "Address to the Third National Conference on Public Security" (11 May 1951), in Wang, *Mao Zedong laodong gaizao sixiang yanjiu*, 163–64. According to UN statistics, Bulgaria had a population of 7.2 million people in 1951. At that time, its workforce was around 5.4 million people. See http://www.un.org/esa/population/publications/worldageing19502050/pdf/054bulga.pdf. This indicates at least five million prisoners in 1951 before the establishment of a labor camp system.

33. Deborah A. Kaple, "Soviet Advisors in China in the 1950s," in *Brothers in Arms: The Rise and Fall of the Sino-Soviet Alliance, 1945–1963*, ed. Odd Arne Westad (Washington, DC: Woodrow Wilson Center Press, 1998), 117–40.

34. "Resolution of the Third National Conference of Public Security" (15 May 1951), in Wang, *Mao Zedong laodong gaizao sixiang yanjiu*, 162.

35. Sun Xiaoli, *Zhongguo laodong gaizao zhidu de lilun yu shijian: Lishi yu xianshi* (Laogai—the Chinese Prison System's Theory and Practices: History and Reality) (Sanhe: Zhongguo zhengfa daxue chubanshe, 1994), 22.

36. See Jean-Luc Domenach, *Der vergessene Archipel: Gefängnisse und Lager in der Volksrepublik China* (Hamburg: Hamburger Edition, 1995), 89.

37. Anne Applebaum, *Gulag: A History* (New York: Doubleday, 2003).

38. The role of the provinces is also emphasized in Domenach, *Vergessene Archipel*, 127–28.

39. Yang, *Laogai faxue cidian*, 24.

40. Oleg V. Khlevniuk, *The History of the Gulag: From Collectivization to the Great Terror* (New Haven: Yale University Press, 2004).

41. Unless otherwise noted, numbers are from Sun, *Zhongguo laodong gaizao*, 23. Harry Wu, *Laogai: The Chinese Gulag* (Boulder, CO: Westview, 1992), 60, gives similar numbers for the camps. His number for inmates is much higher, though.

42. This point is also made in Domenach, *Vergessene Archipel*, 96.

43. An English translation is available in Albert P. Blaustein, ed., *Fundamental Legal Documents of Communist China* (South Hackensack, NJ: F. B. Rothman, 1962).

44. See Mao, *Selected Works*, 4:420.

45. Luo Ruiqing, *Lun renmin gongan gongzuo* (On the People's Public Security Work) (Beijing: Qunzhong chubanshe, 1994), 233.

46. It seems that article 62 was controversial within the leadership, too. Luo Ruiqing spent much time discussing this article in his general introduction of the statute (*Lun renmin gongan gongzuo*, 23).

47. The article was elaborated by the Temporary Statute on the Release of Criminals Completing Their Terms and the Implementation of Job Placement, 7 September 1954. See Wu, *Laogai*, 1, 13–14, 108–10; Domenach, *Vergessene Archipel*, 99–100.

48. The only groups released were convicts who had served terms under two years, old and infirm prisoners, CCP cadres and their children, and those with families in the countryside. See Wu, *Laogai*, 111.

49. Wu, *Laogai*, 111.

50. David R. Shearer, *Policing Stalin's Socialism: Repression and Social Order in the Soviet Union, 1924–1953* (New Haven: Yale University Press, 2009); Sheila Fitzpatrick, *Everyday Stalinism: Ordinary Life in Extraordinary Times. Soviet Russia in the 1930s* (Oxford: Oxford University Press, 1999).

51. Domenach, *Vergessene Archipel*, 89.

52. Sun, *Zhongguo laodong gaizao*, 25.

53. Yang and Zhang, *Zhongguo tese jianyu zhidu yanjiu*, 31.

54. Several internal Chinese documents indicate that there were about two thousand camps in the early 1960s. An average of twenty thousand prisoners per camp would yield a total of forty million prisoners. From several eyewitness reports, however, we know that some camps held more than forty thousand prisoners.

55. Domenach, *Vergessene Archipel*, 58, 215, 248.

56. Giorgio Agamben, *Homo Sacer: Sovereign Power and Bare Life* (Stanford, CA: Stanford University Press, 1998), 169.

57. Christian Gerlach and Nicolas Werth, "State Violence—Violent Societies," in *Beyond Totalitarianism: Stalinism and Nazism Compared*, ed. Michael Geyer and Sheila Fitzpatrick (New York: Cambridge University Press, 2009), 151.

58. Golfo Alexopoulos, "Destructive Labor Camps: Rethinking Solzhenitsyn's Play on Words," in this volume; Mühlhahn, *Criminal Justice in China*, chap. 3.

59. Michael David-Fox, *Crossing Borders: Modernity, Ideology, and Culture in Russia and the Soviet Union* (Pittsburgh: University of Pittsburgh Press, 2015).

60. Tu Wei-ming, "Destructive Will and Ideological Holocaust: Maoism as a Source of Social Suffering in China," in *Social Suffering*, ed. Arthur Kleinman, Veena Das, and Margaret M. Lock (Berkeley: University of California Press, 1997), 167.

CHAPTER 13. THE ORIGINS AND EVOLUTION OF THE NORTH KOREAN PRISON CAMPS: A COMPARISON WITH THE SOVIET GULAG

1. Victor Cha, *The Impossible State: North Korea, Past and Future* (New York: Ecco Books, 2012), 170.

2. David Hawk, *The Hidden Gulag* (Washington, DC: Committee for Human Rights in North Korea, 2012), 27.

3. South Korea granted some two thousand North Korean defectors asylum between the end of the Korean War and 2001; by 2013 that number had increased to twenty-five thousand. For the statistical data on North Korean defections, see Leo Byrne, "North Korean Defection by the Numbers," *NK News* (8 July 2015), https://www.nknews.org/2015/07/north-korean-defection-by-the-numbers/.

4. *Report of the UN Commission of Inquiry on Human Rights in the Democratic People's Republic of Korea* (February 2014), VII, para. 1211, p. 365.

5. Hawk, *Hidden Gulag*, 40.

6. Theda Skocpol, "Doubly Engaged Social Science: The Promise of Comparative Historical Analysis," in *Comparative Historical Analysis in the Social Sciences*, ed. James Mahoney and Dietrich Rueschemeyer (New York: Cambridge University Press, 2003), 412.

7. Ahn Myung-Chul, *Bukkan jeongchibum suyongso kyungbi daewon ui suki* (The Memoir of a Former North Korean Political Prison Guard) (Seoul: Shidae Jungshin, 2007).

8. Chol-hwan Kang and Pierre Rigoulot, *The Aquariums of Pyongyang: Ten Years in the North Korean Gulag* (New York: Basic Books, 2005).

9. Kang was invited to the White House by President Bush in 2005.

10. Since the publication of the first edition in 2003, Hawk has continued to update the report with new information supplied by defectors in 2012, 2013, and 2015. *The Hidden Gulag* and other reports on North Korea's prison camps can be found at the website of the Committee for Human Rights in North Korea, https://www.hrnk.org/publications/hrnk-publications.php.

11. See Kyung-ok Do et al., *White Paper on Human Rights in North Korea 2015* (Seoul: Korean Institute for National Unification, 2015), 114–15.

12. Blaine Harden, *Escape from Camp 14: One Man's Remarkable Odyssey from North Korea to Freedom in the West* (New York: Penguin Books, 2013).

13. Catherine E. Shoichet and Madison Park, "North Korean Prison Camp Survivor Admits Inaccuracies, Author Says," CNN.com, http://www.cnn.com/2015/01/18/asia/north-korea-defector-changes-story/index.html.

14. Although this annual report covers a wide range of human rights issues across North Korea beyond prison camps, still its focus of investigation is on accumulating records of human rights abuses within the camp system.

15. Yoon Yeo-sang et al., *Bukkan jungchibum suyongso ui unyungchegye wa inkwon shiltae* (North Korean Prison Camps' Operational System and Human Rights Situations) (Seoul: Archives of North Korean Human Rights Record, 2011).

16. Aleksandr I. Solzhenitsyn, *The Gulag Archipelago, 1918–1956: An Experiment in Literary Investigation*, trans. Thomas P. Whitney (New York: Basic Books, 1997).

17. For a detailed analysis of satellite images of North Korea's prison camps through Google Earth, see "North Korea's Largest Concentration Camps on Google Earth," http://freekorea.us/camps/.

18. For more details on the variety of facilities for detention and forced labor in North Korea, see David Hawk, *Hidden Gulag VI: Gender Repression and Prisoner Disappearance* (Washington, DC: Committee for Human Rights in North Korea, 2015), 7–9.

19. Oh Kyung-sup, "Bukhan inkwon chimhae ui gujojeok shiltae-e guanhan yeongu" (Analysis of North Korea's Structural Human Rights Violations, with a Focus on Political Prisons) (MA diss., Korea University, 2005); Yoon et al., *Bukkan jungchibum*, 318–32.

20. Hawk's *Hidden Gulag* includes a historical overview, but it offers only brief background information.

21. Oh Kyung-sup, "Soryeon, Bukhan, Jungguk ui jeongchibum suyongso bigyo" (A Comparison of the Soviet, North Korean, and Chinese Political Prisons), in *Research on North Korean Human Rights Policy* (Seoul: Korea Institute of National Unification, 2012), 302–59; Jang Kong-ja, "Bukhan ui Gangje Suyongso wa Dokyil yi Juneun Kyohun" (North Korea's Prison Camps and Lessons from Germany), *Unification Strategy* 11, no. 1 (2011): 121–50.

22. Ken Gause, *Coercion, Control, Surveillance, and Punishment: An Examination of the North Korean Police State* (Washington, DC: Committee for Human Rights in North Korea, 2012), 91.

23. For a more comprehensive analysis of Soviet influence over North Korean state building, see Andrei Lankov, *From Stalin to Kim Il Sung: The Formation of North Korea, 1945–1960* (New Brunswick, NJ: Rutgers University Press, 2002).

24. Available documentary evidence does not reveal much about Pang's pre-Korean past. Lankov collected information from other Soviet Koreans who used to be educators, engineers, and party bureaucrats in the ethnic Korean communities in what was then Soviet Central Asia before being sent, like Pang, as advisers to the emerging North Korean state agencies (*From Stalin to Kim Il Sung*, 128–29).

25. As North Korea's minister of the interior until 1958, Pang was also in charge of carrying out the purge that contributed so strongly to the expansion of the camp system in the 1950s and 1960s. For more detail, see Andrei Lankov, "Pang Hak-Se: Founder of NK Security Police," *Korea Times*, http://www.koreatimes.co.kr/www/news/issues/2016/01/363_105493.html.

26. The statistics vary from 1,679,258 to 1,803,392 depending on the source. For the history of kulak deportations and the special settlements that laid the foundation for Stalin's Gulag, see Lynne A. Viola, *The Unknown Gulag: The Lost World of Stalin's Special Settlements* (New York: Oxford University Press, 2007).

27. Gause, *Coercion, Control, Surveillance, and Punishment*, 126.

28. Jae-Jung Suh, *Origins of North Korea's Juche: Colonialism, War, and Development* (Lanham, MD: Rowman and Littlefield, 2013), 97.

29. See Steven A. Barnes, *Death and Redemption: The Gulag and the Shaping of Soviet Society* (Princeton, NJ: Princeton University Press, 2011), 154.

30. Barnes, *Death and Redemption*, 166.

31. On the power struggles within Soviet camps between the political prisoners and the criminal element, see Fyodor Vasilevich Mochulsky, "Part 2: Gulag from the Inside," *Gulag Boss: A Soviet Memoir*, trans. and ed. Deborah Kaple (New York: Oxford University Press, 2012), 25–64.

32. Barnes, *Death and Redemption*, 213.

33. Andrei Lankov, *The Real North Korea* (New York: Oxford University Press, 2013), 13–14.

34. As noted above, during the Second World War many Red Army soldiers who had been captured by the Germans were sent to the Gulag after being labeled collaborators. These newly arrived prisoners had the combat experience, skills, and courage to confront the prison guards (Barnes, *Death and Redemption*, 203).

35. On the economic costs of the Gulag system, see Paul R. Gregory, "An Introduction to the Economics of the Gulag," in *The Economics of Forced Labor: The Soviet Gulag*, ed. Gregory and Valery Lazarev (Stanford, CA: Hoover Institution Press, 2003), 1–22. On how penal workers in some camps were offered wages and monetary bonuses, thus raising their cost to the state, see Leonid Borodkin and Simon Ertz, "Coercion versus Motivation: Forced Labor in Norilsk," in *Economics of Forced Labor*, 75–104.

36. Miriam Dobson, *Khrushchev's Cold Summer: Gulag Returnees, Crime, and the Fate of Reform after Stalin* (Ithaca, NY: Cornell University Press, 2011), 77.

37. The Gulag system was not fully dismantled until the late 1980s. It contracted but did not disappear. Even today the Russian penal system retains the imprint of the Gulag in its use of prisoner labor in remote locations. See Judith Pallot's chapter in this volume and her other articles, including "Continuities in Penal Russia: Space and Gender in Post-Soviet Geography of Punishment," in *What Is Soviet Now? Identities, Legacies, Memories*, ed. Thomas Lahusen and Peter H. Solomon (Münster: Lit, 2008), 234–56; and "The Topography of Incarceration: The Spatial Continuity of Penality and the Legacy of the Gulag in Twentieth- and Twenty-First Century Russia," *Laboratorium: Russian Review of Social Research* 7, no. 1 (2015): 26–50.

38. For more detail, see Robert Collins, *Marked for Life: Songbun—North Korea's Social Classification System* (Washington, DC: Committee for Human Rights in North Korea, 2012).

39. *White Paper on Human Rights in North Korea* (Seoul: Korean Institute for National Unification, 2007).

40. The group was known as the Gapsan faction because its members had previously served on the Gapsan Operations Committee, an underground organization

that had fought for Korea's liberation from Japanese colonization. See Son Gwang-ju, *Kim Jong-il Report* (Seoul: Bada, 2003), 61–62.

41. See Yoon et al., *Bukkan jungchibum*, 82.

42. Oh, "Bukhan inkwon chimhae," 75.

43. Except for Kim Il-sung, Kim Jong-il was the only member who held three leadership positions at the same time (Gause, *Coercion, Control, Surveillance, and Punishment*, 121).

44. Heo Man-Ho, "Kukje ingwon bub ul kijun uro barabon bukhan ui jungchibum suyongso" (North Korean Political Prison Camps: A View Based on International Norms of Human Rights), *Sahoe gwahak damron gua jungchaek* (Social Science Discourse and Policy) 4, no. 1: 108.

45. For the compilation of records on resistance in North Korea, see Joshua Stanton, "Can They Do It? A Brief History of Resistance to the North Korean Regime," http://freekorea.us/2007/03/06/can-they-do-it-a-brief-history-of-resistance-to-the-north-korean-regime/.

46. Gause, *Coercion, Control, Surveillance, and Punishment*, 127.

47. Oh, "Bukhan inkwon chimhae," 74

48. Ahn Myung-chol, a former prison camp guard in North Korea, describes the merging, closing, and relocating of the camps as a measure to hide their existence from the international community (*Bukkan jeongchibum*, 54–55).

49. Evidence confirms the maintenance of camps 14, 15, 22, 23, and 25 under the administration of the SSD (Oh, "Soryeon, Bukhan, Jungguk," 345).

50. In addition to the exploitation of physical labor, the Soviet leadership and Gulag administration repeatedly employed convicted technical specialists and forced intellectual labor. See Asif Siddiqi's chapter in this volume, as well as Oleg V. Khlevniuk, *The History of the Gulag: From Collectivization to the Great Terror*, trans. Vadim A. Staklo (New Haven: Yale University Press, 2004), 34; and Anne Applebaum, *Gulag: A History* (New York: Anchor, 2004), 73.

51. The Soviet rear faced two interconnected campaigns during the war: the demand for increased labor output with less material input, intensified political exhortations to heroic labor (Applebaum, *Gulag*, 109).

52. Khlevniuk, *History of the Gulag*, 344.

53. Applebaum, *Gulag*, 72.

54. Khlevniuk, *History of the Gulag*, 334–36.

55. Dobson, *Khrushchev's Cold Summer*, 7. For more detailed accounts of the Gulag's economic costs in its final years, see Galina Mikhailovna Ivanova, *Labor Camp Socialism: The Gulag in the Soviet Totalitarian System*, trans. Carol Flath (Armonk, NY: M. E. Sharpe, 1997), 118–19, 124–26; and Alan Barenberg, *Gulag Town, Company Town: Forced Labor and Its Legacy in Vorkuta* (New Haven: Yale University Press, 2014), 122–30.

56. Khlevniuk, *History of the Gulag*, 185.

57. Khlevniuk, *History of the Gulag*, 330.

58. On the manner in which an "intentionalist-functionalist" debate was replicated in the Soviet field, see Michael David-Fox, "On the Primacy of Ideology: Soviet Revisionists and Holocaust Deniers (In Response to Martin Malia)," *Kritika: Explorations in Russian and Eurasian History* 5, no. 1 (2004): 81–106.

59. For the list of commodities produced by North Korean gulags, see Yoon et al., *Bukkan jungchibum*, 334–37.

60. Yoon et al., *Bukkan jungchibum*, 334–37. This book also mentions the specific economic activities of each prison camp in the list.

61. Yoon et al., *Bukkan jungchibum*, 333.

62. Oh, "Soryeon, Bukhan, Jungguk," 345.

63. North Korean defectors said that those who were mobilized for secret projects never returned, implying that they were executed to maintain the secrecy of such projects (Yoon et al., *Bukkan jungchibum*, 430–31).

64. See Kim Sung-bo et al., *Sajin gwa gurim uro bonun bukkan hyundaesa* (North Korea's Modern History in Picture and Painting) (Seoul: Unjin Jishik House, 2009), 145.

65. For the study of how Confucian ideas are reflected in the political discourse to legitimize the Kim family's dictatorship, see Jin-Woong Kang, "Political Uses of Confucianism in North Korea," *Journal of Korean Studies* 16, no. 1 (2011): 63–87.

66. The preface to the North Korean constitution adopted in 1998 lavishes praise on Kim Il-sung for transforming the whole of North Korean society into a single united family. North Korean propaganda and media refer to Kim Il-sung as "fatherly great leader" and the party as "motherly party."

67. Jiyoung Song, *Human Rights Discourse in North Korea: Post-Colonial, Marxist, and Confucian Perspectives* (New York: Routledge, 2011), 176.

68. Jeffrey Brooks, *Thank You, Comrade Stalin! Soviet Public Culture from Revolution to Cold War* (Princeton, NJ: Princeton University Press, 2000), xv.

69. Sheila Fitzpatrick, *Everyday Stalinism: Ordinary Life in Extraordinary Times. Soviet Russia in the 1930s* (New York: Oxford University Press, 1999), 130.

70. See "The Gulag behind the Goose-Steps," *The Economist* (April 2012), http://www.economist.com/node/21553090; and Danielle Kim, "Three Generations of Punishment: The Atrocities Being Committed in North Korea," *Point of View*, http://www.bbnpov.com/?p=904.

71. Ken Gause, *North Korean House of Cards: Leadership Dynamics under Kim Jong-un* (Washington, DC: Committee for Human Rights in North Korea, 2015), 3; Adam Cathcart, "The Fall of Jang Song-Taek," *The National Interest*, http://nationalinterest.org/commentary/the-fall-jang-song-taek-9539.

72. On North Korea's racism as the basis of North Korea's political system, see Bri-

an Myers, *The Cleanest Race: How North Koreans See Themselves and Why It Matters* (Brooklyn, NY: Melville House, 2011).

73. For the testimonies of the hardship and ordeal of North Korean defectors in China, see Mike Kim, *Escaping North Korea: Defiance and Hope in the World's Most Repressive Country* (Lanham, MD: Rowman and Littlefield, 2010), 61–81.

74. See Roberta Cohen, "China's Forced Repatriation of North Korean Refugees Incurs United Nations Censure," *International Journal of Korean Studies* 18, no. 1 (2014), http://www.brookings.edu/research/opinions/2014/07/north-korea-human-rights-un -cohen; and "UN North Korea Report Main Findings," *BBC News*, http://www.bbc .com/news/world-asia-26223180. For the testimonies of North Korean defectors, see Hawk, *Hidden Gulag VI*.

75. In a similar context, the banishment of disabled people to the camps in North Korea can be considered another major difference from the Soviet system. In the Gulag, disabled people were not imprisoned merely for being disabled. The US Department of State's *Human Rights Report for North Korea* for 2013 mentions people with physical and mental disabilities being sent from Pyongyang to internal exile, quarantined within camps, and forcibly sterilized.

76. Balázs Szalontai, *Kim Il Sung in the Khrushchev Era: Soviet-DPRK Relations and the Roots of North Korean Despotism, 1953–1964* (Stanford, CA: Stanford University Press, 2006), 16.

77. Szalontai, *Kim Il Sung in the Khrushchev Era*, 217. For a detailed account of the Soviet Union's reinvention of class structure in the 1920s and 1930s, see Sheila Fitzpatrick, "Ascribing Class: The Construction of Social Identity in Soviet Russia," *Journal of Modern History* 65, no. 4 (1993): 745–70.

78. For the testimony of a former guard, see Ahn, *Bukkan jeongchibum*.

79. The Soviet Union criticized the cult of personality in North Korea in the Khrushchev era, which Pyongyang perceived as an attempt to intervene in its domestic politics. The Soviet-North Korea relationship recovered in the mid-1960s, which worsened the Sino-North Korean relationship during the Cultural Revolution, when China criticized Pyongyang for its "revisionist" tendency to move closer to the Soviet Union. See Lee Jong-seok, *Hyundae bukkan ui yihae* (An Understanding of Modern North Korea) (Seoul: Yeoksa Bipyeongsa, 2001), 154.

80. Song, *Human Rights Discourse in North Korea*, 25.

81. Song, *Human Rights Discourse in North Korea*, 143.

82. Hannah Arendt, *The Origins of Totalitarianism* (New York: Harcourt, Brace, and World, 1968), 438.

83. Skocpol, "Doubly Engaged Social Science," 414.

84. On the "cultural turn" in penology and its relevance to Russia's history of punishment, see Judith Pallot's chapter in this volume.

CHAPTER 14. THE GULAG AS THE CRUCIBLE OF RUSSIA'S TWENTY-FIRST-CENTURY SYSTEM OF PUNISHMENT

1. Liudmila Ivanovna Granovskaia, "From *Aelita's Notes*," in *Remembering the Darkness: Women in Soviet Prisons*, ed. and trans. Veronica Shapalov (Lanham, MD: Rowman and Littlefield, 2001), 246–47.

2. The interview was conducted as part of a UK Economic and Social Research Council project. This name and all others in the text have been changed.

3. Judith Pallot, "Russia's Penal Peripheries: Space, Place, and Penalty in Soviet and Post-Soviet Russia," *Transactions of the Institute of British Geographers* 30, no. 1 (2005): 98–112; Dominique Moran, Pallot, and Laura Piacentini, "The Geography of Crime and Punishment in the Russian Federation," *Eurasian Geography and Economics* 52, no. 1 (2011): 79–104.

4. See, respectively, Michael Jakobson, *Origins of the Gulag: The Soviet Prison Camp System, 1917–1934* (Lexington: University of Kentucky Press, 1993); Peter H. Solomon, "Soviet Penal Policy, 1917–1934: A Reinterpretation," *Slavic Review* 39, no. 2 (1980): 195–217; Jeffrey S. Hardy, "'The Camp Is Not a Resort': The Campaign against Privileges in the Soviet Gulag, 1957–61," *Kritika* 13, no. 1 (2012): 89–122; and Roy D. King, "Russian Prisons after Perestroika: End of the Gulag?" *British Journal of Criminology* 34 (1994): 62–82.

5. See Lev Ponomarev, "Revival of the Gulag: Putin's Penitentiary System," http://www.bu.edu/iscip/vol18/ponomarov.html; and Bret Stephens, "Putin's Torture Colonies," *Wall Street Journal*, http://online.wsj.com/article/SB120277726156660765.html. Among historians of the Gulag, the relationship between the Gulag and Russia's failed democracy is discussed in Oleg V. Khlevniuk, *The History of the Gulag: From Collectivization to the Great Terror* (New Haven: Yale University Press, 2004).

6. Jakobson, *Origins of the Gulag*.

7. Michel Foucault, *Discipline and Punish: The Birth of the Prison*, trans. Alan Sheridan (London: Allen Lane, 1977).

8. Jan Plamper, "Foucault's Gulag," *Kritika: Explorations in Russian and Eurasian Studies* 3, no. 2 (2002): 255–80.

9. Andrew A. Gentes, *Exile to Siberia, 1590–1822* (Basingstoke: Palgrave Macmillan, 2008); Gentes, *Exile, Murder, and Madness in Siberia, 1823–61* (Basingstoke: Palgrave Macmillan, 2010).

10. Paul M. Hagenloh, "'Socially Harmful Elements' and the Great Terror," in *Stalinism: New Directions*, ed. Sheila Fitzpatrick (London: Routledge, 2000), 286–305; Hagenloh, *Stalin's Police: Public Order and Mass Repression in the USSR, 1929–1941* (Baltimore: Johns Hopkins University Press, 2009); David R. Shearer, *Policing Stalin's Socialism: Repression and Social Order, 1924–1993* (New Haven: Yale University Press, 2009).

11. Maria Los, "The Technologies of Total Domination," *Surveillance and Society* 2, no. 1 (2004): 15–34; Steven Pfaff, writing on the German Democratic Republic (GDR), shows the limits of surveillance's disciplinary powers ("The Limits of Coercive Surveillance: Social and Penal Control in the GDR," *Punishment and Society* 3, no. 3 [2001]: 381–407). Oleg Kharkhordin, *The Collective and the Individual in Russia: A Study of Practices* (Berkeley: University of California Press, 1999) makes a similar argument to Los in relation to the 1950s dormitory. Svetlana Boym, "The Banality of Evil, Mimicry, and the Soviet Subject: Varlam Shalamov and Hannah Arendt," *Slavic Review* 67, no. 2 (2008): 342–63, uses Foucault, Carl Schmitt, and Giorgio Agamben to examine the blurring of the distinction between the enlightenment subject and Stalinism.

12. Los, "Technologies of Total Domination," 35.

13. Georg Rusche and Otto Kirchheimer, *Punishment and Social Structure*, with introduction by Daria Melossi (New Brunswick, NJ: Transaction Publishers, 2009 [1939]).

14. See, e.g., Valery Lazerev, "Conclusions," in *The Economics of Forced Labor*, ed. Paul R. Gregory and Lazerev (Stanford, CA: Hoover Institution Press, 2003), 190.

15. John Pratt and Anna Eriksson, *Contrasts in Punishment: An Explanation of Anglophone Excess and Nordic Exceptionalism* (London: Routledge, 2013).

16. David Garland, *The Culture of Control: Crime and Social Order in Contemporary Society* (Oxford: Clarendon, 2001); John Pratt et al., eds., *The New Punitiveness: Trends, Theories, Perspectives* (Cullompton: Willan, 2005). The "new punitiveness" has been noted even in countries that traditionally have been penologically liberal, including Canada (Dawn Moore and Kelly Hannah-Moffat, "The Liberal Veil: Revisiting Canadian Penality," in *The New Punitiveness*, 85–100) and the Nordic countries (Pratt and Erikson, *Contrasts in Punishment*, 209; Yvonne Jewkes and Jamie Bennett, *Dictionary of Prisons and Punishment* [Cullompton: Willan, 2007], 202).

17. The United States, with an imprisonment rate of 716 per 100,000, tops the list, followed by several small island states, Rwanda, and Russia. More than 50 percent of countries have an imprisonment rate of under 150 per 100,000. For the complete list, see Roy Walmsley, *World Prison Population List*, 10th ed. (Colchester: International Centre for Prison Studies, 2013, http://www.apcca.org/uploads/10th_Edition_2013 .pdf).

18. Garland, *Culture of Control*; David Garland, *Punishment and Modern Society: A Study in Social History* (Chicago: University of Chicago Press, 1990).

19. Judith Pallot, Laura Piacentini, and Dominique Moran, "Patriotic Discourses in Russia's Penal Peripheries: Remembering the Mordovan Gulag," *Europe-Asia Studies* 62, no. 1 (2010): 1–33.

20. Philip Smith, *Punishment and Culture* (Chicago: University of Chicago Press,

2008). For Garland's critique, see David Garland, "A Culturalist Theory of Punishment?" *Punishment and Society* 11, no. 2 (2009): 259–68.

21. Sharyl M. Corrado, "The 'End of the Earth': Sakhalin Island in the Russian Imperial Imagination, 1849–1906" (PhD diss., University of Illinois, 2010).

22. Sarah Davies, *Popular Opinion in Stalin's Russia: Terror, Propaganda, and Dissent, 1934–1941* (Cambridge: Cambridge University Press).

23. Miriam Dobson, *Cold Summer: Gulag Returnees, Crime, and the Fate of Reform after Stalin* (Ithaca, NY: Cornell University Press, 2009), 165.

24. Garland, "Culturalist Theory of Punishment."

25. Works I find particularly useful include Nanci Adler, "Life in the 'Big Zone': The Fate of Returnees in the Aftermath of Stalinist Repression," *Europe-Asia Studies* 51, no. 1 (1999): 5–19; Golfo Alexopoulos, "Amnesty 1945: The Revolving Door of Stalin's Gulag," *Slavic Review* 64, no. 2 (2005): 274–306; Steven A. Barnes, *Death and Redemption: The Gulag and the Shaping of Soviet Society* (Princeton, NJ: Princeton University Press, 2011); Nick Baron, *Soviet Karelia: Policies, Planning, and Terror in Stalin's Russia, 1920–1939* (Abingdon: Routledge, 2007); Wilson T. Bell, "Was the Gulag an Archipelago? De-Convoyed Prisoners and Porous Borders in the Camps of Western Siberia," *Russian Review* 72, no. 1 (2013): 116–41; and Cynthia A. Ruder, *Making History for Stalin: The Story of the Belomor Canal* (Gainesville: University Press of Florida, 1998).

26. Gresham M. Sykes, *Society of Captives: A Study of a Maximum Security Prison* (Princeton, NJ: Princeton University Press, 1958).

27. James Q. Whitman, *Harsh Justice: Criminal Punishment and the Widening Divide between America and Europe* (Oxford: Oxford University Press, 2003).

28. Jakobson, *Origins of the Gulag.*

29. Bruce F. Adams, *Politics of Punishment: Prison Reform in Russia, 1863–1917* (DeKalb: Northern Illinois University Press, 1996); Andrew W. Gentes, "Katorga: Penal Labor and Tsarist Siberia," in *The Siberian Saga: A History of the Russian Wild East*, ed. Eva-Maria Stolberg (Frankfurt am Main: Peter Lang, 2005), 73–85; Alan Wood, "Crime and Punishment in the House of the Dead," in *Civil Rights in Imperial Russia*, ed. Olga Crisp and Linda Edmondson (Oxford: Clarendon, 1989), 215–33.

30. Whitman, *Harsh Justice*, 13–15.

31. The first conducted interviews with 115 prisoners, 25 ex-prisoners, and about 12 personnel in correctional colonies in European Russia. The results are published in Pallot and Piacentini, *Geography, Gender, and Punishment.* The second has interviewed twenty-five wives, mothers, and daughters of prisoners currently serving sentences in Russian colonies.

32. The section title comes from Mark Finnaine, *Punishment in Australian Society* (Oxford: Oxford University Press, 1997), 13.

33. Michel Foucault, *History of Madness*, ed. Jean Khalfa, trans. Jonathan Murphy (London: Routledge, 2006), 110.

34. Stephen Castles and Alistair Davidson, *Citizenship and Migration: Globalization and the Politics of Belonging* (London: Routledge, 2000).

35. Adams, *Politics of Punishment*, 73; Stephen P. Frank, *Crime, Cultural Conflict, and Justice in Rural Russia, 1856–1914* (Berkeley: University of California Press, 1999), 237.

36. Gentes, *Exile to Siberia*, 10–13. Gentes also refers to *katorga* as a form of exile. He conceptualizes these overlaps as evidence of exile and imprisonment's "coevality."

37. Plamper, "Foucault's Gulag," 265–66.

38. Jakobson, *Origins of the Gulag*, 39–40; Dmitri Volkogonov, *Lenin: A New Biography*, trans. Harold Shukman (New York: Free Press, 1997), 197.

39. Hardy, "'Camp Is Not a Resort,'" 103.

40. For a cartographic representation of the Gulag's expansion in space and time, see my web resource, http://www.Gulagmaps.org.

41. Bell, "Was the Gulag an Archipelago?"; Oxana Klimkova, "Special Settlements in Soviet Russia in the 1930s–50s," *Kritika: Explorations in Russian and Eurasian History* 8, no. 1 (2007): 105–39; Lynne Viola, *The Unknown Gulag: The Lost World of Stalin's Special Settlements* (New York: Oxford University Press, 2007).

42. Barnes, *Death and Redemption;* Kate Brown, "Out of Solitary Confinement: The History of the Gulag," *Kritika: Explorations in Russian and Eurasian History* 8, no. 1 (2007): 67–103.

43. Laura Piacentini and Judith Pallot, "'In Exile Imprisonment' in Russia," *British Journal of Criminology* 54, no. 1 (2014): 20–37.

44. Foucault, *Discipline and Punish*, 264.

45. Pallot and Piacentini, *Gender, Geography, and Punishment*, chap. 6; Dominique Moran, Laura Piacentini, and Judith Pallot, "Liminal Transcarceral Space: Prison Transportation for Women in the Russian Federation," in *Carceral Spaces: Mobility and Agency in Imprisonment and Migrant Detention*, ed. Moran, Nick Gill, and Deirdre Conlan (Farnham: Ashgate, 2014), 109–26; Moran, Piacentini, and Pallot, "Disciplined Mobility and Carceral Geography: Prisoner Transport in Russia," *Transactions of the Institute of British Geographers* 37, no. 3 (2012): 446–60.

46. Anne Applebaum, *Gulag: A History of the Soviet Camps* (London: Allen Lane, 2003), 6, 169–70.

47. Ibid., 172.

48. Alexander Solzhenitsyn, *The Gulag Archipelago, 1918–1956: An Experiment in Literary Investigation*, trans. Thomas P. Whitney (Glasgow: Collins/Fontana, 1974), 1, pt. 2:494–99. See also Lynne Viola, "The Question of the Perpetrator in Soviet History," *Slavic Review* 72, no. 1 (2013): 1–23.

49. Finnaine, *Punishment in Australian Society*, 13.

50. Wood, "Crime and Punishment," 200.

51. Solzhenitsyn, *Gulag Archipelago* (1978), 3, pt. 6:340.

52. Elena Katz and Judith Pallot, "Prisoners' Wives in Post-Soviet Russia: 'For My Husband I Am Pining!'" *Europe-Asia Studies* 62, no. 2 (2014): 204–24.

53. "Rebenok ot ZK," http://forumtyurem.net/lofiversion/index.php/t86-100.html.

54. Zoia Eroshek, "Novye dekabristki," *Novaia gazeta*, no. 44 (25 April 2011), http://www.novayagazeta.ru/data/2011/044/00.html?print=201103070927.

55. Aleksei Tikhonov, "The End of the Gulag," in *Economics of Forced Labor*, 67–73.

56. Kharkhordin, *Individual and the Collective in Russia*, 300–305.

57. Kseniia Dmitrievna Medvedskaia, "Life Is Everywhere," in *Remembering the Darkness*, 227.

58. Anatoly T. Marchenko, *My Testimony*, trans. Michael Scammell (Harmondsworth: Penguin, 1971).

59. V. M. Anisimkov, *Rossiia v zerkale ugolovnykh traditsii tiur´my* (St. Petersburg: Iuridicheskii tsentr press, 2003); Iu. M. Antonian and E. N. Kolyshnitsyna, *Motivatsiia povedeniia osuzhdennykh* (Moscow: Iuniti—Zakon i pravo, 2009); Anton N. Oleinik, *Organized Crime, Prison, and Post-Soviet Societies* (Aldershot: Ashgate, 2003).

60. Joera Mulders, "Legal Reforms: Medvedev's Achievements," RussiaWatchers: Getting Russia Right blog (25 April 2011), http://russiawatchers.ru/daily/legal-reforms.

61. Adams, *Politics of Punishment*, 110.

62. "Kontseptsiia razvitiia ugolovno-ispolnitel´noi sistemy Rossiiskoi Federatsii do 2020, utverzhdena rasporiazheniem Pravitel´stva Rossiiskoi Federatsii ot 14-ogo oktiabria 2010 g. no. 1772-R," http://fsin.su/document/index.php?ELEMENT_ID=6663.

63. V. I. Seliverstov, "Kontseptsiia razvitiia ugolovno-ispolnitel´noi sistemy dolzhna byt´ izmenena," in *Ugolovno-ispolnitel´naia politika, zakondatel´stvo i pravo*, ed. Seliverstov and V. A. Utkin (Moscow: Iurisprudentsiia, 2014), 163.

64. "Rossiiskie tiur´my ukhodiat ot traditsii GULAGA," *Zakoniia* (17 December 2010), http://www.zakonia.ru/news/72/60468. Reimer was removed from his post by Putin on 26 June 2012 and replaced by Gennadii Kornienko, a Federal Security Service professional and Putin associate.

65. "Justice Minister: Russian Penitentiary System Reminiscent of GULAG," *Eurasian Law: Breaking News* (22 September 2011), http://eurasian-law-breaking-news.blogspot.co.uk/2011/09/justice-minister-russian-penitentiary.html.

66. "Kontseptsiia razvitiia ugolovno-ispolnitel´noi sistemy Rossiiskoi Federatsii."

67. Iubileinyi arkhiereiskii sobor Rossiiskoi pravoslavnoi tserkvi, "Osnovy sotsial´noi kontseptsii Russkoi pravoslavnoi tserkvi," 9: "Prestupnost´, nakazanie, ispravlenie," IX.3, https://mospat.ru/ru/documents/social-concepts/ix.

68. Iu. V. Golik, "Reforma posle Reformy," in *Ugolovno-ispolnitel´naia politika*, 78–93.

69. Andrei Babushkin, "Nakonets-to sostoialos´ pervoe zasedanie Komissii po korrektirovke reformy ugolovno-ispolnitel´noi," blog (23 January 2014), http://an -babushkin.livejournal.com/102871.html.

CHAPTER 15. THE GULAG: AN INCARNATION OF THE STATE THAT CREATED IT

1. Felix Schnell, "Der Gulag als Systemstelle sowjetischer Herrschaft," in *Welt der Lager: Zur "Erfolgsgeschichte" einer Institution*, ed. Bettina Greiner and Alan Kramer (Hamburg: Hamburger Edition, 2013), 134.

2. Norman Davies, "Preface," in *Gulag*, ed. Tomasz Kizny (Buffalo, NY: Firefly, 2004), 9.

3. Schnell, "Gulag," 135, 136.

4. David R. Shearer, "The Soviet Gulag—An Archipelago?," *Kritika: Explorations in Russian History* 16, no. 3 (2015): 722.

5. Kate Brown, "Out of Solitary Confinement: The History of the Gulag," *Kritika: Explorations in Russian and Eurasian History* 8, no. 1 (2007): 77–78.

6. Most research on different camp systems follows what might be called an en- cyclopedic approach. A well-known example is Joël Kotek and Pierre Rigoulet, *Das Jahrhundert der Lager: Gefangenschaft, Zwangsarbeit, Vernichtung* (Berlin: Propyläen, 2001). A more comparative view focusing on questions of the dynamic development of camps and the radicalization of the institution was, within German scholarship, first taken by Peter Reif-Spirek and Bodo Ritscher, eds., *Speziallager in der SBZ: Gedenkstätten mit "doppelter Vergangenheit"* (Berlin: Christoph Links, 1999). As of late, this line of research was strengthened by Greiner and Kramer, *Die Welt der La- ger*, and Christoph Jahr and Jens Thiel, eds., *Lager vor Auschwitz: Gewalt und Integra- tion im 20. Jahrhundert* (Berlin: Metropol, 2013).

7. See Alan Kramer, "Einleitung," in *Welt der Lager*, 17.

8. Joshua A. Sanborn, "Unsettling the Empire: Violent Migration and Social Di- saster duing World War I," *Journal of Modern History* 77, no. 2 (2005): 318.

CONTRIBUTORS

GOLFO ALEXOPOULOS is associate professor of Russian/Soviet history at the University of South Florida in Tampa and the author of *Stalin's Outcasts: Aliens, Citizens, and the Soviet State, 1926–1936* (2003). Her research on Stalin's forced labor camp system, under contract for publication, has been supported by the Hoover Institution and the National Endowment for the Humanities.

DANIEL BEER is senior lecturer in Modern European history at Royal Holloway College, University of London, and the author of *Renovating Russia: The Human Sciences and the Fate of Liberal Modernity, 1880–1930* (2008). His next book, *Prison Empire: Siberian Exile under the Tsars*, is due to appear in 2016.

WILSON T. BELL is assistant professor of history and politics at Thompson Rivers University. His work on the Gulag has appeared in *Canadian Slavonic Papers, Gulag Studies, The Russian Review*, and, most recently, *The Journal of the History of Sexuality*. His book manuscript, *Stalin's Gulag at War: Forced Labour, Mass Death, and Soviet Victory in World War II*, is currently under review.

DIETRICH BEYRAU is professor emeritus at the Institut für Osteuropäische Geschichte und Landeskunde, Universität Tübingen. His many publications include *Schlachtfeld der Diktatoren: Osteuropa im Schatten von Hitler und Stalin* (Battlefield of Dictators: Eastern Europe in the Shadow of Hitler and Stalin [2000]) and "Mortal Embrace: Germans and (Soviet) Russians in the First Half of the Twentieth Century," in *Fascination and Enmity: Russia and Germany as Entangled Histories, 1914–1945*, ed. Michael David-Fox, Peter Holquist, and Alexander M. Martin (2012).

SUNGMIN CHO, a PhD student in government at Georgetown University, is writing his dissertation on authoritarian regimes' counterstrategy to the promotion of Western democracy.

MICHAEL DAVID-FOX is professor in the School of Foreign Service and Department of History at Georgetown as well as academic supervisor at the International Centre for the History and Sociology of World War II and Its Consequences at the National Research University—Higher School of Economics in Moscow. His most recent book is *Crossing Borders: Modernity, Ideology, and Culture in Russia and the Soviet Union* (2015). He is currently working on a book project, "Smolensk under Nazi and Soviet Rule."

AIDAN FORTH, assistant professor of British history at Loyola University in Chicago, is currently completing *Barbed Wire Imperialism: Britain's Empire of Concentration Camps, 1876–1903*.

AGLAYA GLEBOVA is assistant professor in the Department of Art History and the Department of Film and Media Studies, as well as the PhD Program in Visual Studies, at the University of California, Irvine. She is currently at work on her first book, which examines Soviet propaganda photographs of the White Sea-Baltic Canal by the avant-garde photographer Aleksandr Rodchenko.

BETTINA GREINER works for the Hamburg Institute for Social Research and is coordinator of the Berlin Colloquia on Contemporary History and the Berlin Center for Cold War Studies. She is the author of *Suppressed Terror: History and Perception of Soviet Special Camps in Germany* (2014) and the editor, with Alan Kramer, of *Die Welt der Lager: Zur "Erfolgsgeschichte" einer Institution* (The World of the Camps: On the "Success Story" of an Institution [2013]). Her current research project concerns refugee camps and policies of political identity in postwar Germany.

DANIEL HEALEY, professor of modern Russian history at St. Antony's College, University of Oxford, is the author of several works on the history of sexuality, gender, and medicine in Russia and the Soviet Union. He is currently at work on a history of medicine in the Stalinist Gulag.

OLEG V. KHLEVNIUK is leading research fellow at the International Center for the History and Sociology of World War II and Its Consequences, National Research University Higher School of Economics (Russian Federation). He is the author of *The History of the GULAG: From Collectivization to the Great Terror* (2004); *Cold Peace: Stalin and the Soviet Ruling Circle, 1945–1953* (2004), with Yoram Gorlizki; *Master of the House: Stalin and His Inner Circle* (2008); and *Stalin: New Biography of a Dictator* (2015).

EMILIA KOUSTOVA is associate professor of Russian studies and fellow at GEO (Strasbourg University) and associate fellow at CERCEC (EHESS). She has published several articles, most recently "Sovetskii prazdnik 1920-kh godov v poiskakh mass i zrelishch" (Soviet Celebrations in the 1920s in Search of Masses and Spectacles), *Neprikosnovennyi zapas* 100, no. 2 (2015); and "Spetskontingent kak diaspora: Litovskie spetspereselentsy na peresechenii mnozhestvennykh soobshchestv" (The Special Contingent as a Diaspora: Lithuanian Special Settlers at the Intersection of Multiple Communities), *Novoe literaturnoe obozrenie* 127, no. 3 (2014). Her ongoing research projects are "Becoming Soviet: Surveillance, Integration, and Sovietization of the Victims of Stalinist Deportations" and "Soviet Military Journalists during World War II."

KLAUS MÜLHAHN is professor of the history and culture of China, deputy director of the Graduate School for East Asian Studies at the Freie Universität Berlin, and vice-president of the Freie Universität Berlin. His *Criminal Justice in China* (2009) won the John K. Fairbank Prize for East Asian History of the American Historical Association.

PROFESSOR JUDITH PALLOT is official student (fellow) of Christ Church College and senior research fellow in Russian and East European studies in the School of Interdisciplinary Area Studies, University of Oxford. Her most recent book (co-authored with Laura Piacentini) is *Gender, Geography, and Punishment: Women's Experiences of Carceral Russia* (2012); she is currently in the final stages of preparing a monograph examining prisoners' relatives that will be published in 2016.

DAVID R. SHEARER, professor of history at the University of Delaware, specializes in Soviet and Russian history. He is the author of, among other works, *Policing Stalin's Socialism: Social Order and Mass Repression in the Soviet Union, 1924–1953* (2009); and *Stalin and the Lubianka: A Documentary History of the Political Police and Security Organs in the Soviet Union, 1922–1953* (2015), with Vladimir Khaustov.

ASIF SIDDIQI, professor of history at Fordham University, is completing a book provisionally titled *Science, Expertise, and the Stalinist Gulag*. His many books on the history of Soviet science include *The Red Rockets' Glare: Spaceflight and the Soviet Imagination, 1857–1957* (2010) and *Into the Cosmos: Space Exploration and Soviet Culture* (2011), co-edited with James T. Anderson. In addition, he is beginning a project on secrecy in Soviet life.

NOTE: Page numbers in *italics* refer to figures.

absolute loyalty, 281, 282
Administration for Corrective Labor Camps and Colonies (UITLK), 62, 63
Afrikaners, 212, 214, 217
Agamben, Giorgio, 116, 301; concentration camps and, 14, 132, 133–34, 266; enlightenment/Stalinism and, 410n11; hypothesis of, 134; state of exception and, 132, 133, 384n35
agriculture, 117, 143, 255, 264; collectivization of, 7, 168
Ahn Myung-chul, memoir of, 270
Alexander I, 174, 176, 177, 196
Alexander II, 163, 176, 193–98
Alin, D. E., 124, 129–30, 360n48
Andaman Islands, 201, 206
Anglo-Boer War, 17, 201, 212, 215
Anglo-Indian War (1857), 201
apartheid, 2, 211, 228–30, 231–33, 237
Applebaum, Anne, 62, 67, 68, 279, 300, 325n5, 374n9; Gulag and, 280; mortality rates and, 346n76; prisoner releases and, 60
Arendt, Hannah, 212, 214, 216, 251, 291; totalitarianism and, 284–85
Arkhangel´sk, 34, 78, 82
artels, 188, 192, 304; loyalty to, 189, 190; name swapping at, 190–91
Article 58ers, 106–7, 120, 125, 241, 339n9, 359n23, 360n39, 360n53, 361n53
Auschwitz, 4, 215, 224, 227, 228, 233, 234, 242, 284, 314
Aussonderung, 229, 390n27
authoritarianism, 38, 41, 199, 204, 223, 252, 285, 292, 295, 416

Bakhtin, Mikhail, 293, 294
Baltic states, 142, 159; deportation from, 137, 139, 140

Banderites, 149, 159
Barenberg, Alan, 7, 11, 31, 120
Barnes, Steven, 120, 299; Gulag and, 49, 116, 123; Karlag and, 122
barracks, 33, 98, 208, 226, 233, 236, 248, 272, *305*, 308; control of, 246; courtyard of, *310;* labor camp, 293
Bartini, Robert L., 97, 355n72
Bashkir ASSR, 129, 362n70
Bauman, Zygmunt, 202, 360n51, 382n1, 382n4
Belbaltlag, 61, 239
Benkendorf, Count, 186
Bentham, Jeremy, 163, 297
Beria, Lavrentii P., 50, 76, 101, 102, 104, 354n58; cleansing by, 354n56; Gulag and, 47, 246; MVD and, 107; NKVD and, 97, 129; OTB and, 100; prison labor and, 80–81, 341n31; prison science system and, 97; sharashka system and, 100, 109; Stalin and, 99, 100, 103
Berlin, Isaiah: Counter-Enlightenment and, 6
Berman, Matvei Davydovich, 61, 73, 74
biopolitics, 11–12, 65, 67, 68; disability and, 84–86; food distribution and, 79–80; Gulag, 12, 68, 69–70
biopower, 65, 68, 69, 72, 84, 86, 340n20
Bodaibo, 152, 155, 156
Boer War, 9, 224, 318
Boers, 212, 213, 214, 387n67
Boichuk, Mykhailo, 168
Bolshevik revolution, 21, 274
Bolsheviks, 91, 92, 93, 108, 220, 226, 242, 315; liberation by, 240; socialism and, 238–39
Bolshevism, 14, 15
Bolshevo, 100, 101, 102, 354n51
Bombay, 210, 211
Bombay Presidency camps, 207, 384n29
Borodkin, Leonid, 120
Brezhnev, Leonid, 45, 87

British Government of India, 207
Brown, Kate, 3, 90, 128, 299, 315
Browning, Christopher, 251
Bukharin, Nikolai, 91
bureaucracy, 25, 369n47, 399n16; mass campaigns and, 256–57; penal, 290
Butyrka Prison, 93, 101, 102, 303

camp leaders, 213, 233, 237, 246, 300
camp personnel, 234, 235–38, 246–49; prisoners and, 237, 238
camp systems, 16, 134, 231, 414n6; Chinese, 252; dissolution of, 244; Nazi, 249; North Korean, 268–76, 277, 278, 281–84; origin of, 269, 273–76; privatization of, 275; purpose of, 252; Soviet, 132, 249, 252, 269–70, 276, 318, 288n2, 321n2, 388n2
Camp Xifeng, 20
Campaign to Suppress Counterrevolutionaries, 255, 256
camps: agricultural, 118, 127, 204; banditism, 246; black African, 217; Boer, 217; British, 133, 199, 201–14, 214–23; children's, 226; Chinese, 20; colonial, 213, 216; conditions in, 53, 210, 217, 223, 230–31, 232; contract, 129; criminal tribe, 205–8, 217, 220; death, 227, 237; detention, 199, 210, 248; development of, 5, 203, 212, 213, 225, 414n6; dormitory, 210; famine, 208–11, 214, 217, 218, 220; filtration, 240; forced labor, 230, 276; forestry, 54, 334n60; frameworks for, 223; future, 216; ghetto, 229; internment, 222, 224, 230; invalid, 59, 76–79, 80, 83–84; island, 206–7; justice, 230; management of, 5; mass character of, 55; military, 212; modern, 223; motivation for, 212; Nazi, 133, 215, 216, 235; network of, 13; North Korean, 21, 285, 403n10, 404n17; pioneer, 226; plague, 208–11, 209, 214, 218, 220; POW, 224, 230, 231, 232, 241, 245, 248, 319; recovery, 83; reeducation, 224; rehabilitation, 223; satellite, 232; segregation, 202, 208; South African, 214, 387n63; Soviet, 201, 214–23, 241, 405n31; special, 135, 240, 274; Stalinist, 42, 43,

45, 314; standardization of, 212; summer, 248; training, 248; underlife in, 245–46; venereal disease, 348n105; vigilance inside/outside, 166, 168; wartime, 214; work, 204, 230; youth, 226, 248. *See also* extermination camps; labor camps; prison camps; sharashki
Cape Town, 210, 211
capitalism, 67, 209, 220, 273
category 1 prisoners, 336n74, 336n81, 349n112; labor for, 48, 49, 50, 55–56
category 2 prisoners, 336n74, 336n75, 336n81, 349n112; labor for, 48, 49, 50, 54, 56, 57, 58
category 3 prisoners, 336n74, 336n75, 349n112; labor for, 48, 49, 50, 54, 56
category 4 prisoners, 50
Catherine the Great, 17, 174
CCP. *See* Chinese Communist Party
Central Committee, 95, 276, 341n33, 352n37; criticism by, 277
Central Design Bureau-29 (TsKB-29), 102; home of, *103*
Central Design Bureau-39 (TsKB-39), *96, 96,* 351n24
Central Political Committee (Korean Worker's Party), 277
Cheka, 9, 32, 38, 1080, 242, 272
Chekhov, Anton, 197–98, 294
Cheremkhovo, 143, 147
Chickering, Roger, 115
Chinese Communist Party (CCP), 251, 266, 402n48; state/law and, 253; violence/terror by, 257
Chinese leadership, Gulag and, 259–60
citizenship rights, 134, 202
civilizing missions, 207, 208
class enemies, 239, 242, 257
class struggle, 14, 255, 257, 267
classification system, 71, 242, 277
closed cities, 90, 111, 356n93
coercion, 7, 17, 20, 90,. 107, 110, 128, 138, 141, 200, 202, 207, 225, 226, 227, 239, 265, 267; mass, 108; societal, 240
Cold War, 110, 269, 278, 387n79
collaboration, 140, 240, 275

collective farmers, 147, 148, 240
collective farms, 143, 159, 168, 368n21, 370–71n64
collective work, 136, 148, 149, 165
collectivism, 21, 140, 297, 311, 312; as harsh punishment, 304–7; penal, 308–9; transportation and, 304
collectivization, 2, 7, 149, 168, 250, 257, 315; campaigns, 243; consequences of, 8; Stalin-era, 274
Colonial Office, 214
colonies, 13, 205, 214; locally administered, 358n12; population concentration and, 318; strict-regime, 298
colonization, 17, 34, 203, 212, 216, 288, 311, 320; demands of, 174; internal, 328n31; Japanese, 406n40; penal, 197, 378n50; racial, 15
communal living, 305, 306
communication, 252; camp, 114; suspension of, 302; telegraphic, 336n82
communism, 4, 7, 19, 20, 265, 284, 289
concentration camps, 6, 9, 14, 20, 46, 133–34, 210, 227, 231–33, 242, 244, 245, 275, 296, 317; Boer, 217; British, 17, 18, 199, 212, 214, 215, 221, 386n58; comparative history of, 4; expansion of, 228; figures of, 237; Gulag and, 14, 116, 314; military function of, 213–14; model/blueprint, 219; Nazi, 208, 215, 216, 228, 239, 241, 244, 268, 283, 318, 329n43, 384n35, 386n55, 388n2; North Korean, 268, 272, 279; prisoners at, 228, 230; productivizing, 236; satellite camps for, 229; South African, 201, 212–24; term, 200; totalitarianism and, 284–85; war and, 132, 214; writing about, 266
Conception for the Development of the Penal System to 2020: 310–11, 312
Confucianism, 270, 281, 282, 284, 285
construction projects, 45, 46, 285
convicts, 176; deportation of, 175, 378n50; free, 263; health of, 195; transportation of, 298. *See also* prisoners
Cossacks, 9, 178, 179, 180, 185
counterrevolutionaries, 134, 241, 264, 283; campaigns against, 254, 257, 258, 262–63;

collaboration and, 275; definition of, 320; democratic leadership and, 253–54; killing, 254, 256, 400n25; offenses by, 26, 131; sentences for, 55
crimes, 133, 215, 263, 283, 293, 299; fight against, 328n36; ideological, 278; mass, 252, 266; nonpolitical, 27; petty, 34, 45; political, 55, 70, 206, 282; social roots of, 267; statutory, 202; war, 395n90
criminal classes, 203, 204, 209
Criminal Code, 59, 61, 63, 304; criminal correction code, 298–99
criminal groups, 43, 208, 306
criminal justice system, 28, 116, 242, 266, 294, 295, 296; changes in, 309–10; discussing, 299
Criminal Tribes Act (1871), 207
criminals, 201, 220, 233, 234, 245, 405n31; battling, 246; becoming, 208; career, 61, 306, 307; common, 296; conviction of, 206; corruption chains and, 248; habitual, 207; labor-shirking, 247; political, 282, 285
cult of personality, 277, 282, 408n79
Cultural-Educational/Enlightenment Department. *See* Siblag
Cultural Revolution, 95, 108, 265, 277, 320, 408n79
culture, 154, 209, 293, 316, 387n79; bourgeois, 91; camp, 123; Confucian, 284, 285; criminal, 311; ideology and, 284; institutional, 110; metropolitan, 222; national, 292; North Korean, 269, 282; penal, 293, 310, 313; political, 265, 318; power and, 294; punishment, 291; Western, 200

Dachau, 242, 314
dangerous classes, 203, 207, 211, 214
de-Stalinization, 10, 37, 69, 329n46
death penalty, 254, 255
death rates, 124, 234, 243; eliminating, 59–63; prisoner, 275, 284; releases and, 60. *See also* mortality rates
Decembrists, 184, 291, 302–3
defectors, North Korean, 273, 280, 281, 282, 403n3, 408n73
degradation rituals, 297, 299–300

dehumanization, 45, 283
dekabristki, 302, 303, 304
dekulakization, 140, 274
democracy, 202, 292, 305; prisoner, 308
democratic dictatorship, 262, 263; counter-
    revolutionaries and, 253–54
Department of Corrective Labor Colonies
    (OITK), 63, 118
depersonalization, 232, 244
deportation, 43, 146, 148, 157, 160, 174,
    177, 185, 187, 249, 263, 370n57, 378n50;
    children, 366n4; chronological proximity
    of, 139; death and, 196; ethnic, 291; expe-
    rience of, 140–42, 175, 197; forced labor
    and, 258; kulak, 291, 404n26; large-scale,
    137, 144; mass, 138, 265, 266; modern-
    ization of, 193–98; punishment and, 139,
    174; subversion of, 191; victims of, 136,
    138
deportation convoys, 16, 17, 174–76, 178, 195,
    197, 286, 287, 300; dangers of, 183, 194;
    shared sovereignty in, 188–91; special
    settlers and, 158; women/children in,
    191–93. See also marching convoys
deportees, 136, 140, 147, 150, 156, 159; dis-
    crimination against, 160, 161; integration
    of, 142; journey of, 148; living conditions
    for, 146; MGB and, 148; research on, 138;
    return of, 159–60, 161; testimony of, 141
despotism, 41, 227, 239
Destructive Labor Camps (istrebitel' no-tru-
    dovye lageria), 10, 42, 43, 64, 121, 218,
    359n28361n53. See also Solzhenitsyn,
    Alexander
disabled, 72, 342n35; biopolitics of, 84–86;
    camps for, 83–84; classification of, 71;
    separation of, 76–77, 85–86
discipline, 67, 175, 203, 227, 238, 307
Discipline and Punish: The Birth of the Prison
    (Foucault), 67, 227, 290
discrimination, 36, 40, 156, 159, 160, 161,
    231, 241; facing, 29, 373n109; indirect,
    158; political, 28
Dmitlag, 61, 74, 77
dokhodiagi, 60, 63, 75, 244. See also Goners
dormitories, 102, 144, 210, 288, 305, 306;
    communal, 304, 308, 312

Doroshevich, Vlas, 163; illustration from, 164
Dostoevskii, Fedor, 190
Durkheim, Émile, 289, 293, 311
Dzerzhinskii, Feliks, 166, 168

economic activities, 109, 126, 266, 312
economic issues, 108, 115, 126, 146, 262, 269,
    276
economic production, 121, 122, 316; Gulag,
    120, 125, 127, 134, 247; punishment and,
    248
economics, 152, 209, 281
education, 136, 146, 226, 295; cultural, 260;
    hygienic, 260; ideological, 260; political,
    156, 260; social life and, 157; socialization
    and, 156
emancipation, 71, 137, 138, 139
enemies of the people, 253, 254, 257, 275
engineers, 88; imprisonment of, 108, 110
Enisei River, 176, 180, 181, 186
Enlightenment, 200, 223, 382n1
epidemics, 60, 86, 221, 237
Ertz, Simon, 120, 358n18
Escape from Camp 14 (Shin), 271
ethnic groups, 133, 155–56, 246, 275
Etkind, Alexander, 6, 45
exception, state of, 132, 133, 220, 222, 266,
    384n35
exceptionalism, 4, 292
exclusion, 226; racial, 220; regulation by, 291;
    social, 211, 220
executions, 236, 400n25, 400n26; Chinese,
    258; civil, 174; mass, 40, 43, 280, 400n24;
    photographing, 162; public, 236, 257, 292
exile, 17, 36, 137, 174–75, 187, 196, 301–4;
    administration, 185–88; impact of,
    297–98; imperial, 163–64; imprisonment
    and, 299; internal, 37; journey into, 148;
    kulak, 156; prerevolutionary, 300; return
    from, 139; sentence to, 190; Siberian, 198;
    symbolic penal response of, 299
exile system, 16, 21, 183, 186; cost cutting
    with, 195; opposition to, 197
exiles, 134, 174, 180, 180–81, 188; camp
    industries and, 248; death of, 177, 196;
    deportation of, 176, 177; feeding/clothing
    of, 177; illustration of, 182; penal labor

and, 183; Polish, 381n118; Siberian, 173, 377n21; transportation of, 177, 195; travails of, 183

exploitation, 12, 52–53, 55; economic, 273; labor, 56, 235, 277; meting out, 249; physical, 44, 48–52; prisoner, 45, 48–52, 58

extermination camps, 5, 19, 199, 238, 248, 315; labor at, 228; Nazi, 200, 212, 221, 224, 285, 384n35; Soviet camps and, 4

Ezhov, Nikolai, 98, 99, 354n56

famine, 59, 72, 200, 208, 209, 212, 215, 249; administration, 210; emergency legislation of, 213

famine camps, 214, 220; British Indian, 208–11, 217, 218

Far North, 16, 304, 370n57

Federal Prison Service, 39, 300

Filtzer, Donald, 52, 79, 82, 86

First Circle, The (Solzhenitsyn), 87–88, 104, 355n74

First Five-Year Plan, 7, 92, 100, 239, 262

Fleishmaker, Director, 74, 77

food, 117, 118, 124, 127, 150, 248; consumption/rituals, 244; deprivation of, 245; distribution of, 11, 79–80, 217, 244; producing, 115

forced labor, 3, 31, 35, 59, 65, 127, 131, 138, 160–61, 164, 206, 224, 225, 227, 229, 230, 245, 248, 314; civilian population and, 319; deportation and, 258; economics of, 144; free labor and, 126, 128, 135, 362n73, 363n89; Gulag and, 7, 33, 97; inefficiencies of, 13; mobilization of, 9, 116; profitability of, 84; Soviet society and, 238–41; Stalinist, 69; using, 8, 218, 226, 266, 280; war and, 13, 18, 115

forest brothers, 140, 149

forest settlements, 143, 144

Foucault, Michel, 28, 65, 68, 227, 293; biopolitics and, 67, 69, 340n20; on capitalism, 67; enlightenment/Stalinism and, 410n11; forced labor and, 127; Gulag and, 290; liberal governmentality and, 222; punishment and, 361n62; rejection of, 389n12; sovereign/ disciplinary power and, 84; theory of, 290, 291, 292

Fourth International Penitentiary Congress, 16, 163

Fourth Special Department (NKVD), 104, 106, 107, 355n72

free labor, 7; forced labor and, 126, 128, 135, 362n73, 363n89; Red Army and, 130

Gapsan Operations Committee, 277, 405–6n40

GARF. *See* State Archive of the Russian Federation

Garland, David, 292, 293, 294

genocide, 6, 19, 138, 215–16, 230, 285, 386n58

Gentes, Andrew, 174, 291, 378n35, 412n36

Gerlach, Christian, 7, 230, 266

Gestapo, 228, 272

Ginzburg, Eugenia/Evgeniia, 43, 67, 303, 331n8, 339n16

GKO. *See* State Committee on Defense

Goffman, Erving, 226, 233, 249; rejection of, 389n12; total institution and, 227

Goners, 10, 42, 45, 60, 63, 75, 232, 244, 315. See also *dokhodiagi*

Gorbachev, Mikhail Grigor´evich, 121, 357n4

Göring, Herman, 216

Gor´kii, Maksim, 11, 227, 243

Gornoshorlag, 116, 118

GPU, 1, 97, 162

Graham, Loren, 13

Granovskaia, Liudmila Ivanovna, 287, 289, 297, 313

Granovskaia, Sonia, 287, 288, 289, 297, 313

Great Break, 69, 91

Great Leap Forward, 281

Great Purge, 328n36

Great Reforms, 17, 174, 197

Great Siberian Highway, 175, 176, 178, 179, 184

Great Terror (1936–1938), 13, 14, 37, 40, 41, 75, 76, 78, 89, 91, 100, 103, 108, 241, 296, 298, 316; beneficiaries of, 38–39; execution of, 36, 37, 38, 274–75; industrialization and, 238; NKVD and, 99; prison camps and, 97

Grigorovich, Dmitrii P., 93, 94, *96*, 351n23

Grossman, Vasilii, 236

guards, 34, 96, 207, 283, 405n34; colony spaces and, 307; concentration camp, 235;

guards (*cont.*), female, 238; nonpolitical prisoners as, 32; security, 248; SS, 238
guerrillas, 213, 252
Gulag: censorship of, 36, 37; concentration camps and, 14, 116, 314; conditions in, 54–59, 215, 295, 296, 297, 314; crisis in, 59–60; cultural factors of, 10, 285; demise of, 41, 109, 113, 206, 276, 299, 405n37; destructive elements of, 42, 45, 162; divergence by, 276–79; economic function of, 31, 79, 105, 106, 120, 276, 280, 405n35; expansion of, 2, 19, 37, 54–55, 105, 216, 275, 277, 279, 298, 317, 412n40; exploitation at, 44–45, 55; foundation myths of, 310; functions of, 14, 115, 116, 123, 270, 280, 343n46; health records, 44; history of, 1, 3, 9–10, 25–26, 31, 90, 162, 165, 215, 272, 275, 280, 285, 409n5; inefficiency of, 110, 135; institution building in, 109; interpretation of, 39; as model, 33–36; nature of, 6–7, 9, 14; operations of, 72, 135; population of, 26, 30–31, 40, 134; resistance in, 275–76; secrecy at, 58–59; social ladder of, 26; statistics on, 165, 245; strata, 36–40; totalitarian model and, 238; traits of, 277; trajectory of, 266–67
Gulag administration, 406n50; archives, 65; disabled prisoners and, 72
Gulag Archipelago, The (Solzhenitsyn), 1, 37, 44, 66, 114, 200, 202, 206, 287, 372n89
Gulag commandants, 47, 73, 79
Gulag financial planners, 78, 80, 85
Gulag Handbook (Rossi), 42
Gulag studies, 2, 4, 25–26, 42–43, 119, 218, 272, 273, 299, 316, 317, 318; transnational agenda in, 9
Guomindang, 20, 253
GUPVI. *See* Main Administration for Prisoners of War and Internees
gypsies, 230, 234

Habitual Criminals Act (1869), 203, 207
Hadleigh Work Camp, 204, *205*
Harrison, Mark, 59, 131
Hawk, David, 271, 403n10

health care, 12, 44, 46, 54, 55, 58, 133, 208; civilian, 52; lack of, 295; prisoners and, 51, 125–26, 127; public, 86
Health Commissariat, 69, 71
Heidegger, Martin, 226
Hidden Gulag, The (Hawk), 271, 403n10
Himmler, Heinrich, 229, 230, 238; prisoner functionaries and, 233–35
Hitler, Adolf, 47, 199, 216, 229, 238
Höß, Rudolf, 237
Holocaust, 5, 314, 318
hospitals, Gulag, 344n53, 345n61, 348n105
housing, 81, 84; absence of, 146; communal, 21
human rights violations, 273, 281, 403n14; addressing, 285; North Korean, 268, 270, 271, 272, 278, 279, 282, 283, 284
human trafficking, 245, 282
humaneness, social position and, 52–54, 58
humanitarian concern, 71, 200, 206, 207, 209, 221
hunger, 175, 243–44, 246; war and, 141, 240
hygiene, 68, 228, 232, 260, 310

Iagoda, Genrikh, 92
identity, 111; ethnic, 213; illicit trade in, 191; national, 142, 213, 309
ideology, 220, 237, 249; culture and, 156, 284, 331n11; liberal, 200; locally developed, 285; political, 285; remolding, 267
illnesses/diseases, 50, 59, 60, 61, 63, 71, 113, 130, 146, 184, 192, 197, 200, 220, 221, 228; chronic, 57; exhaustion through, 65; faked, 343n43; labor and, 51; neurological, 83; for prisoners, 48, 49; reducing, 53
imprisonment, 36, 200, 201, 210, 211, 224, 243, 266, 404n18; conventional, 304; exile and, 29, 299, 301–4; mass, 3–4, 40, 280; maximum conditions of, 297; pains of, 296; physical, 222, 302; rate of/US, 410n17; solitary, 295; spatial, 206, 235, 237, 266; threat of, 30
industrial economy, 93, 106, 128, 232
Industrial Party show trial, 13, 92, 93, 94
industrial settlements, 143, 217
industrialization, 5, 46, 71, 92, 115, 202, 217,

264, 266, 279; forced, 13, 342n37; Great Terror and, 238; Gulag and, 280, 281, 285; penal labor and, 20; Stalin-era, 21
intelligentsia, 88, 90, 92, 95, 105; purge of, 13; scientific/technical, 91, 93, 108, 109; Soviet, 91, 96, 111; technical, 91, 351n16
Internal Watch, 178, 179, 192
invalids, 48, 49, 50, 54, 56, 57, 58, 61, 71–72, 81, 84, 342n35, 349n112; chronic, 82; classification of, 80; complete, 60; homeless, 71; labor and, 77, 80; management of, 73–79; medicalization of, 86; prisoners as, 70–73; rates, 124; release of, 124; separate camps for, 76–79
Irkutsk, 15, 151, 176, 181, 185, 187, 188, 195
Irkutsk Exile Office, 187, 188
Irkutsk oblast, 140, 149, 154; deportees in, 150; special settlers in, 143, 144, *145*, 145, 148, 153
Irkutsk Province, 177, 178
isolation, 217, 218, 245, 278; social, 209
Isupov, V. A., 61, 62, 132

Jews, 230, 234; genocide of, 230, 285
juche ideology, 270, 283, 284
justice, 254, 258, 395n90

Kaganovich, Lazar´, 95, 98, 353n43
Kalmyks, 130, 134
Kang Chul-hwan, 270–71, 403n9
Karaganda Camp, 112, 339n11
Karlag, 117, 327n24
katorga, 17, 163, 173–74, 191, 215, 221, 240, 298, 374n8, 412n36; visual mythology of, 164
Kazakhstan, 47, 112, 117, 134, 199
Kazan, 102, 103, 176, 193, 196
Kennan, George, 163, 190, 198
Kerber, Leonid, 89, *96*, 102
KGB: deportation and, 137; Lithuanian, 159, 160, 373n104
Khabarovsk krai labor camps/colonies, 58, 62, 336n81
Khrapko, Mikhail, 100–101, 102, 104, 354n65
Khrushchev, Nikita S., 354n60; Gulag and, 38, 270; secret speech of, 277; Stalin and, 279; Thaw and, 1, 37

Khurges, Lev Lazarevich, 78, 79
Kim Il-sung, 269, 283, 406n43, 407n66; camp system and, 268, 284; Confucian concepts and, 281; cult of personality and, 277; death of, 278–79; detentions by, 275; dissidents and, 282; industry and, 277; internal security apparatus and, 277; political enemies and, 275; power for, 278; purge by, 276; secret police and, 277; Stalin and, 270, 274–75; terror and, 279; transformation by, 282; WPSK and, 276
Kim Jong-il, 277, 278, 279, 406n43
Kim Jong-un, 269, 279, 282
Kim regime, 273, 279, 280; legitimacy of, 278; loyalty to, 283, 284; rule of, 269, 270
Kitchener, Lord, 213, 214
Kniazev, Grigorii Vlasovich, 77, 78
Kogan, Lazar´ Iosifovich, 48, 74
kolkhozes, 30, 35, 142
Kolyma, 2, 79, 101, 126, 239, 358n18; camps in, 67, 115; medical services in, 339n15, 348n102; transports to, 346n75
Komi, 34, 62, 81, 302
Komsomol, 151, 156, 157, 158, 372n98
Kondrashev, Aleksandr, 124, 125, 360n51
Kontrimaité, Maryté, 142, 152, 156, 157; recollections of, 153–54
Kopaev, G. N., 122, 125, 129
Korean War, 274, 275, 276, 403n3
Korean Workers' Party, 275, 277, 282
Korolev, Sergei P., *98*, 112–13, 356n92
Krasnoiarsk, 112, 116, 176, 181, 185, 186, 195, 196, 360n39
Kravchenko, Valentin A., 101, 354n56, 355n79
Krest´ianskaia gazeta, 35
Kresty, 98, 99, 100, 290
Krivoshchekovsk, 122, 124, 127
Kruglov, Sergei N., 55, 57, 158, 335n71
Kuibyshev, Valerian, 92
kulaks, 29, 34, 130, 149, 158, 168, 239, 240, 244, 274, 328n36, 369n47, 370n60; deportation of, 156, 226, 291; Gulag and, 26
Kuznetsov, Aleksei Kirilovich, 163, 374n8
Kybartas, Antanas, 142, 156, 157, 160; interview with, 136–37

labor, 146, 201, 215, 305, 310, 311; balance, 72, 73, 76; capability, 51, 60, 218; capacity, 71, 74; civilian, 231, 323n21; extermination through, 228, 235; factory, 223; fitness for, 132; foreign, 230, 231; general, 66, 72, 80; Gulag, 8, 14, 42, 49, 108, 120, 128, 132, 134; hard, 17, 102, 188, 254, 298; heavy, 54, 55–56, 57, 58, 65, 73, 74, 199, 208, 218; ideology of, 217; indentured, 298, 300; individualized, 56, 81, 82, 336n74; intellectual, 90; light, 51, 54, 56, 73; management of, 146; as matter of honor, 242–45; medium, 56, 73; mobilization of, 132, 211; penal, 126–27, 173–74, 181, 183, 187, 188, 190, 191, 192–93, 217, 232, 259, 262, 264, 280, 288, 298; physical, 46, 47, 48, 49, 50, 51, 52, 54, 55–56, 57, 58, 60, 63, 64, 73, 132, 267; reform through, 43, 217, 258–65; scientific/technical, 87; skilled, 152; slave, 8, 42, 44, 45; using, 72, 122, 232, 335n73; "voluntary," 226. See also forced labor; penal labor; prisoner labor
labor battalions, 240
Labor Camp no. 1, 236, 237
labor camps, 5, 42, 58, 62, 101, 210, 222, 227, 231, 234, 252, 308, 401n32; barracks of, 293; British, 199; civilian, 232; corrective, 43, 116, 240, 242, 317, 358n11; creation of, 44; criminals at, 61; death rates at, 65, 265; described, 202–5; destructive, 43, 59, 64, 121; employment at, 263; forced, 65, 229, 248; function of, 320; health crises in, 54; human exploitation at, 48–52; information about, 270–73; North Korean, 269, 270–73, 275, 279, 280, 281, 284; production process at, 45–46; reform of, 84; segregation in, 199; system, 251, 259; violence at, 266. See also camps
labor classification, 48, 49–50, 51, 64, 74, 80, 332n23, 343n47, 359n28; multiple regimes for, 73
labor colonies, 63,116, 203, 210, 308, 325n1; children's, 114; corrective, 118, 121, 122, 132, 215, 221, 240, 242, 358n11
labor forces, 30, 34, 86, 239, 333n36; degradation of, 33; economic utility of, 280; Gulag

and, 18, 279; mobilization of, 280; petty criminals and, 45
labor laws, 130, 134, 362n80, 364n108
labor output, 55, 60, 110, 406n51
labor shortages, 142, 143–44, 146, 369n41; addressing, 224–25; skilled, 245
labor therapy, 71, 81, 82, 86
labor utilization rates, 48, 51, 56, 57
Land Reform Movement, 255, 400n24
Laogai, 5, 285, 320; farms, 262; formation/ evolution of, 19, 20; infrastructure projects and, 262; institutions, 260, 261, 262, 264; job placement and, 263; labor/reeducation within, 261; organization of, 260; reform/labor and, 258–65; state enemies and, 263; studies on, 252–53; workforce, 264–65
Latvians, 168, 235
Law Code (1649), 174
Lenin, Vladimir, 45, 91; concentration camp system of, 46; Gulag and, 199, 215; harmful insects and, 298; terror and, 37
Leningrad, 100, 112, 120, 354n51
leper colonies, 211
liberalism, 200, 214, 221, 222
List of Illnesses, 10, 48–52, 55, 56, 315, 333–34n37; criticism of, 53–54; Gulag exploitation and, 52–53; labor utilization rates and, 57; physical condition and, 53
Lithuanians, 4, 15, 36, *154, 155*, 157, 371n77, 372–73n99; dancing by, 153–56; deportation of, 137, 139, 148, 149, 150, 160; exile of, 151, 153–56; loggers, *152*
Liu Shaoqi, 259, 401n31
living conditions, camp, 53, 55, 80, 139, 143, 144, 145–47, 151, 153, 160–61, 215, 296, 297
logging sector, 54, 144, 147, 152, 369n41, 370n51; labor for, 46, 369n42; output of, 33
Loidin, D. M., 50, 53, 54, 60
Los, Maria, 291, 305
Lubianka, 98, 101, 102, 374n10; files, 164, 165
Luo Ruiqing, 256, 261, 263, 402n46
Lysenkoism, 89

Main Administration for Prisoners of War and Internees (GUPVI), 240, 319
Majdanek, 4, 224, 227, 228, 314

malnutrition, 48, 50, 65, 71, 79, 146, 224, 228, 240, 243, 244, 246

Mao Zedong, 250, 254, 259, 399n8; counterrevolutionaries and, 400n25, 400n26; democratic dictatorship and, 262; enemies of the people and, 254; revolutionary justice and, 254; on state apparatus, 253

Maoism, 7, 252

Marchenko, Anatoly, 305, 306

marching convoys, 173, 175, 177, 179–81, 183–86, 188–95, 197, 198; illustration of, *182. See also* deportation convoys

Marfino sharashka, 105, 112

Marxism-Leninism, 220, 283, 284

mass campaigns, 239, 252, 255–58, 265; bureaucracy and, 256–57

mass death, 43, 265, 266, 315

mass trials, 255, 257, 258, 400n24

Mazower, Mark, 47, 133

medical care, 51, 66–67, 73, 74, 231, 339n10, 339n15, 348n102, 349n112; civilian, 66; prisoner-patients and, 85

medical commissions, 46, 50, 51–52, 71, 72, 344n49

medical policing, 211, 218

medicine, 72, 209, 382n1, 343n45; industrial, 85; military, 80, 85; penal, 12, 340n19

Medvedev, Dmitrii, 310, 311, 312

mental illnesses, 83, 295, 348n105

MGB, 148, 158, 325n5, 326n8

Miasishchev, Vladimir M., 97, 356n92

migration, penal, 176, 191, 196

Miliauskas, Juozas, 149, 151, 153

Military Court (Municipal Military Control Committee), 256

military production, 105, 110, 111, 118, 121

mining, 46, 106, 173, 181, 185, 231, 374n8, 376n12

Ministry of Public Security, 260, 261

Ministry of the Interior, 187, 194

Mironov, L. G., 352n29, 352n34

mobilization, 9, 120, 317, 280, 320, 364n106; labor, 226; mass, 13, 116, 132, 267, 281, 317; total, 357n5

modernism, 4, 6, 16, 168, 252

modernity, 5, 7, 8, 9, 293; anti-modern forces of, 6; penality and, 289–92; political, 200,

202, 216, 225; shared/alternative, 323n23; social, 200, 216; Stalinist, 168–69

modernization, 91, 112; Stalinist, 38–39; theory, 289, 290, 291–92

Moldovans, 140, 151

Molotov, Viacheslav, 108

Mordovian camp, 287; sentry point at, *288*

mortality rates, 5, 12, 14, 42, 76, 86, 123, 221, 231, 232, 245, 315, 346n76; camp, 122; civilian, 79; falsification of, 60; Gulag, 10, 43, 59, 60, 61, 63, 65, 124, 126, 361n53; inmate population and, 59; official, 60; peak, 79; reducing, 53; urban area, 130; in western Siberia, 126. *See also* death rates

Morukov, Mikhail: on Gulag, 109, 110

Moscow 2042 (Voinovich), 59

Moscow-Volga River Canal, 74

Moscowrep, 59

Mosenergo, 96

movement, freedom of, 227, 230, 235

munitions production, NKVD and, 121

Muselmänner, 232, 244

Mutiny (1857), 201, 206

MVD, 1, 31–32, 33, 34, 43, 46, 55, 58, 61, 63, 69, 105, 106, 158, 160, 240, 319, 325n5, 328n35; Beria and, 107; deportation and, 137; forced labor and, 84; industrial enterprises, 32; mortality rates and, 60; prisoner categories and, 336n75; special settlers and, 146–47, 154

MVD-Gulag leadership, 56, 57, 58, 63

MVD Order no. 00418, 55, 58

Nakonechnyi, Mikhail, 60, 62

Napoleonic Wars, 18, 179, 201

Narkomtiazhprom. *See* People's Commissariat of Heavy Industry

Nasedkin, Viktor Grigor'evich, 50, 81, 347n98; List of Illnesses and, 53–54; Order no. 00640 and, 53

National Socialism, 4, 15, 19, 133, 226, 275

nationalities policy, reform of, 36

nationalization, 251, 257

Nerchinsk, mining in, 173, 181, 185, 374n8, 376n12

New China, 250, 251

New Economic Policy (NEP), 16

New York World's Fair (1939), 168

Nicholas I, 174

Nizheudinsk Mining District, 185

Nizhnii Novgorod, 193, 194, 195, 196

NKVD, 1, 6, 8, 20, 31, 33, 39, 46, 61, 63, 69, 78, 84, 103, 109, 124, 125, 130, 239, 240, 319; NKVD Administration, 98; Beria and, 97; camp staff and, 246; camp zones and, 275; executions and, 162; expansion of, 99; Fourth Special Department of, 104, 106, 355n72; Gulag, 43, 44, 51; mortality rates and, 60; munitions production by, 121; NKVD Order no. 00640, 53, 55; physical labor and, 49, 122; prison camps and, 97, 102; sharashka system and, 100; specialist prison system and, 101; Terror and, 99

non-Gulag, 40, 118, 126, 128; food distribution and, 11; freedom and, 27; Gulag and, 3, 10, 15, 18, 21, 28, 29, 30, 31, 32–33, 34, 41, 69, 90, 139, 141, 315; return to, 30–31

Noril´sk, 79, 101, 120, 121, 126, 245

North Korean constitution (1948), 274, 407n66

North Western Provinces, 210

Norvals' Point, 219

Notes from the House of the Dead (Dostoevskii), 190

Novosibirsk, 115, 116, 129, 131, 132, 134, 359n33, 362n70, 363n91, 364n92, 364n106; camps, 53; evacuees in, 126; prisoners in, 122, 130; Siblag and, 118

Novosibirsk Oblast Camp and Colony Administration, 118, 119, 123, 124, 127, 132

Novosibirsk party, 121–22, 123–24

Ob´ River, 127, 141, 194

OGPU, 43, 46, 61, 63, 74, 92, 96, 325n5, 326n8, 351n20, 352n25; camp staff and, 246; leadership of, 97; OGPU Collegium, 95; old specialists and, 93; sharashka and, 94, 95

OITK. *See* Department of Corrective Labor Colonies

OKB. *See* Special Design Bureau

Okhrana, 163

Operation Priboi, 144, 145, 150

Operation Vesna, 144, 150

OPP. See *ozdorovitel´nyi-profilakticheskii punkt*

Ordzhonikidze, Sergo, 94, 95, 97, 98, 352n27

Organic Regulations of People's Tribunals, 255

Organisation Todt, 230

Ostarbeiter, 230, 231, 244

OTB. *See* Special Technical Bureau

ozdorovitel´nyi-profilakticheskii punkt, 82, 83

Pang Hak-se, 21, 274, 404n24, 404n25

Panopticon, 163, 293

Paris International Exposition, 168

Party Plenum (1933), 168

Paulauskaité, Elena, 141, 150, 151, 152–53

Pechora Camp, 47, 348n110, 360n39

penal battalions, 18

penal colonies, 197, 205–8, 220, 300, 304, 315, 378n50; collectivist ethos of, 307

penal economy, Gulag, 68, 69, 345n61

penal infrastructure, 176, 203, 207, 221, 310

penal labor, 31, 42, 332n20; industrialization and, 20; as punishment, 308

penal practices, 16, 21, 260, 262, 289, 294, 309

penal system, 180, 290, 295; harshness of, 296; NKVD and, 99; Russian, 4, 313, 405n37; Soviet, 95, 304, 314; Stalinist, 325n2

penality, 298; modernity and, 289–92

Peng Zhen, 256, 259

penitentiary system, 39, 230, 301

penology, 297, 307; cultural turn in, 292–95

People's Commissariat of Heavy Industry (Narkomtiazhprom), 95, 97, 98, 353n39

People's Commissariat of Munitions Combine no. 179: 122, 124, *128;* award for, 127; prisoners at, 129, 130

People's Commissariat of the Navy, medico-sanitary services of, 66

People's Commissariat of the Railroads, medico-sanitary services of, 66

People's Commissariat of War, medico-sanitary services of, 66

People's Liberation Army, 258

People's Tribunal, 255, 258

Perm´, 39, 80, 176, 193, 194, 196

Permanent Medical Commission, 72

personhood, 287, 296

Peter the Great, 17, 174

photo albums, 165, *166, 167,* 374n19

photography: handpainted, *166;* Stalinist, 169; unruly, 165–66

physicians, 46, 72; Gulag, 3, 10, 52, 73, 81, 86; prisoner-, 11, 66; subordination of, 10

Pioneers, 157, 158

plague, 212, 215; emergency legislation about, 213; outbreak of, 210–11; segregation, 208

Plamper, Jan, 68, 298

Pogarskiy, Yaroslav, 159, 160

Polikarpov, Nikolai N., 93, 94, 351n23

Polish rebellion (1863), 381n118

Politburo, 95, 123, 129, 274, 278, 320

Political Criminal Detention Center 16: 278

political enemies, 219, 220, 228, 323n21

political prisoners, 27, 120, 233, 275–76, 279, 281, 405n31; Gulag and, 276; isolation of, 217; organized activities and, 276; release of, 276–77; social activism of, 37; treatment of, 387n79

politics, 116, 149, 220, 241, 312, 340n24; society and, 265

Poor Law (1834), 203

poverty, 29, 193

POW camps, 224, 230, 231, 232, 241, 248, 319; memories of, 245

power, 1, 96, 238, 278, 318; absolute, 227, 235; culture and, 294; disciplinary, 69, 84; dispersal of, 175; establishment of, 237, 239; labor, 82; penal, 289, 307; punitive, 289; sovereign, 84, 340n24; state, 198, 267; totalitarian aspirations to, 245; wartime paradigms of, 133

POWs. *See* prisoners of war

prison camps, 230, 403n14; closing, 276; economic function of, 279–81; establishment of, 87, 277; expansion of, 278, 280, 281, 285; labor utilization at, 46; last wave of, 104–13; North Korean, 20–21, 268,

269, 271, 272, 273, 277–81, 283; political function of, 279–81; project-driven nature of, 96; scientific/technical work and, 87; second wave of, 97–104; Soviet, 279–81; women/children at, 332n14

prison design bureaus, 102

Prison Medical Service, 340n19

prison officers, 19, 103, 293

prison science system, 97, 103–4, 108

prison sector, 259, 264

Prison Service, 308, 311, 312

prison staff, 233–35, 305, 306

prisoner labor, 8, 72, 84, 358n18; civilian labor and, 323n21; exploitation of, 12; Soviet economy and, 33

prisoners: aristocracy of, 82; breaking, 301; brutalization among, 227; camp personnel and, 237, 238; corruption chains and, 248; dead, 320, 373–74n2; dehumanization of, 230, 231, 283; disabled, 54, 61–62, 63, 70, 72, 79–84; discarded, 60–61, 64; ethnic diversity of, 275; exploitation of, 47, 48–52, 58, 63, 84; as hangmen/executioners, 236; marginalization of, 137; movement, 78; non-political, 26; nonprisoners and, 129–30, 134; nonworking, 70, 75, 80, 84, 349n112; number of, 55, 228, 320, 402n54; perceptions of, 208, 283–84; photo of, *31, 32;* physical condition of, 53; physical labor of, 46, 47; physically inferior, 56; as raw material, 46; releasing, 18, 60, 61, 62–63; relocation of, 279; self-guarding of, 248; sick, 46, 61–63, 75–76, 81, 133, 334n49; spatio-temporal control of, 306; stress among, 306; treatment of, 296; weak, 73, 79–84; women, 191–93, 287, 301–2, 332n14, 348n105; *See also* convicts; invalids; political prisoners; women prisoners

prisoners of war (POWs), 130, 241, 247, 318; death of, 240; emotional distress for, 248; Estonian, 396n104; French, 231; German, 240, 243, 244, 248; labor by, 240; material situation for, 230; North Korean, 275; recollections by, 246; Soviet, 229, 230, 231, 240. *See also* POW camps

prisonization, 290, 292, 297, 298

prisons, 184, 222, 230, 264, 293, 325n1; birth of, 309–13; cellular, 307; construction of, 197; high-security, 311; imperial, 163–64; maintenance of, 89; normal, 102; organizational strength of, 248–49; over-crowded, 259, 287; transit, 192, 196, 304; urban, 78

privacy, deprivation of, 225, 296, 306, 312

propaganda, 108, 165, 166, 168, 216, 285; camp, 121, 122, 123; Chinese, 260; Gulag, 164; North Korean, 407n66; reeducation, 243; Soviet, 16, 163; Stalinist, 163; war-time, 122

Public Security Bureau, 256, 261

punishment, 21, 36, 201, 225, 236, 247, 312–13, 361n62, 372n98; administering, 248, 249, 295, 297, 308; collective, 28; as communicative process, 294; corporal, 189, 221; criminal, 289; deportation and, 139; economic production and, 248; explanations for, 292; forms of, 294, 295, 298; harsh, 295–97, 300, 301–4, 304–7; humanitarian, 295–97, 311; individual, 290, 344n51; modalities, 292, 311; penal labor as, 291, 308; politics of, 26–27; prisonization as, 297; public, 255; Rus-sian, 289, 292–95; social and, 295; social hierarchy and, 296; spaces of, 287; as state instrument, 175–76; transportation as, 297–99; welfare-based systems of, 289

purges, 13, 36, 108, 165, 255, 276, 278, 280, 328n36

Pussy Riot, 299

Putin, Vladimir, 10, 22, 288

Pyongyang, 21, 273, 275, 278, 279, 280

racial difference, 19, 211, 220, 222

racial domination, 19, 230

radicalization, 216, 317

rations, 78, 215, 230, 248, 361n59; famine-camp, 218; Gulag/non-Gulag, 29, 29 (table); prisoner, 51, 199, 218, 287, 326n18

Ravensbruck Women's Camp, 236

re-Stalinization, 10, 37, 38

recovery stations, 82, 83

recovery teams, 73, 73–76, 82

Red Air Force, 94

Red Army, 115, 121, 122, 129, 134, 240, 247; food for, 118; free labor and, 130; growth of, 127; prisoner death rates and, 275; soldiers/capture of, 405n34; special set-tlers and, 364n106; surgeons/priority for, 81

reeducation, 225, 243, 254, 261, 264, 266, 267, 298, 304, 308–9; prisoner, 327n21; role of, 317; social/political, 201

reform, 17, 36, 174, 187, 197; labor and, 43, 217, 258–65; labor camp, 84, 259; land, 250, 255, 257, 400n24; penal, 133, 290, 298, 309–10; rhetoric of, 264; Siberian, 176–79, 179–81, 183–84; social, 203, 211

refugees, 213, 224, 265, 301

Regulation on Exile Transfer with Siberian Provinces, 179, 181, 183

rehabilitation, 90, 213, 215, 217, 221, 223, 295, 304, 330n51, 387n79; British, 201; individ-ual, 344n51; labor and, 43; rhetoric of, 264

religion, 153, 365n108

repression, 40, 104, 105, 140, 164; political, 55, 269, 273; Stalinist, 41, 90, 162, 165, 168, 169, 294, 314

resistance, 234, 275–76; Baltic/Ukrainian, 241; collective, 381n118

resocialization, 139, 309

Resurrection (Tolstoi), 198

riots, prison, 276, 277, 276, 312

Rodchenko, Aleksandr, 168

Rossi, Jacques, 27, 42

RSFSR Criminal Procedural Code, 61

Ruciński, Justynian, 173, 176, 192

rule-of-law restraints, 68

Russian Civil War, 238, 241, 242, 298

Russian Federation, 21, 287, 297, 311, 330n51; prison reform in, 309–10

Russian Orthodox, 307, 312

Russkaia mysl', Chekhov in, 198

Ruzgys, Rimgaudas, 155, 372n97, 373n107

St. Petersburg, 163, 175, 178, 184, 186, 187, 192, 198

Sakhalin Island, 163; penitentiary colony, 190, 294

Sakhalin Island (Chekhov), 198
samizdat literature, 87
sanitation, 43, 53, 86, 162, 200, 232, 307
Sanitation Department, 11, 46, 50, 53, 58, 60,
  74, 335n73; List of Illnesses of, 10, 48;
  problems for, 44
Sanotdel, 66, 67, 68, 69, 70, 77, 82, 83, 86,
  338n6, 340n19, 345n61, 345n63, 347n96,
  348n98; authority for, 85; camp hospitals
  and, 81; decree by, 76; problems for, 84
Savitskii, I. M., 363n81, 363n91
Schmitt, Carl, 14, 133, 226, 254, 265, 410n11
science, 87, 91, 111, 316; normative, 89; technology and, 100
scientists, 88; imprisonment of, 108, 110
Scott, James C., 252
Second Five-Year Plan, 95, 97
secret police, 8, 77, 165, 277–78, 314
security, 277, 278; national, 283; public, 258,
  260; state, 105, 125
security apparatus, 43, 109, 258, 274, 325n3;
  North Korean, 278, 279
segregation, 199, 202, 218; plague, 208; social,
  204; spatial, 237; technologies of, 209
self-organization, 288, 305
self-organization committees, 306–7, 308
self-policing, 189, 291
semistations, 179, 184, 185
sentences, 55, 190, 255; death, 131; reducing,
  123, 131
Sevzheldorlag, 345n64, 347n91
sexual activities, 231, 235, 244
sexually transmitted diseases, 83, 348n105
Shakhty trial, 92
Shalamov, Varlam, 2, 79, 339n11, 339n15;
  documentary fiction of, 67; on labor
  camps, 64
sharashka system, 3, 12, 13, 33, 89, 90, 91,
  94, 99, 101, 102, 104, 106, 107, 108, 111,
  112, 316, 350n12, 356n92; civil society
  and, 113; as coercive phenomenon, 109;
  history/work of, 110; inmates of, 103; ;
  institutional memory and, 109; interwar,
  105; NKVD and, 100; OGPU and, 94, 95;
  origins of, 91–97, 111–12
Shavrov, B. V., 93, 352n25
Shavrov, Vadim, 97, 353n40

Shearer, David R., on Gulag, 315, 323n22,
  328n36
shortages: food, 55; general economy of, 248;
  labor, 142, 143–44, 146, 224–25, 245,
  369n41; wartime, 124
show trials, 13
Siberia and the Exile System (Kennan), 163
Siberian Administration of Camps of Special
  Significance (SibULON), 116
Siberian Military District, 122, 359n33
Siblag, 74, *85,* 116, 117, 121, 122–23, 126, 128,
  360n36; central administration of, 118;
  data from, 118–19; labor supply and, 129;
  prisoners at, 362n67; subdivisions, *117*
Sixth Party Congress, 278
Sixth Plenum (Korean Workers' Party Central
  Committee), 276
Skolkovo complex, 109
slave labor, 8, 42, 44, 45
Slavs, 230, 234
SLON. *See* Solovki
Smith, Philip, 312, 387n67; punishment and,
  293–94, 299, 311
social control, 209, 267, 291
social danger, 215, 222
Social Darwinism, 249
social disorder, 108, 206, 299
social hierarchy, punishment and, 296
social life, 157, 258; special settlers and, 153–56
social logic, role of, 146
social mobility, 137, 138, 156
social parasites, imprisonment of, 30
social practices, 153, 154
socialism, 8, 14, 35, 37, 168, 238–39, 248, 259,
  266, 267; Bolsheviks and, 238–39; Chinese, 250, 251; construction of, 226, 264;
  enemies of, 253
Socialist Realism, 16, 168, 169
socialist reconstruction, 91, 308
socialist state, 108, 265
socialist system, 250, 251
socialization, 156, 248
society: apartheid, 228–30, 231–33; center
  of, 236; Chinese, 320; civil, 113, 197, 221;
  cleansing, 228; North Korean, 283; politics and, 265; Russian, 36; state control of,
  251. *See also* Soviet society

Society of Former Political Prisoners and Exiles, 164

Sofsky, Wolfgang, 227, 231, 389n12

solidarity, 153, 232, 234–35, 245, 249

Solovki, 1–2, 12, 69, 72, 116, 165, 241, 244, 332n23, 333n33, 333n37, 343n45, 374n7

Solzhenitsyn, Alexander, 10, 37, 43, 87–88, 162, 218, 241, 298, 301, 302, 375n12; camp of, 112; convoy guards and, 300; Gulag and, 1, 2, 26, 54, 272; on higher-ups, 62; on human beings as raw material, 46; impact of, 42, 44; labor camps and, 121; medical care and, 12, 52, 66–67; metaphor of, 3; on prisoner utilization, 47; social position/humaneness and, 54; systemic approach and, 321n1; writing of, 104

South African War (1899–1903), 116, 133, 213, 216, 382n3

Soviet economy, 82, 92, 143; forced labor and, 33; sharashka system and, 110; state and, 40

Soviet life, history of, 139–42

Soviet society, 16, 26, 31, 70–73, 84, 156–59; camps and, 238–41; depoliticization of, 368n23; deportees and, 161; development of, 241–42; disabled and, 86; discipline/punishment and, 220; ethnic groups and, 156; forced labor in, 238–41; free elements in, 139; Gulag and, 33, 36, 115; non-Gulag and, 27; poverty of, 29; repression of, 40; rules of, 137; sociopolitical evolution of, 36; state and, 34

Soviet system, 126, 408n75; Gulag and, 8, 33, 190

Sovietization, 137, 142, 143, 148, 274

Special Design Bureau (OKB), 98, 99, 355n72

special settlements, 6, 138, 159, 239, 249, 274, 300, 325n1, 372n95; conditions in, 160–61; leaving, 141, 150–51; life in, 139, 140, 142–43, 148, 160

special settlers, 4, 15, 36, *147, 154,* 159, 239; conditions for, 139, 145–47, 153; economic function of, 143; encouragement for, 151; life of, 150–53, 153–56; mobilization of, 364n106; MVD and, 146–47, 154; as other, 156–61; policy making and,

146; rejection of, 158–61; social mobility of, 138; stories of, 139–142; supervision of, 146–47

Special Technical Bureau (OTB), 99, 100, 106, 107, 353n48, 356n95

specialist prison system, 95, 101, 105, 110, 112

specialists, 88, 90; bourgeois, 13, 91; old, 92, 93; red, 92, 93; sanitation, 66

Speranskii, Mikhail Mikhailovich, 17, 179, 183, 186; exiles and, 181; reforms by, 187; vision of, 180

Speranskii's Regulation on Exiles, 179, 183, 189

SS, 6, 233, 234, 235, 236, 238, 241; concentration camps and, 228

SSD. *See* State Security Department

SSSR na stroike (journal), 52, 168

Stakhanovites, 151, 243

Stalin, Iosif (Joseph), 7, 26, 34, 35, 101, 104, 108, 220, 225, 243, 283, 397; Beria and, 99, 100, 103; camps of, 27, 44, 59, 61, 325n2; counterrevolutionaries and, 275; criticism of, 277; cult of personality and, 282; death of, 11, 30, 33, 36, 54, 66, 70, 84, 107, 135, 151, 270, 276, 287; exploitation and, 58; Gulag and, 2, 8, 12–13, 19, 25, 39, 40, 42, 45, 47, 54, 60–61, 63, 111, 133, 199, 215, 247, 270, 276, 284, 348n106, 404n26; health care system and, 52; intelligentsia and, 13, 95; Khrushchev and, 279; Kim and, 270, 274–75; on kulaks, 168; nationalities policy and, 36; nonworking prisoners and, 75; penal policies of, 55; political/economic enemies and, 323n21; power for, 1, 238; prison labor and, 31, 45, 47, 48, 49; prisoner health and, 319; repression by, 41, 162, 165, 168, 169, 294, 314; rule of, 9, 28, 39, 270; secret police and, 74; sharashka system and, 91, 94, 106; socialism and, 8, 168; specialist prison system and, 105; terror and, 37, 274–75, 279; totalitarian surveillance and, 291

Stalinism, 1, 5, 11, 16, 20, 21, 34, 36, 40, 41, 42, 45, 69, 88, 91, 105, 108, 165, 166, 168, 239, 249, 252, 263, 320; brutality of, 28; criticism of, 10, 37, 38; enlightenment and, 410n11; forced labor and, 314; Gulag

and, 8, 11, 36, 38; legacy of, 35; Maoism
and, 7; moral decay and, 107; political
apparatus of, 25; political violence and, 6;
rehabilitation and, 43; repression by, 104;
Soviet history and, 267; transition from,
137–38; war and, 14–15
Stammlager, 229, 230
starvation, 71, 79, 81, 127, 218, 315
State Archive of the Russian Federation
(GARF), 137, 165
State Committee on Defense (GKO), 100, 131
State Security Department (SSD), 272, 278,
279, 406n49
State Senate, 178, 192
Stepa, Uncle, 156, 372n90
stereotypes: gender, 309; historical, 304, 306
stigmatization, 156, 158, 242
Stolypin carriages, 293, 301, 303
Supreme Council of the National Economy
(VSNKh), 351n20, 352n27
surveillance, 260, 279, 291, 311
survivors, 46–47; memoirs of, 66; mindset
of, 38

Talagi Invalid Camp, 78, 80, 82
Tashkent, 131; camp system, 84; as evacuation
destination, 364n91
Tatars, 140, 239–40
technology, 13, 87, 89; camps and, 202; sci-
ence and, 100
terror, 90, 251, 254, 255–58; establishment of,
227; mass, 37; political, 37; reigns of, 279;
Stalinist/post-Stalinist, 38; stemming, 41;
victims of, 38. *See also* Great Terror
Thaw, 1, 37
Third Department to the Ministry, 105, 185
Thomson, S. J., 210, 214
Timashev, Aleksandr Egorovich, 186, 195
Tiumen´, 136, 160, 176, 180, 189, 194, 195
Tobol´sk, 176, 179, 180, 181, 184, 186, 187,
188, 194; convoys in, 189
Tobol´sk Exile Office, 181, 186–87, 189, 194
Tobol´sk Transit Prison, 181, 196
Tolstoi, Lev, 198
Tomsk, 114, 115, 116, 118, 132, 176, 178, 179,
181, 186, 187, 192, 194, 195; plant, 121;
prisons of, 196

Tomsk Corrective Labor Colony, 121, 122
torture, 226, 228, 232, 236–37, 245, 268, 271,
292, 296, 299
total war, 115, 213, 214, 357n5; Gulag and,
126–35; Soviet, 131, 132
totalitarianism, 89, 273; concentration camps
and, 284–85; origins of, 284–85; Stalinist,
267
Trans-Siberian Railway, 117
transportation, 74, 78, 177, 192, 195, 224, 286,
312, 346n75; availability of, 150; collectivism and, 304; penal, 287; as punishment,
297–99; terrors of, 299–307
Treblinka, 4, 228, 315
Treblinka Labor Camp no. 1, 236, 237
tribunals, 210, 255, 258, 337n98, 399n16
Trotskii, Lev, 9, 91, 216
Trotskyists, 241
TsKB. See Central Design Bureau-29; Central
Design Bureau-39
tuberculosis, 48, 50, 71, 79, 80, 81, 83, 184,
287, 312, 347n94
Tupolev, Andrei N., *88,* 90, 97, 100, 354n51,
356n92; arrest of, 102; aviation designers
and, 102; manuscript of, 349n6; prison
camps and, 87; sharashka of, 105, 112
Tupolevskaia sharaga, 87, 102
Tushino, 100, 101, 104, 354n51

UITLK. *See* Administration for Corrective
Labor Camps and Colonies
Ukhta, 75, 81, 302
Ukrainians, 4, 36, 140, 141, 151, 235
UNHRC. *See* United Nations Human Rights
Council
United Nations Human Rights Council
(UNHRC), 268, 271
Untermenschen, 236
Usol´lag, *39, 39,* 40, 80; anniversary of, *40*
Usova, Zinaida Danilovna, 78, 80, 82,
348n103

venereal disease, 192, 348n105
vigilance, 166, 168
Viola, Lynne, 2, 15, 148, 150
violence, 40, 72, 226, 227, 239, 245, 307,
315; archaeology, 200; calculated, 251;

violence (*cont.*), camp, 266; developmental, 7; ethnic, 202; excessive, 257; excisionary, 291; exhaustion through, 65; forced labor and, 238; Gulag, 221; institutionalized, 45; mass, 251–52, 265; Nazi, 236; organized, 251; physical, 232; political, 6, 8, 202, 212, 214, 253; public use of, 251; regulated, 237; relationships of, 237; resorting to, 252; Soviet, 221; sphere of, 228; spread of, 265; state, 35, 38, 40, 41, 212, 252, 331n7; targets of, 213; threats of, 227; torture and, 232

Vladimir, 176, 194

Vlasov, Vasilii, 193, 196

Volga Germans, 130–31, 134, 140, 239

Volksdeutsche, 235

Volksgemeinschaft, 225, 226, 248

volost´ courts, 298

Vorkuta, 11, 77, 120, 126, 341n31

Voroshilov, Kliment, 94, 95, 109, 352n27, 353n39

vrachebnye-trudovye ekspertnye komissii (VTEK), 71, 72

VSNKh. *See* Supreme Council of the National Economy

VTEK. *See vrachebnye-trudovye ekspertnye komissii*

vydvizhentsy, 29, 39

war: absolute, 357n5; concentration camps and, 132; forced labor and, 13; Gulag and, 13–14, 49, 79–84, 104, 114, 115, 116, 119–35, 246, 357n2; hunger and, 141, 240, 243–44. *See also* total war

waystations, 184, 185, 186, 189, 190, 193, 195; decline of, 196; separation at, 192

weak-prisoner teams, 73–76, 78, 82

Wehrmacht, 231, 241, 319

Weiner, Amir, 133, 134, 367n16

welfare, 217, 289; colonial, 211; postwar, 292; social, 200, 201

western Siberia: convoys and, 184; economic growth of, 115; forced labor in, 131; Gulag in, 14, 114, 115, 116–19, 123, 135; labor soldiers in, 131; mortality rates in, 126; prisoners in, 121, 132, 134

western Ukraine, 145, 159; deportation from, 137, 139, 140

Weyler, Valeriano, 213, 382n3

White Sea-Baltic Canal, 99, 165, 239, 243, 279–80, 281, 332n20, 374n7, 375n10; Belomor Canal, 16; labor for, 48; overfulfilling quota for, 52

Winter War, 121, 128

women prisoners, 191–93, 287, 301–2, 332n14; amnesty for, 348n105; transportation of, 302

women's colonies, 309

Workers Party of South Korea (WPSK), 276

workhouses, 210, 218, 220, 222; described, 202–5

working classes, legitimate, 205

workshops, prison, 87

Wyabalenna Reserve, 205

Yanan faction, 276

Yan´an period, 259

Yeon-an group, 275

yeon-jwa-je, 269, 282

ZATOs, 90, 111–12, 356n93

Zemskov, V. N., 366n5, 372n98

Zhukov, Pavel, 104, 112, 354n65